FROM GUTENBERG TO THE INTERNET

FROM GUTENBERG TO THE INTERNET

FREE SPEECH, ADVANCING TECHNOLOGY, AND THE IMPLICATIONS FOR DEMOCRACY

THIRD EDITION

Russell L. Weaver
Professor of Law and
Distinguished University Scholar
University of Louisville, Louis D. Brandeis School of Law

CAROLINA ACADEMIC PRESS
Durham, North Carolina

Library of Congress Cataloging-in-Publication Data

Names: Weaver, Russell L., 1952- author.
Title: From Gutenberg to the internet : free speech, advancing technology, and the implications for democracy / by Russell L. Weaver.
Description: Third edition. | Durham, North Carolina : Carolina Academic Press, [2025] | Previous edition: 2019. | Includes bibliographical references and index.
Identifiers: LCCN 2025000479 | ISBN 9781531032890 (paperback) | ISBN 9781531032906 (ebook)
Subjects: LCSH: Communication in politics—Technological innovations. | Internet—Political aspects. | Freedom of speech. | Communication—Technological innovations—History.
Classification: LCC JA85 .W43 2025 | DDC 320.01/4—dc23/eng/20250123
LC record available at https://lccn.loc.gov/2025000479

Carolina Academic Press, LLC
700 Kent Street
Durham, North Carolina 27701
(919) 489-7486
www.cap-press.com

Printed in the United States of America

To Laurence, Ben and Kate, with love, RLW

CONTENTS

ACKNOWLEDGMENTS

The author wishes to express appreciation to the University of Louisville's Distinguished University Scholar program for providing financial support for his research, as well as to his magnificent research assistants, Mr. Andrew Denning, Mr. Kenneth Schwalbert, and Mr. Timothy Hamilton, who provided valuable assistance.

FROM GUTENBERG TO THE INTERNET

CHAPTER 1

EARLY COMMUNICATION

The history of free expression is inextricably linked to advances in speech technology.[1] Prior to the 1400s, society had very limited communications technologies at its disposal.[2] Indeed, with some exceptions (*e.g.*, the use of carrier pigeons or smoke signals), information generally moved at the pace at which people moved.[3] As a result, when an important battle was fought in a distant part of the Roman Empire, the Emperor might wait days, if not weeks, to hear the outcome of the battle. Without telephones, telegraphs or the internet, the "news" regarding the outcome would be transported to Rome by a person traveling on foot, chariot, horseback or ship.[4] Necessarily, information did not move quickly at that time.

---

1. *See* David Crowley & Paul Heyer, Communication in History: Technology, Culture, Society (5th ed. 2007); Irving Fang, A History of Mass Communication: Six Information Revolutions (1997); Lucien Febvre & Henri-Jean Martin, The Coming of the Book: The Impact of Printing 1450–1800 (1976); Marshall McLuhan, The Gutenberg Galaxy (1962); Charles T. Meadow, Making Connections: Communication Through the Ages (2002); Russell L. Weaver, Understanding the First Amendment 245–272 (8th ed. 2023).

2. *See* A History of Mass Communication, *supra* note 1, at 11–12.

3. *See id.*

4. *See id.*, at 15 (because Roman emperors "wanted to receive intelligence and send out orders quickly," they maintained an extensive road and postal system. Also noting that less prominent citizens sent letters in other ways: "For long journeys, the writer had to rely upon traders and ship captains. Over short distances, private messengers or servants, usually slaves, carried letters. It was a dangerous duty, for a slave risked loss of limb or life if he was caught by the master's enemies but, if he failed to deliver the letters promptly, faced a similar fate at home.").

A. EARLY METHODS OF COMMUNICATION

Of course, "communication" (in a broad sense) has existed since the beginning of time.[5] Prehistoric humans communicated primarily through oral means, but also created representations in the form of cave drawings,[6] figurines,[7] and other symbols.[8]

Even though the alphabet (as such) did not exist until about 1700 B.C.,[9] some date the existence of writings to even earlier periods[10] and indeed question whether the alphabet is superior to hieroglyphics.[11] Nevertheless, the creation of the alphabet and writing involved a major step forward in communication,[12] enabling "the civilizations who employed them to achieve unparalleled size and complexity."[13]

Early peoples had limited technologies available for producing and reproducing the documents that they created.[14] For many centuries, written documents were laboriously prepared by hand, and there was no mechanism for easily copying or reproducing those works.[15] Many of the

---

5. *See* Communication in History, *supra* note 1, at 2 ("Communication is an exchange of information. It is an activity. About 100,000 years ago our early ancestors communicated through nonverbal gestures and an evolving system of spoken language.... The later prehistoric period, from about 50,000 to 10,000 B.C., has recently begun to yield impressive evidence of both communication and communications.").

6. *See* A History of Mass Communication, *supra* note 1, at 1–2; *see also* Hillary Rosner, *Spotted Horses in Cave Art Weren't Just a Figment, DNA Shows, The New York Times*, at D3 (Nov. 8, 2011).

7. *See* Communication in History, *supra* note 1, at 2.

8. Alexander Marshack, *The Art and Symbols of Ice Age Man*, printed in Communication in History, *supra* note 1, at 5 (noting that, even though "history began with writing," communication preceded history: "man began making images and keeping symbolic records more than 25,000 years before the invention of true writing.").

9. *See* A History of Mass Communication, *supra* note 1, at 1–2.

10. *See* Andrew Robinson, *The Origins of Writing*, in Communication in History, *supra* note 1, at 38 ("The earliest Egyptian writing dates from 3100 B.C., that of the Indus Valley from 2500 B.C., that of China from 1200 B.C., that of Central America from 600 B.C. (all dates are approximate).").

11. *Id.*, at 40.

12. *See* Communication in History, *supra* note 1, at 44.

13. *Id.*

14. *See* Harold Innis, *Media in Ancient Empires*, in Communication in History, *supra* note 1, at 23.

15. *See* A History of Mass Communication, *supra* note 1, at 1–17.

earliest writings (aside from ancient tokens[16]) were made on papyrus[17] using brushes.[18] Included were ancient Greek writings such as the *Iliad* and the *Odyssey*.[19]

Because of the limited availability of papyrus,[20] non-Egyptians eventually developed a substitute material, parchment, from the skins of sheep, calves and goats.[21] Although "paper" was created in China in the second century,[22] Europe did not have a paper factory until the twelfth century,[23]

---

16. *See id.*, 1–2 ("But we must look to the Fertile Crescent, particularly to Mesopotamia, for the long trek to reproducing and storing spoken language, which began about 8,000 B.C. in Sumer. Small clay triangles, spheres, cones, and other tokens were molded to represent sheep, measures of grain, jars of oil, and other trading goods[.] The shape of the token carried its meaning."); COMMUNICATION IN HISTORY, *supra* note 1, at 3 ("before the emergence of writing, several Old World societies were recording economic transactions through the use of fired clay tokens 1 to 3 centimeters in size.").

17. *See* A HISTORY OF MASS COMMUNICATION, *supra* note 1, at 4:

> Ancient Egyptians found it in the Nile river delta, the reed called *papyrus*, growing 10 feet high along its banks. Workers split the reed into thin strips, placed one layer crosswise over another in close-set rows, hammered them gently for a couple of hours, and let them dry in the sun. A seashell or piece of ivory was used to smooth the resulting sheets. The product of this effort weighed little, but lasted for years. Glue fastened the sheets end to end to make a scroll. It could be rolled up for convenient transport and storage. Scribes could fasten the papyrus sheets to form a single piece 30 feet or more in length, which they rolled around a cylinder of wood, metal or ivory. Scribes also tied smaller sheets together by passing a string through holes along one margin, an early form of bookbinding.

See also Innis, *supra* note 14, at 23.

18. *See* Innis, *supra* note 14, at 23.

19. *Id.*, at 8:

> The gathering of knowledge in a way that might be characterized as an information revolution had its faint beginnings in the Hellenic world during the eighth century B.C., when the Phoenician alphabet took root in Aegean soil. It was the period after the Greek emergence out of the Dark Ages. Because of the alphabetic script and the availability of papyrus, the *Iliad* and the *Odyssey*, the epic poems of Homer, recalled and repeated orally for the previous four centuries by storytellers, were at last written down.

20. *Id.*, at 6 ("Papyrus had its limitations. Manuscripts ... eventually turned brittle and disintegrated.... A further limitation, papyrus came from one source, Egypt.").

21. *Id.*, at 6 ("The skin was scraped clean to remove the hairs, rubbed smooth with pumice stone, then dressed with chalk and lime. Ancient writers also used vellum, the thin and supple skin of unborn lambs or kids.").

22. *Id.*, at 7 & 20.

23. *Id.*, at 22.

and paper was not widely used in Europe prior to the development of the printing press.[24]

For centuries after writing became possible, communication methods remained painfully inefficient by modern standards, and both the powerful and the poor encountered significant difficulties in communicating with large numbers of people over long distances. There was no shortage of effort to develop more effective systems of communication. Some nations established "relay systems" that moved information more quickly.[25] For example, the ancient Greeks used "runners" to carry important news from place-to-place,[26] and also employed a torch system that allowed them to signal information between distant towers.[27] Some societies used flags and pennants to communicate,[28] and various groups (*e.g.*, the Scots, French and English) used fires to send messages.[29] During the Revolutionary War, Americans (and their French allies) used torches, flares and heavy guns.[30] In France, a mechanical system was developed

---

24. *Id.*, at 23 ("In any event, paper did not find wide use in Europe until printing was invented. Low literacy kept demand down. If paper made printing effective, it was printing that introduced paper to most Europeans.").

25. *See* Innis, *supra* note 14, at 23 ("Persians under Cyrus, Darius and Xerxes established relay stations of horses throughout the empire. They could not have been popular because the public was forbidden to use the service, yet nearby communities were forced to support each station with horses, food, and labor.").

26. *See* A History of Mass Communication, *supra* note 1, at 15 ("The most famous, we know, was the youth who ran so hard to carry the news of the victory at Marathon that he fell dead after delivering the message 'nike!'—'victory.'").

27. *See* Communication in History, *supra* note 1, at 118.

28. *See* Daniel Headrick, *The Optical Telegraph*, in Communication in History, *supra* note 1, at 119., at 123.

29. *See id.*, at 121, noting that various societies used fire to communicate information. The French, for one, had a fire-based system. So did the Scots and English: "Of the Scots, Geoffrey Wilson wrote: 'An Act of the Scottish parliament in 1455 laid down that on the approach of English invaders one bale or faggot could be set ablaze. Two on first would signify that the English were 'coming indeed' and four that they were in great force.' In 1588, when the Spanish Armada was sighted off the coast of Cornwall, fires relayed the news to the English fleet at Plymouth and to the rest of England." *Id.*

30. *Id.* ("And during the American Revolutionary War, General Lafayette used a variety of prearranged signals: shots from a heavy gun, flashes from torches or flares, even "the sun's rays, although no definite code for sending messages appears to have been in operation.").

that could convey messages from the south of France to Paris in less than four hours.[31] Some societies used carrier pigeons to convey information.[32]

Despite these inventions, for most of human history, ordinary people had limited avenues available to them for disseminating their ideas, or for engaging in political discourse.[33] Roman and Greek citizens, and their medieval counterparts throughout Europe, could speak to each other individually, and could communicate with larger audiences by giving speeches.[34] During medieval times, individuals often received information about the outside world orally from "itinerant monks, soldiers, peddlers, couriers, and the pardoners who traveled from town to town selling absolution from sin."[35] However, the information brought by outsiders was second, "third and fourth hand,"[36] with the accuracy problems attendant with distant oral communications.

From a mass communication standpoint, oral methods of communication had inherent limitations because even the loudest orators could only communicate with a relatively small number of people. Benjamin Franklin recounted the example of an eighteenth century evangelist orator (presumably, one with extremely powerful lungs) who Franklin calculated was able to project his voice to an audience as large as 30,000 people,[37] and

31. *Id.* (Describing a French system, "called the *Chappe telegraph*, messages of several sentences could be sent from the south of France to Paris in under four hours.").

32. *See* K.K. DuVivier, *Neuro-Linguistic Programming and Writing: A New Era of Communication—Part I*, 28-SEP. COLO. L. 45 (1999); Marianne D. Short & Jodene Pope, *History and Scope of the Press' Right of Access to Foreign Battlefields*, 41 NAVAL L. REV. 1, 4 n.22 (1993).

33. *See* Adrienne J. Marsh, *Fair Use and New Technology: The Appropriate Standards to Apply*, 5 CARDOZO L. REV. 635, 635 n.1 (1984) (concluding that Gutenberg's invention of the printing press "brought books and the written word to the masses."); Richard J. Zecchino, *Could the Framers Ever Have Imagined? A Discussion on the First Amendment and the Internet*, 1999 L. REV. MICH. ST. U. DET. C. L 981, 983.

34. *See* David J. Pfeffer, *Depriving America of Evolving Its Own Standards of Decency? An Analysis of the Use of Foreign Law in Eighth Amendment Jurisprudence and Its Effect on Democracy*, 51 ST. LOUIS U.L.J. 855, 865 (2007) ("In the Hellenic democracy, free citizens engaged directly with one another in the public sphere to better achieve an understanding of truth in the community.").

35. *See* A HISTORY OF MASS COMMUNICATION, *supra* note 1, at 19.

36. *Id.*

37. *See* H.W. Brands, The First American: The Life and Times of Benjamin Franklin 148 (2000) (hereafter THE LIFE AND TIMES OF BENJAMIN FRANKLIN):

he cited ancient reports that some Roman generals were able to address as many as 25,000 troops at one time.[38] Nevertheless, few people had a voice adequate to make themselves heard by so many people, and most people reached far fewer people through oral communication methods.

B. THE MONASTIC TRADITION

From the demise of the Roman Empire until the invention of the printing press, most books produced in Europe were handwritten.[39] As a result, for "nearly a thousand years, from the fall of Rome" the "monasteries kept the sputtering flame of knowledge alive and continued to produce handwritten manuscripts."[40] Monks, hunched over their scriptorium desktops, painstakingly hand lettered and painted manuscripts magnificently to produce books for libraries and cathedrals."[41] For the monks, the work was spiritually satisfying because they felt that the work brought them

---

> One evening he [George Whitefield] spoke from the top of the steps of the Philadelphia courthouse, in the middle of Market Street on the west side of Second [in Philadelphia].... "I had the curiosity to learn how far he could be heard," Franklin wrote. Franklin was already at the rear of the crowd; he walked slowly back in the direction of the river. He could hear Whitefield's "loud and clear voice" distinctly until he came to Front Street, where some street noise obscured it. Taking the distance from Front Street to Second as radius, he mentally constructed a semi-circle and filled it with listeners, allowing two square feet to each. In this way, he calculated that Whitefield might be heard by an audience of more than thirty thousand.

38. *Id.* ("'This [the story recounted in the prior footnote] reconciled me to the newspaper accounts of his [George Whitefield] having preached to 25,000 people in the fields, and to the ancient histories of generals haranguing whole armies, of which I had sometimes doubted.'").

39. *See* A History of Mass Communication, *supra* note 1, at 24; *see also Id.*, at 7 ("In Europe, now began centuries of monastic responsibility for knowledge and information. As monasteries were built in Europe during the dark ages of western civilization, monks, chiefly Benedictines, took up the profession of scribe. Among their tasks, they were charged with the duty of transcribing the crumbling old papyrus manuscripts in the libraries onto fresh parchment that was prepared in or near the monastery. To be a scribe was no longer a mean calling. It was to do the work of God.").

40. *See* Nicholas Wade, *In Dusty Archives, A Theory of Affluence, The New York Times*, at F1 (Aug. 7, 2007) (reviewing Gregory Clark, A Farewell to Alms: A Brief Economic History of the World (2008).

41. *See* A History of Mass Communication, *supra* note 1, at 24.

closer to God.[42] Since monks usually wrote in Latin, and focused on copying religious texts, their works were not widely accessible by the masses who did not speak or read Latin.[43] Moreover, rather than creating original content, monks generally copied existing religious scripts.[44]

Before Johannes Gutenberg's development of the printing press, most written manuscripts were created by hand, a process that was extremely slow.[45] Moreover, most people in the Middle Ages were unable to write. Since only a small number of people, usually monks,[46] were literate enough and able to devote the time needed to create manuscripts, much less, multiple copies of manuscripts,[47] "the monasteries and other ecclesiastical establishments associated with them ... enjoyed an almost complete monopoly of book production and so of book culture."[48]

During this period, the absence of books was less critical because most people were illiterate. Indeed, in the middle ages, even many nobles and some kings, including the Emperor Charlemagne,[49] could not read or write.[50] Ordinary people were often consumed with the task of mak-

---

42. *Book Curses*, Virginia Commonwealth Univ. Libraries, http://www.library.vcu.edu/preservation/curse.html.

43. *Id.*, at 22–23; *see also See* Rogelio Lasso, *From the Paper Chase to the Digital Chase: Technology and the Challenge of Teaching 21st Century Law Students*, 43 Santa Clara L. Rev. 1, 4 n.2 (2002).

44. *See* Lasso, *supra* note 43, at 4 n.2; Peter K. Yu, *Of Monks, Medieval Scribes and Middlemen*, 2006 Mich. St. L. Rev. 1, 7.

45. *See* Lasso, *supra* note 43, at 4 n.2 (noting that, prior to development of the printing press, printed documents were handwritten by monks who functioned as scribes); Yu, *supra* note 44, at 7 ("Notwithstanding the Church's active participation, the production of knowledge remained parochial. The copying of books was also slow, tedious, and very time- consuming; it took years for a scribe to complete "a particularly fine manuscript with colored initials and miniature art work.").

46. *See* Katie Lula, *Neither Here Nor There But Fair: Finding an International Copyright Legal System Between East and West, Past and Present*, 8 Asian-Pac. L. & Policy J. 96, 101 (2006); Jay H. Perlman & Lawrence T. Greenberg, *The Internet Reformation: Gutenberg and Martin Luther on Wall Street*, 4 Wall Street Lawyer 9 (2000).

47. *Id.*

48. *See* Febvre & Martin, *supra* note 1, at 15.

49. *See* A History of Mass Communication, *supra* note 1, at 20.

50. *Id.*, at 19 ("Most nobles, even kings, could neither read nor write. Medieval bishops encouraged civil illiteracy. The Bible could not be translated into the vernacular, and only the clergy could possess copies, in Latin.").

ing a living,[51] and providing themselves and their families with adequate food, clothing and shelter, and rarely could devote the time necessary to create (or, for that matter, read) written works even had they been literate.[52] Despite the creation of the printing press, and the rise of secular printers, Monks continued writing manuscripts until well into the sixteenth century.[53]

C. THE SPREAD OF BOOKS

Despite the absence of sophisticated reproduction technologies, intellectual life was beginning to spread well beyond the walls of monasteries by the thirteenth century as universities came into being (Bologna (1088), Salamanca (1134), Paris (by 1150), and Oxford (by 1167)), and started producing their own manuscripts and books[54] about diverse subject such as law, medicine, theology, and the arts.[55]

At this point in history, university books were also handwritten,[56] often by artisans or craftsmen,[57] but differed from monastic texts because of their focus on secular subjects (*e.g.*, course texts, reference books and commentaries) rather than religion.[58] Since books were not readily available for purchase, universities started hiring scribes to create copies by hand,[59] and some richer university students hired scribes to produce copies of important books for them.[60] In Paris, secular scribes reproduced

---

51. *See* Wade, *supra note* 40.

52. *See id.* ("For thousands of years, most people lived in abject poverty, first as hunters and gatherers, then as peasants or laborers. But with the Industrial Revolutions, some societies traded this ancient poverty for amazing affluence.").

53. *See* Febvre & Martin, *supra* note 1, at 18–19.

54. *See id.*, at 19.

55. INCUNABULA, Library of Congress, https://www.loc.gov/ghe/cascade/index.html?appid=580edae150234258a49a3eeb58d9121c

56. *See* A HISTORY OF MASS COMMUNICATION, *supra* note 1, at 24–25 ("Inevitably, errors crept into the copied and recopied books. Not until Gutenberg were books consistent from volume to volume." Their works were written by "secular copyists known as *scriveners*. . . .").

57. *See* Febvre & Martin, *supra* note 1, at 19.

58. *See* A HISTORY OF MASS COMMUNICATION, *supra* note 1, at 9–10.

59. *See* Febvre & Martin, *supra* note 1, at 19.

60. *See id.* at 19.

works by classical authors in "pure Latin prose style."[61] By this time, books were also being produced for recreational reading with a focus on popular and recreational literature.[62] While many of these books were very expensive,[63] others were inexpensive because writers began using a tracing technique that allowed them to create multiple copies at once.[64] Today, more than 2,000 copies of Aristotle's works remain that were created in the thirteenth and fourteenth centuries.[65]

As cities grew bigger and wealthier, and more and more universities were founded, and as literacy increased, so did the private demand for books.[66] Eventually, booksellers and libraries came into being,[67] and secular book producers gradually became more important, copying and decorating books.[68] Indeed, some churches even began employing secular workers,[69] who functioned as scribes (copiers) rather than creators of original content.[70] Since they were "mere laborers," they "received little

---

61. *See id.* at 21–22.

62. *See id.* at 22–27.

63. *See* Carlo M. Cipolla, Before the Industrial Revolution: European Society and Economy 1000–1700 148 (3rd ed. 1973) ("Before [Gutenbeg] books were so expensive that only a few wealthy people could afford to buy them. In Spain in around 800, a book cost about as much as two cows.").

64. *See* Febvre & Martin, *supra* note 1, at 27 ("The supreme luxury article, a work of art in itself, designed for admiration rather than use—like the sumptuous books belonging to the Duc de Berry, the greatest bibliophile of his day—too months if not years of work and cost a fortune. But many other books were also being turned out ... which were within reach of clients of modest means.").

65. *See id.* at 22.

66. *See* A History of Mass Communication, *supra* note 1, at 9–10.

67. *See* Febvre & Martin, *supra* note 1, at 20–21.

68. *See* A History of Mass Communication, *supra* note 1, at 9–10 ("With the changing lifestyle and the emergence of new educational institutions, it became more and more common for people to want to own books themselves, whether students seeking textbooks or noble women desiring to own beautifully illuminated Psalters. By 1200 there is quite good evidence of secular workshops writing and decorating manuscripts for sale to the laity. By 1250 there were certainly bookshops in the big university and commercial towns, arranging the writing out of new manuscripts and trading in second-hand copies. By 1300 it must have been exceptional for a monastery to make its own manuscripts: usually, monks bought their books from shops like anyone else, although this is not quite true of the Carthusians or of some religious communities in the Netherlands.").

69. *See id.*

70. *See id.*, at 10 ("[Mediaeval scribes continued to be treated as mere laborers, rather than content creators or knowledge producers. Worse still, they 'received little pay for

pay for [their] work"; sometimes working as many as three days per week to earn the amount that a common foot-soldier might earn in a day.[71] Over time, universities developed rules regulating the work of the copyists, which were designed to establish "minimum requirements of formal presentation and substantial correctness, and to prescribe the selling price of duly certified copies."[72]

The spread of books was enhanced by advances in the development of paper.[73] Although paper was not introduced in Europe until the eleventh century, it was widely used in subsequent centuries and virtually replaced parchment by the fourteenth century.[74] Paper was lighter which meant that parchment books were heavier, and more expensive to produce.[75] Medieval paper was not perfect because it "was more fragile than parchment, had a rougher surface, and was less impervious to ink and less amenable to the pigments used by the illuminators."[76] However, paper was less costly than parchment and began being produced in much greater quantities.[77] Plus, paper was more efficient than parchment since the latter was created from animal skin, and a significant size book could require a substantial number of animal skins.[78]

Because hand written production processes were so slow, it could take years to create a single book, and many decades to create a relatively modest number of books,[79] with most books being religious rather than political in nature.[80] When Gutenberg created the printing press in the mid-1500s, the total number of books numbered in the thousands,[81]

[their] work'; '[t]he average scribe in the later Middle Ages [for example] had to work three to seven days for the sum earned in one day by a common foot-soldier slogging through Scotland in King Edward's army.'").

71. *See id.*

72. *See id.*

73. *See* Febvre & Martin, *supra* note 1, at 30–32.

74. *See id.*

75. *See id.*

76. *Id.*

77. *Id.* at 17.

78. *Id.* at 18 (calculating that each volume of the Gutenberg Bible that was printed on vellum required 1,000 animal skins).

79. *See* Yu, *supra* note 43, at 7.

80. *See Id.*

81. *See* Incunabula, *supra* note 55.

and individual libraries had very limited collections of books. For example, in 1050, Exeter Cathedral had only five books in its entire library.[82] Although Exeter's Bishop established a group of skilled workers to create more books, they managed to produce only sixty-six books over the next twenty-two years.[83] Similarly, Cambridge University library "had a remarkable collection of 122 books in 1424."[84]

Even though books were spreading, they remained the reserve of the wealthy. The masses were still not literate, and generally could not afford books. As a result, even though book publishing became much more common, ordinary people saw little improvement in their ability to communicate with each other, to choose the works that were created, or their ability to propagate ideas.[85]

---

82. Yu, *supra* note 44, at 7.

83. *Id.*

84. *Id.*

85. *See Id.*, at 9–10 ("'Monastic libraries [soon] found it more and more difficult to keep their collections up to date, and they began employing secular scribes and illuminators to collaborate in book production.' Meanwhile, schools became independent from cathedrals, to which they were originally attached, and guilds of lecturers and students gathered to form universities.").

CHAPTER II

THE GUTENBERG REVOLUTION

The first revolutionary breakthrough in communications technology occurred in the fifteenth century when Johannes Gutenberg developed the printing press.[1] Gutenberg's invention was preceded by the development of primitive printing presses in China, centuries earlier.[2] However, the early Chinese presses were primitive and required the printer to laboriously engrave a block of wood.[3] Once the block was engraved, the printer could use it to create multiple copies of documents. By the fourteenth century, Europeans were using similar engraving techniques to create similar "block books."[4] Most of these books were religious in

---

1. *See* David Crowley & Paul Heyer, Communication in History: Technology, Culture, Society 82 (5th ed. 2007) (noting that some commentators believe that printing "was the major cultural/technological transformation in the history of the West," and that "printing, along with numerous other developments, marked the transition between the end of the Middle Ages and the dawn of the modern era.").

2. *See* Charles T. Meadow, Making Connections: Communication Through the Ages 64–65 (2002) ("Johannes Gutenberg did not invent the printing press. Nor was he the first to use movable type but he brought the movable-type printing press into existence in the western world. Printing of a sort, was known in China as far back as the seventh century C.E. This was printing from wood blocks into which reverse images of written ideographs were carved.... It is something like using a large rubber stamp.").

3. *See* Irving Fang, A History of Mass Communication: Six Information Revolutions 26 (1997).

4. *Id.* ("Xylographic printing, which impressed an entire page from an engraved block of wood, preceded movable type. Sheets of cloth or vellum or paper, printed on one side and folded over or bound back to back were assembled into 'block books.'"); *see also* Luc-

nature, involving sometimes elaborate pictures of legends, saints or biblical characters,[5] with text being inserted later by hand.[6]

A. GUTENBERG'S INVENTION

During Gutenberg's time, many Europeans were striving to develop a better printing press.[7] However, Gutenberg was the first European to succeed, and his idea involved the creation of movable type.[8] Essentially, Gutenberg forged lead pieces representing every letter of the alphabet, both lower-case and upper-case[9] from lead.[10] The task was complicated because he was forced to test different types of metals.[11] He undoubtedly profited from the fact that he had been a goldsmith with a working knowledge of metals.[12] Gutenberg was also forced to invent his own ink since existing inks were designed for printing on wood, and did not work well with metal.[13] Gutenberg's invention was preceded by the development of

---

IEN FEBVRE & HENRI-JEAN MARTIN, THE COMING OF THE BOOK: THE IMPACT OF PRINTING 1450–1800 46 (1976).

5. *See also* Febvre & Martin, *supra* note 4, at 46.

6. *See* A HISTORY OF MASS COMMUNICATION, *supra* note 3, at 26.

7. *See also* Febvre & Martin, *supra* note 4, at 52–54.

8. *See id.*, at 29.

9. *See* A HISTORY OF MASS COMMUNICATION, *supra* note 3, at 40 ("The early cases in which printers kept their type were divided horizontally, with the capital letters stored in the upper case and the small letters in the lower case.").

10. *See* CONNECTIONS: COMMUNICATION THROUGH THE AGES, *supra* note 2, at 65 (2002) ("The plan was to design and make a piece of type for each character to be printed. These had to be of the same height, to a fine tolerance.").

11. *See also* Febvre & Martin, *supra* note 4, at 57:

> To begin with, there was the problem of making type sorts. Not only did the printer need a foolproof method of making them with the aid of punches and molds, but he had to find metals and alloys tough enough not to damage the punch when struck, and a matrix that would not melt when the alloy was in the fluid state and on the point of fusion. It was vital, too, that the alloy-produced characters should accept ink and not quickly wear out with use.... The letters themselves present similar problems. Did the invertors immediately hit upon an alloy tough enough not to wear out quickly?

12. *See id.*, at 50–51.

13. *See* COMMUNICATION THROUGH THE AGES, *supra* note 2, at 65.

movable type in Korea.[14] Although scholars debate the issue, there is no indication that he was aware of the Korean invention.[15]

Once Gutenberg created movable type, he then created special cases that separated the lower-case letters from the upper-case letters.[16] He then used the lead type to "compose" pages by arranging a line of type in a "composing stick" and inserting the composed type into wooden boxes the size of a printed page, thereby laying-out full pages that were ready to be printed.[17] Once a page was composed, Gutenberg would apply ink to the letters, place a paper over the top, and slowly crank the press down onto the paper in order to make an impression on the paper.[18] Gutenberg would then crank the press back up, remove the paper, and hang it up to dry. By repeating this process multiple times, he could create multiple copies of a single page.

Even though the Gutenberg press was slow by modern standards, the invention represented a dramatic advance in communications technology. Rather than being forced to laboriously carve a block of wood (which could then be used to print multiple copies of the carved work), but which usually did not contain written words, or laboriously handwrite each page of a book, Gutenberg's invention allowed printers to type set a page, thereby enabling them to much more quickly produce multiple copies of writings, and by allowing them to print posters, newspapers, and books in their own languages.[19] Using this process, Gutenberg could create a newspaper or book by repeating this process for subsequent pages, and then assembling the completed pages, and (for books) binding them.[20] Printers

---

14. *See id.*, at 65 ("A form of movable type was developed in Korea in the late fourteenth century CE, but there is no indication that Gutenberg did not conceive of movable type on his own.").

15. *See* A HISTORY OF MASS COMMUNICATION, *supra* note 3, at 64–65.

16. *See id.*, at 40 ("The early cases in which printers kept their type were divided horizontally, with the capital letters stored in the upper case and the small letters in the lower case.").

17. *See* Febvre & Martin, *supra* note 4, at 61; *see also* Peter Linzer, *From the Gutenberg Bible to Net Neutrality—How Technology Makes Law and Why English Majors Need to Understand It*, 39 MCGEORGE L. REV. 1, 4–5 (2008).

18. *See id.*, at 64.

19. *See* A HISTORY OF MASS COMMUNICATION, *supra* note 3, at 40.

20. *See* Febvre & Martin, *supra* note 4, at 104 (suggesting that Medieval bindings were superior to modern bindings).

were constricted only by the fact that they had only a limited quantity of type at their disposal, and therefore could not lay out more than a few dozen pages at a time.[21]

The absence of high literacy rates meant that it did not matter quite so much that society lacked sophisticated technologies for reproducing documents. Moreover, even if ordinary citizens had succeeded in creating multiple copies of a document, they would have faced nearly insurmountable barriers in trying to mass distribute them. There were no mass distribution networks like those used by modern newspapers. Although a postal service eventually developed, it was costly to send even a single letter, much less a book (or multiple copies of newspapers or books).[22] Of course, individuals could create posters, and place them in public squares all over a country, but that tactic also required great effort. In order to place posters in public squares, someone had to physically carry the posters to each city or village and hand post them. As a result, posters did not become commonplace until much later.

B. THE PRINTING PRESS'S IMPACT ON SOCIETY

Despite the fact that the Gutenberg press was relatively slow by modern standards, and despite the distribution problems, Gutenberg's invention was revolutionary,[23] and had an extraordinary impact on society.[24] Not only did the printing press allow printers to more quickly create books, newspapers, fliers, pamphlets and other documents, it allowed them to do so in their own languages.[25] The ability to create books was no longer

---

21. *See* H.W. BRANDS, THE FIRST AMERICAN: THE LIFE AND TIMES OF BENJAMIN FRANKLIN 20 (2000) (hereafter THE LIFE AND TIMES OF BENJAMIN FRANKLIN).

22. Peter K. Yu, *Of Monks, Medieval Scribes and Middlemen*, 2006 MICH. ST. L. REV. 1, 29.

23. *See* A HISTORY OF MASS COMMUNICATION, *supra* note 3, at 64–65.

24. *See* Febvre & Martin, *supra* note 4, at 105.

25. *See* Rogelio Lasso, *From the Paper Chase to the Digital Chase: Technology and the Challenge of Teaching 21st Century Law Students*, 43 SANTA CLARA L. REV. 1, 4 n.2 (2002):

> Before the invention of the printing press, works of literature had to be reproduced by hand, and thus were not readily available. The lack of accessible literature was one factor that contributed to extremely low literacy rates in Europe at the time. Additionally, the books that were in print, most notably the Bible, were written in Latin—a language that the majority of society could neither read nor

the sole province of monks and university scribes,[26] and printing presses rapidly spread across Europe,[27] becoming relatively commonplace.[28] Encouraged by the support of wealthy individuals, ecclesiastics and businessmen,[29] printing presses could be found in more than one hundred cities by the year 1480.[30] By 1482, Venice had become the virtual capital of printing, producing 156 book editions in a two year period.[31] Overall, during the first half century of its existence, the Gutenberg press led to

---

understand. As a result, large segments of the population had to rely upon those who could read Latin, such as the Roman Catholic clergy, to interpret the Bible for them and communicate the meaning of God's word. The end result was that the priestly class exercised a great deal of power over many individuals' religious beliefs and practices.

Johannes Gutenberg's invention of metal movable type in the mid-fifteenth century made the printing press possible, which in turn caused books and other written materials to become widely available for the first time. More importantly, the literature that was mass-produced was printed in languages that more people could read and understand—a trend that fueled literacy. As literacy increased, so too did individuals' ability to determine for themselves the word of God, thus forever changing the relationship between churches and their flocks. Indeed, salvation could become an individual's own responsibility.

26. *See* Febvre & Martin, *supra* note 4, at 105.

27. *See id.*, at 167–215.

28. *Id.* at 181:

> It may appear to the 20th century reader, accustomed to technical revolutions, that printing spread very slowly. Yet when we think of the innumerable problems posed for the 15th century by slow communications and a rudimentary technology; when we consider that in the years between 1450 and 1460 only a handful of men based in a few workshops in Mainz were acquainted with the secrets of printing, itself a craft of considerable technical sophistication by contemporary standards; when we remember the multiple difficulties that those who established new workshops had to overcome if they were to gather together the necessary raw materials (to take but one example—steel for the punch, copper for the moulds, a mixture of lead and of tin for the type); when we take into account the shortage of technicians, of engravers for the punch, of type founders and of compositors—then it becomes evident that the spread of printing was far from slow.

29. *Id.* at 167–180.

30. *Id.* at 182; *see also* Carlo M. Cipolla, Before the Industrial Revolution: European Society and Economy 1000–1700 148–149 (3rd ed. 1973).

31. *See* Febvre & Martin, *supra* note 4, at 182–183.

the creation of some 1,821 book editions, with total production of 15 to 20 million copies.[32]

Although Gutenberg himself went bankrupt,[33] and even though it took decades for press owners to figure out how to profit from his device,[34] the Gutenberg press is widely regarded as "the major cultural/technological transformation in the history of the West," and it "marked the transition between the end of the Middle Ages and the dawn of the modern era."[35] Indeed, "the printed book was something more than a triumph of technical ingenuity"; it was "one of the most potent agents of change in western civilization because it brought "together the scattered ideas of representative thinkers."[36]

Even though only a small quantity of books existed prior to 1450, the printing press led to a dramatic increase in the quantity of books.[37] The Gutenberg press spread rapidly across European states—with each major state having at least one printing press, and many having several by the 1490s.[38] As a result, the number of books increased dramatically,[39] and the cost of books decreased as well.[40]

The printing press transformed society by enabling mass communication by people other than monks, governmental officials and universities, who previously had a monopoly on the creation of written works,[41] as well as because it gave private individuals the chance to control the means of communication. As one commentator observed, the "introduction of

---

32. *Id.* at 186.

33. *See* Robert Pinsky, *Start the Presses: A Revisionist History of the First 150 Years of the Age of Print, The New York Times Book Review*, at 15 (Aug. 15, 2010).

34. *Id.*

35. See COMMUNICATION IN HISTORY, *supra* note 1, at 82.

36. *See* Febvre & Martin, *supra* note 4, at 10.

37. Yu, *supra* note 22, at 7.

38. *See id.*, at 11 .

39. *See* Michael Brandon Lopez, *Creating the National Wealth: Authorship, Copyright and Literacy Contracts*, 88 N. DAKOTA L. REV. 161, 168 (2012).

40. *See id.*, at 168.

41. *See* Richard J. Zecchino, *Could the Framers Ever Have Imagined? A Discussion on the First Amendment and the Internet*, 1999 L. REV. MICH. ST. U. DET. C. L 981, 983 ("The introduction of the printing press by Gutenberg in the fifteenth century marked a new era. For the first time in history, reproducing the printed word became a thing of ease and, as a consequence, books and newspapers soon began to flourish").

movable type marked a new era."[42] Just "as the full-rigged ship opened up vast new geographical horizons to the Europeans, so the press with movable characters opened up vast new horizons and opportunities in the fields of knowledge and education."[43]

As the printing press spread beyond Germany to other countries, it profoundly influenced society.[44] Although handwritten books did not quickly disappear, printed works assumed an increasingly important role,[45] even though some regarded printed works as "vulgar" in comparison to hand-written works.[46] Nevertheless, by 1499, some 2,500 European cities had printing presses,[47] and the quantity of books (and other printed media) had risen dramatically to some 15 million books, representing thirty thousand book titles,[48] and the printing press had also spread to the Far East[49] and Eastern Europe,[50] with some 20 million books being printed between 1450 and 1500;[51] an extraordinary number given that there were only 100 million inhabitants in Europe at the time.[52] Some 30,000 to 35,000 of the editions that were printed between 1450 and 1500 survive to this day, representing some 10,000 to 15,000 different texts.[53]

42. *See* Cipolla, *supra* note 30, at 148.

43. *Id.*

44. *See* Yu, *supra* note 22, at 11 ("Shortly after the invention, the technology of the printing press was spread quickly throughout Europe. '[B]y the 1490s each of the major states had one important publishing centre and some had several.'").

45. *See id.*, at 12.

46. *See id.*, at 13.

47. *See* Joseph Karl Grant, *Shattering and Moving Beyond the Gutenberg Paradigm: The Dawn of the Electronic Will*, 42 U. Mich. J. L. Reform 105, 111–112 (2008).

48. *See id.*

49. *See* Febvre & Martin, *supra* note 4, at 212–215.

50. *Id.*, at 198–207.

51. *Id.*

52. *Id.*, at 249.

53. *Id.*, at 248.

C. THE IMPACT OF PRINTING

The Gutenberg printing press led to a flowering of information and knowledge among the citizenry,[54] and to the development of a new type of intellectual.[55] Over time, the nature of books expanded from primarily religious to a variety of subjects.[56] The change did not happen immediately. Early books and texts were reproductions of existing (mainly religious) works.[57] Indeed, Gutenberg is particularly well known for printing the Gutenberg Bible, but "texts on the new science and philosophy would soon become a major aspect of the printing industry."[58] Although 77% of books published between 1450 and 1500 were written in Latin, and 45% of those dealt with primarily religious subjects,[59] 30% of the remaining books were devoted to literature, 10% to law, and 10% to scientific subjects.[60]

Over time, the printing press began to alter the "entire fabric of society," "encourag[ing] literacy" and "broaden[ing] knowledge,"[61] as it knitted together "the scattered ideas of representative thinkers" by "transmitting results from one researcher to another."[62] The printing press was impactful because it promoted a "world of ideas by making knowledge widely available and creating a space in which new forms of expression could flour-

54. *See* Febvre & Martin, *supra* note 4, at 66 ("[The] spread of books in Gutenberg's day was astonishing for the times. The world has never been the same since and probably never will be again.").

55. *See* Communication in History, *supra* note 1, at 83 (noting that "printing brought forth a new class of intellectuals, so-called men of letters. Previously those who produced knowledge worked under the auspices of the Church or acquired a patron from the nobility or wealthy merchant class. The printer became a new kind of patron, one linked to a growing market economy. As a result the nature of texts changed.").

56. *Id.*

57. *Id.*

58. *Id.*

59. *Id.*, at 249.

60. *Id.*, at 249.

61. *See* A History of Mass Communication, *supra* note 3, at 46 ("After 1800, swiftly changing technology in the printing industry helped to alter the entire fabric of society. Religion on both sides of the Atlantic had been the major impulse to teach men and some women to read, but printing further encouraged literacy, broadened knowledge, and involved ordinary people in public affairs to a greater extent than ever before.").

62. *See* Febvre & Martin, *supra* note 4, at 10.

ish."[63] Ultimately, the printing press is credited with contributing to the Renaissance, the Scientific Revolution, and the Protestant Reformation.[64]

1. THE PRINTING PRESS AND THE PROTESTANT REFORMATION

The Protestant Reformation involved a direct challenge to the Roman Catholic church which, alongside monarchy, was one of the two dominant institutions in medieval Europe.[65] The Reformation began on October 31, 1517, when Martin Luther nailed a one-page document with grievances to the door of the Castle Church in Wittenberg, Germany.[66] Although some of the attacks against the church involved oral communications,[67] or visual depictions such as woodcuts and copper plates,[68] the printing press played a crucial role in that it led to the creation of books[69] that "unleashed the strongest passions," led to "a propaganda campaign con-

---

63. *See* COMMUNICATION IN HISTORY, *supra* note 1, at 82.

64. *See* Lasso, *supra* note 25, at 4 n.2 ("Printing changed every aspect of the human condition—from thinking, learning, and language, to science, religion, and government." "The 17th century became known as 'the century of genius' in large part due to the explosion of creativity and new ideas fueled by printing. Creativity is often the result of a combination of intellectual activities. For example, reading two books on separate topics and combining their themes in one mind produces a creative interaction. Increased output of printed works led first to the combination of old ideas, and later to the creation of entirely new systems of thought."); George Paul & Jason Baron, *Information Inflation: Can the Legal System Adapt?*, 13 RICH. J. L. & TECH. 1, 8 (2007) ("There has been only one transformative advance in the original writing technology. Circa 1450 Johannes Gutenberg invented the movable type printing press, which dramatically lowered the cost of producing written records. The printing press allowed mass production of information and thus contributed to the Renaissance, the Scientific Revolution, and the Protestant Reformation.").

65. *See* COMMUNICATION IN HISTORY, *supra* note 1, at 82 (noting the Catholic Church's prior "monopoly on written communication.").

66. *See* Richard J. Evans, *The Monk Who Shook the World: A Pugnacious Wit and the New Technology of Print Made Luther One of History's First Media Stars, The Wall Street Journal* C5 (April 1–2, 2017) (reviewing LYNDAL ROPER, MARTIN LUTHER (2017)).

67. *See* Harvey J. Graff, *Early Modern Languages*, in COMMUNICATION IN HISTORY, *supra* note 1, at 106 ("The ideas of the Reformation were spread through various channels. One way was through personal contact. Luther and his supporters were responsible for some of the diffusion, but more significant were itinerant middlemen—preachers, salesmen, and journeymen.

68. *See id.*

69. *See id.* ("The message was also disseminated through print and writing—the distribution of books, manuscripts, pictures, personal letters, and songs.").

ducted through the medium of the press,[70] and revealed the press' ability to "influence thought and mold public opinion."[71]

Followers of Martin Luther used the printing press with "great skill," and their printings took a number of different forms.[72] Some translated Luther's handwritten theses into German, and reproduced and circulated them in a format that allowed book distributors to distribute them to a broad audience.[73] Others created posters to advertise reformation events,[74] or printed pamphlets that caricatured the church fathers and monks.[75]

German printing presses churned out numerous publications related to the Reformation.[76] After Luther posted his attack on indulgences in 1517,[77] printers reproduced his writings in "flysheets" that were distributed throughout Germany.[78] Luther's "Sermon on Indulgences and Grace" went through 25 printings, and his works were responsible for 20% of all publications in Germany between 1500 and 1530.[79] Of some 70 German printers, at least 45 worked for Luther, including all of the printers in Wittenberg, 6 of 8 printers in Strasbourg, and 9 out of 12 in Augsburg.[80] As Reformation publications made their way into the countryside, they were

---

70. *See* Febvre & Martin, *supra* note 4, at 288.

71. *Id.*

72. *Id.*

73. *See* Febvre & Martin, *supra* note 4, at 192 ("Large numbers of printing firms published Luther in hundreds of thousands of copies; his translations, sermons, polemics were pirated and reprinted in the towns supporting the Reformation. German presses from this time concentrated on producing cheap pamphlets and propaganda tracts in the vernacular, a literature of revolt spread far and wide by pedlars."); Graff, *supra* note 67, at 105 ("Luther's own writings were in demand, and he and his colleagues produced more and more literature in the vernacular, hoping to reach the widest audience possible. In support and response came pamphlets caricaturing the church fathers and monks. More important, the number of books printed in Germany rose quickly. The presses of Germany were kept busy with the business of the Reformation until well past mid-century.").

74. *Id.* at 289 ("Before every big event in the Reformation there was a poster to advertise it, a poster which served to give the event general importance.").

75. *Id.*

76. *Id.*

77. *Id.*

78. *Id.* at 289–290.

79. *See* Evans, *supra* note 66, at C-5.

80. *See* Febvre & Martin, *supra* note 4, at 292.

credited with stimulating the Peasants Revolt.[81] Luther also translated the Bible into German so that it was accessible by ordinary people.[82]

2. THE PRINTING PRESS AND THE AMERICAN REVOLUTION

The printing press also played an important role in the American Revolution, as well as in the drafting of the U.S. Constitution. The first printing office was opened in the British Colonies in the Americas by 1638; only twenty years after the Pilgrims founded the Massachusetts Bay Colony.[83] Although print shops were "few and far between" in the Americas in the seventeenth century, shops were established in Boston, New York, Maryland and Virginia by the end of that century.[84] However, printing did not really take off in the colonies until the advent of newspapers.[85] Between 1691 and 1820, more than 2,120 newspapers were published in thirty colonies and states, and 461 of these newspapers lasted for more than ten years."[86] The number of newspapers increased dramatically in the eighteenth century.[87] American newspapers were supplemented by books that were shipped from England, and this was a period of substantial political ferment in Europe.[88]

At the time of the American Revolution, most European countries were ruled by monarchs some of whom claimed (or had claimed) to rule by Divine Right—the idea that kings were placed on their thrones by God, and were carrying out God's will on earth. Influenced by European philosophers, writers were beginning to challenge the notion of Divine Right. Thomas Paine, who was British born, but who was in the American colonies during the Revolution, expressed serious reservations regarding the British monarchy's claim to rule by Divine Right: "no man in his senses can say that their claim (the British monarchs' claim to the throne) under William the Conqueror is a very honorable one. A French bastard

81. *Id.* at 293.
82. *Id.* at 294.
83. *See id.*, at 209.
84. *Id.* at 210.
85. *Id.* at 210–211.
86. *Id.* at 211.
87. *Id.*
88. *Id.* at 210.

landing with an armed bandetti, and establishing himself king of England against the consent of the natives, is in plain terms a very paltry rascally original—It certainly hath no divinity in it."[89]

European political thought powerfully influenced American thinkers. In the U.S. Declaration of Independence, Thomas Jefferson (the principal drafter) articulated an entirely different vision of people and their relationship to government, decreeing that "Governments are instituted among Men, deriving their just powers from the consent of the governed."[90] Jefferson implicitly rejected Divine Right by declaring that Americans had the right to break away from England, because of alleged grievances against the English King, and to establish their own form of government.[91] It is tempting to view the Declaration as a novel document, that sprang full-blown from the genius of Jefferson[92] and his collaborators.[93] The likely explanation for the document's contents, even though legend has it that Jefferson consulted no book or pamphlet in drafting the Declaration,[94] is that the contents were indirectly attributable to Gutenberg's invention of the printing press. Books from the European Enlightenment crossed the Atlantic Ocean,[95] were read by Thomas Jefferson, and influenced his drafting of the Declaration.[96] As one commentator noted:

---

89. *See* Thomas Paine, Common Sense 13–14 (1776) (Dover ed. 1997).

90. U.S. Declaration of Independence (July 4, 1776).

91. *Id.*

92. *See* Dumas Malone, Jefferson: The Virginian 221 (1948) ("Jefferson was asked to draft it . . . [H]e appears to have submitted his draft first to Adams and then to the ailing Franklin. . . .").

93. *See* John D. Bessler, The Celebrated Marquis: An Italian Noble and the Making of the Modern World 197 (Carolina Academic Press 2018) ("On June 11, 1776, the Continental Congress had appointed a committee of five men—John Adams of Massachusetts, Benjamin Franklin of Pennsylvania, Thomas Jefferson of Virginia, Robert R. Livingston of New York, and Robert Sherman of Connecticut—to draft a declaration of independence."). However, Jefferson was the primary drafter. *Id.* at 219 (stating that Jefferson "was the primary drafter of the landscape-changing Declaration of Independence."); Malone, *supra* note 92, at 219.

94. *See* Malone, *supra* note 92, at 220.

95. *See* Febvre & Martin, *supra* note 4, at 222 ("There were only two forms of transport available, boat and wagon, so that books risked being ruined by the seawater at the bottom of a ship's hold or by rainwater in a carrier during bad weather.").

96. *See* Bessler, *supra* note 93, at 197 ("Except for Dr. Franklin, all of the members of the committee [to draft the Declaration of Independence] were lawyers, and all five—as highly educated men—were familiar with Enlightenment texts. . . .").

> Despite the efforts that have been made to discount the "glittering generalities" of the European Enlightenment on eighteenth-century Americans, their influence remains, and is profoundly illustrated in the political literature. It is not simply that the great *virtuosi* of the American Enlightenment—Franklin, Adams, Jefferson—cited the classic Enlightenment texts and fought for the legal recognition of natural rights and for the elimination of institutions and practices associated with the ancien régime. They did so; but they were not alone. The ideas and writings of the leading secular thinkers of the European Enlightenment—reformers and social critics like Voltaire, Rousseau, and Beccaria as well as conservative analysts like Montesquieu—were quoted everywhere in the colonies, by everyone who claimed a broad awareness. In pamphlet after pamphlet the American writers cited Locke on natural rights and on the social and governmental contract, Montesquieu and later Delolme on the character of British liberty and on the institutional requirements for its attainment, Voltaire on the evils of clerical oppression, Beccaria on the reform of criminal law, Grotius, Pufendorf, Burlamaqui, and Vattel on the laws of nature and of nations, and on the principles of civil government.[97]

Thus, even though the Declaration was revolutionary for its time, Jefferson stood on the shoulders of European philosophers.[98] As even Jefferson said, he was not aiming at "originality of principle or sentiment" even

---

97. Bernard Bailyn, The Ideological Origins of the American Revolution 16–17 (1967) (he goes on to note that the "pervasiveness of such citations is at times astonishing.").

98. *See* Donald L. Doernberg, *"We the People": John Locke, Collective Constitutional Rights, and Standing to Challenge Government Action*, 73 Cal. L. Rev. 52, 57, 64–65 (1985) (concluding that it "would be difficult to overstate John Locke's influence on the American Revolution and the people who created the government that followed it."); David Konig, *Thomas Jefferson's Armed Citizenry and the Republican Militia*, 1 *Alb. Gov't. L. Rev.* 250, 262 (2008) (noting that "Jefferson followed Locke in justifying for the American colonies of 1776 the right of armed resistance."); Malone, *supra* note 92, at 175 ("If he did not draw on John Locke in the first place but got the ideas of that noted writer secondhand, he certainly had his very phraseology by heart in 1776.").

though the Declaration was not "copied from any particular and previous writing."[99]

European writings also influenced the structure of the U.S. government.[100] Even though the framers of the Declaration of Independence embraced the concept of democracy, as well as the idea that the power to govern is rooted in the "consent of the governed," many in the founding generation were highly distrustful of governmental power.[101] Illustrative were the views of Thomas Paine who argued that, "Society in every state is a blessing, but government even in its best state is but a necessary evil; in its worst state an intolerable one."[102]

In the United States, there may have been three separate and distinct reasons for this distrust of government. First, the new Americans were highly independent people, having emigrated from Europe to the colonies, many at a time when the voyage and the living were arduous and dangerous. Second, they had just revolted against the British empire, and claimed their independence, because of alleged abuses by the British monarch, and were wary about creating a powerful central government.[103] Third, many of the new Americans had emigrated to the American col-

---

99. Malone, *supra* note 92, at 220.

100. *See* Bessler, *supra* note 93, at 207 ("Early American political leaders read a lot of history and political philosophy and they were conversant in economics, literature and the literary arts. John Adams read many English writers—from John Locke (1632–1704) to Algernon Sidney (1623–1683) and from James Harrington (1611–1677) to Thomas Hobbes (1588–1679).").

101. *See* Ralph Ketcham, The Anti-Federalist Papers and the Constitutional Convention Debates: The Clashes and the Compromises That Gave Birth to our Form of Government at xv (1986) ("Uncertain that any government over so vast a domain as the United States could be controlled by the people, the anti-federalists saw in the enlarged powers of the central government only the familiar threats to the rights and liberties of the people.").

102. *See* Paine, *supra* note 89, at 3 (1776). In full, the quotation reads as follows:

> Society in every state is a blessing, but government even in its best state is but a necessary evil; in its worst state an intolerable one; for when we suffer, or are exposed to the same miseries by a *government*, which we might expect in a country *without government*, our calamity is heightened by reflecting that we furnish the means by which we suffer....

103. *See, e.g.*, U.S. Declaration of Independence (July 4, 1776) (listing grievances against the English King (although, in fact, some of the offenses had been committed by the British Parliament rather than the King)).

onies in order to escape religious persecution in Europe.[104] In particular, they were seeking to escape "established" religions that required everyone to support those religions, and aggressively persecuted those who tried to practice other religions.[105] Given this confluence of factors, it is hardly surprising that the people were distrustful of government.

Despite Jefferson's grand statements regarding the "consent of the governed" in the Declaration of Independence, the early Americans did not unequivocally embrace democracy; on the contrary, they sought to limit and constrain governmental power. The U.S. Constitution was written at a time when Europe was dominated by monarchies, and Americans were influenced by the philosophical writers of the time who detailed the risks that monarchies posed.[106] For example, Thomas Paine argued that monarchs become "poisoned by importance" and ultimately are "the most ignorant and unfit of any throughout the dominions."[107] He goes

---

104. *See Everson v. Board of Education*, 330 U.S. 1, 8–9 (1947):

> A large proportion of the early settlers of this country came here from Europe to escape the bondage of laws which compelled them to support and attend government favored churches. Catholics had persecuted Protestants, Protestants had persecuted Catholics, Protestant sects had persecuted other Protestant sects, Catholics of one shade of belief had persecuted Catholics of another shade of belief, and all of these had from time to time persecuted Jews. In efforts to force loyalty to whatever religious group happened to be on top and in league with the government of a particular time and place, men and women had been fined, cast in jail, cruelly tortured, and killed. Among the offenses for which these punishments had been inflicted were such things as speaking disrespectfully of the views of ministers of government-established churches, nonattendance at those churches, expressions of non belief in their doctrines, and failure to pay taxes and tithes to support them.

105. *Id.*

106. *See* Paine, *supra* note 89, at 8 ("But there is another and greater distinction for which no truly natural or religious reason can be assigned, and that is, the distinction of men into KINGS and SUBJECTS. Male and female are the distinctions of nature, good and bad the distinctions of heaven, but how a race of men came into the world so exalted above the rest, and distinguished like some new species, is worth enquiring into, and whether they are the means or happiness or misery to mankind."). He goes on to argue that: "As the exalting one man so greatly above the rest cannot be justified on the equal rights of nature, so neither can it be defended on the authority of scripture; for the will of the Almighty, as declared by Gideon and the prophet Samuel, expressly disapproves of government by kings." *Id.* at 9.

107. *Id.* at 15 ("Men who look upon themselves born to reign, and others to obey, some grow insolent; selected from the rest of mankind their minds are early poisoned by

on to note, "*How came the king by a power which the people are afraid to trust, and always obliged to check?* Such a power could not be the gift of a wise people, neither can any power, *which needs checking*, be from God; yet the provision, which the [British] constitution makes, supposes such a power to exist."[108]

In an effort to limit and control the actions of governmental officials, the Framers of the U.S. Constitution embraced the ideas of a French philosopher, Baron de Montesquieu, who is credited with articulating the doctrine of separation of powers.[109] In his landmark *The Spirit of the Laws*, he articulates the theory:

> [There] is no liberty [if] the judiciary power be not separated from the legislative and executive. Were it joined with the legislative, the life and liberty of the subject would be exposed to arbitrary control; for the judge would be then the legislator. Were it joined to the executive power, the judge might behave with violence and oppression.
>
> There would be an end of everything, were the same man or the same body, whether of the nobles or of the people, to exercise those three powers, that of enacting laws, that of executing the public resolutions, and of trying the causes of individuals.[110]

Citations to Montesquieu's arguments regarding separation of powers, appear in the Federalist Papers[111] and the debates at the constitutional convention,[112] as well as in many other writings from the period.[113] More importantly, the doctrine of "separation of powers" is incorporated throughout

importance; and the world they act in differs so materially from the world at large, that they have but little opportunity of knowing its true interests, and when they succeed to the government are frequently the most ignorance and unfit of any throughout the dominions.").

108. *Id.* at 7; *see also* Bessler, *supra* note 93, at 207 ("Montesquieu and Beccaria—both from *civil law* countries—shaped Adams' views in important ways, too ...").

109. Baron de Montesquieu, The Spirit of Laws 151–152 (Cosimo Edition 2011).

110. *Id.* at 152.

111. *See* James Madison, Alexander Hamilton & John Jay, The Federalist Papers (The Classic Original Edition), at 139 (*citing* Federalist No. 47 (Jan. 30, 1788)).

112. *See* Ketcham, *supra* note 101, at 85, 237, 249, 253, 260, 288, 339 & 360.

113. *See id.* at 159–160, 163, 166–167, 240, 247, 259–260 & 357; *see also* Bessler, *supra* note 93, at 211–212 ("... the Continental Congress's October 26, 1774 letter ... put

the U.S. Constitution.[114] For example, even though Congress was given the power to enact legislation, the Constitution required the President's signature as a prerequisite to enactment (unless Congress overrides the President's veto or the President allows the act to become law without his signature).[115] Likewise, although Congress and the President jointly enact legislation, the judiciary is frequently charged with interpreting that legislation, and sometimes in striking it down.[116] Moreover, many powers, such as the foreign affairs power, are shared between the President and Congress.[117] For example, the Senate is charged with ratifying treaties, which the Constitution charges the President with the power to negotiate and make,[118] but only the entire Congress can declare war,[119] and the President is integrally involved in other foreign affairs issues as well.[120] In addition, the Framers created different terms of office for different officials so that a single election could not dramatically shift the course and direction of government.[121]

Montesquieu and Beccaria front and center.... The writings of Beccaria and Montesquieu were, in reality, among the most quoted of the 1770s.").

114. *See* Ketcham, *supra* note 101, at xv ("Also, mindful of colonial experience and following the arguments of Montesquieu, the idea that the legislative, executive, and judicial powers had to be 'separated,' made to 'check and balance' each other in order to prevent tyranny, gained wide acceptance."); MALONE, *supra* note 92, at 176 (noting that Jefferson had read Montesquieu's *Esprit des Lois*, and further noting that "he had copied into his notebook in the French numerous quotations from Montesquieu, with summaries and reflections of his own.").

115. U.S. CONST., Art. I, Sec. 7 [3] ("Every Order, Resolution, or Vote to Which the Concurrence of the Senate and House of Representatives may be necessary (except on a question of Adjournment) shall be presented to the President of the United States; and before the Same shall take Effect, shall be approved by him, or being disapproved by him, shall be repassed by two thirds of the Senate and House of Representatives, according to the Rules and Limitations prescribed in the Case of a Bill.").

116. *See Marbury v. Madison*, 5 U.S. (1 Cranch) 137 (1803).

117. *See United States v. Curtiss Wright Export Corp.*, 299 U.S. 304 (1936).

118. U.S. CONST., Art. II, Sec. 2 [2] ("He [the President] shall have Power, by and with the Advice and Consent of the Senate, to make Treaties, provided two thirds of the Senators present concur....").

119. U.S. CONST., Art. I, Sec. 8 [11] ("[1] The Congress shall have Power... [11] declare War....").

120. *See United States v. Curtiss Wright Export Corp.*, 299 U.S. 304 (1936).

121. *See* U.S. CONST., Art. I, Sec. 2 [1] ("The House of Representatives shall be composed of Members chosen every second Year by the People of the several States....); U.S. CONST., Sec. 3 [1] ("The Senate of the United States shall be composed of two Senators from

New ideas and political theories ultimately transformed the entire fabric of European society and government as well. Even though monarchy was the dominant form of government in Europe during the Middle Ages,[122] most monarchies were eventually overthrown and replaced by democratic governments, or their powers were severely restricted, by the early twentieth century.[123] The Bourbon dynasty fell not long after the American Revolution,[124] although there were brief monarchical restorations in the nineteenth century,[125] and the Hapsburg dynasty fell in the early twentieth century.[126] Of the monarchies that remained (*e.g.*, the British monarchy), the monarchs were largely transformed into figureheads (the last British monarch to refuse consent to an act of Parliament did so in 1707).[127]

An interesting side note is that, when the Declaration of Independence was adopted, the revolutionaries knew that they desperately needed support and assistance from the King of France, Louis XVI, the king who was beheaded during the French Revolution. Had he seriously thought about the implications of the language in the Declaration, or had he had any inkling regarding his own future, one might surmise that King Louis XVI would have refused to assist the revolutionaries in their bid for independence. Presumably, either he was unaware of the contents of the Declaration, or perhaps his dislike for the English overrode all else. In any event,

---

each State, chosen by the Legislature thereof, for six Years. . . ."); U.S. Const., Art. II, Sec. 1 [1] ("The executive Power shall be vested in a President of the United States of America. He shall hold his Office during the Term of four Years. . . ."); *see also* Ketcham, *supra* note 101, at xvii ("Thus, for example, even though an upper and a lower house might each eventually derive from the people, different districts, different terms of office, different modes of election, and different definitions of authority would create balances of power.").

122. *See* J. Hampden Jackson, A Short History of France: From Early Times to 1972 19–24 (2nd ed. 1980).

123. *Id.* at 159.

124. *Id.* at 109–112.

125. *Id.* at 136–158.

126. *See* Andras Inotal, *Past, Present and Future of Federalism in Central and Eastern Europe*, 1 New Europe L. Rev. 505, 506 (1993).

127. *See* Howard R. Sklamberg, *The Meaning of "Advice and Consent": The Senate's Constitutional Role in Treatymaking*, 18 Mich. J. Int'l L. 445, 448 (1997).

Louis XVI ignored the Declaration's "radical ideas," unable to anticipate the fate that would befall him some thirteen years later.[128]

3. THE PRINTING PRESS' IMPACT ON COMMUNICATION IN OTHER FIELDS

The Gutenberg press also had a profound impact on science and industry. Even though scientific books had limited impact on scientific theory in the first century after the print press was invented,[129] publications eventually developed that focused on the natural sciences, anatomy and astrology.[130] However, since printers and booksellers were primarily interested in profit, they sought out "works which were of interest to the largest possible number of their contemporaries."[131] Scientific books generally did not meet that criteria.

The printing press also had a major impact on the development of language.[132] Over time, the use of Latin gave way to the use of national languages,[133] and the press brought about consistency of usage in those languages, including consistency of spelling.[134]

Even though books proliferated in the centuries following Gutenberg's invention, and even though the press encouraged the development of newspapers,[135] the presses of that time continued to use Gutenberg's movable type.[136] Newspapers and printing presses continued to have a significant impact on political thought and the broader social fabric. During

---

128. Curiously enough, the City of Louisville is named for Louis XVI. Louisville was founded after the American Revolution, but before the French Revolution, and the founders wanted to express gratitude towards Louis XVI for his assistance during the American Revolution. Also, curiously, Louisville is one of the few cities in the world with a prominently displayed statute of Louis XVI (a gift from Louisville's Sister City, the City of Montpellier, France).

129. *See* Febvre & Martin, *supra* note 4, at 259.

130. *Id.*, at 277.

131. *Id.* at 260.

132. *Id.* at 319 ("Just as printing favoured the growth of the Reformation, so it helped mould our modern European languages.").

133. *Id.* at 320.

134. *Id.* at 319.

135. *See* John B. Thompson, *The Trade in News*, in COMMUNICATION IN HISTORY, *supra* note 1, at 114.

136. When Benjamin Franklin was printing in the eighteenth century, he used essentially the same process that Gutenberg had used:

the American Revolution, printers reproduced (and, ultimately, disseminated) the writings of Europeans, including *Cato's Letters*,[137] as well as the thoughts of political philosophers such as Locke,[138] Paine[139] and Baron de

---

> In fact Ben served very well [as an apprentice printer]. Printing turned out to be ideally suited to his peculiar combination of manual and intellectual dexterity. The physical process of printing was straightforward, if somewhat involved. The printer set the handwritten type in text, placing the cast-metal letters (imported, during this period, from England) in rows that would yield the lines of printed text. These lines were held in place by rectangular frames corresponding to the printed pages; typically four pages were set and framed at once. The letters were inked, paper was laid over them and pressed against them, and the sheet of four pages was hung or laid aside to dry. As many sheets were pressed as copies the customer ordered. After the last impressions were made and had dried, the sheets were cut into their separate pages, which were collated and bound.

See The Life and Times of Benjamin Franklin, *supra* note 21, at 20.

137. *See* Michael Kent Curtis, *St. George Tucker and the Legacy of Slavery*, 47 Wm. & Mary L. Rev. 1157, 1206 (2006) ("If an inconsistency exists here, it is an old one. Cato's Letters were a series of essays on liberty that were widely circulated in the colonies and the United States both before and after the Revolution."); Dan Friedman, *Tracing the Lineage, Textual and Conceptual Similarities in the Revolutionary-War Era State Declarations of Rights of Virginia, Maryland and Delaware*, 33 Rutgers L.J. 929 (2002) ("The description of the freedom of the press as a 'bulwark of liberty' apparently originates with Cato's Letters, a series of essays by two English pamphleteers, widely reprinted and quoted in the American colonies...."); Paige Gold, *Fair Use and the First Amendment: Corporate Control of Copyright is Stifling, Documentary-Making and Thwarting the Aims of the First Amendment*, 15 U. Balt. Intellectual Property L.J. 1, 12 (2006) ("John Trenchard and Thomas Gordon, two widely-read British political thinkers whose essays were published in the colonies as *Cato's Letters*, identified three central values that the right of free speech is designed to advance....").

138. *See* Doernberg, *supra* note 178, at 64–65 (concluding that it "would be difficult to overstate John Locke's influence on the American Revolution and the people who created the government that followed it."); David Konig, *supra* note 98, at 262 (noting that "Jefferson followed Locke in justifying for the American colonies of 1776 the right of armed resistance.").

139. *See* Allen Edward Shoenberger, *Connecticut Yankee in Europe's Court: An Alternative Vision of Constitutional Defamation Law to New York Times v. Sullivan?*, 28 Quinnipiac L. Rev. 431, 432 (2010) ("Free speech, such as that exemplified by the speeches and pamphlets of the revolutionary firebrand Thomas Paine, has been at the center of American civil rights.") (citing Harvey J. Kaye, Thomas Paine: Firebrand of the Revolution (2000)).

Montesquieu,[140] all of which helped shape American political thought.[141] In addition, the printing press provided revolutionaries with a way to communicate with each other,[142] and was used to create and mass distribute copies of the Declaration of Independence,[143] and ultimately the Federalist Papers.[144] The printing press also played a role in the French Revolution with posters being placed in village squares.[145]

The printing press's impact on the American Revolution is, in some respects, counterintuitive. In the eighteenth century, literacy rates were quite low. Indeed, until the Industrial Revolution, most ordinary people lacked the ability to read and write,[146] and therefore were unable to prepare or read letters, circulars, petitions or newspapers.[147] Only in the nineteenth century did literacy rates rise sufficiently so that ordinary peo-

---

140. *See* Douglass Adair, *That Politics May Be Reduced to a Science: David Hume, James Madison and the Tenth Federalist*, reprinted in FAME AND THE FOUNDING FATHERS 93, 94–95 (1974).

141. *See* A HISTORY OF MASS COMMUNICATION, *supra* note 3, at 49 ("Over the course of a century that began with the Industrial Revolution, the American Revolution and the French Revolution, the Western World underwent a tremendous alteration. Printing played a significant role in all three revolutions.... Pamphlets such as Tom Paine's *Common Sense* spread the revolt to the American Revolution. And printing awakened France and shook all of Europe with its *Declaration of the Rights of Man*.").

142. *See also id.*, at 51.

143. *See also Id.* ("Newspapers would now [late eighteenth century], more than ever, be a force for freedom. It should not be surprising that the concept of a printing press unfettered by government leads the Bill of Rights, nor that Thomas Jefferson, who once wrote that if forced to choose he would choose newspapers over government...."); *Id.*, at 67–68 ("In terms of content, the early American political tradition featured a series of succinct readable democratic self-government. From Thomas Paine's Common Sense to the Declaration of Independence to the Federalist Papers to the Constitution itself, important materials circulated far and wide among the American population, often as reprints in newspapers publications to engage the populace with an opportunity to participate in deliberative and reflective or as pamphlets.").

144. *See* Philip J. Weider, *The Ghost of Telecommunications Past*, 103 MICH. L. REV. 1671, 1675 (2005).

145. *See* A HISTORY OF MASS COMMUNICATION, *supra* note 3, at 47.

146. *See A Theory of Affluence, supra* note 44.

147. *See* Geoffrey Nunberg, *Reading, Writing and Thinking, The New York Times*, at A3 (Dec. 13, 1981) (discussing SYLVIA SCRIBNER & MICHAEL COLE, THE PSYCHOLOGY OF LITERACY (1981), which suggests the importance of literacy to society, but noting that universal literacy came relatively late in history).

ple could read and write.[148] Before that time, most ordinary people communicated orally,[149] and written communication was the domain of the higher classes.[150] Despite these circumstances, the printing press seems to have had a significant impact on society and politics even among the illiterate. During the American Revolution, even though print runs for newspapers were often quite low by modern standards—a single newspaper might produce only 400 copies per day—newspapers had a greater impact than the extent of their press runs might indicate because they were read by more than one person, and were also read out loud in communal settings like taverns.[151] During the French Revolution, when many ordinary Frenchmen could not read or write,[152] posters were placed in public squares,[153] and a literate person might read the contents to a group of listeners.[154]

Following Gutenberg's invention of the printing press, and the beginning of the Industrial Revolution, the printing press changed little for centuries.[155] Printers continued to set type by hand, to use screw presses, and to produce only a relatively small number of pages per hour.[156] Indeed, even as late as the eighteenth century, when Benjamin Franklin acquired his

---

148. *See id.*

149. *See* A History of Mass Communication, *supra* note 3, at 19 ("Most information reached the brain through the ear, via gossip, morality plays, sermons, narrative ballads and tales....").

150. *See id.*

151. *Id.*, at 115.

152. *Id.*, at 47 ("Most people in Europe and North America could not read, let alone write. Beyond the few that were educated, most skilled craftsmen knew their letters, while most women, unskilled laborers, and peasants did not.").

153. *Id.*, at 47.

154. *Id.* ("The French Revolution depended on the printed word to get out the message of liberty, equality, and fraternity. To seize power the revolutionaries had to fortify a lower class enfeebled by centuries of misery. Most peasants were illiterate, but they could look at posters and they could listen to others read.").

155. *See* A History of Mass Communication, *supra* note 3, at 47; Febvre & Martin, *supra* note 4, at 11–12 & 67.

156. *See id.* ("It would seem reasonable that the burst of technology that gave western Europe and then the world a system of printing would continue its pace of invention and innovation to meet the excited demand. Yet, between 1450 and 1800 surprisingly little changed in the printing industry. Printers continued to set type by hand. A typical screw press impressed no more than 100 to 150 sheets of paper an hour. At the start of the Industrial Revolution, printing was done much as it had been accomplished in Gutenberg's day."); The Life and Times of Benjamin Franklin, *supra* note 21, at 20.

first printing press, Franklin used Gutenberg's lead type, and he traveled to England to try to purchase the type. Although the trip proved to be a failure (because Franklin's sponsor failed to provide the necessary letter of credit), the "technology" that he sought to acquire was essentially Gutenberg's movable type.[157] Printers did make a number of refinements, not only to the printing press, but also regarding the quality of paper needed to make good copies, but the basic technology remained unchanged.[158]

Printing technology did not advance significantly until the dawn of the Industrial Revolution which led to the creation of much more sophisticated printing presses that allowed printers to produce thousands of pages per hour.[159] By that time, advances in technology coupled with other events were beginning to transform society. In particular, the development of public school systems led to a much higher literacy rate, and to a populace that was capable of taking advantage of the publications being churned out by the new printing technologies.[160] Printing production was limited only by a scarcity of paper, as well as by the limitations of lead type that tended to break down under the intense pressure imposed by more modern printing technology.[161] These processes were subsequently enhanced by electrotyping and lithography.[162]

---

157. *See* The Life and Times of Benjamin Franklin, *supra* note 21, at 20.

158. *See also* Febvre & Martin, *supra* note 4, at 65–83.

159. *See* A History of Mass Communication, *supra* note 3, at 48:

> Iron presses, easier to operate and making better impressions, replaced wooden presses around the turn of the nineteenth century. The lever press replaced the ancient method of pressing pages by twisting a screw. A steam press was operating in 1810. Richard Hoe's rotary cylinder press, making use of the rolls of newsprint from the Fourdrinier machines, replaced the flatbed press, multiplying newspaper production manifold and increasing circulation. Pages came off the presses at the rate of 1,100 sheets per hour per side. Friederich Koenig hooked two presses together, so that they printed both sides of the sheet at once. By 1827, output on the most modern presses was 7,000 sheets an hour, although this technology was spreading slowly and flatbed newspaper printing presses still required muscles and patience.

160. *Id.* (" Society had changed, too. An emphasis on basic education for all brought literacy to many of the common folk of Europe and the United States for the first time in history.... Now the printing press would have a mass market for its mass production capability. By the end of the century, huge Hoe presses were printing 72,000 copies an hour.").

161. *Id.*

162. *Id.*, at 48–49.

CHAPTER III

THE EMERGENCE OF "GATEKEEPERS": PUBLIC AND PRIVATE

Even though the Gutenberg printing press had a profound impact on medieval society, it's impact was limited by two factors. First, many governments sought to limit and control the ability of private individuals to use the printing press. Second, there were private gatekeepers who controlled the ability of others to harness printing technology.

A. A HISTORY OF GOVERNMENTAL REPRESSION

Throughout history, as new forms of speech technology were developed, governments have tried to restrict or control their use.[1] That was certainly true of Gutenberg's printing press. Even though many governments might have been happy to utilize the printing press for their own purposes, they were not keen to allow private people to use print technology to propagate their own ideas, or to communicate with each other.[2] Justifiably fearful

1. *See* Elizabeth Townsend Gard, *Conversations with Renowned Professors on the Future of Copyright*, 12 Tul. J. Tech. & Intell. Prop. 35, 101 (2009) ("From monks transcribing Aristotle, to Gutenberg's printing press, to the photocopier, to the Betamax, we have seen striking similarities in the way various societies have feared the effects of new technologies and then created law in reaction to these fears.").

2. There were some exceptions, notably Italy and Germany, which gave the press greater latitude to discuss events occurring in other countries: "In the states and principalities of Germany and Italy the degree of official control varied from one state to another,

that the press might be used to undermine their monarchical authority (as ultimately happened), many kings took steps to restrain its "evils"[3] and to impose restrictions on the ability of individuals to access print technologies.[4] "Official restrictions were the official response to the new, disquieting idea that this invention would provide a means for mass communication."[5]

Restrictions on the printing press took various forms. Realizing that printing was facilitating discussion and debate, "printers and booksellers were always the most vulnerable to victimization, at the mercy of inquiries which might commit them to prison and often the stake."[6] As one commentator noted, "What better way to root out heresy than to punish severely those who initiated the publication of suspected books?"[7] As a result, French Protestant printers were forced to flee to other countries,[8] and publishers of Reformation literature were persecuted in Saxony.[9]

---

but newspapers were generally allowed more leeway in reporting foreign news than in discussing domestic politics." DAVID CROWLEY & PAUL HEYER, COMMUNICATION IN HISTORY: TECHNOLOGY, CULTURE, SOCIETY 2 (5th ed. 2007)

3. *See First National Bank of Boston v. Bellotti*, 435 U.S. 765, 800–801 (1978) ("Soon after the invention of the printing press, English and continental monarchs, fearful of the power implicit in its use and the threat to Establishment thought and order-political and religious-devised restraints, such as licensing, censors, indices of prohibited books, and prosecutions for seditious libel, which generally were unknown in the pre-printing press era. Official restrictions were the official response to the new, disquieting idea that this invention would provide a means for mass communication."); *see also* William T. Mayton, *Seditious Libel and the Lost Guarantee of a Freedom of Expression*, 84 COLUM. L. REV. 91, 97–98 (1984); NORMAN L. ROSENBERG, PROTECTING THE BEST MEN: AN INTERPRETIVE THEORY OF THE HISTORY OF LIBEL (U. N. Carolina Press, 1986); M. LINDSAY KAPLAN, THE CULTURE OF SLANDER IN EARLY MODERN ENGLAND (Cambridge U. Press 1997).

4. *See First National Bank of Boston v. Bellotti*, 435 U.S. 765, 800–801 (1978) ("Soon after the invention of the printing press, English and continental monarchs, fearful of the power implicit in its use and the threat to Establishment thought and order-political and religious-devised restraints, such as licensing, censors, indices of prohibited books, and prosecutions for seditious libel, which generally were unknown in the pre-printing press era.").

5. *Id.*

6. *See* LUCIEN FEBVRE & HENRI-JEAN MARTIN, THE COMING OF THE BOOK: THE IMPACT OF PRINTING 1450–1800 150 (1976).

7. *Id.*

8. *Id.*

9. *Id.* at 192.

Throughout Europe, publishers were fined,[10] executed,[11] or imprisoned with some offending French publishers being imprisoned in the Bastille.[12] Indeed, there was a period when publishing "was in total subjection to authority," and "originality was shunned."[13] "Both printers and booksellers were under surveillance by the Church, or rather by both the Catholic and the new Protestant Churches, and also by numerous secular authorities who often came to contradictory conclusions, making it difficult for even the most orthodox printer, however obedient, to avoid the rigours of censorship."[14] Some were forced into exile where they continued to publish pamphlets criticizing the government that forced them to flee.[15]

Restrictions on press freedom varied from country-to-country. Prior to the French Revolution, the French government imposed licensing restrictions and censorship.[16] A 1563 edict required that all books be licensed prior to publication, and gave governmental authorities discretionary power to censor material.[17] As a result, some books were banned.[18] Although French presses were relatively free for a brief period following the Revolution,[19] Napoleon later imposed press restrictions.[20] Censorship was also imposed in Italy with Catholic Church officials being involved in the repression.[21]

In Germany, governmental authority was intertwined with the church which gave the Catholic Church the power to censor publications and to prohibit "heretical" works.[22] As a result, the Archbishop of Mainz instructed two priests to examine all books, and prohibited the publica-

10. *Id.* at 115.

11. *Id.* at 150–151.

12. *Id.* at 155

13. *Id.* at 153.

14. *Id.* at 154.

15. *Id.* at 155–156.

16. *See* John B. Thompson, *The Trade in News*, in DAVID CROWLEY & PAUL HEYER, COMMUNICATION IN HISTORY: TECHNOLOGY, CULTURE, SOCIETY 116 (5th ed. 2007) ("In France, a centralized and highly restrictive system of licensing, supervision and censorship existed until the Revolution").

17. *See* Febvre & Martin, *supra* note 6, at 246.

18. *Id.* at 304.

19. *See* Thompson, *supra* note 16, at 116

20. *Id.* (noting that Napoleon "instituted a strict system of censorship and control").

21. *Id.* at 245.

22. *See* Febvre & Martin, *supra* note 6, at 244.

tion of any book without his prior approval.[23] For example, in response to Martin Luther's attack on indulgences, Emperor Charles V commanded that all of Luther's writings be burned.[24]

Attempts at repression were not always effective. Charles V's edict against Luther's writings spurred great interest and almost "desperate eagerness" in reading everything that Luther wrote.[25] Thus, even though Luther's attack on indulgences was banned, thousands of copies were printed, some of which ridiculed the Pope.[26] 4,000 copies of one pamphlet were distributed within three weeks, and the pamphlet ultimately went through thirteen to twenty-five editions.[27] Reformation works were printed even in cities that were primarily Catholic.[28] Although the Catholic Church tried to suppress these "heretical" writings, enforcement of church imposed prohibitions were dependent on enforcement by secular officials who did not always cooperate.[29] There were some successful prosecutions in places like Leipzig.[30] Nevertheless, "books defending the Catholic faith were few in number in comparison to the flood-tide of works hostile to Rome."[31]

During the fifteenth to the eighteenth centuries, governmental repression led to the creation of an underground book trade.[32] Banned books were highly sought after and commanded high prices,[33] and the sale of contraband literature was "an everyday feature of the city scene at that time."[34] In the sixteenth century, a royal decree only allowed a small number of Parisian printers to publish books.[35] However, the decree was never enforced and more books were published in the year after the decree than

23. *Id.*

24. *Id.* at 290.

25. *Id.*

26. *Id.* at 291 ("To ridicule the Pope and the monks, pamphlets entitled *Pope Donkey* and *Cow Monk* were produced.").

27. *Id.*

28. *Id.*

29. *Id.* at 245.

30. *Id.* at 293.

31. *Id.*

32. *See* Febvre & Martin, *supra* note 6, at 240.

33. *Id.* at 238.

34. *Id.*

35. *Id.* at 310.

the year before.[36] A 1547 decree prohibited the sale of any book that had not previously been submitted to governmental censors.[37]

In the sixteenth century, the book trade flourished even though "many street vendors were burned at the stake because they were caught selling heretical books,[38] and even though the French king forbade the printing of banned books "on pain of death by hanging."[39] In seventeenth and eighteenth century France, "many were sent to the Bastille for having sold pamphlets hostile to the royal authority."[40] Despite the persecutions "banned books continued to circulate more or less everywhere with the same ease."[41] For book sellers, the banned books attracted considerable interest and substantial profits.[42] However, some publishers, fearful of prosecution, set up operations just outside of France and shipped banned publications into the country.[43] Imported books easily moved past governmental officials, even into monasteries and seminaries.[44] French publishers frequently omitted their addresses from the title pages of banned books that they published.[45]

---

36. *Id.*

37. *Id.* at 311.

38. *Id.* at 238–239 & 309 ("November 1534 saw the first series of spectacular executions. On the 10th it was a printer who was burned, for having printed and bound the 'false works" of Luther, and on the 19th it was the turn of a bookseller.").

39. *Id.* at 310.

40. *Id.* at 238–239.

41. *Id.* at 238–246.

42. *Id.* at 304.

43. *Id.* at 247 & 298–299 (noting that Reformation French-language publications were created in Germany and Belgium and smuggled into France. "Such books printed just beyond the borders of France, often at the instigation of Frenchmen, entered France in large numbers and with ease." Indeed, an underground network developed.).

44. *Id.* at 316 (noting that "heretical books poured into France. Not simply in a few isolated cases, but in hundreds at a time in packing cases, in the baggage of a merchant or the wagon of a colporteur. As there was no effective police force the risks of being caught on the road were few, except perhaps by watchmen at the city gates. But how were watchmen to find the crate or crates of books among all the other crates of legitimate merchandise, especially if, as a further precaution, the books were concealed under other goods?").

45. *Id.* at 307 ("The truth is that French booksellers were able in many cases to go on selling and printing heterodox literature in response to the demands of their eager clients without running any serious risk, so long as they acted prudently and adopted a few elementary subterfuges.... Thus editions of doubtful orthodoxy multiplied despite all the condemnations.").

The English restricted press freedom through licensing schemes.[46] The government limited the total number of printing presses that could exist.[47] The goal was to control the flow of information by limiting the number of people who could print.[48] Under the Printing Act of 1662, the British Parliament went further and "prescribed what could be printed, who could print, and who could sell."[49] The Act required a printer to obtain a license to print, and (of course) allowed the government to withhold permits from those whose views it found objectionable (often materials critical of the government).[50] The British licensing scheme also prohibited the publication of any book or pamphlet without a license specifically authorizing publication, and required those who wished to obtain a license to submit their work for review.[51] Of course, if a proposed publication contained material that the censor deemed objectionable, the license could be denied.[52] Under the Stamp Act of 1712, taxes were levied on each page as well as on each advertisement that a newspaper contained.[53]

Perhaps the most draconian restriction on printing involved the British Star Chamber's 1606 decision in *de Libellis Famosis*.[54] That decision

46. *See Thomas v. Chicago Park District*, 534 U.S. 316, 320 (2002).

47. *See* Edward Lee, *Guns and Speech Technologies: How the Right to Bear Arms Affects Copyright Regulations of Speech Technologies*, 17 WM. & MARY BILL RIGHTS J. 1037, 1072 (2009).

48. *See Thomas v. Chicago Park District*, 534 U.S. 316, 320 (2002) (*quoting* William T. Mayton, *Toward a Theory of First Amendment Process: Injunctions of Speech, Subsequent Punishment, and the Costs of the Prior Restraint Doctrine*, 67 CORNELL L. REV. 245, 248 (1982)).

49. *See Lovell v. City of Griffin*, 303 U.S. 444. 451 (1938) (*quoting Toward a Theory of First Amendment Process, supra* note 48, at 248).

50. *See Thomas v. Chicago Park District*, 534 U.S. 316, 320 (2002); *Lovell v. City of Griffin*, 303 U.S. 444 (1938).

51. *See Thomas v. Chicago Park District*, 534 U.S. 316, 320 (2002); *see also* F. SIEBERT, FREEDOM OF THE PRESS IN ENGLAND, 1476–1776 240 (1952).

52. *See Lovell v. City of Griffin*, 303 U.S. 444. 451 (1938); *see also City of Lakewood v. Plain Dealer Publishing, Co.*, 486 U.S. 750, 757 (1988); *Lowe v. Securities & Exchange Commission*, 472 U.S. 181, 205 (1985).

53. *See* Thompson, *supra* note 16, at 2 ("The Stamp Act of 1712 required newspaper proprietors to pay one penny for every printed sheet and one shilling for every advertisement. Subsequent acts increased the amounts and broadened the basis for the application of the law. The Stamp Acts were bitterly opposed and became a rallying point in the struggle for the freedom of the press.").

54. 77 Eng.Rep. 250 (Star Chamber 1606).

created the crime of seditious libel, which replaced, in part, the criminal offense of constructive treason,[55] and made it a crime to criticize the government or governmental officials (and, at one point, the clergy as well).[56] The crime was enforced by "threats of punishment, litigation costs, and stigma,"[57] and was justified by the notion that criticism of the government "inculcated a disrespect for public authority."[58] "Since maintaining a proper regard for government was the goal of this new offense, it followed that truth was just as reprehensible as falsehood" and therefore was not a defense.[59] Indeed, truthful criticisms were punished more severely than false criticisms because it was assumed that true criticisms were potentially more damaging to the government.[60]

In the American colonies, there were similar efforts to control printing. "Often colonial governors distrusted printers and hesitated to give them permission to establish themselves, keeping a very close watch on them after they had done so."[61] There were also attempts to censor publications.[62] Although licensing expired in England in the late eighteenth century,[63] the British maintained restrictions on speech in the American colonies.[64] British restrictions on speech were believed to have been

---

55. *See* William T. Mayton, *Toward a Theory of First Amendment Process: Injunctions of Speech, Subsequent Punishment, and the Costs of the Prior Restraint Doctrine*, 67 CORNELL L. REV. 245, 248 (1982).

56. *Id.* Indeed, in *de Libellis Famosis,* the defendants had ridiculed high clergy.

57. *Id.*

58. *Id.* at 103; *see also* Matt J. O'Laughlin, *Exigent Circumstances: Circumscribing the Exclusionary Rule in Response to 9/11*, UMKC L. REV. 707,720–21 (2002) (referring to the seditious libel prosecution of John Wilkes during the reign of George III: (1760–64) LJ 426, (1761–64) CJ 674).

59. *Id; see also* William R. Glendon, *The Trial of John Peter Zenger*, 68 N.Y. ST. B.J. 48 (1996).

60. *See* Stanton D. Krauss, *An Inquiry into the Right of Criminal Juries to Determine the Law in America*, 89 J. CRIM. L. & CRIMINOLOGY 111, 183 n.290 (1998); *see also* Glendon, *supra* note 59, at 48.

61. *See* Febvre & Martin, *supra* note 6, at 210.

62. *Id.*

63. For a discussion of the history of seditious libel, *see* Law Commission Working Paper No. 72, Treason, Sedition and Allied Offences (1977); Judith Schenck Koffler & Bennett L. Gershman, *The New Seditious Libel*, 69 CORNELL L. REV. 816 (1984).

64. *See* RUSSELL L. WEAVER, ANDREW T. KENYON, DAVID F. PARTLETT & CLIVE P. WALKER, THE RIGHT TO SPEAK ILL: DEFAMATION, REPUTATION AND FREE SPEECH 6–7 (2006) (hereafter "THE RIGHT TO SPEAK ILL").

a motivating factor behind the demand by American colonists for free expression protections in the United States Constitution.[65] In the colonies, the British appointed censors who were required to approve the content of newspapers prior to publication;[66] leading to objections from the American colonists.[67] Perhaps the most famous seditious libel prosecution in the colonies involved John Peter Zenger.[68] Zenger, a New York publisher, had published stories mocking the royal Governor and his administration, and was prosecuted for seditious libel.[69] Zenger languished in jail for 10 months awaiting trial, and the Governor arranged for the disbarment of his lawyers for stating exceptions on Zenger's behalf.[70] When the case was finally tried, Zenger's lawyer admitted that Zenger had published the allegedly libelous statements, and offered to concede the libel if the prosecution could prove that the allegations were false. When the prosecution declined, the lawyer offered to prove that the statements were true. Although the court disallowed the evidence, on the then valid basis that truth was immaterial, Zenger was acquitted in what was viewed as an early and significant exercise of jury nullification.[71]

Also in the American colonies, James Franklin (Benjamin's brother), who published *The Courant*, was jailed at one point for showing "disrespect" to governmental officials.[72] Because James had a tendency "to mock religion and bring it into disrespect," a court ordered that "'James Franklyn, the printer and publisher [of the Courant], be strictly forbidden by this court to print or publish the New England Courant' unless

---

65. *See Thomas v. Chicago Park District*, 534 U.S. 316, 320 (2002).

66. *See* H.W. Brands, The First American: The Life and Times of Benjamin Franklin 31 (2000) ("Declaring that the tendency of the *Courant* was 'to mock religion and bring it into disrespect,' the General Court ordered that 'James Franklyn, the printer and publisher thereof, be strictly forbidden by this court to print or publish the New England Courant' unless he submitted each issue of the paper to the censor for prior approval.").

67. *See Thomas v. Chicago Park District*, 534 U.S. 316, 320 (2002).

68. *Id.*

69. *See* Elizabeth I. Haynes, *United States v. Thomas: Pulling the Jury Apart*, 30 Conn. L. Rev. 731 (1998).

70. *See Cohen v. Hurley*, 366 U.S. 117, 140 (1961) (Black, J., dissenting).

71. *See* Haynes, *supra* note 69, at 731.

72. *See* The Life and Times of Benjamin Franklin, *supra* note 37, at 30 (he was ultimately imprisoned for about 30 days).

he submitted each issue of the paper to the censor for prior approval."[73] James was also prosecuted for printing a fake letter to the editor (fake in the sense that James was the real author, but he attributed the letter to someone else) that implied that the authorities were not pursuing pirates (operating off the New England coast) with sufficient vigor.[74] In that letter, James reported (sarcastically) that the captain (heading up the expedition against the pirates) "will sail sometime this month, if wind and weather permit."[75] James was jailed for publishing this letter, and Ben was questioned, but ultimately released.[76] Many believed that the arrest was politically motivated, and was designed simply to silence James for his stinging political commentaries.[77] While his brother was in prison, Benjamin Franklin continued publishing the newspaper.[78] When Benjamin Franklin left Boston for New York and (ultimately) Philadelphia, he was motivated in part by a fear of prosecution by Boston's elite.[79] Subsequently, well aware of what had happened to his brother, Benjamin Franklin was sometimes cautious about using his newspaper to provoke the authorities.[80]

---

73. *Id.*, at 31.

74. *See* THE LIFE AND TIMES OF BENJAMIN FRANKLIN, *supra* note 66, at 29–30.

75. *Id.*

76. *Id.*, at 30.

77. *Id.* ("A commonly accepted explanation was that ever since the smallpox scuffles [in which James Franklin had opposed Cotton Mather], the court had been seeking an excuse to silence the turbulent pressman; this was simply the excuse that fell to hand.").

78. *Id.*

79. *Id.*, at 34:

> Consequently Ben saw no recourse but flight—which recommended itself on other grounds as well. To a curious boy, Boston had been an exciting place; to an independent-minded young man, it was starting to stifle. The Mathers did not say such threatening things about Ben as about James, but it was clear they and their supporters had doubts about the younger Franklin too.... Now might be a good time to leave, before the clerics and judges came after him as they had come after James. "It was likely I might if I stayed soon bring myself into scrapes."

80. *Id.*, at 114:

> ... Some journalists enter their profession from a zeal to right wrong and oppose entrenched authority; this was what had motivated Franklin's brother James—and landed James in jail. Ben Franklin certainly learned from James's experience and from his own experience on James's paper. He had no desire to publish from prison, and even less desire to *not* publish from prison or anywhere else. Journalism for him was a business rather than a calling, or perhaps with a

Claims of repression continue even in modern times. For example, in 2020 in Algeria, after a reporter wrote about a protest movement, he was charged with, and convicted of, "inciting an unarmed gathering" and "endangering national unity."[81] In 2023, a Kansas newspaper was raided by the police who seized computers and phones.[82] While prosecutors sought to justify the raid and seizures on the basis that there was evidence of identity theft and computer crimes, the raid was condemned by news organizations who viewed the actions as indicative of governmental repression.[83] Interestingly, many local citizens were not sympathetic to the paper, viewing its coverage as "negative" in tone.[84]

B. PRIVATE "GATEKEEPERS"

In addition to governmentally-imposed restrictions on printing, there have always been private "gatekeepers" who sought to exercise control over, and access to, print technology. Although technology has advanced too quickly for any single individual or corporation to exert monopolistic control over speech technology for long periods of time,[85] there have

---

calling that could call only so long as the business beneath it flourished. Unlike James, Ben Franklin would not provoke the authorities into closing him down. If nothing else, such rashness would lose him his primary contract with the provincial government.

81. *See* Adam Nossiter, *Journalist in Algeria Sentenced for Reporting on Protest Movement, The New York Times* A10 (Aug. 22, 2020).

82. *See* Kevin Draper, *Raided Paper Hailed from Afar Is Too Negative for Some Locals, The New York Times* A1 (Aug. 20, 2023).

83. *Id.*

84. *Id.*

85. *See* Ruth Schwartz Cohen, *The Social Shape of Electronics,* in COMMUNICATION IN HISTORY, in DAVID CROWLEY & PAUL HEYER, COMMUNICATION IN HISTORY: TECHNOLOGY, CULTURE, SOCIETY 319 (5th ed. 2007) ("From the invention of wireless telegraphy in the late nineteenth century to the creation of an electronic superhighway in the late twentieth, no one individual, and no one institution, has succeeded in controlling for very long the American market for electronic components or electronic devices or even the content of what is communicated by those devices."); *Id.*, at 311–312:

> [T]here are many surprises for individuals and organizations that think they can remain in control of the business of communications. Just when an inventor, after years of painstaking work, would begin to count his royalties in the millions of dollars, along came another inventor with a patent on a new, slightly better device, stealing his thunder and his plans for future wealth. Or just when

always been individuals or companies in "gatekeeper" positions who were able to limit or control the ability of average people to use their technologies. The printing press was one of the technologies governed by gatekeepers.

Although the printing press had the undeniable effect of enhancing the capacity for communication, and of enabling significant numbers of individuals to engage in mass communication, Gutenberg's invention was not readily accessible by ordinary people. The owners of printing presses, especially the owners of newspapers, could readily use the technology to communicate their ideas and their criticisms of government to their fellow citizens.[86] Examples of these anti-government criticisms abound. For example, John Peter Zenger of New York[87] published "anti-British song-sheets and mock advertisements describing an associate of the royal governor as 'a large Spaniel, of about 5 feet 5 inches high ... lately strayed

---

> a company, after years of complex maneuvering, would begin to exert almost complete control over some marketplace, along came another company with a new idea to compete for market share. Control of electronic industries—by individuals, by companies, even by governments—has been from the very beginning evanescent, transitory, fleeting. Individuals and companies have had their moment in the sun, but eventually they have all lost monopolistic control of the market that had once proven so profitable.

See also Associated Press, *TW Cable Net Income Declines: Seeks Growth in Web Video, The Courier-Journal*, at B8 (Oct. 28, 2011) (noting that overall cable television revenue was declining as consumers shifted to internet-based services).

86. While the printing press had the undeniable effect of increasing the number of communicators, and of enabling some private individuals to engage in mass communication, Gutenberg's invention was not readily accessible by the masses. The owners of printing presses, especially the owners of newspapers, had easy access to the technology, and could easily communicate their ideas to their fellow citizens and could criticize government. Examples of these anti-government criticisms abound. For example, John Peter Zenger of New York published "anti-British song-sheets and mock advertisements describing an associate of the royal governor as 'a large Spaniel, of about 5 feet 5 inches high ... lately strayed from his kennel with his mouth full.'" *See* The Life and Times of Benjamin Franklin, *supra* note 66, at 168 (Noting that Franklin's position as a printer gave him a "crucial advantage" in attempting to convey information or sway public opinion: "[John] Bartram and [Cadwallader] Colden [who promoted ideas similar to those espoused by Franklin] might—and did—communicate between themselves and with a small circle of correspondents, but Franklin could reach hundreds or thousands through his printing press."); *see also id.*, at 182 & 182–184 (noting how Franklin was able to move the public to action in contributing money for a battery of guns).

87. *See* Glendon, *supra* note 59, at 48.

from his kennel with his mouth full of fulsome panegyrics,' and also described the associate as a 'monkey ... lately broke from his chain and run into the country.'"[88] As noted, James Franklin of Boston, Massachusetts,[89] Benjamin Franklin's brother, published an article suggesting that colonial authorities were not pursuing pirates with sufficient vigor.[90] Even Benjamin Franklin joined the fray as a teenager when he ran his brother's newspaper during the latter's imprisonment for criticizing governmental officials.[91] Later, when Franklin owned his own press, he sometimes used it to comment on society,[92] and to critique and challenge government.[93] For example, when the Pennsylvania Assembly was considering whether to issue paper currency, Franklin used his printing press to wade into the fray,[94] and his position seemed to align with his economic interests.[95]

Nevertheless, the number of people who could use the printing press to convey their ideas was comparatively small. Few people were wealthy enough to own or operate their own printing presses.[96] Printing required

---

88. *See* Haynes, *supra* note 69, at 731.

89. *See* The Life and Times of Benjamin Franklin, *supra* note 66, at 25 (referring to James Franklin's newspaper as "lively, opinionated, and not averse to challenging the establishment."); *see also id.*, at 181.

90. *See id.*, at 29–30.

91. *Id.*, at 30–31.

92. *Id.*, at 144 (recounting how Franklin weighed in on religious issues of the day. Included among his comments were some fairly derogatory remarks regarding Presbyterian clergy:

Asses are grave and dullish animals,
Our authors are grave and dull animals; therefore
Our authors are grave, dull, or if you will, *Rev. Asses.*

Id. He went on to comment that those involved in the controversy fell into one of three categories: "first, the men of honesty who wanted sense; secondly, the men of sense who wanted honesty; and lastly, those who had neither sense nor honesty."); *Id.*, at 145.

93. *Id.*, at 188 ("there was an obvious, almost inevitable progression from [Franklin's deciding to act] independently of government to acting against government."), & 284–285 (noting, among other things, that "Franklin relished a good fight in the press."), & 294–295 (noting Franklin's attempt to influence British public policy through the press).

94. *Id.*, at 133–135 (noting that Franklin published an essay entitled *A Modest Enquiry into the Nature and Necessity of a Paper-Currency*).

95. *Id.*, at 135 ("Franklin doubtless hoped that if the assembly could be persuaded to authorize another paper issue, he would receive the contract for the printing; as always, he expected that what was good for Pennsylvania would be good for him. In fact his arguments, joined to those of others of like mind, did carry the day....").

96. *See id.*, at 41.

specialized printing equipment,[97] including a printing press and lead type, and an aspiring press owner might be forced to work for many years in order to save up enough capital to buy a printing press.[98] Benjamin Franklin, who made a name for himself as a printer, among other things, initially found it difficult to obtain the necessary funds to acquire a printing press.[99] At one point, Franklin believed that he had secured a wealthy benefactor (Pennsylvania's provincial governor, William Keith) who would loan him the money to buy a press, and who would direct governmental printing business his way in order to ensure that Franklin's new business would be a success.[100] Unfortunately for Franklin, Keith's promises turned out to be puffery, and Franklin did not realize this fact until he had traveled to London, England, to purchase the lead type necessary to establish his business.[101] Franklin found himself stranded in London, lacking the means to purchase the press, initially without employment, and without the funds for a return trip to Philadelphia.[102] So, he was forced to work in London to support himself and pay for his return trip.[103] Franklin did not acquire a press until later, after he had returned to the colonies, when his partner's father agreed to underwrite the purchase of a printing press.[104] A press (and the necessary lead type) became available

97. *See id.*, at 88 ("The printing trade was fairly comparatively capital intensive, requiring specialized equipment that had to be purchased. Whether he [Benjamin Franklin] bought an existing business—Keimer's, for instance—or started his own from nothing, he would have to find the funds to purchase the equipment. Such funds were precisely what he lacked.").

98. *Id.*, at 51 ("Franklin did not doubt his own talents, but he painfully felt his lack of capital. Without money for a press and related equipment, not even the most gifted printer could set up shop. At his present pay he might put aside sufficient funds to purchase equipment in several years, but hardly before then.").

99. *Id.* ("An older man with an established reputation might borrow money, but who would lend to a lad just arrived from distant parts—a lad who, as the governor evidently knew from Roberts Homes, had fled his contractual obligations there.").

100. *Id.*, at 55–63.

101. *Id.*, at 63.

102. *Id.* ("This lesson in human nature [Governor Keith's failure to follow through on his promises] came as a shock. When he had awakened that morning, Franklin fancied himself an independent artisan about to embark on a brilliant career [with a new printing press and governmental business]. Now he was simply an out-of-work journeyman a very long way from home, with no place to stay and no friends within three thousand miles.").

103. *Id.*

104. *Id.*, at 88–90 .

only because Franklin's former employer was unable to run his newspaper profitably, and was willing to sell the press for a "trifle."[105]

Even those who had the means to buy printing equipment sometimes found that market forces limited their choice of location as well as their ability to operate a profitable enterprise. Benjamin Franklin, who ultimately settled in Philadelphia (after leaving Boston), reputedly wanted to settle in New York City.[106] However, he decided that New York could not support another newspaper.[107] Since Benjamin could not find suitable employment in New York City, he moved on to Philadelphia.[108] In Philadelphia, he initially had difficulty finding employment.[109]

In many U.S. cities, prominent families controlled the newspaper business. Families such as the Ochs-Sulzbergers (New York), Binghams (Louisville) and Chandlers (Los Angeles) became press "lords."[110] The Medill dynasty began when Joseph Medill, the patriarch of the family, bought a one-third interest in *The Chicago Tribune* and eventually acquired a controlling interest. Other Medills became, variously, the publisher of *The Chicago Tribune*,[111] the founder of *The Daily Post* in New York,[112] the editor and eventual purchaser of *The Washington Herald*,[113] which was later

---

105. *Id.*, at 103 ("Neither party disclosed the sale price; Franklin called it a 'trifle'—which was about what the new owners got for their money: a few score subscribers and a name.").

106. *Id.*, at 41.

107. *Id.*

108. *Id.* After arriving in New York City, Benjamin found that his prospects for employment as a printer were very limited: "The ship's eventual arrival in New York overturned Franklin's expectations in another respect. For all their commercial energy—perhaps because of it—the Dutch merchants and tradesmen in Manhattan evinced scant interest in the services of printers. The town lacked a newspaper.... The single printer who kept a shop in New York, William Bradford, had no difficulty supplying the town's needs with the helpers he already had. There was no room for Franklin." *Id.*

109. *Id.*, at 46.

110. *See* Joseph Epstein, *Dynasts of the Daily Press*, reviewing Megan McKinney, *The Magnificent Medills: America's Royal Family of Journalism During a Century of Turbulent Splendor* (2011); Amanda Smith, *Newspaper Titan: The Infamous Life and Monumental Times of Cissy Patterson* (2011), *The New York Times* Book Review Section, at 17 (Oct. 16, 2011).

111. *Id.*, at 14 (Robert Rutherford, Medill's grandson, eventually became the publisher of the newspaper.).

112. *Id.* (Joseph Medill Patterson, a grandson of Joseph Medill).

113. *Id.* (Eleanor Medill Patterson, a granddaughter of Joseph Medill).

combined with the *Washington Times* to create the *Washington Times-Herald*,[114] and the editor of *Newsday*.[115] At one point, the Medills owned the three largest circulation dailies in three of the most important cities in the United States.[116]

In terms of media power, few could rival the Hearst empire. George Hearst acquired the *San Francisco Examiner* in exchange for a bad debt, and proceeded to lose money operating the paper.[117] His son, William Randolph Hearst, took over the paper in 1887 when George was elected to the U.S. Senate,[118] and later built a media juggernaut that included *The New York Morning Journal*,[119] *Das Morgen Journal* (a German language newspaper that he acquired along with *The New York Morning Journal*),[120] the *Los Angeles Examiner*,[121] the *Detroit Times*,[122] the *Boston Herald American*,[123] the *Seattle Post-Intelligencer*,[124] the *Washington Times*,[125] the *Washington Herald*,[126] the *Houston Chronicle*,[127] the *San Antonio Light*,[128] and the *Baltimore News American* (among others).[129]

---

114. *Id.*

115. *Id.* (Alicia Patterson Guggenheim, a great-grandchild of Joseph Medill).

116. *Id.*, at 14 .

117. *See* W.A. SWANBERG. CITIZEN HEARST 26 & 40 (1961) (hereafter "CITIZEN HEARST").

118. *Id.*, at 43–44 & 47.

119. *Id.*, at 100.

120. *Id.*

121. *See* Richard W. Stevenson, *The Media Business: Hearst to Cease Publication of the Los Angeles Herald, The New York Times*, at D21 (Nov. 2, 1989).

122. See Frank Boles, *Michigan Newspapers: A Two Hundred Year Review*, 2010 MICH. HIST. REV. 31.

123. *See* Geraldine Fabrikant, *Hearst's Eight-Year Buying Spree, The New York Times*, at A4 (Apr. 26, 1987).

124. *See* Richard Perez-Pena, *Hearst's Seattle Paper May Move to Web, The New York Times*, at B5 (Mar. 6, 2009).

125. *See* Burton Crane, *Hearst Built Corporate Empires in Newspapers, Magazines, Radio and Real Estate, The New York Times*, at 21 (Aug. 15, 1951).

126. *See* Epstein, *supra* note 110.

127. *See* Fabrikant, *supra* note 123.

128. *Id.*

129. *Id.*

In recent decades, the media has been dominated by a relative handful of media corporations.[130] The Hearst Corporation continues to control scores of newspapers, but also has expanded to other forms of communication, including magazines (Redbook, Esquire, Cosmopolitan, Cosmopolitan Living, Connoisseur, Country Living, Victoria, House Beautiful, Harper's Bazaar, and Popular Mechanics), radio and television stations, and cable television systems (including Arts & Entertainment and Lifetime), as well as various book printing companies (Avon Books & William Morrow and Co.).[131] Time, Inc.[132] publishes (or published) Time, Fortune, Fortune Small Business, People, Business 2.0, Cottage Living, Southern Accents and Life, Sports Illustrated and Money magazines.[133] The Gannett Company owns (or owned) some 93 newspapers, a movie studio, and a television programming production property.[134]

News Corp., founded and controlled by Rupert Murdoch,[135] is one of the largest media companies in the world with total revenues in excess of $1 billion per year, and ownership of various newspapers, including *The Times of London*, *The Sun* (London), *The Wall Street Journal*, and formerly *The News of the World*.[136] News Corp. also controls a broadcasting network (Fox News), cable companies, and a movie studio (20th Century Fox).[137] In addition, News Corp. aspired to take control of British Sky Broadcasting (BSkyB).[138] There is also Comcast which received approval to purchase

130. *See* Laurence Zuckerman, *Questions Abound As Media Influence Grows for a Handful, The New York Times*, at C6 (Jan. 13, 2000).

131. *Id.*

132. *Id.*

133. *See* Stephanie Clifford, *Time Inc. Is Expected to Eliminate More Jobs, The New York Times*, at B3 (Oct. 30, 2009).

134. *See Company News: Ex-NBC Head in Gannett Venture, The New York Times*, at D4 (Dec. 16, 1986). http://www.nytimes.com/1986/12/16/business/company-news-ex-nbc-head-in-gannett-venture.html?scp=1&sq=media%20conglomerate%20gannett&st=cse.

135. *See News Corporation, The New York Times* (Nov. 21, 2011). http://topics.nytimes.com/top/news/business/companies/news_corporation/index.html?scp=3&sq=media%20conglomerates&st=cse (last access on Feb. 22, 2012).

136. *Id.*

137. *Id.*

138. *Id.*

NBC.[139] CNN, long one of the dominant cable news broadcasters, is now faced with competition from the likes of Fox News and MSNBC.[140]

Unlike the newspaper magnates, who could publish whatever they wanted in their own newspapers, ordinary individuals could publish their ideas only with the consent of those who controlled the newspapers and printing presses. Although non-owners could pay printing press owners to print their ideas (assuming, of course, that licensing restrictions did not prevent the publication when licensing restrictions applied), this avenue of communication was not available to many because of the cost.[141] Even individuals who could afford to pay to have books or posters printed were confronted by substantial distribution costs that were beyond the means of average individuals.[142] For example, if someone wanted to print a poster and distribute it throughout England (or throughout New England in the American colonies), and to reach a substantial majority of the population, distribution costs could be enormous. The net effect was that, even though the press revolutionized speech technology, the elite (*e.g.*, governmental officials, newspapers, universities and the rich who owned and controlled presses) were the primary beneficiaries of the new technology,

---

139. *See* Bob Garfield, *Comcast Gets the Okay to Buy NBC*, National Public Radio, On The Media (Jan. 21, 2011), http://www.onthemedia.org/2011/jan/21/comcast-gets-the-okay-to-buy-nbc/.

140. *See* Bob Garfield, *The Cable News Wars*, National Public Radio, On the Media (Oct. 8, 2010), http://www.onthemedia.org/2010/oct/08/the-cable-news-wars/transcript/. Despite this concentration of media power, the Federal Communications Commission recently proposed to ease a rule prohibiting ownership of both a television station and a newspaper in large media markets. *See* Amy Schatz, *FCC Aims to Ease Media Rule, The Wall Street Journal*, at B3 (Dec. 23, 2011).

141. *See* Adrienne J. Marsh, *Fair Use and New Technology: The Appropriate Standards to Apply*, 5 CARDOZO L. REV. 635, 635 (1984).

142. *See* Markenzy Lapointe, *Universal Service and the Digital Revolution: Beyond the Telecommunications Act of 1996*, 25 RUTGERS COMPUTER & TECH. L.J. 61, 80 (1999) ("When Gutenberg developed the first moveable printing press and published his famous Bible in 1445, a communications revolution was greatly anticipated. However, this momentous invention failed to immediately ignite the expected information revolution. For centuries, books were available primarily to the rich, the academics, and the clerics. It was not until the creation of institutions like public libraries, which made books more accessible and the technological enhancement of the printing press, which allowed the production of books to become more affordable, that a true revolution finally began to take place.").

and were the ones who were most able to use the printing press to disseminate their ideas.[143]

Those who did not own printing presses could try to persuade the owners or editors of newspapers or magazines to publish their ideas (*e.g.*, by writing op-ed pieces or persuasive articles) in their newspapers, and to distribute their ideas through their newspaper distribution networks. However, the editors (and reporters) of newspapers served as "gatekeepers" in the sense that they could decide whether or not to publish the ideas of others, and could reject ideas that they did not like. A writer could (in theory, at least) pay a newspaper owner to publish his ideas, but few could afford to do so, and the publisher always retained the authority to reject the payment and the publication. The net effect was that ordinary individuals did not have assured access to the print medium for disseminating their ideas. If the gatekeepers of the print media refused a publication request, and the speaker could not afford to pay a printer to publish his ideas, the speaker was left with only more primitive methods of communication (*e.g.*, oral and handwritten methods).

All too often, the press lords (and modern media conglomerates) were inclined to use their newspapers to push their own political views.[144] For example, during World War II, the Medills advocated for an isolationist position that some attributed to their dislike for President Franklin Delano Roosevelt.[145] William Randolph Hearst aggressively used his newspapers to campaign for causes that he supported,[146] as well as to promote his preferred views and positions.[147] Prior to the American Revolution, there

---

143. *See* Peter K. Yu, *Of Monks, Medieval Scribes and Middlemen*, 2006 MICH. ST. L. REV. 1, 11 ("The initial demand for printed books came from universities, the clergy, monasteries and convents, the Civil Service, the feudal nobility (and their ladies), lawyers and physicians, and schoolboys and their teachers. There was also "a wide market for prayer-books, missals, almanacs, calendars, prognostications, broadsides, and other printed matter." In fact, the demand and supply for printed materials varied considerably from one geographical region to another.").

144. *See* Epstein, *supra* note 110, at p. 14 ("The Medill grandchildren viewed journalism as purveying entertainment while enhancing their social positions and spreading their political views.").

145. *See id.*, at 14.

146. *See* CITIZEN HEARST, *supra* note 117, at 100 & 119–127.

147. *See* Jerome A. Barron, *Access to the Media—1967 to 2007 and Beyond: A Symposium Honoring Jerome A. Barron's Path-Breaking Article "Access Reconsidered,"* 76 GEO. W. L. REV. 826, 832 (2008).

is evidence that printers similarly used their presses to pursue the interests and positions that they preferred. For example, James Franklin (Benjamin Franklin's brother) was opposed to positions taken by prominent Bostonian Cotton Mather who (to James) represented the Boston "establishment."[148] When Mather advocated for mass inoculations against smallpox,[149] Franklin opposed Mather even though he "knew next to nothing of the etiology of smallpox."[150] He did know that "he despised Mather for what James judged the eminent minister's smugness and his inordinate influence over the life of Boston. If Mather advocated inoculation, the *Courant* [James Franklin's newspaper] must oppose it—and did."[151] Benjamin Franklin, who initially agreed with his brother and joined the attack against Mather, later became a proponent of inoculation, mourning the fact that he failed to inoculate his own son who died in a smallpox epidemic at a young age.[152]

The gatekeeper role of editors and owners of newspapers and magazines, and the evidence of their potential biases, continues even today. To its credit, *The Courier-Journal* (Louisville, Kentucky) seems to make no bones about its bias. In an article published in 2009, the newspaper's then Publisher and President Arnold Garson flatly admitted that his newspaper generally has a liberal bias: "*The Courier-Journal's* Democratic or liberal perspective for its editorials extends through all 140 years of its existence, evolving through three different ownerships, a dozen or so different publishers and a like number of editors. Today, there certainly are exceptions, including occasional endorsements of Republican candidates. But on a day-to-day basis, our editorials fall pretty consistently on the liberal side."[153] Garson is no apologist for that bias: "We do hear from

---

148. *See* THE LIFE AND TIMES OF BENJAMIN FRANKLIN, *supra* note 66, at 25.

149. *Id.* ("The occasion of the attack [by James Franklin against Mather] was an epidemic of smallpox, the first in nearly two decades,—which hiatus was a primary cause of the virulence of this outbreak, in that an unexposed generation had little or no resistance to the disease. For all his obsession with the supernatural, Mather had maintained his youthful interest in the natural, and he advocated the novel technique of inoculation to combat the contagion.").

150. *Id.*

151. *Id.*

152. *Id.*, at 154–155.

153. *See* Arnold Garson, *Editorial: The Politics of a Newspaper*, *The Courier-Journal*, at H4 (Aug. 2, 2009).

readers who are dismayed by this [the newspaper's liberal bent]. But, as explained above, our choices are very limited if we're going to be relevant to the political debate of the day. We have to be either liberal or conservative, and either way, we're going to find ourselves at odds with a significant portion of our readers."[154]

Bias is also evident elsewhere. *Time* ran a cover in which it depicted Trump confronting a crying two-year old girl who had purportedly been separated from her mother.[155] The difficulty with the cover was that the girl was not actually separated from her mother.[156] *Time* later issued a clarification, stating that the mother and daughter had been taken away together, Time stood by the cover of the magazine.[157]

Of course, as a private entity, a newspaper or magazine is free to adopt whatever political perspectives it chooses to adopt, and to shape its news coverage in the way that it prefers. If the public feels that the paper's coverage is too slanted in one direction, its remedy is to refuse to buy the newspaper and thereby ignore its news coverage. However, the fact remains that many newspapers have historically served as gatekeepers of information in their communities, and have attempted to exercise influence or control over the public debate.

In the final analysis, the Gutenberg printing press was an extraordinary invention that dramatically reshaped much of the world, including religion, science and government. The potential of the press was limited by governmental repression as well as by gatekeepers who limited the ability of ordinary people to access the technology. Nevertheless, the printing press had a profound influence on society and communication.

---

154. *Id.*, at H4.

155. *See* Lauretta Brown, *Time Magazine Stands by Cover Art Despite Massive Correction to Story on Family Separations at Border, Townhall* (June 22, 2018).

156. *Id.*

157. *Id.*

CHAPTER IV

THE DEVELOPMENT OF ELECTRICITY BRINGS AN EXPLOSION OF NEW COMMUNICATIONS TECHNOLOGIES

Communications technologies began to move beyond Gutenberg's lead type with the invention of electricity in the eighteenth century.[1] Electricity led to an explosion of new technologies premised on the ability to communicate information through electrical impulses.[2] Electricity was transformational because it allowed information to move much more quickly than people could move, and to move quickly over long distances.

1. *See* DAVID CROWLEY & PAUL HEYER, COMMUNICATION IN HISTORY: TECHNOLOGY, CULTURE, SOCIETY 118 (5th ed. 2007) ("With the advent of harnessable electricity, a major shift occurred: The telegraph and telephone became the first wave of a new communications revolution.").

2. *See* COMMUNICATION IN HISTORY, *supra* note 1, at 118 ("With the advent of harnessable electricity, a major shift occurred: The telegraph and telephone became the first wave of a new communications revolution.").

A. THE TELEGRAPH

Electricity initially led to the invention of the telegraph in the 1840s,[3] and to the development of a national telegraphic network.[4] The Morse Code converted electrical impulses into a compact decipherable communication system based on dots and dashes, and therefore made it possible to understand the meaning of electrical impulses.[5]

The telegraph enabled individuals to send information over long distances at extraordinary speed.[6] No longer was it necessary to send information in the same way, or at the same speed, at which people and goods were transported (*e.g.*, over roads, or by train, horse, or water). Instead, information could be transmitted instantaneously over electrical lines,[7] and individuals could receive almost "real-time information" from distant locations.[8]

---

3. *See* Charles T. Meadow, Making Connections: Communication Through the Ages 77–83 (2002). The telegraph may actually have been invented earlier, but some argue that Samuel F.B. Morse can and should receive much credit because he successfully demonstrated and implemented the technology with his assistant, Alfred Vail. *Id.*, at 78. He describes their early efforts:

> His original receiving equipment consisted of a pen attached to one end of a pivoted arm, with a magnet pulling at a piece of iron attached to the arm. A windup clock motor drew a paper tape under the pen, which marked the tape according to the current flowing through the electromagnet. Morse and Vail continued to improve the device. Eventually, Vail invented a system that used a click key at the transmitter, and a receiver that indented a pattern of dots and dashes on a moving paper tape. Because the instrument made enough noise so the operator could hear the message, the paper tape was abandoned. *See Id.* at 77–83.

4. *See* Communication in History, *supra* note 1, at 118.

5. *Id.*

6. *See* Daniel Headrick, *The Optical Telegraph*, in Communication in History, *supra* note 1, at 119, at 123 (noting that the electrical telegraph could send as many 60 characters per minute, and could operate both night and day.).

7. *See* James W. Carey, *Time, Space and Telegraph*, in Communication in History, *supra* note 1, at 119. The article goes on to note that the telegraph had the effect of diminishing "space as a differentiating criterion in human affairs."

8. *See* Irving Fang, A History of Mass Communication: Six Information Revolutions 77 (1997). As one commentator noted: "The telegraph changed the way that information moved through society. Previously limited to a minuscule bit of news at the distance of a human voice could shout, or the flash of a mirror in the sun, complex messages carried by wire traveled thousands of miles in less time than a horse could be saddled." *See* Tom Standage, *Telegraphy—The Victorian Internet*, in Communication in History, *supra* note 1, at 130.

Telegraph usage expanded rapidly,[9] expanding from 40 miles in 1846 to 2,000 miles in 1848 and 12,000 miles in 1850.[10] Whereas the Pony Express had previously required ten days to transport a message from St. Joseph, Missouri, to Sacramento, California, using a relay system involving horses and riders,[11] the telegraph could transmit a message across the country in a matter of seconds.[12] By 1861, the transcontinental telegraph extended across the entire United States,[13] and led to a swift demise of the Pony Express system.[14] The telegraph system was eventually extended across the Atlantic Ocean.[15] The laying of trans-Atlantic cables involved a major engineering feat in its own right.[16] The telegraph also transformed newspapers and traditional publishing because it allowed newspapers (even small-town newspapers) to report on distant events relatively contemporaneously.[17]

Telegraph technology, like the printing press, was not freely accessible by ordinary people.[18] Following the Civil War, only two major telegraph companies remained, and one of those two (Western Union) was bought by its competitor in order to create a monopoly.[19] Moreover, the telegraph

---

9. *See* Standage, *supra* note 8, at 130 ("The growth of the telegraph network was, in fact, nothing short of explosive; it grew so fast that it was almost impossible to keep track of its size.").

10. *Id.*

11. *Id.*, at 130–131 ("Before the [intercontinental telegraph] line was completed, the only link between East and West was provided by Pony Express, a mail delivery system involving horse and rider relays. Colorful characters like William "Buffalo Bill" Cody and "Pony Bob" Haslam took about 10 days to carry messages over the 1,800 miles between St. Joseph, Missouri, and Sacramento.").

12. *See id.*, at 130.

13. *Id.*

14. *Id.*

15. *See* Communication in History, *supra* note 1, at 118.

16. *See* Standage, *supra* note 8, at 134–136 (noting the technical difficulties involved in finding a coating for the wires that would not deteriorate in salt water, the fact that water distorted the electrical impulses, and other problems, including difficulties financing the project.).

17. *Id.*, at 130 ("In the growth and strengthening of smaller newspapers, the telegraph gave a clear example of how the diffusion of a tool of communication created more information producers, because it was no longer necessary to read a large city newspaper to acquire fresh news from beyond the community.").

18. *See id.*, at 79–80.

19. *Id.*, at 79.

generally could not be used in private homes because it required literacy, as well as mastery of the Morse Code.[20] As a result, the technology was used primarily by government, business, or rich individuals,[21] including newspapers and other publishers who could afford to use it to transmit or receive news and content.[22]

In theory, a private individual could also send a telegram although the process was complicated. Except for the wealthy, who could afford to have telegraph lines in their homes, an individual who wanted to send a telegram was forced to take the message to the telegraph office,[23] which would transmit the message to a telegraph office where the recipient lived, and then the recipient telegraph company would arrange delivery.[24] While the telegraph could be used by ordinary individuals, the cost was relatively high for the time (fifty cents for 10 words).[25] Because of the high cost, even newspapers were forced to economize in their use of telegraphic communications,[26] and few private individuals (except the wealthy) could use the telegraph as a routine or ordinary means of communication.[27] Moreover, because of its point-to-point nature, the telegraph was not an effective mass communications technology.

---

20. *See* Communication in History, *supra* note 1, at 119.

21. *Id.*

22. *See* A History of Mass Communication, *supra* note 8, at 81–82.

23. *See* Standage, *supra* note 8, at 132 ("Sending a message was a matter of going into the office of one of the telegraph companies and filling in a form giving the postal address of the recipient and a message expressed as briefly as possible, since messages were charged by the word, as well as by the distance from the sender to the receiver. Once the message was ready to go, it would be handed to the clerk, who would transmit it up the line.").

24. *Id.* ("Once received at the nearest telegraph office, the message was transcribed on a paper slip and taken on foot by a messenger boy directly to the recipient. A reply, if one was given, would then be taken back to the office; some telegraph companies offered special rates for a message plus a prepaid reply.").

25. *Id.*, at 81.

26. *Id.* ("To economize, reporters attempted to shorten their stories by coding news dispatches. This produced expert coders and decoders, but it also produced blunders, and led to retaliatory tactics by the telegraph companies, such as counting every three letters as one word.").

27. *See id.*, at 132 ("Sending and receiving messages—which by the early 1850s had been dubbed 'telegrams'—soon became part of everyday life for many people around the world. But because this service was expensive, only the rich could afford to use the network to send trivial messages; most people used the telegraph strictly to convey really urgent news.").

B. TYPEWRITER

By the late nineteenth century, technological innovations were beginning to follow each other with surprising rapidity. The typewriter, a new invention that did not initially require electricity, was invented in 1868,[28] and was followed by the invention of linotyping.[29] The typewriter was rapidly employed in business contexts, and was widely used by private individuals in their homes.[30] Although the quantity of typed materials was dwarfed by the quantity of printed materials, the typewriter had the advantage of ease and accessibility, and could be used in the home.[31] Mark Twain was an early user of the typewriter.[32]

The typewriter involved a major communications advance because it was "democratic" in the sense that it was relatively inexpensive, did not come with the traditional gatekeepers, and therefore could be accessed by almost everyone. As a result, individuals could create printed works even though they did not own a printing press. However, the typewriter was limited as a method of mass communication. While an individual could create extra copies of a typewriter-produced document by using carbon paper,[33] it was difficult to produce sufficient quantities for mass distribution until copy machines (and, later printers) were developed in the mid-twentieth century.[34] Even then, a writer might encounter daunting distribution problems. An individual could hand out petitions or posters on public streets or at city hall. However, without large scale collaboration, it was extremely difficult to launch a statewide, regional or national campaign armed with nothing more than a typewriter. Distribution difficulties were overwhelming except for large, well-staffed, and disciplined organizations. In other words, average people could not readily engage in mass communication using only a typewriter.

---

28. *See* Communication Through the Ages, *supra* note 3, at 66.
29. *Id.*, at 66–67.
30. *Id.*
31. *Id.*
32. *Id.*
33. *Id.*
34. *See* A History of Mass Communication, *supra* note 8, at 75–76.

C. THE TELEPHONE

The telephone, developed by Alexander Graham Bell in 1876, was the next major advance in communications technology.[35] The telephone was distinguished by the fact that it allowed people to orally communicate with each other even though they were separated by great distances.[36] Of course, the telephone's impact on communication was directly proportional to the number of people who owned telephones,[37] and telephone usage in the 1880s was primarily limited to the wealthy.[38] By the dawn of the twentieth century, as people began to appreciate the telephone's potential,[39] they began to use it more frequently, causing the price of a phone line to decline, and telephone usage became commonplace throughout society.[40]

The major advantage of the telephone is that it provided direct communication between two people. Moreover, the telephone was free of gatekeepers because people could simply dial a number and speak directly to another person. As a result, the telephone allowed ordinary individuals to engage in enhanced communication in the sense that a single person, on behalf of a cause or a political campaign, could call lots of people to try to encourage or persuade them to support the person or campaign.

---

35. *See id.*, at 84; Claude S. Fischer, *The Telephone Takes Command*, in COMMUNICATION IN HISTORY, *supra* note 1, at 119.

36. *See* Stephen Kern, *Wireless World*, in COMMUNICATION IN HISTORY, *supra* note 1, at 209 ("The telephone had an even broader impact and made it possible, in a sense, to be in two places at the same time. It allowed people to talk to one another across great distances, to think about what others were feeling and to respond at once without the time to reflect afforded by written communication. Business and personal exchanges suddenly became instantaneous instead of protracted and sequential.").

37. *See* A HISTORY OF MASS COMMUNICATION, *supra* note 8, at 85.

38. *See* COMMUNICATION IN HISTORY, *supra* note 1, at 119.

39. *Id.*, at 83 ("Before the invention of the telephone, people could not talk to anyone they could not see.... To summon the fire department, someone had to gallop on a horse or run on foot. No one called a doctor or a hospital or the police department. Business communication was by letter, messenger, or personal visit. Living alone posed a special danger, particularly in a rural area.... Construction upward was also restricted by a lack of communication. Skyscrapers awaited the telephone.").

40. *See* A HISTORY OF MASS COMMUNICATION, *supra* note 8, at 85 ("By 1878, New Haven, Connecticut, became the first city to have a commercial telephone exchange, with a switchboard of eight lines and 21 telephones. Within two years of the awarding of Bell's patent, some 10,000 Bell telephones were in use.").

However, the telephone's utility as a political device was limited by a variety of factors. For one thing, in the early days, the cost of using a phone was subject to monopolistic pricing which made it expensive.[41] In addition, the telephone initially allowed people to connect with only one or a small number of people at a time (at least until more sophisticated conferencing capabilities were developed). Although there were some efforts at mass communication (*e.g.*, a concert might be sent via phone lines from one place to another or a phone might be hooked up to a speaker system),[42] so that the phone enabled some mass communication, the telephone was a far less effective communications device than other later developed technologies.

At one point, telephone companies offered customers a telex service that allowed them to transmit documents.[43] The telex was eventually replaced by fax machines which made it possible for individuals to transmit documents over long distances using their own phone lines.[44] One commentator described the fax as essentially "a photocopier linked to a telephone."[45] Although the fax machine was actually invented in 1842,[46] it did not come into widespread use until the 1960s.[47] The fax was eventually used by newspapers to facilitate the transmission of information throughout the country.[48]

---

41. *See* Fischer, *supra* note 35, at 144–148.

42. *See* Kern, *supra* note 36, at 207–209.

43. *Id.*, at 89.

44. *Id.*, at 227 ("The modern facsimile machine transmits what is on a page by scanning it using a light source, like a laser beam, to read the dark and light points, which are converted into digital data then sent over a phone line to the receiving machine, where the page is reproduced.").

45. *Id.*, at 227.

46. *Id.*

47. *Id.*, at 228 ("The fax popularity explosion began after a court ruling in 1968, the Carterphone Decision, that allowed customers to connect fax machines and other non-Bell devices to the Bell System. Improvements in technology plus the agreement on a single worldwide standard for transmission did the rest.").

48. *Id.*, at 220 ("Facsimile technology, which has been spreading year by year, has given the United States a truly national press when pages of major newspapers can be transmitted by satellite to regional printing plants so Wednesday's edition is available on Wednesday, not only in New York City and Washington, D.C., but in cities across the United States and overseas.").

With fax machines, it became possible for individuals to transmit documents or political position papers over phone lines, and to have those documents received within seconds.[49] Initially, documents had to be faxed one at a time. Nevertheless, the fax was a significant improvement for ordinary individuals over earlier technologies because it allowed documents to be sent almost simultaneously over long distances. However, it could be extremely difficult and time consuming (not to mention expensive, if long-distance calls were involved) to communicate with a large number of people.

D. WIRELESS TECHNOLOGY AND THE DEVELOPMENT OF THE RADIO

The invention of the telephone was followed by the development of wireless technology in the early nineteenth century,[50] which led to the invention of various other communications technologies, including the radio which was developed in the 1920s.[51] Radio technology was a major advance because it did not require point-to-point communication (in other words, it did not require transmission lines to be constructed between the communicators),[52] and permitted the dissemination of sound over long distances through the utilization of radio waves.[53] Radio obviated the need for telegraphic lines,[54] and therefore dramatically expanded communication possibilities,[55] permitting communications to move quickly over

49. *See* A History of Mass Communication, *supra* note 8, at 226.

50. *See id.*, at 90.

51. *See* Communication in History, *supra* note 1, at 204.

52. *See* Susan J. Douglas, *Early Radio*, in Communication in History, *supra* note 1, at 207–208.

53. *See Red Lion Broadcasting Co. v. FCC*, 395 U.S. 367 (1969).

54. *See* Communication in History, *supra* note 1, at 91–93. Guglielmo Marconi invented wireless technology. *Id.; see also* Communication in History, *supra* note 1, at 204. Marconi viewed the wireless primarily as a way to accomplish point to point communication, and did not have a strong interest in developing the technology's general broadcast potential. *See* A History of Mass Communication, *supra* note 8, at 89; Communication in History, *supra* note 1, at 204.

55. Early radios were difficult to install. For one thing, they did not come pre-assembled. *See* Douglas, *supra* note 52, at 207–208.

long distances.[56] The communications potential of wireless technology was dramatically illustrated in 1912 when the *Titanic*, the doomed and sinking ocean liner, sent out frantic calls for help.[57]

Radio had a profound impact on society.[58] During World War II, President Franklin Delano Roosevelt used it to communicate with the American people through his famous "Fireside Chats,"[59] thereby transforming "the president from an abstraction in people's lives to a presence in their homes."[60] The Japanese government used radio transmissions to wage psychological warfare on American troops stationed in the Pacific region.[61]

Radio was an extraordinary advance because it allowed audiences to hear the sound of events in real time.[62] Americans who remained at home during World War II were able to experience the sounds of a distant war through their radios.[63] Reporter Edward R. Murrow broadcast the horror of the German aerial bombardment of London during the Battle of Britain: "Night after night from the rooftop above his studio, Murrow's microphone picked up the sounds of anti-aircraft fire as Murrow painted word pictures of the bombing. Across the Atlantic in a nation still at peace, listeners eagerly awaited his CBS Radio reports, which helped to shift American sentiment from the isolationist wish to avoid war to a feel-

56. *See Red Lion Broadcasting Co. v. FCC*, 395 U.S. 367 (1969).

57. *See* Communication in History, *supra* note 1, at 204; Kern, *supra* note 36, at 207–208.

58. *See* A History of Mass Communication, *supra* note 8, at 189–190 ("Radio during its golden years, the decades of the 1930s and 1940s, acted to bring Americans together as a nation, to speak a common language with a common accent so far as possible, to share moral values, and to survive the Depression and World War II.").

59. Audio recordings of the Fireside Chats can be found at the University of California's The American Presidency Project. The recordings can be found online at the following URL: http://www.presidency.ucsb.edu/fireside.php

60. *See* Matt Bai, *Pushing the Presidential Message Into the Broadband Age, The New York Times*, at A12 (Jan. 25, 2011) (noting, also, "Presented with the new primacy of radio, for instance, Franklin D. Roosevelt developed the "fireside chats" that many Americans remembered long after his death").

61. A discussion of Tokyo Rose can be found on the Public Broadcasting System's History Detectives at the following URL: http://www.pbs.org/opb/historydetectives/investigations/705_tokyorose.html

62. *See* A History of Mass Communication, *supra* note 8, at 163–164 ("Instead of simply describing an event, audio technology allowed radio to bring an audience of millions to the event itself. . . .").

63. *Id.* at 164.

ing of wanting to come to the aid of the beleaguered English populace."[64] Unlike ancient Roman Emperors, the American people did not have to wait days or weeks to hear the outcome of an important battle in a distant place. They received nightly updates almost in real time. Over time, radio broadcasters developed their own information and news networks.[65]

In modern times, talk radio, especially AM (short for "Amplitude Modulation") talk radio, has become a major political influence. Rush Limbaugh wielded enormous political influence through his radio show beginning in the 1990s.[66] During that time, he reached some 20 million listeners on approximately 600 radio stations, and he delighted conservatives and infuriated liberals as he talked about race, gender, and a variety of hot button political issues.[67] In addition, he blazed a path for later conservative talk show hosts like Laura Ingraham,[68] Mark Levin,[69] and Sean Hannity of Fox News, whose talk radio shows reach some 13 million listeners.[70]

Not all talk radio is successful. Early in this century, the left tried to respond to Limbaugh (and others on the right) with a show entitled Liberal Air America.[71] Even though the show was staffed with high-profile hosts, the show lasted only 6 years before it descended into bankruptcy.[72] In addition, AM radio may be on its last legs because electric vehicle manufacturers are said to be moving to exclude AM radio from new vehicles because electromagnetic impulses interfere with AM radio frequencies.[73]

---

64. *Id.*

65. *Id.*, at 163.

66. *See* James Varney, *Rush Limbaugh, Voice of American Conservatism, Dead at 70, Washington Times* (Feb. 18, 2021); *Will Electric Vehicles Silence AM Radio? AM Served the Country for 100 Years, The Freeman* (Waukesha, WI) (Aug. 1, 2023); *see also* Perry O. Hooper, Rush Limbaugh was a master communicator, Montgomery Advertiser (Alabama) B9 (Feb. 21, 2021).

67. *See* Varney, *supra* note 66.

68. *Id.*

69. *Id.*

70. *See Will Electric Vehicles Silence AM Radio?, supra* note 66.

71. *See* David Folkenflik, *Liberal Air America Goes Off the Air*, National Public Radio, Talk of the Nation (Jan. 25, 2010).

72. *Id.*

73. *See* Marc Fisher, *Era of AM Radio Crackles Off Into the Sunset, The Washington Post* A1 (May 14, 2023).

E. CB RADIOS

Individuals have also been able to use private equipment to broadcast using citizens' band radios (so-called "CB" radios).[74] CB technology allows ordinary people to communicate with each other, but is limited by the fact that only a small percentage of the population has the technology to receive citizens band communications, and waves can only be transmitted over short distances. Since the audience for CB communications is relatively small and constricted, the potential impact of CB communications has been likewise limited.

F. TELEVISION

Radio technology was followed by the development of television which allowed individuals to not only receive the spoken word, but also to see pictures of events occurring far away. In the words of one commentator, television provided a "compelling demonstration of simultaneity and co-presence."[75] Although television had its roots in technology developed during the early nineteenth century,[76] the first television sets were not sold to the public until the 1930s,[77] and television technology was still regarded as novel enough to be displayed in "The World of Tomorrow" exhibit at the New York World's Fair in 1939.[78] The first regular television broadcasts began that same year.[79]

In the ensuing decades, television transformed society. Television achieved significant market penetration because those who could not

---

74. *See Id.*, at 151 (noting that CB radios have largely been replaced by cellphone technology). *See* A HISTORY OF MASS COMMUNICATION, *supra* note 8.

75. COMMUNICATION IN HISTORY, *supra* note 1, at 243.

76. *See* A HISTORY OF MASS COMMUNICATION, *supra* note 8, at 154 ("*Television* means *seeing at a distance*. Its roots reach back to at least 1817, when Swedish scientist Jon Berzelius discovered that selenium, a sulfur-like chemical element that is a byproduct of copper refining, conducted electricity, depending upon how much light shone upon it. In 1873, an Irish telegraph operator, Joseph May, by exposing a selenium resistor to light, sent a signal across the ocean on the Atlantic telegraph cable. Two years later, American engineer Philip Carey proposed a means of television using a camera containing an array of selenium cells, each wired to a light bulb in a matching array in a receiver. . . .").

77. *Id.*, at 156.

78. *Id.*

79. *See* COMMUNICATION IN HISTORY, *supra* note 1, at 242.

afford to purchase radios or televisions went to their neighbors' houses to listen to radio broadcasts and view television programs.[80] Over time, television became a fixture in almost every home as more than one million television sets were manufactured in the United States in 1948, and nearly 10 million more were produced in 1950.[81] As time passed, televisions became quite commonplace,[82] and were viewed by the average American for several hours every day.[83] Although some commentators believed that the development of television might render radio technology obsolete,[84] broadcast radio has survived quite nicely as an alternate method of communication.[85]

Over time, television news reporting became a staple of modern communication. By the early 1960s, television news programs began broad-

80. *See* A History of Mass Communication, *supra* note 8, at 158 ("In the 1920s, neighbors gathered around the first radio on the block. As television sets were sold across the nation during the late 1940s and 1950s, people without sets would crowd into a neighbor's home or stand in front of shop window displays....").

81. *Id.*, at 156–157.

82. *Id.*, at 153 ("A color television set sat in 98% of all American homes in the 1990s. More homes have TV sets than bathtubs or telephones, and far more homes than are on newspaper delivery routes.").

83. *Id.*, at 152 ("The average American television set is on for 7 hours 45 minutes a day. Drive along any avenue in the United States or any other industrialized nation and you will see the bluish glow from television sets in darkened rooms of house after house.").

84. *See id.* ("With the rapid spread of television, radio broadcasting seemed on a one-way road to ruin. Station and network assets fled eagerly to the new medium, taking staff, talent and energy with it. In the home, the old Philco console was moved out of the parlor to make way for the RCA "); Peter Fornatale & Joshua E. Mills, *Radio in the Television Age*, in Communication in History, *supra* note 1, at 207–208 ("Radio jokes abounded in the early 1950s: one cartoon showed a young boy dusting off a radio in the attic and asking his dad, 'What's that?' Americans had seen icemen put out of work, ice chests discarded for refrigerators, and silent pictures give way to talkies. It was against memories like these—recent memories—that many people gauged radio's chances against television.").

85. *See* A History of Mass Communication, *supra* note 8, at 150 ("Today there are far more radio stations than at the start of television broadcasting. By 1992, with 11,338 radio stations and 576 million radios in use—5.6 radio sets for every household on average—and radios in 19 of every 20 cars in the United States alone, on average Americans listened to the radio 3 hours 20 minutes a day."); Tovia Smith, *NPR Sees Spike in Audience*, National Public Radio, All Things Considered (Mar. 24, 2009), http://www.npr.org/templates/story/story.php?storyId=102306369; Jay Caspian Kang, *Mike Francesa Still Believes in the Power of Radio, The New York Times Magazine* 54 (Aug. 26, 2018).

casting in color, and network news programs increased in length.[86] While television news was not well received initially, and many of the best reporters shunned the medium,[87] attitudes changed as television news outlets effectively covered major news events (*e.g.*, the assassination of President John F. Kennedy[88] and the Civil Rights movement of the 1960s),[89] and journalists began to see how television could influence the political process. Richard Nixon's poor performance in his televised debate with John F. Kennedy in the televised 1960 presidential election is widely viewed as swaying the election against him.[90]

G. CABLE TELEVISION

In recent decades, radio and television have been supplemented by other methods of mass communication. Although cable television had its roots in the nineteenth century,[91] cable technology did not have a major impact until the twentieth century.[92] By the 1990s, cable television was present in two-thirds of American homes,[93] and was enhanced by the development of fiber optics.[94]

---

86. *Id.* at 164.

87. *Id.* at 165.

88. *Id.* ("Attitudes changed on November 22, 1963, the day of the assassination of John F. Kennedy. The murder of the President under mysterious circumstances, followed by the murder of his alleged assailant, both shown as they happened, led not to angry citizens taking to the streets, but to a citizenry glued to television sets to watch the drama that unfolded over more than three days. All programming, all commercials, and all other news vanished. Television news pictures hypnotized viewers as night and day the unfolding events were told and shown over and over.").

89. *Id.* ("The capacity of television news to generate emotion surfaced frequently during the coverage of the Civil Rights movement in the South.").

90. *See* Marshall McLuhan, *Understanding Radio*, in COMMUNICATION IN HISTORY, *supra* note 1, at 235 ("In the Kennedy-Nixon debates, those who heard them on the radio received an overwhelming idea of Nixon's superiority. It was Nixon's fate to provide a sharp, high-definition image and action for the cool TV medium that translated that sharp image into the impression of a phony."); *see also Pushing the Presidential Message, supra* note 558.

91. *See* A HISTORY OF MASS COMMUNICATION, *supra* note 8, at 170.

92. *Id.*, at 172–174.

93. *See id.*, at 169.

94. *Id.*, at 205–206.

Cable technology was fundamentally similar to broadcast technology because it offered both images and sound, but it used cables to transmit the programming rather than broadcast waves.[95] Cable was advantageous because it made it possible for subscribers in remote areas to receive clear pictures, as well as because it offered cable viewers far more programming than they could receive over the broadcast medium.[96] Cable had a major impact on television, claiming a significant market share, while the market for television declined.[97] By 1994, cable television revenues exceeded $23 billion per year.[98]

Unlike the early days of broadcast television, which tended to unify the country, in the sense that everyone was watching similar programming, cable television had a tendency to segment the viewing audience by offering viewers far more programming options, and by allowing individuals to gravitate to those programs and viewpoints that interested them or that aligned with their beliefs.[99] Cable television eventually developed its own news and information systems with some stations offering twenty-four hour news coverage. But the divergence of reporting continued with some programs on the left and others on the right.

However, there is evidence that cable television has entered a period of decline.[100] The decline has hit not only cable companies, but also many streaming services.[101] Some suggest that there were concerns that CNN's political coverage was too partisan.[102]

---

95. *Id.*

96. *Id.*

97. *See id.*, at 162 ("As cable choices expanded, the audience for the Big Three American networks shrank from more than 90 percent of the total television audience to about 60 percent.... The American commercial networks battled over a thinning share of the total audience.").

98. *Id.*, at 203.

99. *Id.*, at 169–170 ("Cable was supposed to bring us together. In fact, the proliferation of channels has had the exact opposite effect as viewers select from an ever thicker menu.").

100. *See* Joseph De Avila, *Lay-Offs as CNN Tightens Its Belt, Australian* 18 (Dec. 2, 2022).

101. *Id.*

102. *Id.*

H. SATELLITES

Even though radio and television technology helped reshape communication, subsequent technologies transformed communication even further. By 1965, the first communications satellite was launched into orbit,[103] and other satellites were soon launched by a quasi-government corporation, with strong corporate support and participation.[104] Satellites employed "transponders" that allowed them to receive and transmit information,[105] and they functioned like wireless technologies because they enabled communicators to circumvent existing cable and telephone lines, and to communicate directly through the medium of electronic signals.[106] By the 1990s, the satellite communications industry had achieved significant market penetration and was beginning to challenge the cable industry.[107]

Satellite technology created enhanced communication possibilities as contrasted with existing technologies and could be combined with those

---

103. *See* Ruth Schwartz Cohen, *The Social Shape of Electronics*, in COMMUNICATION IN HISTORY, in DAVID CROWLEY & PAUL HEYER, COMMUNICATION IN HISTORY: TECHNOLOGY, CULTURE, SOCIETY 313 (5th ed. 2007).

104. COMMUNICATION IN HISTORY, *supra* note 1, at 313 ("The first several satellites were constructed and rocketed into orbit by Intelstat (the International Space Communications Consortium); 60 percent of the shares in Intelstat belonged to COMSAT, an American corporation which—like RCA—had been created by Congress as a profit-making, investor-owned business, belonging equally to four American corporations (AT&T, ITT, RCA, and Western Union.").

105. *See* Cohen, *supra* note 103, at 313 ("Communications satellites contain electronic devices (called transponders) that amplify and transmit electromagnetic signals. Because the satellites are located high above the earth's surface and because their orbits are synchronous with the earth's rotation, communications satellites can receive and transmit signals from and to virtually anyplace on the surface of the globe; connecting a production studio in Texas, let us say, with a receiving antenna in Cairo.").

106. *Id.* ("Communications satellites made it possible for cable companies to stop paying AT&T for the use of its phone lines, and it also made it possible for some of the cable companies to begin thinking of creating national, even international, networks, beaming programs from one location to receiving antenna all over the country, if not all over the world.").

107. *See* A HISTORY OF MASS COMMUNICATION, *supra* note 8, at 169 (noting that satellite television "produced a financial bonanza [for cable television] by attracting huge urban audiences with a variety of cable-delivered channels, but in the 1990s it loomed as cable's competition because of direct broadcast satellite technology, which can bypass both local stations and cable to deliver those same channels directly from a source transmitter to the viewer.").

other technologies.[108] For example, during the first Persian Gulf War, CNN (Cable News Network) reporters used satellite and cable technology to broadcast live images of the war to businesses and homes around the world. At the outset of that war, United States viewers were riveted to CNN, which used satellites to broadcast live images of U.S. cruise missiles descending on Baghdad, thereby allowing viewers to "witness" these events (over their cable networks) in real time from the comfort of their living rooms.[109] Cable TV led to online news, sports, etc.

I. THE INTERNET

Of course the most potent communications technology, and one that was also based on electricity, is the internet. But more on that later.

---

108. *See* David Pogue, *State of the Art: Satellite Radio Extends Its Orbit*, *The New York Times*, at G1 (Dec. 18, 2003).

109. *See* Walter Goodman, *WAR IN THE GULF: TV CRITIC'S NOTEBOOK, On Television, the Theater of War*, *The New York Times*, at A19 (Jan. 17, 1991) ("Television achieved the excitement of old-time radio reporting last night as war began in the Persian Gulf.").

CHAPTER V

ELECTRONIC (NON-INTERNET) GATEKEEPERS

Just as the printing press was subject to governmental repression and "gatekeepers," the new electronics-based technologies were also subject to repression and gatekeepers (essentially private individuals or governmental entities) that could limit or control access to those technologies.

A. GOVERNMENTAL CONTROL OF THE BROADCAST MEDIA

As new mediums of communication were developed in later centuries, including broadcast technology, governments sought to restrict their uses in various ways.[1] While both radio and television dramatically expanded communications possibilities, both technologies suffered from numerous restrictions. In a number of countries, governments did not allow private individuals or corporations to hold radio or television licenses, or to use those technologies to broadcast. On the contrary, government retained control of broadcast frequencies. As a result, governments in those countries were able to control the content that was broadcast over radio and

1. *See FCC v. Pacifica Foundation*, 438 U.S. 726 (1978) (upholding FCC order relating to a radio station's broadcast of George Carlin's *Filthy Words* satire); *Red Lion Broadcasting Co. v. FCC*, 395 U.S. 367 (1969) (commenting on the scarcity of broadcast licenses).

television networks, and radio and television did not enable ordinary people to mass communicate.

1. MEDIA REGULATION IN THE UNITED STATES

In the United States, Congress allowed private entities to operate television and radio broadcasting stations, but it created the Federal Communications Commission (FCC) to exercise jurisdiction over wire and radio transmissions.[2] Under the FCC's mandate, the government maintains ownership of all radio waves, but has created a licensing scheme designed to allocate the use of those airwaves to private parties.[3] In addition, Congress gave the FCC the power to control wire and radio transmissions as needed for the public interest, convenience and necessity,[4] and FCC's regulatory authority extends not only to questions of *who* may communicate over the airwaves, but to some extent *what* they can communicate.[5]

Even in countries that permit private ownership of radio and television stations, governments have imposed restrictions on the content of radio and television broadcasts. For example, in some authoritarian countries, governments go to great lengths to regulate and control the content of radio and television broadcasts. During the revolt in Egypt that was part of the so-called Arab Spring, President Hosni Mubarak exercised tight control over what was published in the print media, repressing and try-

2. 47 U.S.C. § 151.

3. 47 U.S.C. § 301.

4. 47 U.S.C. § 303.

5. For example, Congress has imposed the requirement that broadcasters allot equal time to all qualified political candidates. 47 U.S.C. § 315. At one point, the FCC also imposed the so-called Fairness Doctrine which imposed content-based restrictions on broadcasters. 47 U.S.C. § 315(a). The Doctrine contained two separate and distinct components. The first, the political attack prong, required broadcasters to provide a right of reply to any person or group that was attacked. 47 U.S.C. § 315(a). Although there were exceptions to the rule, the rule imposed stringer procedural and reply restrictions on broadcasters. The Fairness Doctrine also contained a requirement that broadcasters give adequate coverage to public issues, and required that this coverage must accurately reflect opposing views. In *Red Lion Broadcasting Co. v. Federal Communications Commission*, 395 U.S. 367 (1969), the Court upheld the Fairness Doctrine, suggesting that the broadcast media could be treated differently than the print media because of the limited number of broadcasting bands available, and the fact that those who allocated frequencies are treated as trustees. The Court refused to apply strict scrutiny, and simply asserted the public's right "to receive suitable access to social, political, esthetic, moral, and other ideas."

ing to silence traditional journalists,[6] and he was able to arrange to have newspaper articles published that were designed to scare the population with rhetoric about the violence that might result if he resigned.[7] Egyptian authorities also took repressive action against the satellite-based television network Al Jazeera.[8]

Even in countries that permit private ownership of broadcast licenses, governments have imposed limitations on the ability of people to use that technology. Some of the limitations are inherent in the nature of broadcast technologies.[9] Since radio and television signals can reach much farther than the human voice, and there are a limited number of broadcast waves, there is the potential for interference if too many people attempt to use the same broadcast waves at the same time.[10] As the U.S. Supreme Court recognized in *Red Lion Broadcasting Co. v. F.C.C.*,[11] although a "lack of know-how and equipment may keep many from the air," "only a tiny fraction of those with resources and intelligence can hope to communicate by radio at the same time if intelligible communication is to be had, even if the entire radio spectrum is utilized."[12] If multiple people try to broadcast on the same air waves at the same time, the potential for signal interference would become a "massive reality."[13]

Because of the limited number of broadcast waves, and because of the potential for interference, the U.S. Congress enacted the Radio Act of 1927[14] and the Communications Act of 1934. Basically, Congress subdivided the broadcast spectrum so that it could be used for a variety of

6. *See* Jeremy W. Peters & J. David Goodman, *Reporters Beaten and Cameras Smashed in Struggle to Control the News From Cairo, The New York Times*, A8 (Feb. 4, 2011).

7. *See* Michael Slackman, *A Brittle Leader, Appearing Strong, The New York Times*, at A1 (Feb. 12, 2011) ("Mr. Mubarak resorted to the tried and proven tactics that have been a hallmark of his authoritarian regime. He unleashed the full force of the police, tried to manage the message by shutting down the Internet and censoring news reports, insisted the people in the street were manipulated by foreigners or Islamists, and presented a stark either-or equation—if he did not remain in power, the alternative would be far worse.").

8. *See* Brian Stelter, *Televising the Revolution: Al Jazeera Hopes Reports from Egypt Open Doors in U.S., The New York Times*, at B8 (Feb. 7, 2011).

9. *See Red Lion Broadcasting Co. v. FCC*, 395 U.S. 367 (1969).

10. *Id.* at 387–388.

11. 395 U.S. 367 (1969).

12. *Id.* at 388.

13. *Id.*

14. *Id.*

purposes: "public broadcasting and for other important radio uses such as amateur operation, aircraft, police, defense, and navigation; and then the subdivision of each portion, and assignment of specific frequencies to individual users or groups of users."[15] In other words, Congress limited the number of radio and television broadcast licenses that could exist, and in the U.S. (at least) allowed the FCC to allocate those licenses among private interests.[16] The net effect of this regulatory scheme is that only a few were awarded broadcast licenses, and those few were given the power to decide who could broadcast on their radio and televisions.

Because only a few individuals could obtain broadcast licenses, Congress and the courts have treated those individuals as fiduciaries of the air waves, and the FCC has been given enhanced authority to regulate those who broadcast.[17] For example, at one point, the FCC imposed the so-called Fairness Doctrine on broadcast media which treated those who received broadcast licenses as fiduciaries of the broadcast waves that they had been allocated, required them to give adequate coverage to public issues, and mandated that the coverage accurately reflect opposing viewpoints.[18] In other words, the broadcaster must handle public issues "fairly" with due regard for opposing points of view. The FCC also imposed the political attack rule on broadcasters. Under that rule, if a media outlet attacked a political candidate, it was required to give the person attacked the opportunity to respond.

Interestingly, had Congress attempted to impose a limitation like the Fairness Doctrine or the political attack rule on the print media, the restriction would have been struck down as unconstitutional. In general, the government cannot force newspapers to provide a "right of reply" to those that it attacks.[19] Moreover, government is not allowed to exercise control over the content or viewpoints articulated in the print media[20] (with limited exceptions—for example, it may prohibit child pornography,[21]

15. *Id.*
16. *Id.*
17. *Id.* at 389.
18. *Id.*
19. *See Miami Herald Publishing Co. v. Tornillo*, 418 U.S. 241 1974).
20. *See R.A.V. v. City of St. Paul*, 505 U.S. 377 (1992).
21. *See New York v. Ferber*, 458 U.S. 747)1982).

true threats[22] and obscenity[23]). The Fairness Doctrine clearly involved a viewpoint-based restriction on speech. The political attack rule required media outlets to provide a right of reply to those who are attacked.

The broadcast media was also subject to other restrictions. For example, in *F.C.C. v. Pacifica Foundation*,[24] the Court held that content-based restrictions could be imposed on "indecent" speech. That case involved a George Carlin monologue entitled "Filthy Words," which was aired by a radio station as part of a program regarding contemporary society's attitude towards language. In his monologue, Carlin focused on (and repeatedly uttered) the seven words that one is not allowed to say on the radio. Although the *Pacifica* decision did not hold that these "indecent" (but not obscene) words could be banned, it did hold that such programs could be restricted to late night hours when children were less likely to be listening. Again, this involves a variance from the print media. Although the print media can be prohibited from publishing obscene speech, it cannot prohibited from publishing "indecent," "offensive,"[25] or vulgar speech.[26]

2. MEDIA REPRESSION AND REGULATION OUTSIDE THE UNITED STATES

In some countries, broadcasting has been limited to government-owned and government-controlled entities. In that situation, as well as when private interests own radio and television stations, there has been much regulation and control. During the Tunisian revolt, in an effort to control content, the government closed down a private television station.[27] Interestingly, after the Tunisian government was ousted, the interim government shut down another Tunisian television channel.[28] Egyptian authorities also took repressive action against the satellite-based television network Al Jazeera.[29] In South Africa, the government proposed to

22. *See Virginia v. Black*, 538 U.S. 343 (2003).

23. *See Miller v. California*, 413 U.S. 15 (1973).

24. 438 U.S. 726 (1978).

25. *See Cohen v. California*, 403 U.S. 15 (1971).

26. *Id.*

27. *See* David D. Kirkpatrick, *Government of Tunisia Shuts Down TV Channel*, *The New York Times*, at A4 (Jan. 24, 2011).

28. *See id.*

29. *See Televising the Revolution*, *supra* note 8, at B8.

impose new criminal penalties on the media.[30] In North Korea, journalists have been jailed.[31]

In Iraq, during the 2013 uprising, Iraq's government revoked the operating licenses of Al Jazeera and nine other television stations.[32] Iraq sought to justify the revocation on the basis that the channels had broadcast "misinformation, hype and exaggeration" which had encouraged "hatred on the basis of national or ethnic or religious identities that can incite discrimination, hostility or violence."[33] The government also suggested that the channels were trying to incite a revolution in favor of Al Qaeda.[34] Prior to the revocation, these channels had devoted a significant amount of air time to the Sunni protests, and critics alleged that Iraq revoked the licenses in order to silence its critics and cover up governmental misconduct.[35] Because of an explosion of new technologies, the revocations did not force all of these stations off the air.[36] For example, Al Jazeera operated on satellite channels outside of Iraq, and was able to continue broadcasting by satellite.[37] However, the revocation did limit the ability of Al Jazeera journalists to report from within Iraq, rendering their newsrooms inside Iraq quiet.[38]

B. PRIVATE GATEKEEPERS

Just as there were private gatekeepers who controlled the use of the Gutenberg printing press, gatekeepers have controlled electronic communications technologies as well. In the case of the electronic media, some of the gatekeepers were monopolists who tried to exercise market control

30. *See* Celia W. Dugger, *Proposed Restrictions on the News Media Cause Alarm in South Africa, The New York Times*, at A4 (Aug. 23, 2010).

31. *See* Brian Stelter, *A World of Risk for a New Brand of Journalist, The New York Times*, at B1 (June 15, 2009).

32. *See* Tim Arango, *Iraq Revokes Licenses of Al Jazeera and Other TV Channels Amid Sunni Uprising, The New York Times* A6 (Apr. 29, 2013).

33. *Id.*

34. *Id.*

35. *Id.*

36. *Id.*

37. *Id.*

38. *Id.*

over a particular communications technology (radio or television).[39] Over time, no one individual or corporation has been able to exert monopolistic control over communications for long periods of time. Technology has advanced too quickly for that to happen.[40] Nevertheless, there have always been individuals (or groups of individuals) or companies in "gatekeeper" positions who tried to control the ability of the populace to use certain communications technologies.

Although broadcast technology was revolutionary in terms of its speech potential, in the sense that it allowed the spoken word and pictures to be transmitted very quickly over very long distances, so that it was possible to reach large audiences simultaneously, the mass communications potential of broadcast technology was muted because not everyone could obtain a broadcast license. There were a limited number of airwaves, and it was costly to acquire, establish and operate a radio or television station.[41] Those who did hold broadcast licenses effectively

---

39. *See* Ruth Schwartz Cohen, *The Social Shape of Electronics,* in COMMUNICATION IN HISTORY, in DAVID CROWLEY & PAUL HEYER, COMMUNICATION IN HISTORY: TECHNOLOGY, CULTURE, SOCIETY 311–319 (5th ed. 2007).

40. *Id.*, at 318 ("From the invention of wireless telegraphy in the late nineteenth century to the creation of an electronic superhighway in the late twentieth, no one individual, and no one institution, has succeeded in controlling for very long the American market for electronic components or electronic devices or even the content of what is communicated by those devices."); *Id.*, at 311–312:

> [T]here are many surprises for individuals and organizations that think they can remain in control of the business of communications. Just when an inventor, after years of painstaking work, would begin to count his royalties in the millions of dollars, along came another inventor with a patent on a new, slightly better device, stealing his thunder and his plans for future wealth. Or just when a company, after years of complex maneuvering, would begin to exert almost complete control over some marketplace, along came another company with a new idea to compete for market share. Control of electronic industries—by individuals, by companies, even by governments—has been from the very beginning evanescent, transitory, fleeting. Individuals and companies have had their moment in the sun, but eventually they have all lost monopolistic control of the market that had once proven so profitable.

See also TW Cable Net Income Declines, supra note 429, at B8 (noting that overall cable television revenue was declining as consumers shifted to internet-based services).

41. *See Red Lion Broadcasting Co. v. FCC*, 395 U.S. 367 (1969) (commenting on the scarcity of broadcast licenses); *see also* Jerome A. Barron, *Access to the Media—1967 to 2007 and Beyond: A Symposium Honoring Jerome A. Barron's Path-Breaking Article "Access Reconsidered,"* 76 GEO. W. L. REV. 826, 832 (2008) ("Technology and patterns of media con-

became gatekeepers of the technology for those who did not. As with newspapers, radio broadcasters had the power to decide what would (and, more importantly, would not) be aired.

The U.S. Supreme Court has recognized that those who hold broadcast licenses can exercise editorial discretion over what they broadcast. *Columbia Broadcasting System, Inc. v. Democratic National Committee,*[42] involved a suit by the Democratic National Committee (DNC) and the Business Executives' Move for Vietnam Peace (BEM), a national organization that opposed U.S. involvement in the Vietnam conflict, both of which wanted to run paid advertisements on television. The Federal Communications Commission (FCC) held that, a broadcaster that otherwise meets its obligation to provide full and fair examination of public issues, is not required to accept editorial advertisements. While the Court recognized that broadcasters do not have as much freedom as newspaper publishers, it nonetheless held that they retain a "large measure of journalistic freedom,"[43] and are not required to "make regular programming time available to those holding a different view."[44]

However, there are limits to their editorial discretion. In, for example, *CBS, Inc. v. Federal Communications Commission,*[45] the FCC found that the major television networks failed to provide "reasonable access" to their networks as required by the governing statute. In that case, the Carter-Mondale Presidential Committee wanted to air a documentary outlining the accomplishments of the Carter administration. In upholding the FCC order, the U.S. Supreme Court concluded that legally qualified federal candidates are entitled to "reasonable access" that can be invoked once a federal campaign has commenced. In rendering its decision, the Court

centration had combined to place a few companies with the power to control access to the content to which the majority of the population was exposed.'); Elaine B. Gin, *2004 International Copyright Law: Beyond the WIPO and Trips Debate*, 86 J. PAT. & TRADEMARK OFF. SOC'Y 763, 777–778 (2004) ("Advanced democracies have well-developed market-based media channels, which are often large conglomerates. Because of their economic power, these media conglomerates may impede meaningful democratic rule, by monopolizing media access.").

42. 412 U.S. 94 (1973).

43. *Id.* at 110.

44. *Id.* at 124.

45. 453 U.S. 367 (1981).

purported to balance the First Amendment rights of federal candidates against the rights of the public and broadcasters.

In other countries, governments have exercised significant control over television broadcasting.[46] In some countries, television broadcasting is either government-owned or government controlled. In the United States, television stations are generally controlled by private individuals rather than being government owned,[47] and television broadcasters are regarded as exercising a public privilege to broadcast even though they been given fairly broad authority to control what is broadcast on their stations.[48] Although ordinary individuals have the right to listen to the broadcasts provided by the owners of television stations, they have not historically had the right to broadcast their own content or ideas over the airwaves except with the permission or consent of the owners or operators of television stations.

The net effect was that a non licensee's ability to access the air waves was subject to the whims of those who held the licenses. A non licensee could create an op-ed piece, or might even try to offer an advertisement, but the holder of the radio or television license was not required to broadcast either of them.[49]Although some broadcasters allowed (and allow) private individuals to air op-ed pieces, just as some newspapers publish op-eds or letters to the editor, the broadcaster's editor or producer retained discretion about whether to air a particular op-ed.

---

46. *See* Irving Fang, A History of Mass Communication: Six Information Revolutions 90 (1997). ("As a source of information, radio has been universally powerful, although in many nations today radio remains strictly under government control.").

47. *Id.*, at 158 ("Television developed as a private business in the United States, unlike most other countries....").

48. *Compare Red Lion* with *CBS* decisions; *see also* William Boddy, *Television Begins*, in *See* David Crowley & Paul Heyer, Communication in History: Technology, Culture, Society 244 (5th ed. 2007) ("Broadcast regulation in the United States has been founded upon two opposing principles: that the federal license confers a privilege, not a right, to the broadcaster to operate in "the public interest" using public airwaves, and the license establishes and protects the broad *de facto* property rights of private operators of television and radio stations under restricted oversight of network operations and programme content.").

49. *See Columbia Broadcasting System, Inc. v. Democratic National Committee*, 412 U.S. 94 (1973) ("Congress opted for a system of private broadcasters licensed and regulated by Government.... A broadcast licensee has a large measure of journalistic freedom but not as large as that exercised by a newspaper.").

At various points in history, broadcasters have stridently attempted to use their media power to try to influence public opinion, in much the same way that newspaper owners and editors have done, and they have not necessarily served as honest brokers of information and news. On the contrary, some have used their broadcast licenses to air or discuss issues only in ways that comport with their political or social beliefs. For example, some have alleged that Fox News has a decidedly conservative bias that it uses to try to influence public opinion.[50] Interestingly, a number of actual and possible Republican presidential candidates (Mike Huckabee, Rick Santorum, Newt Gingrich and Sarah Palin) were Fox News employees in 2010, and were contractually precluded from appearing on other news channels.[51] In addition, at times, Fox News personalities (non-political candidates) have made campaign appearances with Republican candidates.[52] For example, Sean Hannity campaigned with Donald Trump during the 2018 mid-term elections.[53] On the left, MSNBC is viewed as having a decidedly left-wing bias.

Likewise, National Public Radio (NPR) has a decidedly left-wing bias. The allegations against NPR began when it fired commentator Juan Williams, for making comments about Muslims.[54] The firing sparked protests,[55] and prompted one commentator to claim that NPR was being run

---

50. See Timothy Noah, *Fox News Admits Bias! Its London Bureau Chief Blurts Out the Political Slant That Dare Not Speak its Name*, Slate (May 31, 2005). http://www.slate.com/id/2119864/.

51. *See* Bob Garfield, *A Fox Presidential Primary?*, National Public Radio, On the Media (Oct. 1, 2010), http://www.onthemedia.org/2010/oct/01/a-fox-presidential-primary/transcript/.

52. *See* Jim Rutenberg, *Sharing the Stage With Trump, Fox News Stars Flout an Ideal, The New York Times* A1 (Nov. 7, 2018).

53. *Id.*

54. *See* Brett Zongker, *NPR's Williams Is Fired After Muslim Remarks, The Courier-Journal*, A2 (Oct. 22, 2010).

55. *See* Michelle Martin, *NPR Fires Juan Williams, Journalists React*, National Public Radio, Tell Me More (Oct. 22, 2010), http://www.npr.org/templates/story/story.php?storyId=130751882 ("National Public Radio was widely criticized for firing news analyst Juan Williams.... He was fired Wednesday after comments he made about Muslims in an appearance on FOX News' "The O'Reilly Factor." Those comments and NPR's response to them have generated a controversy that has engulfed both networks and the blogosphere. For example, by midmorning today, some 15,000 messages have been blogged about this on NPR's home page.").

by "left-wing Nazis."[56] The Williams firing even led to an effort to cut off public funding for NPR,[57] but that effort failed.[58] There was also an incident involving NPR's then-fundraiser, Mr. Ron Schiller, who was videotaped making disparaging remarks about conservatives.[59] The airing of the videotape led Schiller to resign,[60] as well as to the resignation of NPR's Senior Vice President,[61] and its President and CEO, Vivian Schiller (no relation).[62]

The Williams and Schiller incidents may constitute isolated examples, but there is ample evidence of left-wing bias at NPR. Perhaps the

---

56. *See* David Folkenflik, *Fox News CEO Ailes: NPR Execs Have Nazi Attitude*, National Public Radio, Morning Edition (Nov. 19, 2010), http://www.npr.org/2010/11/19/131436212/fox-news-ceo-ailes-npr-execs-have-nazi-attitude ("'But in the piece published Thursday, Ailes spoke of NPR executives: 'They are, of course, Nazis. They have a kind of Nazi attitude. They are the left wing of Nazism. These guys don't want any other point of view.'").

57. *See* Brian Stelter and Elizabeth Jensen, *Criticism of Firing by HPR Heightens as Broadcaster Defends the Decision, The New York Times*, at B3 (Oct. 23, 2010) ("many conservatives have seized on his firing to resurrect their war against public broadcasting.").

58. *See* Frank James, *Effort to Block NPR's Funding Fails*, National Public Radio, It's All Politics (Nov. 18, 2010), http://www.npr.org/blogs/itsallpolitics/2010/11/18/131428963/effort-to-block-npr-s-public-funding-fails.

59. *See* Associated Press, *NPR Chief Executive Quits Over Hidden Camera Video*, National Public Radio (Mar. 9, 2011), http://www.npr.org/blogs/thetwo-way/2011/03/10/134388981/npr-ceo-vivian-schiller-resigns (Schiller made the following statement: "'The current Republican Party is not really the Republican Party. It's been hijacked by this group that is... not just Islamophobic but, really, xenophobic,' Ron Schiller said in the video, referring to the tea party movement. 'They believe in sort of white, middle America, gun-toting—it's scary. They're seriously racist, racist people.'"); Mark Memmott, *In Video: NPR Exec Slams Tea Party, Questions Need for Federal Funds*, National Public Radio, The Two-Way (Mar. 8, 2011), http://www.npr.org/blogs/thetwo-way/2011/03/09/134358398/in-video-npr-exec-slams-tea-party-questions-need-for-federal-funds (he also stated that "'Tea Party is fanatically involved in people's personal lives and very fundamental Christian—I wouldn't even call it Christian. It's this weird evangelical kind of move." The videotape also suggests that Schiller had no reaction when told that the group with which he was meeting was sponsored by Egypt's Muslim Brotherhood); David Folkenflik, *NPR Exec: NPR Would Be Better Off Without Federal Support*, National Public Radio, All Things Considered (Mar. 8, 2011), http://www.npr.org/2011/03/08/134371393/NPR-Exec-NPR-Would-Be-Better-Off-Without-Fed-Support.

60. *See* Mark Memmott, *NPR CEO Vivian Schiller Resigns After Board Decides She Should Go*, National Public Radio, The Two-Way (Mar. 9, 2011), http://www.npr.org/blogs/thetwo-way/2011/03/10/134388981/npr-ceo-vivian-schiller-resigns.

61. *See* David Folkenflik, *N.P.R. V.P. Resigns, CEO Rebuked Over Williams' Firing*, National Public Radio, Morning Edition (Jan. 7, 2011), http://www.npr.org/2011/01/07/132726894/npr-v-p-resigns-ceo-rebuked-over-williams-firing.

62. *See NPR CEO Vivian Schiller Resigns*, *supra* note 60.

most obvious evidence of that tendency is revealed by the reporting of NPR Morning Edition commentator Steve Inskeep. When the nation was debating whether to enact health care legislation in 2009, Inskeep conducted an aggressive, hostile and almost rude interview with Republican National Committee Chairman Michael Steele, during which Inskeep frequently interrupted Steele,[63] and made it difficult for Steele to articulate his position.[64] For an interesting contrast, about that same time, NPR host Lianne Hanson lobbed softballs to an advocate for providing illegal immigrants with health care benefits.[65] Hanson made absolutely no effort to ask the interviewee any tough questions about why it might not be desirable to extend coverage to illegals. The contrast between the two interviews was striking.

With Inskeep, there are lots of other examples of biased interviewing. In 2018, he conducted an extremely biased interview with Senator Marco Rubio. During that interview, Inskeep was absolutely determined to focus on whether President Trump should be removed from office under the Twenty-Fifth Amendment to the U.S. Constitution for mental unfitness.[66] Even though Rubio flatly rejected the suggestion, stating "That's a stretch,"[67] and even though Rubio dismissed the factual basis for the

---

63. *See* Steve Inskeep, *Steele: Don't Raid Medicare to Fund Health Changes*, National Public Radio, Morning Edition (Aug. 27, 2009), http://www.npr.org/templates/story/story.php?storyId=112281170.

64. *Id.*

65. *See* Lianne Hanson, *The Intersection of Health Care and Immigration*, National Public Radio, Weekend Edition Sunday (Sept. 30, 2009), http://www.npr.org/templates/story/story.php?storyId=113005541.

66. *See* Steve Inskeep, *Rubio: Congress Should Constrain President, Not "Anonymous" Staffer*, National Public Radio, Morning Edition (Sept. 7, 2018). https://www.npr.org/2018/09/07/645459797/rubio-congress-should-constrain-president-not-anonymous-staffer:

> INSKEEP: This op-ed writer describes a president who's so erratic that there were quote "whispers in the cabinet about applying the 25th Amendment," which is a way to remove a president who seems unable to perform his duties. Late in the presidency of Ronald Reagan, his then-chief of staff, Howard Baker—it's a matter of history—conducted an examination, even talking to the president himself to try to determine, is there a 25th Amendment problem here? Should John Kelly be doing that?

67. *Id.* ("Oh, that's a stretch.").

suggestion,[68] Inskeep persistently pursued the line of questioning, asking the same question in four different ways four different times.[69] Inskeep, apparently committed to the idea that Trump was unfit for office and should be removed, was simply unwilling to take "no" for an answer.[70] A few days later, in an interview with Ken Starr about Starr's conduct of the Clinton special counsel investigation, Inskeep tried repeatedly to shift the focus away from Clinton to Trump.[71] Thus, even though Starr was being interviewed to discuss the Clinton investigation, and even though Starr repeatedly rejected the comparison of Trump to Clinton, Inskeep doggedly pursued the line of questioning, spending the last half of the interview focused almost entirely on Trump.[72] Again, Inskeep was determined to make his points rather than to listen to the interviewee.

---

68. *Id.*:

RUBIO: We're talking here more about a behavioral issue in terms of what some people claim anonymously. They don't like temperament. And that's a very different situation. I've never heard John Kelly or, frankly, anyone in the administration come to me and said (sic) any of the things that have been reported in the last 72 hours.

69. *See id.*

70. *See id.*

71. *See* Steve *Inskeep, 2 Decades Later, Starr Writes Memoir "Contempt" on Clinton Impeachment*, National Public Radio, Morning Edition (Sept. 10, 2018). https://www.npr.org/2018/09/10/646213925/2-decades-later-starr-writes-memoir-contempt-on-clinton-impeachment.

INSKEEP: ... What have you thought about, now that Republicans—the same party—have become overwhelmingly supportive of a president who's been documented making thousands of false statements?

STARR: (Laughter).... But here's a key distinction. At least as far as we know, Donald Trump has not lied under oath. As far as we know, he's not intimidated witnesses. As far as we know, in my view, he has not obstructed justice. So ...

72. *See id:*

INSKEEP: You described the Clintons as fundamentally dishonest. Is our current president fundamentally dishonest?

* * *

INSKEEP: I noticed in the book you were upset at Janet Reno, the attorney general at the time, because she failed to publicly support your work. She didn't trash your work, so far as I know. But she didn't speak up. And you found that to be cowardly, which does make me wonder—what do you think now that President Trump publicly calls the investigation surrounding him a witch hunt, regularly calls it that on a regular basis?

* * *

If such hard-hitting questioning were the norm at NPR, one could perhaps dismiss Inskeep's interviewing of Steele, Rubio and Starr as simply a reflection of his style. However, when it serves left-wing interests, NPR might ignore even the most basic questions that one might expect a reasonably competent journalist to ask. For example, during the confirmation proceedings of Judge Brett Kavanaugh to the U.S. Supreme Court, questions arose regarding whether Kavanaugh (an admittedly conservative jurist) had committed sexual assaults against women. These allegations were extremely important to our society and to our democratic system. If Kavanaugh engaged in such conduct, he simply should not have been appointed to the nation's highest court. On the other hand, if he was innocent of the alleged conduct, and the allegations were simply part of a Democratically led smear campaign, NPR had an ethical and journalistic obligation to expose that fact. NPR failed miserably in its reporting on the issue.

In regard to the allegations by the first witness, Dr. Christine Blasey-Ford, following the hearing, questions were raised regarding whether Dr. Blasey-Ford testified truthfully that she did not know much about polygraph tests, or how to game them. Afterwards, a former boyfriend alleged that she had helped prepare a friend to take a polygraph exam.[73] The claims were later denied by the friend.[74] On the day that the allegations about the polygraph exam broke, there was no mention of them on NPR. Instead, NPR aired a segment on someone who knew Kavanaugh in college, who wanted to give a statement to the FBI, but who was never

---

INSKEEP: Why do you think large majorities of Republicans, at least, think it's fine? They approve of the President's performance at least.

* * *

INSKEEP: Isn't that kind of dissembling, though, Mr. Starr, because that is the heart of his presidency, is what he says publicly and the attitude he strikes?

* * *

73. *See* Gregg Re & John Roberts, *Christine Blasey Ford ex-boyfriend says she helped friend prep for potential polygraph; Grassley sounds alarm*, Fox News Channel (Oct. 3, 2018) https://www.foxnews.com/politics/christine-blasey-ford-ex-boyfriend-says-she-helped-friend-prep-for-potential-polygraph-grassley-sounds-alarm.

74. *See* Brooke Singman, *Christine Ford's friend denies being helped on polygraph, fires back at new claims*, Fox News Channel (Oct. 4, 2018) https://www.foxnews.com/politics/christine-fords-friend-denies-being-helped-on-polygraph-fires-back-at-new-claims.

interviewed.[75] There was no mention of the polygraph allegations the following morning on NPR's Morning Edition either.[76]

At one point, *The New Yorker* magazine published explosive allegations from a second woman (Ramirez) who charged Kavanaugh with sexual assault for sticking his penis in her face. There was lots of room for skepticism regarding the validity of the accuser's story. For one thing, she admitted that she was really drunk at the party where the assault allegedly occurred, and that she was initially unable to state whether Kavanaugh was the perpetrator (or whether someone else had done it).[77] Ms. Ramirez also admitted that she contacted former Yale classmates to ask whether they recalled the incident, and told some of them that she did not remember whether Kavanaugh was the one who had exposed himself, and inquired whether they remembered.[78] Only after six days of discussions with lawyers and psychologists was she able to definitely identify Kavanaugh as the perpetrator.[79] In the meantime, those who she identified as being at the party (who purportedly witnessed the alleged events) denied that such an incident had occurred at all.[80] Because of these problems with the Ramirez allegations, *The New York Times* initially decided not to publish the allegations. *The Times* had interviewed several dozen people over the prior week in an attempt to corroborate her story, and could find no one with firsthand knowledge who would state that the event actually happened. Ramirez also made clear that she was a Democrat, who worked for social justice, and was opposed to the Kavanaugh nomination.[81] In other words, her sudden ability to identify Kavanaugh may have had more to do with her political convictions than with the truth of the matter.

---

75. *See* Mary Louise Kelly, *What Happened When A College Friend Of Kavanaugh Tried To Talk To The FBI*, National Public Radio, All Things Considered (Oct. 4, 2018). https://www.npr.org/2018/10/04/654518406/what-happened-when-a-college-friend-of-kavanaugh-tried-to-talk-to-the-fbi.

76. *See* https://www.npr.org/programs/morning-edition/2018/10/05/654659772/morning-edition-for-october-5-2018?showDate=2018-10-05.

77. *Id.*

78. *Id.*

79. *Id.*

80. *Id.*

81. *Id.*

From listening to NPR, it would have been difficult to learn most of these extremely important details.[82] The NPR Morning Edition interview was conducted with the authors of the piece and they were largely sympathetic to the allegations, stating that they believed the allegations were true, that there was one confirmatory witness, and that they felt that there should be an investigation. They emphasized that Ramirez was "calling for an FBI investigation, which they believed was appropriate and necessary.[83] NPR never bothered to conduct an in-depth examination of the serious deficiencies in Ramirez's allegations. Although NPR's All Things Considered talked about the story later that same day, it did not bother to mention the deficiencies in her story either. Apparently, NPR's commitment to consider "all things" did not extend to consideration of the problems with the woman's allegations. Instead, NPR emphasized that this claim involved a second woman making claims against Kavanaugh, and suggested that the evidence was mounting against Kavanaugh, but that Republicans seem determined to push ahead with the Kavanaugh nomination.[84] On the following day, rather than discuss the deficiencies in the second woman's allegations, NPR aired stories about a woman who had previously supported Kavanaugh but does no longer,[85] and about Professor Anita hill's belief that the Judiciary Committee was proceeding unfairly.[86] By contrast, when *The New York Times* finally decided to publish something regarding the allegations, it included information related the flaws in the allegations.[87]

---

82. Rachel Martin, "*New Yorker* " *Publishes Another Sexual Misconduct Allegation Against Kavanaugh*, National Public Radio, Morning Edition (Sept. 24, 2018). https://www.npr.org/2018/09/24/651030769/new-yorker-publishes-another-sexual-misconduct-allegation-against-kavanaugh.

83. *Id.*

84. *See* Scott Detrow, *Lawmakers Debate Next Steps For Kavanaugh As Second Woman Comes Forward*, National Public Radio, All Things Considered (Sept. 24, 2018). https://www.npr.org/2018/09/24/651221310/lawmakers-debate-next-steps-for-kavanaugh-as-second-woman-comes-forward.

85. *See* Audie Cornish, *Kavanaugh Supporter Now Has Second Thoughts*, National Public Radio, All Things Considered (Sept. 25, 2018). https://www.npr.org/2018/09/25/651571233/kavanaugh-supporter-now-has-second-thoughts.

86. *See* Merit Kennedy & Bill Chappell, *Anita Hill Says Kavanaugh Hearing Cannot "Be Fair,"*, National Public Radio, All Things Considered (Sept. 25, 2018). https://www.npr.org/2018/09/25/651489805/anita-hill-says-kavanaugh-accuser-hearing-cannot-be-fair.

87. *See* Stephanie Saul, Robin Pogrebin, Mike McIntire & Ben Protess, *In a Culture of Privilege and Alcohol at Yale, her World Converged with Kavanaugh's, The New York Times*

When a third woman came forward with claims against Kavanaugh, NPR reiterated Ramirez's allegation and again failed to mention the concerns about those allegations.[88] Even on Thursday, the day on which the Judiciary Committee hearing was held, NPR was still referring to three accusers, but was still not providing essential details.

Of course, NPR's concealment of the facts is very troubling. As a *Washington Post* journalist commented on *The New Yorker* story, ultimately, the believability of journalists depends on their credibility.[89] The writer noted that she was originally of the opinion that, if a second accuser came forward, the Kavanaugh nomination should not go forward. However, after reading the Ramirez allegations, she reached the opposite conclusion: that she must "discard my prewritten thesis and start fresh."[90] After recounting all of the problems with Ramirez's allegations, she concluded that "given the thinness of the evidence, I'm frankly surprised *The New Yorker* ran the article." So, instead of demanding that Kavanaugh withdraw, on the basis that "a second allegation would be stronger, not weaker, than the first," she found herself making "a sudden shift toward the view that Republicans must take the matter at least through a hearing. Otherwise, nominee after nominee would go down to a string of unverifiable allegations."[91] To

---

(Sept. 25, 2018) (" Ms. Ramirez initially told friends she had memory gaps and was not certain that Judge Kavanaugh was the person who exposed himself, as she related to Mr. Roche and some other old classmates last week. But, after six days of assessing her memories, The New Yorker reported, she said she was confident that Judge Kavanaugh was the man who had humiliated her."). https://www.nytimes.com/2018/09/25/us/politics/deborah-ramirez-brett-kavanaugh-allegations.html?action=click&module=Top%20Stories&pgtype=Homepage.

88. *See* Scott Detrow, *Third Woman Comes Forward With Allegations of Sexual Misconduct Against Kavanaugh*, National Public Radio, All Things Considered (Sept. 26, 2018). https://www.npr.org/2018/09/26/651918647/third-woman-comes-forward-with-allegations-of-sexual-misconduct-against-kavanaug; Ryan Lucas, *Judiciary Committee Reviews New Sexual Misconduct Allegations Against Kavanaugh*, National Public Radio (Sept. 26, 2018). https://www.npr.org/2018/09/26/651797758/judiciary-committee-review-new-sexual-misconduct-allegations-against-kavanaugh.

89. *See* Megan McArdle, *#Me Too depends on the credibility of the journalists who report it, The Washington Post* (Sept. 25, 2018). https://www.washingtonpost.com/opinions/metoo-depends-on-the-credibility-of-the-journalists-who-report-on-it/2018/09/25/02ddc35c-c104-11e8-9005-5104e9616c21_story.html?utm_term=.2b9be7686e1e.

90. *Id.*

91. *Id.*

her, the Ramirez allegations reminded her of another journalistic fiasco: "When Rolling Stone failed to check allegations about gang rape at the University of Virginia, the magazine both smeared innocent young men and caused other victims to be treated more skeptically." She concluded that "when a weak story breaks into an already raging political conflagration, it not only creates skepticism under which future abusers can shelter but also threatens to turn #MeToo into yet another divide in the culture wars."[92] Of course, the journalism she was criticizing in the Ramirez case was *The New Yorker's* decision to air the allegations at all. By contrast to NPR, *The New Yorker* at least had the journalistic integrity to explain the main flaws in Ramirez's allegations. NPR's Morning Edition made only vague references to the flaws in her contentions. On the morning of the Judiciary Committee hearing, NPR did not mention the concerns about Ramirez's allegations.[93]

If the Ramirez reporting were an isolated incident, one might be inclined to give NPR a pass on the bias question. The difficulty is that NPR followed its reporting about the Ramirez allegations with shoddy reporting about the third accuser's allegations.[94] In that accusation, a woman by the name of Julie Swetnick claimed that she had attended many parties during a two year period at which she saw women purportedly drugged and gang raped (with guys being lined up to rape them). In those interviews, NPR again failed to ask some of the most basic questions that one might have expected even a moderately competent journalist to have asked. The most obvious question was, if the woman was aware that women were being drugged and gang raped at these parties, why in the world would she have attended them at all, much less many of them? Moreover, if she knew that woman were routinely being gang raped, why did she not notify the police? Suddenly, given that the woman was making allegations against a conservative, NPR decided to play soft ball with its reporting.

The program *On the Media* (OTM), which is produced by NYC, provides perhaps the most obvious and pristine example of left-wing bias; the program seems to make almost no pretense of being neutral and objec-

92. *Id.*

93. *See* https://www.npr.org/programs/morning-edition/2018/09/26/651707416?-showDate=2018-09-26.

94. *See Third Woman Comes Forward, supra* note 88.

tive, and indeed makes Fox News appears to be neutral, objective and unbiased in comparison. The producers of OTM air programs that talk about the "myth" of individuals pulling themselves up by their bootstraps, they hammer away at their perception of racism, and rarely approach hot button issues with any sort of objectivity or balance. Following the Kavanaugh judiciary hearing involving Professor Blasey-Ford, OTM showed outright venom towards Kavanaugh and Trump with commentator Brooke Gladstone, the left's response to Rush Limbaugh, on full-scale attack against Kavanaugh (and, to a lesser extent, Trump).[95] Even the introduction to the program suggested Gladstone's bias. She began by positing the following questions: "How long since naked id has been displayed so brazenly to a nation's people, and embraced as rectitude by its most powerful men? How long since a country's professed values, its principles, even its deodorizing pieties and hypocrisies, have been so swiftly repealed?"[96] Throughout the program, Gladstone presented Kavanaugh as a sexual predator and did not display even a pretense of journalistic objectivity.[97] However, OTM's bias does not show up only in regard to Kavanaugh. During the uproar over bias at NPR, rather than interviewing NPR's critics, OTM did a lengthy interview with an NPR personality about whether NPR is biased.[98] Amazingly enough, the NPR personality did not perceive that NPR is biased![99] And, of course, OTM did not deem it necessary to interview any of NPR's critics.

Of course, the image that the media is biased and political is sometimes obvious. For example, at the annual White House Correspondents' Association Dinner, comedian Michelle Wolf savaged Trump and his aides in "vicious and occasionally vulgar terms that predictably caused the media's

---

95. *See* Brooke Gladstone, *Having It Both Ways With Kavanaugh*, On The Media (Sept. 28, 2018). https://www.wnycstudios.org/story/having-it-both-ways-kavanaugh?tab=summary.

96. *See id.*

97. *See id.*

98. *See* Brooke Gladstone, *The Bias Bias*, National Public Radio, On the Media (Mar. 11, 2011), http://www.onthemedia.org/2011/mar/11/the-bias-bias/transcript/ (interviewing NPR commentator Ira Glass).

99. *See id.* (quoting NPR commentator Ira Glass: "As somebody who works in public radio, it is killing me that people on the right are going around trying to basically rebrand us, saying that it's biased news, it's—it's, you know, it's left wing news, when I feel like anybody who listens to the shows knows that it's not. And we are not fighting back.").

enemies to trumpet that journalists are no more dignified than the president whose decency they lament."[100] Wolf also shamed White House press correspondent, Sarah Huckabee Sanders, for her appearance.[101] Even a journalist lamented the fact that "every caricature thrust upon national press—that we are culturally elitist, socioeconomically detached and ideologically biased—is confirmed by this train wreck of an event."[102] As one commentator noted, the media was held in low regard even before Trump began his attacks.[103]

Of course, in a free society, the broadcast and newsprint media can and should have journalistic license and discretion, and therefore should have freedom to report on issues in the way that they deem to be most appropriate. The point is that, during most of the twentieth century, the average individual had few affordable and effective means of mass communication. As before the invention of the printing press, individuals could give speeches, and could draft arguments and position papers, but could not readily or easily harness the communications potential of the print media, or of radio and television, to communicate their political and social ideas. If the media suffered from bias, the media has the opportunity and ability to shape the public debate.

The media's gatekeeper function has limited the ability of third party and insurgent candidates to participate in the political process. The media generally tends to focus on the "front runners" which, of course, usually means that they focus on the candidates who represent the two major political parties. Third party candidates are frequently ignored. For example, at one point, allegations were being made that Ron Paul's presidential campaign was being ignored by National Public Radio.[104] While the NPR Ombudsman argued that Paul had received considerable coverage from NPR, he also concluded that any limitations on coverage might have been appropriate given that Paul was an "also ran" candidate.[105] As will be dis-

---

100. *See* Frank Bruni, *The News Isn't Fake. But It's Flawed, The New York Times, The New York Times*, Opinion 3 (May 20, 2018).

101. *Id.*

102. *Id.*

103. *Id.*

104. *See Is NPR Ignoring Ron Paul*, NPR Ombudsman (Jan. 30, 2008). http://www.npr.org/blogs/ombudsman/2008/01/is_npr_ignoring_ron_paul.html

105. *See id.*

cussed more fully below, Paul was ultimately able to circumvent these restrictions using modern communication technologies.

Even though both radio and television have historically been subject to gatekeepers, some political and social movements have used those systems to bring about change. For example, in the 1960s, the counterculture movement received significant coverage from the media, both print and broadcast.[106] Indeed, at times, there was a "flood of coverage" regarding the movement.[107] However, individual protestors could not mandate that television and radio broadcasters air such images, but could only hope that broadcasters would be sufficiently intrigued with the concepts presented to broadcast information about their cause.

Cable television,[108] and satellite radio and television, have also come with gatekeepers. Those technologies have dramatically increased the number of viewing and listening options, sometimes increasing station availability by hundreds of times, and have also expanded the number of perspectives available in the information marketplace.[109] Moreover, cable television has gained an increasingly large market share, now approaching 50 percent,[110] and has expanded communication possibilities in important respects. When so-called "shock jock" Howard Stern was threatened by the Federal Communications Commission's (FCC) new indecency policies, he had an easy option available to him: leave traditional radio and

---

106. *See* Aniko Bodroghkozy, *The Sixties Counterculture on TV*, in COMMUNICATION IN HISTORY, *supra* note 48, at 268 ("Nevertheless, a surprisingly large amount of commentary about the hippie phenomenon during its heyday was tentatively positive. A largely sympathetic *Time* magazine cover story that ran in July of the 'Summer of Love' concluded by arguing that 'in their independence of material possessions and their emphasis on peacefulness and honesty, hippies lead considerably more virtuous lives than the great majority of their fellow citizens.'").

107. *Id.*, at 270 ("As the hippie scene in the Haight-Ashbury began to gain more and more media attention through 1967, both the networks and local public stations flooded the airways with news reports and documentaries on the new phenomenon.").

108. *See Turner Broadcasting System, Inc. v. FCC*, 512 U.S. 622 (1994).

109. *See* Cohen, *supra* note 39, at 313 (noting that "cable television exercised a powerful, decentralizing force, creating new means by which independent points of view could be heard.").

110. *See* Brian Stelter, *Cable Networks Trying to Build on Their Gains in Ratings*, *The New York Times*, at C5 (May 26, 2008) ("Cable channels have been eroding broadcast viewership for years, and comparisons between them are inexact. This television season, though, the shifts are especially sharp.").

broadcast his program on a satellite radio station.[111] Since satellite communications are not regulated by the FCC, Stern could broadcast more freely through that medium.[112]

Potential gatekeepers come in many different forms. One form is cable companies which now provide many individuals with their internet service.[113] As more and more content is streamed over the internet, there is a significant risk that the role of cable companies as content providers will be eroded.[114] Since most people remain connected to their cable systems as internet providers,[115] cable companies have the potential to favor certain content over other content as it is funneled through their systems.[116] If that happens, cable companies may be able to exercise gatekeeper control by favoring their content over other content.[117] This possibility may be undercut by the development of new "smart" televisions that allow direct streaming to televisions without the need for cable boxes.[118]

As important as the development of cable and satellite mediums might have been, they did not dramatically increase the ability of average individuals to access the media or participate in freedom of expression. Increasingly, cable television has been dominated and controlled by large corporations,[119] and many of these corporations own multiple types of media.[120] Even though some cable companies have established local access channels,[121] thereby providing ordinary people with some access to this

---

111. *See* David Wilkerson, CBS.MarketWatch.com. Details can be found at: http://www.topsatelliteradio.com/howard-stern/fcc-indecency-ok.html.

112. Although Stern was free of FCC restrictions, he could still be prosecuted for obscenity if one of his programs met the constitutional requirements imposed in *Miller v. California*, 413 U.S. 15 (1973).

113. *See* Brian Stelter, *The TV-Internet Nuptials: Distributors Ponder Their Roles in a Time of Transition, The New York Times*, at B1 (Jan. 10, 2011).

114. *Id.*

115. *See* Matt Richtel & Brian Stelter, *In the Living Room Hooked on Pay TV: It's Cable Fees Vs. Online Shows; So Far People Would Rather Pay, The New York Times*, at B1 (Aug. 23, 2010).

116. *See The TV-Internet Nuptials, supra* note 705.

117. *Id.*

118. *Id.* at B5.

119. *See* A History of Mass Communication, *supra* note 46, at 203–204.

120. *Id.*, at 204.

121. *See* John J. O'Connor, *How Much Access Have We to Public Access?; Television, The New York Times*, Sec. 2, at 17 (Jun. 3, 1973).

new medium, the overwhelming majority of the hundreds of cable and satellite channels were (and remain) controlled by media conglomerates.

In the final analysis, even though speech technology improved dramatically between the fifteenth century and the twentieth century, the ability of ordinary people to mass communicate did not improve much. With limited exceptions, most mass communications technologies were accompanied by gatekeepers who exercised control over those technologies, who exercised discretion about who could access those technologies, and (in some instances) what they could say. As a result, mass communication remained the purview of the rich and the powerful, as well as of government, but not of the common man. At the end of the twentieth century, communications technology began to evolve in a decidedly more democratic direction.

CHAPTER VI

THE INTERNET

Recent technological innovations, personal computers (PCs) and smart phones) and the invention of the internet,[1] which dates to 1969,[2] have provided the most significant advances in communication.[3]

Early computers[4] were quite large machines (a/k/a "mainframe computers") that filled entire rooms,[5] and were used almost exclusively by

---

1. The internet's roots are generally traced back to September 2, 1969. *See* Anick Jesdanun, *Internet at 40: Midlife Crisis? Barriers Threaten, Openness, Growth, The Courier-Journal*, at D5 (Sept. 6, 2009).

2. *See* Ira Flatow, *Happy Birthday Internet*, National Public Radio, Talk of the Nation (Oct. 30, 2009), http://www.npr.org/templates/story/story.php?storyId=114319703 (dating the development of the internet to 1969); Guy Raz, *40 Years Later, Looking Back at the Internet's Birth*, National Public Radio, All Things Considered (Nov. 1, 2009), http://www.npr.org/templates/story/story.php?storyId=114376728.

3. *See Happy Birthday Internet, supra* note 2.

4. The first computer was designed as a calculation device. *See* Ruth Schwartz Cohen, *The Social Shape of Electronics*, in COMMUNICATION IN HISTORY, in DAVID CROWLEY & PAUL HEYER, COMMUNICATION IN HISTORY: TECHNOLOGY, CULTURE, SOCIETY 315 (5th ed. 2007) ("In 1942, an engineer on the faculty of the Moore School of Engineering at the University of Pennsylvania, John Mauchly, suggested ... that he could build an electronic calculator based on high-speed vacuum tube devices which would solve the trajectory equations in a matter of seconds, rather than hours.... Unfortunately for the war effort, ENIAC which stood for electronic numerical integrator and computer, took three years to build."). Some believe that a British mathematician, Charles Babbage, who lived during the nineteenth century, may have been the first person to conceive of a computer and develop blueprints. *See* John Markoff, *It Started Digital Wheels Turning: In the Age of Steam, a British Mathematician Brainstormed a Contraption That Inspired Dreams of Computers. Experts in London Intend to Spend a Decade Piecing It Together, The New York Times*, Science Times, at D1 (Nov. 8, 2011). However, he did not actually build his contraption. *Id.*

5. COMMUNICATION IN HISTORY, *supra* note 4, at 316 ("When it was done, ENIAC contained more than 17,000 vacuum tubes; it weighed thirty tons, had cost roughly

large corporations and governmental entities.[6] One of the early machines, the IBM 1401, was as large as a two-car garage.[7] These early machines were subject to tight security controls,[8] and corporate personnel were often forced to share time on the systems.[9] However, even these bulky, early, computers were much faster than prior technologies.[10]

By the 1970s, inventors had created so-called "personal computers" (PCs) and were beginning to mass market them.[11] Development of the PC was preceded by development of microchip technology,[12] which enabled manufacturers to create smaller computers,[13] with quite powerful com-

---

$450,000 to build, and filled a room the size of a squash court.").

6. *See* David Crowley & Paul Heyer, Communication in History: Technology, Culture, Society 298 (5th ed. 2007) ("Computers got their start in large organizations, aiding administration, scientific research, and the military."); *see also* John Markoff, *Business Technology; Improving a Computer Network's Efficiency*, *The New York Times*, at D7 (March 29, 1989).

7. *See 40 Years Later, supra* note 2.

8. *See* Communications in History, *supra* note 1, at 298 ("In the past, computer power has been centralized in large mainframe computers locked in specially controlled rooms. Users gained access remotely through terminals.").

9. *See id.* ("As computer networks become more complex, users who want time on another computer in the network to perform a specialized task often discover that several people are ahead of them. These traffic jams can waste valuable computer time as well as burden users with bothersome coordination chores.").

10. *See* Communication in History, *supra* note 6, at 316 ("[The first computer] could calculate very fast, multiplying 333 ten-digit numbers a second, finishing one of the trajectory equations, which had previously taken hours to complete, in twenty seconds.").

11. *See* Stuart Kauffman, *Re-Imagining Society: Are We Trapped by Old Ideas?*, National Public Radio, Cosmos and Culture (Nov. 1, 2010), http://www.npr.org/blogs/13.7/2010/11/01/130976163/?print=1 ("the invention and wide sale of the main frame computer enabled the invention and wide sale of the personal computer which in turn enabled the invention and wide sale of word processing, which enabled the storing of computer files, whose wide use enabled the storage and sharing of files, which enabled the invention and wide use of the Web, which enabled selling things on the Web, which enabled content on the Web, which enabled Google.").

12. *See* Janet Abbate, *Popularizing the Internet*, in Communication in History, *supra* note 6, at 327.

13. *See* Peter H. Lewis, *The Executive Computer; Can There Be Too Much Power?*, *The New York Times*, at A9 (Dec. 31, 1989) ("Gordon Campbell, chief executive of Chips and Technologies Inc., had some ideas about what computers would be like in the 1990's. As he spoke, he held up a pair of circuit boards, each about the size of a credit card. The two cards together held all the components that used to be found on the magazine-sized

ponents.[14] "Newer" computers were so small that they that could fit on a desk,[15] and virtually everyone could eventually have PCs in their homes.

In 1976, Steve Jobs shipped the "Apple 1" PC to customers for only $666.66.[16] What separated the Apple 1 from its predecessors was that it came preassembled, and did not have to be soldered together.[17] Thereafter, computer technology went through a period of rapid innovation and development in which each "generation of computers was better, faster, more powerful, more flexible, and less expensive, than the generation that came before it.[18] Indeed, new computers were being developed so quickly that "generations" of computers emerged in years rather than decades.[19]

The personal computer was a dramatic breakthrough because it allowed individuals, especially those who could not afford to own or operate printing presses, to quickly and easily create quality content at home

---

motherboard of the original I.B.M. PC-XT. "Eventually we'll get this down to a single-chip architecture," he said.").

14. *See id.* ("Each human brain cell can store the equivalent of 10,000 bits of information, and the brain has about 10 billion brain cells, according to The Body Almanac. The memory capacity of the brain, therefore, is estimated at 100 trillion (100,000,000,000,000) bits, or slightly more than 10 terabytes. Each brain cell can discharge an electrical impulse about 200 times a second. By computer standards, the brain is astonishingly slow.").

15. *See id.* (the following "futuristic" prediction was made: "Today's microcomputers send out instructions millions of times a second. At the current pace of technological development, it seems fairly certain that sometime in the 1990's scientists will produce a computer the size of the human brain (a fist-sized unit weighing about three pounds) with about 10 terabytes of storage capacity and much greater processing speed-hundreds of millions of instructions per second, known as mips. Bits and bytes and mips have no life spark, of course, so it is far-fetched to say that science is close to creating computers that can rival the human brain. But processing speed is one measure of how far computers have come in the last decade and where they are likely to go in the next.").

16. *See* Nick Bilton, *For Sale: A $160,000 Apple Computer, The New York Times*, Bits (blog) (Nov. 11, 2010) ("According to the auction Web site, this version of the Apple computer is number 82 of those made, was hand built by Steve Wozniak and then "dispatched from the garage of Steve Jobs' parents' house—the return address on the original packaging present here.") http://bits.blogs.nytimes.com/2010/11/11/for-sale-a-16000-apple-computer/?scp=1&sq=apple's%20first%20computer&st=cse.

17. *See id.*

18. *See* Cohen, *supra* note 4, at 317–318.

19. *See id.*

using their own equipment.[20] When coupled with a printer, the prices of which had dropped dramatically, the PC enabled ordinary people to print their own content.[21] While people may have previously been able to create typed documents using typewriters or other techniques, the PC allowed individuals to create high quality documents with exceedingly high quality graphics, and to print multiple copies of the documents that they created,[22] thereby effectively enabling individuals to engage in "desktop publishing."[23]

The internet functioned by sending packets of information from one computer to another through an electronic address system.[24] In some instances, a single communication was sent in multiple packets that were reassembled into a single communication at the point of reception.[25] The first internet message processor was extremely large (the size of two full-size gym lockers, or roughly 100 times larger than the modern router).[26]

---

20. *See* George Paul & Jason Baron, *Information Inflation: Can the Legal System Adapt?*, 13 RICH. J. L. & TECH. 1, 9 (2007):

> [Q]uite recently there has been an evolutionary burst in writing technology—a jagged punctuation on a 50 century-long sine wave. A quick succession of advances clustered or synced together, to emerge into a radically new and more powerful writing technology. These include digitization; real time computing; the microprocessor; the personal computer, e-mail; local and wide-area networks leading to the Internet; the evolution of software, which has "locked in" seamless editing as an almost universal function; the World Wide Web; and of course people and their technique. These constituents have swirled into an information complex, now known as the "Information Ecosystem." In such a system, the whole exhibits an emergent behavior that is much more than the sum of the parts. Critically for law, such systems cannot be understood or explained by any one person. As a result, writing has now grown into something akin to a new "form of life." Because of its long-standing stasis and the importance of writing as a global technology, such a development may legitimately be said to herald a new phase of civilization.

21. *See id.* ("With the emergence of the personal computer, an individual working at home now has access to information-processing capacities that previously had been the sole preserve of large institutions.").

22. *See* IRVING FANG, A HISTORY OF MASS COMMUNICATION: SIX INFORMATION REVOLUTIONS 196 (1997).

23. *See id.*, at 195–196.

24. *See Happy Birthday Internet, supra* note 2.

25. *Id.*

26. *See 40 Years Later, supra* note 2.

While the internet originated in the United States as ARPANET,[27] the system began to have worldwide impact as other nations connected their information systems to the network.[28] While these multinational connections did not occur until the 1970s,[29] they were soon followed by privately developed systems,[30] and eventually the World Wide Web developed as new software systems were created.[31]

The internet solved the distribution problem for documents created with PCs. Historically, if someone created a printed work, they would either have to distribute it themselves in hard copy, pay someone else to distribute it (*e.g.*, the United States Postal Service), post it in a public square, or try to disseminate it through newspapers, or radio and television networks. Unless the individual could get free distribution through an existing media outlet, distribution costs (either in terms of personal effort or monetary cost) could be daunting. Using the internet, ordinary people could bypass traditional methods of communication for the first time in history and distribute content themselves directly to their readers. Indeed, individuals could instantaneously disseminate their ideas all over the world through the click of a computer mouse. Not only could individuals send e-mails and create websites, they could also communicate through chat rooms, list serves and blogs. They could also send text messages and communicate in lots of other (new) ways. In other words, PCs and the internet created completely new communication possibilities for ordinary individuals,[32] enabling them to mass communicate without having to go through the traditional gatekeepers of mass

27. *See id.*, at 323.

28. *Id.*

29. *Id.* ("By the mid 1970s, state-run networks were being built in a number of countries, including Canada, Germany, Norway, Sweden, Australia, New Zealand, and Japan.... In addition to these national networks, there were several efforts to build multinational networks across Europe in support of the creation of a European Union. These included the European Informatics Network (established in 1971) and its successor, Euronet. Some of the networks were, like the ARPANET, designed for research and education; other provided commercial network services.").

30. *Id.*, at 325–326.

31. *Id.*, at 325–327.

32. *See Reno v. American Civil Liberties Union*, 521 U.S. 844 (1997).

communication.[33] As a result, the internet was widely accessed by all age groups and people of all political persuasions, in almost every country, and began to radically transform mass communication.[34]

E-mail, for example, differed radically from broadcast communications. Like the telephone, e-mail and the internet allowed people to communicate without leaving the comfort of their homes.[35] The recipient of an e-mail could read and respond to the e-mail within seconds.[36] Unlike a telephone, an e-mail could be distributed to a very large group of people in far-flung places, and the communication could take place almost instantaneously.

PCs and the internet were also different from other forms of mass communication because the barriers to access were extremely low. Broadcast technologies required not only a government license, but also sophisticated technologies. By contrast, an individual could access the internet simply by purchasing a personal computer and obtaining an internet connection, and both a PC and an internet connection could be obtained relatively cheaply. Those who lacked the means to buy a computer could gain inexpensive access through a cyber café,[37] a library or a university,[38] or with a handheld device. Indeed, a number of businesses (*e.g.*, Starbucks, McDonald's and Barnes & Noble) routinely offer free internet connections as a way of encouraging business. The result is that millions upon millions of people can regularly engage in speech and communication through the medium of the internet.

---

33. *See* Communication in History, *supra* note 6, at 298.

34. *See* Teddy Wayne, *Digital Habits Shift Across Age Groups*, *The New York Times*, at B3 (Dec. 14, 2009) ("Children aren't the only ones whiling away hours on the Internet; people of retirement age now spend even more time online than youngsters.").

35. *See* A History of Mass Communication, *supra* note 22, at 225.

36. *Id.*

37. *See* Virginia Heffernan, *The Cybercafe Lives*, *The New York Times* (Nov. 7, 2008) (discussing how the reporter accessed a cyber café in Tokyo, Japan); Ramen Jaleshgari, *At a Café, Internet and Coffee*, *The New York Times* (Feb. 16, 1997) (discussing the development of cyber cafés).

38. *See* Gretchen Ruethling, *Almost All Libraries Offer Free Web Access*, *The New York Times*, at A14 (Jun. 24, 2005).

Of course, there are limits to the communications potential of the internet. In some areas, even though Broadband access is crucial to the modern economy, in some areas (particularly rural areas) broadband access has not historically been available and many users were relegated to dial-up systems.[39] Although more than 65% of urban households had high-speed internet access, only about 51% of rural households had similar access at one point.[40] As a result, 24.7 million Americans lack broadband access, and 162.8 million people do not access the internet at broadband speeds.[41] The federal government has sought to remedy this deficiency by devoting $7.2 billion in stimulus funds toward the development of DSL, cable modem, fiber optic, and fixed wireless technologies in rural areas.[42] In addition, large internet companies (e.g., Microsoft) are working to improve internet access.[43]

The PC and the internet have subsequently been supplemented and complemented by a plethora of new technologies that help facilitate communication, and that have made PCs and e-mail relatively old school. Indeed, new technologies seem to emerge almost daily so that individuals are no longer required to own PCs to access the internet. PCs were supplemented by laptop computers,[44] and they were followed by a variety of handheld devices that made text messaging possible.[45] Handheld devices, such as Apple's iPhone, allowed individuals to connect to the internet even though they were away from their PCs (and, indeed, almost no matter where they were located). Mobile phone makers have created touch screen phones with communication applications that help users access

---

39. *See* John Curran, *Dial-Up Doldrums: Broadband Access Is Still Just a Dream in Many Rural Areas, but Stimulus Funds Are Invigorating Projects, The Courier-Journal*, at A3 (Jan. 20, 2011).

40. *Id.*

41. *See* Steve Lohr, *The Gap in Broadband Access, The New York Times* B7 (Dec. 5, 2018).

42. See Curran, *supra* note 39, at A3.

43. *See* Lohr, *supra* note 41, at B7.

44. *See* Matt Bai, *D.I.Y. Populism, Left and Right, The New York Times*, at WK.1 (Oct. 31, 2010).

45. *See Handheld Devices: Most Popular, The New York Times* (Nov. 23, 2010), http://topics.nytimes.com/top/news/technology/products/handhelds/popular.html.

social media platforms.[46] Indeed, handheld devices are powerful enough to send e-mails and text messages, access Facebook pages, and do a multitude of other things. By 2010, market penetration for handheld devices (including cell phones) had reached 96 percent of young people in the United States.[47]

Handheld devices (*e.g.*, the iPhone) have been complimented by new platforms designed to enhance electronic communication. Included are Web search and communications apps such as e-mail, listservs, Facebook,[48] Instagram,[49] Snapchat,[50] Google,[51] blogs,[52] YouTube,[53] Flickr, Twitter (now X,[54] which was 18 years old in 2024[55]), 3-D panorama, streaming services, and other more modern methods of communication,[56] including LinkedIn, Tumblr, and Reddit.[57] MySpace, which once held a preeminent place among social media technologies, has virtually disappeared having lost more than nine million users in a single year and having been

46. *See* Tim Bradshaw, *Handsets to Boost Facebook's Mobile Status, Financial Times*, at 24 (Feb. 10, 2011).

47. *See* Steve Inskeep, *Survey: 96 Percent of Young Adults Own Cellphones*, National Public Radio, Morning Edition (Oct. 18, 2010), http://www.npr.org/templates/story/story.php?storyId=130639028.

48. See www.facebook.com.

49. See www.instagram.com.

50. See www.snapchat.com.

51. *See Happy Birthday Internet, supra* note 2

52. *See* Adam Nagourney, *Gathering Highlights Power of the Blog, The New York Times*, at A10 (June 10, 2006); Jim Rutenberg, *Liberal Groups are Flexing New Muscle in Lobby Wars, The New York Times*, at A1 (Mar. 1, 2009) (describing how liberal bloggers are trying to assist the Obama administration in achieving its legislative priorities).

53. *See* http://www.youtube.com/; *see also Happy Birthday Internet, supra* note 2.

54. Twitter has been described as perhaps the fastest way to share information around the world and has been referred to as the new "water cooler." *See* Andy Carvin, *Welcome to the Twitterverse*, Weekend Edition Saturday (Feb. 28, 2009); *see also* Michael Liedtke, *Tweets Could be Sweet Revenue Source at Twitter; Service Hasn't Pushed for Profits, but Features are Promising, The Courier-Journal*, D5 (Feb. 22, 2009).

55. *See* Jennifer Szalai, *The Men Who Made Twitter, Then Proceeded to Unmake It, The New York Times* C3 (Feb. 22, 2024).

56. *See* Jenna Wortham, *The Inauguration Will be Televised—and Tweeted and Flickr'd, The New York Times* (Jan. 19, 2009) (blog), http://bits.blogs.nytimes.com/2009/01/19/the-inauguration-will-be-televised-and-twitter-streamed-flickrd/.

57. *See* Tim Arango, *A Hot Social Networking Site Cools as Facebook Flourishes, The New York Times*, at A1 (Jan. 12, 2011).

forced to reduce its staff by 50%.[58] My Space has largely been replaced by platforms such as SnapChat. Although the presence of gatekeepers on the internet will be analyzed more fully in the following chapters, the internet, PCs, and handheld devices are revolutionary because they enabled ordinary individuals to communicate directly with each other without always having to go through the historical gatekeepers of communication (except, perhaps, when they access social media platforms). As a result, new technologies have reshaped the communications landscape. Not only does the internet allow individuals to convey information, it allows them to make phone calls, and even to see each other through video phones and through software such as Skype, Facetime, or Google Chat.[59]

Although Twitter (now "X") communications involve only 140 characters,[60] 20 million people now use the service,[61] producing more than 100 million "tweets" (now referred to as "posts") per day,[62] and two billion posts per month.[63] In a 24-hour news cycle, in which electronic media can disseminate information quickly, X is much faster,[64] and posts can even be used by reporters to solicit information from possible sources.[65] By mid-2010, Facebook (now Meta) had more than 500 million users worldwide.[66]

"Livestreaming," in which people stream themselves and events online, has also become a phenomenon.[67] Twitch has long dominated livestreaming, but social media platforms like Kick (which has 21 million accounts)

---

58. *See id.*, at A1.

59. *See* Olivia Barker, *See and Be Seen on Video Calls: Technology Not Limited to Business Use, The Courier-Journal*, at D5 (Apr. 18, 2010).

60. *See Welcome to the Twitterverse, supra* note 54.

61. *See* Bob Garfield, *Evan Williams*, National Public Radio, On the Media (Nov. 26, 2010), http://www.onthemedia.org/2010/nov/26/evan-williams/transcript/.

62. *See id.*

63. *See* Bob Garfield, *The Point of Twitter*, National Public Radio, On the Media (Nov. 26, 2010), http://www.onthemedia.org/2010/nov/26/the-point-of-twitter/transcript/.

64. *Id.*

65. *Id.*

66. *See* Bob Garfield, *The Facebook Effect*, National Public Radio, On the Media (Aug. 20, 2010), http://www.onthemedia.org/2010/aug/20/the-facebook-effect/transcript/.

67. *See* Kellen Browning, *Kick Flourishes as Livesteaming's New Cowboy, The New York Times* A6 (Dec. 3, 2023).

have gained ascendance.[68] Some of these livestreams have been controversial and political. For example, on Kick, there was a fake interview with North Korean Leader Kim Jong-un (the interviewee was not Kim, but rather a lookalike).[69] But livestreaming is also used to show non-political things such as individuals playing slot machines (banned on Twitch), an individual shooting at cartoon enemies, and even chats with viewers.[70]

Blogs have also become commonplace. As one commentator noted, one "of the great things about the blogosphere is that it is very open and meritocratic. For very little money, anyone can start a blog and post their thoughts on the internet,"[71] and there are lots of other communications options, including online commentary and so-called "viral videos."[72]

In different countries, social media platforms have evolved in very different ways. For example, in China, where Facebook and Twitter are banned, alternate social networking systems have developed.[73] These include renren.com, which has more than 160 million registered users, and Kaixin001.com, which has more than 93 million users.[74] Although it is possible for the Chinese to connect to Facebook and Twitter, connection speeds can be quite slow on those networks,[75] and many Chinese have gravitated to China-based social media sites.[76]

The internet has also transformed radio communications. Early radio broadcasts were sent solely over broadcast waves, and the finite quantity of waves limited the number of radio stations that could exist. If too many people tried to broadcast on the same broadcast waves, they

---

68. *Id.*

69. *Id.*

70. *Id.*

71. *See* Micah Sifry, *The Gatekeepers Are Gone*, National Public Radio, Soap Box (Aug. 21, 2008), http://www.npr.org/blogs/sundaysoapbox/2008/08/the_gatekeepers_are_gone.html.

72. *See* Liane Hansen and Davar Iran Ardalan, *Looking at the Future of "E-Politics,"* National Public Radio (June 29, 2008), http://www.npr.org/templates/story/story.php?storyId=91963952.

73. *See* Mark Lee, *Chinese Social Sites Fill Facebook's Void, International Herald Tribune*, at 14 (Feb. 10, 2011).

74. *Id.*

75. *Id.*

76. *Id.*

would interfere with each other's broadcasts. As a result, governments required a license in order to broadcast, and they limited the number of broadcast licenses that could be issued. The internet has altered that equation because an unlimited number of radio stations can broadcast over the internet,[77] and a seemingly limitless number of internet radio stations can exist.

---

77. *See* A HISTORY OF MASS COMMUNICATION, *supra* note 22, at 151 ("Except for satellite feeds, the networks, and shortwave broadcasts, radio is local. The appearance of radio channels on the World Wide Web promises to change that. Because Web sites do not require F.C.C. approval and occupy no space in the electromagnetic spectrum, the number of stations is potentially unlimited except by commercial considerations.").

CHAPTER VII

THE IMPLICATIONS OF THE INTERNET FOR DEMOCRACY

Although the traditional gatekeepers of speech continue to play a prominent role in society—in that they control the print and broadcast media—the internet has changed the dynamics of speech in ways that are giving ordinary people much greater access to communications technologies. As a medium, the internet is extraordinarily democratic in the sense that individuals are free to write about the issues that move them,[1] and to disseminate their ideas to a wide range of people without having to invest in printing presses or radio and television stations. As the Chief Executive of Snapchat, Evan Spiegel, stated, "this ability for any random person to have their own channel to reach millions of people, is totally unprecedented."[2]

The internet and associated technologies (*e.g.*, PCs and handheld devices) have dramatically expanded the scope of communication,[3]

1. *See Reno v. American Civil Liberties Union*, 521 U.S. 844 (1997).

2. *See* Ross Sorkin, *Social Media and Standards Regulations Don't Yet Match Reality, The New York Times* C6 (Nov. 6, 2018).

3. Of course, the new technologies are used for a variety of purposes, some of which have nothing to do with political expression. *See* Donna Gordon Blankenship, *For Some, Facebook Is Route to New Kidney: Washington Man's Online Quest Shows Organ Donation Trend, The Courier-Journal*, A3 (Jan. 2, 2012).

thereby allowing people to directly engage in the democratic process.[4] In the past, ordinary people could directly participate in the political process by talking to others, distributing campaign literature, going door-to-door making political pitches, or by sponsoring or attending campaign rallies and gatherings; activities that required substantial time and effort. But, in order to communicate on a mass scale, ordinary people were usually forced to beseech the media gatekeepers to publish their ideas. With the development of the internet, ordinary people could engage in politics from the comfort of their homes and could reach thousands if not millions of other people. As one commentator noted, "What we are finally seeing ... is a realization of that ideal that Adams and Jefferson and Paine and before him Voltaire and Plato had [—] that ideal of having everybody have a shot at participating in this discussion."[5] The internet has allowed individuals with common interests, including common political interests, to more easily locate each other and directly communicate between themselves (although it also creates the potential for "echo chambers" if people communicate only with like-minded others).[6] This potential for communication has been enhanced by advancing technologies.[7] In the process, the internet has given the populace a fuller opportunity to directly participate in, and influence, the political process.[8] Individuals can now parody

4. *See* Anthony Kuhn, *In Malaysia, Web's Popularity Breaks a Grip on Power*, National Public Radio, All Things Considered (Nov. 22, 2010), http://www.npr.org/2010/11/22/131512384/in-malaysia-web-s-popularity-breaks-a-grip-on-power ("In established democracies, the Internet has become a powerful political tool used for mobilizing, fundraising and advertising.").

5. *See* Liane Hansen & Davar Iran Ardalan, *Looking at the Future of "E-Politics,"* National Public Radio (June 29, 2008), http://www.npr.org/templates/story/story.php?storyId=91963952.

6. *See* Irving Fang, A History of Mass Communication: Six Information Revolutions 225 (1997).

7. *See* Jessica Mintz, *The Future Is Closer Than You Think*, *The Courier-Journal*, at D5 (Dec. 27, 2009).

8. *See* Markenzy Lapointe, *Universal Service and the Digital Revolution: Beyond the Telecommunications Act of 1996*, 25 Rutgers Computer & Tech. L.J. 61, 87 (1999) (discussing how online communication can be used to bring pressure on legislators).

and satirize,[9] as well as organize mass protests,[10] entirely online. No longer are individuals forced to have their communicative messages filtered through newspaper editors, or radio and television producers.[11]

The other distinguishing feature of the internet is that the gatekeepers of communication are less able to control communications.[12] As will be discussed in the next chapter, there are gatekeepers on the internet, especially on social media platforms. However, the internet has in many respects allowed ordinary people to use cheap and affordable technologies to convey their ideas to others all over the world.[13] As a result, ordinary individuals are beginning to directly communicate with each other on a scale that was not possible before, and the result has been a free speech revolution that has affected not only the United States, but the entire world. In the broad sweep of history, mass communication has never been as possible for ordinary people as it is today.

Because of the development of new technologies, including smart phones and social media platforms, mass political communication is no longer the sole purview of the rich and powerful. Indeed, at times, there is a complex synergy between ordinary individuals and the media. Ordinary people can use the internet to prompt and stimulate media cover-

---

9. *See* Matt Frassica, *Twicky Tweets: Twitter Parodies Bring Online Laughs for Followers, The Courier-Journal*, E1 (Nov. 21, 2010) (discussing how Twitter is being used to parody commercial entities, and (of course) suggesting how similar tactics can be used against political candidates).

10. *See* David Carr, *Digitally, Location Is Where It's At, The New York Times*, at B1 (Mar. 22, 2010) (discussing Foursquare and Gowalla technologies which can be used to coordinate the mass movement of people. In the article, the author refers to how those technologies are used to coordinate parties, but they can also be used to coordinate protest movements).

11. *See* Dan Klepal, *Abramson Faces Rising Criticism Amid Budget Cuts, The Courier-Journal*, at A8 (Jan. 18, 2009) (commenting on the fact that Louisville's "Mayor for Life," Jerry Abramson, has been subject to more criticism in recent years because "there are more outlets for it—such as blogs or comments at the end of online media stories.").

12. Professor Richard L. Hasen laments this new era as permitting "cheap speech," which he claims leads to a variety of societal ills, and he proffers various solutions designed to rescue society from this situation. *See* Richard L. Hasen, *The Price of 'Cheap Speech,' The New York Times* 6 (Mar. 13, 2022).

13. *See* Micah Sifry, *The Gatekeepers Are Gone*, National Public Radio, Soap Box (Aug. 21, 2008), http://www.npr.org/blogs/sundaysoapbox/2008/08/the_gatekeepers_are_gone.html. ("But if you want to join in the conversation online, it's a lot easier than, say, getting yourself published on a newspaper's op-ed page. The gatekeepers are gone.").

age of issues.[14] For example, early videos of anti-government protests in Tunisia were distributed by individuals over the internet using images captured on their smart phones.[15] These images led to unrest in other parts of Tunisia and encouraged the media to begin covering the story.[16] Afterwards, some media companies began monitoring internet postings,[17] even though those communications were directed at individuals rather than at media companies.[18]

Sites like Facebook, TikTok, and Bambuser, a Swedish social media platform, provide ordinary individuals with a mechanism for streaming online videos,[19] some social rather than political.[20] Moreover, generational differences have developed regarding internet use with older individuals more inclined to use e-mail and younger people more likely to text or use handheld devices.[21] In addition, Snapchat, which has 150 million users (compared to Facebook's 1.2 billion users), is heavily used by people in their twenties.[22] The platform is revolutionary because it is designed so

---

14. *See* Jennifer Preston & Brian Stelter, *Cellphone Cameras Become World's Eyes and Ears on Protests Across the Middle East, The New York Times*, at A11 (Feb. 19, 2011).

15. *Id.*

16. *Id.* ("In Tunisia, cellphones were used to capture video images of the first protests in Sidi Bouzid in December, which helped spread unrest to other parts of the country. The uploaded images also prompted producers at Al Jazeera, the satellite television network, to begin focusing on the revolt, which toppled the Tunisian government in mid-January and set the stage for demonstrations in Egypt.").

17. *Id.* ("Now, news organizations regularly seek out, sift and publish such images. Authenticating them remains a challenge, since photos can be easily altered by computers and old videos can resurface again, purporting to be new. YouTube is using Storyful, a news aggregation site, to help manage the tens of thousands of videos that have been uploaded from the Middle East in recent weeks and to highlight notable ones on the CitizenTube channel.").

18. *Id.* ("But journalists are not the only conduits [of internet information]. Cellphone images are increasingly being shared between users on mobile networks and social networking sites, and they are being broadly consumed on Web sites that aggregate video and images.").

19. *Id.*

20. *See* Taylor Lorenz, *Hungry for Connection, The New York Times* B1 (Aug. 16, 2021) (describing a woman who was excluded from a friend's birthday party and used the event to connect with others).

21. *See* Matt Richtel, *In Youthful World of Messaging, E-Mail Gets Instant Makeover, The New York Times*, at A1 (Dec. 21, 2010).

22. *See* Farhad Manjoo, *How Snapchat Transformed Social Networks, The New York Times* B1 (Dec. 1, 2016).

that content disappears in a short period of time.[23] Snapchat is also different because posts are played in chronological order, like a story, rather than in reverse order as on most other platforms.[24]

The internet revolution has the potential to dramatically reshape both society and the political process—for better, as well as for worse. For one thing, even people in remote parts of the world are able to connect, and their communications are not as subject to the control of traditional media, the government or others (except, of course, in countries that maintain tight internet censorship).[25] Of course, some media observers have lamented the decline of the traditional media, and the fact that a number of investigative journalists have been forced to seek alternate careers.[26] They argue that newspapers (and other media outlets) have traditionally served as the "watchdog" of democracy, in the sense that they investigate and challenge government, and these observers worry about how the retreat or demise of traditional media will affect society. While there is some validity to this concern (which will be discussed more fully in a later chapter), a strong argument can be made that democracy is enhanced by the rise of the internet, and the enhanced communications possibilities that have come with its development.

The rise of the internet generally supports freedom of expression, which is a necessary and essential building block for a democratic system of government,[27] and is critical to the effective functioning of the political process.[28] Indeed, even in some countries that do not have a written con-

---

23. *Id.*

24. *Id.*

25. *See* Anton Troianovski, *Internet Awakens Russians in a Place No Roads Lead To, The New York Times* A4 (Oct. 21, 2019).

26. *See* David Folkenflik, *Investigative Reporters Move Outside Newsrooms*, National Public Radio, Morning Edition (July 2, 2009), http://www.npr.org/templates/story/story.php?storyId=106168383.

27. *See* C. Edwin Baker, *Scope of the First Amendment Freedom of Speech*, 25 U.C.L.A. L. Rev. 964 (1978); Robert H. Bork, *Neutral Principles and Some First Amendment Problems*, 47 Ind. L.J. 1 (1971);Thomas I. Emerson, *Toward a General Theory of the First Amendment*, 72 Yale L.J. 877 (1963); Alexander Meiklejohn, *The First Amendment as an Absolute*,1961 Sup. Ct. Rev. 245; *see also* Russell L. Weaver, Understanding the First Amendment 261–276 (Carolina Academic Press, 8th ed., 2023).

28. *Id; see also* Russell L. Weaver, Catherine Hancock & John C. Knechtle, The First Amendment: Cases, Problems and Materials 7–14 (Carolina Academic Press, 7th ed., 2023).

stitution, or that have a written constitution but do not provide explicit protections for free speech, freedom of expression is valued.[29] For example, although the Australian Constitution is premised upon the notion of parliamentary supremacy,[30] and even though the framers explicitly decided not to include a bill of rights,[31] Australian High Court decisions have implied a constitutional right to free speech for matters related to the political process.[32] Australia has also provided enhanced protections to publishers against defamation liability.[33] Even Britain, which has his-

---

29. For example, England functions without a written constitution, and without a constitutional bill of rights, although it has adopted a statutory bill of rights. *See* Clive Walker & Russell L. Weaver, *The United Kingdom Bill of Rights 1998: The Modernisation of Rights in the Old World*, 33 U. Mich. J. Law Reform 497 (2000). Even in countries that function under a written constitution, without a constitutionally imposed bill of rights, free speech considerations have shaped judicial decisions. *See Reynolds v. Times Newspapers* [2001] 2 A.C. 127 (HL). For a discussion of *Reynolds'* impact, *see* Russell L. Weaver, Andrew T. Kenyon, David F. Partlett & Clive P. Walker, The Right to Speak Ill: Defamation, Reputation and Free Speech 131–150 (2006) (hereafter "The Right to Speak Ill").

30. *See* Neil F. Douglas, *Freedom of Expression Under the Australian Constitution*, 16 UNSW L.J. 315, 320–21 (1993) ("By not including ... as constitutional guarantees, the rights and freedoms in the United States Bill of Rights, it was intended that the courts could not invalidate legislation on the ground of inconsistency with a particular right or freedom); Russell L. Weaver & Kathe Boehringer, *Implied Rights and the Australian Constitution: A Modified New York Times, Inc. v. Sullivan Goes Down Under*, 8 Seton Hall Const. L.J. 459 (1998).

31. *See* Leslie Zines, *A Judicially Created Bill of Rights?*, 16 Sydney L. Rev. 166, 182 (1994) (noting that the Australian Constitution was based on British concepts. He goes on to note that: "British political notions, backed up by British constitutional history, pointed to Parliament as the protector of liberties and to the electorate as the ultimate check on Parliament.").

32. *See Australian Capital Television Pty. Ltd. v. The Commonwealth* (1992) 177 C.L.R. 106 (the essence of the majority position, with the exception of Justice McHugh, was that the principle of representative democracy provides the basis for the constitutional implication of a right to freedom of political discussion); *Nationwide News Pty. Ltd. v. Wills* (1992) 177 C.L.R. 1; *see also Stephens v. Western Australian Newspapers Ltd.* (1994) 182 C.L.R. 211 (justices Deane and Toohey relied on the doctrines of representative democracy and responsible government which they viewed as grounded in the "thesis that all powers of government ultimately belong to, and are derived from, the government."); *Theophanous v. The Herald & Weekly Times Ltd.* (1994) 182 C.L.R. 104.

33. *See* Russell L. Weaver & David F. Partlett, *Defamation, the Media & Free Speech: Australia's Experiment with Expanded Qualified Privilege*, 36 Geo. Wash. Int'l. L. Rev. 377 (2004).

torically been far less protective of free speech than the United States,[34] and which has historically cut the balance between freedom of speech and protection against defamation much more decisively in favor of reputation,[35] now provides greater protection for speech, and has imposed limitations on defamation liability.[36]

A. POLITICAL IMPACTS OUTSIDE THE UNITED STATES

The internet has had a profound political impact even in countries with repressive attitudes towards free speech.[37] In some countries, governments have historically tried to maintain tight control over the traditional media,[38] including retaining state-control over newspapers, as well as radio and television, in an effort to control political discourse and dissent, as well as the flow of information that reaches their people.[39] However, with the advent of the internet, as well as of satellite television, it has become much more difficult for governments to tightly control the flow of information. Both the internet and satellite television allow information to flow freely across international borders, and the internet allows people to directly communicate with each other, as well as to exchange ideas, without having to go through the government-controlled media.[40] Like citizens of the U.S., people outside the U.S. are using a variety of methods to communicate with each other, including e-mails, texts, blogs, X,

---

34. *See* Russell L. Weaver, *The N. Ireland Media Ban: Some Reflections on Judicial Review*, 22 VAND. J. OF TRANSNAT'L LAW 1119 (1989).

35. *See* THE RIGHT TO SPEAK ILL, *supra* note 29.

36. *See* Russell L. Weaver, Andrew Kenyon, David F. Partlett & Clive C.P. Walker, *Defamation Law & Free Speech: Reynolds v. Times Newspapers and the English Media*, 37 VAND. J. TRANS-NAT'L LAW 1255 (2005).

37. *See, e.g.*, Michael Sullivan, *The War Vietnam Wants to Forget*, National Public Radio's *Morning Edition* (March 2, 2009), http://www.npr.org/templates/story/story.php?storyId=101329709.

38. *See* Deborah Amos, *Social Media Revolution Hits Saudia Arabia*, National Public Radio, All Things Considered (Jan. 26, 2011), http://www.npr.org/2011/01/26/133212623/social-media-revolution-hits-saudi-arabia.

39. *See* Michael Slackman, *A Brittle Leader, Appearing Strong*, *The New York Times*, at A1 (Feb. 12, 2011) (hereafter "*A Brittle Leader*").

40. *See id.* ("Satellite television and the Internet meant the state could no longer control what people knew, and so its narrative was often ignored or even mocked.").

Meta and WhatsApp.[41] In Saudi Arabia alone, nearly ten million people were using the internet in 2011, more than a million of whom were using Facebook, and large numbers using Twitter,[42] Snapchat and WhatsApp.[43] WhatsApp has become popular in many nations as a way for "political parties, religious activists and others to spread information."[44]

1. THE INTERNET IN VARIOUS COUNTRIES

Individuals in many countries are using the internet to express their ideas, and the internet is having considerable political impact in a number of countries. For example, in Iran in 2009, protestors uploaded images of the death of a young woman to YouTube.[45] Elsewhere in the Middle East, a blogger "angered the Muslim cyberworld by promoting atheism, displaying spoofs of Koranic verses, skewering the lifestyle of the Prophet Muhammad, and chatting online using the sarcastic name God Almighty."[46] One of his blog posts, entitled "Why I Left Islam," describes the Muslim God as a "primitive, Bedouin and anthropomorphic God," and claimed that the Prophet Muhammad was a "sex addict" who bent his own rules "to appease his voracious desire."[47] In England, a single tweet managed to set off "a frenzy of vitriolic attacks and counterattacks."[48]

In Belgium, when there was growing discontent over the inability of politicians to form a government due to tensions between Dutch speakers in the north and French speakers in the south,[49] students protested the lack of a government through the internet using the label "shame."[50] The

---

41. *See The War Vietnam Wants to Forget, supra* note 37.

42. *See Social Media Revolution Hits Saudia Arabia, supra* note 38.

43. *See* Ben Hubbard, *Young Saudis Find Freedom on Smartphones, The New York Times*, International 6 (May 24, 2015).

44. *See* Alexandra Stevenson, *Facebook Admits Role Platform Had in Fueling Violence in Myanmar, The New York Times* B2 (Nov. 7, 2018).

45. *See Cellphone Cameras Become World's Eyes and Ears on Protests, supra* note 14.

46. *See* Isabel Kershner, *A Blogger's Irreverence Infuriates West Bank Muslims, The New York Times*, at A5 (Nov. 16, 2010).

47. *Id.*

48. *See* Sarah Lyall, *A Tweet Read Across Britain Unleashes a Cascade of Vitriol on a User, The New York Times*, at A8 (Nov. 2, 2009).

49. *See* Stephen Castle, *Belgians Take to the Streets to Protest the Government (a Lack of One, That Is), The New York Times*, at A4 (Jan. 24, 2011).

50. *Id.*

protests ultimately led to street demonstrations, involving some 30,000 plus protestors.[51]

In the UK, social media platforms are being used by political parties to build support and organize voters.[52] At Momentum, a pro-Labour group, a team of 15 people produces memes, videos, and other content in support of the Labour party.[53] There is also online political advertising from new groups whose financial support is unclear.[54]

Elsewhere in Europe, a new political party, the Pirate Party, emerged on the internet.[55] The party's goals were to alter copyright laws in order to permit greater sharing of audio and video files, eliminate patents, and guarantee increased online privacy.[56] The party organized online,[57] conducted an online convention,[58] and spent just 500,000 Euros on European elections.[59] Nevertheless, because of the ease of internet communication, the party was able to carry on a dialogue with its supporters,[60] including through a blog that one of the organizers wrote from home.[61] By 2009, the party was able to claim 47,000 members with half of those under the age of 26,[62] and it forced more traditional parties to increase their online presence, as well as their political agendas.[63] In some European countries, the Pirate Party recorded modest electoral successes. For example, in Sweden, the Party managed to capture a seat in the European Parliament.[64] In

51. *Id.*

52. *See* Adam Satariano & Amie Tsang, *In Britain, Disinformation Ahead of Vote Comes Largely From Within, The New York Times International* A13 (Dec. 11, 2019).

53. *Id.*

54. *Id.*

55. *See* Stephen Castle, *Freewheeling Internet Pirates Hijack Dull E.U. Vote in Sweden, International Herald Tribune*, at 1 (June 5, 2009).

56. *Id.*, at 2.

57. *Id.*, at 3.

58. *Id.*, at 1.

59. *Id.*

60. *Id.* at 3.

61. *Id.*

62. *Id.*

63. *Id.*

64. *See* Renee Montagne, *Pirate Party Wins Seat in European Parliament, National Public Radio*, Morning Edition (June 9, 2009), http://www.npr.org/templates/story/story.php?storyId=105145034.

Germany, the party won 8.5% of the vote in one election,[65] and captured three seats in Parliament.[66]

The internet has also been used to fuel political violence.[67] An American who converted to Islam, but who had rarely set foot in Egypt, encouraged Egyptian protests against "globalization."[68] In particular, he suggested that Egyptians attack "restaurants, banks, mobile phone shops and other corporate outposts."[69] Believing that non-violent protests are "futile," he encouraged attacks on empty business institutions.[70] While he encouraged his followers not to use explosives, and not to harm civilians, six bombs were set off and two people were killed.[71] His messages were followed and forwarded by activists and militant groups.[72]

In 2015, Palestinian protestors used social media to fuel the intifada, their protest over Israel's occupation of Palestinian territories.[73] Using social media platforms like Twitter and Facebook, protestors were able to mobilize protests, disseminate information, and fuel outrage against Israel.[74] In addition, Palestinians posted photos, videos, and commentary.[75] The posts included pictures of bloody knives and an injured Palestinian.[76]

In Malaysia, the internet was used by a political protest movement to promote its objectives. In that country, individuals used the internet to circumvent the traditional media, as well as to foster free discussion of

---

65. *See* Eyder Peralta, *Pirate Party Wins Seats in Berlin Election*, National Public Radio (Sept. 19, 2011), http://www.npr.org/blogs/thetwo-way/2011/09/19/140604853/pirate-party-wins-seats-in-berlin-elections.

66. *See* Jennifer Collins, *Pirates Surprise in Berlin Elections, National Public Radio*, NPR Berlin Blog (Sept. 20, 2011), http://www.npr.org/blogs/nprberlinblog/2011/09/19/140611428/pirates-surprise-in-berlin-election-results.

67. *See* David D. Kirkpatrick, *American Agitator Helps Fuel Attacks in Egypt, The New York Times* A1 (Feb. 28, 2015).

68. *Id.*

69. *Id.*

70. *Id.*

71. *Id.*

72. *Id.*

73. *See* Shira Rubin, *Social Media Feed Palestinian Intifada, USA Today* B1 (Oct. 15, 2015).

74. *Id.*

75. *Id.*

76. *Id.*

important social and political issues.[77] Interestingly, Malaysia's handling of the internet differed significantly from its regulation of newspapers which were (at the time) required to obtain print licenses.[78] Print licenses were difficult to acquire because they were issued for only a year at a time, and were usually awarded only to people "who are friendly to the government."[79] Because the internet is subject to far less governmental intervention, many Malaysians sought their news from Web-based sources, including the news website *Malaysiakini*,[80] which attracted 300,000 visitors a day and was published in some of the multiple languages spoken in Malaysia.[81] The website was created in response to Malaysia's print restrictions,[82] and it frequently wrote about sensitive issues,[83] and was one of the few places where Malaysians could find frank discussion of such topics.[84] The website wielded considerable influence since 50 percent of Malaysia's population had internet access in 2010, and was accustomed to receiving its news through that medium.[85] Opposition parties won two-thirds of the

---

77. *See* Kuhn, *supra* note 4.

78. *Id.*

79. *Id.*

80. *Id.* ("When mainstream media will not or cannot cover important political stories, many Malaysians click toward *Malaysiakini*, or Malaysia Now, the nation's most popular news website.").

81. *Id.* ("The site attracts 300,000 visitors a day to its text and video content in English, Bahasa, Chinese and Tamil. The languages reflect the main ethnic groups of Malaysia's 28 million people: roughly 54 percent ethnic Malays, 24 percent ethnic Chinese and 7 percent ethnic Indians.").

82. *Id.* ("'We came about mostly because of the fact that we were unable to get a print license,' recalls *Malaysiakini* editor Steve Gan. 'To do print, you need to get a license from the government, and that license is renewable every year, which puts a lot of print publications on a pretty short leash. And the license is only given to people who are friendly to the government.'").

83. *Id.* ("*Malaysiakini* quickly made a name for itself by daring to write about the politics of race and religion in Malaysia, areas where Gan says few conventional media dare to tread. 'We've been told time and again by the ruling coalition that all these issues are sensitive issues,' he says, '[that] it shouldn't be debated and discussed out in the open, it should be discussed behind closed doors by the ruling parties, and they will come up with solutions.'").

84. *Id.* (Quoting Azmi Sharom, a legal scholar at the University of Malaya in Kuala Lumpur, who stated that websites and blogs constituted "the only method where criticism of the government could be expressed freely.'").

85. *Id.*

seats in Malaysia's parliament, at least in part because of internet-based communications.[86] Interestingly, the internet thrived in Malaysia because the government announced a no internet censorship policy in an effort to attract business.[87]

The internet has also had a significant impact on political discourse in Myanmar. When governmental officials in that country cut off internet access, in an effort to prevent the publication of videos showing anti-government protests, videos were posted from outside the country.[88] Presumably, those videos originated from sources within the country.

The internet has also been used to organize international migrations.[89] For example, in the run-up to the 2018 U.S. mid-term elections, Facebook and WhatsApp were used to recruit participants for a caravan which planned to march from central America to the U.S.[90] They chose to march together for safety reasons. Not only did potential migrants learn about the caravan from social media, they used social media to coordinate the group.[91] Once the caravan actually began to form, it received significant coverage on traditional media, and video was live streamed on Facebook.[92] The "explosion of media coverage" and the "viral social media posts" ultimately led to an "explosion in the number of migrants."[93] The caravan grew from a small number of people (30) to hundreds within a matter of hours.[94]

The internet has also been used by politicians to heap abuse on political opponents. For example, in England, after a politician suggested that it was time for a vote of no confidence in Britain's then Prime Minister,

86. *Id.*

87. *Id.*

88. *See* J.J. Sutherland, *Myanmar Shuts Down Internet Access*, National Public Radio, The NPR News Blog (Sept. 28, 2007) (noting that posts were made from England).

89. *See* Kevin Sieff & Joshua Partlow, *How the Migrant Caravan Became So Big and Why Its Continuing to Grow, The Washington Post* (Oct. 23, 2018) https://www.washingtonpost.com/world/the_americas/how-the-migrant-caravan-became-so-big-and-why-its-continuing-to-grow/2018/10/23/88abf1a6-d631-11e8-8384-bcc5492fef49_story.html?utm_term=.5f85cd66e2aa.

90. *Id.*

91. *Id.*

92. *Id.*

93. *Id.*

94. *Id.*

Theresa May, the politician was pilloried on the internet with the hashtag #CurseReesMogg.[95] The tweets blended "sarcasm, a touch of cruelty and self-derision," and some were "rude, crude and obscene."[96]

In Brazil, a #NotHim movement emerged against presidential candidate Jair Bolsonaro who made a number of derogatory remarks about women.[97] Despite the movement, Bolsonaro was elected anyway. In Taiwan, the then president was using Twitter to keep the nation relevant in the international conversation.[98]

2. THE INTERNET AND THE ARAB SPRING UPRISINGS

Perhaps the most striking illustration of the power of the internet is the upheaval in the Middle East which was referred to as "The Arab Spring." There were numerous factors underlying the protests, including the fact that many Arab nations had large numbers of young people who were suffering from high poverty and unemployment rates, and there were significant gaps between rich and poor.[99] As one commentator noted, "the social contract between the state and citizens" has broken down, and there are increasing demands "for freedom, democracy, social justice, rule of law and economic equality."[100] In some cases, the protestors sought to change existing governmental structures, and to adopt constitutions limiting monarchial authority.[101] As tensions began to build, some feared that the unrest would sweep the Middle East.[102]

---

95. *See* Palko Karasz, *Why Twitter Is Cursing A British Conservative Who's Not Named May, The New York Times* A9 (Nov. 18, 2018).

96. *Id.*

97. *See* Shasta Darlington, *Candidate in Brazil Faces Women's Calls: #NotHim, The New York Times International* A10 (Sept. 25, 2018).

98. *See* Chris Horton, *Taiwan's President Embraces Twitter, The New York Times International* 4 (July 8–9, 2017).

99. *See* Harry Smith, *Wael Ghonim and Egypt's New Age Revolution*, 60 Minutes, CBSNews (Feb. 13, 2011) ("Egypt is an ancient civilization with a youthful population—nearly two-thirds of them are 30 years old or under. Many of them are educated but unemployed and angry."); *A Brittle Leader, supra* note 39.

100. *See A Brittle Leader, supra* note 39.

101. *See* Michael Slackman & Mark Landler, *Bahrain Turmoil Poses Fresh Test for White House, The New York Times*, at A1 (Feb. 18, 2011).

102. *See* Michael Slackman & Mona El Naggar, *Tunisia Casts Shadow on Arab Meeting, The New York Times*, A13 (Jan. 20, 2011).

The internet played a critical role in the first uprising in Tunisia. There, the internet helped the people topple the Tunisian government.[103] Indeed, the initial impetus for the uprising may have been WikiLeaks' internet disclosure of diplomatic cables revealing corruption in the Tunisian government.[104] WikiLeaks apparently coordinated with a Tunisian group, TuniLeak, which posted the cables online on the same day that WikiLeaks posted the documents.[105] Although the WikiLeaks/TuniLeak disclosures may have laid the groundwork for the uprising, the spark came when a 26-year-old college graduate, a fruit vendor who had been harassed by the police, and who faced dismal employment prospects, committed suicide by setting himself on fire.[106] The man's death "unleashed the pent-up anger of Tunisia's educated and unemployed youth, and soon that of others as well."[107]

During the uprising, the internet provided ordinary individuals with the means to organize, mobilize and protest.[108] Traditional media, in particular the popular Arab news outlet Al Jazeera, also played a role, complementing internet-based tools.[109] For example, Tunisian protestors recorded the uprising on their cell phones,[110] and posted pictures and videos on the internet through various sites, including Facebook, Twitter,[111]

---

103. *See* Eleanor Beardsley, *Social Media Gets Credit for Tunisian Overthrow*, National Public Radio, Weekend Edition Sunday (Jan. 16, 2011), http://www.npr.org/2011/01/16/132975274/Social-Media-Gets-Credit-For-Tunisian-Overthrow ("Two days ago, Tunisia's president fled the country—many reasons are being cited for his overthrow. But many credit the Internet and young, educated bloggers, tweeters and Facebook users for bringing down the regime.").

104. *See* David Kirkpatrick, *Beyond Tunisia Unrest, Rage Over Wealth of Ruling Family, The New York Times*, at A10 (Jan. 14, 2011).

105. *Id.*

106. *See* David D. Kirkpatrick, *Amid Rioting, Tunisia Closes Universities and Schools, The New York Times*, at A4 (Jan. 11, 2011) ("He had been trying to sell a container of fruits and vegetables, and the police confiscated his merchandise because he had no work permit.").

107. *See id.*

108. *See* Jennifer Preston, *Movement Began With Outrage and a Facebook Page That Gave It an Outlet, The New York Times*, at A10 (Feb. 6, 2011).

109. *See* Bob Garfield & Brooke Gladstone, *Tunisia's Twitter Revolution*, National Public Radio, On the Media (Jan. 21, 2011), http://www.onthemedia.org/2011/jan/21/tunisias-twitter-revolution/transcript/.

110. *See Cellphone Cameras Become World's Eyes and Ears on Protests, supra* note 14.

111. *See Movement Began With Outrage, supra* note 108.

and Frog,[112] and they also distributed videos and pictures through their smart phones and other handheld devices.[113] A YouTube video, depicting police corruption, was viewed more than 500,000 times.[114] As the protests continued, internet postings continued to drive political dissent[115] through various social media platforms[116] such as Facebook.[117] Some of these postings explicitly called for the ouster of Tunisia's President.[118]

Trying to suppress the revolt, the Tunisian government sought to restrict internet and cellular telephone communications,[119] particularly those depicting governmental violence,[120] and the government even imprisoned bloggers.[121] However, tech-savvy citizens found ways to evade governmental controls.[122] As one commentator noted, "'This is a generation that is educated, is well-informed, that will be more demanding of their rights to participate, to have a civic role in their state, and not to sit through gerrymandered elections and lack of participation in the econ-

112. *See Cellphone Cameras Become World's Eyes and Ears on Protests, supra* note 14.

113. *See* Beardsley, *supra* note 103 ("Everyone in Tunisia was connected to the Internet, to the site of the bloggers, to the site of Facebook, to Twitter, to organize the revolution." (quoting Mohamed Ben Hazouz, a software engineer and blogger)).

114. *Id.*

115. *See* Eleanor Beardsley, *Tunisians Watch Egypt, Tend Their Own Revolution*, National Public Radio (Jan. 30, 2011), http://www.npr.org/2011/01/30/133348376/Tunisians-Watch-Egypt-While-Tending-Their-Own-Revolution ("President Zine El Abiding Ben Ali ruled Tunisia with an iron first for 23 years, until the people rose up and overthrew him. Their anger at corruption, repression and poverty spread on the Internet, fomenting the revolt.").

116. *See Beyond Tunisia Unrest, supra* note 104 ("Throughout a month of demonstrations, protestors have relied on Facebook and other social media to advertise and coordinate their actions....").

117. *See Movement Began With Outrage, supra* note 108, at A10.

118. *Id.*

119. *Id.* ("The government had attempted to control the internet by blocking sites like YouTube. Nevertheless, the Web played a principle role in the Tunisian peoples revolution.").

120. *Id.* ("President Ben Ali tried to block the cell phone videos of the first killings of protesters in the south of the country.").

121. *Id.*

122. *Id.* ("'I think there is definitely a generation who have understood the technology of how to circumvent banned websites. The moment something is banned, somebody in this country is breaking through it and going around it. So it's been counterproductive in recent years in terms of a control strategy.'" (Quoting Dr. Claire Spencer, Head, Middle East and North Africa Program, Chatham House)).

omy.'"[123] Traditional media outside the country, which was given limited access to Tunisia, monitored internet postings as a way of tracking the uprising.[124] Ultimately, Tunisia's president was forced to step down.[125]

The Tunisian revolution was the catalyst for anti-government protests in Egypt.[126] Although Egyptians had protested before the Tunisian revolt, the fall of the Tunisian government convinced many Egyptians that change was possible in their country as well.[127] Tunisian protestors collab-

123. *Id.* (Quoting Dr. Claire Spencer, Head, Middle East and North Africa Program, Chatham House).

124. *See* Brian Stelter, *Televising the Revolution: Al Jazeera Hopes Reports from Egypt Open Doors in U.S., The New York Times*, at B8 (Feb. 7, 2011) ("In the Arabic newsroom [of Al Jazeera], a group of volunteers scoured Facebook and YouTube for newly uploaded material. The uprising in Tunisia, where Al Jazeera was not allowed to have a bureau, resulted in the 'biggest use yet of citizen video' by the network, Mr. Souag [Al Jazeera's news director] said.").

125. See NPR Staff & Wires, *Tunisia's President Departs Amid National Turmoil*, National Public Radio (Jan. 14, 2011), http://www.npr.org/2011/01/15/132925632/angry-demonstrators-march-on-tunisian-capital.

126. *See* Anthony Shadid & David R. Kirkpatrick, *Military Struggles Amid Fears of Chaos*, at A1 (Jan. 31, 2011) ("In scenes as tumultuous as any since the uprising began, Dr. El-Baradei defied a government curfew and joined thousands of protestors in Liberation Square, a downtown landmark that has become the epicenter of the uprising and a platform, writ small, for the frustrations, ambitions and resurgent pride of a generation claiming the country's mantle."); Scott Simon, *Egyptian Streets Fill with Protestors, Tanks*, National Public Radio, Weekend Edition Saturday (Jan. 31, 2011), http://www.npr.org/2011/01/29/133327911/Egyptian-Streets-Fill-With-Protesters-Tanks ("Egypt stands at the edge of history today as President Hosni Mubarak faces the most serious challenge to his long, authoritarian regime.... Protestors are back on the streets of Cairo demanding Mr. Mubarak to step down."); Liz Sly, *Jubilation—and New Determination—Sweep Across Egypt as Thousands Rejoice, The Courier-Journal*, at A3 (Feb. 12, 2011) ("When they called the first major protest Jan. 25, they tapped into a public inspired by Tunisia's revolt and thousands turned out, beyond even the organizers' expectations.").

127. *See* Scott Simon, *Unrest Spreads Through the Middle East*, National Public Radio, Weekend Edition Saturday (Jan. 29, 2011), http://www.npr.org/2011/01/29/133327917/Unrest-Spreads-Through-Middle-East ("I think that if you look at Egypt, this has been an extremely turbulent decade. But the problem is that each time they started to crest and they started to put pressure, they got beaten back.... Literally beaten back. And you remember very clearly the journalists, the protestors, the bloggers, being beaten up and arrested. And there was this sense of almost like a tide coming in. And the waves would hit the beachhead but it would never quite be enough. I think the difference this time is the demonstration effect from Tunisia and the idea that this is actually possible.") (quoting Mr. Marc Lynch, Director, Middle East Studies, George Washington University) ; *Tunisians Watch Egypt, supra* note 115 ("And the Tunisian revolt inspired the Egyptian.").

orated with Egyptian protestors, using social network sites to discuss tactical issues, including how to evade surveillance, deal with rubber bullets, and counteract tear gas.[128] As in Tunisia, the desire to protest was inflamed by social divisions between rich and poor,[129] and was further aggravated by the beating and killing of a dissident (Khaled Said).[130]

Even though a relatively small number of Egyptians had internet access at the time (roughly, 20% of the population),[131] the internet played a major role in the Egyptian revolution.[132] Protestors took smart phone photos of Khaled Said lying in the morgue,[133] and posted the photos on Facebook and YouTube.[134] In addition, protestors used the internet to disseminate a message of nonviolence.[135] Bloggers and Twitter users also participated.[136]

Since Egypt had some five million Facebook users at the time, that platform provided a particularly effective medium by which to inform

---

128. *See* David D. Kirkpatrick & David E. Sanger, *A Tunisian-Egyptian Link That Shook Arab History, The New York Times*, at A1 (Feb. 14, 2011) ("As protestors in Tahrir Square faced off against pro-government forces, they drew a lesson from their counterparts in Tunisia: 'Advice to the youth of Egypt: Put vinegar or onion under your scarf for tear gas.' The exchange on Facebook was part of a remarkable two-year collaboration that has given birth to a new force in the Arab world—a pan Arab youth movement dedicated to spreading democracy in a region without it.... They fused their secular expertise in social networks....").

129. *See* David D. Kirkpatrick & Mona El-Naggar, *Elite Areas Attacked as Class War Explodes, The New York Times*, A6 (Jan. 31, 2011) ("As the government of Egypt shakes from a broad-based uprising, long simmering resentments have burst into open class warfare" and "tensions between rich and poor [have] exploded.").

130. *See Movement Began With Outrage and a Facebook Page, supra* note 108, at A10.

131. *See* Margaret Warner, *Social Media and Satellite TV: A One-Two Punch Against Mubarak*, Public Broadcasting Service, The News Hour (Feb. 14, 2011). http://www.pbs.org/newshour/bb/world/jan-june11/egypt2_02-14.html.

132. *See Jubilation—and New Determination, supra* note 126, at A3 (Feb. 12, 2011) ("The protests were started by a small core of secular, liberal youth activists organizing on the Internet who only a few months earlier struggled to gather more than 100 demonstrators at time."); *see also* Brooke Gladstone, *Tweeting From Egypt's Tahrir Square*, National Public Radio, On the Media (Feb. 4, 2011), http://www.onthemedia.org/2011/feb/04/tweeting-from-egypts-tahrir-square/.

133. *See Movement Began With Outrage and a Facebook Page, supra* note 108, at A10.

134. *Id.*

135. *Id.*

136. *See* Deborah Amos, *Blogging and Tweeting, Egyptians Push for Change*, National Public Radio (Aug. 26, 2010). http://www.npr.org/templates/story/story.php?storyId=129425721.

Egyptians about the uprising,[137] as well as to organize protests.[138] Google, YouTube, and smart phones were also used "to capture and share video."[139] At the time of the revolt, some 473,000 users had accessed Said's Facebook page, and that page was being used to facilitate communication between the protestors.[140] The site proposed a day of protests on January 14 (known in Egypt as "Police Day" because it commemorates a police fight against British colonialism) provided that 50,000 people would commit to participate.[141] In fact, more than 100,000 people signaled their intent to participate.[142] The Facebook postings were supplemented by traditional print posters that advertised the protests.[143] Tens of thousands of protestors ultimately turned out to protest and many shouted slogans suggested on the Facebook page.[144]

Other internet-based sites also facilitated the protests, including Twitter. At one point, some 11,000 Tweets regarding Hosni Mubarak were posted in a single hour (although, to put the quantity into perspective, a Twitter feed entitled "icantdateyou" generated 274,000 postings in that

---

137. *See A Tunisian-Egyptian Link, supra* note 128:

> The result was a Facebook group Mr. Ghonim set up: We Are All Kalid Said, after a young Egyptian who was beaten to death by police. Mr. Ghonim—unknown to the public, but working closely with Mr. Maher of the April 6 Youth Movement and a contact from Mr. ElBaradei's group—said that he used Mr. Said's killing to educate Egyptians about democracy movements.
>
> He filled the site with video clips and newspaper articles about police violence. He repeatedly hammered home a simple message: "This is your country; a government official is your employee who gets his salary from your tax money, and you have your rights." He took special aim at the distortions of the official media, because when the people "distrust the media then you know you are not going to lose them," he said.

138. *Id.*, at A10; *see also Jubilation—and New Determination, supra* note 126, at A3 ("But their work on Facebook and other social network sites over the past few years built a greater awareness and bitterness among Egyptians over issues like police abuse and corruption.").

139. *See Movement Began With Outrage and a Facebook Page, supra* note 108; *see also* Kareem Fahim & Mona El-Naggar, *Across Egypt, Protests Direct Fury at Leader, The New York Times*, A8 (Jan. 26, 2011).

140. *See Movement Began With Outrage and a Facebook Page, supra* note 108, at A10.

141. *See A Tunisian-Egyptian Link, supra* note 128.

142. *Id.*

143. *Id.*

144. *Id.*

same hour).[145] Protesters responded by taking to the streets.[146] On one site, Bambuser, which hosts streaming video images, postings increased dramatically from 800 to 10,000 postings a day during the protests.[147]

Egyptian protests were also facilitated by the April 6 Youth Movement which coordinated street protests through Facebook.[148] The group's organizational efforts prompted more than 90,000 protestors to sign up on April 6th's Facebook page, and tens of thousands of protestors turned out to rally in Egypt's streets.[149] After developing a plan for the protests (which involved gathering after Friday prayers to march on Liberation Square), the organizers distributed the plan through e-mail, Twitter and text messages.[150] In addition, one protestor used Facebook to disseminate information regarding the brutality of Egyptian police.[151] The protestors were able to coordinate the participation of Mohamed ElBaradei, a diplomat and Nobel laureate who supported the protests, by recommending the mosque that he should attend on the day of the protests.[152] As the protests grew in strength, the uprising began to be covered by the mainstream media, and became a major news story in its own right.[153] Protestors streamed into Cairo and camped out in Tahrir Square[154] with traditional technologies (*e.g.*, bullhorns) being used at the rallies themselves.[155]

---

145. *See* Natasha Singer, *Why Some Twitter Posts Catch On, and Some Don't, The New York Times*, at A4 (Feb. 6, 2011).

146. *See Across Egypt, Protests Direct Fury at Leader, supra* note 139, at A8.

147. *See Cellphone Cameras Become World's Eyes and Ears on Protests, supra* note 14.

148. *See* David Kirkpatrick & Mona El-Naggar, *Protest's Old Guard Falls in Behind the Young, The New York Times*, at A1 (Jan. 31, 2011).

149. *Id.*

150. *Id.*, at A1 ("They decided to follow a blueprint similar to Tuesday's urging protestors to converge on the central Liberation Square. So they drew up a list of selected mosques around Cairo where they asked people to gather at Friday Prayer before marching together toward the square. Then they distributed the list through e-mail and text messages, which spread virally."); *See Wael Ghonim and Egypt's New Age Revolution, supra* note 99 ("[The Egyptians] 18 day revolution began not with terrorism and tanks, but with Twitter and texts and satellite TV broadcasts").

151. *See Wael Ghonim and Egypt's New Age Revolution, supra* note 99.

152. *See Protest's Old Guard Falls in Behind the Young, supra* note 148, at A1.

153. *Id.*

154. *See* Kareem Fahim & Anthony Shadid, *Quiet Acts of Protest on a Noisy Day, The New York Times*, at A10 (Feb. 2, 2010).

155. *See* Lolita C. Baldor, *U.S. Urges Democracy for Egypt: Clinton: Avoid Another Iran, The Courier-Journal*, at A1 (Jan. 31, 2011).

Once the Egyptian government realized that the internet was being used to coordinate the revolt, it moved to shut down Egyptian internet providers,[156] as well as cell phone service providers[157] and Twitter.[158] Vodafone, for example, was ordered to shut down its service to selected areas in Egypt,[159] as were other internet service providers.[160] Because of these governmental actions, Facebook saw a dramatic drop in activity.[161] The government even jailed a Google official for assisting with internet organizing.[162]

Since Egypt had only a limited number of internet service providers (some reports suggested there were only four), it was relatively easy for the government to shut down the internet,[163] thereby cutting-off internet, cell phone and SMS communications.[164] These actions reduced data traffic by 90 percent.[165] Amazingly, in a nation of some 80 million people and 20 million internet users, Egypt was able to shut down 90% of internet access in a matter of minutes.[166] The government could do so because a state-owned company, Telecom Egypt, controlled virtually all of the

---

156. *See* Scott Simon, *Egypt's Stone Age Response to 21st Century Media*, National Public Radio, Weekend Edition Saturday, Simon Says (Jan. 29, 2011). http://www.npr.org/2011/01/29/133325987/egypts-stone-age-response-to-21st-century-media.

157. *See* Soraya Sarhaddi Nelson, *Lawlessness Could Hijack Egypt's Popular Uprising*, National Public Radio (Jan. 31, 2011) http://www.npr.org/2011/01/31/133363676/lawlessness-could-hijack-egypts-popular-uprising (as the unrest grew, "the government took the unprecedented step of shutting down the Internet and cell phones across the country to stop protestors from communicating with each other or the outside world.").

158. *See Across Egypt, Protests Direct Fury at Leader, supra* note 139, at A1 (Jan. 26, 2011) (noting various restrictions, including the fact that Twitter had confirmed that its site had been blocked in Egypt).

159. *See* James Glanz, *Egypt Autocracy Found Internet's "Off" Switch, The New York Times*, at A1 (Feb. 16, 2011) ("Vodafone expressed extreme reluctance to shut down but was told that if it did not comply, the government would uses its own "off" switch via the Telecom Egypt infrastructure—a method that would have be much more time consuming to reverse."); Matt Richtel, *Egypt Halts Most Internet and Cell Service, and Scale of Shutdown Surprises Experts, The New York Times*, at A13 (Jan. 29, 2011).

160. *See Egypt Autocracy Found "Off Switch", supra* note 159.

161. *Id.*

162. *See Wael Ghonim and Egypt's New Age Revolution, supra* note 99.

163. *See Lawlessness Could Hijack Egypt's Popular Uprising, supra* note 157.

164. *See Egyptian Streets Fill with Protestors, supra* note 126 (quoting National Public Radio Correspondent Soraya Sarhaddi Nelson).

165. *See Egypt Halts Most Internet and Cell Service, supra* note 159, at A10.

166. *See Egypt Autocracy Found "Off" Switch, supra* note 159; *See Egypt Halts Most Internet and Cell Service, supra* note 159, at A13.

fiberoptic bandwidth that carried internet traffic.[167] Nevertheless, some people remained connected, especially those connected to smaller ISPs, and land-based phone lines continued to work so that information could be transmitted by telephone.[168] Within a day or so after the internet shut down, there were reports that some internet service had been restored.[169] During this period, Al Jazeera (the satellite television network) continued to broadcast,[170] and some protestors were able to connect to dial-up internet services in other countries.[171] Moreover, and more importantly, even during the internet shutdown, the protestors pushed ahead.

Whether the government's decision to shut down the internet was a smart move is debatable. Clearly, the internet was being used to organize and promote the protests, and therefore the shut down hindered that effort. The difficulty is that, in modern societies, many people have become addicted to the internet. At one point, Karl Marx suggested that religion is the opiate of the masses. Today, the internet has become the new opiate. Although the Egyptian protests had grown quite large, undoubtedly some Egyptians were oblivious, happily surfing the internet for work or pleasure. Once the government shut the internet down, these individuals had nothing to do. As a result, the protests swelled.[172] Indeed, many Egyptians were offended by the government's decision to shut down the internet,[173] and decided to join the street protests,[174] interpreting the

---

167. *See Egypt Autocracy Found "Off" Switch, supra* note 159, at A10.

168. *See Tweeting From Egypt's Tahrir Square, supra* note 132 (quoting Mona Seif, described as an "activist, blogger and post-graduate student" at Cairo University) ("By chance, one of our friends still had Internet connection. She was so scared to admit it because she didn't want to get it shut down. She had her wireless provided by one company, which had all the stuff on financial exchanges, so the government were not ready to shut down this—").

169. *See Egypt's Stone Age Response, supra* note 156.

170. *See* Robert F. Worth, *On Al Jazeera, a Revolution Televised Despite Hurdles, The New York Times*, A8 (Jan. 29, 2011).

171. *See Egypt Halts Most Internet and Cell Service, supra* note 159.

172. *See id.*; *See* Noan Cohen, *Egyptians Were Unplugged, and Uncowed, The New York Times*, at B3 Feb. 21, 2011).

173. *See Egyptians Were Unplugged, supra* note 172, at B3; *Egypt Autocracy Found "Off" Switch, supra* note 159.

174. *See Egypt Halts Most Internet and Cell Service, supra* note 159; *Egyptians Were Unplugged, supra* note 172, at B3.

government's efforts to restrict speech as a sign of weakness and fear.[175] In addition, some who had been supporting the protests online might have decided to move from the internet to the streets.

Ultimately, the internet shut down was ineffective. Some fifteen days after the protests began, online activists still used the internet to coordinate demonstrations,[176] and were using their smart phones to capture pictures and video,[177] as well as to post video and information on social networking sites like Facebook and Twitter.[178] Interviews with the organizers of a Facebook protest page openly encouraged Egyptians to join the protests.[179]

During the shutdown, Egyptian protestors found creative ways to circumvent internet restrictions. For example, some protestors used their smart phones to piece together communications and post tweets using a system called @speak2tweet,[180] which correlated to a second account,

---

175. *See* Scott Shane, *Technology Helps Ignite Chain (as in Tunisia). Except When It Bolsters Oppression (as in Iran), The New York Times*, Week in Review, at 1 (Jan. 30, 2011) ("But by cutting off Egypt's Internet and wireless service late last week in the face of huge street protests, President Hosni Mubarak betrayed his own fear—that Facebook, Twitter, laptops and smartphones cold empower his opponents, expose his weakness to the world and topple his regime.").

176. *See* David D. Kirkpatrick, *As Egypt Protest Swells, U.S. Sends Specific Demands, The New York Times* A1 (Feb. 9, 2011) ("Many in the crowd, for example, said they had turned out because organizers had spread the word over loudspeakers and online media for demonstrators to concentrate their efforts on just Tuesdays and Fridays, enabling their supporters to rest in between.").

177. *See Across Egypt, Protests Direct Fury at Leader, supra* note 139, at A1.

178. *See As Egypt Protest Swells, supra* note 176, at A1 (showing a photograph of Egyptian youths using laptop computers, and containing the following description of their activities: "In Cairo, Egyptian youths used laptops to post video they had shot earlier Tuesday in Tahrir Square. The group has been collecting accounts of the demonstrations and videos of the protestors, putting them on social networking sites like Facebook and Twitter.").

179. *See id.*, at A12 ("Many in the crowd—some protesting for the first time—said that they were newly inspired by the interview Monday night with Wael Ghonim, a Google executive, who had been the anonymous administrator of a Facebook group that enlisted tens of thousands to oppose the Mubarak government by politicizing a young Egyptian's beating death at the hands of its reviled police force.").

180. *See* Christine Hauser, *New Service Lets Voices From Egypt Be Heard, The New York Times*, A14 (Feb. 2, 2011) ("Unedited, raw, anonymous and emotional, Egyptian voices are trickling out through a new service that evades attempts by the authorities to suppress them by cutting Internet services. There is still some cellphone service, so a new social-media link that marries Google, Twitter and SayNow, a voice-based social media platform,

@AliveinEgypt, that transcribed the phone messages to text, and sent them to an internet radio station, egypt.periszkopradio.hu, that played the recordings.[181] That service provided a way for ordinary Egyptians to express their views,[182] and quickly picked up 8,000 subscribers.[183] Other Egyptians found other ways to circumvent the shutdown, including using older communications systems.[184]

Protestors were also able to use the internet to dispute false governmental claims. When the Egyptian government tried to quell the protests by announcing that consensus had been reached regarding how to proceed, protest organizers quickly refuted the claim over the internet.[185] Traditional journalists, whose equipment had been seized by governmental officials, used platforms like Twitter to continue to report on events,[186] based in part on information obtained from WikiLeaks.[187]

The Egyptian protests continued for the next eighteen days, escalating in both size and intensity.[188] By the end, hundreds of thousands of Egyp-

---

gives Egyptians three phone numbers to call and leave a message, which is then posted on the Internet as a recorded Twitter message. The messages are at twitter.com/speak2tweet and can also be heard by telephone."); *see also* Michael Liedtke, *Google Got Egypt to Twitter, The Courier-Journal*, D4.(Feb. 6, 2011).

181. *See Google Got Egypt to Twitter, supra* note 180.

182. *Id.* ("The result is a story of a revolution unfolding in short bursts. Sometimes speaking for just several seconds, other times for more than a minute, the disembodied voices convey highly charged moments of excitement or calm declarations of what life is like in Egypt, the Arab world's most populous country, as it seeks to remove its leader.").

183. *Id.*

184. *See Egypt Autocracy Found "Off" Switch, supra* note 159 ("When he, too, noticed that domestic fiber-optic cables were open, he had a moment of exhilaration, remembering that he could link up servers directly and establishing messaging using an older system called Internet Relay Chat. But then it dawned on him that he had always assumed that he could download the necessary software via the Internet and had saved no copy.... [H]e decided to risk having a driver bring $7,000 in satellite equipment, including a four-foot dish, from Cairo, and somehow he was connected internationally again by Monday evening.").

185. *See* David D. Kirkpatrick & David E. Sanger, *Mubarak's Aides Meet Opposition, a First for Egypt, The New York Times*, at A9 (Feb. 7, 2011).

186. *See* Jeremy W. Peters & J. David Goodman, *Reporters Beaten and Cameras Smashed in Struggle to Control the News From Cairo, The New York Times*, A8 (Feb. 4, 2011).

187. *See* Elisabeth Bumiller, *Ally's Stability Hinges on a Secretive Military, The New York Times*, at A1 (Feb. 6, 2011) (discussing Egypt's defense minister).

188. *See* David D. Kirkpatrick & Kareem Fahim, *Mubarak's Backers Storm Protestors as U.S. Condemns Egypt's Violent Turn, The New York Times*, at A1 (Feb. 3, 2011).

tians were protesting in public places,[189] and many protestors remained in public places around the clock.[190] By that time, the protests included not only the young and tech-savvy, but also a broad cross-section of Egyptian society.[191] Ultimately, Mubarak was forced to resign the Presidency,[192] and transfer his powers to a military council.[193]

Before he stepped down, Mubarak went to great lengths to hold on to power, including trying to use police power against Egyptian citizens,[194] repressing and trying to silence traditional journalists,[195] shutting down communication systems, and trying to scare the population with rhetoric about the violence that might ensue if he resigned.[196] He even offered to amend the Egyptian Constitution to reduce his autocratic authority,[197] promised to shuffle his cabinet,[198] appointed Mr. Suleiman as Vice President,[199] ceded power to Suleiman,[200] and offered not to run for reelection

---

189. *See Jubilation—and New Determination, supra* note 126, at A3 ("Hundreds of thousands marched throughout the day in cities across Egypt as soldiers stood by, besieging his [Mubarak's] palaces in Cairo and Alexandria.").

190. *See A Brittle Leader, supra* note 39.

191. *See* David D. Kirkpatrick, *Egypt's Army Renounces Use of Force, and Vice President Offers to Talk, The New York Times,* at A10 (Feb. 1, 2011).

192. *See* Mona El-Naggar, *The Legacy of 18 Days in Tahrir Square, The New York Times,* at 4 (Feb. 20, 2011).

193. *See* David D. Kirkpatrick, *Mubarak Out, The New York Times,* at A1 (Feb. 12, 2011).

194. *See Across Egypt, Protests Direct Fury at Leader, supra* note 139, at A1; *see also* Kareem Fahim, *Hopes of Egyptians, Poor and Wealthy, Converge in Fight for Cairo Bridge, The New York Times,* A9 (Jan. 29, 2011) (suggesting that Egyptian police used tear gas and water cannons on Egyptian protestors).

195. *See Reporters Beaten and Cameras Smashed, supra* note 186.

196. *See A Brittle Leader, supra* note 39 ("Mr. Mubarak resorted to the tried and proven tactics that have been a hallmark of his authoritarian regime. He unleashed the full force of the police, tried to manage the message by shutting down the Internet and censoring news reports, insisted the people in the street were manipulated by foreigners or Islamists, and presented a stark either-or equation—if he did not remain in power, the alternative would be far worse.").

197. *See* Anthony Shadid & David D. Kirkpatrick, *Fears of Violence in Standoff, The New York Times,* A1 (Feb. 11, 2011).

198. *See* David D. Kirkpatrick, *Mubarak Orders Crackdown, With Revolt Sweeping Egypt, The New York Times,* A1 (Jan. 29, 2011).

199. *See* David D. Kirkpatrick, *Mubarak Names Intelligence Chief as Vice President, The New York Times,* A1 (Jan. 30, 2011).

200. *See* Hamza Hendawi & Sarah El Deeb, *Mubarak Stays, Cedes Powers: Gives Authority to VP—Without Stepping Down, The Courier-Journal,* A1 (Feb. 11. 2011).

at the end of his term (but indicated that he would remain in office until elections could be held the following September).[201] He also shut down train service and closed roads in order to prevent Egyptians from flooding into Cairo.[202] In the final analysis, nothing worked as the protesters became furious[203] and emboldened,[204] and the Egyptian military refused to intervene on Mubarak's behalf.[205] Indeed, Mubarak's efforts to hold on to power seemed to inflame the populace,[206] and incite violence.[207] After eighteen days of tumult, and only four weeks after the conclusion of the Tunisian revolution, President Mubarak was ousted from power.[208] Less than 1,000 people died in the uprising.[209] Interestingly, in Mubarak's wake, the military asserted control and the protests continued.[210] The one year anniversary revealed a continuation of the protests.[211]

By the end of the Egyptian revolution, unrest was breaking out all over the Middle East,[212] and commentators were beginning to suggest that 2011

---

201. *See* Anthony Shadid, *Mubarak Won't Run Again, But Stays; Obama Urges a Faster Shift of Power, The New York Times*, at A1 (Feb. 2, 2011).

202. *Id.* at A12.

203. *See* Margaret Coker & Charles Levinson, *Calls for Mubarak's Ouster Intensify, The Wall Street Journal*, at 5 (Feb. 1, 2011); *Fears of Violence in Standoff, supra* note 195, at A1.

204. *See Hopes of Egyptians, Poor and Wealthy, supra* note 194, at A9; Nicholas Kulish & Souad Mekhennet, *In Alexandria, Protestors Win After a Day of Fierce Fighting with Riot Police, The New York Times*, A9 (Jan. 29, 2011); *Mubarak Orders Crackdown, supra* note 198, at A1.

205. *See A Tunisian-Egyptian Link, supra* note 128.

206. *Id.* at A1; *see also* Sarah El Deeb & Hadeel Al-Shalchi, *Sept. Exit for Mubarak Not Fast Enough For Foes: His Pledge to Not Seek Re-Election Leaves 250,000 in Cairo Square Jeering, The Courier-Journal*, A1 (Feb. 2, 2011).

207. *See* Hadeel Al-Shalchi, *Egypt Demonstrations Turn Violent, Deadly: Mubarak Supporters, Opponents Trade Fierce Attacks in Cairo, The Courier-Journal*, at A1 (Feb. 3, 2001).

208. *See Jubilation—and New Determination, supra* note 126, at A1.

209. *See A Tunisian-Egyptian Link, supra* note 128.

210. *See* David D. Kirkpatrick, *Egypt's Military Expands Power, Raising Alarms: Reneging on Promises, The New York Times*, at A1 (Oct. 15, 2011).

211. *See* Charles Levinson & Matt Bradley, *Egyptians Show Mix of Jubilation, Anger to Mark Anniversary: Rallies Reflect Political Rifts Amid Joy of Mubarak's Exit, The Wall Street Journal*, at A10 (Jan. 26, 2012).

212. *See* Anthony Shadid, *In Peril: The Arab Status Quo, The New York Times*, Week in Review, at 1 (Jan. 16, 2011); Associated Press, *Thousands of Protesters Fill Streets of Arab World, The Courier-Journal*, A3 (Feb. 26, 2011). By this time, Arab League leaders were clearly concerned about how to deal with the situation. *See Tunisia Casts Shadow on Arab Meeting, supra* note 102.

might be "the year that the status quo in the Middle East proved untenable and began falling apart."[213] One protestor claimed that a "giant tsunami has just hit the Arab world,"[214] and another suggested that, in "the living rooms of ordinary people watching history unfold live on television, there was wonder, amazement and a renewed sense of hope and possibility."[215] There was "stunned silence" from the "halls of power" in the Arab world,[216] as powerful officials watched Mubarak fall from power in less than three weeks when his hold on power had previously seemed unshakeable).[217] Various Arab governments took steps to quell the protests in their own countries.[218]

The internet also played a major role in the events that occurred elsewhere in the Middle East. In the internet era, it is much easier for individuals in one country to be aware of what is happening in other countries. Historically, governments could control the flow of information to their people by manipulating the traditional media (*e.g.*, newspapers, radio and television), and by limiting the quantity of information available to their citizens. In an internet era, such control was no longer possible. Because of the internet, citizens in other Arab countries quickly became aware of what had happened in Tunisia and Egypt,[219] and were inspired by those events.[220] Unrest "spread across the Arab world at breathtaking speed," and raised hopes that "the same Web tools that so many Americans use to keep up with college pals and post passing thoughts have a more noble

---

213. *See In Peril: The Arab Status Quo, supra* note 212.

214. *See Tunisians Watch Egypt, supra* note 115; John Leland, *Some Iraqis See Symptoms of Region's Tumult at Home, The New York Times*, at A9 (Jan. 26, 2011).

215. *See* Liz Sly, *The Arab World: Other Regimes Feel Upheaval's Tremors, The Courier-Journal*, at A1 (Feb. 12, 2011).

216. *Id.*

217. *Id.*, at A2.

218. *Id.* (noting that governments in Algeria, Syria, and Iraq took relatively immediate actions).

219. *See* Anthony Shadid, *Yearning for Respect, Arabs Find a Voice, The New York Times*, A11 (Jan. 30, 2011).

220. *See* Neil MacFarquhar, *Unrest Spreads, Some Violently, in Middle East, The New York Times*, at A1 (Feb. 17, 2011) ("The unrest has been inspired partly by grievances unique to each country, but many shared a new confidence, bred in Egypt and Tunisia, that a new generation could challenge unresponsive authoritarian rule in ways their parents thought impossible."). http://www.nytimes.com/2011/02/18/world/middleeast/18protests.html?_r=2&hp=&pagewanted.

role as well, as a scourge of despotism."[221] In countries like Saudi Arabia, the Tunisian and Egyptian revolutions generated much comment and discussion.[222] Yemen's citizens were inspired as well.[223] Internet-based tools were supplemented by traditional media, including Al Jazeera, the satellite television network.[224] In addition, Tunisian and Egyptian shared their expertise with young people in Libya, Algeria, Morocco and Iran.[225]

The revolts that developed in other Arab countries involved many of the same communications tools that had been used in Tunisia and Egypt. Al Jazeera continued to use traditional broadcast technology in its reporting.[226] Other protestors used social media platforms such as Facebook and Twitter,[227] and it rapidly became apparent that a cross-fertilization of ideas was occurring throughout the Middle East. In Egypt, protest chants mirrored those used in the Tunisian protests, and protestor's waved Tunisian flags.[228] Protestors were clearly inspired by the unfolding events in Tunisia (and, later, Egypt),[229] and their chants indicated that they were well aware

---

221. *See Technology Helps Ignite Change, supra* note 175.

222. *See Social Media Revolution Hits Saudia Arabia, supra* note 38.

223. *See* David Goodman & Nada Bakri, *Yemen's Opposition Goes to Code Pink, The New York Times*, The Lede (blog) (Jan. 27, 2011), http://thelede.blogs.nytimes.com/2011/01/27/yemens-opposition-goes-to-code-pink/?scp=1&sq=yemen's%20opposition%20goes%20to%20code%20pink&st=cse ("The protesters who filled the streets of Sana, the Yemeni capital, on Thursday demanding the resignation of the country's authoritarian leader claimed inspiration from similar large antigovernment protests that have rattled Egypt and toppled the government in Tunisia this month.").

224. *See Televising the Revolution, supra* note 124, at B1 ("Al Jazeera's Arabic- and English-language coverage has provided a worldwide megaphone for the protests that have disrupted the Middle East, first in Tunisia and then Egypt—and to a lesser degree, Yemen, Jordan and Sudan.").

225. *See A Tunisian-Egyptian Link, supra* note 128.

226. *See Yearning for Respect, Arabs Find a Voice, supra* note 219, at A11.

227. *See id.*

228. *See id.* ("The slogan of the revolution, 'The people want to bring down the regime,' adopted from Tunisia, became, 'The People, at last, have brought down the regime.'").

229. *See* Laura Kasinof & J. David Goodman, *Yemeni Youth Square Off With Forces, The New York Times*, at A4 (Feb. 14, 2001) ("While the aims of Yemen's southern secessionist movement are different from the political opposition's in Sana, they too have claimed inspiration from the Tunisian and Egyptian revolutions.").

of the events that were unfolding in those countries.[230] Cross-border communications were common.[231]

Protest demonstrations quickly spread across the Arab world,[232] engulfing Jordan,[233] Lebanon,[234] Libya,[235] Yemen,[236] Morocco,[237] Saudi Arabia,[238] Oman,[239] Syria,[240] Bahrain,[241] Sudan,[242] Qatar,[243] Iraq,[244] Algeria,[245] Iran,[246]

---

230. *See id.* ("'In Egypt they chanted "The people want to expel the system," but we chant "The people want to cut the ties,"' said Wagdy al-Shaaby, a secessionist protestor who marched on Friday in the southern city of Zinjibar.").

231. *See Yearning for Respect, Arabs Find a Voice, supra* note 219, at A11.

232. *See Thousands of Protesters Fill Streets of Arab World, supra* note 212, at A3.

233. *See* Ranya Kadri & Ethan Bronner, *King of Jordan Dismisses His Cabinet, The New York Times*, at A14 (Feb. 2, 2011).

234. *See In Peril: The Arab Status Quo, supra* note 212, at 1.

235. *See* Jack Healy, *Popular Rage Encounters State Violence in Mideast, The New York Times*, A12 (Feb. 18, 2011).

236. *See* Ahmed Al-Haj, *Massive Protests in Yemen Seek to Oust Leader, The Courier-Journal*, A4 (Feb. 4, 2011) ("Tens of thousands of protestors staged unprecedented demonstrations Thursday against Yemen's autocratic president. . . ."); *King of Jordan Dismisses His Cabinet, supra* note 233 ("In Yemen, the government, fearing new protests, offered concessions to the opposition, which promised to call a demonstration every Thursday until March, when it will evaluate whether its demands have been met."); Laura Kasinof, *Deaths and Injuries Reported in Yemeni Protest March, The New York Times*, A9 (May 10, 2011).

237. *See* Steven Erlanger, *In Morocco, Fears of Chaos Temper Calls for Change, The New York Times*, A8 (Feb. 21, 2011).

238. *See* David D. Kirkpatrick, *Egyptians Remain Defiant as the Military Does Little to Quash Protests, The New York Times*, A11 (Jan. 30 2011).

239. *See* Nada Bakri, *Oman Joins Protest Wave, and 2 Die in Clashes with Police, The New York Times*, at A9 (Feb. 28, 2011).

240. *See King of Jordan Dismisses His Cabinet, supra* note 233.

241. *See Bahrain Turmoil Poses Fresh Test for White House, supra* note 101.

242. *See King of Jordan Dismisses His Cabinet, supra* note 233; Sharon Otterman, *Sudan Sees Migration of Unrest to Its Streets, The New York Times*, at A8 (Jan. 31, 2011).

243. *See King of Jordan Dismisses His Cabinet, supra* note 233.

244. *See Popular Rage Encounters State Violence in Mideast, supra* note 235, at A12 (Feb. 18, 2011); Sinan Salaheddin, *12 Dead in Iraqi "Day of Rage" Protest: Thousands March in Cities Nationwide, The Courier-Journal*, A3 (Feb. 26, 2011).

245. *See id.*; Associated Press, *Thousands of Algerians Stage Demonstration, The Courier-Journal*, A12 (Feb. 13, 2011). Some suggested that Algerian protests were more muted. *See* Adam Nossiter, *Amid a Sea of Upheaval, Algeria is Still, The New York Times*, at A4 (Feb. 19, 2011).

246. *See Popular Rage Encounters State Violence, supra* note 235; *see also* William Yong, *Iran Presses Opposition to Refrain From Rally, The New York Times*, A12 (Feb. 11, 2011).

Djibouti[247] and Palestine.[248] King Abdullah II of Jordan, facing demonstrations and protests, dismissed his cabinet.[249] Yemen's leader promised to step down in 2013,[250] and seemed on the verge of resigning after protests continued.[251] In an attempt to prevent similar protests in his country, Saudi Arabia's King decided to give substantial sums of money to his people, but even that gesture did not completely quell dissent.[252]

Throughout the Arab world, social media played a prominent role in the Arab Spring uprisings. Protestors in Bahrain, who were calling for the establishment of a constitutional monarchy,[253] used their smart phones to take pictures of governmental repression, and posted their pictures on the internet.[254] Even though Facebook was officially banned in Jordan, calls for protests were spreading in that country through both Facebook and Twitter.[255] Syrians used Facebook to call for "a day of rage,"[256] as well as to arrange protests,[257] and also relied on YouTube to depict their protests to the rest of the world[258] as well as to attract other Syrians to the

247. *See* Hadell Al-Shalchi, *Bahrain Fires on Protestors: Dozens Injured as Army Tries to Quash Political Uprising, The Courier-Journal*, at A3 ((Feb. 19, 2011).

248. *See King of Jordan Dismisses His Cabinet, supra* note 233.

249. *See id.* ("King Abdullah II of Jordan fired his government on Tuesday after weeks of demonstrations challenging his regime, part of a wave of demands of public accountability sweeping the Arab world....").

250. *See* Laura Kasinof & Nada Bakri, *Facing Unrest, Yemen's Leader Says He Will Step Down in 2013, The New York Times*, A13 (Feb. 3, 2011).

251. *See* Haley Sweetland Edwards & Jeffrey Fleishman, *Yemeni President on Verge of Quitting After Opposition Demands, The Sydney Morning Herald*, at 7 (Mar. 4, 2001).

252. *See* Deborah Amos & Steve Inskeep, *Online Calls Increase For Protests in Saudia Arabia*, National Public Radio, Morning Edition (Mar. 3, 2011). http://www.npr.org/2011/03/03/134221978/Saudi-Reforms.

253. *See* Michael Slackman, *Amid Standoff, Opposition Seeks Dissolution of Bahraini Government, The New York Times*, at A6 (Feb. 21, 2011).

254. *See Cellphone Cameras Become the World's Eyes and Ears, supra* note 14.

255. *See King of Jordan Dismisses His Cabinet, supra* note 233.

256. *See id.*

257. *See* Roula Khalaf, *Syria Crackdown as Unrest Spreads, FT (Financial Times) Weekend*, A1 (Mar. 27, 2011).

258. *See id.*

protests.[259] As tensions mounted, hostilities in the country increased.[260] In Yemen, some of the protests were arranged via text message,[261] which was viewed as preferable to social networking sites like Facebook because of a lower level of internet access in that country.[262] In Sudan, protests were organized through Facebook, Twitter and other internet sites.[263] In Saudi Arabia, online petitions were offered to the government, and some individuals called for a day of protest,[264] as well as for the establishment of a constitutional monarchy.[265] In Morocco, the "February 20 Movement for Change" turned out 10,000 protestors.[266] In Iran, protestors used the internet to report on events,[267] establishing a Facebook page for videos and eyewitness accounts, and they also tweeted.[268]

As in Egypt, Middle Eastern governments tried to control the flow of information available to their people. For example, Sudanese officials moved to shut down protest-related websites.[269] Governments also resorted to violence. Following Egyptian attempts to quell protests

---

259. *See* NPR Staff and Wires, *Syria "Great Friday" Protest Reportedly Turns Bloody*, National Public Radio (Apr. 22, 2011). http://www.npr.org/2011/04/22/135628118/syrian-forces-protesters-face-off-on-great-Friday.

260. *See* Anthony Shadid, *Fear of Civil War Mounts in Syria as Crisis Deepens, The New York Times*, at A1 (Jan. 15, 2012).

261. *See Yemeni Youth Square Off With Forces, supra* note 227 ("The protests, organized largely via text message, were the largest yet by young Yemenis, with more than 1,000 marching.... A text message sent around on Sunday called on Yemenis to 'participate in the student and youth revolution in a demonstration to demand the removal of the leader and to celebrate the Egyptian revolution, tomorrow at 9 a.m. in front of the main gate of Sana University.'").

262. *See id.* ("Protestors also posted messages on Facebook to rally supporters on Sunday, but social networking sites remain less of an organizing tool in Yemen than in Tunisia and Egypt because of low Internet penetration.").

263. *See Sudan Sees Migration of Unrest to Its Streets, supra* note 242.

264. *See Online Calls Increase For Protests in Saudia Arabia, supra* note 252.

265. *See Leading Saudis Call for Constitutional Monarchy, The Sydney Morning Herald*, at 8 (Mar. 1, 2011).

266. *See In Morocco, Fears of Chaos, supra* note 237, at A8.

267. *See* Liz Robbins, *Protests Across Tehran Are Stifled by Security Forces, The New York Times*, A6 (Feb. 21, 2011).

268. *See* Neil MacFarquhar & Alan Cowell, *Iran Uses Force Against Protests as Region Erupts, The New York Times*, at A1 (Feb. 15, 2011).

269. *See Sudan Sees Migration of Unrest to Its Streets, supra* note 242.

through force,[270] Bahrain responded with violence[271] and also sought to restrict citizen access to the internet.[272] Violence was used in a number of other countries, including Libya,[273] Yemen,[274] Bahrain,[275] Iran,[276] and Iraq.[277] Iran jailed opposition figures and their wives.[278] The Syrian response was particularly brutal.[279]

Libya was one of the countries that suffered major upheavals in the wake of the Tunisian and Egyptian revolts,[280] and the government responded to the protests with an extreme level of brutality and violence.[281] The situation rapidly evolved into open warfare.[282] Libya's revolt was clearly influenced by Tunisian events with people chanting "Thank you Tunisia."[283] In Bahrain, protestors were inspired by revolts in other Middle Eastern countries,[284] but Bahrainis were partially subdued when Saudi Arabia

---

270. *See Mubarak Orders Crackdown, supra* note 198, at A1.

271. *See Bahrain Turmoil Poses Fresh Test for White House, supra* note 101, at A1.

272. *See* James Glanz, *Internet Use Restricted, Data Shows, The New York Times*, A11 (Feb. 18, 2011) (noting that Bahrain "severely restricted the access of its citizens to the Internet" during recent protests).

273. *See Popular Rage Encounters State Violence in Mideast, supra* note 235, at A12.

274. *See* Laura Kasinof, *Yemeni Forces Reportedly Heighten Deadly Assault on Protestors in Southern City, The New York Times*, A9 (Nov. 12, 2011).

275. *See Bahrain Fires on Protestors, supra* note 247, at A3.

276. *See Popular Rage Encounters State Violence in Mideast, supra* note 235, at A12.

277. *Id.*

278. *See Iran Jails Opposition Chiefs and Their Wives, The Australian*, at 1, (Mar. 2, 2011).

279. *See* Nada Bakri, *Europe Accuses Iranian Force of Aiding Syrian Crackdown, The New York Times*, at A14 (Aug. 25, 2011); Nour Malas, *Syrian Leader Vows "Iron Fist": Assad Blasts Arab League and Says He Won't Exit, in Address Opponents See as Prelude to Deeper Violence, The Wall Street Journal*, at A7 (Jan. 11, 2012); Michael Slackman, *Syrian Troops Fire on Protestors as Unrest Spreads to More Cities, International Herald Tribune*, at 1 (Mar. 26–27, 2011).

280. *See Popular Rage Encounters State Violence in Mideast, supra* note 235, at A12.

281. *See id.*, at A12.

282. *See* John Lyons, *Fear, Distrust as Gaddafi Fights to Death, The Australian*, at 9 (Mar. 1, 2011).

283. *See* David Greene & Renee Montagne, *Mass Exodus of Foreigners Jams Libya's Borders*, National Public Radio, Morning Edition (Mar. 3, 2011). http://www.npr.org/2011/03/03/134221974/Libya-Border.

284. *See* Ethan Bronner, *State of Emergency Declared in Bahrain: Security Forces Kill 2 in Crackdown, The New York Times*, at A14 (Mar. 16, 2011) (quoting a protestor as stating that "We are not an exact copy of what happened in Egypt, but we have been inspired by it."); Michael Slackman, *Police in Bahrain Clear Protest Site in Early Morning Raid, The New York Times*, at A14 (Feb. 17, 2011) ("Before the events in Egypt and Tunisia, the traditional

sent troops to the country.[285] As with Egypt, Libya tried to sever internet access,[286] but protestors found ways to communicate anyway using satellite technology and by phoning information to sources outside the country.[287] After a prominent Libyan opposition lawyer was released from jail, he established an online communication system.[288] Other protestors used social networks like Facebook and Twitter to issue pleas for help, including medical supplies, to individuals located outside the country.[289]

As protestors occupied important parts of Libya outside of Tripoli, the country dissolved into civil war, and the Libyan government resorted to brutal repression against the residents of Tripoli.[290] Some army commanders defected to the protestors with their troops,[291] and the protestors vowed to liberate Tripoli.[292] Despite the protests, Mummar Qaddafi continued to claim that the Libyan people "loved him," and he blamed Al Qaida for the unrest.[293] Ultimately, as outside countries intervened with air support for the rebels,[294] the Qaddafi government was forced from

---

opposition made little progress in pushing its demands. But the success of those popular, peaceful uprisings inspired a change of tactics here, and young people led a call for a Bahrani 'Day of Rage' on Feb. 14.").

285. *See* Michael Slackman & Ethan Bronner, *Saudis, Fearful of Iran, Send Troops to Bahrain to Quell Protests, The New York Times*, at A1 (Mar. 15, 2011).

286. *See* David D. Kirkpatrick & Mona El-Naggar, *Son of Qaddafi Says Libya Faces "Civil War" Fear, The New York Times*, A7 (Feb. 21, 2011).

287. *Id.*

288. *Id.*

289. *Id.* ("And Egyptians, with the help of Libyans living abroad, were organizing aid convoys to the border.").

290. *See* Sarah El Deeb, *Libyan Forces Again Fire on Citizens: More Than 200 Believed Killed in 5 Days, The New York Times*, at A1 (Feb. 21, 2011); David D. Kirkpatrick, *Qaddafi Is Using Ruthless Force to Hold Capital, The New York Times*, at A1 (Mar. 4, 2011).

291. *See* Jason Koutsoukis, *"I Cannot Live With Any Man Who Would Be Prepared to Kill His Own People," The Sydney Morning Herald*, at 8 (Mar. 1, 2011).

292. *See* Jason Koutsoukis, *Next We Liberate Tripoli, Say Rebels, The Sydney Morning Herald*, at 8 (Mar. 1, 2011).

293. *See They Love Me, Says "Delusional" Gaddafi, The Australian*, at 1 (Mar. 2, 2011).

294. *See U.N. OKs No-Fly Zone for Libya: Security Council Acts to Protect Civilians, The Courier-Journal*, A1 (Mar. 18, 2011).

power after weeks of military hostilities.[295] Qaddafi was ultimately captured and killed.[296]

In Iran, protestors were able to send information out of the country through Twitter[297] and Facebook,[298] and were remarkably adept at evading the government's internet censors.[299] When the Iranian government prohibited television stations from broadcasting information regarding the protests, individual protestors took pictures with their smart phones and posted those pictures on the internet.[300] Following one protest, there were so many "tweets" from Iran that the event was the most talked-about news story of the day.[301] Using devices like Twitter, protestors pressured CNN into expanding its coverage of the protests.[302] In response to CNN's lack of coverage, protestors circulated on the internet a Channel 4 (England) report on events occurring in the country.[303]

In theory, governments can "shut down" the internet to preclude internal information from being disseminated to the outside world. In reality, as the situations in Iran and Egypt reveal, governments are reluctant to completely shut down the internet.[304] It is too important for commerce

---

295. *See* Kareem Fahim & David D. Kirkpatrick, *Rebels Pour Into Central Tripoli Square, Declaring Victory: Opposition Claims It Captured Two of Qaddafi's Sons, The New York Times*, at A1 (Aug. 22, 2011).

296. *See* Anthony Shadid, *Death of Qaddafi Revives Opposition in Syria, The New York Times*, at A1 (Oct. 22, 2011).

297. *See* David Carr, *After a Year of Ruin, Some Hope, The New York Times*, at B1 (Dec. 21, 2009) ("... on Twitter, the elections in Iran outranked Michael Jackson, who came in second, according to What the Trend?, a site that ranked topics in 2009 (whatthetrend.com/zeitgeist. In an age that is ridiculed as chronically unserious, a life-and-death struggle for freedom on the other side of the world is the story that rang the bell on Twitter.").

298. *See* Jim Lehrer, *In Iran, Political Protests Move Online*, PBS News Hour (June 17, 2009) (quoting Lindsey Hilsum).

299. *See* Kelly Niknedjad, *Iran Protests Play Out Online*, PBS News Hour (June 26, 2009).

300. *See* Lehrer, *supra* note 298.

301. *Id.*

302. *See* Brian Stelter, *Real-Time Criticism of CNN's Iran Coverage, The New York Times*, at B5 (June 15, 2009) ("Untold thousands used the label 'CNNfail' on Twitter to vent their frustrations.... For a time, new criticisms were being added on Twitter at least once a second.").

303. *Id.* ("Some Americans relied on British networks. A report from Channel 4 was spread widely on the Internet.").

304. *See* Niknedjad, *supra* note 299.

and other non protest activities (*e.g.*, staying in touch with family and friends).[305] Although some commentators questioned whether social media and Twitter were actually being used to coordinate and activate protests in Iran,[306] or that smart phones and text messaging were used for that purpose,[307] the evidence suggests otherwise. Iranians used social media to communicate with friends and family who were located outside of Iran,[308] and the recipients posted the communications on social media platforms in their own countries.[309]

As the Middle East revolts reveal, after succeeding in overthrowing the pre-existing regimes, the revolutionaries faced the daunting task of forming stable governments. Following the overthrow of Tunisia's president, that country went through a period of instability. A similar problem occurred in Egypt,[310] and Egyptians continued to protest against Mubarak's successor, the military.[311] Of course, the autocratic regimes in those countries had severely repressed the opposition, and the protest movements did not have established leaders who were ready to govern the countries.[312]

Interestingly, the Arab protests did not extend to peoples in sub-Saharan Africa.[313] In the opinion of one writer, the same "combustible conditions" ("grinding poverty, masses of jobless people, students glued to Facebook, and a leader who refuses to step down after more than two

---

305. *See* David Tafuri, *Egypt's Assault on the World Wide Web, The New York Times*, at A19 (Feb. 10, 2011).

306. *See* Frank James, *Which Tweets From Iran Are True?*, National Public Radio, The Two Way (June 17, 2009) http://www.npr.org/blogs/thetwo-way/2009/06/which_tweats_from_iran_are_tru.html; Frank James, *Twitter, Social Media Role in Iran is Hyped: Expert*, National Public Radio, The Two Way (June 19, 2009) (quoting Professor Ethan Zuckerman, Harvard University, for the proposition that the Iranian protestors are not communicating with each other primarily through social media). http://www.npr.org/blogs/thetwo-way/2009/06/twitter_social_media_role_in_i.html.

307. *Id.*

308. *Id.*

309. *See Which Tweets From Iran Are True, supra* note 306.

310. *See The Legacy of 18 Days in Tahrir Square, supra* note 192, at 4.

311. *See* Sarah El Deeb, *Egypt Showdown: U.S., Protesters Press Military to Hand Over Power to Civilians, The Courier-Journal*, at A1 (Nov. 25, 2011).

312. *See* Kareem Fahim & Mona El-Naggar, *Some Fear a Street Movement's Leaderless Status May Become a Liability, The New York Times*, at A6 (Feb. 4, 2011).

313. *See* Jeffrey Gettleman & Josh Kron, *Arab Spark Unlikely to Ignite Uganda's Combustible Elements, The New York Times*, at A4 (Feb. 18, 2011).

decades of power") were present in countries like Uganda, but the people did not revolt.[314] However, the internet may have helped lead to the immigrant and refugee crisis sweeping Europe by encouraging large number of individuals to migrate to Europe.

The internet has also been prominent in the "me too" movement.[315] In Mexico, for example, the movement started when a woman posted messages on Twitter regarding a young writer having beaten and abused women.[316] The post led to an avalanche of social media messages by women regarding harassment.[317]

In 2019, a German youth produced a video critical of German Chancellor Angela Merkel's policies.[318] His criticisms, which extended to such issues as social inequality, pollution, war, and internet censorship, was produced with first-rate sound effects, graphs, and style.[319] The video was widely viewed and became a public relations crisis for Merkel's government, and forced her to respond.[320] The video prompted other German political parties to produce their own videos.[321]

3. INTERNET ACTIVISM IN RUSSIA

In Russia, as well, ordinary people have used the internet to challenge governmental authority and governmental decisions. As in many other countries, the Russian government tried to maintain relatively tight control over the traditional media.[322] However, with some sixty million Russians connected to the internet by 2012 (approximately 40 percent

---

314. *Id.*

315. *See* Paulina Villegas, *Weekend Tweet Puts New Spotlight on Sexual Harassment in Mexico, The New York Times* A9 (Mar. 29, 2019).

316. *Id.*

317. *Id.*

318. *See* Christopher F. Schuetze, *Video Sets Off a Storm In Germany by Taking Aim at Merkel's Party, The New York Times* A10 (May 28, 2019).

319. *Id.*

320. *Id.*

321. *Id.*

322. *See* Scott Shane, *In Russia, Echoes of Revolution, The New York Times*, at 4 (Jan. 15, 2012) ("Mr. Putin devised a new model of media management, keeping tight control of national television and most newspapers while allowing free rein to a few Moscow outlets (the newspaper Novaya Gazeta and the radio station Ekho Moskvy), providing a steam valve to the intelligentsia and a display of tolerance to foreign critics.").

of the population), the internet has been increasingly used to challenge the Russian establishment.[323] Some ordinary Russians have used blogs (including LiveJournal which was once described as Russia's most popular blogging site) and Twitter, as well as social media sites such as Facebook and Vkontakte.[324] One Russian launched a project entitled "A Country Without Stupidity," and another created a movement entitled "Blue Buckets" (established to challenge the use of blue sirens that allows drivers to ignore traffic laws).[325] When a local mayor offered cash to veterans in exchange for votes, an individual recorded the offer on his smart phone and posted it on YouTube.[326] The video led to the mayor's conviction for violating Russian election rules.[327] When a Russian police officer discussed police corruption in a YouTube video, it received some two million hits and sparked public anger.[328]

The internet also sparked challenges to Vladmir Putin's decision to run for another presidential term,[329] and has also prompted street protests.[330] Facebook and Twitter were used to organize and coordinate these protests,[331] and the protests turned out tens of thousands (perhaps as many as 120,000) of protestors.[332] Russians have also used YouTube to produce "comic Putin put-downs, including a mash-up of Russian politics and the movie 'Titanic,' with Putin and Medvedev as the doomed lovers—and Russia in the role of the sinking ship,"[333] and they also produced another YouTube video entitled F****** Amazing Russia.[334] Russian bloggers fre-

323. *Id.*

324. *See* Julia Ioffe, *The Blog Society: As Recent Protests Show, Russians Are Discovering How Powerful a Tool Online Activism Can Be, The Financial Times*, 9 (Dec. 18, 2011).

325. *Id.*

326. *See* Michael Schwartz, *In Russia, Viral Videos Make Electoral Politics a Bit Cleaner, The New York Times*, at 1 (Nov. 25, 2011).

327. *Id.*

328. *See* Clifford J. Levy, *Videos Rouse Russian Anger Toward Police: Officer Stirs Debate on Rituals of Corruption, The New York Times*, at A1 (July 28, 2010).

329. *See In Russia, Echoes of Revolution, supra* note 322, at 4.

330. *Id.*

331. *See The Blog Society, supra* note 324.

332. *See* Ellen Barry & Michael Schwirtz, *Putin Opponents Hold Vast Rally, Promising More: A Push for Momentum: With Election in March, A Struggle to Become a Political Force, The New York Times*, at A1 (Dec. 25, 2011).

333. *See In Russia, Echoes of Revolution, supra* note 322.

334. *See The Blog Society, supra* note 324.

quently attack the ruling party, describing it as "the party of swindlers and thieves."[335] When then-Prime Minister Putin was booed at a sporting event, a video clip of the event was posted online.[336] In addition, believing that Putin was rigging elections, Russians created websites where ordinary Russians could post complaints about election fraud.[337] Even though Putin remained in power, Putin's party suffered an electoral setback at the end of 2011.[338] After a Russian blogger was released from jail, he used online resources to continue his protests.[339]

During the Ukrainian conflict, Russia tried to use the internet to propagandize, not only outside of Russia, but also within. However, Russia's efforts to control the flow of information to its people was undercut by several factors. Russians who had emigrated to other countries had the ability to inform Russians who did not emigrate regarding the facts and can undercut governmental propaganda.[340]

In an effort to avoid detection and retaliation, some Russian protestors installed VPN (virtual private networks) software on their computers.[341] VPNs, which allow users to hide their identities and locations, have been downloaded by Russians at the rate of hundreds of downloads per day.[342] VPN use accelerated after Russia began asserting greater control over media outlets, forcing them to "tow the official line" regarding the war.[343] Daily downloads in Russia of the 10 most popular VPNs surged

335. *See In Russia, Viral Videos, supra* note 326, at 4.

336. *Id.*

337. *Id.*, at 4.

338. *See* Alan Greenblatt, *Russian Voters Send Putin a Message*, National Public Radio (Dec. 5, 2011), http://www.npr.org/2011/12/05/143146036/russian-voters-send-putin-a-message.

339. *See* David M. Herszenhorn, *Freed Blogger Puts Protest in Overdrive in Russia, The New York Times*, at A5 (Dec. 22, 2011).

340. Robert C. Thornett, *Open and Closed: From Russia to China to America, the Largest Societies Are Pushing Their Limits, moderndiplomacy* (May 28, 2022), https://moderndiplomacy.eu/2022/05/28/open-and-closed-from-russia-to-china-to-america-the-largest-societies-are-pushing-their-limit.

341. *VPN Use Skyrockets in Russia During Ukraine Invasion*, Aljazeera (May 7, 2022). https://www.aljazeera.com/news/2022/5/7/vpn-use-skyrockets-in-russia-during-ukraine-invas; Chris Stokel-Walker, *How Russians are Dealing with an Internet That's Gone Dark, Time* (Mar. 10, 2022) https://time.com/6156639/russia-internet-dissent.

342. Thornett, *supra* note 340.

343. Aljazeera, *supra* note 341.

from about 15,000 before the war to 475,000, and continued at a rate of nearly 300,000 a day.[344] Indeed, one report suggested that interest in VPNs within Russia had soared nearly 1,000 percent.[345]

VPNs are not a foolproof solution for Russian dissidents because it is still possible for Russian officials to track down individuals who use that technology,[346] and therefore Russians who use VPNs risk discovery and repression.[347] Indeed, some worry that "VPNs may have backdoor access for Russian authorities" and that "Russia may have advanced techniques for examining how internet traffic flows through a VPN, which could put users at risk."[348] In addition, some Russians find it difficult to access VPNs as Google suspended all ad sales and Play Store billing, and Visa and MasterCard shut down international transactions for Russian account holders, and consumer brands ranging from Coke to McDonald's to Starbucks have been closing up shop in Russia.[349] In addition, Russia has purportedly blocked a number of VPN services.[350]

An interesting aspect of Russia's crackdown is that pro-Russian bloggers have begun attacking Putin for his failures on the battlefield.[351] At the outset of the war, those bloggers cheered Russia's battlefield successes, and pushed narratives consistent with Russia's messaging.[352] However, as Russia began to suffer battlefield defeats, the bloggers purportedly turned on Putin for his failures.[353] One blogger attacked Putin for celebrating City Day (which celebrates the founding of Moscow) despite the losses in Ukraine where Russian soldiers were doing without: "NO thermal imag-

344. *Id.*

345. Stokel-Walker, *supra* note 341.

346. *Id.*

347. *Id.*

348. *Id.*

349. Albert Fox Cahn, *Tech Bans Hurt Russian Dissidents More Than They Help Ukraine*, Wired (Apr. 11, 2022), https://www.wired.com/story/tech-bans-hurt-russian-dissidents-more-than-they-help-ukraine/.

350. *Id.*

351. *See* Aljazeera, *supra* note 341; Andrew Stanton, *Putin Faces Backlash from Russian Bloggers Amid Retreat: 'Horrible Failure,' Newsweek* (Sept. 11, 2022). https://www.newsweek.com/putin-faces-backlash-russian-bloggers-amid-retreat-horrible-failure-1741872.

352. *Id.*

353. *Id.*

ers, NO bulletproof vests, NO reconnaissance equipment, NO secure communications, NO enough copters, NO first aid kits."[354] Another pro-Russia blogger purportedly lamented that Russia losses were "large" and "cannot be ignored."[355] One blog purportedly criticized the defense ministry for its "deathly silence."[356]

4. THE INTERNET IN CHINA

Even in China, a country in which the government has engaged in aggressive internet censorship, the internet has begun to significantly reshape society. In 2009, China had some 298 million internet users, as well as some 70 million bloggers,[357] and its bloggers repeatedly found ways to avoid governmentally-imposed internet restrictions.[358] For example, some bloggers posted their writings under pseudonyms.[359] In an effort to avoid the impact of internet filters, bloggers employed alternate names for the issues and things that they were discussing (*e.g.*, instead of saying that military "tanks" were involved in an incident, a blogger might refer to "tractors").[360] Using the internet, some called for protests and for a "Jasmine Revolution."[361]

The internet was also used to undercut Chinese propaganda during the Covid-19 pandemic.[362] For example, when China imposed lockdowns, the Chinese government painted a rosy picture suggesting that the Chinese government had the will to "confront, and hold back, the virus."[363] However, people who were upset with the lockdown, which they viewed as leading to "food shortages, delayed medical care, shoddy quarantine

---

354. *Id.*

355. *Id.*

356. *Id.*

357. *See* Anne Stopper, *China Appears to Tighten Internet Access Around Tiananmen Anniversary*, PBS News Hour (June 1, 2009).

358. *Id.*

359. *Id.*

360. *Id.*

361. *See* Andrew Jacobs, *Calls For Protests in China Draw Government Attention, The New York Times*, at A8 (Feb. 21, 2011) (noting "anonymous calls for protestors to stage a 'Jasmine Revolution" [that] went out over social media and microblogging outlets.").

362. *See* Vivian Wang, Paul Mozur & Isabelle Qian, *Agonizing Lockdown Tests the Limits of China's Propaganda, The New York Times* A4 (Apr. 28, 2022).

363. *Id.*

conditions and even physical fencing" around homes, pushed back.[364] Although Chinese governmental officials tried to censor critical online posts, and responded on social media with positive stories, the people pushed back with their own narrative.[365] Deleted video and other content were reposted with such speed that they overwhelmed the ability of censors to keep up.[366] For example, when someone posted a video showing "residents chanting for the government to provide supplies, of a son begging for his sick father to be admitted to a hospital, of a tearful official explaining to a frustrated caller" that she was also frustrated and helpless," the people reposted the videos following governmental censorship: "posting it upside down, embedding it within separate images or adding its audio atop unrelated clips."[367] The video was even displayed on a cartoon computer watched by SpongeBob SquarePants in the back of the Krusty Krab.[368] Analysts suggested that there was simply too much material being posted for the censors to keep up.[369]

Some protest messages were issued from outside of China, in particular the U.S., using services like Twitter.[370] Within China, attempts to protest were met with what one newspaper referred to as "a mass show of force."[371] When a prominent dissident repeated threats that had been made against him by Chinese officials,[372] the threats were quickly repeated on the Chinese microblogging website Sina Weibo.[373]

As new technologies have taken hold, people have been able to challenge (and, sometimes, even to mock) Chinese government-controlled media reports.[374] Even though the government had gone to great lengths

---

364. *Id.*

365. *Id.*

366. *Id.*

367. *Id.*

368. *Id.*

369. *Id.*

370. *See* Jacobs, *supra* note 361, at A8.

371. *Id.*

372. *See* Josh Chin, *After Beijing Lets Dissident Leave, He Spurs and Internet Catchphrase, The Wall Street Journal*, A7 (Jan. 20, 2012) (the official stated that the Chinese government "could round up all significant dissidents and 'bury them alive.'").

373. *Id.*

374. *See A Brittle Leader, supra* note 39.

to tightly regulate and control internet use,[375] the internet has had a significant impact on political discourse because there are some 800 million internet users, and more than 1 billion WeChat accounts, which the Chinese use for work and leisure and to keep up with current events.[376] The Chinese also use Weibo which is the Chinese equivalent of Twitter.[377] For example, during the Covid-19 pandemic, Chinese citizens heaped scorn on governmental officials.[378] Likewise, following a major train crash, the Chinese Railways Ministry through the state-controlled television and news media gave the public only limited information about what had happened.[379] Bloggers and individuals filled that void using weibo, quickly revealing the extent of the disaster, and posting some 26 million messages on the subject.[380] Similarly, when the Chinese government claimed that air quality was improving in Chinese cities, disbelieving environmental activists purchased air quality monitors and posted environmental readings on the internet.[381] Those readings revealed serious pollution problems.[382] As pollution data began to mount, Chinese citizens began to demand environmental improvements, and air quality standards were strengthened.[383]

Using the internet, even a single individual can have a significant impact. Li Ying, a Chinese painter and art school graduate living in Milan,

---

375. *Id.*

376. *See* Li Yuan, *A Billion Reasons to Use WeChat in China, The New York Times* B5 (Jan. 10, 2019).

377. *See id.*

378. *See* Raymond Zhong, *On Social Media, Anger Over Virus Spreads in China, The New York Times* B1 (Jan. 26, 2020).

379. *See* Michael Wines & Sharon LaFraniere, *In Baring Facts of Train Crash, Blogs Erode China Censorship, The New York Times*, at A1 (July 29, 2011).

380. *Id*; *see also* James T. Areddy & Josh Chin, *Chinese Media Resist Curbs on Coverage of Train Crash, The Wall Street Journal*, at A7 (Aug. 1., 2011) ("The Internet has been the primary channel for calls to get to the bottom of the accident, especially the popular Weibo microblog service, which was flush with submissions tacitly criticizing Friday night's propaganda order.").

381. *See* Sharon LaFraniere, *Activists Crack China's Wall of Denial About Air Pollution, The New York Times*, at A4 (Jan. 28, 2012).

382. *Id.*

383. *Id.* (The Chinese government decreed "that about 30 major cities must begin monitoring the particulates this year, followed by about 80 more next year. The Ministry of Environmental Protection also promised to set health standards for such fine particulates 'as soon as possible.'").

Italy, became a virtual "clearinghouse" for information in China.[384] Using Twitter, even though it was banned in China, he distributed photos, videos and witness accounts of the pandemic that would otherwise have been banned in China.[385] His following rapidly climbed to 500,000, eventually to 1.4 million, and he had over 300 million views in a two-week period.[386] Some of his posts made it into China through virtual private networks.[387] However, he paid a stiff price in the sense that his Chinese bank accounts were frozen, he lost his job in Italy (due to a letter from the Chinese Embassy), and he was subjected to death threats.[388]

5. THE INTERNET IN INDIA

Indian political parties have been accessing the internet and using social media in their campaigns for some time.[389] Beginning in 2014, Prime Minister Narinda Modi used two social media platforms, WhatsApp and Facebook, to reach potential voters.[390] When he succeeded, opposing political parties began using similar techniques,[391] although there were concerns about disinformation.[392] By the time of the 2019 elections, Indian politicians were using WhatsApp to connect with thousands of social media groups that they had created.[393] These groups were designed to reach out to Indians of different castes, income levels and religions.[394] Many of those in rural areas connected only through mobile phones.[395] And disinformation was rampant, with hundreds of

384. *See* Li Yuan, *China's Rebel Influencer Is Still Paying a Price, The New York Times* B1 (Dec. 19, 2023).

385. *Id.*

386. *Id.*

387. *Id.*

388. *Id.*

389. *See* Suhasini Raj, *In India, One Website Battles Rampant Online Misinformation, The New York Times* B1 (Sept. 27, 1992).

390. *Id.*

391. *Id.*

392. *Id.*

393. *See* Newley Purnell, *Fake News Roils WhatsApp in India, The Wall Street Journal* A1 (Apr. 7, 2019).

394. *Id.*

395. *Id.*

deceptive posts per day, on such things as the dates of elections and information about politicians.[396]

In India, the B.J.P. party, which controls the national and state governments, decided to hand out $71 million worth of free smart phones to the Indian people.[397] By constructing more cell phone towers, and distributing free phones, the government's goal was to create a "Digital India."[398] Although the phones were distributed by the government, the B.J.P. used the phones to reach out and target potential B.J.P. voters.[399] In addition, the phones actively promoted a B.J.P. politician by posting his likeness as the background image on the phones, and the phones contained two B.J.P. campaign apps.[400]

B. DEMOCRATIC IMPLICATIONS WITHIN THE UNITED STATES

Within the United States, ordinary individuals, and grassroots organizations have routinely used the internet (and internet-related technologies) to directly advance their political or social objectives, as well as to influence other people and governmental policies.

1. ATTEMPTS TO INFLUENCE GOVERNMENT AND THE POLITICAL PROCESS (OUTSIDE OF POLITICAL CAMPAIGNS)

The technologies used in the United States mirror those used in Tunisia, Egypt and elsewhere, and the possibilities are endless. Using social media platforms, individuals and groups have been able to influence society in many different ways.

Some uses of the internet are not necessarily political in nature. For example, individuals have used the internet to produce so-called "Flash

---

396. *Id.*

397. *See* Vindu Goel & Suhasni Raj, *Handing Out Free Phones Then Calling to Get Votes: A Party's New Campaign Tactic in Rural India, The New York Times* B1 & B4 (Nov. 19, 2018).

398. *Id.* at B4.

399. *Id.*

400. *Id.*

Mobs" to protest (or, for that matter, just to frolic).[401] The internet has also been used to vent about local issues,[402] or to organize future protests.

One of the most interesting developments has involved the use of local social media sites to address local issues.[403] These sites have developed even in areas that might be regarded as less online oriented (*e.g.*, Amish communities).[404] In New Jersey, for example, student protests erupted when voters rejected school budgets, thereby forcing potential budget cuts that negatively affected class sizes and offerings.[405] The protests were attributed to a Facebook posting that led to a gathering of some 18,000 student protestors.[406]

On campuses, a fair number of students are using an app known as Sidechat which allows them to anonymously communicate with their fellow students.[407] The platform has turned into a virtual commons where students can articulate their views on a range of issues, but the app requires a university email address to enroll.[408] There has been much discussion on Sidechat about the Israel-Hamas war.[409] A similar app, YikYak (later taken over by Sidechat), also allows individuals to post anonymously.[410] The app, which had millions of users at one point, has generally fallen out of favor.[411]

---

401. *See* Robert Siegel, *Planning a Flash Mob? Better Keep It Quiet*, National Public Radio, All Things Considered (Dec. 20, 2010). http://www.npr.org/2010/12/20/132205587/planning-a-flash-mob-better-keep-it-quiet; Ian Urbina, *Mobs Are Born as Word Grows By Text Message, The New York Times*, at A1 (Mar. 25, 2010).

402. *See* Susan Dominus, *Via Listserv, Parents Clash in Harlem, The New York Times*, A16 (Aug. 10, 2010) (discussing venting about gentrification).

403. *See* Grace Schneider, *S. Ind. Deaths Turn Spotlight on Topix.com: Social Network for Small Towns Can be a Harsh World, The Courier-Journal*, A1 (Feb. 13, 2011).

404. *See* Noam Cohen, *Online News Can Be Like an Amish Paper, The New York Times*, at B3 (Sept. 21, 2009).

405. *See* Winnie Hu, *In New Jersey, A Civics Lesson in the Internet Age: Inspired by a Facebook Message, Students Rally Against School Budget Cuts, The New York Times*, at A19 (Apr. 28, 2010).

406. *Id.*

407. *See* Zachary Schermale, *Students Love Sidechat; Colleges Don't, The Courier-Journal* 13A (Mar. 10, 2024).

408. *Id.*

409. *Id.*

410. *Id.*

411. *Id.*

In Louisville, Kentucky, a local organization "8664.org" (the term "86" means to throw away or get rid of and "64" referred (in this case) to a highway, Interstate 64). The group sought to alter traffic routes in order to create a more livable city by converting river front downtown land (currently used for the highway) for scenic and recreational purposes. The group's plan was to reroute I-64, which goes right through downtown Louisville along the river front,[412] thereby reducing traffic congestion,[413] and saving money.[414] The organization conducted an aggressive online campaign,[415] and also used traditional media.[416] For example, it maintained a strong presence on Facebook[417] and YouTube,[418] and arranged public fora to promote its ideas.[419] Although the effort failed, the effort garnered considerable local support (the organization claimed 10,000 members),[420] and demonstrated how an organization can effectively use the internet to convey its ideas to the public and create a movement.

Likewise, a group of Old Louisville (Kentucky) residents, who were seeking to preserve a historic firehouse, filed suit over the City's decision to close the firehouse.[421] As part of its effort, the group used traditional media,[422] as well as online resources.[423] Although the residents ultimately

412. *See* www.8664.org ;http://www.youtube.com/watch?v=eMFkK419XIk.

413. *See* www.8664.org

414. *See id.*

415. *See* www.8664.org ; http://www.youtube.com/watch?v=eMFkK419XIk.

416. *See* Marcus Green, *$341 Million for Bridges OK'ed, The Courier Journal* (Mar. 25, 2008).

417. *See* http://www.facebook.com/group.php?gid=2204733437

418. *See* http://www.youtube.com/watch?v=eMFkK419XIk

419. *See* Marcus Green, *8664 Organizers Push Proposal with the Public, The Courier-Journal* (Nov. 29, 2007) ("The founders of a movement to raze part of Interstate 64 along the city's waterfront urged supporters at a public forum last night to mobilize behind what they say is a better and cheaper vision for the $4.1 billion Ohio River Bridges Project."). http://www.courier-journal.com/apps/pbcs.dll/article?AID=/20071129/NEWS01/711290452.

420. *See id.*

421. *See Old Louisville Residents Sue City*, Leo Weekly (Jan. 9, 2009); *see also* http://fatlip.leoweekly.com/2009/01/09/old-louisville-residents-sue-city/.

422. *See* Jessie Halladay, *Court Hearing Set Next Week in Effort to Reopen Firehouse, The Courier-Journal* (Jan. 13, 2009).

423. *See Request to Reopen Old Louisville Firehouse is Denied*, WHAS11.com (Jan. 23, 2009) http://www.whas11.com/topstories/stories/whas11_topstory-090123-firehouseruling.21329492.html.

lost the battle to save the firehouse, they generated a lot of controversy and attention.[424] For example, the local newspaper covered the effort, and its article generated lots of online comments about the issue.[425]

In New Jersey, when a teacher removed a seven-year-old female student's hijab, the mother protested on Facebook.[426] The posting ignited a strong online reaction which included a post from an Olympic medalist from the same area who fences in a hijab.[427] The fencer had 340,000 followers.[428] The posts eventually cascaded "across the internet, drawing news crews and police cars to the front of the elementary school."[429] There were also posts on Reddit, Twitter, and Instagram.[430]

Not surprisingly, given that the young are often more adept at using modern technologies, teenagers have effectively used the internet and social media to weigh in on social and political issues. In Boston, for example, a 16-year-old high school junior worked to push Massachusetts politics to the left.[431] She and her friends campaigned online in favor of U.S. Senator Edward J. Markey in his defeat of then U.S. Representative Joseph P. Kennedy, III, a primary challenger.[432] In that effort, they managed to portray Markey as a "left-wing icon" and Kennedy as a right winger.[433] Their tactics included the use of group chats, direct messages and texts. They also engaged in opposition research as part of their effort.[434] For example, they dug up off-color Twitter posts by one candidate (who lost), and attacked another candidate (who withdrew from the race) for criticizing the Black Lives Matter movement.[435] They also investigated and

---

424. *See* Jessie Halladay, *Judge Rules Engine 7 Firehouse Will Stay Closed, Louisville The Courier-Journal* (Jan. 24, 2009).

425. *See id.*

426. *See* Tracey Tully, *Online Furor Over a Student's Hijab Engulfs a New Jersey Town, The New York Times* A17 (Oct. 22, 2021).

427. *Id.*

428. *Id.*

429. *Id.*

430. *Id.*

431. *See* Ellen Barry, *'Army of 16-Year-Olds' Presses Democrats a Tweet at a Time, The New York Times* SeeMicA1 (May 20, 2021).

432. *Id.*

433. *Id.*

434. *Id.*

435. *Id.*

kept records regarding donors to political campaigns.[436] Because of their effectiveness, one campaign hired one of the youngsters to coordinate his digital outreach (although the candidate lost).[437] Some question whether the adolescents treated candidates fairly, and many of their efforts have been unsuccessful.[438] Interestingly, the group turned on Markey after he blamed the Israeli-Palestinian conflict on both sides of the dispute.[439]

The internet has also been used to stimulate protests and issue calls for action. The internet was used to energize and galvanize both the Black Lives Matter protests and anti-Covid-19 lockdown protests.[440]

In Kenosha, Wisconsin, after a 29-year-old was shot by police, protestors took to the streets and the protests resulted in burning buildings.[441] In response, an individual posted a Facebook call for Kenosha residents to "take up arms to defend our City tonight from the evil things."[442] His post produced 4,000 Facebook responses, and allegedly prompted a number of individuals to go to the streets with military-style weapons (although how many of those with weapons responded to the post is unclear).[443] One of the individuals (with military weapons) killed two protestors.[444]

The internet is also being used by white supremacists to reach out to potential sympathizers and recruits.[445] For example, The Daily Stormer[446] posted information about African-Americans committing crimes against Caucasians.[447] In addition, Stormfront.org[448] is an online discussion forum which attracts some 40,000 visitors a day.[449] There is also a weekly

436. *Id.*

437. *Id.*

438. *Id.*

439. *Id.*

440. *See* Neil MacFarquhar, *When a Vigilante's Call to Action Is Only a Facebook Post Away, The New York Times* A23 (Oct. 17, 2020).

441. *Id.*, at A1.

442. *Id.*

443. *Id.*, at A1 & A23.

444. *Id.*

445. *See* Michael Wines & Stephanie Saul, *Supremacists Extend Reach With the Web, The New York Times* A1 (July 6, 2015).

446. https://dailystormer.in/section/us/

447. *See Supremacists Extend Reach With the Web, supra* note 445 at A1.

448. https://www.stormfront.org/forum/

449. *See Supremacists Extend Reach With the Web, supra* note 445 at A1.

internet radio program,[450] as well as a variety of other online sites, including the Council of Conservative Citizens, the League of the South, and the Occidental Observer.[451] Daily page views for these sites can range between 1,000 and 40,000.[452]

Teenagers at Marjory Stoneman Douglas in Parkland, Florida, where there were mass shootings in 2018 that killed 17 people and wounded 17 others, actively use social media to keep the tragedy at the center of public discussions.[453] The students have built a social media presence, attracted coverage from traditional media, raised funds, connected with elected officials, and worked to pass gun control legislation.[454] The students frequently use Twitter to mock their opponents and push their message,[455] They also use "quote Tweets" which allow a user to repost a tweet but with a comment about the original tweet.[456] They like "quote Tweets" because they believe that it encourages dialogue with their ideological opponents.[457]

Online challenges to establishment interests are hardly limited to local issues. For example, various interest groups (e.g., African-Americans and transgendered individuals) have used Twitter to communicate their views.[458] Indeed, it is alleged that African-Americans are overrepresented on Twitter compared to other races, and that they have weighed in on issues like the Oscars and other prominent public issues (e.g., the Trayvon Martin case).[459]

Public outrage over the Transportation Security Administration's (TSA) more intrusive body scan machines, and invasive patdowns, pro-

---

450. *Id.*

451. *Id.*

452. *Id.*

453. *See* Jonah Engel Bromwich, *The Social Media Warriors of Parkland, The New York Times* A13 (Mar. 11, 2018).

454. *See* Aubri Juhasz, *'Glimmer of Hope' Provides a Blueprint for Launching Social Change*, National Public Radio (Oct. 23, 2018). https://www.npr.org/2018/10/23/659474008/glimmer-of-hope-provides-a-blueprint-for-launching-social-change.

455. *See The Social Media Warriors of Parkland, supra* note 453, at A13.

456. *Id.*

457. *Id.*

458. *See* Sarah L. Jackson, *Twitter Made Us Better, The New York Times*, Sunday Review 3 (Dec. 29, 2019).

459. *Id.*

duced virtual protests designed to alter TSA security screening policies.[460] The protest movement was sparked when the TSA decided to introduce new scanners designed to improve traveler security and thwart potential terrorists.[461] Because the scanning machines emit radiation, TSA decided to allow airline travelers to opt out of the scans in favor of patdown searches.[462] However, in order to ensure that dangerous materials would not be carried onto airplanes, TSA conducted thorough and invasive patdowns, involving using the front of the hands, instead of the back, and probing the groin area.[463]

Opposition to the scans and pat-downs came to a head when John Tyner, a would-be airplane passenger, refused a groin pat down at the San Diego airport, and ended up in a heated exchange with TSA officials.[464] When Tyner recorded the exchange and posted it on the internet,[465] his actions quickly sparked an internet-based campaign calling for a "National Opt-Out Day" on the busiest airline travel day of the year, the day before a national holiday (Thanksgiving).[466] The idea was that, if enough travelers opted out of the scans, and forced the TSA to pat them down, the airline travel system would descend into chaos, and TSA would be forced to alter its scanning/pat down policy.[467]

460. *See* Joe Sharkey, *Screening Protests Grow as Holiday Crunch Looms, The New York Times*, On the Road (blog) (Nov. 15, 2010), http://www.nytimes.com/2010/11/16/business/16road.html?ref=transportation_security_administration.

461. *Id.*

462. *Id.*

463. *Id.*

464. *Id.*

465. *Id.* The video can be viewed at the following website: http://abcnews.go.com/Video/playerIndex?id=12153460.

466. *See Screening Protests Grow as Holiday Crunch Looms*, *supra* note 460.

467. *Id.* ("Mr. Pistole [TSA Administrator] was specifically worried about the internet-based campaign encouraging fliers who opposed the new machines to observe a "national opt-out day" on Nov. 24, the day before Thanksgiving. Any passenger can opt out of a scan that creates an image of the naked body and choose a full-body pat down instead. Only a tiny percentage of passengers now do, the T.S.A. says. But if enough people choose to do so on one of the busiest travel days of the year, checkpoints could become crowded and disorderly.").

Although the National Opt-Out Day protest was a failure,[468] in the sense of persuading travelers to "opt-out" of the scans on the day in question, there was evidence indicating that the scanners and the protests (or a combination of the two) might have discouraged some travelers from flying at all.[469] Nevertheless, from a communications perspective, the protest was a major success, and demonstrated how Web-based advocacy could generate extensive media coverage,[470] as well as how information could move very quickly on the internet. In the old (pre-internet) days, opposition to the TSA's policies might have built up very slowly, and would have depended on the traditional media and the historical gatekeepers of the media deciding to publicize the issue. Because of the internet, the furor over TSA's policies erupted quickly and came to a head within days.

---

468. *See* Associated Press, *Airport Protest Never Takes Off, Few Delays Seen*, National Public Radio (Nov. 25, 2010), http://www.npr.org/templates/story/story.php?storyId=131327045, ("The big Opt-Out looked like a big bust Wednesday as most of the Thanksgiving travelers selected for full-body scans and pat-down searches chose to submit to them rather than create havoc on one of the busiest flying days of the year. In fact, in some parts of the U.S., bad weather was shaping up as a bigger threat to travelers' hopes of getting to their destinations on time."); Kevin Fagan & Will Kane, *TSA Security Checks Cause Anxiety, Not Resistance, San Francisco Chronicle*, SFGate (Nov. 24, 2010) ("'It's kind of creepy, and I wish they didn't have to do any of it,' Hanchak, 25, said while advancing in a security line on her way to New York. 'But they have to do what they have to do, even though it's an invasion of privacy.' That's pretty much the take of most people flying this holiday, the busiest air-travel time of the year, according to interviews with passengers and airport security officials.") http://www.sfgate.com/cgi-bin/article.cgi?f=/c/a/2010/11/24/MNI81GGK9D.DTL&type=travel; Mary Louise Kelly, *Air Travelers Cope During Busiest Travel Season*, National Public Radio, All Things Considered (Nov. 24, 2010), http://www.npr.org/templates/story/story.php?storyId=131575222, ("The day before Thanksgiving is one of the busiest days of the year for airports; throw in threatened protests over passenger screening methods and the result could be chaos. But the so-called opt-out day has not caused chaos."); *Holiday Airport Lines Move Smoothly in Louisville, Nationwide, The Courier-Journal* (Nov. 24, 2010) http://www.courier-journal.com/article/20101124/NEWS01/311240047/1008/NEWS01/Holiday+airport+lines+move+smoothly+in+Louisville++nationwide; Staff & Wire Dispatches, Michael Tarm, *Despite Furor Over Full-Body Scans, Airport Protest Never Takes Off, Lines Move Smoothly, The Baltimore Sun.*(Nov. 25, 2010) http://www.baltimoresun.com/news/maryland/sns-ap-us-airport-security,0,6816284.story.

469. *See* Michael Tarm, *Opt-Out Fizzles As Airport Security Lines Flow Smoothly*, Boston Herald (Nov. 25, 2010) ("At least some people said they decided not to fly at all, in part because of the airport screening procedures.") http://www.timesheraldonline.com/ci_16710496?source=rss_viewed.

470. *See Screening Protests Grow as Holiday Crunch Looms, supra* note 460.

Tyner posted his video on the Web on November 13,[471] and it was picked up by the traditional media and broadcast nationally the next day.[472] The National Opt-Out Day was declared for only ten days later, November 24. Through the Web, enhanced by widespread coverage in the traditional media, people all over the country were quickly informed about the protest,[473] which received widespread coverage in the blogosphere, as well as in political cartoons.[474] Although the idea of a boycott was advertised online by a single person,[475] the idea was endorsed by two Philadelphia men who created a Facebook page,[476] as well as by a mobile app developer who promised that those who opted out would be given the chance to win an iPod.[477] The protest attracted such a high level of attention that the TSA's Administrator was forced to respond in media interviews.[478]

---

471. *See, e.g.*, Robert J. Hawkins, *Who Is John Tyner and Why Is He Upsetting the TSA?*, Signon San Diego (Nov. 16, 2010) http://www.signonsandiego.com/news/2010/nov/16/who-john-tyner-and-why-he-upsetting-tsa/; Scott Mayerowitz, *Is TSA Security Patdown Sexual Molestation? New TSA Search is Far More Physical Than Previous Airport Security Checks*, ABC World News with Diane Sawyer (Nov. 15, 2010) http://abcnews.go.com/Travel/john-tyner-tsa-security-check-sexual-molestation/story?id=12153388 ; Alexandra Petri, *TSA and John Tyner—Usually This Sort of Thing is Preceded by Dinner*, The Washington Post, ComPost (Nov. 15, 2010) http://voices.washingtonpost.com/compost/2010/11/tsa_and_john_tyner_--_usually.html.

472. *Id.*

473. *See, e.g.*, Associated Press, *National Opt-Out Day: Placards, Kilts and More*, Boston Herald.com (Nov. 24, 2010) http://www.bostonherald.com/news/national/general/view/20101124national_opt-out_day_placards_kilts_and_more/; Daniel Rubin, *Opt Out of TSA Opt-Out*, Philadelphia Inquirer Nov. 23, 2010) http://www.philly.com/inquirer/breaking/news_breaking/20101123_Opt_out_of_TSA_Opt-Out.html.

474. *See, e.g.*, Michael Cavna, *DON'T TOUCH MY JUNK: Best of the TSA Body Search Cartoons*, The Washington Post (Nov. 22, 2010) http://voices.washingtonpost.com/comic-riffs/2010/11/dont_touch_my_junk_best_of_the.html?tid=wp_ipad.

475. *See* http://www.optoutday.com/.

476. *See* Sara J. Welch, *T.S.A. Screening Measures Draw Virtual Protests, The New York Times*, In Transit (blog) (Nov. 19, 2010), http://intransit.blogs.nytimes.com/2010/11/19/t-s-a-screening-measures-draw-virtual-protests/?src=twrhp. The Facebook page can be found at: http://www.facebook.com/optoutday.

477. *See Opt-Out Day Promotion: Let TSA Touch You, Win an IPod*, Center for Media and Democracy (Nov. 18, 2010). http://prwatch.org/node/9637.

478. *See* Associated Press, *TSA Chief: Screening Should Be Minimally Invasive*, National Public Radio (Nov. 21, 2010), http://www.npr.org/2010/11/21/131492663/tsa-chief-no-change-in-screening-policy?ft=1&f=1001,("The head of the agency responsible for airport security, facing protests from travelers and pressure from the White House, appeared to give ground Sunday on his position that there would be no change in policies regard-

So, why did the National Opt-Out protest fail? The failure cannot be attributed to the communications technologies used by the organizers. The organizers' online efforts sparked a major national controversy. Of course, the most important factor in the success of any protest movement is the soundness and wisdom of its ideas. Although the internet can empower ordinary people to communicate their political and social ideas, there is no guarantee that those ideas will be good ones or that they will be accepted by the public. In the case of the proposed National Opt-Out Day, there is reason to believe that the public supported the TSA's new security measures, because they wanted enhanced public safety, as well as because they believed that those measures were appropriate given the terrorist threat.[479] In addition, there was significant editorial opposition to the protests. For example, a *Slate* article urged the public to reject the idea of an opt out:

> Ignore these imbeciles. Their plan would clog security lines and ruin your holiday for no good reason. They don't understand the importance of the electronic scans. They're wrong about the scanners' safety. And from the standpoint of dignity, their advice

---

ing invasive passenger screening procedures."); Brian Naylor, *TSA Chief Defends Airport Screening Procedures*, National Public Radio, Morning Edition (Nov. 17, 2010), http://www.npr.org/2010/11/16/131373145/tsa-chief-defends-airport-screening-procedures?ps=rs, ("The head of the Transportation Security Administration is defending controversial screening procedures at the nation's airports that have everyone from civil liberties groups to airline pilots upset.").

479. *See* J. David Goodman, *Travelers' Report: Better Than Expected, The New York Times*, at A24 (Nov. 25, 2010) ("George Oberle, 50, a Lutheran minister who flew to New York for Thanksgiving from his home in Detroit, said he gladly submitted to a scan, not worried in the least that his modesty was compromised. 'If it's going to keep me and others safe, I'm all for it,' he said. 'Besides, I'm 50. I'm proud of what I've got.'"); Rick Green, *National Opt-Out Day—Will You Say No to Naked Scanning?*, CT Confidential (Nov. 12, 2010), http://blogs.courant.com/rick_green/2010/11/national-optout-day-will-you-s.html; (I can't believe some folks think this is the debate we should be having when we left liberty on the side of the road way back in the Bush Administration. Actually, I think the scans do a better job of making me feel better about flying than the two waste-of-lives-and-money wars we are fighting in Iraq and Afghanistan. With the body scans, at least I'll know the guy next to me doesn't have a toner cartridge packed with explosives."); Campbell Robertson, *Passengers Unmoved by Protests Against Scan, The New York Times*, at A24 (Nov. 25, 2010).

> is insane. If you opt out of the scan, you'll get a pat-down instead. You'll trade a fast, invisible, intangible, privacy-protected machine inspection for an unpleasant, extended grope. In effect, you'll be telling TSA to touch your junk.[480]

The *Slate* article goes on to reject the protestor's ultimate objectives:

> And for what? If Opt-Out Day grinds air travel to a halt and forces the government to withdraw the scanners, WWF's next goal is to abolish TSA. It claims the agency isn't 'agile' enough to match al-Qaida. That's hilarious. Naked scanners are exactly the kind of agile response al-Qaida requires. Last year's underwear

---

480. *See* William Saletan, *This Junk Won't Fly: The Idiocy of Airport-Scanner "Opt-Out" Day*, Slate (Nov. 22, 2010) http://www.slate.com/id/2275681/ The article goes on to state that:

> It's hard to know where to start with this idiocy. The body scanners aren't dangerous. Their safety has been certified by the Food and Drug Administration, the Johns Hopkins University Applied Physics Laboratory, and other scientific reviewers. You get more radiation from being at flying altitude for two minutes than you do from a scan.
>
> Second, a "virtual strip search" is nothing like a real one. According to We Won't Fly, the fact that airport scans "are automated and mechanical in no way changes the fact that when a government agent looks beneath your clothing you are being strip searched." Are you kidding? It changes everything. In an airport scan, the only person who sees your naked body (it looks like this on the viewing screen) is an officer in a room away from where you're standing. He or she never sees your face and has no idea whose body is on the screen. Conversely, the officer who's standing in front of you, awaiting word that you've passed the scan, never sees you naked. This separation of your identity from your nude image is what protects your privacy. In a pat-down, there's no separation. The same officer who looks you in the eye slides his hand up your groin.
>
> Did I mention the cost in time? A scanner can clear you in 10 seconds. A pat-down can take four minutes—or longer, if you accept TSA's offer of a private screening room. Imagine how long you'll have to wait at the airport Wednesday if half the people in front of you refuse to be scanned. TSA "won't have the manpower to reach into everyone's crotch," exults a WWF co-founder. The group urges followers to "jam TSA checkpoints by opting out" and "slowing down their security theater."

Id.

> bomber showed that metal detectors can't handle nonmetallic explosives concealed on the passenger. Hence the scanners.[481]

In addition, there were online editorials opposing the protests. One commentator argued that "If activists want to make changes, doing it while at the airport in the security lane is not the appropriate place."[482] While "it is all well and good to make a stand ... you need to make this stand by consistently contacting your elected officials in Washington. Write your Congressional representative, your two Senators and write to the House & Senate Committees that oversee the TSA."[483]

Without the internet, it is not clear that the National Opt-Out Day controversy would have arisen. Tyner could have taken his video of the TSA incident to a newspaper, or a radio or television outlet, and talked to them about the possibility of airing it, but there is no assurance that they would have agreed to do so. The media might have picked up on the incident as politically significant, or it might have decided that the incident was trivial and uninteresting (or it could have rejected the story for a multitude of other reasons). Alternatively, Tyner could have tried to organize a mass demonstration, in order to draw attention to his cause,

---

481. *Id.*

482. *See* Steve Frischling, *National Opt-Out Day ... Why I Am Not Supporting It*, Flying With Fish: The Blog For Those Who Fly and Those Who Want to Fly Smarter (Nov. 15, 2010) ("The security lane is the front line of the TSA, where screeners have a job to do. If you refuse the scanner, then refuse the pat down, you'll simply be denied access to the airport and miss your flight.") http://boardingarea.com/blogs/flyingwithfish/2010/11/15/national-opt-out-day-%e2%80%a6-why-i-am-not-supporting-it/; Jonah Goldberg, National Opt Out Day, The Corner (Nov. 24, 2010) ("I gotta say, I'm pretty skeptical about the idea. Among other concerns it could backfire terribly. If I was late for my flight, I wouldn't be cheering-on the folks slowing things down.") http://www.nationalreview.com/corner/253882/opt-out-day-jonah-goldberg; Joe Smith, *Opt Out of National Opt Out Day*, Dissident Voice (Nov. 16, 2010) ("I can't agree with the plan. For one thing, you're not likely to find a lot of support for the idea of asking people to protest by delaying their own travel, particularly on a day that's difficult enough and already prone to delays, and even more especially when their primary concern at that moment will be simply getting home for the holidays. So the protest itself will be relatively weak, because relatively few will join in, compared to the underlying number of people who would be far more willing to participate in the protest if it were called for a more favorable date.") http://dissidentvoice.org/2010/11/opt-out-of-national-opt-out-day/.

483. *Id.*

but without any way to mass publicize his ideas, the protest might or might not have been successful. Because of the internet, Tyner could post the video clip online, thereby allowing others to view the clip and provide their own comments and exhortations (*e.g.*, some decided to declare a National Opt-Out Day), as well as the pro and negative responses that followed. In other words, both Tyner and his responders could discuss the issue even though they did not have access to the traditional media. Then, because of the internet, the traditional media concluded that the story was interesting enough to air.

During the debate about whether Judge Brett Kavanagh should be confirmed to the U.S. Supreme Court, many used the internet to discuss issues related to sexual abuse. The #MeToo movement—involving individuals who claimed to have been sexually assaulted or harassed—emerged on the internet.[484] During the hearings, after questions were raised regarding Dr. Christine Blasey Ford's failure to come forward earlier with her accusations against Kavanagh, a new hashtag emerged: #WhyIDidntReport.[485] As one commentator noted, it "may take a survivor a while to process that trauma, and even to identify what has happened," and many women explained that they were also dissuaded from reporting by "fear, anger and shame."[486] Another hashtag, #BelieveWomen, also emerged.[487] These hashtag movements were significant because they encouraged other women to step forward and identity themselves as being victims of sexual assault and harassment.[488]

The internet has also been used by PragerU which produces conservative videos designed to influence the culture wars.[489] Using a legion of 6,500 high school and college students, and a staff of 50, PragerU videos generated some one billion views in a single year.[490] The videos have

484. *See* Jacey Fortin, *After Trump Tweet, Women Share Stories of Assault, The New York Times* A19 (Sept. 25, 2018).

485. *Id.*

486. *Id.*

487. *See* Maya Salam & Niraj Chokshi, *#BelieveWomen: Support for Kavanaugh's Accusers, The New York Times* A19 (Sept. 25, 2018).

488. *See* Fortin, *supra* note 484.

489. *See* Nellie Bowles, *It's Fox News for Generation Z, In Five-Minute Videos Online, The New York Times* A1 (Jan. 5, 2020).

490. *Id.*

titles like "Why Socialism Never Works," "Fossil Fuels: The Green Energy," "Where are the Moderate Muslims?," and "Are Some Cultures Better Than Others?"[491] PragerU operates on the assumption that today's youth have been heavily indoctrinated into left-wing views.[492] Funded by conservative donors, PragerU distributes its videos through Facebook and YouTube.[493]

A conservative "attack" blogger, James O'Keefe, used the internet to arrange a "sting" of National Public Radio's (NPR) then-fund-raiser, Mr. Ron Schiller.[494] The sting involved two men who posed as members of a fictitious Muslim organization (the Muslim Education Action Center Trust) during a meeting with Schiller. A videotape of the meeting (taken by O'Keefe) showed Schiller making disparaging remarks about conservatives and questioning whether NPR needs or should receive federal funding.[495] The posting of the videotape led Schiller to resign,[496] and, coupled with other missteps (*e.g.*, NPR's firing of commentator, Juan Williams),[497]

491. *Id.*

492. *Id.*

493. *Id.*

494. *See* Mark Memmott, *NPR CEO Vivian Schiller Resigns After Board Decides She Should Go*, National Public Radio, The Two-Way (Mar. 9, 2011), http://www.npr.org/blogs/thetwo-way/2011/03/10/134388981/npr-ceo-vivian-schiller-resigns.

495. *See* Associated Press, *NPR Chief Executive Quits Over Hidden Camera Video*, National Public Radio (Mar. 9, 2011), http://www.npr.org/blogs/thetwo-way/2011/03/10/134388981/npr-ceo-vivian-schiller-resigns (Schiller made the following statement: "'The current Republican Party is not really the Republican Party. It's been hijacked by this group that is ... not just Islamophobic but, really, xenophobic,' Ron Schiller said in the video, referring to the tea party movement. 'They believe in sort of white, middle America, gun-toting—it's scary. They're seriously racist, racist people.'"); Mark Memmott, *In Video: NPR Exec Slams Tea Party, Questions Need for Federal Funds*, National Public Radio, The Two-Way (Mar. 8, 2011), http://www.npr.org/blogs/thetwo-way/2011/03/09/134358398/in-video-npr-exec-slams-tea-party-questions-need-for-federal-funds (he also stated that "'Tea Party is fanatically involved in people's personal lives and very fundamental Christian—I wouldn't even call it Christian. It's this weird evangelical kind of move." The videotape also suggests that Schiller had no reaction when told that the group with which he was meeting was sponsored by Egypt's Muslim Brotherhood) http://www.npr.org/blogs/thetwo-way/2011/03/09/134358398/in-video-npr-exec-slams-tea-party-questions-need-for-federal-funds; David Folkenflik, *NPR Exec: NPR Would Be Better Off Without Federal Support*, National Public Radio, All Things Considered (Mar. 8, 2011), http://www.npr.org/2011/03/08/134371393/NPR-Exec-NPR-Would-Be-Better-Off-Without-Fed-Support.

496. *See NPR CEO Vivian Schiller Resigns*, *supra* note 490.

497. *See* Brooke Gladstone, *The Firing of Juan Williams*, National Public Radio, On the Media (Oct. 22, 2010) http://www.onthemedia.org/2010/oct/22/the-firing-of-juan

led NPR's Board of Directors to force NPR's then-President and CEO, Vivian Schiller (no relation) to resign.[498] Even though an NPR report suggested that parts of the video were taken out of context,[499] the dismissal appears to have been prompted a congressional effort to cut off federal funding to NPR ($430 million per year at the time), partly in response to the video.[500] O'Keefe also did a sting of ACORN (Association of Community Organizations for Reform Now).[501] The sting created a stir because it showed video clips in which Acorn officials purportedly advised an individual who was posing as a pimp being provided with advice by ACORN.[502]

Another "sting" was directed at Planned Parenthood, and led some congressmen to try to cut off funding to that organization (Planned Parenthood was receiving approximately $75 million per year for family planning purposes, and additional funding for other purposes).[503] Although Planned Parenthood had been a target of anti-abortion groups for years, the effort to cut-off funding was prompted by an internet video posted by a group called "Live Action," which showed undercover videotapes in which [Planned Parenthood] employees are seen answering questions from a man posing as a trafficker of underage sex slaves.[504] Live Action claimed that a Planned Parenthood clinic manager advised the man how to make his operation seem legitimate.[505] The video prompted "Concerned Women for America" to establish a Web site entitled "Expose Planned Parenthood."[506] The video also prompted a congressman to assert that Planned Parenthood had "a pattern of apparent fraud and abuse" and

-williams/transcript/; *NPR Chief Executive Quits*, *supra* note 495 (Williams was fired after stating that he feels uncomfortable when he sees people in Muslim garb on airplanes).

498. *See NPR Chief Executive Quits*, *supra* note 495; *NPR CEO Vivian Schiller Resigns*, *supra* note 490.

499. *See* David Folkenflik, *Elements of NPR Gotcha Video Taken Out of Context*, National Public Radio, (Mar. 14, 2011). http://www.npr.org/2011/03/14/134525412/Segments-Of-NPR-Gotcha-Video-Taken-Out-Of-Context.

500. *See NPR Chief Executive Quits*, *supra* note 495.

501. *See In Video: NPR Exec Slams Tea Party*, *supra* note 495.

502. *See* David Carr, *Journalist, Provocateur, Maybe Both*, *The New York Times*, The Media Equation, at B1 (July 26, 2010).

503. *See* Eric Eckholm, *Planned Parenthood Funding Is Caught in Budget Feud*, *The New York Times*, at A17 (Feb. 18, 2011).

504. http://liveaction.org/blog/planned-parenthood-aids-sex-ring/.

505. *Id.*

506. http://exposeplannedparenthood.net/.

to conclude that "the time has come to deny any federal funding" to the group.[507] Planned Parenthood responded on the Web,[508] encouraging supporters to call and e-mail Congress on its behalf.[509] Live Action followed with an e-mail challenging Planned Parenthood's response.[510]

As an outgrowth of the Occupy Wall Street movement, which is discussed more fully below, students have protested tuition hikes at public universities.[511] Governmental funding for universities has declined in recent years, and universities have increasingly sought to charge students higher and higher tuition rates, prompting some students to protest.[512] When police on the University of California at Davis's campus used pepper spray to disperse protestors, a video of the police action was posted on the Web and was ultimately viewed by hundreds of thousands of people.[513]

The internet has also been used to satirize or parody public officials and governmental figures.[514] For example, anonymous Twitter posts have made fun of prominent individuals and governmental officials.[515] These fake Twitter postings are complimented by internet publications like Fishbowl DC which mines Twitter feeds for embarrassing information about prominent people.[516]

---

507. *See Planned Parenthood Funding Is Caught in Budget Feud, supra* note 503, at A17.

508. *See* https://secure.ppaction.org/site/SPageServer?pagename=pp_ppol_ws_I_Stand_with_PP&s_src=istandwithPP_home&__utma=1.342759001.1298948404.1298948404.1298948404.1&__utmb=1.3.10.1298948404&__utmc=1&__utmx=-&__utmz=1.1298948404.1.1.utmcsr=bing|utmccn=(organic)|utmcmd=organic|utmctr=planned%20parenthood&__utmv=-&__utmk=28745404.

509. *See Planned Parenthood Funding Is Caught in Budget Feud, supra* note 503, at A17.

510. *See id.*, at A17 ("The answer for poor women is not a corporation that is happy to help sex traffickers and that has enabled the sexual abuse and exploitation of countless girls and young women.").

511. *See* Jennifer Medina, *California's Campus Movement Digs in Their Heels, The New York Times*, at A17 (Nov. 22, 2011).

512. *Id.* ("It has become something of an annual tradition on California college campuses, in what is perhaps the most prestigious state university system in the country: the state makes large cuts in public universities, they in turn raise tuition, and students respond with angry protests.").

513. *Id.*

514. *See* Ashley Parker, *#newwashingtontonguesguessinggame: Fake Twitter Personalities Mock Politicians and Journalists in the Capital, International Herald Tribune*, at 14 (Feb. 10, 2011).

515. *Id.*

516. *See* Parker, *supra* note 514, at 3; https://twitter.com/FishbowlDC.

When groups on the right believed that Google was unduly biased in favor of left-wing interests, they resorted to the internet to attack Google.[517] Not only did they attack Google online, but they attempted to organize a boycott.[518] They later expanded their criticisms to other websites, including Patreon, Airbnb, and PayPal.[519] Likewise, from the opposite political perspective, when a transplant from New Hampshire to Naples, Florida, became concerned regarding environmental issues (specifically, the state of sea life), she began using her cellphone to take videos which she posted on the internet.[520] To ward off claims that she was doctoring the photos, she began posting live pictures.[521]

Crossroads GPS, a conservative political action group, began a new website, Wikicountability.org.[522] The website focused on freedom of information requests against the Obama administration.[523] In some instances, website posters have uploaded the results of their own FOIA requests to the site.[524] In other instances, they have analyzed information obtained by others.[525] The group claims that its goal is to make government accountable.[526]

The Occupy Wall Street movement which began in New York on September 17, 2011,[527] and took up residence in Zuccotti Park in New York City,[528] also uses the internet to organize and protest. The movement consisted of a diverse group of individuals, many from the left side of the polit-

517. *See* Kevin Roose, *The Alt-Right Finds a New Enemy in Silicon Valley, The New York Times* B6 (Aug. 10, 2017).

518. *Id.*

519. *Id.*

520. *See* Jim Rutenberg, *Filling in for TV News With Just an iPhone, The New York Times* B1 (Dec. 3, 2018).

521. *Id.*

522. *See* Noam Cohen, *A Wiki Takes Aim at Obama, The New York Times*, Link by Link, at B1 (Apr. 4, 2011); https://www.crossroadsgps.org/.

523. *Id.*

524. *Id.*, at B8.

525. *Id.*

526. *Id.*

527. David Carr, *A Protest's Ink-Stained Fingers, The New York Times*, The Media Equation, at B1 (Oct. 10, 2011).

528. *Id.*, at B3.

ical spectrum, and many of whom were unemployed.[529] The movement purported to represent what they claimed was the 99% of the population that was disadvantaged by the current political and economic system.[530] Occupy Wall Street did not have an organized plan of action or specific demands.[531] Indeed, given its anarchic roots, the Occupy movement seemed reluctant to embrace specific leaders or specific policy positions.[532] The movement had an aversion to hierarchy, and to formal leaders, but a strong commitment to democratic principles.[533] It did share a level of anger regarding societal wealth disparities,[534] special interests and the political system.[535] Other issues seem to have bubbled to the surface in various protests.[536] Unemployment, coupled with high levels of student debt, also seemed to be motivating factors for Occupy protestors.[537]

The Occupy movement pulled in various other groups, including labor unions, but the role of these other groups was unclear given that

---

529. *See* Chris Arnold, *Frustration Over Jobs Unites "Occupiers" in Boston*, National Public Radio, Morning Edition (Oct. 20, 2011), http://www.npr.org/2011/10/20/141509639/frustration-over-jobs-unites-occupiers-in-boston; Jocelyn Noveck, *We're Just Like You, Protestors Tell the World: Occupy Wall Street Diverse in all Things, The Courier-Journal*, at A3 (Oct. 9, 2011).

530. *See* Steven Greenhouse & Cara Buckley, *Unions, Seeking New Energy, Join a Protest Against Wall St., The New York Times*, at A23 (Oct. 6, 2011).

531. *See* Todd Gitlin, *The Left Declares Its Independence, The New York Times*, at S.R.4 (Oct. 9, 2011); N.R. Kleinfield & Cara Buckley, *Wall Street Occupiers, Protesting Till Whenever, The New York Times*, at A1 (Oct. 1, 2011).

532. *See The Left Declares Its Independence, supra* note 531; Laura Sullivan, *What Do Occupy Wall Street Protestors Want?*, National Public Radio, All Things Considered (Nov. 6, 2011), http://www.npr.org/2011/11/06/142079828/what-do-occupy-wall-street-protesters-want.

533. *See Unions, Seeking New Energy, supra* note 530, at A23.

534. *See* Cara Buckley & Rachel Donadio, *Rallies Across the Globe Protest Economic Policies: A Day of Demonstrations, Mixed in Their Messages but the Most Peaceful Part, The New York Times*, A4 (Oct. 16, 2011) ("Yet despite the difference in language, landscape and scale, the protests were united in frustration with the widening gap between the rich and the poor."); Marc Lacey, *Countless Grievances, One Thread: We're Angry, The New York Times*, A1 (Oct. 18, 2011); *The Left Declares Its Independence, supra* note 531.

535. *See* Reuters Report, *A Manifesto For Protestors, The New York Times*, at B2 (Oct. 6, 2011).

536. *See Countless Grievances, supra* note 534, at A1 (*e.g.*, education, the environment, and the wars in Iraq and Afghanistan).

537. *See Rallies Across the Globe Protest Economic Policies, supra* note 534.

the Occupy Movement was adverse to the concept of declared leaders,[538] and given that individual occupiers articulated different and sometimes conflicting messages.[539] While most of the Occupy protests were peaceful, some turned violent, and some protestors were arrested for trespass.[540] Some viewed the Occupy protestors as the beginning of a long-term social movement (which it did not turn out to be).[541]

The Occupy movement had a strong online presence. The Movement was alleged to have originated with the Adbusters organization,[542] and attracted adherents through e-mail[543] and Web-based social media.[544] It maintained live streaming over the internet of all of its proceedings,[545] and raised nearly $300,000 through the Web.[546] The website Pastebin, originally created as a way for computer programmers to share information, was used by some Occupy protestors to convey information about the Movement,[547] and it achieved that goal through individual Web postings since there was no "official" leader of the Movement.[548] Using modern production technology, the movement also produced a high-quality newspaper (*The Occupied Wall Street Journal*) in both English and Spanish,

538. *Id.*

539. *Id.* ("But just as the rallies in New York have represented a variety of messages—signs have been held in opposition to President Obama yards away from signs in support of him—so did Saturday's protests contain a grab bag of sentiments, opposing nuclear power, political corruption and the privatization of water.").

540. *See id.*, at A4.

541. *See* Jeffrey D. Sachs, *The New Progressive Movement, The New York Times*, at 6–7 (Nov. 13, 2011).

542. *See* Martin Kaste, *Exploring Occupy Wall Street's "Adbuster" Origins*, National Public Radio, Morning Edition (Oct. 20, 2011), http://www.npr.org/2011/10/20/141526467/exploring-occupy-wall-streets-adbuster-origins ("*Adbusters* is an anti-consumerism magazine based in Vancouver, British Columbia. This summer, it proposed a Sept. 17 "occupation" of Wall Street, and the idea caught fire.").

543. *See* Greenhouse & Buckley, *supra* note 530, at A1.

544. *See We're Just Like You, supra* note 529.

545. *See A Protest's Ink-Stained Fingers, supra* note 527; Jennifer Preston, *Occupy Video Showcases Live Streaming, The New York Times*, at B1 (Dec. 12, 2011).

546. *See* Verena Dobnik, *Protestors Flex Their Muscles: Peaking? Or Just Getting Started?, The Courier-Journal*, at A2 (Oct. 17, 2011).

547. *See* Noam Cohen, *A Fluid Protest Movement Finds a Forum to Match, The New York Times*, Link By Link, at B3 (Oct. 10, 2011) ("Lately, Occupy Wall Street is generating many of the most-viewed posts, as the Arab Spring protests did before.").

548. *Id.*

that looked a lot like *The Wall Street Journal*,[549] and distributed it at the protests.[550] The Movement solicited financial support for the newspaper over the Web.[551] Although the Movement initially hoped to raise $12,000 to pay for the print run, it actually raised more than $75,000.[552] Finally, protestors documented the Occupy movement through Web postings[553] that were distributed via Twitter and through sites like TheStreet.com.[554]

Through the traditional media and the Web, information about the Occupy Wall Street Movement spread rapidly around the globe. Initially, traditional media sources were slow to report on the movement.[555] That soon changed,[556] and the traditional media ultimately reported extensively about the movement.[557] Although the worldwide protests were not coordinated, online resources were used to coordinate individual protests,[558] and some protestors were inspired to join the protests after reading about them online.[559] Protests spread quickly to Madrid,[560] London,[561] Berlin,[562] and across Asia, Europe, and the Americas,[563] and involved thousands of

549. *See A Protest's Ink-Stained Fingers*, *supra* note 527, at B3.

550. *See id.*, at b1 (noting that the Movement produces "a professionally produced, four-color, four-page document of the demonstration, which began on September 17th."). A PDF of the paper was available at bit.ly/qio5ls.

551. *Id.*

552. *Id.*

553. *See* Andy Newman & Al Baker, *Two Police-Protester Flare-Ups Gain Fuel Online*, *The New York Times*, A15 (Oct. 15, 2011) ("Amid the chaos in Lower Manhattan on Friday morning as the Occupy Wall Street protesters marched through the streets, there were two encounters between protesters and the police that were captured, however imperfectly, on video and then ricocheted across the internet.").

554. *Id.*

555. *See* Brian Stelter, *Occupy Wall Street Occupies Headlines*, *The New York Times*, Media Decoder (blog) (Oct. 12, 2011), http://mediadecoder.blogs.nytimes.com/2011/10/12/occupy-wall-street-occupies-headlines/?scp=1&sq=occupy%20wall%20street%20occupies%20headlines&st=cse.

556. *See id.*

557. *See Protestors Flex Their Muscles*, *supra* note 546.

558. *See Rallies Across the Globe*, *supra* note 534.

559. *See id.*, at A4 ("Kelly Mears, 24, a former software engineer, said he was despondent about the direction of the country and was inspired to join the protest after following the one in New York on Twitter and other social media.").

560. *See id.*

561. *See id.*; *Countless Grievances*, *supra* note 534, at A3.

562. *See Rallies Across the Globe*, *supra* note 534.

563. *See id.*

people.[564] In the United States, some 1,500 people turned up for an Occupy Orlando protest,[565] and the protests spread to various U.S. cities, including Phoenix,[566] Portland,[567] Louisville,[568] Los Angeles,[569] Chicago,[570] Tucson,[571] Boston,[572] Atlanta,[573] Oakland,[574] Philadelphia,[575] Albany,[576] Berkeley,[577] Nashville,[578] Tampa,[579] St. Petersburg,[580] the District of Columbia,[581] Salt Lake City,[582] Honolulu,[583] Raleigh,[584] Trenton,[585] Wilmington,[586] Lynchburg,[587] and Bloomington.[588]

---

564. *Id.*

565. *See Protestors Flex Their Muscles, supra* note 546, at A2.

566. *See Countless Grievances, One Thread, supra* note 534, at A1.

567. *See* Terrence Petty, *Police Move on Occupy Portland: Defiant Protestors Hit Streets After Eviction From Parks, The Courier-Journal*, A3 (Nov. 14, 2011).

568. *See* Elizabeth Kramer, *Occupy Louisville Takes Issues to Street: Two Events Launch Week of Solidarity, The Courier-Journal*, at B1 (Nov. 14, 2011) (protestors were occupying Jefferson Square Park, and one event that they decided to hold was entitled "Seven Days of Solidarity.").

569. *See Countless Grievances, supra* note 534, at A3.

570. *Id.*

571. *Id.*

572. *Id.*

573. *Id.*

574. *See* Terry Collins, *Oakland Rally Halts Port Operations, The Courier-Journal*, A3 (2011).

575. *Id.*

576. *Id.*

577. *See* Associated Press, *Occupy Activists to Converge on UC Berkeley Campus*, National Public Radio, (Nov. 15, 2011), http://www.npr.org/templates/story/story.php?storyId=142331943.

578. *See* Travis Loller, *Officials Back Protestors: Removal Thwarted in Tenn., New York, The Courier-Journal*, A3 (Oct. 31, 2011).

579. *See Occupy Wall Street Occupies Headlines, supra* note 555.

580. *See id.*

581. *See* Associated Press, *Latest Developments in the Occupy Protests*, National Public Radio (Nov. 7, 2011), http://www.npr.org/templates/story/story.php?storyID=142074678

582. *Id.*

583. *Id.*

584. *Id.*

585. *Id.*

586. *Id.*

587. *Id.*

588. *Id.*

The internet has also been used to promote social activism. For example, in 2015, a lion was lured off of a sanctuary in Zimbabwe and killed.[589] As it turned out, the lion was a local "favorite," was collared, and was part of a study.[590] Once it was known that a dentist from Minnesota had killed the lion, he was targeted online for the killing and protestors descended on his office.[591]

Of course, the mere fact that an issue receives substantial social media attention does not guarantee that it will have popular support.[592] After an old photo surfaced of then Virginia Governor Ralph Northam in black face, there was substantial criticism and demands for his resignation.[593] However, a poll indicated that a majority of voters, both black and white, believed that Governor Northam should not resign.[594]

In one of the more unusual uses of modern technology, inmates at a Georgia prison used cell phones to coordinate a nonviolent work strike.[595] The objective of the strike was to obtain better living conditions, as well as to push for higher pay for inmate work.[596] The protest was interesting, not only because it was illegal for prisoners to possess cell phones, but also because they used those phones to conduct interviews with the media.[597]

---

589. *See* Christina Capeechi & Katie Rogers, *Killer of Cecil the Lion Finds Out That He Is a Target Now, of Internet Vigilantism, The New York Times* A11 (July 30, 2015).

590. *Id.*

591. *Id.* (One Facebook page was titled "Shame Lion Killer Dr. Walter Palmer and River Bluff Dental").

592. *See* Nate Cohn & Kevin Quealy, *Liberals on Twitter Don't Speak for Quiet Majority, The New York Times* A1 (Apr. 10, 2019).

593. *Id.*

594. *Id.*

595. *See* Sarah Wheaton, *Inmates in Georgia Prisons Use Contraband Cellphones to Coordinate Protests, The New York Times*, at A13 (Dec. 13, 2010).

596. *Id.*

597. *Id.*

2. NON-CANDIDATES' USE OF THE INTERNET TO INFLUENCE THE OUTCOME OF POLITICAL CAMPAIGNS

The internet has also been used to influence political campaigns.[598] Illustrative is Moveon.org, a group of liberal activists who have actively sought to influence political debate through the internet,[599] and who have tried to involve increasing numbers of liberal voters in the political process.[600] In 2003, the group claimed 1.4 million members, and even held a mock presidential primary to pick a challenger to President Bush.[601] The movement used internet-based techniques to raise very substantial amounts of money, including raising $700,000, within a matter of hours, to support candidates who opposed the Iraq War.[602] Following the nomination of then-Governor Sarah Palin for vice-president of the United States, MoveOn.org raised $1.2 million in a 24-hour period for a pro-Obama, pro-Biden, advertising campaign.[603]

Like MoveOn.org, a number of "liberal bloggers" have teamed-up with Democratic interests (*e.g.*, labor unions and MoveOn.org) in an attempt to push the Democratic Party further to the left. One such group is "Accountability Now."[604] In addition to soliciting donations, these bloggers have tried to recruit more leftist candidates to challenge centrist incumbent Democrats.[605] As one of the founders stated, "We're going to be about targeting incumbents to make space for Obama to be more progressive."[606]

---

598. *See* Linton Weeks, *Politics in the Social Media Age: How Tweet It Is*, National Public Radio (Oct. 29, 2010), http://www.npr.org/templates/story/story.php?storyId=130873983

599. *See* Linton Weeks, *Ten Years Later, MoveOn Is 4.2 Million Strong*, National public Radio (Sept. 22, 2008), http://www.npr.org/templates/story/story.php?storyId=94882173.

600. *See* Terence Smith, *Plugged-In Politics*, Public Broadcasting System, The News Hour (Aug. 5, 2003), http://www.pbs.org/newshour/bb/media/july-dec03/internetpolitics_8-5.html.

601. *See id.*

602. *See* Michael Luo, *Obama Hauls in Record $750 Million for Campaign, With Plenty Left to Spend, The New York Times*, A29 (Dec. 5, 1998); *Ten Years Later, MoveOn Is 4.2 Million Strong, supra* note 599.

603. *See Ten Years Later, MoveOn Is 4.2 Million Strong, supra* note 599.

604. *See* Jim Rutenberg, *Bloggers Seek Candidates to Push Democrats to Left, The New York Times*, at A19 (Feb. 27, 2009).

605. *Id.*

606. *Id.*

On the right side of the political spectrum, the internet movement started more slowly, but quickly gained momentum. Townhall.com launched in 1995 with hundreds of commentators and 9,000 grassroots bloggers.[607] Perhaps the most prominent movement on the right was the Tea Party which mushroomed quickly, rapidly gained momentum,[608] and had a significant impact (both positive and negative) on the 2010 elections. While the Tea Party did not have a firm platform, the movement seemed to be motivated by several broad themes.[609] David Brooks, a columnist for *The New York Times*, explained that the Tea party "is a large, fractious confederation of Americans who are defined by what they are against. They are against the concentrated power of the educated class. They believe big government, big business, big media and the affluent professionals are merging to form a self-serving oligarchy—with bloated government, unsustainable deficits, high taxes and intrusive regulation."[610] The Tea Party aggressively used Twitter and other online media, and it set up a Twitter group called #TCOT (Top Conservatives on Twitter).[611] At one point, more Americans had a more positive view of the Tea Party movement than they had of either the Democratic or Republican parties.[612]

The Tea Party also targeted Republicans that it regarded as too "liberal."[613] For example, during the 2010 election cycle, the Tea Party targeted and defeated Senator Robert F. Bennett of Utah (one of the nation's more conservative senators), and replaced him with a more conservative

---

607. *See* Hansen & Ardalan, *supra* note 5.

608. *See* Robert Smith, *Tax Day Tea Parties*, National Public Radio (April 15, 2009), http://www.npr.org/templates/story/story.php?storyId=103143657.

609. *See* Kate Zernike, *Tea Party Gets Early Start on G.O.P. Targets for 2012, The New York Times*, at A16 (Jan. 30, 2011) ("[T]heir complaints often boil down to nothing more specific ... than 'we want this or that stopped, or there is spending, big government.'").

610. *Id.*

611. *See* Bob Garfield, *A Tea Party Primary*, National Public Radio, On the Media (Sept. 17, 2010), http://www.onthemedia.org/2010/sep/17/a-tea-party-primary/ ("Well, they definitely use Facebook, Ning, which is a lesser-known social network but is really the home page for a lot of these Tea Party groups. You have huge e-mail lists.").

612. *See Tea Party Gets Early Start, supra* note 609 ("According to the NBC News/Wall Street Journal poll, 41 percent of Americans have a positive view of the tea party movement. Only 35 percent of Americans have a positive view of the Democrats and only 28 percent have a positive view of the Republican Party.").

613. *See id.*, at A16.

Republican.[614] In the 2012 election cycle, there was talk that it would target other senators (Olympia Snowe of Maine, Orrin Hatch of Utah and Richard Lugar of Indiana).[615] Although the primary challenge against Orrin Hatch fizzled,[616] the Tea Party did manage to defeat Richard Lugar[617] and to encourage Olympia Snowe not to run for re-election.[618]

The Tea Party produced counter responses. For example, a former Obama special adviser created the "American Dream Movement" as a liberal response to the Tea Party, and that organization soon claimed more than 100,000 members.[619] At its convention, Restoring American Democracy, the party hoped to promote dialogue between liberals and conservatives.[620] Another group, the so-called Coffee Party USA, was also formed in response to the Tea Party.[621] The Coffee Party favored dialogue rather than "slogans and revolutionary flags," and believed that the nation's problems were "too complex to solve by simply slashing taxes and cutting the size of government."[622] The Coffee Party claimed that 500,000

---

614. *Id.*

615. *Id.*

616. *See* Jack Healy, *Hatch Is Tested in Utah, but Tea Party Anger Cools, The New York Times*, Politics (June 25, 2012) ("Recent polls have given Mr. Hatch a double-digit lead over Daniel R. Liljenquist, the former state senator and Tea Party favorite who is his opponent. Mr. Hatch has a commanding cash advantage, raising some $10 million this election cycle compared with Mr. Liljenquist's $800,000. That advantage has allowed Mr. Hatch to spend millions on grass-roots organizing and advertisements trumpeting his political power and conservative credentials.") https://www.nytimes.com/2012/06/26/us/politics/utahs-orrin-hatch-faces-less-anger-from-tea-party-in-primary.html.

617. *See* Paul Kane, *Richard Lugar loses primary nomination to conservative challenger Richard Mourdock, The Washington Post* (May 5, 2012). https://www.washingtonpost.com/politics/richard-lugar-loses-primary-nomination-to-conservative-challenger-richard-mourdock/2012/05/08/gIQANcJjBU_story.html?noredirect=on&utm_term=.0a84e94de123.

618. *See* Dana Bash & Paul Steinhauser, *Citing Partisanship, Maine's Snowe Says She'll Leave the Senate*, CNN Politics (Feb. 28, 2012). https://www.cnn.com/2012/02/28/politics/senate-snowe-retiring/index.html.

619. *See* Guy Raz, *Former Obama Adviser Brews a Different Tea Party*, National Public Radio (July 31, 2011), http://www.npr.org/2011/07/31/138867706/former-obama-adviser-brews-a-different-tea-party.

620. *Id.*

621. *See* Joseph Gerth, *Tea Party Alternative Meets in Louisville: Coffee Party USA Will Hone Message, The Courier-Journal*, at A1 (Sept. 24, 2010).

622. *Id.*

people friended it on the party's Facebook page.[623] The Coffee Party's one agreed-upon platform position involved opposition to the idea of allowing corporations to spend limitless amounts on campaign finance.[624] Consistent with its emphasis on dialogue, the Coffee Party believed that the nation's rhetoric has become angry and mean spirited.[625] However, the Coffee Party seemed to have had less impact than the Tea Party.

The internet has sometimes produced unintended consequences for politicians. For example, Ronald Vitiello, who was chosen by President Trump to head Immigration and Customs Enforcement (ICE), was forced to deal with his prior Twitter posts.[626] In those posts, he had referred to the Democratic Party as the "liberalcratic party of NeoKlanist Party."[627] Senate Democrats grilled him about those statements.[628]

Web-based political and social movements have also had a significant impact on political campaigns. For example, an internet-based challenge by MoveOn.org is widely credited with causing Senator Joseph Lieberman (a former Democratic vice-presidential candidate) to lose his bid for re-nomination to the United States Senate in 2006.[629] Lieberman, who in the view of his critics had failed to adequately oppose the war in Iraq, was challenged from the left in the primary.[630] Although Lieberman lost the primary, he ultimately decided to run in the general election as an Independent.[631] With support from Republicans, who realized that they could not otherwise defeat the Democratic candidate, and who evidently felt that Lieberman was a preferable alternative, Republicans voted for

---

623. *Id.*, at B4.

624. *Id.*, at A1.

625. *Id.*, at B4.

626. *See* Ron Nixon, *Immigration Pick Grilled About Child Detentions And an Insult on Twitter, The New York Times* A14 (Nov. 16, 2018).

627. *Id.*

628. *Id.*

629. *See* Michael Russo, *Are Bloggers Representatives of the News Media Under the Freedom of Information Act?*, 40 Colum. J. L. & Soc. Prob. 225, 225–26 (2006); *Bloggers Seek Candidates, supra* note 1270, at A19.

630. *See id.*

631. *See* William Yardley, *Lieberman Plans Independent Bid if Primary Fails, The New York Times*, at A1 (July 4, 2006).

Lieberman who prevailed in the general election.[632] The net effect was that the internet-based challenge did not oust Lieberman, but did have the effect of shifting Lieberman's political affiliation from Democrat to Independent. Lieberman, who was therefore less beholden to Democratic party interests, endorsed John McCain over Barrack Obama in the 2008 presidential election.[633] Interestingly, in the next election cycle, Lieberman decided not to run for reelection, acknowledging that he would face substantial opposition.[634]

During the contentious battle over whether to seat U.S. Supreme Court nominee Brett Kavanagh, three activists groups (Be A Hero Team, Maine People's Alliance, and Mainers for Accountable Leadership) began raising money in an effort to pressure Maine Senator Susan Collins to vote "no" on Kavanagh.[635] The effort raised more than $3 million, including more than $50,000 that was donated during Collins' announcement regarding her vote.[636] Although Collins did not have an opponent at the time, the money gave potential opponents a strong incentive to challenge Collins.[637] Nevertheless, Senator Collins was easily re-elected.

The Web-based group, Americans Elect, functions entirely online.[638] The group disclaimed any aspiration to organize a new political par-

---

632. *See* Kate Zernike, *Allied with Democrats, Lieberman Easily Aligns with Republicans, The New York Times*, at A18 (Feb. 8, 2007).

633. *See* Liz Holloran, *Sen. Lieberman: Why Should We Toe the Party Line?*, National Public Radio (Jan. 21, 2010), http://www.npr.org/2011/01/21/133095715/sen-lieberman-why-should-we-toe-the-party-line ("I felt at the time that [McCain] was just plain the best prepared to be the president we needed at that time," Lieberman said. "Enjoying the independence I had, as an independent, I did what I thought was best for the country at the time.").

634. *See* Craig Lemoult, *Connecticut Sen. Lieberman Won't Seek Re-Election*, National Public Radio, All Things Considered (Jan. 19, 2011), http://www.npr.org/2011/01/19/133058807/Sen-Lieberman-Wont-Seek-Re-Election.

635. *See* Crystal Hughes, *$3 million Raised for Sen. Susan Collins' Opponent Amid Outcry on Kavanaugh Vote, USA Today* (Oct. 5, 2018). https://www.usatoday.com/story/news/politics/onpolitics/2018/10/05/susan-collins-yes-Kavanagh-leaves-2-million-donated-opponent/1537749002/.

636. *Id.*

637. *Id.*

638. *See* Peter Oversby, *Nonprofit Seeks to Be New Political Force*, National Public Radio (Nov. 2, 2011), http://www.npr.org/2011/11/02/141921051/nonprofit-seeks-to-be-new-political-force.

ty,[639] but it sought to organize a national online political primary.[640] In addition, it posted online questionnaires designed to help voters decide which issues were important to them,[641] and which were designed to help and allow voters to select prospective presidential candidates.[642] In addition, voters could sign-up as "delegates" to Americans Elect.[643] Little was known regarding the sources of Americans Elect's funding.[644]

TikTok, which uses a short video format,[645] has 1 billion users, many of whom are young politicians, particularly Democrats and left-leaning independents, who are using the platform to reach potential voters.[646] For example, Senator Ed Markey (Massachusetts) posted a video showing him making pasta for Rigatoni Day, and he also posted a video about the Green New Deal.[647] In their 2020 campaigns, then senatorial candidates John Fetterman and Jon Ossoff successfully used the platform to reach voters.[648] Representative Tim Ryan wanted to post his views on infrastructure legislation, as well as some of his speeches on the floor of the U.S. House of Representatives.[649] In an effort to encourage potential voters to watch the videos, he played a Taylor Swift song in the background.[650] He viewed the videos as a way to reach "an audience that wasn't watching political talk shows or watching the news."[651] TikTok was also used to target a Trump rally.[652] In an effort to disrupt the rally, anti-Trump individuals

---

639. *Id.*

640. *See* https://www.americanselect.org/.

641. *See Nonprofit Seeks to Be New Political Force, supra* note 638.

642. *Id.*

643. *Id.*

644. *Id.*

645. *See* Meghan Bobrowsky, *Salvador Rodriguez, Sarah E. Needleman & Georgia Wells, TikTok's Stratospheric Rise, The Wall Street Journal* B1 (Nov. 5–6, 2022).

646. *See* Anna F. Kambhampaty, *Trying to Trend, Politicians Take On The TikTok Challenge, The New York Times* 10 (Mar. 20, 2022).

647. *Id.*

648. *See* Anjali Huynh, *Using TikTok, Biden Courts Tough Crowd, The New York Times* A1 (Mar. 27, 2024).

649. *See Trying to Trend, Politicians Take On The TikTok Challenge, supra* note 646, at 10.

650. *Id.*

651. *Id.*

652. *Id.*

requested tickets to the rally.[653] Although more than one million tickets were requested, only 6,200 people showed up.[654]

Kentucky's Senate Democrats, who hold a super-minority in the chamber, have resorted to TikTok as a way to reach out to voters, especially younger voters, and convey their messages.[655] Former state senator Morgan McGarvey, who is now a U.S. Congressman, regularly posted videos on TikTok when he was in Kentucky's Senate.[656] The videos, which showed him lip-synching and dancing, were viewed more than 1 million times, received 147,000 likes, 1,334 comments, and were shared 1,854 times.[657] McGarvey believed that he reached far more potential voters on TikTok than on other social media sites.[658] There were numerous videos created by McGarvey and other Kentucky Senate Democrats which have (in total) received 541,000 likes and 2.4 million views.[659] Kentucky House Democrats have followed their lead and begun posting on TikTok.[660] Climate activists have also used TikTok to reach out.[661] TikTok has also been used by federal politicians. For example, U.S. representatives Alexandria Ocasio-Cortez and Jeff Jackson have built substantial followings on the platform.[662]

Others have used the internet in other ways. For example, Steve Bannon, a former adviser to President Trump, operated a so-called "War Room" where he produced podcasts.[663] These podcasts allowed Bannon to push political issues and politicians that might not receive coverage from more mainstream outlets like Fox News.[664] In addition, Bannon has used the internet to help Republican politicians raise money.[665]

---

653. *Id.*

654. *Id.*

655. *See* Joe Sonka, *State Senate Democrats Are TikTok Stars, The Courier-Journal* 2A (Aug. 17, 2021).

656. *Id.*, at 2A.

657. *Id.*

658. *Id.*

659. *Id.*

660. *Id.*

661. *Id.*

662. *See* Anjali Huynh, *Using TikTok, Biden Courts Tough Crowd, The New York Times* A1 (Mar. 27, 2024).

663. *See* Annie Karni, *In a Cavelike D.C. Studio, Bannon Sows Chaos, The New York Times* A7 & A14 (Oct. 6, 2003).

664. *Id.*

665. *Id.*

3. THE INTERNET IN POLITICAL CAMPAIGNS

The internet has also been used by candidates to fuel political campaigns.[666] Web-based political activism has surfaced on both sides of the political spectrum, and has had a significant impact on political campaigns.

Increasingly, political blogs are being used by candidates to promote their messages,[667] and candidates are working with media groups like *Politico*, *Talking Points Memo* and *Real Clear Politics* to promote blogging regarding their campaigns.[668] In 2012, *Politico* tripled its staff and established a website (2012 Live) related to the campaign.[669] The goal was for the website to function like a blog on a campaign bus.[670]

The big advantage of the internet is that it allows candidates to end-run the media gatekeepers, and take their message directly to their constituents.[671] Individual candidates have accomplished this objective through internet platforms such as Facebook, Twitter and YouTube, and they have also used the internet to organize and rally supporters.[672] Social media also provides a method for a candidate's supporters to articulate and show their support, and help recruit other like-minded individuals.[673]

Social media advocacy is much cheaper for campaigns than buying advertisements on traditional media, and can be targeted at voters in specific electoral districts.[674] Although some question the extent to which social media actually persuades voters to support a particular candidate,[675] noting the existence of candidates who have failed in their efforts to ride social media to victory,[676] the internet seems to correlate to successful political campaigns in that electoral winners often have more Facebook

666. *See How Tweet It Is, supra* note 598.

667. *See* Jeremy W. Peters, *Political Blogs Are Ready to Flood the Campaign Trail, The New York Times*, at A1 (Jan. 30, 2011).

668. *Id.*

669. *Id.*

670. *Id.*

671. *See How Tweet It Is, supra* note 598.

672. *Id.*

673. *Id.*

674. *Id.* ("'In particular, we've seen a real explosion of Facebook advertising, because it's typically relatively cheap and it's very easy to target at residents in a particular district, meaning that you don't waste ads and money.'").

675. *Id.*

676. *Id.*

engagement than their opponents.[677] Of course, a candidate's internet success may have more to do with the candidate him/herself than to the use of social media.

Facebook advertisements played a significant role in the 2018 midterm elections.[678] Some commentators believe that some of the advertisements were "inflammatory and polarizing,"[679] and that Facebook's system tends to reward "extreme messaging" by charging lower rates for advertisements that grab a viewer's attention, and advertisements can be shared by users free of charge.[680] Facebook denies that its criteria encourages inflammatory advertising.[681] However, some commentators do not view Facebook as a vehicle for persuading people to particular political positions, but rather as a mechanism for motivating voters.[682] Facebook has taken steps to ensure that those backing Facebook advertising are more transparent.[683]

In individual elections, social media may have influenced the outcome. In 2006, when Senator George Allen made a disparaging remark to a questioner, a video of the remark was posted on YouTube and used against him in his reelection campaign (which he ultimately lost).[684] Then Republican Senatorial candidate Scott Brown used the internet (as well as a wave of public discontent over President Obama's then pending health care legislation) to win the late Senator Edward M. Kennedy's seat in the United States Senate.[685] Brown's win was shocking given that the seat had

---

677. *Id.*

678. *See* Georgia Wells & Deepa Seetharaman, *Campaign Ads to Flood Facebook, The Wall Street Journal* A4 (Sept. 1–2, 2018).

679. *Id.*

680. *Id.*

681. *Id.*

682. *Id.*

683. *Id.*

684. *See Campaign Ads to Flood Facebook, supra* note 678, at A4 ("In 2006, a YouTube video made by an aide from his Democratic opponent's campaign captured Republican Sen. George Allen of Virginia on the campaign trail referring to that young Indian-American man as 'macaca.' The incident became an embarrassment for Allen and helped cost him re-election.").

685. *See* Frank James, *Republican Scott Brown Wins Kennedy (or People's) Senate Seat*, National Public Radio, The Two Way (Jan. 19, 2010), http://www.npr.org/blogs/thetwo-way/2010/01/republican_scott_brown_wins_ke.html ("In a staggering blow to President Barack Obama and Democrats nationally, Scott Brown, a little known Republican Mas-

been held by Democrats for nearly half-a-century, and given that Massachusetts is very left-leaning.[686] Brown's victory raised substantial concerns for President Obama and the Democrats regarding their ability to enact their legislative platform.[687]

Brown's campaign was enhanced by the internet where he was able to raise a significant amount of money.[688] In addition, Brown used the internet to mobilize grass-roots support, particularly Tea Party support, both inside and outside of the State of Massachusetts.[689] Brown was also aided by support from traditional Republican interests and media advertising.[690] Through these diverse tactics, Brown managed to pull off what could only be regarded as a stunning upset in the bluest of states, and his victory threw President Obama's legislative agenda into disarray.

Another striking example of the internet's impact is illustrated by the campaign of Rand Paul who was elected to a seat in the United States Senate from the Commonwealth of Kentucky. Paul, son of the former Republican Representative and presidential candidate, Ron Paul, aggressively used the internet in his campaign.[691] Paul entered the race after then incumbent U.S. Senator Jim Bunning, a baseball Hall of Famer, was pushed out of the seat by the Republican hierarchy. When Bunning decided to resign, it was widely assumed that Senator Mitch McConnell (the Republican minority leader in the Senate and the senior Senator from Kentucky) intended to replace Bunning with Kentucky Secretary of State Trey Grayson. McConnell did not anticipate that Rand Paul would use internet-based fundrais-

---

sachusetts state senator, won a special election to replace the Democratic icon late Sen. Edward Kennedy.").

686. *Id.* ("The stunning result in a blue state cast doubts on Obama's ability to get his agenda enacted, especially health care reform, and seemed a repudiation, especially by independent voters, of much of what the president has done so far.").

687. *Id.*

688. *See* Madeline Brand, *Dick Armey: Massachusetts Results Not Unique*, National Public Radio, All Things Considered (Jan. 20, 2010), http://www.npr.org/templates/story/story.php?storyId=122777071; *see also* Gwen Ifill, *Browns Senate Victory Endangers Democrats" Agenda*, Public Broadcasting System, The News House (Jan. 20, 2010).

689. *Id.*

690. *See Republican Scott Brown Wins, supra* note 685 ("Brown also got help from the national Republican Party which helped him saturate the airwaves with ads in the final weeks of the campaign. And he raised a lot of money on the Internet, too.").

691. *See* Joseph Gerth, *Paul Takes Lead in Fundraising, The Courier-Journal*, at B1 (Feb. 2, 2010).

ing techniques to gather more campaign donations than Grayson ($1.8 million to $1.7 million, and $652,958 to $443,266 in the fourth quarter of 2009),[692] or that Paul—capitalizing on Tea Party sentiment—would overtake Grayson (once a "prohibitive favorite") in public opinion polls.[693] In a single day, Paul raised more than $400,000.[694] In the run-up to the primary election, Paul led Grayson by 15 to 19 percentage points even though he had never run for public office, and despite the fact that Grayson had won two statewide races.[695] Ultimately, Paul defeated Grayson by a comfortable margin (14 percentage points) in the primary.[696]

Despite the fact that Paul made some controversial remarks during the general election campaign,[697] and even though some difficult issues were raised regarding his past,[698] either of which might have derailed an ordinary candidate, Paul easily defeated his Democratic rival, Attorney

692. *See Id.*; *see also* Joseph Gerth, *Ron Paul Touts Son for Senate in Ky. Visit, The Courier-Journal*, at B4 (Jan. 31, 2010) ("The campaign does most of its fundraising on the Internet instead of using traditional fundraising events.").

693. *See* Joseph Gerth, *Rand Paul: This Year's Political Surprise, The Courier-Journal*, at A1 (Feb. 14, 2010).

694. *See* Roger Alford, *Paul Fundraiser Nets $172,000: Using Father's Online Strategy, The Courier-Journal*, at B5 (June 30, 2010).

695. *See* Joseph Gerth, *Mongiardo, Paul Lead in Senate Primaries; Double-Digit Margins Built on Strong Showings Throughout Kentucky, The Courier-Journal*, at A1 (Mar. 7, 2010); *Id.*, at A1.

696. *See* Ken Rudin, *Rand Paul Is Big Winner in Ky. GOP Senate Primary; Conway Wins*, National Public Radio, It's All Politics (May 18, 2010), http://www.npr.org/blogs/politicaljunkie/2010/05/18/126961563/rand-paul-is-big-winner-in-kentucky-gop-senate-primary-conway-leads-dems.

697. *See* Roger Alford, *Drug-Fight Funding Stance May Cost Paul: He Insists E. Ky. Will Side With Him, The Courier-Journal*, at B1 (Aug. 14, 2010); Joseph Gerth, *Paul Draws Questions From East and West, The Courier-Journal*, Political Notebook, at B1 (July 12, 2010); Ken Rudin, *Rand Paul in Civil Rights Bill Firestorm*, National Public Radio, It's All Politics (May 20, 2010), http://www.npr.org/blogs/politicaljunkie/2010/05/20/127009788/kentucky-gop-unity-rally-on-saturday-mongiardo-d-won-t-seek-recanvass ("[S]upporters of Paul and defeated opponent Trey Grayson, the secretary of state, don't like each other. But right now, Paul seems to have other, more pressing problems. He has gotten himself in a growing controversy over his views about the 1964 Civil Rights Act.").

698. *See* Andrew Wolfson, *Paul Taps Anti-Washington Fervor: Republican's Limited-Government Message Resonates with Voters, The Courier-Journal*, A1 (Oct. 17, 2010) (Paul's campaign was potentially complicated by the fact he had belonged to a society in college that was sacrilegious and blasphemous—a potentially difficult complication in a religiously conservative state).

General Jack Conway.[699] Conway had raised more money than Paul at one point,[700] although some of that money involved a personal loan to his own campaign.[701] Paul used both traditional and online fundraising techniques to raise a substantial amount of campaign funds.[702] Despite Conway's loans to himself, Rand Paul was still able to outspend Conway.[703]

Almost immediately following the primaries, Paul jumped to an early lead in public opinion polls,[704] and he continued to lead throughout the general election campaign, despite aggressive opposition from the Louisville newspaper, *The Courier-Journal.*[705] Paul ultimately defeated Conway by 12 percentage points.[706] Part of that gap may have been created by Conway's aggressive and negative advertising that may have alienated voters[707] and that lowered Conway's public approval ratings.[708] Conway may have been motivated to air those advertisements because he was trailing in public opinion polls.

As noted, the Tea Party aggressively used the internet in political campaigns, but Tea Party support for political campaigns did not always

---

699. *See The New York Times*, Election 2010, Election Results, Kentucky, at p. 96 (Nov. 3, 2010) (showing that Paul defeated Conway by 56% to 44%).

700. *See* Joseph Gerth, *Conway War Chest Nearly Twice the Size of Paul's: Democratic U.S. Senate Candidate Reports $703,013, The Courier-Journal*, at B1 (July 16, 2010).

701. *See* Joseph Gerth, *Conway Raised $1.4 Million in Last Quarter: He Surpassed Paul, But Total Includes $400,000 Loan to Self, The Courier-Journal*, at B1 (July 14, 2010).

702. *See Paul Fundraiser Nets $172,000, supra* note 694.

703. *See* Bruce Schreiner, *Rand Paul Spent $7.5 Million to Win Senate Seat, The Courier-Journal*, at B3 (Dec. 12, 2010).

704. *Rand Paul Leads Jack Conway in Kentucky Senate Race, The Courier-Journal*, A1 (May 29, 2010).

705. *See* James R. Carroll, *Conway's Potential Was Seen Early: Mentors Urged Him to Run for Office, The Courier-Journal*, at A1 (Oct. 10, 2010: Andrew Wolfson, *Rand Paul Has Long History of Controversial Views, The Courier-Journal* (Jun. 17, 2010).

706. *See* Joseph Gerth, *Paul Win Sends a Message: Part of GOP Wave, He Champions Small Government, Few Business Limits, The Courier-Journal*, K3 (Nov. 3, 2010) (showing that Paul amassed 751,664 votes (56%) to Conway's 597,685 votes (44%).

707. *See* Renee Montagne, *Kentucky Senate Race Heats Up Over Attack Ad*, National Public Radio, Morning Edition (Oct. 20, 2010), http://www.npr.org/templates/story/story.php?storyId=130690590.

708. *See* Real Clear Politics, Kentucky Senate—Paul v. Conway (showing that, following the airing of Conway's attack advertisements, Paul's lead expanded to double digits in some polls, and double digits in other polls), http://www.realclearpolitics.com/epolls/2010/senate/ky/kentucky_senate_paul_vs_conway-1148.html.

produce winning candidates.[709] In Delaware, Christine O'Donnell, a Tea Party candidate, pulled off a stunning upset in the Republican primary against a more establishment Republican candidate,[710] but then proceeded to make a number of gaffes in the general election campaign,[711] and lost the election by double digits.[712] Likewise, in Nevada, Sharon Angle rode the Tea Party movement to victory in the GOP primary,[713] but then lost the general election to Senate Majority Leader Harry Reid who was regarded as highly vulnerable.[714]

However, the internet has helped some candidates achieve victory. Allen West, a then Republican candidate for the U.S. House of Representatives from Florida, aggressively used the internet in his campaign. He posted a YouTube video in which he complained about the "tyranny" of the federal government,[715] and he urged citizens to "get your musket, fix your bayonet."[716] Although Democratic opposition researchers hoped

709. *See* Don Gonyea, *Tea Party Favorite Upsets Del. GOP Senate Primary*, National Public Radio, Morning Edition (Sept. 15, 2010), http://www.npr.org/templates/story/story.php?storyId=129874286 ("Virtually unknown a month ago, Christine O'Donnell rode a surge of support from Tea Party activists to victory in Delaware's Republican Senate primary Tuesday night. The results deal yet another setback to the GOP establishment in a campaign season full of them.").

710. *See id.*

711. *See* Frank James, *Christine O'Donnell Stuns Audience with 1st Amendment Gaffe*, National Public Radio, It's All Politics (Oct. 19, 2010), http://www.npr.org/blogs/itsallpolitics/2010/10/19/130671265/christine-o-donnell-stuns-crowd-with-1st-amendment-ignorance.

712. *See* Frank James, *Chris Coons Defeats Christine O'Donnell in Delaware: CNN, AP*, National Public Radio, It's All Politics (Nov. 2, 2010), http://www.npr.org/blogs/itsallpolitics/2010/11/02/131023701/chris-coons-defeats-christine-o-donnell-in-delaware-cnn.

713. *See* Ken Rudin, *A Super Tuesday for Women Nationwide*, National Public Radio, It's All Politics (June 9, 2010), http://www.npr.org/blogs/politicaljunkie/2010/06/08/127583381/super-tuesday-for-women?print=1.

714. *See* Carrie Johnson, *SENATE: Democrats Retain Control Amid GOP Gains* (Nov. 3, 2010). http://www.npr.org/templates/story/story.php?storyId=131020739.

715. *See* Kate Zernike, *For G.O.P., Tea Party Wields Double-Edged Sword, The New York Times*, at A11 (Sept. 6, 2010).

716. *Id.*

to use West's statements against him,[717] he nonetheless prevailed in the general election.[718]

Of course, the Web can be both beneficial and risky for politicians and political candidates. Former New York congressman Anthony Weiner, who used Twitter effectively to attack others,[719] was forced to resign his seat[720] after it became known that he used his Twitter account to send sexually suggestive Tweets to a college student.[721] Also in New York, although candidate Mark Cenedella, a candidate for the state Senate—who appeared to be a very promising candidate (Ivy-league credentials, successful businessman, and the ability to put substantial resources into his races)[722]—found that the internet undermined his campaign. His campaign was hampered by postings under his name on a Website,[723] with titles such as "Sexy vs. Shanky," "Dating Advice for Girly Girls," "He Stole My Weed," and "High Quality Dope."[724] The candidate denied that the postings came from him.[725]

Candidates increasingly have also used email in their campaigns. For example, House Speaker Mike Johnson used emails to raise money for Republican campaigns.[726] He sent an email complaining about the "radical left" which he claimed was engaged in a "coordinated" and "preplanned"

717. *Id.*

718. *See* Jennifer Steinhauer, *Allen West to Switch Districts, The New York Times* (Jan. 31, 2012) (blog), http://thecaucus.blogs.nytimes.com/2012/01/31/allen-west-to-switch-districts/?scp=1&sq=allen%20west%20florida&st=cse.

719. *See* Ashley Parker, Congressman, *Sharp Voice on Twitter, Finds It Can Cut 2 Ways, The New York Times* A18 (May 31, 2011).

720. *See* Steve Inskeep, *Scandal Forces Rep. Anthony Weiner to Leave Office*, National Public Radio, Morning Edition (June 17, 2011), http://www.npr.org/2011/06/17/137241349/scandal-forces-rep-anthony-weiner-to-leave-office.

721. *Id.; See also* Anthony Weiner, *The Audacity of the Dalliance*, National Public Radio, It's All Politics (June 7, 2011), http://www.npr.org/blogs/itsallpolitics/2011/06/07/137028441/anthony-weiner-the-audacity-of-the-dalliance.

722. *See* Raymond Hernandez, *Under the Name of a Senate Hopeful, Blog Posts on Sex and Drugs, The New York Times*, at A15 (Jan. 23, 2012).

723. *Id.*

724. *Id.*

725. *Id.*

726. Email from House Speaker Mike Johnson sent through proudrep.com (Nov. 6, 2023).

attack against him.[727] Email campaigns have also gotten increasingly creative. For example, Congressman Andy Barr sent out an email entitled "I'm Just a Dad."[728] In that email, he shows a picture of himself with his two daughters, explains that he takes his family "to church on Sundays and make sure my daughters get to school on time," but that he is being "buried" in fundraising and needs help (in the form of donations). Congresswoman Michelle Steel sent out a fundraising email entitled "This is my promise to you" in which she touts her background as a Korean woman and claimed that she is "a mom, wife, immigrant, Conservative, and Biden's TOP target."[729]

Campaigns now routinely use text messaging.[730] In the 2018 mid-term election cycle, political candidates sent text messages to potential supporters asking for their votes.[731]In Tennessee, voters received text messages that attacked two Republican candidates for governor.[732] It is unclear whether these messages were sent by a messaging app or in another way.[733] Candidates have also begun sending personalized campaign text messages to the phones of potential voters.[734] Both Democrats and Republicans are texting through mass messaging apps.[735]

Of course, the use of text messages in political campaigns is not entirely new. Barrack Obama announced his vice-presidential candidate by text message, and both Hillary Clinton and Donald Trump used text messages "to raise money, promote local events and get voters to the poll."[736] What is new is that political candidates are aggressively using text messaging to avoid crowded social media platforms and crowded email in boxes.[737] As a result, by 2022, candidates were flooding potential supporters and

727. Email from House Speaker Mike Johnson sent through "proud rep" (Nov. 7, 2023).

728. Email from proudrep.com (Nov. 12,2023).

729. Email from Congresswoman Michelle Steel sent thought "proudrep" (Nov.7, 2023).

730. *See* Kevin Roose, *Candidates Enter The Texting Era With a Plea: Will U Vote 4 Me? The New York Times* B4 (Aug. 2, 2018).

731. *Id.*, at B1.

732. *Id.*

733. *Id.*

734. *Id.*

735. *Id.*

736. *Id.*

737. *Id.* at B4.

donors with text messages.[738] They were able to do so because the laws prohibiting robocalls don't apply to text messages.[739] In October, 2022, some 1.29 billion political text messages were sent, and many contained language suggesting that the situation was urgent.[740] Many included divisive or deceptive content.[741]

Text messaging is advantageous for candidates because it allows them to "carry on thousands of individual text conversations, keep track of replies and answer questions from voters in real time."[742] While bulk text messaging may be prohibited, so-called "peer-to-peer texts" are unregulated.[743] These texts are sent individually even though a program automates the process of selecting the recipient, fills in the message with pre-prepared texts, and requires the sender only to push the send button.[744] Once sent, the text can lead to a two-way communication between the campaign and the text recipient.[745] Individual candidates have used these systems to send millions of text messages to constituents.[746]

Campaigns can also use text messaging apps to inform voters regarding their polling places, and to help "get out the vote."[747] While text messaging systems are not free (frequently charging between 10 cents and 30 cents per message), they are cheaper and more effective than printed mailers, and they produce an 8% higher rate of campaign donations.[748] However, some recipients are offended when they receive unsolicited campaign messages.[749]

There are two apps, VoteWithMe and OutVote, that allow individuals to determine whether their friends have voted, and lets them encourage

---

738. *See* Natasha Singer, *Political Texts Gone Wild, The New York Times* B1 (Nov. 7, 2022).

739. *Id.*

740. *Id.*

741. *Id.*

742. *See Candidates Enter The Texting Era With a Plea: Will U Vote 4 Me?, supra* note 730, at B4.

743. *Id.*

744. *Id.*

745. *Id.*

746. *Id.*

747. *Id.*

748. *Id.*

749. *Id.*

the friends to vote.[750] These apps access governmental voting records, repackage the information for viewing through apps,[751] and enable individuals to send text messages to friends with words of encouragement (*e.g.*, "You gonna vote?").[752] In addition, the apps can be used to enlist individuals to encourage others to vote *(e.g.*, be sending the message "I know you're gonna vote on November 6 DUH, but make sure to remind your friends too!").[753] Some believe that the apps create social pressure to vote because they reveal whether an individual has or has not voted, and social science data suggests that individuals are more likely to vote when they feel that they are being observed by family, friends or neighbors.[754]

Exhortations to vote may have particular force when they come from someone who knows that the recipient failed to vote in the prior election.[755] However, there is no clear evidence regarding a correlation between the app's messages and voting behavior.[756] VoteWithMe, which favors Democratic candidates, has presets which reveal likely Democratic voters.[757] In order to see the voting preferences of other individuals, the user must change the settings.[758] However, some apps are non-partisan.[759]

Republicans have created uCampaign which involves multiple apps designed to promote interaction between conservatives.[760] These apps allow candidates to collect various types of information from their supporters, including their names, addresses, phone numbers and email addresses.[761] The system can also collect information regarding a user's friends, and can ask users to provide information allowing their friends

---

750. *See* Natasha Singer, *Did Your Friends Vote? Apps Check Their Records and Offer Reminders, The New York Times* A21 (Nov. 5, 2018).

751. *Id.*

752. *Id.*

753. *Id.*

754. *Id.*

755. *Id.*

756. *Id.*

757. *Id.*

758. *Id.*

759. *Id.*

760. *See* Natasha Singer & Nicholas Confessore, *Let's Talk Politics, No Liberals Allowed, Conservative Apps Build Networks Unhindered By Social Media Giants, The New York Times* B3 (Oct. 22, 2018).

761. *Id.*

to be contacted.[762] uCampaign led to RumbleUp, a peer-to-peer texting program for conservative campaigns.[763]

Internet techniques have led to a high level of engagement between candidates and potential voters. During the 2018 elections, Democrats, especially Democrats running for seats in the House of Representatives, enjoyed a sizeable lead in terms of voter engagement on platforms such as Facebook and Instagram (15.1 million interactions for Democrats versus 5.4 million interactions for Republicans).[764] While Instagram has younger and more politically-involved participants, Facebook users tend to be older, more rural, and less educated.[765] Some believe that this higher level of Democratic engagement is directly attributable to a significant increase in small dollar donations to Democratic candidates which "allowed them to spend more on digital campaigning and advertising."[766]

Democratic engagement may have been more focused on prominent Democratic candidates.[767] Some 86% of Democratic interactions on Facebook, and 92% of Instagram interactions, involved prominent politicians such as Elizabeth Warren, Bernie Sanders and Beto O'Rourke (O'Rourke had more than 600,000 followers on Facebook and Twitter, and another 250,000 on Instagram).[768] Each of those politicians had personas "which are punchy, passionate and tailor-made to resonate with fired-up progressive audiences online," and they have "dedicated digital staff members and sophisticated tools to create custom content and test various messages for impact."[769] Smaller campaigns often have much smaller resources at their disposal,[770] and the Democrats' advantage over Republicans did not exist there (although an 8% Democratic advantage still remained).[771]

---

762. *Id.*

763. *Id.*

764. *Id.*

765. *See* Kevin Roose & Kevin Collins, *Who's Winning the Social Media Midterms? Sizeable Lead for Democrats in Engagement With Voters, The New York Times* A14 (Oct. 20, 2018).

766. *Id.*

767. *Id.*

768. *Id.*

769. *Id.*

770. *Id.*

771. *Id.*

It is not clear how much significance should be attributed to social media interactions. While most candidates recognize that social media engagement is absolutely necessary in an internet era, because it produces "more eyeballs than anywhere else," the data on engagement is potentially misleading for a variety of reasons. For one thing, at one point, it was possible to "buy" Twitter followers.[772] In addition, negative comments left on a candidate's website can be treated as voter "engagement" even though it is unlikely that the critic will vote for that candidate.[773] Nevertheless, social media interactions can provide an indication of the level of a candidate's support,[774] but do not guarantee victory. Despite his huge following on social media, Beto O'Rourke lost his bid to upset Senator Ted Cruz.[775]

The data on social media interactions shows that Democrats have generally been more effective on Instagram while Republicans have been more effective on Facebook.[776] In addition, in some hotly-contested races, Republicans have fared better than Democrats.[777] For example, even though Georgia Democratic gubernatorial candidate Stacey Abrams had more Facebook followers, her opponent, Republican candidate Brian Kemp, had more interactions.[778]

In the 2020 elections, Facebook advertisements played a significant role.[779] A political activist and commentator posted her views on George Floyd.[780] That post was viewed 80 million times.[781] A Democrat who was challenging Senator Lindsey Graham spent $500,000 on Facebook advertisements over a 7-day period.[782] In addition, the Congressional Black

---

772. *See* Nicholas Confessore, Gabriel J.X. Dance & Rich Harris, *A Twitter Purge? Followers Abruptly Exit, The New York Times* B1 (Feb. 1, 2018).

773. *See Who's Winning the Social Media Midterms?, supra* note 765, at A14.

774. *Id.*

775. *Id.*

776. *Id.*

777. *Id.*

778. *Id.*

779. *See* Shane Goldmacher, *Biden Spends Millions on Facebook Ads, Far Eclipsing Trump's Record, The New York Times* A13 (June 9, 2020).

780. *Id.*

781. *Id.*

782. *Id.*

Caucus PAC spent $222,000 on Facebook ads in an effort to further the challenge to Graham.[783]

An increase in Republican social media interactions was particularly evident following the Kavanagh confirmation hearings when Republican social media interactions increased by 64%, and by 94% in the most tightly contested U.S. Senate races.[784] Tennessee Republican senatorial candidate Marsha Blackburn had 77,000 more interactions than her Democratic opponent against whom she ultimately prevailed.[785] Before the Kavanagh hearings, Republican senatorial candidate Mike Braun was trailing his opponent in interactions, but that changed following the hearings, and Braun ultimately unseated Donnelly.[786]

So-called "viral" video clips are increasingly being used by activists to influence the outcome of political campaigns.[787] The liberal organization, Media Matters for America, combs through media streams looking for statements that they can call out as absurd, and its blog posts are sometimes viewed millions of times.[788] Likewise for the right which has NewsBusters and @RNCResearch which have also attracted millions of views.[789] Some of these so-called "clippers" (because they "clip" and replay video) sometimes omit crucial facts in their presentations.

Following the election of Joe Biden as President in 2020, online posters believed that the election had been stolen.[790] As a result, one twenty-year-old started a Facebook group entitled Win the Win with the goal of overturning the election results.[791] He quickly obtained 440 comments and 1,500 likes, and 60,000 followers.[792]

---

783. *Id.*

784. *Id.*

785. *Id.*

786. *Id.*

787. *See* Simon J. Levien, *How Viral Clips Became Campaign Currency, The New York Times* A12 (June 24, 2024).

788. *Id.*

789. *Id.*

790. *See* Stuart A. Thompson & Charlie Warzel, *How Facebook Incubated the Insurrection, The New York Times* A2 (Jan. 17, 2021).

791. *Id.*

792. *Id.*

The January 6th Capitol rioters also made extensive use of social media,[793] vowing on Facebook to prevent Congress from certifying Joe Biden's 2020 election victory.[794] Some rioters announced in advance of Jan. 6th that they would be at the Capitol, and one even declared that "chaos is coming."[795] Indeed, they communicated so much on social media that the prosecution was able to cull their social media accounts in order to convict them for break-ins at the Capitol, or to seek enhanced sentences.[796] One individual hosted a Facebook group with 61,000 members.[797]

The internet can also be used to undercut the political process by spreading disinformation.[798] For example, in the 2016 election, one man tried to trick Democratic voters into believing that they could cast their votes by text messages on their phones rather than by going to the polls.[799] At least 4,900 voters tried to text vote for presidential candidate Hillary Clinton.[800] The man was criminally charged under a civil rights law.[801]

4. THE INTERNET AND PRESIDENTIAL POLITICS

The internet has also revolutionized presidential politics. Historically, presidential campaigns have been heavily influenced and controlled by media gatekeepers. For minor candidates, the political trail has often been harsh and treacherous. Not only do minor candidates face difficulties generating enough money to be competitive, they are frequently refused admission to presidential debates, and rarely attract sufficient media coverage to be competitive with major party candidates.

The internet has significantly altered this equation. The first signs of change came with Senator John McCain's 2000 presidential campaign.

---

793. *See* Michael Kunzelman, *Social Media Haunts Jan. 6 Rioters, The Courier-Journal* 15 A (Dec. 12, 2021).

794. *See* Alan Suderman & Joshua Goodman, *Facebook Had Its Own Insurrection Jan. 6, Courier-Journal* 15A (Oct. 24, 2021).

795. *See Social media haunts Jan. 6 rioters, supra* note 793, at A15.

796. *Id.*; see also Elizabeth Williamson, *Star Witnesses Against Rioters: Their Online Boasts, The New York Times* A16 (Apr. 7, 2021).

797. *See How Facebook Incubated the Insurrection, supra* note 790, at 2.

798. *See* Nicole Hong, *Twitter Troll Is Charged With Fooling 2016 Voters, The New York Times* A22 (Jan. 28, 2021).

799. *Id.*

800. *Id.*

801. *Id.*

Although McCain did not succeed in that campaign, he used the internet to enlist 142,000 volunteers and raise $6.4 million.[802] In that same election cycle, other candidates also tried to harness the internet in their campaigns, including Representative Richard Gephardt, Senator Joseph Lieberman,[803] Senator John Kerry and Senator John Edwards.[804] One internet-based group even tried to lure a noncandidate, General Wesley Clark, into the presidential race.[805]

Internet usage accelerated in 2003, and began to reshape presidential politics, with Howard Dean's unsuccessful presidential campaign. Dean created 89 Web sites and 326 online discussion groups, including two in Spanish, and he also employed the blogosphere.[806] Through these techniques, Dean managed to raise significant amounts of money over the internet—$2 million in eight days, and one-half of his $7.5 million total campaign funds during a single quarter.[807] In addition, Dean aggressively used the internet to attract tens of thousands of supporters to his campaign,[808] to coordinate in-person meetings through the internet,[809] and to appear at multiple campaign gatherings simultaneously through video

802. *See* Terence Smith, *Harnessing the Power of the Web*, PBS News Hour (Aug. 5, 2003) http://www.pbs.org/newshour/bb/media/july-dec03/internetpolitics_8-5.html.

803. *See id.* ("For example, on the campaign site of Congressman Dick Gephardt, there is an appeal to Spanish-speaking voters. Senator Joe Lieberman's site utilizes video, including a diary from the campaign which the candidate narrates.").

804. *See id.* ("Senator John Kerry's features 'virtual precincts,' where supporters can trade information and organize their friends to vote for Kerry, while Senator John Edwards features his schedule, so people can see where he's going and what he's doing; Senator Bob Graham does the same.").

805. *See id.*

806. *See id.*

807. *See id.*

808. *See id.* ("The self-appointed political elite—pundits, the media, and insiders from both major parties—never anticipated the former Vermont governor could attract such early national attention. But he has, largely by computer-assisted grassroots organizing and fund-raising. Once a month, his campaign promotes what it calls 'meet-ups' online. The concept is simple: The Dean campaign uses the Web site Meetup.com, which organizes groups of people with similar interests, from poodles to politics.").

809. *See id.* ("Generated by the Internet, these 'smart mobs,' as they're coming to be known, gather at a designated place. On this night, some Dean supporters meet up at the University of Iowa in Iowa City, and at a Cajun restaurant in Denver, and in 310 other cities across the country.").

connections.[810] Dean also leveraged his campaign by enlisting supporters who used their own e-mail lists to disseminate his message.[811] Even though Dean lost, the internet allowed him to build a sense of cohesion among his supporters,[812] and proved that internet-based techniques could powerfully influence the political process.

Perhaps the most dramatic illustration of the power of the internet was President Obama's 2008 campaign for the presidency. Obama's staff was more technologically savvy than the staff of previous campaigns and skillfully used text messaging[813] and internet fundraising techniques to propel his campaign effort,[814] as well as to connect with and mobilize voters.[815] At one point, Obama tried to raise a million dollars in a single minute.[816] During a single month, he was able to raise $150 million,[817] and overall he raised nearly three-quarters of a billion dollars for his campaign.[818]

Without the internet, it is difficult to believe that candidate Obama could have defeated then Senator Hillary Rodham Clinton, his rival for the Democratic nomination. When the primary race began, Clinton held

---

810. *See id.*

811. *See id.*

812. *See id.*

813. *See* http://www.sfgate.com/cgi-bin/article.cgi?f=/n/a/2008/08/20/politics/p003612D15.DTL&hw=tv&sn=056&sc=212; http://www.youtube.com/watch?v=OOX-6I0Zj4E.

814. *See* James R. Carroll, *"Game Change" Insightful and Lively*, *The Courier-Journal*, Forum Section, A7 (Jan. 30, 2010) ("Under the radar, the [Obama] campaign was raising money off the Web with ferocity—positioning Obama to capitalize on his victories while Clinton scrambled to keep up."); Michael Luo, *Obama's September Success Recasts the Fund-raising Landscape*, *The New York Times*, at A21 (Oct. 20, 2008); *see also* Michael Luo, *Small Online Contributions Add Up to Huge Fund-Raising Edge for Obama*, *The New York Times*, Feb. 20, 2008, at A18; Michael Luo & Jeff Zeleny, *Reversing Stand, Obama Declines Public Financing*, *The New York Times*, at A1 (Jun. 20, 2008).

815. *See* Darlene Superville, *Obama Turns to YouTube Event*, *The Courier-Journal*, at A6 (Feb. 2, 2010).

816. *See "Obama Minute" Looks to Raise a Million in a Minute,* National Public Radio, The NPR News Blog (April 21, 2008).

817. *See Small Online Contributions Add Up*, *supra* note 814, at A18; Peter Overby, *Obama Raises Stunning $150 Million in September*, National Public Radio (Oct. 19, 2008), http://www.npr.org/templates/story/story.php?storyId=95876276.

818. *See* Peter Overby, *Could Big Donors Break Obama's Fundraising Record?*, National Public Radio (Nov. 7, 2009), http://www.npr.org/templates/story/story.php?storyId=120191096.

significant advantages over Obama.[819] With a former President as her spouse, Clinton had obtained major financial donations from prominent Democratic supporters, and was able to garner major endorsements.[820] Obama, who aggressively used the internet, was able to overcome Clinton's advantages, to create his own advantages, and ultimately to prevail in the primary campaign.

Although Obama was able to attract large donors,[821] his campaign was propelled by small donations gathered over the internet. These small donations provided Obama with a significant advantage over Clinton.[822] She was more dependent on "large" donors with nearly half of her donors reaching their maximum permissible contribution levels.[823] The result was that Obama ultimately raised three times as much money as Clinton.[824] Given the significant headwind facing Republican candidates in that election cycle (*e.g.*, an unpopular incumbent President, a severe economic recession, and wars in Iraq and Afghanistan), had it not been for the internet, Hillary Clinton might well have become the first female President of the United States.

The internet also influenced the outcome of the 2008 general election campaign. As during the primaries, Obama relied heavily on the internet in his general election campaign, especially on social media.[825] In addition to using Facebook and Twitter, he also used text messages and

---

819. *See* David K. Kirkpatrick, *Clinton Campaign Shows Fundraising Edge*, *The New York Times*, at A18 (Apr. 2, 2007).

820. *See Clinton Exceeds Obama in Summer Fundraising*, National Public Radio (Oct. 2, 2007), http://www.npr.org/templates/story/story.php?storyId=14898146 ("Hillary Rodham Clinton outpaced all of her rivals for the Democratic presidential nomination by raising $22 million this summer for her primary campaign, reporting more new donors than even Barack Obama.").

821. *Id.*

822. Peter Overby, *Presidential Fundraising: 2003 x 2*, NPR News Blog, National Public Radio (Feb. 12, 2008).

823. *Id.*

824. *See Obama Out-Fundraises Clinton 3-1 in Indiana in March*, National Public Radio, NPR News Blog (April 22, 2008).

825. *See* Ari Shapiro, *Obama No Longer Leads the Pack on Social Media*, National Public Radio, All Things Considered (Jan. 26, 2011), http://www.npr.org/search/index.php?searchinput=obama+no+longer+leads+the+pack&tabId=all&dateId=0&programId=0&topicId=0.

YouTube.[826] More importantly, because of Obama's internet fundraising prowess, candidate Obama was able to dramatically outspend his Republican Challenger John McCain who agreed to accept public financing for his campaign, faced spending limits and was ultimately able to spend only about $84 million on his campaign.[827] Obama rejected public financing and raised hundreds of millions of dollars for his campaign.[828] Indeed, Obama was able to raise more than had ever been raised in a single month, and he raised more than $750 million during the course of the campaign.[829] Indeed, when the campaign ended, Obama had unspent money.[830]

Obama's fundraising prowess provided him with a huge financial advantage during the general election campaign. Because of that advantage, Obama was able "to overwhelm the McCain campaign with a flood of advertising."[831] As one observer noted, Obama was able to promote his campaign "not only in old-school venues such as television and Web sites," but also in "innovative spaces such as video games" and he even "purchased a 30-minute time slot on several networks to air an infomercial."[832] Obama was able to "meet McCain's negative ads one for one," and to "run positive advertising as well."[833] Obama's fundraising advantages also allowed him to maintain substantial campaign networks in every state, even states that might have been regarded as unwinnable for him,[834]

---

826. *See id.*

827. *See Public Funding on the Ropes, The New York Times*, at A20 (June 20, 2008); Peter Overby, *Obama's Fundraising Skyrockets After Slow May*, National Public Radio (July 17, 2008), http://www.npr.org/templates/story/story.php?storyId=92627339; Peter Overby & Renee Montagne, *Obama Campaign Shatters Fundraising Record*, National Public Radio (Dec. 5, 2008), http://www.npr.org/templates/story/story.php?storyId=97843649.

828. *Id.*; *see also* Peter Overby, *Obama Finished Campaign With Money to Spare*, National Public Radio, All Things Considered (Dec. 5, 2008) http://www.npr.org/templates/story/story.php?storyId=97877948; Linton Weeks, *Did Obama Kill Public Campaign Finance?*, National Public Radio (Oct. 22, 2008), http://www.npr.org/templates/story/story.php?storyId=97877948.

829. *See Obama Hauls in Record $750 Million, supra* note 602.

830. *See Obama Finished Campaign With Money to Spare, supra* note 828.

831. *See id.*

832. *See id.*

833. *See id.*

834. *See Did Obama Kill Public Campaign Finance, supra* note 828.

and also allowed him to bolster his on site networks in every state.[835] In the final analysis, Obama's fundraising gave him the opportunity to maintain "a vast grass-roots organizations and run several TV ads for every one run by McCain.[836] A striking example of the effect of Obama's money was his ability to capture the State of Indiana which had previously been regarded as a reliably "red" state.[837] Obama achieved that objective by literally "flooding" Indiana with television advertisements and campaign workers.[838] Interestingly, in the 2010 congressional elections, Indiana returned to its Republican roots.[839]

In what was a relatively tight popular vote (even though the electoral vote was a "landslide"),[840] it is difficult to believe that Obama's $8 to $1 financial advantage over McCain did not play a significant role in deciding the election. One cannot begrudge Obama the additional funds since much of his money came from small donors.[841] Indeed, the campaign generated more than 6,000 new donors in a single month, each of which gave

---

835. *See id.* ("While McCain is pulling out of states such as Michigan that he sees as unwinnable, Obama's money allows him to wade into states such as Utah and West Virginia that Democrats heretofore had considered to be lost causes. At the same time, Obama is bolstering his organization in traditionally Republican strongholds where the race has narrowed this year, such as Missouri, Virginia and North Carolina.").

836. *See id.*

837. *See Could Big Donors Break Obama's Fundraising Record, supra* note 818.

838. *See id.* ("Just one example: Indiana, a state that had been reliably Republican until 2008. State Republican Chairman Murray Clark was staggered by what the Obama money was able to buy—TV ads and campaign workers flooding his state. 'I hate to keep going back to money,' he told NPR in October of 2008. 'But I think it's hard for campaign and political veterans to fathom what kind of money the Obama campaign has.'").

839. *See* Carrie Johnson, *supra* note 714 ("Republicans picked up six seats—in Indiana, Illinois, Arkansas, North Dakota, Pennsylvania and Wisconsin. And they held on in several other races with strong showings from a few candidates with strong ties to the Tea Party."); *see also* Don Gonyea, *Obama Slips in Indiana, Site of 2008 Upset Win*, National Public Radio, Morning Edition (Jan. 20, 2010), http://www.npr.org/templates/story/story.php?storyId=122730741.

840. *See* CNN Election Center 2008 (Obama-Biden received 53% of the popular vote to McCain-Palin's 46%). http://www.cnn.com/ELECTION/2008/results/president/ The variance of seven percent of the popular vote is relatively small given the fundraising discrepancy.

841. *See* Overby & Montagne, *supra* note 827 ("[Obama] got small donors on the Internet like no one has ever seen before."); Weeks, *Did Obama Kill Public Campaign Finance?*, *supra* note 828.

less than $100 each, and each of which was prohibited from giving more than $2,300.[842] In other words, the donations reflected the campaign's popular appeal.[843]

In the 2008 election cycle, the internet also played a role in other presidential campaigns. For example, Republican presidential candidate Ron Paul effectively used the internet in his unsuccessful campaign for the Republican nomination for President.[844] Using YouTube, Paul generated seven million clicks,[845] and he used other internet-based techniques to attract a significant level of excitement to his effort.[846] Like Obama, Paul was able to raise significant amounts of money over the internet, and he surprised everyone when he was able to raise $4.2 million in a single day.[847] He later followed that effort by raising $10 million on another

842. *See id.* ("The Obama campaign reports it had 632,000 new donors in September, and the average gift was less than $100.").

843. *See id.* ("In an essay titled, 'Money in the 2008 Presidential Elections: A Collapse of the Campaign Finance Regime?' Thomas E. Mann of the Brookings Institution [who notes] the rise in the number of small donors, investments in grass-roots campaigning, and 'signs that suggest fundraising is more an indicator than a cause of interest, energy, and electoral appeal,' he writes.").

844. *See* Katharine Q. Seelye & Leslie Wayne, *The Web Finds Its Man, and Takes Him for a Ride*, *The New York Times*, at A30 (Nov. 11, 2007).

845. *See* http://www.npr.org/blogs/ombudsman/2008/01/is_npr_ignoring_ron_paul.html.

846. *See* Seelye & Wayne, *supra* note 844 ("If his [Ron Paul's] campaign had taken place in the pre-Internet era, it might have gone the way of his 1988 Libertarian campaign for president, as a footnote to history. But because of the Internet's low-cost ability to connect grass-roots supporters with one another—in this case, largely iconoclastic white men—Mr. Paul's once-solo quest has taken on a life of its own. It is evolving from a figment of cyberspace into a traditional campaign, with yard signs, direct mail and old-fashioned rallies, like one here on Saturday attended by a few thousand people under cold, gray skies.").

847. *See* Leslie Wayne, *Ron Paul's Tight-Fisted Campaign,*, *The New York Times*, The Caucus (blog) (Nov. 20, 2007), http://thecaucus.blogs.nytimes.com/2007/11/20/ron-pauls-tight-fisted-campaign/?scp=1&sq=ron%20paul%204.2%20million%20day&st=cse.

day,[848] and $6 million on a third day.[849] Paul referred to the internet as "a strong political equalizer."[850]

As the Lieberman, Obama, and Paul examples suggest, the internet has the potential to reshape the nature of public debate and political campaigns, but it is not clear whether the internet is actually reshaping political opinion as opposed to simply giving campaigns the ability to connect with like-minded voters. Some commentators argue that Obama's fundraising prowess was a dramatic exception to ordinary fundraising rules, that Obama was simply "riding a wave,"[851] and that future candidates might find it difficult to replicate his success.[852] Indeed, some commentators questioned whether Obama himself would be able to repeat his fundraising success when he ran for reelection in 2012.[853]

Following the 2008 campaign, there were reasons to question whether internet-based fundraising techniques would reshape future presidential elections campaigns. If future candidates believed that they could raise significant amounts of money through the internet, they might follow Obama's lead (from the 2008 presidential campaign) and opt out of federal election funding. Indeed, given the huge funding disparities between

848. *Id.* ("How much the Paul campaign had snowballed on the Internet became evident last week when supporters independent of the campaign raised $4 million online and an additional $200,000 over the phone in a single day, a record among this year's Republican candidates.").

849. *Ron Paul Raises $6 Million in a 24-Hour Period*, National Public Radio, The NPR News Blog (Feb. 12, 2010).

850. *Id.*

851. *See id.* (a Democratic policy strategist opined that "For the run of the mill candidates who think that they are going to raise a lot of money, it's overly optimistic." He went on to note that: "Obama is such a unique candidate.... He's almost like a movement. He's not the regular mainstream candidate. I don't think John Kerry could have done this. Or Al Gore or even Bill Clinton."); *How Tweet It Is, supra* note 598 ("And so, for politicians, the lesson may be clear: The media is not always the message.").

852. *See Ron Paul Raises $6 Million, supra* note 849 ("Mann [Thomas E. Mann of the Brookings Institution] notes that the 'The success of small-donor fundraising in this election cycle will be difficult to match in years without strong national political tides and by candidates without Obama's star quality.'").

853. *See id.* (Oct. 22, 2008) ("After he [Obama] has been a president for four years and perhaps is seen as a member of the establishment and no longer a fresh-faced leader or a movement, will he again want to eschew federal funding as he has this time around? Or, if he sees that his wave has crested and the fervor has died down, will he reach out and grab federal funding with both hands in 2012 like a long-lost friend?").

Obama and McCain, future candidates could hardly be expected to engage in the functional equivalent of unilateral disarmament by accepting the paltry sums available under the federal campaign financing scheme, and by ending up running against a challenger who has multiple times as much money. Interestingly, as we shall see, money was not the determinative factor in the 2016 presidential campaign.

By the time of the 2010 midterm elections, Obama's internet magic seemed to have disappeared, and some were questioning whether the problem was Obama's message or a failure to effectively communicate.[854] By that time, Obama's public opinion ratings had dipped and nearly 60% of voters expressed a lack of confidence in his ability to handle the nation's problems.[855] Indeed, the magic probably disappeared much earlier as Republicans and Tea Party activists began mobilizing against Obama's legislative agenda, including against Obama's economic stimulus package, his health care legislation, and his proposed cap and trade legislation.[856] Although independent voters had decisively supported Obama in the 2008 presidential election, those same voters broke solidly against the Democrats in the 2010 elections.[857] Public opinion polls showed that 40% of independent voters disapproved of Obama's job performance, and an astounding 29% of independent voters indicated that they would vote against Democratic congressional candidates as a protest against Obama.[858]

In a stinging electoral rebuke, the Democrats lost sixty seats in the U.S. House of Representatives, thereby shifting control to the Republicans, and

---

854. *See* Jeff Zeleny, *A Failure to Communicate or the Wrong Message, The New York Times*, at A15 (Jan. 27, 2010).

855. *See* Dan Balz & Jon Cohen, *Poll: Confidence in Obama Falls to New Low, The Courier-Journal*, at A2 (July 13, 2010).

856. *See* Mara Liasson, *The Political Difficulties Facing President Obama*, National Public Radio, All Things Considered (Sept. 28, 2010), http://www.npr.org/templates/story/story.php?storyId=130194249.

857. *See* Frank James, *Obama Makes Beeline for Independent Voters*, National Public Radio, It's All Politics (Nov. 15, 2010), http://www.npr.org/blogs/itsallpolitics/2010/11/15/131330580/obama-makes-beeline-for-independent-voters ("So all the action is really with the independents, who just two weeks ago were decisive in helping Republicans win the House, just as they helped Obama win in 2008 and aided Democrats to gain control of Congress ion 2006.").

858. *See* Frank James, *Independents Give Republicans Big Edge: Pew Survey*, National Public Radio, It's All Politics (Sept. 23, 2010), http://www.npr.org/blogs/itsallpolitics/2010/09/23/130077866/independents-give-republicans-big-edge-pew-survey.

they lost another six seats in the United States Senate.[859] The results may have been affected by President Obama's low approval rating, which at the time was below 50%, rivaling that of his predecessor, President George W. Bush.[860] Political commentators opined that the election results were affected by the downbeat economic situation, but were also influenced by public disapproval of Obama's alleged "big government" solutions to problems in the United States.[861] Indeed, in multiple attack advertisements, Republicans successfully linked Democratic senatorial and congressional candidates with Obama, as well as with then Speaker of the House Nancy Pelosi and then Senate Majority Leader Harry Reid.[862] Those same themes were evident in other Republican campaign efforts as well.[863] If Obama had been able to "control" the electorate through the internet, rather than simply use the internet to ride a political wave, one would have expected to have seen quite different results in the 2010 elections.

Some commentators have suggested that the internet is simply more challenger-friendly and more geared toward disrupting "the existing

---

859. *See* Barbara Bradley Hagerty, *HOUSE: Republicans Recapture Control*, National Public Radio, (Nov. 3, 2010), http://www.npr.org/templates/story/story.php?storyId=131020615.

860. *See* Frank James, *George Bush Ties Barack Obama in Public Approval: Poll*, National Public Radio, It's All Politics (Oct. 8, 2010), http://www.npr.org/blogs/itsallpolitics/2010/10/08/130436247/george-bush-now-ties-barack-obama-in-public-approval-poll.

861. *See* Hagerty, *supra* note 859 ("In 2010, it's a counterwave election, in which Republican are snatching back the victories that Democrats won in 2006 and 2008. This wave was propelled by the view—articulated most vehemently by the populist Tea Party movement—that the Obama administration has driven the economy in the wrong direction by pushing through health care reform, the financial bailout and the economic stimulus plan. The health care law is particularly unpopular: Recent polls suggest that more than half of Americans oppose it, and 51 percent are in favor of repealing it.").

862. *See* Ari Shapiro, *Obama Takes a Starring Role in GOP Campaign Ads*, National Public Radio, Morning Edition (Sept. 16, 2010), http://www.npr.org/templates/story/story.php?storyId=129891256 ("Two years ago, virtually every Democrat included Obama in campaign materials. Today, if you want to see Obama with his arm around a Democratic candidate, the best place to look is a Republican ad.").

863. *See* Joseph Gerth, *Paul Fires Up Tea Party Crowd: Says Conway Must "Run" from Obama, The Courier-Journal*, at B1 (July 11, 2010) (Paul claimed that his opponent, Jack Conway, would "have to run away from President Barack Obama and his policies. 'I don't think he can run fast enough,' Paul told a cheering crowd of several hundred people at the tea party's Freedom Festival 2010.").

power structure."[864] As one commentator opined, "Inherently speaking, a decentralized online movement is going to be frustrating to people who have the power, and the White House is the very definition of power."[865] While a political campaign might allow a candidate to stake out strong political positions that appeal to his base, the process of governing requires compromises that can alienate the elected candidate's base.[866] For the general public, social media platforms provide a vehicle for dissenters to disseminate information regarding the administration's positions and views.

Of course, the 2010 election was affected by other factors as well. For one thing, the Tea Party showed surprising strength, although it had both positive and negative impacts on Republican results. As noted, the Tea Party helped to elect Senator Rand Paul of Kentucky and Senator Scott Brown of Massachusetts,[867] but its intervention led to Republican defeats in Nevada and Connecticut,[868] with those defeats directly attributable to the nomination of less desirable candidates.[869] In Nevada, the Tea Party candidate deprived the Republican Party of the coup of toppling the highly vulnerable Senate Majority Leader.[870] Following the 2010 election, the Tea Party continued to wield considerable influence. For example, the Tea Party's opposition to so-called "earmarks" (the legislative procedure used to direct budgetary expenditures to particular recipients) led someone who had been a strong proponent of earmarks, Kentucky Senator Mitch McConnell, to oppose them.[871]

---

864. *See Obama No Longer Leads the Pack on Social Media, supra* note 825.

865. *Id.* (quoting Mr. Patrick Ruffini, a digital media consultant).

866. *Id.* (noting that the Obama administration sent out e-mails urging a liberal base to support positions that it might not like regarding tax cuts and federal employee pay).

867. *See Republican Scott Brown Wins, supra* note 685.

868. *See* John Nichols, *The Nation: How the Tea Party Saved the Democrats*, National Public Radio (Nov. 5, 2010), http://www.npr.org/templates/story/story.php?storyId =131092263.

869. *See id.*

870. *See id.*

871. *See* Frank James, *GOP Senate Leader Mitch McConnell Folds on Earmarks*, National Public Radio, It's All Politics (Nov. 15, 2010), http://www.npr.org/blogs/itsallpolitics /2010/11/15/131337312/gop-senate-leader-mitch-mcconnell-folds-on-earmarks.

The 2010 election may also have been affected by the U.S. Supreme Court's decision in *Citizens United v. Federal Election Commission*.[872] That decision overturned prior precedent, in particular the Court's holdings in *McConnell v. Federal Election Commission*[873] and *Austin v. Michigan Chamber of Commerce*,[874] and limited Congress' ability to restrict participation by corporations in the political process. Neither *Citizens United*, nor *Austin*, involved the Court's first attempt to define the free speech rights of corporations.[875] *Austin* was not even the Court's first decision regarding the free speech rights of corporations in the political process. In *FEC v. Massachusetts Citizens for Life, Inc.*[876] (MCFL), the Court struck down portions of a federal statute requiring corporations to make independent political expenditures only through special segregated funds (rather than from their general corporate treasuries) as a violation of a corporation's free speech rights.[877] For present purposes, the significance of *Citizens United*

---

872. 558 U.S. 310 (2010).

873. 540 U.S. 93 (2003).

874. 494 U.S. 652 (1990).

875. In a number of decisions, the Court had held that corporations have free speech rights. For example, in the Court's landmark decision in *New York Times Co. v. Sullivan*, 376 U.S. 254 (1964), the Court constitutionalized the tort of defamation and held that free speech considerations limit the ability of state courts to award defamation damages. The Court reached that conclusion in a suit against a corporation, *The New York Times Co.* Likewise, in *Globe Newspaper Co. v. Superior Court*, 457 U.S. 596 (1982), as well as in other decisions, the Court held that the press (in many instances, the corporate press) has a free speech right of access to observe judicial proceedings. *See Press Enterprise Co. v. Superior Court*, 478 U.S. 1 (1986); *Columbia Broadcasting System, Inc. v. Democratic National Committee*, 412 U.S. 94 (1973); *see also Turner Broadcasting System, Inc. v. FCC*, 512 U.S. 622 (1994); *Seattle Times Co. v. Rhinehart*, 467 U.S. 20 (1984). In *Cox Broadcasting Corp. v. Cohn*, 420 U.S. 469 (1975), the Court held that the First Amendment barred a damage award against a corporation for publishing the name of a dead rape victim.

876. 479 U.S. 238 (1986).

877. In *MCFL*, the Court reasoned that a small nonprofit corporation would face significant organizational and financial burdens if it were required to establish and administer a segregated political fund. *Id.*, at 255. The law included a requirement that the corporation appoint a treasurer for its segregated fund, to keep records of all contributions, to file a statement of organization containing information about the fund, and to update that statement periodically. In addition, the corporation was permitted to solicit contributions to its segregated fund only from "members," and could not accept contributions from other persons. The Court held that these hurdles "impose[d] administrative costs that many small entities [might] be unable to bear" and "create[d] a disincentive for such organizations to engage in political speech." *Id.*

was that it allowed non candidates to raise and spend significantly more money in the 2010 election, and some believe that this change allowed Republicans to spend more than their Democratic counterparts.[878] In other words, just as Obama's internet fundraising may have shaped the 2008 election, it is arguable that *Citizens United* may have helped shape the 2010 elections. It is difficult to know the extent to which corporate funding was raised over the internet, or whether that decision actually affected the outcome of that election. Under current campaign finance laws, those who raised and spent that money were not required to divulge their funding sources.[879] Nevertheless, Obama's attempt to control the electorate through internet communications seemed to fall flat in the 2010 election cycle.

Despite the problems faced by Democrats in the 2010 mid-term election, the Obama campaign effectively used the internet to propel his 2012 re-election effort. His campaign created a relatively slick app that allowed Obama supporters to do a variety of things: "follow campaign news, volunteer, canvas voters and promote campaign messages on social media."[880] Social media was also used by Republican candidates. Mitt Romney announced his candidacy on a Web video, and Jon Hunstman was chagrined to learn that a Democratic activist had purchased the website jonhuntsman.com.[881]

But candidates frequently used a variety of media to promote themselves and their messages. Sarah Palin, a former vice-presidential candidate and someone who was once regarded as a possible 2012 presidential candidate, aggressively used the internet as a method of communica-

878. *See* Juan Williams, *Republicans Benefit from Influx of Corporate Funds*, National Public Radio, Morning Edition (Oct. 19, 2010), http://www.npr.org/templates/story/story.php?storyId=130665397 ("As midterm elections , it is Republican candidates that are benefitting from an influx of campaign contributions.... So you have a situation where lots of money is sloshing around. It's hard to understand exactly what's happening because things are happening quickly, and disclosure is moving slowly.").

879. *See Citizens United v. Federal Election Commission*, 558 U.S. 310 (2010).

880. *See* Singer & Confessore, *supra* note 760, at B1.

881. *See* Ari Shapiro, *New Media Could Make or Break Presidential Race*, National Public Radio, Morning Edition (Apr. 20, 2011), http://www.npr.org/2011/04/20/135553017/new-media-could-make-or-break-presidential-race.

tion,[882] often using electronic platforms such as Facebook and Twitter.[883] She also appeared on television, including Fox News.[884] When she was criticized for creating a climate that was ripe for political violence, in the wake of the Tucson shooting of congresswoman Gabrielle Giffords, she used both electronic and traditional media to respond by sending an e-mail to Glenn Beck that he read on his television program.[885]

The 2012 Republican presidential candidate, Mitt Romney, did not use social media as effectively as Barrack Obama. Romney, had an app that allowed supporters to take a selfie with a picture of Mitt which had the title: "I'm with Mitt,"[886] but which did not allow Romney's supporters to donate money, post items on social media, or invite friends and family to register to vote.[887] President Obama, by contrast, even went so far as to host a Facebook "town hall" in an effort to reconnect with his social media constituency.[888]

Interestingly, despite the impact of the internet in the 2012 presidential election, social media did not eliminate traditional methods of campaigning. Candidates sought to raise large amounts of money from big donors, purchased huge amounts of traditional media advertising,[889] and blanketed the airwaves with traditional media advertising.[890]

In 2016, the internet continued to play a major role in political campaigns. By that time, Vermont Senator Bernie Sanders had amassed a large digital army that was quite active and aggressive.[891] His supporters

---

882. *See* Jim Rutenberg & Kate Zernike, *Amid Criticism, Palin Lobs Electronic Defense, The New York Times*, at A9 (Jan. 11, 2011).

883. *Id.*

884. *Id.*

885. *Id.*

886. *See* Singer & Nicholas Confessore, *supra* note 760.

887. *Id.*

888. *See* Eyder Peralta, *Kicking Off Social Media Campaign, Obama Hosts Facebook Town Hall*, National Public Radio, The Two-Way (Apr. 20, 2011), http://www.npr.org/blogs/thetwo-way/2011/04/20/135574843/kicking-off-social-media-campaign-obama-hosts-facebook-town-hall.

889. *See* Jeremy W. Peters, *On Pace for a Record Barrage of Ads, The New York Times*, at A12 (Jan. 16, 2012).

890. *Id; see also* Alessandra Stanley, *A Relentless On-Screen Bid to Sell Candidates in Iowa, The New York Times*, The TV Watch, at A14 (Jan. 2, 2012).

891. *See* Matt Flegenhelmer, Rebecca R. Ruiz & Nellie Bowles, *The Underside of Sanders's Colossal Online Base, The New York Times* A1 (Jan. 27, 2020).

actively defended him and lashed out at his foes, allegedly harassing and bullying opponents.[892] In addition, the movement helped Sanders raise funds from small donors.[893] Although Sanders was unable to obtain the Democratic Party's presidential nomination, the internet made him a major contender for the nomination.[894]

By 2016, Donald Trump was the candidate who was using the internet in a transformative way.[895] Trump had a penchant for using Twitter to circumvent the traditional media and communicate directly with potential voters.[896] He also had a knack for ensnaring the broadcast and cable media into reporting extensively about his Twitter messages.[897] As one columnist noted: "the media format that really made him president ... was that old pre-internet standby, broadcast and cable television, and especially TV news."[898] He used his television show, The Apprentice, to bolster his stature, and then he cunningly turned "news channels into infomercials for his campaign."[899] Indeed, Trump enjoyed watching how his tweets altered the news coverage.[900] One commentator estimated that news coverage added as much as $2 billion in free advertising to the Trump campaign.[901] He also exploited the "polarization" created by cable news.[902] Finally, he used Facebook advertising, with approximately $1.4 billion in such advertisements during the 2016 election; a format which is also credited with helping Donald Trump defeat Hillary Clinton.[903]

---

892. *Id.*

893. *Id.*

894. *Id.*

895. *See* Frank Bruni, *Will the Media Be Trump's Accomplice Again?*, *The New York Times*, Sunday Review 1 & 3 (Jan. 13, 2019).

896. *See* Vernon E. Jordan, Jr., *Both Old and New Media Are Failing Voters*, *The Wall Street Journal* A 15 (Nov. 4, 2016).

897. *See* Ross Douthat, *Trump Hacked the Media Right Before Our Eyes*, *The New York Times* (Mar. 21, 2018); Jordan, *supra* note 896, at A15 ("Mainstream media, under pressure from new media, gave the candidate abundant free airtime, because his behavior was good for ratings.").

898. *Id.*

899. *Id.*

900. *See* Maggie Haberman, *Without Twitter, Who Is Donald J. Trump?*, *The New York Times* A11 (Jan. 11, 2021).

901. *Id.*

902. *Id.*

903. *See Campaign Ads to Flood Facebook*, *supra* note 678.

As President, Trump frequently used Twitter to attack his opponents and critics.[904] On one Thanksgiving, Trump tweeted regarding the death of journalist Jamal Khashoggi, and threatened to close the U.S.-Mexican border to prevent a caravan of migrants from entering the country.[905] Trump regularly tweeted regarding special counsel Robert Mueller's Russia investigation, referring to it as a "witch hunt,"[906] and he tweeted derogatory remarks about then Attorney General Jeff Sessions, complaining about Sessions' decision to recuse himself from oversight of special counsel Robert Mueller's Russia investigation.[907] Some argued that Trump's tweets constituted an attempt to obstruct justice, and therefore could be used as evidence against him,[908] or that his Tweets might have been used against him in impeachment proceedings.[909]

In 2018, when a former campaign aide and White House staffer published a tell-all book about her experiences with Trump,[910] Trump referred to her in tweets as a "dog," as a "wacky and deranged Omarosa," and said that she was hated by other White House staffers because she was "vicious" but "not smart."[911] He also tweeted that White House Counsel, Donald McGahn II, was leaving his job—before Trump had spoken to

904. *See* Maggie Haberman, *Trump Tweets on Inquiry: No Mercy for Ex-Lawyer, But Praise for Ex-Adviser, The New York Times* A17 (Dec. 4, 2018) (Trump tweets regarding the potential prison sentence for his ex-lawyer who cooperated with the special prosecutor).

905. *See* Emily Cochrane, *Tweets, Threats and Catapults: Trump's Thanksgiving Menu, The New York Times* A15 (Nov. 23, 2018).

906. *See* Mark Landler, *Trump, Citing a 'Witch Hunt,' Denies Any Collusion with Russia, The New York Times* (May 18, 2017). https://www.nytimes.com/2017/05/18/us/politics/trump-back-on-twitter-complains-of-witch-hunt.html.

907. *See* Michael D. Shear & Eileen Sullivan, *Trump Calls Omarosa Manigault Newman "That Dog" in His Latest Insult, The New York Times* A-1 (Aug. 15, 2018).

908. *Id.*

909. *See* Charles Truax, *Trump Twitter Attack on Sessions Is Serious Impeachment Fodder, The Courier-Journal*, A17 (Sept. 5, 2018).

910. *See* Maggie Haberman, *Trump Campaign Says It Has Filed a Case Against a Tell-All's Author, The New York Times* A12 (Aug. 15, 2018).

911. *See* Shear & Sullivan, *supra* note 907, at A-1.

McGahn about leaving.[912] Of course, his Tweets regarding individual businesses affected those companies share valuations.[913]

In the 2020 presidential campaign, a number of candidates tried to harness the internet and the media in support of their campaigns. Pete Buttigieg and Elizabeth Warren both sought to use the internet, with Buttigieg spending nearly a million dollars and Warren spending $1.1 million on Facebook and Google advertising.[914] Some believe that they outperformed the other 21 Democratic presidential candidates because of their media and internet efforts.[915] In the Iowa primary, Mr. Buttigieg managed to climb from 1% to 14% in the rankings by emphasizing his personal background.[916] Senator Warren saw her percentage of the electorate rise from 9% to 15% based on her policy proposals.[917] Joe Biden spent $1.5 million and Kamala Harris spent nearly $1 million.[918]

Michael Bloomberg, who ran for president in 2020, also tried to harness the internet in support of his campaign.[919] In that effort, he hired hundreds of employees to post messages on their personal social media accounts, as well as to send text messages to their friends.[920] The Bloomberg approach was different than prior campaigns which had encouraged supporters to post favorable statements on their own social media accounts, but did not pay for such statements.[921] By contrast, Bloomberg hired 500 "deputy digital organizers" and paid them $2,500 a month.[922] Bloomberg's staff issued out posts such as "The Fight for Equal Rights Has Been One of the Great

---

912. *See* Julie Hirschfeld Davis, Michael S. Schmidt & Maggie Haberman, *Trump Lawyer Is Ushered Out With a Tweet: White House Counsel Is Key Mueller Witness, The New York Times* A1 (Aug. 30, 2018).

913. *See* Michael D. Shear & Cecilia Kang, *Firms Shudder at Trump's Tweets Mean Business, The New York Times* A1 (Apr. 4, 2018).

914. *See* Reid J. Epstein, *Buttigieg and Warren Tap Power of Social Media and TV to Stand Out, The New York Times* A16 (June 14, 2019).

915. *Id.*

916. *Id.*

917. *Id.*

918. *Id.*

919. *See* Jeff Horowitz & Georgia Wells, *Bloomberg Hires Hundreds to Push Message on Social Media, The Wall Street Journal* A1 (Feb. 20, 2020).

920. *Id.*

921. *Id.*

922. *Id.*

Fights of Mike's Life," touting his support for same-sex marriage,[923] and the campaign tried to interact "with voters everywhere on any platform" where individuals consumed news.[924] The Bloomberg campaign also used Outvote, an app designed to send texts, post to social media, and send data back to the campaign.[925] The app allows users to determine whether their friends have voted.[926] Interestingly, the campaign seemed to skirt Facebook's ad rules. When campaigns post ads, those ads must be labeled as "sponsored." Under the rules, if campaign employees choose to post on their own social media accounts, the "sponsored" label is not required.[927] However, the rules do not make clear what happens when the campaign workers are paid to post messages on their own accounts.[928] The campaign viewed the posts as "political organizing" rather than "paid influencer content."[929] The campaign also contracted with large meme accounts to push Bloomberg.[930] One post was titled: "Ha! Even Republicans think Mike is our best bet to defeat Trump!"[931] Despite the creativity and the massive infusion of money for campaign staffers, the Bloomberg campaign was not as successful as the earlier Obama and Trump campaigns had been.[932] The effort did generate enough support to help Bloomberg qualify for the Democratic primary debates, and raise more money than a number of other candidates.[933]

Because the pandemic made in-person campaigning difficult in 2020, and because media consumption was high, candidate Biden used digital video ads to convey his message.[934] The ads were displayed on Hulu and on ViacomCBS, Incos and Pluto TV with a focus on swing states

923. *Id.*
924. *Id.*
925. *Id.*
926. *Id.*
927. *Id.*
928. *Id.*
929. *Id.*
930. *Id.*
931. *Id.*
932. *Id.*
933. *Id.*
934. *See* Emily Glazer & Patience Haggin, *Campaigns Jump Into Digital-Video Ads, The Wall Street Journal* A4 (Sept. 4, 2020).

such as Arizona and Wisconsin.[935] Then President Trump also used video advertisements on platforms like Hulu.[936] In total, video ads increased six-fold to $1.8 billion during that campaign.[937] The campaigns liked the digital video advertisements, distributed through the internet, because they were less expensive than television advertising and were effective at targeting desired voter groups.[938] TikTok was also used in the 2020 presidential campaign.[939] At the time, TikTok had approximately 24 million users and most were between the ages of 18 and 24.[940] Lots of videos were posted involving candidates such as Donald Trump and Bernie Sanders.[941] Although TikTok bans political advertisements, there was lots of content posted by individual users (rather than by political campaigns).[942]

In 2020, then President Trump and then former Vice-President Biden sought to use social media as well.[943] On Twitter, Trump had some 82.4 million followers and sent some 160 Twitter messages in a single 7 day period, while Biden sent approximately 60 messages to his 6.4 million followers during the same time frame.[944] In addition, Trump's campaign was aided by his followers who retweeted his posts several hundred times a day.[945] The campaigns also made lots of posts on Facebook.[946] Trump made approximately 14 posts on Facebook a day to his some 28 million followers while Biden delivered about 7 posts per day to his 2 million followers.[947] Some concluded that the platforms provided Trump "with a massive platform to connect with supporters and push a message that ignores his vulnerabilities."[948]

---

935. *Id.*

936. *Id.*

937. *Id.*

938. *See Campaigns Jump Into Digital-Video Ads, supra* note 934, at A4.

939. *See* Georgia Wells & Emily Glazer, *TikTok Pulled Into Election Fray As Both Parties Vie for Youth Vote, The Wall Street Journal* A4 (Jan. 6, 2020).

940. *Id.*

941. *Id.*

942. *Id.*

943. *See* Alexandra Jaffee & Amanda Seitz, *Trump, Biden Fight for Primacy On Social Media, Courier-Journal* 19A (July 5, 2020).

944. *Id.*

945. *Id.*

946. *Id.*

947. *Id.*

948. *Id.*

Biden outspent Trump on Facebook advertising, and held virtual fundraisers.[949] In just a few days, Biden spent nearly $5 million on Facebook advertisements, seeking to capitalize on protests against racism and police brutality.[950] Some of the ads depicted then President Trump walking past protestors in riot gear.[951] The advertisement implored watchers to sign a petition condemning Trump.[952] The initial goal was to obtain 1 million signatures on the petition, but that goal was raised to 2.5 million after more than 1.2 million people signed.[953] One of the objectives of the petition campaign was to collect the names, email addresses, zip codes, and mobile numbers of potential Biden supporters.[954] In particular, Biden targeted potential voters under the age of 35.[955] Biden also placed advertisements on Google.[956] Trump held nightly live broadcasts on platforms such as Facebook, Twitter, Instagram, and Twitch.[957] Biden campaign managers argued that his approach was superior to Trump's because, rather than simply trying to stir up anger, Biden was trying to connect with voters.[958]

By 2024, the internet continued to play a major role in the election process. In an effort to reach out to young voters, President Biden tried to connect through TikTok,[959] which is used by 56% of people between the ages of 18 and 34.[960] At the time, Biden was polling poorly with young people because of the war in Gaza, as well as because of his age and the fact that it was "uncool" to support the administration in power.[961] However, the Biden campaign was using the app to post videos and interact with young voters, and confront difficult issues.[962] In addition, the

---

949. *Id.*

950. *See* Shane Goldmacher, *Biden Spends Millions on Facebook Ads, Far Eclipsing Trump's Record, The New York Times* A13 (June 9, 2020).

951. *Id.*

952. *Id.*

953. *Id.*

954. *Id.*

955. *Id.*

956. *Id.*

957. *See Trump, Biden Fight for Primacy On Social Media, supra* note 943, at A19.

958. *Id.*

959. *See* Anjali Huynh, *Using TikTok, Biden Courts Tough Crowd, The New York Times* A1 (Mar. 27, 2024).

960. *Id.*

961. *Id.*

962. *Id.*

Biden campaign partnered with social media "influencers" to promote his campaign.[963] However, the effort was complicated by the fact that TikTok discourages political activity, prohibits political advertising, and prohibit users from receiving payment for political content.[964] Interestingly, Gen-Z for Change, an online group with 1.7 million followers that was created in 2020 to support the Biden campaign, ultimately turned critical of Biden.[965] Whether these tactics would have overcome voter apathy towards the Biden campaign is unclear.[966] We will never know given that that Biden was ultimately forced to withdraw from the campaign because of his declining mental condition.[967]

In 2024, as in 2016, Donald Trump used the internet more creatively and more effectively than his opponent. In addition to using his new social media platform, Truth Social, Trump used the internet to connect with young male voters.[968] Trump, recognizing that more than half of all voters sometimes obtain their news through non-traditional sources (e.g., social media platforms, Facebook, YouTube, Instagram and TikTok),[969] placed much less emphasis on mainstream media interviews, and invested far more effort in podcast interviews designed to reach young males.[970] For example, he did a lengthy three-hour podcast interview with Joe Rogan which netted 45 million views on YouTube,[971] and he also did podcasts with Clay Travis on his "Outkick the Coverage" show,[972] with Logan Paul,

---

963. *Id.*

964. *Id.*

965. *Id.*

966. *Id.*

967. *See* Zolan Kanno-Youngs, Erica L. Green & Nicholas Nehamas, *What's Next for the Harris Campaign, International New York Times* (July 23, 2024); Catie Edmonson, Kellen Browning & Nicholas Nehamas, *Democrats Go Public About Biden Amid Fears of an Electoral Debacle, International New York Times* 15 (July 4, 2024).

968. *See* Shane Goldmacher, Maggie Haberman & Jonathan Swan, *How Trump Won, and Harris Lost, International New York Times* 1 (Nov. 9, 2024).

969. *See* Michael M. Grynbaum & John Koblin, *A Master's Media Instincts Evolved Yet Again in 2024, The New York Times* A15 (Nov. 8, 2024).

970. *Id.*

971. *Id.*

972. *See* Manuel Roig-Franzia, Elahe Izadi &Herb Scribner, *As Trump Joined the Podcast Revolution, Legacy Media Got Left Out, Podcasts Proved Powerful for Trump Manual, The Washington Post* C-1 (Nov. 9, 2024).

a wrestler and social media star,[973] and on Bussin' With the Boys.[974] In the process, Trump was aggressively seeking to reach out to male voters and he connected through YouTube videos by the Nelk Boys,[975] as well as in interactions with Adin Ross (a prominent gamer)[976] and Theo Von.[977] The effort was regarded as risky because young males, particularly young Hispanic and African-American males, were viewed as less likely to turn out on election day.[978] But Trump relied heavily on anti-trans advertisements,[979] and Harris was forced to battle headwinds in the form of negative views about the economy and the Biden Administration's handling of immigration.[980] Kamala Harris also appeared on some podcasts, but was much less aggressive than Trump.[981] She talked about a podcast with Joe Rogan, but it never came to pass.[982]

Another factor fueling Trump's campaign came from the support of Elon Musk.[983] Musk, the owner of the Social Media Platform, X, posted more than 3,000 times in the final month before the election.[984] Not only did Musk strongly support Donald Trump, but it has been alleged that he spread disinformation.[985] Musk's posts were particularly important because his account dominates X and is the most popular account on that platform with 202 million followers.[986] In a single two-week period,

---

973. *See* Kellen Browning, Benjamin Oreskes & Eduardo Medina, *Trump Is Courting Apolitical Young Men. Will It Pay Off?, International New York Times* (Nov. 4, 2024).

974. *See A Master's Media Instincts Evolved Yet Again in the 2024, supra* note 969.

975. *See* John Branch, *Donald Trump Courts the Manoverse, International New York Tines* 1 (Sept. 7, 2024) ("At a time of an immense gender gap in politics among young people—women leaning left, men leaning right—the Trump campaign has been aggressively courting what might be called the bro vote, the frat-boy flank. It's a slice of 18-to-29-year-olds that has long been regarded as unreliable and unreachable, but that Republicans believe may just swing the election this year.").

976. *See A Master's Media Instincts Evolved Yet Again in the 2024, supra* note 969.

977. *Id.*

978. *See Trump Is Courting Apolitical Young Men. Will It Pay Off?, supra* note 973.

979. *See How Trump Won, and How Harris Lost, supra* note 968.

980. *Id.*

981. *See A Master's Media Instincts Evolved Yet Again in 2024, supra* note 969.

982. *Id.*

983. *See* Kate Conger, Aaron Krolik, Santul Nerkar & Dylan Freedman, *Musk Lets His Account Dominate X, The New York Times* B1 (Nov. 5, 2024).

984. *Id.*

985. *Id.*

986. *Id.*

Musk posted 1,220 times and the posts generated an average of 65,000 engagements per post.[987] 1,200 of his posts were reposted some 11 million times.[988] When he posted that "If Trump is NOT elected this will be the last election," the post was viewed 103 million times and reposted nearly 180,000 times.[989] Musk's dominance is no accident since, for those who sign up for X account, X recommends that they follow Musk.[990] In addition, Musk elevated pro-Trump influencers on X, is believed to have provided significant levels of free advertising to Republicans, and helped persuade podcaster Joe Rogan to support Trump.[991] Also, acting through a political action committee (PAC), Musk spent nearly $120 million to support Trump's campaign, much of which was spent on a canvassing operation,[992] as well as a ground team that went door-to-door,[993] and spent $175 million on digital media advertising.[994] In addition, Musk offered voters the opportunity to win $1 million (with awards being made daily) if they signed a petition and provided his PAC with their personal information.[995] Finally, X suppressed news stories critical of Trump.[996]

Finally, supporters of Donald Trump would sometimes use the internet to "troll" his opponents.[997] These often anonymous individuals were sometimes referred to as "Trump's Troll Army."[998] For much of the 2024 campaign, they attacked Florida Governor Ron DeSantis, regarded as Trump's most threatening rival, and denigrated his competence, loyalty, and masculinity.[999] After DeSantis dropped out of the race, the trolls turned on his only remaining opponent Nikki Haley, attacking and mock-

---

987. *Id.*

988. *Id.*

989. *Id.*

990. *Id.*

991. *See* Gabe Kaminsky, *How Elon Musk Helped Will Trump Back to the White House, Gazette* (Colorado Springs) (Nov. 6, 2024).

992. *See Musk Lets His Account Dominate X, supra* note 977.

993. *See How Elon Musk Helped Will Trump Back to the White House, supra* note 985.

994. *Id.*

995. *See Musk Lets His Account Dominate X, supra* note 977.

996. *See* Ryan Mac, *How Twitter Moved Musk to the Right, The New York Times* B1 (Nov. 2, 2024).

997. *See* Jazmine Ulloa & Ken Bensinger, *Army of Trolls Hounds Haley Online and Off, The New York Times* A1 (Feb. 25, 2024).

998. *Id.*

999. *Id.*

ing her.[1000] Some of these trolls showed up at Haley's campaign events in person, trying to undermine her.[1001]

5. THE INTERNET'S INFLUENCE ON DAY-TO-DAY POLITICS

Equally interesting is the issue of how the internet has reshaped day-to-day politics. In recent years, elected officials and their opponents have increasingly turned to the internet to try to influence the outcome of pending issues in Congress, state legislatures, and local councils.

The Republican Party, which came late to the internet revolution, caught up with President Obama in its use of social media techniques,[1002] and aggressively used internet-based tactics to challenge then President Obama's political agenda.[1003] For example, during a session of Congress, former Republican National Committee Chairman Michael Steele sent out an internet appeal to Republican supporters with titles such as "It's Time to Fire Nancy Pelosi,"[1004] which argued that "Nancy Pelosi has gone too far. She is no longer serving the American people and the Constitu-

---

1000. *Id.*

1001. *Id.*

1002. *See Obama No Longer Leads the Pack on Social Media, supra* note 825 (noting that "the reality just two years later [after President Obama's election] is striking: In social media, Republicans have caught up.").

1003. *See, e.g.*, e-mail by Senator John McCain, Chairman, Country First PAC, entitled *Repeal and Replace Obamacare* (Jan. 19, 2011).

1004. E-mail from Mr. Michael Steele, Chairman, Republican Party Committee (Mar. 21, 2010):

> In defiance of the will of the American people, Nancy Pelosi and her Democrat cronies have authorized a government takeover of your health care. She even considered an unconstitutional backdoor process that involved passing the bill without a vote on it before she realized that she could simply cajole, bully, and even buy off members of Congress in order to get enough "yeas" to ram President Obama's socialist scheme down our throats.
>
> Nancy Pelosi has gone too far. She is no longer serving the American people and the Constitution of the United States. She is beholden to left-wing special interests, and does not represent the will of the people. It is time to fire Nancy Pelosi.
>
> In order to fund our efforts to oust Speaker Pelosi, the Republican National Committee is launching a Money Bomb to raise the resources we need to gain 40 House seats. If we gain just 40 House seats, we will fire Nancy Pelosi. Please donate, and then tell your friends to donate, so that we can end the tyrannical

tion of the United States. She is beholden to left-wing special interests, and does not represent the will of the people. It is time to fire Nancy Pelosi."[1005] In another e-mail, the "GOP Action Team" (described in the e-mail as part of the Republican National Committee) sent out an e-mail entitled *40 in 2010 to Fire Pelosi*,[1006] which stated that "The outpouring of support that we've [sic] received has been extraordinary. Just 12 hours after Nancy Pelosi and her cronies on Capitol Hill forced their government takeover of our country's health care through Congress, you and other concerned Americans have responded by donating more than $402,010 to the Fire Nancy Pelosi project of the Republican National Committee, so that we can continue to fight to make your voice heard!"[1007] There were other Republican messages, including e-mails entitled "The Drive to Fire Nancy

---

reign of the most aggressively left-wing Speaker in American history. Donate, so that we can fire Nancy Pelosi!

1005. *Id.*

1006. The text of the e-mail, dated April 16, 2010, read as follows:

Dear Fellow Patriot,

The outpouring of support that we've (sic) received has been extraordinary. Just 12 hours after Nancy Pelosi and her cronies on Capitol Hill forced their government takeover of our country's health care through Congress, you and other concerned Americans have responded by donating more than $402,010 to the Fire Nancy Pelosi project of the Republican National Committee, so that we can continue to fight to make your voice heard!

The Democrats in Washington have abandoned all pretense of representing the will of the American people. They are pursuing their own Leftist agenda in defiance of your will. But this November, you've got the chance to derail that agenda once and for all. We will fire Nancy Pelosi. Only you can make it happen.

The GOP Action Team cannot thank you enough for all of the time, money, and passion that you have put into combating these Beltway Leftists, but in this fight we'll need all of the help we can get. We've set a new goal of $842,010! Now we're asking you to call or e-mail your friends, tell them the stakes, and urge them to give to the Republican National Committee today so that we can work to fire Nancy Pelosi. Together we can win the battle against the Left this November, and take this country back for the American people!

Yours,

The GOP Action Team

A copy of the e-mail is on file with the author.

1007. *Id.*

Pelosi is On. Join Us,"[1008] and "Obama Wants Your Money."[1009] A similar e-mail was sent out by then Republican National Committee Chairman Michael Steele.[1010] Individual Republicans, including Senator and former presidential candidate John McCain, also used the internet during the 2010 election cycle to influence the political process.[1011]

Internet communications between Republicans and their constituents are no longer entirely one way. Republicans have set up websites designed to allow voters to express their opinions and (to a greater or lesser extent) participate in the political process.[1012] Included are such websites as America Speaks Out[1013] and youcut[1014] (for individuals who wish to express an opinion about which government programs should be subject to budget cuts).

Of course, Republicans are not alone in their efforts to use the internet in this way. Not surprisingly, given the way that President Obama was elected, the Democratic National Committee and President Obama aggressively used the internet to try to attempt to shape the national political agenda. Democrats sent out e-mails entitled "Prevention,"[1015] "We Won,"[1016] and "Fight Back in Louisville."[1017] In the e-mail entitled *Fight Back in Louisville*, Jeremy Bird of "Organizing for America," wrote that "There

---

1008. E-mail from Mr. Michael Steele, Chairman, Republican National Committee (Sept. 18, 2010).

1009. E-mail from The GOP Action Team (Mar. 16, 2010).

1010. The e-mail entitled *Its Time to Fire Nancy Pelosi*, and dated March 21, 2010, is quite similar to the GOP Action Team e-mail, and contains similar language: "In defiance of the will of the American people, Nancy Pelosi and her Democratic cronies have authorized a government takeover of your health care." A copy of the full e-mail is on file with the author.

1011. *See, e.g.*, E-mail from U.S. Senator John McCain entitled "Will You Help Decide America's Future" (Sept. 17, 2010); E-mail from U.S. Senator John McCain entitled "26 Days" (July 29, 2010).

1012. *See* Andrea Seabrook, *GOP Seeks Clear Voter Message Amid Clamor*, National Public Radio, Morning Edition (July 28, 2010), http://www.npr.org/templates/story/story.php?storyId=128810085.

1013. *See* http://www.americaspeakingout.com/.

1014. *See* http://republicanwhip.house.gov/YouCut.

1015. E-mail from Michelle Obama (July 20, 2010).

1016. E-mail from Mr. Mitch Stewart, Director, Organizing for America (July 20, 2010).

1017. E-mail from Mr. Jeremy Bird, Deputy Director, Organizing for America (July 20, 2010).

have been some stark reminders this week of exactly what's at stake in the coming elections. It's not just everything that this movement has accomplished—from health reform to the Wall Street reform that we're about to pass—would be in jeopardy. Its who would be in charge if Republicans and their extremist allies prevail."[1018] The Democrats even involved First Lady, Michelle Obama, who sent an e-mail entitled *Prevention* which tried to defend the Democrat's passage of health care legislation.[1019] Mitch Stewart, Director of Organizing for America, sent out a personalized e-mail with the name of the recipient, and a tag line indicating that "we won."[1020] The e-mail extolled the Democrat's passage of financial reform legislation. Following his loss in the race against Rand Paul for the U.S. Senate, Jack Conway announced his intention to run for reelection for the post of Attorney-General by e-mail.[1021]

Interestingly, despite his continued use of the internet, President Obama was unable to rally support as effectively as candidate Obama was able to do. For example, although President Obama and the Democrats were ultimately able to pass health care legislation, they had great difficulty rallying public support for the legislation,[1022] which remained unpopular with the public even after passage,[1023] and undoubtedly contributed to Democratic losses in the 2010 elections.[1024] Because of oppo-

---

1018. The e-mail was dated July 15, 2010 (on file with author).

1019. The e-mail was dated July 20, 2010 (on file with author).

1020. The e-mail was dated July 7, 2010.

1021. E-mail from Attorney-General Jack Conway entitled "Future Plans" (Jan. 21, 2011).

1022. *See* Scott Horsley, *Public Option Feels Pressure Amid Opposition*, National Public Radio, All Things Considered (July 28, 2009), http://www.npr.org/templates/story/story.php?storyId=111208396.

1023. *See* Liz Halloran, *Opposition to Obama's Health Care Overhaul Hardens*, National Public Radio (Sept. 3, 2009) http://www.npr.org/templates/story/story.php?storyId=112514565 ; Julie Rovner, *Opposition to Health Mandate Softens When Details Are Clearer*, National Public Radio, Shots (Mar. 18, 2011), http://www.npr.org/blogs/health/2011/03/18/134654092/opposition-to-health-mandate-softens-when-details-are-clearer ("People don't like the idea of being required to have health insurance.").

1024. *See* Julie Rovner & Steve Inskeep, *Republicans Renew Calls to Repeal Health Care Law*, National Public Radio, Morning Edition (Nov. 3, 2010), http://www.npr.org/templates/story/story.php?storyId=131033008 ("After big wins in Tuesday's elections, Republicans are again calling for the repeal of Obama's health care overhaul."); *see also* Frank James, *Health Care Law Even Losing Support Among Democrats*, National Public Radio, It's

sition, Democrats were ultimately forced to abandon key components of the proposed legislation, including the public option. Obama's failure to rally support came as a bit of a surprise. Given how President Obama tapped into the internet's potential during his presidential campaign, one might have expected him to continue to tap that potential in support of his legislative agenda. Nevertheless, President Obama was relatively ineffectual in his attempts to rally support for his legislation.

Obama's lack of success was hardly due to a lack of effort. President Obama continued to use the internet and other "new media" forms of communication following his election. For example, Obama was the first president to do a YouTube interview.[1025] In addition, following his 2011 State of the Union address, Obama scheduled interactive online events, including one on YouTube,[1026] and he uploaded video clips of his weekly radio address (a practice that other presidents had used with traditional broadcast media).[1027] However, Obama was criticized for not using modern technologies—including Twitter, e-mail and blogs—more aggressively.[1028]

Liberal bloggers also tried to harness the internet in support of Obama's legislative agenda.[1029] Although the health care legislation passed, there was widespread opposition. Moreover, there was a widely held percep-

---

All Politics (Oct. 28, 2011), http://www.npr.org/blogs/itsallpolitics/2011/10/28/141792652/health-care-law-even-losing-support-among-democrats.

1025. *See* Superville, *supra* note 815, at A6.

1026. *See Pushing the Presidential Message, supra* note 558.

1027. *Id.*

1028. *Id.*:

> Answering questions online, however, really just amounts to the same kind of televised town hall that presidents have been doing since the dawn of the broadcast era, except that now you watch it on a different kind of screen. Like his predecessors, Mr. Obama interacts from time to time with a few highly motivated voters at such events, but he has yet to find a way to make himself accessible or compelling to the wider electorate online.
>
> It's significant because history suggests that presidents who govern at times of sweeping technological change have a rare opportunity to make the presidency more immediate and more powerful....

1029. *See* Jim Rutenberg, *Liberal Groups Are Flexing New Muscle in Lobby Wars, The New York Times*, at A1 (Mar. 1, 2009):

> When Newt Gingrich's Congress was moving full-speed in its efforts to shrink the government more than a dozen years ago, Ralph G. Neas, an indefatigable champion of liberal causes, threw up his hands and declared that his side had been outmaneuvered.

tion that the Democrats' efforts to ram through their health care proposal led to Senator Scott Brown's election in Massachusetts,[1030] and damaged the chances of Democratic congressional candidates in the fall 2010 elections.[1031] At the time that the law was enacted, a minority of the population approved of the legislation.[1032]

President Obama's use of social media also did not help his public approval ratings after he took office. By 2009, just a year after his election, Obama's public approval ratings had dropped below 50 percent.[1033] By 2010 and 2011, just slightly more than 40 percent of the population approved of his handling of the economy.[1034] Although his approval rating climbed above 50% in early 2011, it subsequently plummeted to the 30th

---

> Liberals who had grown up pressing their case with marches and old-fashioned door-knocking campaigns, Mr. Neas said, were no match for conservatives with big business allies and a commanding understanding of the new talk-radio, cable-news battlefield, where former President Bill Clinton's signature health care plan lay bleeding.
>
> Recent days have found Mr. Neas in a new perch, preparing to join the coming fight over President Obama's sweeping health care proposals, with plans to coordinate a campaign of television advertisements, "blogger outreach" and community meetings. This time, he is supported by his own phalanx of big business backers, including the Exelon power company and Giant food stores.

1030. *See* Ifill, *supra* note 679.

1031. *See* Sheryl Gay, *Obama Faces Dour Public, Despite Gains in Congress: Legislative Success Fail to Convince Voters That He is Acting in Their Interest*, *International Herald Tribune*, at 1 (July 17–18, 2010):

> ... Mr. Obama's legislative success poses a paradox: While he may be winning on Capitol Hill, he is losing with the American public at a time of economic distress, and he soon may be forced to scale back his ambitions.
>
> But as he has done so [passed health care legislation, a fiscal stimulus and financial regulation reform] the political context has changed around him. Today, with unemployment remaining persistently double digits despite the scale of the stimulus program and the BP oil spill having raised questions about his administration's competence, Mr. Obama's signature legislation is providing ammunition to conservatives who argue that government is the problem, not the solution.

1032. *See Id.*, at 8.

1033. *See* John Harwood, *As Obama's Poll Numbers Fall, Criticism of Multitasking Rises*, *The New York Times*, at A17 (Dec. 7, 2009).

1034. *See Obama Faces Dour Public*, *supra* note 1001, at 8 ("In Mr. Obama's case, people are up in arms over the economy. Just over 40 percent of Americans now approve of Mr. Obama's handling of the economy, the CBS News poll found.").

percentile.[1035] By that time, Republicans appeared to be winning the public relations battle. As one commentator noted, "What Mr. Obama and his allies portray as a progressive, activist government has been framed by his opponents as overreaching and profligate when it comes to the economy."[1036] The President's stimulus package, and his handling of the economy, were also met with public disapproval.[1037]

As President, Donald Trump frequently attempted to use the internet to affect the public debate, there were allegations that Trump's Twitter communications were avidly watched by fringe racist groups.[1038] These groups purportedly reviewed Trump's tweets for evidence that he supported their positions, and they circulated Trump's comments through sites like 4chan, Reddit and Gab.[1039] They also circulated ideas through private channels, such as Discord, or through encrypted systems like Telegram and Wire or on podcasts like White Rabbit Radio.[1040] As a result, when Trump tweeted that protesters at the Kavanagh hearings were funded by Soros and others, some viewed the Tweet as supporting their views regarding the existence of a global Jewish conspiracy.[1041] Some believe that there is two-way communication between Trump and his supporters in the sense that online posts can affect the public debate and influence Trump's views.[1042]

However, Trump was not always successful in his efforts to control the public debate through Twitter. For example, as Covid-19 emerged as a public threat, Trump tried to respond to it through Twitter,[1043] attempting to portray Covid-19 as a partisan political issue and suggesting that the

---

1035. *See id.*

1036. *See id.*, at 1.

1037. *See id.*, at 8 ("In one of the most striking findings, nearly two-thirds said the President's economic policies had no effect on them personally—just 13 percent said they had helped them.").

1038. *See* Kevin Roose & Ali Winston, *Web's Far Right Can Hear Itself as Trump Talks: Cheering the Spread of Once-Fringe Views, The New York Times* A17 (Nov. 5, 2018)

1039. *Id.*

1040. *Id.*

1041. *Id.*

1042. *Id.*

1043. *See* Peter Baker, *Twitter Pulpit Is No Match for Viral Foe, The New York Times* A1 (Mar. 9, 2020).

media was simply trying to make him look bad.[1044] Trump's effort was not successful.[1045]

Increasingly, government agencies are using the internet to reach out to the public. For example, the New York Police Department has aggressively used social media to connect with its constituencies.[1046] The Department used IdeaScale to solicit tips and concerns from locals which are available for everyone to see.[1047] The Department also used Twitter to announce arrests, provide information about transportation delays, and seek information about possible suspects.[1048] Because of these efforts, the department learned about a situation in which individuals were causing noise problems by revving the engines on their all-terrain vehicles.[1049] Overall, the Department hopes that its use of social media will improve and encourage interaction between the citizenry and the police, especially with groups that have not historically interacted with the police.[1050]

Websites have also been created to facilitate citizen communication with government. For instance, there is a website called http://seeclickfix.com/citizens. The purpose of the website is to increase communication between citizens and local government:[1051] "SeeClickFix users post complaints about problems that occur within a set of boundaries on a Google Map, like graffiti at a bus stop or potholes on a busy street, and the site communicates the problem to the appropriate government agency and highlights the problem on a map. Users can comment on the issue or label it resolved. Government agencies can post on the site to respond to residents, and journalists can use the site to communicate with readers and see

1044. *Id.*

1045. *Id.*

1046. *See* Benjamin Mueller & Jeffrey E. Singer, *Police to Use Social Media to Connect With Residents, The New York Times* A17 (Mar. 26, 2015).

1047. *Id.*

1048. *Id.*

1049. *Id.*

1050. *Id.*

1051. *See* Daniel E. Slotnik, *News Sites Dabble with a Tool for Nudging Local Officials, The New York Times*, at B1 (Jan. 4, 2010).

which issues are most pressing to people."[1052] Other similar websites exist, including EveryBlock.com, CrimeReports.com, and FixMyStreet.com.[1053]

Governmental officials also sometimes use devices like Twitter to weigh in on the issues of the day. For example, when a podcast "Pros and Joes" criticized University of Kentucky sports fans, suggesting that their collective IQ was 120, and referring to the fan base as "annoying," U.S. Senator Mitch McConnell responded on Twitter: "Watch your mouth, fellas."[1054] McConnell has also used Twitter to weigh in on other issues.[1055]

6. A NEW PARADIGM?

In the final analysis, the internet may have created a new paradigm that will affect the political process forever. The Tea Party provides, perhaps, a good example of this new paradigm. During the 2010 elections, the Tea Party was able to effectively mobilize the electorate at times, including mobilizing large numbers of ordinary people.[1056] It is likely that some of the mobilized individuals had not previously been involved in political movements. So, the internet may be attracting new and different types of voters.

The more interesting question is whether these new voters will take the country in new and different directions. For example, the Tea Party presented an interesting challenge to the Republican party hierarchy which welcomed the energy and enthusiasm of the Tea Party, but was concerned regarding whether the Republican party could control and direct that energy and enthusiasm. Interestingly, since that time, the Tea Party has faded to insignificance.

However, internet-fueled action is hardly limited to political contexts. For example, Google employees organized a protest designed to

---

1052. *Id.*

1053. *Id.* ("SeeClickFix is not unique in its hyperlocal focus. Other sites, like EveryBlock.com and CrimeReports.com, post data from government organizations and news outlets. FixMyStreet.com features discussion between residents and government officials, but only in Britain.").

1054. *See* Thomas Novelly, *McConnell's Twitter Blasts Barstool Sports, The Courier-Journal* 8A (Aug. 3, 2018).

1055. *Id.*

1056. *See* Dale Moss, *They're Just Normal But Want Change: Hoosier Tea Party Tyros Unite, The Courier-Journal*, at B4 (Apr. 4, 2010).

challenge the company's protection of individuals charged with sexual harassment.[1057] Interestingly, in promoting their protests, Google employees specifically used various Google products, including Google Groups and Docs and the ability to provide comments.[1058] In other words, Google employees sought to "flex the skills that a lot of them had developed at Google—their program management skills, their marketing skills, their PR skills" in pursuit of their protests.[1059]

The internet has also affected international diplomacy. For example, during the Trump administration, a tweet led to an in-person meeting between then President Donald Trump and North Korean leader Kim Jong-un.[1060]

1057. *See* Farhad Manjoo, *When Tech Workers Raise Their Voices: The Google Walkout Shows How Leverage Can Be Maximized to Move an Industry, The New York Times*, State of the Art B1 (Nov. 8, 2018).

1058. *Id.* at B3.

1059. *Id.*

1060. *See* Michael Crowley and David E Sanger, *After Twitter Overture, Trump and Kim Meet on North Korean Soil, The New York Times* A1 (July 1, 2019).

CHAPTER VIII

THE INTERNET, GOVERNMENTAL REPRESSION, AND THE EMERGENCE OF NEW GATEKEEPERS

As noted in earlier chapters, since the 1500s, governments and gatekeepers have controlled (or, at least, attempted to control) the ability of ordinary individuals to access and use speech technologies.[1] After Gutenberg invented the printing press, governments did not willingly or readily embrace its use by private citizens.[2] On the contrary, many monarchs, fearing that the printing press might undermine their legitimacy, as it ultimately did, sought to restrain what they regarded as its "evils."[3]

1. *See* Elizabeth Townsend Gard, *Conversations with Renowned Professors on the Future of Copyright*, 12 Tul. J. Tech. & Intell. Prop. 35, 101 (2009) ("From monks transcribing Aristotle, to Gutenberg's printing press, to the photocopier, to the Betamax, we have seen striking similarities in the way various societies have feared the effects of new technologies and then created law in reaction to these fears.").

2. There were some exceptions, notably Italy and Germany, which gave the press greater latitude to discuss events occurring in other countries: "In the states and principalities of Germany and Italy the degree of official control varied from one state to another, but newspapers were generally allowed more leeway in reporting foreign news than in discussing domestic politics." David Crowley & Paul Heyer, Communication in History: Technology, Culture, Society 2 (5th ed. 2007).

3. *See First National Bank of Boston v. Bellotti*, 435 U.S. 765, 800–801 (1978) ("Soon after the invention of the printing press, English and continental monarchs, fearful of the power implicit in its use and the threat to Establishment thought and order-political and religious-devised restraints, such as licensing, censors, indices of prohibited books, and prosecutions for seditious libel, which generally were unknown in the pre-printing press

Moreover, there were private gatekeepers (the owners and publishers of newspapers) who controlled what could be published on their presses.

As impactful as Gutenberg's printing press might have been, the internet comes with much greater potential. Unlike the Gutenberg press, which could only be owned and operated by a privileged few, the internet has broad democratic potential in the sense that it can be accessed by almost everyone. In addition, as we have seen, the internet can be (and has been) used to organize protest movements and challenge governments. At the outset, the most important feature of the internet is that it functioned largely free of gatekeepers. However, in recent years, concerns have been raised regarding governmental repression of internet communications, even in the U.S., as well as about the emergence of internet gatekeepers.

Governments have an easy pretext for justifying internet regulation: the potential harms that can result from internet communications. In addition to using the internet to engage in legitimate discourse, individuals can use the internet to disseminate potentially harmful content, including disinformation,[4] child pornography[5] and hate speech,[6] and the internet can be used by sexual predators,[7] fraudsters, and gamblers. There has also been a significant increase in the number of Holocaust deniers

---

era. Official restrictions were the official response to the new, disquieting idea that this invention would provide a means for mass communication."); *see also Seditious Libel and the Lost Guarantee, supra* note 245, at 97–98; Norman L. Rosenberg, Protecting the Best Men: An Interpretive Theory of the History of Libel (U. N. Carolina Press, 1986); M. Lindsay Kaplan, The Culture of Slander in Early Modern England (Cambridge U. Press 1997).

4. *See* Kevin Roose, *Facebook Had a Good Election, But It Can't Let Up on Vigilance, The New York Times*, The Shift B1 (Nov. 8, 2018) ("digging up large-scale misinformation on Facebook was as easy as finding baby photos or birthday greetings.").

5. *See Ashcroft v. Free Speech Coalition*, 535 U.S. 234 (2002); *Ferber v. New York*, 458 U.S. 747 (1982).

6. *See* Russell L. Weaver, Nicholas Delpierre & Laurence Boissier, *Governmentally Imposed Truth: An Examination of France's Holocaust Denial Law*, 41 Texas Tech. U. L. Rev. 495 (2009); *see also* Ian Lovett, *U.C.L.A. Student's Video Rant Against Asians Fuels Firestorm, The New York Times*, at A21 (Mar. 16, 2011) (referring to a negative portrayal of Asians posted on YouTube by a student).

7. *See* Max Fisher & Amanda Taub, *On YouTube's Digital Playground, a Gate Left Wide Open for Pedophiles, The New York Times International* A6 Jun 4, 2019).

in recent years[8] because the internet makes it much easier for deniers to communicate with others.[9] In addition, the internet is accessible, not only by political activists, but by terrorists.[10] The risk is that governments will focus on dangerous speech as a pretext for restricting legitimate internet communications, especially speech related to the political process, in much the same way that earlier governments sought to restrict the printing press through licensing restrictions and the crime of seditious libel.

A. GOVERNMENTAL RESTRICTIONS (OUTSIDE THE US)

Governments have tried with varying levels of success to regulate and control the flow of information over the internet, especially when social tensions are high.[11] In theory, it is difficult for governments to control internet communications because there is often no single point of control similar to those that exist for systems like telephone networks.[12] "The routing of internet data packets is handled by a web of computers known as routers, so that in principle each packet might take a different route." The complete message or document may ultimately be reassembled at the receiving end.[13] Nevertheless, in some countries, internet traffic passes through centralized exchange points that give governments the

8. *See* http://www.ihr.org/books/harwood/dsmrd01.html; *see also* Raffi Berg, *The Fight Against Holocaust Denial*, http://news.bbc.co.uk/1/hi/world/europe/4436275.stm (hereafter "The Fight Against Holocaust Denial").

9. *See Id*; Christopher Wolf, *A Comment on Private Harms in the Cyber-World*, 62 WASH. & LEE L. REV. 355, 360 (2005) (As one commentator noted, "hate has gone high tech. Hatemongers used to meet in dingy basements; now they meet online. And instead of sending their propaganda in plain brown wrappers to a limited audience, they use the Internet to distribute graphic racist images, Holocaust denials, and venomous music around the globe.").

10. *See* Russell L. Weaver, *Brandenburg in the Cyber Village*, 80 MISS. L.J. 1263 (2011) (forthcoming) (discussing the fact that terrorists, and others intent on inciting civil and social disobedience, have and are likely to continue to try to use the internet).

11. Matt Richtel, *Egypt Halts Most Internet and Cell Service, and Scale of Shutdown Surprises Experts, The New York Times*, at A13 (Jan. 29, 2011).

12. *See* James Glanz, *Egypt Autocracy Found Internet's "Off" Switch, The New York Times*, at A1 (Feb. 16, 2011).

13. *Id.*

possibility to "monitor, filter or in dire cases completely stop the flow of internet data."[14]

Although restrictions have varied from country-to-country, with more autocratic regimes imposing more severe restrictions,[15] most countries have imposed restrictions on internet access. One way they achieve that objective is by banning particular apps, which is a tactic that is sometimes more effective than trying to block websites.[16] For example, China required Apple to remove the *New York Times* app from its App Store, and Russia banned Apple and Google from providing the LinkedIn app.[17] The U.S. tried to ban TikTok.

But countries have also imposed lots of other restrictions on internet access. Thailand imposed severe restrictions,[18] especially on those critical of the monarchy.[19] India recently adopted rules prohibiting all Web content that might be regarded as "disparaging," "harassing," "blasphemous," or "hateful,"[20] and has pressured tech companies regarding censorship, as have Myanmar and Turkey.[21] Moreover, Indian Prime Minister Narenda Modi has pressured Twitter to take down posts critical of his government.[22] Twitter initially rebuffed Modi, but relented and permanently blocked 500 accounts when its Indian employees were threatened with seven years' imprisonment,[23] but Twitter refused to block accounts as-

---

14. *Id.*

15. *See* Anick Jesdanun, *Internet at 40: Midlife Crisis? Barriers Threaten, Openness, Growth, The Courier-Journal*, at D5 (Sept. 6, 2009).

16. *See* Farhad Manjoo, *Censors Delight in the World's Reliance on App Stores, The New York Times* B1 (Jan. 19, 2017).

17. *Id.*

18. *See* Thomas Fuller, *Thailand Blocks Users' Access to YouTube, The New York Times*, at C12 (Apr. 5, 2007) ("Thailand's military-appointed government blocked access to YouTube and several other Internet sites on Wednesday in a crackdown on material that denigrates the country's monarch.").

19. *See* Hannah Beech, *Facebook Plans to Sue Thais Over Order to Restrain Critic, The New York Times* A2 (Aug 26, 2020).

20. *See* Vikas Bajaj, *India Put Tight Leash on Internet Free Speech, The New York Times*, at B3 (Apr. 28, 2011).

21. *See id.*

22. *See* Karan Deep Singh, *Twitter Blocks Accounts in India As Modi Pressures Social Media, The New York Times* B4 (Feb. 11, 2021).

23. *Id.*

sociated with journalists, politicians, activists, or media outlets.[24] India's suppression requests accompanied other repressive actions, including the arrest of journalists and activists, and it pressured media organizations regarding their coverage of the Modi government.[25] Of course, India is a major market for social media platforms given that it has 1.3 billion people.[26]

Nigeria banned Twitter from the country altogether,[27] and Uganda blocked the internet during elections in 2016.[28] Uganda blocked Facebook two days before a national election in 2021 after Facebook removed fake pages linked to the government that criticized the opposition and promoted the government.[29] Uganda also closed or suspended other social media platforms, including WhatsApp, Instagram and Twitter, and blocked more than 100 VPNs (virtual private networks) for fear that they could be used to circumvent the ban.[30] Allegedly, the social media ban came amidst a "crackdown on the political opposition, harassment of journalists."[31]

In the Middle East, there has been a great deal of internet repression. In Tunisia, bloggers have been jailed and harassed, and many social media posts are only visible outside the country.[32] In Algeria, a journalist was convicted for reporting about a protest movement.[33]

During the uprising that overthrew President Mubarak, Egyptian officials arrested and jailed the internet organizers.[34] In Nepal and Myanmar,

---

24. *Id.*

25. *Id.*

26. *Id.*

27. *See* Sa'eed Husaini, *His Nation in Crisis, Leader Banned Twitter, The New York Times* A19 (June 9, 2021).

28. *See* Abdi Latif Dahir, *Uganda Blocks Facebook Two Days Before Election, The New York Times* A 10 (Jan. 14, 2021).

29. *Id.*

30. *Id.*

31. *Id.*

32. *See* Brooke Gladstone, *Tunisian Blogger Lina Ben Mhenni*, National Public Radio, On the Media (Jan. 21, 2011), http://www.onthemedia.org/2011/jan/21/tunisian-blogger-lina-ben-mhenni/transcript/.

33. *See* Adam Nossiter, *Journalist in Algeria Sentenced for Reporting on Protest Movement, The New York Times* A10 (Aug. 22, 2020).

34. *See* David D. Kirkpatrick & David E. Sanger, *A Tunisian-Egyptian Link That Shook Arab History, The New York Times*, at A1 (Feb. 14, 2011) ("When the revolt exploded, the Mubarak government detained him [Wael Ghonim who established the Facebook page

the government used centralized control points to shut down the internet,[35] and Egypt managed to almost completely shut down most internet communications for a brief period during the uprising that toppled President Mubarak.[36] For a period, Syria cut its citizens off from both Facebook and YouTube,[37] and persecuted cyber-activists.[38] A number of Middle Eastern countries have limited citizen access to certain internet sites.[39] Interestingly, the suppression is not entirely one way. For example, YouTube banned Myanmar military channels in the wake of a military coup.[40]

There are numerous other examples of internet suppression in the Middle East. Bahrain blocked access to the Bambuser website where videos can be posted.[41] During uprisings, Iran cut-off cellular phone service, and dramatically slowed internet access in the squares where protests were occurring.[42] In addition, Iran threatened to execute a blogger for communicating with dissidents,[43] and tried to intimidate protestors located outside of Iran (in the U.S., for example) by pressuring their relatives who

---

that helped touch off the Egyptian protests] for 12 days in blindfolded isolation in a belated attempt to stop his work.").

35. Matt Richtel, *Egypt Cuts Off Most Internet and Cell Service, The New York Times* (Jan. 28, 2011), http://www.nytimes.com/2011/01/29/technology/internet/29cutoff.html?scp=1&sq=egypt%20cuts%20off%20most%20internet&st=Search ("Few governments have cut off access entirely; Myanmar did so in 2007, as did Nepal two years earlier.").

36. *See Egypt Autocracy Found "Off" Switch, supra* note 12; *Egypt Cuts Off Most Internet and Cell Service, supra* note 35 ("Some Internet traffic remained flowing on Friday, allowing access to and from the country's stock exchange and some government agencies, according to researchers.").

37. *See* Jennifer Preston, *Syria Restores Access to Facebook and YouTube, Raising Fears of Monitoring Users, The New York Times*, A8 (Feb. 10, 2011).

38. *See* Deborah Amos, *Syrian Activist in Hiding Presses Mission From Abroad*, National Public Radio, Morning Edition (Apr. 22, 2011), http://www.npr.org/2011/04/22/135606445/syrian-activist-in-hiding-presses-mission-from-abroad.

39. *See Egypt Cuts Off Most Internet and Cell Service, supra* note 35 ("But at least 40 countries filter specific Internet sites or services.").

40. *See* Paul Mozur, *YouTube Bans Myanmar Military Channels as Violence Rises, The New York Times* B3 (Mar. 6, 2021).

41. *See* Jennifer Preston & Brian Stelter, *Cellphone Cameras Become World's Eyes and Ears on Protests Across the Middle East, The New York Times*, at A11 (Feb. 19, 2011).

42. *See* Neil MacFarquhar & Alan Cowell, *Iran Uses Force Against Protests as Region Erupts, The New York Times*, at A1 (Feb. 15, 2011).

43. *See* Bob Garfield, *Iran's "Blogfather" Facing Possible Execution*, National Public Radio, On the Media (Sept. 24, 2010), http://www.onthemedia.org/2010/sep/24/irans-blogfather-facing-possible-execution/transcript/.

lived in Iran.[44] Recently, Iran imprisoned social media users for posting "indecent" or "immoral" content.[45]

Iraq has also imposed internet restrictions[46] by attempting to block Web sites, dropping internet speed dramatically,[47] arresting journalists and bloggers,[48] using internet-based tools to track down Web-based protestors,[49] and created an online surveillance center for that purpose.[50] In other words, Iraq has tried to use cyber tools for antidemocratic purposes,[51] in effect creating a "cybersurfing policeman [who] can compile a dossier on a regime opponent without the trouble of the street surveillance and telephone tapping required in a pre-Neb world."[52]

Saudi Arabia enacted regulations requiring all internet users, including bloggers, to register with the government.[53] In addition, Saudi regulations prohibited criticism of Islam or anything that compromises public order, and Saudi Arabia blocked websites that are critical of government, and jailed governmental critics.[54] However, even Saudi Arabia admitted that there are ways to avoid its regulations.[55] For example, internet users could connect their cell phones or other devices to services in other countries.[56]

---

44. *See* Farnaz Fassihi, *Tehran Extends Crackdown to Members of Global Diaspora: Campaign Includes Tracking Social-Networking Activities of Iranians, Identifying Them at Oppositions Protests Abroad, The Wall Street Journal*, at 14 (Dec. 4–6, 2009).

45. *See* Alissa J. Rubin, *Social Media Rules Muffle Iraqi Voices, The International New York Times* B7 (July 17, 2022).

46. *See* Timothy Williams, *Iraq Seeks to Keep a More Watchful Eye on Internet Cafes, Web Sites and Books, The Courier-Journal*, at A1 (Aug. 4, 2009).

47. *See* Jim Lehrer, *In Iran, Political Protests Move Online*, PBS News Hour (June 17, 2009) (quoting Lindsey Hilsum) (quoting Lindsey Hilsum).

48. *See* Rick Gladstone & Artin Afkhami, *Pattern of Intimidation Is Seen in Arrests of Iranian Journalists and Bloggers, The New York Times*, A9 (Jan. 26, 2012).

49. *See* Scott Shane, *Technology Helps Ignite Chain (as in Tunisia). Except When It Bolsters Oppression (as in Iran), The New York Times*, Week in Review, at 1 (Jan. 30, 2011).

50. *Id.*, at 5.

51. *Id.*

52. *Id.*

53. *See* Deborah Amos, *Social Media Revolution Hits Saudia Arabia*, National Public Radio, All Things Considered (Jan. 26, 2011), http://www.npr.org/2011/01/26/133212623/social-media-revolution-hits-saudi-arabia.

54. *See id.*

55. *See id.*

56. *See id.*

As one commentator noted, the big question is "How this authoritarian regime will live with the freedom and chaos that the internet represents."[57]

Russia has also moved to restrict internet dissent.[58] When a Russian police officer exposed police corruption in a video, he was arrested and interrogated.[59] Russian governmental officials have also tried to quell anti-government protests,[60] seized the computers that dissident groups were using to communicate on the internet,[61] forced Microsoft to cooperate in investigating the computers of dissidents,[62] shut down mobile internet access,[63] and installed a monitoring system that allowed it to spy on internet communications.[64] In 2018, Russian leaders blocked the website of an opposition leader (Aeolic A. Navalny) because it included a video accusing a high-ranking Russian official of accepting a bribe from a businessman.[65] The video depicted a deputy prime minister on the businessman's yacht with a "high class escort" and other alleged prostitutes.[66] The order to remove the video extended to YouTube and Instagram, with government orders requiring them to remove some of the accuser's information from their websites.[67] Instagram complied with the request, but YouTube was slow to do so.[68]

---

57. *See id.*

58. *See* Adam Satariano, *Kremlin Steps Up Online Censorship, The New York Times* B1 (Feb. 28, 2022).

59. *See* Clifford J. Levy, *Videos Rouse Russian Anger Toward Police: Officer Stirs Debate on Rituals of Corruption, The New York Times*, at A1 (July 28, 2010).

60. *See* Ellen Barry, *Russia Cracks Down on Antigovernment Protests: Allegations of Fraud Draw a New Generation Into Political Activism, The New York Times*, at A6 (Dec. 7, 2011).

61. *See* Clifford J. Levy, *Using Microsoft, Russia Suppresses Dissent, The New York Times*, at A1 (Sept. 12, 2010).

62. *See Id.*

63. *See* Alan Cullison, *Web Issues Plague Critics in Russia, The New York Times, The Wall Street Journal*, at A6 (Dec. 12, 2011).

64. *Id.*

65. *See* Ivan Nechepurenko, *Russia Blocks Website of Dissident Who Accused Oligarch, The New York Times International* A7 (Feb. 16, 2018).

66. *Id.*

67. *Id.*

68. *Id.*

Russia has also tried to control elections in various ways, including through the suppression of internet content.[69] For example, Russia banned dozens of websites related to the former (now deceased) dissident Alexei Navalny.[70] In addition, Russia pressured Apple and Google to suppress a Navalny-related app that was designed to coordinate protest voting.[71]

Russian censorship increased dramatically following Russia's invasion of Ukraine.[72] For one thing, it started blocking Instagram, and it referred to Instagram's parent company, Meta, as an "extremist" organization.[73] A report by Citizen Lab at the University of Toronto, which monitors online censorship, analyzed court orders against Vkontakte (a Russian social media site) which documented the increase.[74] Prior to the war, the Russian government issued a take down order roughly once every 50 days.[75] After the start of the war, it issued a take down order almost every day.[76] Some of the more recent orders were directed at independent media sites.[77] The government also blocked key words such as lesbian, gay, bisexual, transgender and queer.[78] In addition, it restricted search functions on international sites.[79] The government also sought to block certain community and personal accounts on the website, and cracked down on independent media sites covering the war,[80] and also blocked access to international sites such as Facebook (now Meta) Instagram and Twitter (now X), but not Telegram and YouTube.[81] In some instances (such as the revolt by Yevgeny Prigozhin of the Wagner Group), the censors were slow to react so that there was significant discussion on social media before the

69. *See* Andrew E. Kramer, *How the Kremlin Works to 'Manage' Democracy While Holding Elections, The New York Times* A9 (Sept. 18, 2021).

70. *Id.*

71. *See* Anton Troianovski & Adam Satariano, *Tech Giants Pull Navalny App After Kremlin Level Threats, The New York Times* A1 (Sept. 18, 2021).

72. *See* Paul Mozur, Adam Satariano & Aaron Krolik, *Internet Censorship By Russia Has Soared 30-Fold During War, The New York Times* B4 (July 27, 2023).

73. *Id.*

74. *See id.*

75. *Id.*

76. *Id.*

77. *Id.*

78. *Id.*

79. *Id.*

80. *Id.*

81. *Id.*

government intervened.[82] Despite the censorship, Citizen Lab concluded that there was less censorship than in other speech repressive nations.[83]

However, some within Russia are pushing back against the censorship.[84] A Russian group, Roskomosvoboda (Russian Communications Freedom), has been fighting back against the government's censorship efforts by unblocking websites, filing lawsuits, and revealing governmental disclosures of private information.[85] The group is described as an offshoot of Sweden's Pirate Party which is pro-internet freedom.[86]

Other examples of governmental repression can easily be found. In India, the government harassed journalists who worked for a website, News Click, that was critical of the government.[87] The United Kingdom is considering whether to impose restrictions and monitoring on social media.[88] Likewise, during anti-government protests, Myanmar shut down all internet access within the country.[89] Even Australia, which generally tends to be protective of free expression, has explored the possibility of imposing filters that allow the government to block internet content.[90] The Australian government claims that these filters would only preclude access to banned materials (*e.g.*, child pornography and terrorist materials), but the government refuses to disclose details regarding the filters and their potential impact.[91] Laws in Turkey and Thailand preclude Google from depicting unflattering videos of Turkey's founder and Thailand's

---

82. *Id.*

83. *Id.*

84. *See* Georgi Kantchev, *Web Activists Joust With Kremlin, The Wall Street Journal* A16 (Aug. 23, 2019).

85. *Id.*

86. *Id.*

87. *See* Tripti Lahiri & Shan Li, *Indian Press Cites Government Repression, The Wall Street Journal* A18 (Oct. 19, 2023).

88. *See* Ravi Somaiya, *In Britain, A Meeting on Limiting Social Media, The New York Times*, at A8 (Aug. 26, 2011).

89. *See* J.J. Sutherland, *Myanmar Shuts Down Internet Access*, National Public Radio, The NPR News Blog (Sept. 28, 2007).

90. *See* Meraiah Foley, *Australia to Test Internet Filer to Block Banned Content, The New York Times*, at A7 (Dec. 15, 2008).

91. *See id.*

monarch.[92] Germany and France restrict information that supports or promotes Nazis.[93]

Interrogators in Belarus frequently confront social-media activists regarding statements that they have made on the internet.[94] In Iraq, government agents have posed as internet "activists" in order to extract information from actual activists.[95] During the Egyptian revolt, protestors were instructed to post on certain websites rather than other ones because of a fear of governmental monitoring.[96]

An irreverent blogger in the Middle East was detained by Palestinian authorities, and threatened with execution by private individuals.[97] Palestinian authorities did not allow him to have visitors or an attorney, and refused to release him.[98] He was threatened with prosecution under a law that prohibits defamation of religion.[99] Another blogger was tried under the same law and sentenced to four years in prison.[100]

China has developed "the world's most sophisticated and brutal internet censorship system, called the Great Firewall.[101] China blocks Google, Twitter, Facebook (although the Chinese government uses Facebook outside of China for its own propaganda purposes[102]) and "thousands of other foreign websites."[103] In China, the goal of internet regulation is to create a "harmonious society," including "stability above all," as well as to prevent social unrest.[104] As part of this effort, China has created the "Golden Shield

---

92. *See* Michael Liedtke, *Google Still Must Take on Censors: China Exit Won't Help It Elsewhere, The Courier-Journal*, at D1 (Apr. 4, 2010).

93. *Id.*

94. *Id.*

95. *Id.*, at 5.

96. *Id.*

97. *See* Isabel Kershner, *A Blogger's Irreverence Infuriates West Bank Muslims, The New York Times*, at A5 (Nov. 16, 2010).

98. *Id.*

99. *Id.*

100. *Id.*

101. *See* Li Yuan, *The Infowars Hubbub, And China's Chokehold, The New York Times* B3 (Aug. 13, 2018).

102. *See* Paul Mozur, *Banned by China, but Used for Propaganda by It, The New York Times* B2 (Nov. 9, 2017).

103. *See* Yuan, *supra* note 101, at B3.

104. *See* Andrew Jacobs & Jonathan Ansield, *For China, "Stability Above All": State Pours Resources Into Monitoring Critics and Quelling Dissent, The International Herald Tribune*, at 6 (Dec. 10, 2010).

Project" which involves a national filtering system,[105] and it uses that system to preclude citizens from accessing certain foreign news sources,[106] as well as to block Gmail.[107] In 2017, it issued a list of 68 categories of material that should be censored, including information regarding excessive drinking or gambling, ridicule of China's revolutionary leaders, current members of the army, or police, as well as discussions of "the luxury life," prostitution, rape, masturbation, "unhealthy marital values," and partner swapping.[108] Nevertheless, some Chinese have found ways to avoid governmental blocking and to access banned information.[109] However, they can be held for questioning and detained if discovered.[110] Indeed, even *The New York Times* is blocked on the Chinese internet.[111] Some Google employees protested when they were asked to help Google construct a censored search engine for use in China.[112]

To control its 500 million internet users, China employs some 50,000 internet censors[113] who are asked to monitor and disrupt the actions of dissidents.[114] China has placed restrictions on Web access,[115] blog post-

---

105. *See Egypt Autocracy Found "Off" Switch, supra* note 12.

106. *See Egypt Cuts Off Most Internet and Cell Service, supra* note 35.

107. *See* David Barboza & Claire Cain Miller, *Google Accuses Chinese of Blocking Gmail Service, The New York Times*, at B6 (Mar. 21, 2011).

108. *See* Steven Lee Myers & Amy Cheng, *China Expands Its Internal Web of Online Censors and Forbidden Topics, The New York Times* A7 (Sept. 25, 2017).

109. *See* Yuan, *supra* note 101 (referring to a family which has been "using tools to bypass the Great Firewall for years.").

110. *See* Paul Mozur, *He Was Chained to a Chair in China. What Was His Offense? Posting on Twitter, The New York Times* A1 (Jan. 11, 2019).

111. *See id. See* Yuan, *supra* note 101.

112. *See* Kate Conger & Daisuke Wakabayashi, *Google Employees Protest Secret Work on Censored Search Engine for China, The New York Times* (Aug. 16, 2018).

113. *See* Brook Larmer, *In China, an Internet Joke Is Not Just a Joke. It's a Form of Defiance and the Government is Not Amused, The New York Times Magazine*, at 34–39 (Oct. 30, 2011).

114. *See For China, "Stability Above All", supra* note 104, at 6.

115. *See* David Barboza, *Foreign News Sites Appear to be Blocked in China, The New York Times*, at A8 (Dec. 10, 2010) (noting that Chinese censors have blocked access to the websites of the BBC, CNN and a Norwegian newscaster).

ings,[116] and internet use,[117] including restrictions on political speech,[118] as well as on the websites of international news organizations such as CNN and the BBC.[119] China also requires computer manufacturers to install internet filtering software, and China has shut down more than 700 internet Web sites, including Facebook, Twitter and YouTube.[120] In addition, China prohibits Chinese journalists from reporting unverified information that it finds on the internet.[121] China has pressured Google to filter and limit information that it makes available over the internet in China.[122] In response, Google moved its search engine out of mainland China.[123]

In explaining some of the new restrictions, China's Public Security minister stated that the "Internet has become an important avenue through which anti-China forces infiltrate, sabotage and magnify their

---

116. *See* Andrew Jacobs, *Internet Usage Rises in China, The New York Times* (Jan. 14, 2009), http://www.nytimes.com/2009/01/15/world/asia/15beijing.html?gwh=D0EB55B0418441E2C096AA6054507E69 (noting that, even though China has 298 million Internet users (roughly equivalent to the population of the United States), only 23% of the Chinese population uses the Internet. The article goes on to note that China regularly blocks Web sites and blog postings); *but see* Margaret Warner, *Growing Internet Use in China Reflects Changing Society*, PBS Newshour (May 30, 2008), http://www.pbs.org/newshour/bb/asia/jan-june08/youth_05-30.html (quoting a Chinese blogger who stated that, "I think currently China is more and more open. Now I'm writing some things that I don't think I would write five years ago.").

117. *See* Sharon LaFraniere, *China Imposes New Internet Controls, The New York Times*, at A18 (Dec. 17, 2009).

118. *Id.* ("The authorities say the stricter controls are intended to protect children from pornography; to limit the piracy of films, music and television shows; and to make it hard to perpetuate Internet scams. But the measures also appear devised to enhance the government's already strict control of any political opposition. In various pronouncements, top propaganda and security officials have stressed anew the need to police the Internet on ideological and security grounds.").

119. *See* David Barboza, *Beijing Appears to Block News Sites: CNN and BBC Go Dark as Nobel Ceremony s for Imprisoned Dissident, International Herald Tribune*, at 6 (Dec. 10, 2010); Jeremy Page, *China Steps Up Nobel Response, The Wall Street Journal*, at 10 (Dec. 10–12, 2010).

120. *See China Imposes New Internet Controls, supra* note 117.

121. *See* Michael Wines, *China Rolls Out Tighter Rules on Reporting, The New York Times*, at A7 (Nov. 12, 2011).

122. *See Google Still Must Take on Censors, supra* note 92.

123. *See* James Glanz & John Markoff, *Vast Hacking by a China Fearful of the Web: Cables Depict Google Shock, Censorship and Cyberattacks, The New York Times*, at A1 (Dec. 5, 2010) ("The cables catalog the heavy pressure that was placed on Google to comply with local censorship laws, as well as Google's willingness to comply—up to a point.").

capabilities for destruction. Therefore, it represents a new challenge to the public security authority in maintaining national security and social stability."[124] As a Hong Kong professor of journalism concluded, "The trend in China is toward tighter and tighter control. They are basically improving their censorship mechanisms."[125] For example, China has permanently removed or disabled various blogs,[126] and it monitors the movement of dissidents by cell phone tracking mechanisms.[127] Dissidents have been taken into police custody, and one Tweeter was sentenced to a year in prison for a single three word Tweet.[128] Finally, Web posts have been deleted,[129] but some remain up long enough to be viewed and to have impact,[130] and some internet posters have found creative ways to avoid the censors.

In 2024, China was aggressively trying to portray a rosy view of its economy, and to control critical commentary.[131] Its censorship extended to economists, financial analysts, investment banks, and social media influencers, with critical news stories being removed.[132] China's control even extended to mainstream economic commentary.[133] Some believe that the Chinese effort has reduced confidence in the economy.[134]

As TikTok has become immensely popular, with 53% of English-speaking online news viewers using TikTok, various African countries have moved to ban it.[135] The platform has been blocked in Senegal, and

124. *See China Imposes New Internet Controls*, *supra* note 114.

125. *Id.*

126. *See* Anne Stopper, *China Appears to Tighten Internet Access Around Tiananmen Anniversary*, PBS News Hour (June 1, 2009).

127. *See* Sharon LaFraniere, *Beijing to Stymie Protests By Spying on Mobile Phones*, *Sydney Morning Herald*, at 22 (Mar. 5–6, 2011).

128. *See In China, an Internet Joke Is Not Just a Joke*, *supra* note 113, at 34–39.

129. *Id.*

130. *Id.* ("[Noting that when one individual finished an animation entitled 'Crack Sunflower Seeds,' depicting the detainment of a Chinese dissident, the video was viewed by] a million or so netcitizens.... Then the video began disappearing from Chinese Web sites one by one....").

131. *See* Daisuke Wakabayashi, *China's Censors Target Critics of Its Economy*, *The New York Times* B1 (Feb. 2, 2024).

132. *Id.*

133. *Id.*

134. *Id.*

135. *See* Alexandra Wexler & Stu Woo, *TikTok Battles Against Bans in Africa*, *The Wall Street Journal* B4 (Sept. 22, 2023).

faced proposed bans in Kenya and Somalia.[136] African countries have expressed concern about sexual content on the platform.[137] TikTok survived an effort to ban it in Singapore, and it worked out a deal with Kenya to employ more Kenyan content moderators.[138] Likewise, TikTok and other Chinese apps have been banned in India.[139]

B. U.S. GOVERNMENT CENSORSHIP

Even though there was a period in U.S. history when the U.S. and state governments were able to impose significant restrictions on speech,[140] the U.S. has generally been very pro-free speech, especially relating to internet speech.[141] For example, in the Communications Decency Act of 1996 (CDA), Congress sought to limit and regulate internet speech in an effort to protect children against the dangers of the internet. The CDA prohibited the knowing dissemination of indecent messages to persons under the age of 18 and the knowing dissemination of "patently offensive" messages that would be available to persons under this age. In *Reno v. American Civil Liberties Union*,[142] the Court struck down the CDA and rendered a decision that was highly protective of the internet.[143] In that

136. *Id.*

137. *Id.*

138. *Id.*

139. *See* Maria Abi-Habib, *India Bans Chinese Mobile Apps Like TikTok, The New York Times* B5 (June 30, 2020).

140. *See, e.g., Gitlow v. New York*, 268 U.S. 652 (1925) (conviction for advocacy of illegal action); *Schenck v. United States*, 249 U.S. 47 (1919) (upholding a conviction for distributing circulars urging resistance to the draft); *see also* RUSSELL L. WEAVER, ANDREW T. KENYON, DAVID F. PARTLETT & CLIVE P. WALKER, THE RIGHT TO SPEAK ILL: DEFAMATION, REPUTATION AND FREE SPEECH 5–13 (2006) (hereafter "THE RIGHT TO SPEAK ILL").

141. *See Ashcroft v. Free Speech Coalition*, 535 U.S. 234 (2002) (striking down portions of the Child Pornography Prevention Act of 1996 that prohibited "virtual" child pornography); *Reno v. American Civil Liberties Union*, 521 U.S. 844 (1997) (striking down the Communications Decency Act on free speech grounds).

142. 521 U.S. 844 (1997).

143. In *Reno*, the Court was confronted by the question of whether the internet should be treated like the press (and, therefore, accorded a high level of protection), or like broadcasting (and subject to greater regulatory restrictions), or whether some intermediate model of review should apply. The Court struck down portions of the CDA, concluding that the internet should be treated more like the traditional press. The Court found that the internet was not analogous to broadcasting because scarcity rationale did not apply.

decision, the Court analyzed the development of the internet,[144] and the range of activities that individuals can do on the internet.[145] In the process, the Court recognized that the "Internet can hardly be considered a 'scarce' expressive commodity like the radio and broadcast spectra[146] because it "provides relatively unlimited, low cost capacity for communication of all kinds."[147] "Through the use of chat rooms, any person with a phone line can become a town crier with a voice that resonates farther than it could from any soapbox."[148] "Through the use of Web pages, mail exploders, and newsgroups, the same individual can become a pamphleteer."[149] The Court noted that "this new marketplace of ideas" has gone through "phenomenal" growth, and the Court concluded that the "interest in encouraging freedom of expression in a democratic society outweighs any theoretical but unproven benefit of censorship."[150]

In striking down the law, the Court concluded that the term "indecent" suffered from vagueness and ambiguity,[151] and the Court expressed concern that the CDA would lead to "censorship" of speech and might

---

Unlike broadcasting, in which only a few broadcast spectrum are available, the internet is almost universally accessible through personal computers. Individuals who cannot afford computers and internet access can go online at libraries or cyber-cafes. Moreover, the Court noted a historical absence of governmental regulation, and lack of intrusiveness as with broadcasting, and ultimately concluded that there was no justification for applying a diminished standard of review. Applying strict scrutiny, the Court found a compelling governmental interest in the desire to protect children from exposure to indecent material. Because the CDA could not be enforced against foreign sites, as well as because age is difficult to verify, the Court concluded that the regulatory means were not designed to achieve the stated regulatory purpose. Moreover, the CDA imposed a significant burden on adult users by limiting their right to receive information unsuitable for children. The Court concluded that Congress could use less constitutionally restrictive means, including blocking or filtering software, to achieve its objectives. In addition, the Court held that the term "patently offensive" was unduly vague.

144. *Id.* at 849–850.

145. *Id.* at 850–852.

146. *Id.* at 870.

147. *Id.*

148. *Id.*

149. *Id.*

150. *Id.* at 849–850.

151. *Id.* at 870 ("Regardless of whether the CDA is so vague that it violates the Fifth Amendment, the many ambiguities concerning the scope of its coverage render it problematic for purposes of the First Amendment.").

silence "some speakers whose messages would be entitled to constitutional protection."[152] Although the Court recognized that society has an interest in "protecting children from harmful materials," the Court concluded that this interest does not justify "an unnecessarily broad suppression of speech addressed to adults."[153] As the Court concluded "the level of discourse reaching a mailbox simply cannot be limited to that which would be suitable for a sandbox."[154]

Following the decision in *Reno*, Congress enacted the Child Online Pornography Act (COPA) which was designed to limit children's exposure to indecent materials on the internet. The Child Online Pornography Act (COPA) prohibited knowing communication for commercial purposes of any material that is harmful to minors. In *Ashcroft v. American Civil Liberties Union*,[155] the Court addressed the question of whether COPA's use of the term "community standards," as the basis for determining whether material was harmful, created a problem of substantial overbreadth. The Court concluded that, because COPA applies to significantly less material than the CDA and defines harmful-to-minors by reference to well-established obscenity standards, the community standards provision was not overbroad. Nevertheless, in *Ashcroft*, the Court struck down the Child Pornography Prevention Act (CPPA) which prohibited the visual depiction, including computer or computer-generated images, of a minor engaged in sexually explicit conduct. In striking down the law, the Court emphasized that CPPA did not prohibit just images that appeal to a prurient interest, or that are patently offensive, but also prohibited speech that had serious literary, artistic, political, or scientific value.

Congress responded to the *Ashcroft* decision by enacting legislation prohibiting the distribution and possession of material marketed as child pornography. In *United States v. Williams*,[156] the Court held that such pandering could be criminalized regardless of whether it depicted actual or digital images, rejecting the argument that the law was unconstitutionally vague or overbroad.

152. *Id.* at 874.
153. *Id.* at 875.
154. *Id.*
155. 535 U.S. 234 (2002).
156. 553 U.S. 285 (2008).

There are plenty of examples of internet repression in the U.S. Not only U.S. governmental officials, but also European and Indian governmental officials, have expressed concerns regarding TikTok.[157] They are worried about TikTok's connections to China's government and therefore perceived national security concerns[158] as well as privacy issues.[159] They are also concerned that TikTok's parent company (ByteDance) is being or might be forced by Chinese governmental officials to spy on TikTok users.[160] TikTok denies that it has ever received such a request from the Chinese government and asserts that it would refuse to comply if it did.[161] Critics question whether there is sufficient evidence of governmental interference or meddling.[162] There are also claims that TikTok feeds adolescents a "diet of darkness,"[163] including a focus on eating disorders, body image, self-harm, and suicide.[164] For example, in the U.S., Montana banned TikTok and Google and Apple from making TikTok's app available for download.[165] Subsequently, Congress enacted legislation trying to force the Chinese company (ByteDance) to sell the social media platform TikTok.

There are rumors that officials in the United States are also seeking software that will help them monitor and evaluate information posted on the Web.[166] For example, the Trump Administration required applicants

---

157. *See* Wexler & Woo, *supra* note 135, at B4.

158. *Id.*

159. *Id.*

160. *Id. See* Stu Wo & Meghan Bobrowsky, *Montana Imposes Statewide Ban on TikTok, The Wall Street Journal* A1 (May 18, 2023).

161. *See* Wo & Bobrowsky, *supra* note 162, at A1.

162. *Id.* (citing an ACLU lawyer for the proposition that the "U.S. government hasn't pointed to any specific or direct evidence of national security harm from TikTok–only vague speculation about how Americans' date might be used, or how the Chinese government might be able to promote propaganda.").

163. *See* Julie Jargon, *TikTok Feeds Tenns a Diet of Darkness, The Wall Street Journal* A11 (May 15, 2023).

164. *Id.*

165. *See* Wo & Bobrowsky, *supra* note 162, at A1; *see also* Amy Beth Hansen & Haleluya Hadero, *Montana First State to Ban TikTok, Courier-Journal* 14A (May 19, 2023).

166. *See* Marcus Wohlsen, *U.S. Seeks Software to Monitor Web: Feds Want to Mine Social Media to Predict Events, The Atlanta Journal-Constitution*, at A4 (Feb. 13, 2012).

for visas to disclose their social media profiles.[167] Although the purpose of the requirement was to help uncover potential terrorists, the government later concluded that the information had little efficacy.[168] The collection of such information did have the potential to chill online speech and endanger privacy.[169]

There is also evidence that U.S. governmental officials, while not outright prohibiting internet content (as is done in many other countries), has pressured and threatened social media platforms in an attempt to force them to suppress internet content. The nature of social media platforms, in particular the fact that social media platforms can easily remove posts from their platforms, gives the government a unique opportunity to try to control (and, indeed, suppress) freedom of expression. In particular, government can pressure platforms to suppress speech to which the government objects or disagrees.

The U.S. government's efforts to repress internet content was revealed by the trial court decision in *Missouri v. Biden*.[170] That decision provides a chilling look at the Biden administration's aggressive efforts to control and suppress free speech. Purportedly, in an effort to combat "disinformation," the White House pressured and threatened social media platforms regarding their content-moderation decisions. The *Boston Globe* analogized the government's actions to working "the refs [the content moderators of social media platforms] like an aggressive football coach, hectoring and goading [social media platform] executives into exercising ever-stricter control over what users are permitted to say."[171] Moreover, as we shall see, some of the speech that the White House tried to suppress was not disinformation at all, but simply information that the government wanted to suppress, and sometimes that suppression amounted to disinformation itself.

---

167. See Charles Savage, *Reviewing Social Media in Visa Cases Doesn't Aid Security, Documents Say, The New York Times* A13 (Oct. 6, 2023).

168. *Id.*

169. *Id.*

170. 2023 WL 5841935 (W.D. La. 2023), *affirmed in part, reversed in part, vacated in part, and remanded*, 83 F.4th 350 (5th Cir. 2023), *stay granted sur nom Murthy v. Missouri*, ___ S.Ct. ___, 2023 WL 6763585 (2023).

171. *See* Hiawatha Bray, *We Ignore Musk's 'Twitter Files' at Our Peril, Boston Globe* B (Jan. 20, 2023).

Since they are regarded as private entities, social media platforms are viewed as having independent authority to censor material on their platforms. However, the *Biden* decision details how the Biden Administration routinely attempted to insert itself into the decision making process. There were ongoing and constant communications between the White House (and other governmental officials) and social media platforms regarding censorship of speech, and the government pressured, coerced, and threatened social media platforms regarding their content moderation. The government promulgated a regulation requiring social media platforms to provide the government with information about their censorship decisions.[172] The government then pressured social media platforms to curb disinformation, including going so far as to flag problematic posts, encourage platforms to suppress the spread of certain types of information, to suspend certain users and even to de-platform them.[173] The range of topics on which the government sought censorship covered a wide range of hot button issues, including allegations regarding Hunter Biden's laptop (which will be discussed more fully below),[174] Covid-19,[175] Covid vaccines,[176] Covid lockdowns,[177] climate change,[178] abortion,[179] gen-

172. *Id.*, at 18:

> On March 3, 2022, the Office of the Surgeon General issued a formal Request for Information ("RFI"), published in the Federal Register, seeking information from social-media platforms and others about the spread of misinformation. The RFI indicated that the Office of the Surgeon General was expanding attempts to control the spread of misinformation on social media and other technology platforms. The RFI also sought information about censorship policies, how they were enforced, and information about disfavored speakers. The RFI was sent to Facebook, Google/YouTube, LinkedIn, Twitter, and Microsoft by Max Lesko ("Lesko"), Murthy's Chief of Staff, requesting responses from these social-media platforms. Murthy again restated social-media platforms' responsibility to reduce the spread of misinformation in an interview with GQ Magazine. Murthy also specifically called upon Spotify to censor health information.

173. *Id.*

174. *Biden*, 2023 WL 5841935, at 5.

175. *Id.*

176. *Id.*

177. *Id.*

178. *Id.*, at 36.

179. *Id.*

der discussions,[180] health,[181] and economic policy.[182] As we shall see, some of the information that was suppressed was not disinformation at all.

The *Biden* case details that U.S. government officials constantly interacted with social media platforms through emails, private portals, and meetings.[183] During these interactions, White House officials "made it very clear to social-media companies what they wanted suppressed and what they wanted amplified."[184] For example, the day after the White House Press Secretary made remarks about removing the antitrust exemption from social media companies, White House officials followed up with emails demanding to know what the social media companies were doing about alleged disinformation.[185] Some of the communications were both aggressive and demanding.[186] The communications were so frequent that the platforms and government officials began to refer to themselves as "partners" and as being "on the same team."[187] Indeed, Twitter created a "partner portal" for governmental communications.[188] These communications led social media platforms to aggressively suppress information, even information that did not violate their terms of use policies, and which did not involve disinformation, but which the government wanted

---

180. *Id.*

181. *Id.*

182. *Id.*

183. *Id.*, at 12–19.

184. *Id.*

185. *Id.*, at 31–32:

> The next day, Flaherty followed up with another email to Facebook and chastised Facebook for not catching various COVID-19 misinformation. Flaherty demanded more information about Facebook's efforts to demote borderline content, stating, "Not to sound like a broken record, but how much content is being demoted, and how effective are you at mitigating reach, and how quicky?" Flaherty also criticized Facebook's efforts to censor the "Disinformation Dozen": "Seems like your 'dedicated vaccine hesitancy policy' isn't stopping the disinfo-dozen—they're being deemed as not dedicated—so it feels like that problem likely coming over to groups."

186. *Id.*, at 32 ("Things apparently became tense between the White House and Facebook after that, culminating in Flaherty's July 15, 2021 email to Facebook, in which Flaherty stated: 'Are you guys fucking serious? I want an answer on what happened here and I want it today.'").

187. *Id.*, at 31 ("The White House Defendants used emails, private portals, meetings, and other means to involve itself as "partners" with social-media platforms.").

188. *Id.* (referring to "emails, private portals, meetings").

suppressed.[189] Governmental officials routinely "'flagged' for Facebook and other social-media platforms posts the White House Defendants considered misinformation."[190] The White House followed up by demanding updates and reports from the platforms regarding their handling of the alleged disinformation, and the social-media companies usually complied with these demands.[191]

Governmental officials threatened social media platforms in order to ensure their cooperation. White House officials threatened to remove Section 230 liability protections from platforms that did not do more to censor "misinformation" and "disinformation."[192] These threats were reinforced by "emails, meetings, press conferences, and intense pressure by the White House, as well as by the Surgeon General Defendants."[193] While threats were made against social media platforms under the Trump administration, they increased significantly under the Biden administration.[194] The Biden Administration had extensive interactions with social-media companies and its efforts produced the desired effect: "paired with the public threats and tense relations between the Biden administration and social-media companies, seemingly resulted in an efficient report-and-censor relationship between Defendants and social-media companies."[195] The threats were reinforced by public statements by the President's press secretary regarding potential antitrust actions against the major social media platforms if they did not act to curb disinformation.[196]

---

189. *Id.*

190. *Id.*

191. *Id.*

192. *Id.*, at 12.

193. *Id.*, at 130.

194. *Id.*, at 176 ("Government officials began publicly threatening social-media companies with adverse legislation as early as 2018. In the wake of COVID-19 and the 2020 election, the threats intensified and became more direct.").

195. *Id.*

196. *Id.*, at 31:

> At a White House Press Conference, Psaki publicly reminded Facebook and other social-media platforms of the threat of "legal consequences" if they do not censor misinformation more aggressively. Psaki further stated: "The President's view is that the major platforms have a responsibility related to the health and safety of all Americans to stop amplifying untrustworthy content, disinformation, and misinformation, especially related to COVID-19 vaccinations and elections." Psaki linked the threat of a "robust anti-trust program" with the

Mark Zuckerberg (of Meta) flatly declared that he regarded "the threat of antitrust enforcement [as] 'an existential threat' to his platform."[197] Also, "the White House National Climate Advisor Gina McCarthy ('McCarthy') blamed social-media companies for allowing misinformation and disinformation about climate change to spread and explicitly tied these censorship demands with threats of adverse legislation regarding the Communications Decency Act."[198] Finally, the White House issued a memorandum about disinformation which specifically threatened the platforms with sanctions if they did not do enough to curb disinformation.[199] The U.S. government's efforts were backed up by implied and explicit threats to take action against social media platforms that did not comply with its wishes.

It would be one thing if the U.S. government were seeking to censor unprotected speech, such as obscenity or child pornography, or to censor fraudulent commercial speech. As previously discussed, none of that speech is entitled to First Amendment protection,[200] and can be prohibited and the disseminator may even be subject to criminal prosecution.[201] However, the speech involved in the *Biden* case did not necessarily involve prohibited speech. On the contrary, it involved such topics as climate

---

White House's censorship demand. "He also supports better privacy protections and a robust anti-trust program. So, his view is that there's more that needs to be done to ensure that this type of misinformation; disinformation; damaging, sometime life-threatening information, is not going out to the American public."

197. *Id.*

198. *Id.*, at 13.

199. *Id.*:

On June 16, 2022, the White House announced a new task force to target "general misinformation" and disinformation campaigns targeted at women and LBGTQI individuals who are public and political figures, government and civic leaders, activists, and journalists. The June 16, 2022, Memorandum discussed the creation of a task force to reel in "online harassment and abuse" and to develop programs targeting such disinformation campaigns. The Memorandum also called for the Task Force to confer with technology experts and again threatened social-media platforms with adverse legal consequences if the platforms did not censor aggressively enough.

200. *See New York v. Ferber*, 458 U.S, 747 (1982); *Miller v. California*, 413 U.S. 15 (1973).

201. *Id.*

change,[202] Covid-19,[203] the efficacy and safety of Covid-19 vaccines,[204] and the Hunter Biden laptop story.[205] While some of the statements on those topics might be regarded as "inaccurate" or "disinformation" by some, none of these topics fell within a category of unprotected speech. Thus, the statements were not otherwise prohibitable.

As a general rule, false speech (disinformation) is not necessarily prohibitable under the First Amendment. *United States v. Alvarez*[206] involved an individual's false assertion that he had won the Congressional Medal of Honor. While *Alvarez* recognized that individuals can be prosecuted for false speech in limited and defined circumstances (e.g., perjury in a judicial proceeding or making false statements to a governmental official or agency),[207] the Court held that Alvarez could not be convicted for making a false statement to the effect that he had won the medal. Of course, if an individual disseminates false and defamatory information about another person, it is theoretically possible to recover for defamation.[208] However, it is extremely difficult for public officials to win a defamation action,[209] and equally difficult for public figures to do so.[210] As a result, until recently, defamation litigation was relatively uncommon in the United States.[211] In addition, courts are rarely permitted to enjoin false speech except false commercial speech.[212] So, generally, the First Amendment prohibits government from censoring speech simply because it regards that speech as disinformation.[213] Indeed, the U.S. does not have "truth commissions" or "censorship boards" which are allowed to dictate which ideas and which facts are permissible, and which are not. On the contrary, the U.S. Su-

---

202. *See Biden*, 2023 WL 5841935 , at 36.

203. *See id.*, at 5.

204. *Id.*

205. *Id.*

206. 567 U.S. 709 (2012).

207. *Id.*

208. *See* The Right to Speak Ill, *supra* note 140.

209. *See New York Times Co. v. Sullivan*, 376 U.S. 254 (1964).

210. *See Curtis Publishing Co. v. Butts*, 388 U.S. 130 (1967).

211. *See* The Right to Speak Ill, *supra* note 140, at 85.

212. *See New York Times Co. v. United States*, 403 U.S. 713 (1971); *Near v. Minnesota*, 283 U.S. 697 (1931).

213. *See Cohen v. California*, 403 U.S. 15 (1971); *Tinker v. Des Moines Independent Community School District*, 393 U.S. 503 (1969).

preme Court has been wary of governmental attempts to control the flow of information, and has generally regarded both content-based and viewpoint-based restrictions on speech as presumptively unconstitutional.[214] Ultimately, it is not for government to dictate what people should believe, but rather for the people to decide for themselves. If the legitimacy of our governmental system depends on the consent of the governed, it is inconsistent with that system to give government the power to control, limit, and suppress the range of ideas that the people can hear or consider.[215]

The *Biden* case is particularly disturbing because the government's efforts to squelch disinformation actually resulted in the perpetuation of disinformation, and the Biden Administration effectively coerced social media platforms into collaborating with its efforts to disseminate disinformation. Consider, for example, the Hunter Biden laptop story. Before the story broke, White House officials warned social media platforms that Russia was about to disseminate disinformation.[216] After the laptop story broke, 51 former intelligence officials came forward to label the story as "Russian disinformation."[217] "The FBI additionally likely misled social-media companies into believing the Hunter Biden laptop story was Russian disinformation" because, even though it had control of the laptop and knew that the allegations were true, it suggested that the story was false.[218] Worse, "the FBI was included in Industry meetings and bilateral meetings, and it received and forwarded alleged misinformation to

214. *See R.A.V. v. City of St. Paul*, 505 U.S. 377 (1992).

215. *See Ashcroft v. American Civil Liberties Union*, 535 U.S. 564, 573 (2002).

216. *Biden, supra*, at 28 ("Before the Hunter Biden Laptop story breaking prior to the 2020 election on October 14, 2020, the FBI and other federal officials repeatedly warned industry participants to be alert for "hack and dump" or "hack and leak" operations.").

217. *See* Luke Broadwater, Officials Who Cast Doubt on Hunter Biden Laptop Face Questions, The New York Times (May 16, 2023); Scott Simon, *More Details Emerge in Federal Investigation into Hunter Biden*, Weekend Edition Saturday (Apr. 9, 2022), https://www.npr.org/2022/04/09/1091859822/more-details-emerge-in-federal-investigation-into-hunter-biden ("And then there was this cohort of paid pundits—50 former national security officials, many of them appearing frequently in mainstream media outlets—who came together for a statement saying that this surfacing of the laptop bore all the hallmarks of a Russian misinformation campaign.") (quoting David Folkenflik).

218. *Biden, supra*, at 144.

social-media companies, and actually misled social-media companies regarding the story."[219]

Most reputable news organizations denounced the Hunter Biden laptop story as "fake news," and refused to report the story even though there were allegations of corruption by the Bidens.[220] For example, National Public Radio, in a segment issued just a couple of weeks before the presidential election, dismissed the story as "questionable,"[221] and suggested that the allegations were part of a conspiracy theory pushed by then President Trump and his allies.[222] The Public Broadcasting Service (PBS) similarly dismissed the allegations, suggesting that Trump's allies were pushing "Russian disinformation,"[223] and the *New York Times* suggested that Trump was colluding with the Russians and dismissed the story stating that "Giuliani's dirty tricks are the scandal, not Hunter Biden's hard drive."[224]

On social media networks, including Facebook and Twitter, the story was essentially purged due, in large part, to the government's suppression efforts.[225] Not only did Twitter squelch the story,[226] it blocked users from sharing links to the *New York Post* story and prevented users who had previously sent tweets sharing the story from sending new tweets until

---

219. *Id.*, at 142.

220. *Id.*

221. *See* David Folkenflik, *Analysis: Questionable 'N.Y. Post' Scoop Driven By Ex-Hannity Producer And Giuliani*, National Public Radio (Oct. 17, 2020). https://www.npr.org/2020/10/17/924506867/analysis-questionable-n-y-post-scoop-driven-by-ex-hannity-producer-giuliani.

222. *Id.* ("The story fits snugly into a narrative from President Trump and his allies that Hunter Biden's zealous pursuit of business ties abroad also compromised the former vice president.").

223. *See* Judy Woodruff, *Are Trump Allies Sharing Russian Disinformation About Biden?*, PBS NewsHour (Oct. 16, 2020). https://www.pbs.org/video/warning-signs-1602880956/.

224. *See* Michelle Goldberg, *Is the Trump Campaign Colluding with Russia Again?*, *International New York Times* 26 (Oct. 21, 2020).

225. *See* Simon, *supra* note 217.

226. *See id.* ("First, let's acknowledge social media's role. A number of platforms tamped down on sharing of the Post's story. In the case of Twitter, not only did they try to block sharing of it, they suspended The New York Post's actual Twitter account for sharing its own article. That was a wild overreach, and even Twitter had to acknowledge that.") (quoting David Folkenflik).

they had deleted the previous tweet.[227] Further, Facebook began reducing the story's distribution on its platform pending a third-party fact-check.[228]

Today, reputable news organizations recognize that the Hunter Biden laptop story was not "disinformation," "fake news," or "Russian propaganda." A *New York Times* article, citing reporting by a staff member at Politico, stated that "the most explosive emails from Hunter Biden's purported laptop were entirely genuine" and were not simply Russian-planted disinformation.[229] Even National Public Radio has recognized that the essence of the story regarding the laptop was valid: "much of the mainstream media dismissed a story about Hunter Biden's business dealings. Now emails supporting the story have been authenticated."[230] And the *Boston Globe* questioned the decision to suppress the story.[231] The government's efforts to conceal the truth were troubling. If the government had tried to suppress the story, it would have been regarded as imposing an unconstitutional "prior restraint" on speech. Governments have also attempted to control hate speech with a new website entitled hatecrimehelp.com.[232]

At the state level, there has also been internet repression in the United States. For example, when two individuals issued Tweets that were critical of Pennsylvania Attorney General Tom Corbett, Corbett served a subpoena on Twitter in an attempt to uncover the identity of the Tweeters.[233] Civil rights groups were outraged, claiming that Corbett was trying to suppress dissent.[234] The Attorney General's office disagreed, arguing that the information was being sought in connection with an ongoing crimi-

227. *Id.*

228. *Id.*

229. *See* Bret Stephens, *An Ethically Challenged Presidency, International New York Times* 21 (Oct. 7, 2021).

230. *See* Simon, *supra* note 217.

231. *See* Bray, *supra* note 171 ("Another discovery: There's no evidence of any "deep state" conspiracy behind Twitter's decision to suppress the New York Post's October 2020 story about the contents of a laptop belonging to President Biden's son Hunter. Twitter executives screwed up that decision all by themselves. They chose to believe a false allegation that the data had been stolen by hackers."), 2023 WLNR 2287522.

232. *See* Marc Davis, *Fighting Hate: Website Serves More Than 2,000 in First Year of Reporting Incidents, ABA Journal* 14 (Sept. 2018).

233. *See* John Schwartz, *Twitter Fighting Pennsylvania Subpoena Seeking Names of 2 Tweeters, The New York Times*, at B4 (May 21, 2010).

234. *Id.*

nal investigation.[235] Similarly, the United States has served subpoenas on Twitter related to the WikiLeaks disclosures.[236] Although the government tried to serve "secret" subpoenas, which would have prevented disclosure to the affected individuals or the public, Twitter successfully opposed portions of the secrecy request.[237]

In the final analysis, governmental attempts at repression raises questions regarding whether the internet will remain a powerful vehicle for change. There is hope, though, in that individuals may find ways to circumvent governmental repression. For example, in Egypt, as noted, when governmental officials tried to shut down the internet in an attempt to halt anti-government protests, Egyptian citizens found ways to circumvent governmental controls and continue to communicate, and the number of protestors increased. In an era of tech-savvy citizens, such circumventions are likely. In addition, new internet-based devices are being developed which assist individuals in evading censorship.[238] These include Haystack which allows users to conceal their identity and thereby escape surveillance (although there are questions about whether Haystack really works).[239]

C. GOVERNMENTAL USE OF THE INTERNET FOR PROPAGANDA PURPOSES

At the same time that many governments are attempting to suppress internet speech, they are aggressively trying to use the internet to convey their own propaganda. The situation is similar to the Middle Ages when governments were happy to have the printing press for their own use, but were not keen to allow the people to use it. Today, while engaging in internet repression, many countries use the internet to communicate

235. *Id.*

236. *See* Noam Cohen, *Twitter Shines a Spotlight on Secret F.B.I. Subpoena*, *The New York Times*, at B3 (Jan. 10, 2011).

237. *Id.*

238. *See* NPR Staff, *A New Way Around Internet Censorship?*, National Public Radio, at All Things Considered (July 31, 2011), http://www.npr.org/2011/07/31/138872976/a-new-way-around-internet-censorship.

239. *See* Brooke Gladstone, *Is Haystack Too Good to Be True?*, National Public Radio, On the Media (Sept. 10, 2010), http://www.onthemedia.org/2010/sep/10/is-haystack-too-good-to-be-true/transcript/.

information to their people or to engage in propaganda.[240] For example, in Thailand, the government uses the internet to attack its critics.[241] Likewise, the N.Y. City police department uses social media to respond to criticism of the Department.[242] Likewise, North Korea uses the internet to evade sanctions and allegedly to engage in cybercrime.[243]

While China prohibits its own citizens from using Facebook, it aggressively uses that medium to promote China's interests outside of the county.[244] As a result, China maintains hundreds of English language Facebook posts stressing China's stability and prosperity,[245] and it pays individuals to post pro-government information on websites.[246]

In a similar vein, the U.S. has created an internet "Embassy" that it is using to communicate with ordinary Iranians.[247] There are allegations that Vladimir Putin of Russia has hired bloggers to write in support of his presidential effort.[248] And, as technology gets more sophisticated, the government's ability to propagandize is enhanced.[249] For example, governments can now use AI to determine who is more susceptible to particular governmental messages, and they can also use bots to help spread their messages.[250] Machine learning will only enhance governmental capabilities.[251]

Numerous commentators contend that Russia has used the internet to try to manipulate and control public opinion regarding the Ukraine

---

240. *See* Mozur, *supra* note 102, at B2.

241. *See* Hannah Beech & Sun Narin, *How Autocrat Used Facebook to Smear Critic, The New York Times International* A1 (May 23, 2020).

242. *See* Maria Cramer & Dana Rubinstein, *N.Y.P.D. Officials Use Social Media to Push Back Against Critics, The New York Times* A18 (Apr. 6, 2024).

243. *See* David E. F, *Web Use in North Korea Rises, Evading Sanctions, The New York Times* A11 (Feb. 10, 2020).

244. *See* Mozur, *supra* note 102, at B2.

245. *Id.*

246. *See A Blogger's Irreverence, supra* note 97, at 5.

247. *Internet "Embassy" To Be Set Up for Iranians, The Courier-Journal*, at A3 (Oct. 27, 2011).

248. *See* Alan Cullison, *Web Strike Blamed on Pro-Putin Youth, The Wall Street Journal*, A11 (Feb. 10, 2012).

249. See Richard Fontaine & Kara Frederick, *The Autocrat's New Tool Kit, The Wall Street Journal* C1 (Mar. 16–17, 2019).

250. *Id.*

251. *Id.*

War.[252] If these reports are accurate, they parallel reports regarding Russia's prior use of internet messaging which commentators viewed as highly effective,[253] and which involved a variety of different messaging methods.[254] One commentator described the pre-war Russian messaging as "unstoppable," and characterized President Vladimir Putin as "a master of information warfare."[255] Commentators claim that Russia planted falsehoods on official news outlets as a way of obfuscating facts, defining false narratives, and manipulating audiences.[256] Indeed, some claim that Russia interfered in the U.S.'s 2016 presidential election in an effort to secure Donald Trump's election,[257] and to undermine Democratic candidate Hillary Clinton.[258] Russia allegedly did so by disseminating hash tags such as "#Trump2016" "#TrumpTrain" and "Hillary4Prison."[259] One blog post allegedly referred to Hillary as "pure evil," and one media outlet reported that a Russian operative was reprimanded for not produc-

---

252. *See, e.g.*, Weilong Kong & Timothy Marler, *Ukraine's Lessons for the Future of Hybrid Warfare*, The Rand Blog (Nov. 28, 2022), https://www.rand.org/blog/2022/11/ukraines-lessons-for-the-future-of-hybrid-warfare.html.

253. *See* P.W. Singer, *How Ukraine Won the #Like War, Politico* (Mar. 12, 2022) ("In the arena of information warfare, there was arguably no one more feared over the last decade than Vladimir Putin. Russia's information warriors ran wild for years, hacking democracies by intervening in more than 30 national elections from Hungary and Poland to Brexit and the 2016 U.S. presidential race. They elevated conspiracy theories that ranged from Q-Anon to coronavirus vaccine lies and provided justification for Russian military action everywhere from Georgia to Syria."), https://www.politico.com/news/magazine/2022/03/12/ukraine-russia-information-warfare-likewar-00016562.

254. *See* Jamie Dettmer, *Russia's Disinformation Playbook Ripped Apart*, VOA News (Mar. 15, 2022) ("They have often expressed frustration at how Russian disinformation has gained traction, managing to roil the 2016 race for the U.S. presidency, worsen political divisions in Europe during the 2015–16 refugee crisis and in Syria shaping a narrative linking opponents of Syrian leader Bashar al-Assad, as well as the first-responders the White Helmets, with jihadists and the Islamic State terror group."), https://www.voanews.com/a/russia-disinformation-playbook-ripped-apart/6486203.html; Kong & Marler, *supra* note 252.

255. *Id.*

256. *Id.*

257. *See* Dustin Volz, *Pence Points Finger at Russia for 2016 Election Meddling, The Wall Street Journal* A7 (Aug. 1, 2018).

258. *See* Neil MacFarquhar, *Inside Russia's Troll Factory: Turning Out Fake Content at a Breakneck Pace, The New York Times* A11 (Feb. 19, 2018).

259. *See* Scott Shane, *How Unwitting Americans Encountered Russian Operatives Online, The New York Times* A10 (Feb. 18, 2018).

ing enough posts critical of Clinton.[260] These claims find support in the findings of special counsel Robert Mueller who indicted 12 Russians for masterminding computer attacks designed to undermine the Democratic Party,[261] as well as for paying for online advertisements that encouraged voters to favor then presidential candidate, Donald Trump, or perhaps to vote for presidential candidate Jill Stein.[262] The assumption is that Stein voters would otherwise have voted for presidential candidate Hillary Clinton, and that a vote for Stein would harm Clinton's electoral possibilities. Although some Clinton supporters believe that the Russian efforts tipped the election in Trump's favor,[263] it is not clear how much impact the posts had.[264] There were lots of problems with Clinton's presidential campaign, including Clinton's general unpopularity.[265]

Commentators also claim that Russia tried to destabilize the U.S. political system and "remove faith" in America prior to the Ukraine War.[266] One of the tactics allegedly used by the Russians during the 2016 presidential campaign was to sow discord "among U.S. voters through social media. Russia purportedly achieved that objective by impersonating Americans, as well as by coordinating with unwitting U.S. activists, and even by planning protest rallies.[267] Russians also allegedly tried to weigh

260. *Id.*

261. *See* Tom Schoenberg & Greg Farrell, *U.S. Indicts 12 Russians Before Trump's Meeting with Putin, The United States Law Week* (July 13, 2018); Scott Shane & Mark Mazzetti, *Indictment Bares Russian Network to Twist 2016 Vote: Mueller Chronicles a Social Media War, The New York Times* A1 (Feb. 17, 2018).

262. *See* Jonathan Martin & Maggie Haberman, *Moscow's Hand Swirled in U.S., but Whether It Tipped Election Is Unclear The New York Times* A11 (Feb. 19, 2018) (As Clinton's campaign communications director alleged, "Russia succeeded in weakening her [Clinton] enough so that the Comey letter could knock her off.").

263. *Id.* (As Clinton's campaign communications director alleged, "Russia succeeded in weakening her [Clinton] enough so that the Comey letter could knock her off.").

264. *See id.* ("And the nation's intelligence agencies say they do not have any way to calculate whether the Russian effort swung the election.").

265. *Id.*

266. *See* David W. Hawpe, *Book Review: Hacking America; Counter-Terrorism Expert Argues Putin Intends, With The Help of Cybersecurity Forces and President Trump's Demagoguery, to "Remove Faith in America Itself," The Courier-Journal* 1I (Apr. 1, 2018).

267. *See* Schoenberg & Farrell, *supra* note 261.

in on debates regarding the Affordable Care Act (ACA).[268] In a four year period, Russia allegedly sent out some 600 posts related to the ACA, and some of the accounts on which these messages were posted had more than 100,000 followers.[269] Although there were tweets on both sides of the ACA issue, approximately 80% of the ACA-related tweets offered an anti-ACA perspective.[270]

Some media observers believe that Russian officials conducted these campaigns through the so-called Internet Research Agency (IRA)[271] which was alleged to have created hundreds of fake accounts and pages on social media,[272] and which spent large amounts on social media advertising.[273] Some election observers claim that the IRA also arranged Facebook advertisements, and used Facebook to organize protest rallies beginning in 2015.[274] The IRA allegedly used Twitter, PayPal and YouTube as well.[275]

Media reports claim that the IRA used "trolls" (essentially, Russian individuals who posed as Americans) to weigh in on controversial issues.[276] These "trolls," purportedly numbering in the thousands, worked 12 hour shifts, and were prepped regarding what to say on social media.[277] Each troll was expected to produce at least 80 comments per day and to make at least 20 shares per day.[278] Trolls allegedly forwarded posts to a "countless" number of fake accounts in an effort to create large numbers of "page

---

268. *See* Stephanie Armour & Paul Overberg, *Russian Tweets Target ACA: Nearly 10,000 Twitter Posts Disparaged or Praised—Health Law, New Analysis Shows,* The Wall Street Journal A4 (Sept. 13, 2018).

269. *Id.*

270. *Id.*

271. *See* Georgia Wells & Deepa Seetharaman, *Campaign Ads to Flood Facebook, The Wall Street Journal* A4 (Sept. 1–2, 2018).

272. *Id.*

273. *See* Kenneth Osgood, *The C.I.A.'s Fake News, The New York Times* A19 (Oct. 14, 2017).

274. *See* Sheera Frenkel & Katie Benner, *To Stir Discord, Russians Liked Facebook Most: Indictment Singles Out a Social Network, The New York Times* A1 (Feb. 18, 2018).

275. *Id.*

276. *See* Mike Isaac, *For Social Media, an Election Day Test, The New York Times,* The Week in Tech B3 (Nov. 12, 2018); Anton Troianovski, *A Former Russian Troll Speaks: "It was like being in Orwell's World," The Washington Post* (Feb. 18, 2018).

277. *See* MacFarquhar, *supra* note 258.

278. *Id.*

views."[279] Russia probably used bots as well. One commentator concluded that, at one point, "YouTube had as much traffic from bots masquerading as people as it did from real human visitors."[280] In 2018, Google removed some 42 YouTube channels that it alleged were connected to the IRA,[281] some of which purportedly discouraged minorities from voting in the midterm elections.[282] One of the sites was "Woke Black" which urged African-Americans to stay home from the polls rather than support "the lesser of two evils."[283]

Given Russia's prior successes, one would have expected it to be very successful in its messaging regarding the Ukraine war.[284] At the beginning of the war, Russia allegedly used a variety of tactics, including espionage, cyberattacks, and internet-based disinformation, to soften Ukraine's defenses and groom Ukraine for the invasion.[285] This approach was similar to the approach it used when it annexed Crimea (2014) and during the Russo-Georgian War (2008).[286] Indeed, a Rand Corporation report concluded that Russia has used both technology and media in ways that would have been "inconceivable during the Cold War."[287] Its arsenal of weapons included "the Internet, social media, and the evolving landscape of professional and amateur journalism and media outlets."[288] The Rand report describes Russian messaging as "rapid, continuous and repetitive,"[289] and claims that it was being distributed through "high

279. *Id.*

280. Michael H. Keller, *The Business of Serving Up YouTube Views: Streams Are for Sale, Eyes Not Included, The New York Times* A18 (Aug. 12, 2018); *see also See* Brian X. Chen, *The Internet Trolls Have Won. Get Used to It, The New York Times* B-7 (Aug. 9, 2018).

281. *See* Chen, *supra* note 280, at B-7.

282. *See* Martin & Haberman, *supra* note 262.

283. *Id.*; *see also* Scott Shane, *Some of the Popular Images and Themes the Russians Posted on Social Media, The New York Times* (Dec. 17, 2018). https://www.nytimes.com/2018/12/17/us/russian-social-media-posts.html.

284. *See* Christian Paul & Miriam Matthews, *The Russian "Firehose of Falsehood" Propaganda Model*, Rand Corporation (2016), https://www.rand.org/pubs/perspectives/PE198.html.

285. Kong & Marler, *supra* note 252.

286. *Id.*

287. *Id.*

288. *Id.*

289. *Id.* ("Russian propaganda is produced in incredibly large volumes and is broadcast or otherwise distributed via a large number of channels. This propaganda includes text,

numbers of channels and messages and a shameless willingness to disseminate partial truths or outright fictions."[290] Allegedly, some Russian videos sought to link Ukraine more generally to Nazism, discredit specific Ukrainian leaders, or blame Europe's energy woes and inflation on its support of Ukraine.[291]

The Rand report further alleges that Russia continued to use internet trolls in the Ukraine War, and that it posted in "online chat rooms, discussion forums, and comments sections on news and other websites."[292] Indeed, Radio Free Europe/Radio Liberty claimed that Russia maintained "thousands of fake accounts on Twitter, Facebook, LiveJournal, and vKontakte"[293] using internet trolls who were on duty 24 hours a day, working 12-hour shifts, and producing a daily quota of 135 posted comments of at least 200 characters.[294]

In addition to using internet trolls, Russia used RT (formerly Russia Today), a multimedia news provider, to disseminate its message.[295] RT had a budget of more than $300 million per year, and was able to broadcast in multiple languages (English, French, German, Spanish, Russian, and some Eastern European languages).[296] Some claim that RT has broad influence with more than a billion page views, a view level which would make it the most-watched site on the internet.[297] There are also allegations that Russia had dozens of news sites designed to disseminate Russian messaging although the Russian affiliation might have been "disguised or downplayed" on some sites.[298] In some instances, the Russian messaging was "picked up and rebroadcast by legitimate news outlets."[299] "For exam-

---

video, audio, and still imagery propagated via the Internet, social media, satellite television, and traditional radio and television broadcasting.").

290. *Id.*

291. Loveday Morris & Will Oremus, *Russian Disinformation Is Demonizing Ukrainian Refugees, The Washington Post* (Dec. 8, 2022),. https://www.washingtonpost.com/technology/2022/12/08/russian-disinfo-ukrainian-refugees-germany/.

292. *Id.*

293. *Id.*

294. *Id.*

295. *Id.*

296. *Id.*

297. *Id.*

298. *Id.*

299. *Id.*

ple, in early 2014, German news sources rebroadcast Russian disinformation about atrocities in Ukraine."[300]

Some commentators allege that Russia's messaging made "little or no commitment to the truth."[301] Even though false claims sometimes contain elements of truth,[302] some of the narratives are simply untrue. For example, some commentators claim that "Russian propagandists" hire "actors to portray victims of manufactured atrocities or crimes for news reports, or to fake "on-scene news reporting."[303] In one case, a Russian "reporter" Maria Katasonova was depicted as being on a battlefield in Donetsk, but a media report claimed that she was actually in a darkened room with fake explosion sounds playing in the background (a fact that was purportedly revealed when a light was switched on in the room during the recording).[304]

The U.S. Department of State claims that Russia's Ukraine messaging contained a number of different narratives,[305] all designed to portray Ukraine as the culprit in the war.[306] The first narrative portrayed Russia as "a besieged fortress surrounded by malevolent outsiders."[307] Purportedly, "Russian government officials falsely portrayed Russia as a perpetual victim and its aggressive actions as a forced response to the alleged actions of the United States and our democratic allies and partners."[308] Indeed, the

300. *Id.*

301. *Id.*

302. *Id.*

303. *Id.*

304. *Id.*

305. Office of the Spokesperson, U.S. Department of State, *Fact Sheet: Russia's Top Five Persistent Disinformation Narratives* (Jan. 20, 2022) (hereafter "State Department Fact Sheet"), https://www.state.gov/russias-top-five-persistent-disinformation-narratives/.

306. *Id.*:

> Russian military and intelligence entities are engaging in this activity across Russia's disinformation and propaganda ecosystem, to include malign social media operations, the use of overt and covert online proxy media outlets, the injection of disinformation into television and radio programming, the hosting of conferences designed to influence attendees into falsely believing that Ukraine, not Russia, is at fault for heightened tensions in the region, and the leveraging of cyber operations to deface media outlets and conduct hack and release operations.

307. *See* Paul & Matthews, *supra* note 284 (quoting book author Edward Lucas).

308. State Department Fact Sheet, *supra* note 305.

State Department claims that Russia tried to perpetuate the idea that "the international community's negative reaction to its invasion of an independent country was simply because people feared and hated Russia."[309] The report went on to claim that: "'Russophobia' persist across a range of topics and are employed whenever the Russian government wants to play the victim, when it is actually the aggressor."[310]

The State Department suggested that Russia's second narrative involves "historical revisionism."[311] In other words, when "history does not align with the Kremlin's political objectives," Russia denies "historical events or distort[s] historical narratives to try to cast Russia in a more favorable light and serve its domestic and geopolitical agenda."[312]

A third narrative is the idea that "the collapse of western civilization is imminent.[313] Russia claims that "Western civilization is collapsing because it has departed from "traditional values."[314] Thus, Russia indicts Western societies for working to "ensure the safety and equality of LGBTQI+ people" and promoting "concepts such as female equality and multiculturalism."[315] Russia tries to portray itself as "a counterweight to the 'decadence' of the United States and Western countries."[316] "For example, President Putin has claimed that the West has practically cancelled the concepts of 'mother' and 'father,' and has replaced them with 'parent 1 and 2,' while Foreign Minister Lavrov purportedly wrote that Western students 'learn at school that Jesus Christ was bisexual.'"[317]

The fourth narrative is the idea that the United States sponsors popular anti-government movements within Russia.[318] In other words, when a popular movement is pro-democracy or pro-reform, but is not necessarily in Russia's geopolitical interests, "the Kremlin will often attack its

309. *Id.*
310. *Id.*
311. *Id.*
312. *Id.*
313. *Id.*
314. *Id.*
315. *Id.*
316. *Id.*
317. *Id.*
318. *Id.*

legitimacy and claim that the United States is secretly behind it."[319] As part of this effort, Russia attacks "local and international civil society organizations, as well as independent media that expose human rights abuses and corruption."[320]

The U.S. Department of State claims that Russia creates "false realities" and tries to create confusions when the "truth is not in its interests."[321] The State Department asserts that the recipients do not always recognize that the information is false.[322] Indeed, the State Department claims that falsehoods are more likely to be accepted "when the disinformation is consistent with narratives or preconceptions held by various audiences."[323] Moreover, "Russian faux-news propaganda channels, such as RT and Sputnik, ... look like news programs, and the persons appearing on them are represented as journalists and experts," making listeners "more likely to ascribe credibility to the misinformation these sources are disseminating."[324]

Despite the sophistication of Russia's propaganda campaign, many commentators believe that Russia has not been as successful in pushing its narratives regarding the Ukrainian invasion as it was in its pre-war messaging,[325] and indeed that Ukraine has outmaneuvered Russia.[326] Despite Russia's messaging, the international community has expressed overwhelming support for Ukraine, and has imposed unprecedented economic sanctions on Russia.[327] In addition, many major companies have severed their ties to Russia, and humanitarian organizations have contributed large amounts to Ukrainian relief.[328] Additionally, "Sprawling sanctions from Western governments have sought to isolate the Russian economy and punish the regime."[329] Some corporations have gone further

319. *Id.*
320. *Id.*
321. *Id.*
322. *Id.*
323. *Id.*
324. *Id.*
325. *See* Dettmer, *supra* note 254.
326. *Id.*
327. *Id.*
328. *Id.*
329. Albert Fox Cahn, *Tech Bans Hurt Russian Dissidents More Than They Help Ukraine*, *Wired* (Apr. 11, 1922), https://www.wired.com/story/tech-bans-hurt-russian-dissidents-more-than-they-help-ukraine/.

still, suspending business in ways that go far beyond what the law requires or what governments intended.[330]

Russia's messaging has also been less effective because Ukrainian President Volodymyr Zelensky is "social-media savvy" and does "daily video addresses which have become viral sensations and have helped rally support for his embattled nation."[331] One commentator suggested that Zelensky has "demonstrated a deft ability to pivot and improvise as the circumstances of the crisis shift," and he is viewed as "communicating brilliantly with his own people and citizens across the world."[332] As a result he has purportedly been "inspiring to millions."[333]

There are various other reasons why Russia's messaging might not have been as effective during the Ukraine War. First, there is a large international press corps in Ukraine, which constantly reports about the events taking place there. Second, Ukrainians have used their cell phones to document the war, depicting bombardments and the destructive consequences of the Russian invasion.[334] Third, both Facebook and Twitter have removed Russian and Belarusian disinformation from their platforms and dismantled networks designed to manipulate algorithms and bolster pro-Russian narratives.[335] Fourth, "Russia's disinformation campaign has been severely hampered by the European Union's ban on Russian state-controlled media outlets RT and Sputnik broadcasting to the 27-nation bloc."[336] The EU's top diplomat Josep Borrell told EU lawmakers after the ban was announced: "They are not independent media, they are assets, they are weapons, in the Kremlin's manipulation ecosystem."[337] He added: "We are not trying to decide what is true and what is false. We don't have ministers of the Truth. But we have to focus on foreign actors who intentionally, in a coordinated manner, try to manipulate our information environment."[338]

330. *Id.*
331. Dettmer, *supra* note 254.
332. *Id.*
333. *Id.*
334. *Id.*
335. *Id.*
336. *Id.*
337. *Id.*
338. *Id.*

Another important factor is that Ukraine has been quite successful in promoting its own narratives.[339] Indeed, some commentators claim that Ukraine has outmaneuvered Russia on the social media front.[340] For one thing, Ukraine "prebunked" Russia's alleged justifications for invading Ukraine,[341] and it "managed to boost domestic morale with social media campaigns that exposed Russian war atrocities, rallied international support, and even helped crowd fund for defensive armaments."[342]

Ukraine's messaging seems to have included several different components. First, rather than simply responding to Russian narratives, Ukraine has attempted to refute Russian messages even before they are delivered (prebunking).[343] Second, Ukraine has gone to great lengths to highlight the heroism of its soldiers and people.[344] It has mythologized Ukrainian martyrs, portrayed Vlodomor Zelensky as a "man of the people," amplified civilian harm, magnified civilian resistance, and humanized the Ukrainian story.[345] In some instances, Ukraine has been able to push its own narratives more quickly and effectively than Russia has been able to promote its narratives.[346] Indeed, Ukraine frequently offers rapid responses to Russian narratives.[347] As a result, one commentator believes that: "Ukraine isn't just winning the battle for hearts and minds online, it has already won."[348]

In some cases, Russian narratives have been challenged with scientific data. For example, after Russia purportedly fired shells at a maternity hospital in Mariupol, killing and injuring people, Russia contended that the hospital had previously been converted into a military base, and

339. Singer, *supra* note 253 ("Yet, when it came time for one of Putin's most ambitious and important operations of all, the invasion of Ukraine, Russia failed at the information side of the fight as much as it failed at its plan for a quick seizure of Kyiv. And the stakes could not have been higher.").

340. Kong & Marler, *supra* note 252.

341. *Id.*

342. *Id.*

343. *Id.*

344. *Id.*

345. *Id.*

346. Dettmer, *supra* note 254.

347. *Id.*

348. *Id.*

thereby suggesting that the hospital was a legitimate target.[349] Russia aggressively supported this narrative through information disseminated by "Kremlin-controlled troll factories" as well as by Russian embassies.[350] However, the narrative was undercut when a photograph posted by Russian embassies was geolocated as being ten kilometers from the maternity hospital.[351] "RT, the Kremlin-controlled television channel, disputed the geolocation data."[352]

The German public television network, ZDF, alleged that Russia had disseminated fake news videos.[353] ZDF purportedly "identified dozens of fake news sites and examples of disinformation targeting European audiences, primarily in Germany, and attributed the campaign to Russian origins."[354] Meta took down all the fake sites that it could find.[355] As content moderation increased on the major U.S.-based social platforms, propagandists and extremists have found new outlets.[356] Those include Telegram, the stateless messaging app that has become a leading communications channel in much of Eastern Europe, including Russia and Ukraine.[357]

Even though the Russian narrative may not have been as successful as Russian leaders might have wished, some commentators argue that Russian disinformation is having some impact in Western countries. For example, Russia has tried to undercut European support for Ukrainian refugees who have swarmed (7.8 million) into Western Europe.[358] These commentators contend that Russia has tried to create fear and division within Western European populations, and argue that these Russian efforts have had a measure of success.[359] For example, one commentator alleges that Russia has fostered a strong anti-Ukranian refugee message

349. *Id.*
350. *Id.*
351. *Id.*
352. *Id.*
353. Morris & Oremus, *supra* note 291.
354. *Id.*
355. *Id.*
356. *Id.*
357. *Id.*
358. *Id.*
359. *Id.*

through "a sprawling, coordinated, Russia-based network of fake news websites, Telegram channels, YouTube and Instagram channels, and even Change.org petitions."[360] This message has allegedly been "amplified by armies of fake social media accounts, real pro-Kremlin influencers, and Russian state media accounts across virtually every major social platform."[361] For example, of 219 videos posted on Deutsche Wahrheit in a four month period, 40 percent mentioned Ukrainian refugees.[362] The posts, many of which feature faked or doctored videos that are designed to look like mainstream media reports, implicate Ukrainian refugees in everything from plotting terrorist attacks to bringing monkeypox to Germany.[363] One commentator argues that a fake news clip showed Ukrainian refugees burning down their German hosts' house.[364]

Thus, while most Europeans welcomed Ukranian refugees, one poll suggests that European support for accepting Ukrainians has slipped from 86 percent approval to 74 percent.[365] In addition, there has been anti-refugee pushback in Belarus and Poland which some ascribe to the propaganda.[366] As a result, a "bad vibe" toward refugees has been created in some countries.[367] For example, a German politician accused Ukrainian refugees of "social tourism" in the sense that they were taking advantage of Germany's welfare system while going back and forth to Ukraine.[368] In Germany, where more than a million Ukrainians fled, some immigrants have been subjected to arson attacks and threatening graffiti has been placed on their accommodations and schools.[369] In many cases, Russia purportedly disseminated its messages via the messaging app Telegram, which does far less content moderation than established giants such as Meta's Facebook and Google's YouTube.[370]

---

360. *Id.*
361. *Id.*
362. *Id.*
363. *Id.*
364. *Id.*
365. *Id.*
366. *Id.*
367. *Id.*
368. *Id.*
369. *Id.*
370. *Id.*

Several commentators have suggested that Russia has tried to control public opinion within its own borders. While Russia has tried to exploit the openness of Western liberal democracies, it has relied on the closed nature of its own society as a way of defending against challenges.[371] Thus, there are allegations that Russia has embarked on a massive misinformation campaign within its own country to spread fictions about Neo-Nazis in Ukraine and aggressions by the Ukrainian government (and China is lending a hand by repeating Russian propaganda through its state media and Foreign Ministry).[372] Thus, the war is portrayed as a "preemptive blow," "an unavoidable measure," or a form of "defense against [the North Atlantic Treaty Organization (NATO)]."[373] Russia's information campaign claims that the West is allied against it, and that, in Ukraine, Russia is taking on the combined might of America, Britain, the EU, and NATO. You name it, Russia's fighting it. In other words, setbacks on the battlefield are not the Kremlin's fault, but the handiwork of external enemies.[374]

Russia's internal propaganda seems to have had some success in that a majority of Russians support the actions of the Russian Armed Forces in Ukraine.[375] "In June 2022, 47 percent of Russians 'definitely supported' the actions of the Russian military, while another 28 percent said they 'mostly supported' them."[376] Nevertheless, there are signs of disagreements within Russia. One commentator alleges that there is dissension: "old friends have fallen out; parents and children are no longer on speaking terms; long-married couples no longer trust each another; and teachers and

---

371. Kong & Marler, *supra* note 252.

372. Robert C. Thornett, *Open and Closed: From Russia to China to America, the Largest Societies Are Pushing Their Limits, moderndiplomacy* (May 28, 2022), https://moderndiplomacy.eu/2022/05/28/open-and-closed-from-russia-to-china-to-america-the-largest-societies-are-pushing-their-limits/.

373. Dennis Volkov & Andrei Kolesnikov, *My Country, Right or Wrong: Russian Public Opinion on Ukraine* (Sept. 7, 2022), https://carnegieendowment.org/2022/09/07/my-country-right-or-wrong-russian-public-opinion-on-ukraine-pub-87803.

374. Steve Rosenberg, *Putin Can't Escape Fallout from Russian Retreat in Ukraine*, British Broadcasting Corp. (Nov. 11, 2022), https://www.bbc.com/news/world-europe-63601426.

375. Volkov & Kolenikov, *supra* note 373.

376. *Id.*

students are denouncing each other."[377] Thus, there appears to be "growing conflict within Russian society."[378]

In addition to disseminating its own narrative, Russia has tried to control and stifle internal dissent regarding the war. Russia has purportedly taken a number of different actions, including restricting more than 1,000 internet sites since the beginning of the war, including Facebook, Instagram, and BBC News.[379] In addition, Russia has criminalized dissent, including the spreading of so-called "fake news" within the country."[380] Dissemination of disinformation is punishable by 15 years in jail, or a fine of 1.5 million rubles (roughly $11,500).[381] A British lecturer claimed that Putin's objective was to scare the population into submission.[382] A number of dissenters have been arrested,[383] and others have purportedly been detained, judicially harassed, raided, and subjected to smear campaigns.[384] For example, a prominent Russian opposition figure was sentenced to 8 ½ years in prison after being convicted on charges stemming from his criticism of the Kremlin's action in Ukraine.[385] In addition, criminal cases were brought against two journalists for their reporting on alleged attacks against civilians in Ukraine.[386] Russian authorities also filed similar charges against at least three other non-journalists.[387]

---

377. *Id.*

378. *Id.*

379. *VPN Use Skyrockets in Russia During Ukraine Invasion*, Aljazeera (May 7, 2022). https://www.aljazeera.com/news/2022/5/7/vpn-use-skyrockets-in-russia-during-ukraine-invasion.

380. Chris Stokel-Walker, *How Russians Are Dealing with an Internet That's Gone Dark*, *Time* (Mar. 10, 2022) https://time.com/6156639/russia-internet-dissent/.

381. *Id.*

382. *Id.*

383. *Id.* (Quoting a woman who claimed that "she was arrested earlier this month (along with more than 13,000 others), and bussed to a police station where she was held in a cramped cell.").

384. *Russia: Arrests, Harassment of Ukraine War Dissidents*, Human Rights Watch (March 24, 2022) (hereafter "Human Rights Watch"), https://www.hrw.org/news/2022/03/24/russia-arrests-harassment-ukraine-war-dissidents#.

385. *Russian Politician Sentenced for Ukraine Action Criticism*, AP News (Dec. 9, 2022), https://apnews.com/article/putin-moscow-ukraine-government-ilya-yashin-russia-2967e1e91816f74eaab8cb7cd661eec6.

386. *Human Rights Watch*, *supra* note 384.

387. *Id.*

Essentially, Russia seems to have warned its people not to criticize the Russian army or Russia's president for the difficulties in Ukraine. The message is "do your duty and rally round the flag."[388] The government has also denounced protestors, labeling them as "national traitors."[389] Indeed, the Europe and Central Asia's Director of Human Rights Watch claims that the Russian government regards independent journalists "as traitors and treats them as a threat to the state."[390] and argues that "unidentified assailants ... physically attacked activists and damaged human rights organizations' offices."[391] In March 2022, Russia's criminal investigation service established interagency rapid response groups to deal with "extremist and terrorist activities, unsanctioned protests and provocations," and other "destabilizing" activities.[392] Human Rights Watch claims that Russian authorities have "detained activists across the country and raided their homes, apparently in response to their participation in the peaceful anti-war movement."[393] In addition, some claim that Russian police regularly detain independent journalists reporting on anti-war protests, and have allegedly gone to their homes to harass and threaten journalists not to take part in protests.[394]

The net effect is that the war has allegedly turned Russians against each other.[395] Protestors have been attacked by other Russians: "Unidentified assailants [have] physically attacked activists and damaged human rights organizations' offices."[396] Human Rights Watch claims that activists and journalists have reported that anonymous vandals painted the letter "Z," a symbol of the Russian armed forces in Ukraine, on the doors of their apartments as well as the warning "Don't betray your motherland" and the slur "A traitor lives here."[397] Human Rights Watch also claims that a

---

388. Rosenberg, *supra* note 374.

389. *Human Rights Watch, supra* note 384.

390. *Id.*

391. *Id.*

392. *Id.*

393. *Id.*

394. *Id.*

395. *See* Andy Hayward & Alec Luhn, *Russians Are Snitching On Friends and Family Who Oppose the War in Ukraine,* VICE (Aug. 8, 2022). https://www.vice.com/en/article/xgyyed/russians-snitching-on-russians-ukraine.

396. *Human Rights Watch, supra* note 384.

397. *Id.*

coordinator for Vesna (Spring), which openly speaks out against the war, was attacked and kicked in the face in Moscow.[398] "Russian celebrities who spoke out against the invasion suddenly found their TV shows had vanished from state channel listings."[399] Some claim that even Russians who live in other countries are afraid to speak out fearing retaliation against their loved ones who still live in Russia.[400]

Because of the increasing lack of tolerance for political dissent, some claim that Russian citizens are afraid to express dissenting opinions regarding the war.[401] As one commentator observed, "It is frightening, especially if your whole life, property, family connections, work and everything is in Russia."[402] Some claim that even the conduct of Russian social influencers, who make their living off social media platforms has been affected. For example, influencer Niki Proshin deleted "any videos that could potentially be caught up in Putin's dragnet," including videos from protests in Saint Petersburg."[403] He did so because he was unsure regarding how Russian authorities might view the posts.[404] Commentators allege that big tech platforms like TikTok have ceased operations in the country because of the new law, while others like Instagram have added labels to Russian state-sponsored content and begun demoting its distribution within the app.[405]

Despite the threat of sanctions, in the weeks following the beginning of the Ukrainian war, hundreds of thousands of Russians protested against the war and expressed their discontent with the invasion.[406] Human Rights Watch claims that thousands of these protestors were detained.[407] In addition to the protests, an employee of Russian state-run Channel One interrupted a live broadcast of a nightly news program shouting "Stop the war! No to war!" News staffer Marina Ovsyannikova, whose father is

---

398. *Id.*
399. Stokel-Walker, *supra* note 380.
400. *Id.*
401. *Id.*
402. *Id.*
403. *Id.*
404. *Id.*
405. *Id.*
406. *See Human Rights Watch*, *supra* note 384.
407. *Id.*

Ukrainian, held up a placard in Russian, saying, "Don't believe the propaganda. They're lying to you here." Studio producers rushed to cut her off.[408] In addition, some websites and apps have continued to function. Clubhouse, which functions in Ukranian, Russian, and English, "gives updates on the invasion, discusses the ramifications for the world, and acts as an under-the-radar place to vent for Russians opposed to the war as they speak to the rest of the world about their disgust."[409] Dissent has also been posted to Telegram, where Russian dissidents and opponents of Vladimir Putin have gravitated.[410] Telegram's CEO assured "users that he wouldn't submit to Russian government demands to breach users' privacy by handing over their personal details."[411] Pro-war Russian military bloggers wrote angry messages about the retreat.[412]

Several factors have undercut Russia's efforts to control the flow of information to its people. Russians who emigrated to other countries have informed Russians who did not emigrate regarding the facts and thereby undercut governmental propaganda.[413] In addition, some Russians tried to avoid retaliation by installing VPN (virtual private networks) software on their computers.[414]

D. CONTENT CONTROL BY SOCIAL MEDIA PLATFORMS

Even though governments have imposed restrictions on free expression, private entities have historically posed an even greater threat to free expression.[415] That was true in the past, as we saw when we examined the concept of "gatekeepers," and remains true today. Private threats to internet expression come in many different forms.

---

408. Dettmer, *supra* note 254.

409. Stokel-Walker, *supra* note 380.

410. *Id.*

411. *Id.*

412. Rosenberg, *supra* note 374.

413. Thornett, *supra* note 372.

414. Aljazeera, *supra* note 379; Stokel-Walker, *supra* note 380.

415. *See* Laura Sydell, *Corporations Are Drawn Into WikiLeaks Controversy*, National Public Radio, Morning Edition (Dec. 13, 2010), http://www.npr.org/2010/12/13/131979010/corporations-are-drawn-into-wikileaks-controversy.

Since social media platforms are privately owned, the owners of those platforms have been assumed to possess the right to control and limit speech on their platforms.[416] Since the First Amendment is viewed as a prohibition only against governmentally-imposed restrictions on free speech,[417] and not privately-imposed restrictions,[418] it arguably does not limit the actions of the platforms which are private.[419] Thus, the paradigm outlined in the prior chapter, of the internet allowing everyone to engage in mass communication, has been undercut by social media platforms limiting speech on their platforms.[420]

Of course, private interests have always exercised some control over free expression. Even individuals who were not "gatekeepers" could retaliate against offensive speech. For example, when Megyn Kelly planned to air an interview with Alex Jones, the controversial head of Infowars, JP Morgan Chase decided to withdraw its television and digital advertising support for her program.[421] The company's chief marketing officer stated that she was "repulsed" that Kelly would "give a second of air time to someone who says Sandy Hook and Aurora are hoaxes."[422] Kelly sought to justify the interview on the basis that "Our goal in sitting down with him was to shine a light—as journalists are supposed to do—on this influen-

---

416. *See* Margot E. Kaminski & Kate Klonick, *Speech in the Social Public Square, The New York Times International* 9 (June 25, 2017).

417. *See Manhattan Community Access Corp. v. Halleck*, 587 U.S. 802 (2019).

418. *Id.*

419. *See* U.S. Const., Amdt. I ("Congress shall make no law no law respecting an establishment of religion, or prohibiting the free exercise thereof; or abridging the freedom of speech, or of the press; or the right of the people peaceably to assemble, and to petition the government for a redress of grievances."). During the nineteenth century, most U.S. Supreme Court First Amendment decisions focused on the question of whether that Amendment should be incorporated into the Fourteenth Amendment and applied to the states. *See, e.g., Rice v. Railroad Co.*, 66 U.S. 358, 374 (1861) (trespass); *Withers v. Buckley*, 61 U.S. 84 (1857) (suit regarding state authority to control a navigable waterway); *Slaughter-House Cases*, 83 U.S. 36, 82 (1872); *Murphy v. Stewart*, 43 U.S. 263 (1844) (suit to enforce a promissory note); *Groves v. Slaughter*, 40 U.S. 449 (1841); *Livingston v. Moore*, 32 U.S. 469 (1833) (dispute over a land title). That issue was not affirmatively resolved until the twentieth century. See Gitlow v. New York, 268 U.S. 652 (1925).

420. *See* Kevin Roose, *Candidates Enter the Texting Era With a Plea: Will U Vote 4 Me? The New York Times* B4 (Aug. 2, 2018).

421. *See* Christine Hauser, *GoDaddy Drops Daily Stormer Site, The New York Times* A15 (Aug. 15, 2017).

422. *Id.*

tial figure, and yes—to discuss the considerable falsehoods he has promoted with impunity."[423]

Because of federal law, social media platforms have not been liable for defamatory or other material posted on their websites. Section 230 of the Communications Decency Act of 1996[424] protects websites and internet service providers against civil liability for information posted by third parties.[425] However, some commentators have argued that social media platforms should be liable for their content in the same way that newspapers and other media giants are liable.[426] As UK lawyer Paul Tweed stated, "Facebook can't say, 'we are not a publisher; we are just a platform.' I have been hearing that from them for years, and I never believed it.'"[427] There is a movement afoot in various countries to hold social media sites liable, especially as they begin to engage in content regulation.[428]

Some have called for social media platforms to be regulated in the same way as "mainstream broadcasters and publishers."[429] If social media platforms were regulated like radio and television broadcasters, that would mean that an entity like the U.S. Federal Communications Commission (FCC) might oversee those platforms in the U.S.[430] Social media platforms argue against this approach on the basis that they are not like traditional media companies. As Monica Bickered, Facebook's head of global policy management, argues, "We build technology.... We don't write the news that people read on the platform."[431]

Virtually all social media platforms engage in some level of content-moderation through their imposition of so-called "acceptable use" or

423. *Id.*

424. 47 U.S.C. § 230 (2012).

425. *Id.* ("No provider or user of an interactive computer service shall be treated as the publisher or speaker of any information provided by another information content provider.").

426. *See* David D. Kirkpatrick, *Is Facebook Just a Platform? A Lawyer to the Stars Says No, The New York Times* A1 (May 21, 2018).

427. *Id.*

428. *Id.*

429. *See* Nick Hopkins, *Revealed: Facebook's Internal Rulebook on Sex, Terrorism and Violence, The Guardian* (May 21, 2017); Kaminski & Klonick, *supra* note 431.

430. *Id.*

431. *Id.*

"terms of service" policies;[432] policies that give them broad authority to exclude various types of content or even to terminate or limit service to particular users.[433] Facebook uses its policy to exclude content that it deems inappropriate or unacceptable,[434] and it employs a team of individuals who are authorized to take down content that they deem to be illegal or in violation of Facebook's policy.[435] Twitter (now "X") also had a terms of use policy, and it blocked Tweets from entering countries when the content would violate local law and the government requested the blocking.[436] As a result, Twitter blocked tweets that insult the Thai monarchy, as well as Nazi-related tweets sent to Germany.[437] In general, courts have affirmed the right of social media platforms to enforce these terms of use policies,[438] and have held that they do not have to guarantee "due process" to its users,[439] or provide any right of redress or appeal.[440] That may be changing as European Union law requires platform to provide some process protections to users.

In late 2022, TikTok employed some 40,000 content moderators, and removed approximately 85 million posts deemed to violate its commu-

---

432. *See* Guy Raz, *Hackers Overwhelm WikiLeaks Servers*, National Public Radio, All Things Considered (Dec. 3, 2010), http://www.npr.org/2010/12/03/131790969/Hackers-Overwhelm-WikiLeaks-Servers ("Clay Shirky, who teaches in the Interactive Telecommunications Program at New York University, says terms-of-service agreements give these companies too much power. 'Every corporate counsel at every large organization is basically paid to write a Web terms of service, which reads: "We can do anything at any time with no announcement and no recourse," he said.'").

433. *See* John F. Burns, *PayPal Drops WikiLeaks, Saying Rules Were Broken, International Herald Tribune*, at 7 (Dec. 6, 2010).

434. *Id.*, at 7.

435. *See* Eyder Peralta, *Is Lying on the Internet Illegal?*, National Public Radio, The Two Way (Nov. 15, 2011), http://www.npr.org/blogs/thetwo-way/2011/11/15/142356399/is-lying-on-the-internet-illegal.

436. *See* Somini Sengupta, *When Twitter Blocks Tweets, It's #Outrage, The New York Times*, at A1 (Jan. 28, 2012).

437. *Id.*

438. *See* Robert Burnson, *Twitter Beats Censorship Lawsuit by Banned White Nationalist*, The United States Law Week (Aug. 24, 2018).

439. *See* Kaminski & Klonick, *supra* note 431.

440. *Id.*

nity guidelines.[441] In addition, TikTok encouraged users to flag objectionable content.[442]

Social media platforms take any of a variety of actions regarding content on their platforms. In some instances, they ban or "take down" offending content.[443] In addition, they sometimes ban individuals from posting on their platforms,[444] and they may censor comments in groups that have a record of hate speech.[445] During the January 6th riot, Facebook labeled the U.S. a "Temporary High Risk Location" for political violence.[446]

Despite the significant power that they exercise over social discourse, the decisions made by social media platforms are not transparent. Indeed, the platforms have gone to great lengths to prevent others from learning about their decisions.[447] When New York University enlisted 6,500 volunteers to study Facebook's political ad targeting practices, Facebook demanded that it cease and desist.[448] While Facebook requires certain information about advertisements (e.g., who paid for an ad, when it ran and the geographic location of the people who saw it), the NYU researchers sought to search political ads to determine the audiences that were targeted and to determine how those ads were funded.[449] Facebook argued that "scraping" practices are prohibited, no matter how well-intentioned.[450] Facebook demanded, not only that NYU cease and desist, but that it delete all data that it had collected.[451]

Until relatively recently, it was difficult to gain much insight into how social media platforms make decisions regarding which content to ban (or take down) because their content moderation guidelines. Although

---

441. *See* Jargon, *supra* note 163, at A11.

442. *Id.* (TikTok has stated that it is "open to feedback and scrutiny, and we seek to engage constructively with partners.").

443. *Id.*

444. *See* Alan Suderman & Joshua Goodman, *Facebook Had Its Own Insurrection Jan. 6, The Courier-Journal* 15A (Oct. 24, 2021).

445. *Id.*

446. *Id.*

447. See Jeff Horowitz, *Facebook Fights Research Projects, The Wall Street Journal* B3 (Oct. 24–25, 2020).

448. *Id.*

449. *Id.*

450. *Id.*

451. *Id.*

Facebook actively tried to maintain secrecy regarding the content of its guidelines,[452] those guidelines became public in early 2017.[453] The guidelines indicate that Facebook will take action against posts involving such things as hate speech, terrorist propaganda, graphic violence, adult nudity, sexual activity, child sexual exploitation, revenge porn, credible violence, suicidal posts, bullying, harassment, breaches of privacy, and copyright infringement.[454]

Facebook's guidelines suffer from both vagueness and ambiguity, and its policies on sexual content are "complex and confusing."[455] There are other problems as well. For example, the guidelines suggest that a statement like "Someone shoot Trump" should be deleted because it involves a reference to killing a governmental official,[456] but a statement like "To snap a bitch's neck, make sure to apply your pressure to the middle of her throat" is permissible.[457] Facebook justifies leaving the latter post online by arguing that "people commonly express disdain or disagreement by threatening or calling for violence in generally facetious and unserious ways."[458] Likewise, the statement "fuck off and die" need not be removed.[459] Photos of children being subjected to bullying or non-sexual physical abuse need not be deleted unless there is a "sadistic or celebratory element."[460] Videos of violent deaths are sometimes deleted, but attempts at self-harm need not be deleted.[461] Although photos of animal abuse or mutilation are permissible, they should be marked as "disturbing."[462] Such photos can be removed if they reveal "sadism" which the guidelines define

---

452. *See* Hopkins, *supra* note 444; Kaminski & Klonick, *supra* note 431.

453. *Id.*

454. *See* Alex Hern & Olivia Solon, *Facebook Closed 583m Fake Accounts in First Three Months of 2018: Firm's First Quarterly Moderation Report Also Shows Scale of Spam, Hate Speech and Violence, The Guardian* (May 15, 2018).

455. *See* Hopkins, *supra* note 444.

456. *Id.* The explanation given was that a head of state is in a protected category.

457. *Id.* The explanation given was that the threat could not be regarded as a "credible" threat.

458. *Id.*

459. *Id.* Again, it would not be regarded as a "credible threat."

460. *Id.*

461. *Id.*

462. *Id.*

as "enjoyment of suffering."[463] Child nudity is sometimes permissible but not in the context of the Holocaust.[464]

Platform take down decisions are often difficult. For example, Facebook faced criticism when it failed to remove a video of a father killing his child in Thailand, as well as one of Robert Godwin being killed, but it won acclaim for "disseminating videos of police killings and other governmental abuses."[465] While the guidelines prohibit posts involving child exploitation, Facebook has not fully decided how to handle cartoon images of exploitation.[466] Facebook also banned Senior General Min Aung Hiaing of Myanmar for his Facebook campaign, which used trolls and fake accounts, to foment ethnic hatred and build support for ethnic cleansing.[467]

The ability to make good decisions regarding take downs is aggravated by the fact that Facebook's moderators are "overwhelmed" by the total volume of work.[468] Purportedly, Facebook receives more than 6.5 million reports a week regarding allegations of fake or improper accounts,[469] and Facebook's moderators are sometimes forced to make decisions regarding the permissibility of content in as little as 10 seconds.[470] The net effect is that some content-moderation decisions are sometimes bizarre. For example, a statement that "white paint colors are the worst" was taken down as hate speech.[471] A post condemning Osama Bin Laden was taken down on the basis that it supported terrorism.[472]

Some claim that social media platforms like Facebook exercise too much control over speech on their platforms, and have suggested that these companies should adopt transparent governing procedures.[473] For

463. *See* Kaminski & Klonick, *supra* note 431.

464. *See* Hern & Solon, *supra* note 469.

465. *Id.*

466. *Id.*

467. *See* Jeff Horowitz, *Facebook Documents Reveal Secret Elite Exempt from Its Rules, The Wall Street Journal* A1 (Sept. 14, 2021); Paul Mozur, *Kicked Off Facebook, but Still the Star of a Grandiose Military Museum, the New York Times*, International Section A4 (Nov. 27, 2018).

468. *See* Hern & Solon, *supra* note 469.

469. *Id.*

470. *Id.*

471. *See* Horowitz, *supra* note 482, at A1.

472. *Id.*

473. *See* Hern & Solon, *supra* note 469.

example, the Santa Clara Principles, a guidebook, suggests that social networks "should publish the number of posts they remove, provide detailed information for users whose content is deleted explaining why, and offering the chance to appeal against the decision."[474]

One thing is clear: a large amount of content has been excluded from social media platforms. In the first three months of 2018, Facebook closed some 583 million accounts that it characterized as "fake," and took "moderation action" against another 1.5 billion accounts.[475] Of these 1.5 billion moderation actions, Facebook removed some 2.5 million instances of what it described as hate speech, 1.9 million instances of terrorist propaganda, 3.4 million instances of graphic violence and 21 million instances of adult nudity and sexual activity.[476] YouTube deleted 8.3 million videos in a 3 month period "for beaching its community guidelines."[477]

At one point, Facebook hired a team of 25 news curators to examine "trending" new stories, and gave them the power to suppress offensive stories.[478] In theory, the team was trained in "the art of determining source credibility, ascertaining truth and applying news content."[479] However, Facebook summarily dismissed the team when its existence became public knowledge, and allegations were made that it "routinely suppressed news stories of interest to conservative readers."[480] Following the dissolution, Facebook has used algorithms to ferret our fake content.[481] The nature of those algorithms has not been publicly revealed.[482]

At one point, Facebook employed hundreds of content moderators in Germany who had the power to delete content from Facebook pages.[483] The deletion could be based either on a violation of German law

---

474. *Id.*
475. *Id.*
476. *Id.*
477. *Id.*
478. *See* Nathan Bomey, *How Facebook Fired Workers Who Blocked "Fake News"; Secret Curators Dismissed After Revelation on Blog, USA Today* B3 (May 6, 2018).
479. *Id.*
480. *Id.*
481. *Id.*
482. *Id.*
483. *See* Katrin Bennhold, *Scouring Hate Off Facebook in Germany, The New York Times International* 1 (May 20, 2018).

or a violation of Facebook's "community standards,"[484] and the regulators routinely took down "hate speech," "terrorist propaganda," Nazi symbols and pictures of child abuse.[485] Of course, such repression is consistent with Germany's approach to free speech which allows the government to prohibit the book Mein Kampf, swastikas and speech that involves incitement to hatred or defamatory speech.[486] Facebook is reinforced by Germany's Network Enforcement Law, enacted in 2017, which defines 21 different types of content that are illegal and that platforms are required to remove from their sites.[487]

Some believe that social media platforms have been "conservative and fickle about removing inappropriate comments, largely to maintain their positions as neutral platforms where people can freely express themselves,"[488] and that companies like Facebook do not react quickly enough to remove offensive posts until there is a "major disruption."[489] For example, Facebook became more proactive about content moderation in Myanmar only "after the United Nations and Western organizations accused it of having played a role in spreading the hate and misinformation that contributed to acts of ethnic cleansing."[490]

Increasingly, "content providers and tech platforms" have begun to "vet their communities and set rules and standards for civilized discussion."[491] However, because many news sites have limited resources, they may leave their comment sections unmoderated, leading to "toxic behavior."[492] By contrast, some platforms have established guidelines and restrictions regarding the type of material that can be posted on their sites.[493]

Of course, the ability of social media platforms to prohibit content raises significant concerns. First, there is a risk that decisions to prohibit

---

484. *Id.* at 8.

485. *Id.*

486. *Id.*

487. *Id.*

488. *See* Chen, *supra* note 280, at B7.

489. *See* Max Fisher, *Social Re-engineering, From Myanmar to Germany, The New York Times*, Tech We're Using B3 (Nov. 8, 2018).

490. *Id.*

491. *See* Chen, *supra* note 280, at B7.

492. *Id.*

493. *Id.*

content will be swayed by public opinion.[494] Thus, unlike the First Amendment, under which an individual's free speech rights are not determined by majority vote, public opinion may influence social media platforms as they make take down decisions.[495] There is also a risk that social media platforms will censor speech based on their own political perspectives. For example, conservatives claim that some social media platforms censor conservative viewpoints.[496] They allege, for example, that some types of information (e.g., information regarding those who died from Covid vaccines) are readily available on search engines like DuckDuckGo, but are difficult to find on Google.[497]

Whether social media platforms actually do discriminate against particular political views is unclear. At one time, Facebook claimed that it did not discriminate based on political views,[498] declaring that free speech is "core to both who we are and why we exist,"[499] and asserting that the platform only removes such things as hate speech and violent threats,[500] and specifically that it does not discriminate against conservative views.[501] Others challenge Facebook's assertions. On Facebook's internal messaging system, a senior Facebook engineer posted a statement to the effect that: "We Have a Problem With Political Diversity,"[502] noting that "We are a political monoculture that's intolerant of different views. We claim to welcome all perspectives, but are quick to attack—often in mobs—anyone who presents a view that appears to be in opposition to left-leaning ideology."[503] Regarding certain issues (*e.g.*, diversity and immigration), the post noted, employees "can either keep quiet or sacrifice your reputa-

494. *See* Jargon, *supra* note 163, at A11.

495. *Id.*

496. *See* Stuart A. Thompson, *The Engine That's Fueling Conspiracy Talk: Some Conservative Influencers Who Say That Google Is Suppressing Their Views Are Embracing DuckDuckGo for Searches, The New York Times* B1 (Feb. 23, 2022).

497. *Id.*

498. *See* Roose, *supra* note 4, at B3.

499. *See id.*

500. *See id.*

501. *See id.*

502. *See* Kate Conger & Sheera Frenkel, *Dozens at Facebook Unite to Challenge Its "Intolerant" Liberal Culture, The New York Times* (Aug. 28, 2018).

503. *Id.*

tion and career."[504] Following the Facebook post, more than one hundred Facebook employees decided to form an online group entitled "FB'ers for Political Diversity."[505] The Facebook controversy erupted after Facebook decided to ban Alex Jones and allegedly limited the speech of Senator Ted Cruz and President Trump.[506] Of course, the perception of a liberal bias is reinforced by the fact that Facebook Chief Executive Mark Zuckerberg and its Chief Operating Officer Sheryl Sandberg donated to Democratic politicians and liberal causes.[507] Allegations of bias have also been leveled against other social media platforms, including Google, Patreon and Go Fund Me.[508] For example, congressional Republicans asserted that Twitter was biased against conservative views;[509] a claim that Twitter's then Chief Executive, Jack Dorsey, vigorously denied.[510] Similar allegations were made against Google.[511]

Further, there is evidence that at least one social media platform (Meta (formerly Facebook)) secretly made distinctions between ordinary people and "high-profile" individuals in its content moderation.[512] While Meta would take action against high-profile individuals in extreme situations (e.g., it banned then President Trump from its platform following the January 6th riot),[513] generally it treated high-profile individuals differently than everyone else, exempting them from many of its rules.[514] Facebook used a system that it referred to as "crosscheck" or "Xcheck" to double-check decisions made against high-profile individuals,[515] a group which included

504. *Id.*

505. *Id.*

506. *Id.*

507. *Id.*

508. *See* Kevin Roose, *The Alt-Right Finds a New Enemy in Silicon Valley, The New York Times* B6 (Aug. 10, 2017).

509. *See* Cecilia Kang & Sheera Frenkel, *Republicans Accuse Twitter of Exhibiting Bias: Democrats Say Claims Are For Political Gain, The New York Times* A1 (Sept. 6, 2018).

510. *Id.*

511. *See* Daisuke Wakabayashi, *Leaked Video From Google Shows Bosses Ruing Trump, The New York Times* B4 (Sept. 13, 2018).

512. *See* Horowitz, *supra* note 482, at A1.

513. *See* Kate Conger & Mike Isaac, *Twitter Permanently Suspends Trump's Personal Account, The New York Times* A1 & A13 (Jan. 9, 2021).

514. *See* Horowitz, *supra* note 482, at A1.

515. *See* Meghan Bobrowsky & Ryan Tracy, *Facebook Reviews Double Set of Rules, The Wall Street Journal* A1 (Sept. 22, 2021).

tens of thousands of people and eventually millions.[516] The system was created for public relations reasons: to limit the level of high-profile incidents regarding content moderation.[517] Only about 10% of Xcheck material was ever reviewed.[518] Even when such material was taken down, the system might allow objectionable content to remain up for some time.[519] As a result, some content that violated Facebook's rules were viewed some 16.4 billion times.[520] A post by a prominent soccer player regarding "non-consensual intimate imagery" was left up for some time, as were posts by Donald Trump that violated Facebook rules.[521] While Xcheck was extended to politicians, it did not extend to all, and there was a tendency to include incumbents rather than challengers.[522] In some instances, rather than delete a post, Facebook would reach out to a prominent individual and provide him/her with the opportunity to self-remediate.[523] Although the self-remediation option has purportedly been eliminated, deletion of a prominent person's post required the permission of a senior Facebook executive.[524]

In addition, some Facebook users were "whitelisted," meaning that they were exempt from ordinary Facebook enforcement rules.[525] The system obviously undercut Mr. Zuckerberg's claims of "principled neutrality" regarding content moderation.[526] Facebook claimed that it was trying to eliminate the practice or phase out the Xcheck practice, as well as whitelisting, but it is not clear that it did.[527] It is difficult to track because Facebook is not transparent about its practices.[528]

516. *Id.*, at A6 & A9.
517. *Id.*, at A6.
518. *Id.*, at A9.
519. *Id.*
520. *Id.*
521. *Id.*, at A6.
522. *Id.*
523. *Id.*
524. *Id.*
525. *Id.*, at A9.
526. *Id.*
527. *Id.*, at A6 & A9.
528. *Id.*, at A9.

In addition, Facebook prohibits political advertisements in the final weeks before an election.[529] Recently, Facebook decided to give users the opportunity to opt out of advertisements.[530]

There is also a risk that social media platforms will censor speech because of governmental pressure. For example, the Indonesian government adopted regulations that allow it to demand that social media platforms take down content that the government deems to be harmful to public order or a disturbance to society.[531] Officials have attempted to justify the regulations based on the need to protect privacy, prevent child sexual abuse and terrorism, and make the internet "a welcoming place for all."[532] Some commentators believe that Indonesia is using the new law to stifle protest and dissent.[533] The regulations require social media companies to scan their platforms for offensive content, and to comply with governmental take down requests.[534]

Interestingly, because Facebook was receiving critical commentary, it started a new news feed called "Project Amity."[535] Project Amity was essentially Facebook propaganda and was designed to cast Facebook in a positive light.[536]

The U.S. government has not gone so far as to enact laws requiring social media platforms to conform to the government's wishes regarding content moderation, but the *Biden* case reveals that the Biden Administration has counseled, pressured, and threatened social media platforms to try to force them to suppress certain content on the internet. Likewise, in 2018, Twitter shut down the account of a prominent Iraqi militia

529. *See* Robert McMillan, Alexa Corse & Dustin Volz, *New AI Deepfakes Complicate 2024 Votes, The Wall Street Journal* A4 (Feb. 16, 2024).

530. *See* Mike Isaac, *Hate Political Ads? Opt Out, Facebook Says, The New York Times* B3 (June 17, 2020).

531. *See* Shira Ovide, *A Classic Case of Internet Censorship, The New York Times*, On Tech B5 (Aug. 6, 2022).

532. *Id.*

533. *Id.*

534. *Id.*

535. *See* Ryan Mac & Sheera Frenkel, *Facebook Uses Its News Feed To Fight Critics, The New York Times* A1 (Sept. 20, 2021).

536. *Id.*

leader, Abu Mehdi al-Mohandis, for inciting violence.[537] Al-Mohandis had blamed the U.S. for "directing" the situation in Basra, and shortly thereafter, there was violence against U.S. diplomats.[538] When he was criticized for inciting violence, his account was shut down, and his supporters complained that the shut down was due to U.S. governmental influence.[539] Twitter refused to comment on the ban for privacy and security reasons.[540]

There is also the risk that public opinion will pressure social media platforms into censoring content. For example, before Joe Biden was elected president, he urged his supporters to pressure Facebook regarding its content moderation decisions, and in particular to more aggressively censor Biden's opponent, Donald J. Trump.[541] As part of that effort, the Biden campaign circulated a petition and an open letter to Mark Zuckerberg, Facebook's chief executive.[542] The campaign argued for "real changes to Facebook's policies for their platform and how they enforce them are necessary to protect against a repeat of the role that disinformation played in the 2016 election and that continues to threaten our democracy today."[543]

In response to WikiLeaks' decision to release diplomatic communications that had been stolen from the U.S. government, some online companies decided (perhaps, after prompting from governmental officials) to cut their ties to WikiLeaks and its supporters,[544] and to discontinue carrying WikiLeaks' website.[545] Amazon was one of the companies that decided to exclude WikiLeaks,[546] stating that it was concerned about how

---

537. *See* Michael R. Gordon, *Twitter Boots Iraqi After U.S. Says He Incited Violence, The Wall Street Journal* A11 (Sept. 13, 2018).

538. *Id.*

539. *Id.*

540. *Id.*

541. *See* Cecilia Kang, *A Campaign Prepares to Go Public in Its Attack on Facebook's Speech Policies, The New York Times* A15 (June 12, 2020).

542. *Id.*

543. *Id.*

544. *Id.*

545. *See Hackers Overwhelm WikiLeaks Servers, supra* note 447 ("Now if you've tried to see them for yourself at WikiLeaks.org, you might have run into some problems. In fact, you probably got an error message. That's in part because all the files and website itself have been jumping around several different servers all over the world.").

546. *Id.*; Charlie Savage, *Amazon Cites Terms of Use in Expulsion of WikiLeaks, The New York Times*, at A12 (Dec. 3, 2010) ("In a statement, Amazon—which rents server space to companies in addition to its better-known business of selling books, music and other

the documents being posted online had been obtained and the possible injury that could result.[547] WikiLeaks' website managed to stay online only by switching servers.[548]

WikiLeaks also suffered setbacks regarding its ability to obtain funding. For example, MasterCard, Visa and PayPal decided to stop processing payments to WikiLeaks.[549] A MasterCard representative justified the decision on the basis that: "Given the serious nature of allegations and broad concerns raised by many regarding the activities of this organization, we believe it was prudent to suspend acceptance, and that's what we've done." PayPal justified its action on the basis that "WikiLeaks might be encouraging illegal behavior, and [its conduct] violates PayPal's acceptable-use policy."[550]

In excluding WikiLeaks content, Amazon also relied on its terms of service agreement[551] which provided that posters "represent and warrant that you own or otherwise control all of the rights to the content."[552] Since WikiLeaks was trying to publish documents that had been stolen from the U.S. government, Amazon concluded that this restriction had been violated.[553] In addition, the Amazon terms of service contract provides that content that "could cause injury" could also be banned,[554] and Amazon

---

products online—said that it had canceled its relationship with WikiLeaks not because of 'a government inquiry,' but because it decided that the organization was violating the terms of service for the program.").

547. *Id.* ("'When companies or people go about securing and storing large quantities of data that isn't rightfully theirs, and publishing this data without ensuring it won't injure others, it's a violation of our terms of service, and folks need to go operate elsewhere,' the company said.").

548. *Id.*; *WikiLeaks Turns to Swiss Party for Help With Web Address, as Options Dwindle, The New York Times*, at A12 (Dec. 6, 2010).

549. *Id.*

550. *Id.; see also PayPal Drops WikiLeaks, Saying Rules Were Broken, supra* note 445, at 7.

551. *Id.; see also Amazon Cites Terms of Use in Expulsion of WikiLeaks, supra* note 561, at A12 ("In a statement, Amazon—which rents server space to companies in addition to its better-known business of selling books, music and other products online—said that it had canceled its relationship with WikiLeaks not because of 'a government inquiry,' but because it decided that the organization was violating the terms of service for the program.").

552. *See id.*

553. *Id.* (An Amazon spokesman stated that "'it's clear that WikiLeaks doesn't own or otherwise control all the rights to this classified content.'").

554. *Id.*, at A12.

expressed concern that "WikiLeaks was not exercising sufficient caution in redacting names from the documents before disclosing them."[555]

The WikiLeaks situation demonstrates that online entities will not necessarily receive the same level of deference and protection as traditional newspapers and media outlets.[556] For example, some commentators have expressed doubt about whether Mastercard, Visa or PayPal would have taken similar actions against a traditional news organization that had broken a major investigative story.[557]

Some social media platforms have even banned particular individuals from posting on their platforms. Under ordinary free speech principles, an individual might be prosecuted for making illegal statements (e.g., subversive advocacy that violates the *Brandenburg* standard[558] or disseminating child pornography).[559] However, the individual would not be denied the right to speak at all. Not true with social media platforms which sometimes ban individuals completely from their platforms, sometimes including politicians.[560] For example, YouTube prohibited Senator Rand Paul's videos alleging that face masks are ineffective in preventing the spread of Covid-19.[561]

---

555. *Id.*

556. *See* Ray Somaiya & Alan Cowell, *WikiLeaks Founder Said to Fear "Illegal Rendition" to U.S., The New York Times*, B8-9 (Jan. 12, 2001) ("WikiLeaks certainly isn't being afforded the same protection we give other media outlets in free countries. It has come under significant attack as PayPal, Amazon and Visa have all tried to bar WikiLeaks from their services, a move that would seem unthinkable had it been made against mainstream newspapers (Can you imagine the outcry if a credit card company decided to cut off The Washington Post because it didn't like what was on the front page?)").

557. *See id.* ("WikiLeaks certainly isn't being afforded the same protection we give other media outlets in free countries. It has come under significant attack as PayPal, Amazon and Visa have all tried to bar WikiLeaks from their services, a move that would seem unthinkable had it been made against mainstream newspapers (Can you imagine the outcry if a credit card company decided to cut off The Washington Post because it didn't like what was on the front page?)").

558. *See Brandenburg v. Ohio*, 395 U.S. 444 (1969).

559. *See New York v. Ferber*, 458 U.S. 747 (1982).

560. *See* Krista Johnson, *Paul Says He'll Longer Post to YouTube, Courier-Journal* 4A (Jan. 5, 2022).

561. *Id.*

In 2020, social media platforms took the extraordinary step of limiting and controlling the speech of a sitting president, Donald Trump.[562] Following the January 6th riot at the U.S. Capitol, both Facebook and Twitter barred then President Trump because they believed that he had broken their rules against incitement of violence.[563] Two Trump posts were at the heart of the suspension.[564] Twitter was concerned about Trump's use of the term "American Patriots" in the following tweet which they viewed as glorifying violence: "The 75,000,000 great American Patriots who voted for me, AMERICA FIRST, and MAKE AMERICA GREAT AGAIN, will have a GIANT VOICE long into the future. They will not be disrespected or treated unfairly in any way, shape or form!!!"[565] Twitter was concerned that the following Tweet would glorify violence as well: "To all those who have asked, I will not be going to the inauguration on January 20th."[566] Since Trump was the sitting president, China denounced the ban as a coup.[567] The Facebook ban was upheld by the Company's Oversight Board.[568] Facebook declared that the risks involved in allowing Trump to continue to use the platform were "simply too great."[569] Trump was also banned on Snapchat and Twitch, and YouTube imposed strict election misinformation guidelines which would allow it to suspend Trump.[570]

562. *See* Kate Conger & Mike Isaac, *Adding Fact-Checking Labels, Twitter Defies the President, The New York Times* B1 (May 29, 2020); Kate Conger & Davey Alba, *Admirers Follow President Into Battle With Twitter, The New York Times* B1 (May 28, 2020).

563. *See* Nathaniel Popper, *Social Networks Without The Power of Big Tech, The New York Times* B1 (Jan. 27, 2021).; *see also* Mike Isaac & Kate Conger, *Facebook Bans Trump to Term's End, The New York Times* B1 (Jan. 8, 2021).

564. *See* Kate Conger & Mike Isaac, *Citing Risk of Violence, Twitter Permanently Suspends Trump, The New York Times* A1 (Jan. 9, 2021).

565. *Id.*, at A13.

566. *Id.*

567. *See* Li Yuan, *Whataboutism Goes Global In Wake of Trump's Muzzling; China's Censored Internet Takes the Side Of the President in His Clash With Big Tech, The New York Times* B1 (Jan. 15, 2021).

568. *See* Mike Isaac, *Facebook Oversight Board Upholds Social Network's Ban on Trump, The New York Times* A1 & A20 (May 6, 2021).

569. *See* Kevin Roose, *Corporate America Reaches Its Limit: Megaphone to Masses Goes Silent, The New York Times* B1 (Jan. 8, 2021).

570. *See* Mike Isaac & Kate Conger, *Facebook Bans President Through the End of His Term, The New York Times* B5 (Jan. 8, 2021).

Earlier, Twitter added warning labels (fact-checking labels suggesting that something was false) to two of then President Donald Trump's tweets.[571]

Facebook has also banned less prominent individuals. For example, Kevin Matthewson was banned for life after making a post while riots were occurring in his city (Kenosha, Wisconsin).[572] Matthewson called for residents to "take up arms to defend our City tonight from the evil things."[573] Although it is unclear whether individuals responded to Matthewson's post, individuals with military weapons showed up on Kenosha streets that evening, and ultimately two of the protestors were killed.[574] Matthewson was banned from both his personal and professional pages, losing 13 years of photos and videos that included his son and daughter.[575]

Facebook also shut down online pages linked to the "Muslim Cyber Army."[576] The allegedly neo-Nazi web site, The Daily Stormer, was banned by GoDaddy after it mocked a young woman, Heather Heyer, who was killed during a white nationalist rally that occurred in Charlottesville, Virginia, in 2017.[577] GoDaddy claimed that the article might incite violence and therefore violated its terms of service.[578] GoDaddy claimed that it was not engaging in "censorship," and that it supported a "free and open internet."[579] The Daily Stormer then moved its website to Google which banned it for violating its terms of service.[580] Facebook and Instagram

---

571. *See* Kate Conger & Davey Alba, *Admirers Follow President Into Battle With Twitter, The New York Times* B1 (May 28, 2020).

572. *See* Neil MacFarquhar, *When a Vigilante's Call to Action Is Only a Facebook Post Away, The New York Times* A23 (Oct. 17, 2020).

573. *Id.*, at A1.

574. *Id.*

575. *Id.*, at A23.

576. *See* Fisher, *supra* note 504, at B3.

577. *See* Bill Chappell, *Neo-Nazi Site Daily Stormer Is Banned By Google After Attempted More From GoDaddy*, National Public Radio, The Two-Way (Aug. 14, 2017) (GoDaddy announced that it had "informed the Daily Stormer that they have 24 hours to move the domain to another provider, as they have violated our terms of service."). https://www.npr.org/sections/thetwo-way/2017/08/14/543360434/white-supremacist-site-is-banned-by-go-daddy-after-virginia-rally; Hauser, *supra* note 436.

578. *Id.*

579. *Id.*

580. *Id.*

have also moved to block white nationalism content on the basis that it constitutes "hate speech."[581]

Likewise, Hamas (the alleged terrorist organization) was banned from Facebook, YouTube, Instagram, and TikTok.[582] Both Hamas and Hezbollah (both of which are labeled "terrorist organizations by the U.S. State Department) were banned from Twitter.[583] In announcing the ban, Twitter proclaimed that there "is no place on Twitter for illegal organizations and violent extremist groups."[584] As a result, in the first six months of 2019, Twitter shut down 116,000 accounts that it viewed as promoting terrorism.[585] Twitter acted in response to governmental pressure.[586] About the same time, Facebook announced that it would deplatform terrorist organizations.[587] Likewise, TikTok took down videos posted by the Islamic State.[588]

Twitter considered whether to ban "dehumanizing" speech which did not involve direct threats of violence, or hate speech,[589] but it struggled to find a suitable definition for the term "dehumanizing."[590] Twitter expressed concern that such speech might lead to violence.[591] As a result, Twitter was forced to decide whether to allow things like anti-immigrant speech as well as whether to allow rape victims to relate their experiences.[592] Twitter struggled to find suitable policies for a platform that brought "together world leaders, celebrities, journalists, political activists and conspiracy

---

581. See Patrick Thomas, *Facebook to Block White Nationalism Content on Its Sites, The Wall Street Journal* A5 (Mar. 28, 2019).

582. *See* Stuart A. Thompson & Mike Isaac, *Hamas's Social Media Ban Isn't Stopping its Message, The New York Times* A-9 (Oct. 19, 2023).

583. *See* Sarah E. Needleman & Bowdeya Tweh, *Twitter Halts Accounts Linked to Hamas, Hezbollah, The Wall Street Journal* A8 (Nov. 5, 2019).

584. *Id.*

585. *Id.*

586. *Id.*

587. *Id.*

588. *Id.*

589. *See* Sara Salinas, *Twitter Permanently Bans Alex Jones and Infowars Accounts,* CNBC (Sept. 6, 2018). https://www.cnbc.com/2018/09/06/twitter-permanently-bans-alex-jones-and-infowars-accounts.html.

590. *Id.* at B6.

591. *Id.*

592. *Id.*

theorists."[593] Even though Twitter's guiding light had been free expression, it eventually shifted to suggesting that "safety" should come first.[594] In an effort to protect its "safety team" against trolls, Twitter asked that the members not be identified.[595]

Leading social media companies have also banned other right wing individuals.[596] Twitter banned Milo Yiannopoulos allegedly for an online harassment campaign against an actress, as well as Chuck Johnson, a Breitbart writer, for alleged threats against a civil rights activist.[597] Twitter also banned organizations such as the American Nazi Party and Golden Dawn.[598] They have also deplatformed the right-wing social media platform, Parler.[599] Apple and Google removed Parler from their app stores, and Amazon refused to continue hosting the app.[600]

Many fundraising sites, including PayPal, Patreon and GoFundMe, have also banned individuals on the right,[601] including Hunter Wallace, described as a white nationalist blogger, and Kyle Chapman, a/k/a Based Stickman, described as an alt-right personality.[602] In addition, Amazon, Apple and Google halted collaboration with Parler, claiming that it had

---

593. *Id.* at B6.

594. *Id.* at B1.

595. *Id.*

596. *See The Alt-Right Finds a New Enemy in Silicon Valley, supra* note 523, at B6:

> The alt-right isn't necessarily wrong when it claims, as its followers often do, that Silicon Valley is steeped in social liberalism. These are companies that emerged out of Bay Area counterculture, that sponsor annual floats in gay pride parades and hang "Black Lives Matter" signs on the walls of their offices. Silicon Valley's policy preferences aren't always liberal, but tech executives routinely side with progressives on hot-button social issues like immigration, the Paris climate accords, and President Trump's recent decision to bar transgender people from military service. In today's political climate, these are partisan positions, and it's no big shock that they have drawn suspicions from the other side.

597. *See* Fisher, *supra* note 586, at B5; *see also* Debra J. Sanders, *@Nero fiddles, Twitter burns, San Francisco Chronicle* (July 22, 2016).

598. *Id.*

599. *See* Jack Nica & Davey Alba, *How Parlier, A Chosen App of Trump Fans, Became a Test of Free Speech, The New York Times* A1 (Jan. 11, 2021).

600. *See* Jack Nicas & Davey Alba, *How Parler, A Chosen App of Trump Fans, Became a Test of Free Speech, The New York Times* (Jan, 10, 2021).

601. *See The Alt-Right Finds a New Enemy, supra* note 523.

602. *Id.*

not done enough to censor violent content.[603] Airbnb cancelled bookings for far right individuals related to a rally in Charlottesville, Virginia (one that ultimately resulted in violence).[604] YouTube, which is owned by Google, placed special restrictions on "controversial religions or supremacist content."[605] Facebook banned "Britain First" which has been described as a far right group in the UK.[606]

In addition to banning certain content and individuals, social media platforms sometimes intentionally hamper efforts by political groups to organize.[607] The goal is to make it difficult for those that the platforms deem to be "harmful communities" to gain "traction."[608] For example, following the January 6th riot at the Capitol, individuals tried to launch the "Patriot Party" as an alternative to the Republican Party.[609] Fearing that the backers involved white nationalists or militias who had been involved in the riot, Facebook attempted to stifle the organizational attempt.[610] In particular, Facebook made it more difficult for the group to share content, and it restricted groups associated with the movement, and made it difficult to recruit new members.[611] Facebook even complimented itself for being able to nip the party's organizational efforts "in the bud."[612]

Three internet companies (Google, Apple and Facebook) moved aggressively to remove content produced by Alex Jones, and his Infowars site, as "hate speech."[613] Infowars was described by one newspaper as a "right-wing conspiracy site."[614] Jones is the founder of the New Century Foundation which (according to the Southern Poverty Law Center) "purports to show

---

603. *See* Popper, *supra* note 578, at B1.

604. *Id.*

605. *Id.*

606. *See* Nikaj Chkshi, *Facebook Blocks Far-Right Group in Britain, The New York Times International* A8 (Mar. 15, 2018).

607. *See* Jeff Horowitz & Justin Scheck, *Facebook Increasingly Ats to Squelch Political Groups, The Wall Street Journal* A1 (Oct. 23–24, 2021).

608. *Id.*

609. *Id.*

610. *Id.*

611. *Id.*

612. *Id.*

613. *See* Yuan, *supra* note 101, at B3.

614. *See* Chen, *supra* note 280, at B-7.

the inferiority of blacks to whites."[615] One newspaper referred to Jones as someone "who became famous for his spittle-flecked rants and far-fetched conspiracy theories, including the idea that the Sandy Hook massacre was an elaborate hoax promoted by gun-control supporters."[616] Jones also referred to the 9/11 attacks as an "inside job" and he helped spread the "Pizzagate" controversy (which involved allegations that Hillary Clinton was in cahoots with others to run a child sexual abuse ring out of a pizza parlor in Maryland).[617] In regard to the 9/11 attacks, Jones stated that "Now 9/11 was an inside job, but when I say inside job it means criminal elements in our government working with Saudi Arabia and others, wanting to frame Iraq for it."[618] Other sites—including YouTube, Pinterest, and MailChimp—also banned Infowars. Facebook also banned Boogaloo which it regarded as a movement that encourages violence.[619]

Although Twitter chose to leave Mr. Jones' posts alone for a while,[620] it eventually changed course and banned both Jones and Infowars from its platforms for allegedly violating its terms of use policy.[621] Twitter expressed concern that Jones was harassing a CNN reporter.[622] Jones responded that the reporter is a "public figure" who has been attempting to "bully" tech companies into banning Jones.[623] Interestingly, 13 of Jones's most popular tweets involved reposts of Tweets by President Trump.[624] Apple, Inc. removed links to most of Infowars podcasts, but initially left the Infowars app on its site.[625] Facebook banned, not only Alex Jones, but also various

---

615. *See* Burnson, *supra* note 453.

616. *See* Christine Hauser, *Megyn Kelly Calls Alex Jones's Sandy Hook Denial "Revolting," but Still Plans to Air Interview, The New York Times* (June 12, 2017); Kevin Roose, *After the Ban On Infowars, What's Next?, The New York Times* B1 (Aug. 10, 2018).

617. *See id.*

618. *Id.*

619. *See* Tiffany Hsu & Mike Isaac, *Count Us Out, Facebook, The New York Times* B1 (July 1, 2020).

620. *See* Yuan, *supra* note 101.

621. *See* Burnson, *supra* note 453; *See* Kate Conger & Jack Nicas, *Twitter Bars Alex Jones and Infowars, Citing Harassing Messages, The New York Times* B1 (Sept. 7, 2018).

622. *See* Conger & Nicas, *supra* note 636.

623. *Id.*

624. *Id.*

625. *See* Salinas, *supra* note 604. https://www.cnbc.com/2018/09/06/twitter-permanently-bans-alex-jones-and-infowars-accounts.html.

other individuals, including Paul Joseph Watson (an Infowars contributor) and Paul Nelson (a white nationalist).[626]

In addition, there is lots of other censorship of right wing actors. For example, the platform Gab has been unable to access Apple or Google.[627] One social media platform, Parler, was denied access to Apple, Google and Amazon.[628] When GoDaddy Inc. and Alphabet revoked the Daily Stormer's internet registration, the Daily Stormer moved its content to the Dark Web.[629]

Even though social media platforms have actively suppressed both content and particular individuals, it is important to remember that the internet is extremely resilient. Platforms like Facebook and Twitter are hardly the only platforms available. Indeed, social media platforms are ever changing. For example, Meta's use by teenagers has been declining for years, and is expected to drop another 45%.[630] Instagram, which had been growing and which offset Meta's decline, is declining in its competition with platforms like TikTok.[631] Similarly, MySpace has been described by one commentator as a "ghost town."[632]

Organizations like Infowars find ways to circumvent social media bans.[633] For example, when Facebook decided to ban Infowars, Infowars private groups and messaging apps continued to proliferate on Facebook.[634] Through these outlets, which involved both "closed" and "secret" groups, Infowars could function without much oversight or review.[635] Thus, even though Infowars video and podcasts have been removed from various platforms, it has become one of the most popular apps, sometimes

---

626. *See* Mike Isaac & Kevin Roose, *Facebook Bars 7 Fiery Voices, Mostly Rightist, The New York Times* A1 & A17 (May 3, 2019).

627. *Id.*

628. *Id.*

629. *See* Jim Finkle, *Neo-Nazi Group Moves to 'Dark Web' After Website Goes Down, The New York Times* A1 (Aug. 15, 2017).

630. See Kevin Roose, *Facebook Is Weaker Than We Knew, The New York Times*, The Shift B1 (Oct. 5, 2021).

631. *Id.*, at B4.

632. *Id.*

633. *See* Kevin Roose, *To the Fringe, Being Barred By Facebook Isn't the End, The New York Times* B1 (Sept. 4, 2018).

634. *Id.* at B2.

635. *Id.*

on those very platforms.[636] Twitter responded that it would take action to prevent Jones and Infowars from circumventing its ban.[637]

Interestingly, Infowars has played up its role as a "martyr" by slapping "censored" labels on a number of its videos and initiating a "forbidden information" marketing campaign.[638] Jones, through another Twitter account, turned the ban into a public relations coup, claiming that "They're scared of us. They're scared of the populist movement."[639] Not only did Infowars remain readily available on the internet,[640] Jones had an 8% bump in his Twitter followers (which translated to about 70,000 followers).[641] Today, while individuals can still access the Infowars site directly, some believe that the social media ban will mean that Jones and Infowars will have trouble attracting new followers.[642]

Likewise, even though *The Daily Stormer* was banned from various websites, it remains readily available on the internet.[643] Indeed, like Infowars, *The Daily Stormer* has used the GoDaddy and Google bans to tout itself as the "most censored" publication.[644] U.S. Senator Rand Paul, who was censored by YouTube, moved his communications to Rumble.[645] Paul then indicated that Rumble is the only place that he would make posts.[646]

Some commentators believe that Facebook's decision to ban Trump from its platform made it difficult for him to amplify his message,[647] as

636. *See* Yuan, *supra* note 101 ("days after Google, Facebook and Apple removed video and podcasts from Infowars from their sites, its app became one of the hottest in the United States. Among news apps on Wednesday, Infowars was No. 3 on Apple and No. 5 on Google, above all mainstream news organizations.").

637. *See* Conger & Nicas, *supra* note 636.

638. *See* Roose, *supra* note 4, at B3.

639. *See* Conger & Nicas, *supra* note 636.

640. After reading a series of articles about how Infowars had been banned, the author ran an internet search for the site on August 28, 2018, and the site readily popped up. *See* https://www.infowars.com/.

641. *See* Conger & Nicas, *supra* note 636.

642. *Id.*

643. https://dailystormer.name/.

644. *Id.*

645. *See* Johnson, *supra* note 575, at 4A.

646. *Id.*

647. *See* Maggie Haberman, *Without Twitter, Who Is Donald J. Trump?*, *The New York Times* A 11 (Jan. 11, 2021).

well as to raise money,[648] and might imperil his effort to remain the leader of the Republican Party.[649] They viewed Facebook as a "vital weapon" in a political campaign, and argue that it has the ability to help a candidate build out a voter base, and "juice small-dollar online-fund-raising numbers into the millions."[650] Moreover, few politicians had tapped Facebook's potential as effectively as Trump.[651] Trump used Twitter, they concluded, to be "an agenda-setter for the day's coverage, a weapon against his rivals, a way of firing aides and cabinet secretaries, a grenade he could throw at Republican lawmakers who had crossed him and reporters whose coverage he hated, a window into his psyche, and most of all, an unfiltered pipeline to his supporters."[652] One commentator referred to Twitter as Trump's "battering ram."[653] However, as the 2024 presidential election reveals, Trump has done just fine.

The conventional wisdom is that the bans limited Trump's ability to disseminate his views, as well as his ability to raise money.[654] *The New York Times* argued that the Facebook ban was important because that platform had become "the most vital weapon in a political campaign's arsenal, with its ability to juice members into the millions, expand and acquire contact information, help build out data on a campaign voter's file and provide the most sophisticated advertising platform available."[655] Some claim that Trump had been the most successful at using Facebook, sending millions of different hyper-targeted political ads to small slices of the population," and using the platform to turn out supporters for his rallies.[656] In the 2020 presidential election, Trump had a nine figure budget for Facebook advertising.[657] During Trump's first impeachment trial, he flooded Facebook

---

648. *Id.*

649. *See* Nick Corasaniti & Shane Goldmaher, *Ban Hits Trump Where It Hurts: Messaging and Money, The New York Times* A20 (May 6, 2021).

650. *Id.*

651. *Id.*

652. *See Without Twitter, Who Is Donald J. Trump? supra* note 662, at A 11.

653. *See* Kevin Roose, *Corporate America Reaches Its Limit: Megaphone to Masses Goes Silent, The New York Times* B1 (Jan. 8, 2021).

654. *See Ban Hits Trump Where It Hurts, supra* note 664, at A20.

655. *Id.*

656. *Id.*

657. *Id.*

with ads criticizing the impeachment as a hoax and as a subversive effort by far-left Democrats.[658]

Without Twitter, the question was whether Trump could dominate without his so-called bullhorn.[659] Or, as another commentator concluded, Trump's "megaphone" went silent.[660] Before Donald Trump was banned, he purportedly had 150 million followers across all social media platform with 35 million followers on Facebook and 88 million on Twitter.[661] After the ban was imposed, Mr. Trump received 88% fewer mentions on Facebook, Twitter and Instagram.[662]

While some recognized that Trump might gravitate to smaller right-wing platforms, they believed that he would not have as much impact: "So he goes to Parler. Who cares? The major platforms have already demonstrated the undeniable value of network and reach beyond the narrow confines of an affinity group."[663]

For a short time, the Twitter ban forced Trump to communicate in more traditional ways, including going on television programs like Fox News.[664] But, despite the dire predictions, Donald Trump fared quite well. Trump considered several options for creating his own social media platform.[665] The potential partners considered Trump an appealing partner because he originally had some 89 million followers on Twitter.[666] Interestingly, despite the ban, some social media companies were willing to sell political advertisements to Trump, including Facebook, although some prohibited using actual footage or Trump or his voice.[667] In 2022, Trump opted to create a new social media platform, Truth Social, which was billed as a place where free speech could survive "without the constraints

---

658. *Id.*

659. *Id.*

660. *See Megaphone to Masses Gone Silent, supra* note 668, at B5.

661. *See* Michael C. Bender & Georgia Wells, *Ban Hasn't Hurt Trump, Social Media, The Wall Street Journal* A4 (Jan. 10, 2022).

662. *Id.*

663. *See Megaphone to Masses Gone Silent, supra* note 668, at B5.

664. *Id.*

665. *See* Keach Hagley, *Trump Weighing Online Partners, The Wall Street Journal* A4 (May 15–16, 2021).

666. *Id.*

667. *See* Bender & Wells, *supra* note 676, at A4.

imposed by Big Tech."[668] And, indeed, things can be posted on Truth Social that would be banned on other social media platforms.[669] Some have characterized that platform as "slow and clunky,"[670] and Trump has far fewer followers on Truth Social (one million) than he had on Twitter (89 million).[671] Moreover, Truth Social has far fewer active users (448,700) as compared to X (74.3 million). Some commentators have speculated that, if Musk imposes fewer content rules on X (the former Twitter), Truth Social's reason for existing (as an alternative venue for conservatives being censored on other social media platforms) might disappear.[672]

Even in the absence of an alternative platform, it is not clear that social media platforms bans have had a debilitating impact on Trump. Trump continued to be present on Facebook and Twitter because his supporters would pick up his posts and post them on their own accounts.[673] "Before the ban, Mr. Trump's posts got 22.1 million likes and shares; after the ban, his posts earned 1.3 million likes and shares across Twitter and Facebook.[674] Some of the more prominent posting supporters were Breitbart News, the President Donald Trump Fan Club (on Facebook), Fox News, and a lawyer who made regular appearances as Trump's representative.[675] Regarding one Trump repost, those four sites had 159,500, 48,200, 42,000, and 36,700 likes and shares respectively.[676] There was a drop in online engagement (e.g., "likes") from a high of 272,000 to 36,000, but 11 of his 89 statements "after the ban attracted as many likes or shares as the median post before the ban, if not more."[677] When Trump criticizes con-

---

668. *See* Matthew Goldstein & Ryan Mac, *Trump's Social Platform Will Join a Crowded Field, The New York Times* B1 (Feb. 21, 2022); *See* Matthew Goldstein, Kenneth Vogel & Ryan Mac, *A Musk Takeover of Twitter Could Endanger Trump's Truth Social, The New York Times* B3 (Apr. 23, 2022).

669. *See* Matthew Goldstein, David Yaffe-Bellamy & Stuart A. Thompson, *Truth Social Is Relying on Niche Market Ads, The New York Times* B1 (Aug. 9, 2024).

670. *Id.*

671. *Id.*

672. *Id.*

673. *See* Davey Alba, Ella Koeze & Jacob Silver, *After Trump's Social Media Ban, His Supporters Stepped Up, The New York Times* B1 (June 10, 2021).

674. *Id.*, at B6.

675. *Id.*

676. *Id.*

677. *Id.*

servatives, his messages may be picked up by both the left and the right.[678] One Trump post criticizing Senator Mitch McConnell was shared 345,000 times.[679] In the final analysis, "deplatforming doesn't 'solve' disinformation," but it does potentially "disrupt harmful networks and blunt the influence of harmful individuals."[680]

In addition to using Truth Social, Trump maintained large email and phone number lists that he used to contact supporters.[681] Some commentators claimed that the Facebook ban made it more difficult for Trump to grow the size of his supporter list.[682] Nevertheless, he used his existing list to text supporters to request donations.[683] He also posted his thoughts on his own website under "From the Desk of Donald J. Trump" site.[684] Trump supporters typically reproduce his thoughts on their social media platforms.[685] As a result, he is still regarded as having "the largest megaphone in the world."[686]

After Trump was banned by certain social media platforms, two of Trump's followers used conservative websites (Trash Regan and Gateway Pundit) to criticize a Twitter executive for his tweets critical of the president and other republicans.[687] The posts quickly spread to "dozens of Facebook groups, Reddit forums and YouTube videos."[688] Interestingly, Facebook's labels reduced the public's belief in the veracity of Trump's posts by only 13% points.[689] About the same time, Reddit banned certain online communities, including The_Donald, which had 800,000 subscribers, and was dedicated to following then President Trump.[690] Reddit

678. *Id.*
679. *Id.*
680. *Id.*
681. *See* Davis, *supra* note 232.
682. *Id.*
683. *Id.*
684. *Id.*
685. *Id.*
686. *Id.*
687. *Id.*
688. *Id.*
689. *Id.*
690. *See* Kevin Roose, *Reddit's C.E.O., on Why He Banned the Subreddit 'The_Donald,' The New York Times* B5 (July 1, 2020).

took this action in an effort to limit hate speech on its platforms.[691] In addition to continuing to be present on Facebook and Twitter, many of Trump's supporters moved to other apps such as LBRY, Minds and Sessions.[692] When YouTube removed videos created by Way of the World, those videos were moved to LBRY.[693]

Just as Trump found alternate ways to project his views, others on the right have started circumventing traditional social media bans by starting their own apps and their own platforms.[694] Whether social media platforms will be able to continue to control speech is unclear. Some, objecting to the control exercised by the existing platforms, are endeavoring to establish alternate internet communication systems independent of big tech.[695] This effort brings together a variety of people including technology experts and investors.[696] One effort attempts to use Bitcoin principles which employ a broad and disparate network of computers to create social media networks that are not governed by a central authority,[697] and are hard to control.[698] After then President Donald Trump was banned from various social media platforms, dozens of new social media platforms sprung up which attracted millions of users.[699] One was the network Minds which hosts a number of right-wing groups that were banned from other networks.[700] After Social Truth was announced, several conservative platforms promised more open platforms as well. Gettr, a Twitter alternative, promoted itself as a bastion against censorship.[701] Parler, also a Twitter alternative, along with a couple of Facebook alternatives (MeWe and CloutHub) promised to promote "speech without restraint."[702] There

691. *Id.*

692. *See* Popper, *supra* note 578, at B1.

693. *Id.*

694. *See* Natasha Singer & Nicholas Confessore, *Let's Talk Politics, No Liberals Allowed, Conservative Apps Build Networks Unhindered By Social Media Giants, The New York Times* B3 (Oct. 22, 2018).

695. *See* Popper, *supra* note 578, at B1.

696. *Id.*

697. *Id.*

698. *Id.*

699. *Id.*

700. *Id.*

701. *Id.*

702. *Id.*

is also Rumble, a YouTube competitor,[703] which has 39 million monthly active users.[704] Rumble is much smaller than YouTube with $7 million in revenue (which contrasts with $9 billion for YouTube).[705] Nevertheless, alternative social media platforms have signed up tens of millions of users.[706] However, many who gravitated to alternative networks remain active on Meta and X.[707] For example, some of the new platforms (e.g., Gettr, Parler and Rumble) use X to announce changes or new roll outs on their platforms.[708] These alternate platforms frequently ignore the content guidelines imposed by the major social media platforms.[709] For example, Unloved, a private discussion group on the messaging site Discord, hosts misogynistic content.[710] One of the rules of Unloved is "Do not respect women."[711] Not only are there posts regarding the attractiveness of particular women, the site has small text chat groups that talk about topics like rape.[712] There are also gaming sites that contain hate speech.[713]

Some commentators are concerned by the large number of impressionable young people on these sites.[714] Included are games like Call of Duty, Minecraft, and Roblox.[715] Roblox, for example, allows individuals to create virtual worlds, and some have created fake Nazi concentration camps.[716] Gaming platforms are trying to respond to, and take down, this content, with some using automatic detection systems.[717]

A Bitcoin millionaire created the Freedom Phone designed to appeal to conservatives.[718] The phone contains apps for right-wing websites, a

---

703. *Id.*
704. *Id.*, at B2.
705. *Id.*
706. *Id.*
707. *Id.*
708. *Id.*
709. *See* Steven Lee Myers & Kellen Browning, *Extremism at Home in Gamer Chat Rooms, The New York Times* B1 (May 19, 2023).
710. *Id.*
711. *Id.*
712. *Id.*
713. *Id.*
714. *Id.*
715. *Id.*
716. *Id.*
717. *Id.*
718. *See* Jack Nicas, *Selling Freedom In a Phone, The New York Times* B1 (Sept. 7, 2021).

"free speech" video site (which essentially replicates YouTube but for conservatives), and includes seven conservative social media platforms.[719] One social media platform on the phone, Parler, was denied access to Apple, Google, and Amazon.[720] Another, Gab, has been unable to access Apple or Google.[721] However, there were questions about the quality of the phone.[722] Millions of users have signed up for these alternate websites.[723]

There are also conservative apps that support the NRA, or that support particular candidates such as Donald Trump or Ted Cruz.[724] The Great America app hosts enthusiastic posts about Trump, pictures of puppies, descriptions of illegal immigrants, and "Fake News Friday" which encourages media bashing.[725] The apps provide a way for conservative candidates to interact with their bases.[726]

Many of these platforms are not curated or controlled in the same way as traditional social media platforms,[727] and they give users the option of posting on Twitter or Facebook using pre-scripted conservative messages.[728] Although the Democrats also have their own apps, many of these apps are focused on encouraging individuals to volunteer in political campaigns.[729] Although anyone can access the conservative apps, app controllers can ban individuals who post messages challenging conservative viewpoints.[730]

In an effort to avoid social media platform content moderation, some have moved to encrypted messaging apps such as Signal and Telegram.[731] Because of fears over WhatsApp's privacy policy, Telegram added 25 mil-

---

719. *Id.*

720. *Id.*

721. *Id.*

722. *Id.*

723. *See* Stuart A. Thompson & Matthew Goldstein, *Truth Social's Influence Grows Despite Its Business Problems, International New York Times* 1 (Nov. 8, 2022).

724. *See* Singer & Confessore, *supra* note 710, at B1.

725. *Id.* at B3.

726. *Id.*

727. *Id.* at B1.

728. *Id.*

729. *Id.*

730. *Id.* at B3.

731. *See* Jack Nicas, Mike Isaac & Sheera Frenkel, *Millions Flee to Chat Apps Behind Walls of Encryption, The New York Times* B1 (Jan. 14, 2021); Popper, *supra* note 578, at B1.

lion users and Signal added 1.3 million users in just three days.[732] While messaging apps allow users to avoid content-moderation, the decentralized nature of the messaging apps makes it harder for them to have as much impact.[733] Right-wing groups that were barred from various social media platforms such as Facebook and Twitter following the January 6th riots have increasingly resorted to such apps.[734] The decentralized nature of such apps makes it difficult for the government or the platforms to respond to misinformation.[735] The network IPFS has been used to give people access to content that has been censored by social media platforms or even companies.[736]

When YouTube banned radio and Fox News commentator Dan Bongino for making allegedly false claims regarding Covid-19 (he alleged that cloth and surgical masks were ineffective in preventing the spread of Covid-19),[737] he continued to make similar claims on another YouTube channel until YouTube terminated his accounts.[738] He then shifted to Rumble, where he had twice as many followers, to explain what had happened.[739] YouTube also banned other anti-vaccine commentators.[740] Facebook moved to quash posts relating to anti-quarantine protests.[741]

Likewise, Hamas has found ways to circumvent the social media bans. Even though Hamas is banned from TikTok, Instagram, Facebook, and YouTube, its content frequently appears (sometimes temporarily) on those websites.[742] In addition, although some of Hamas's content has

---

732. *Id.*

733. *See* Popper, *supra* note 578, at B1.

734. *See* Brian X. Chen & Kevin Roose, *Reclaiming Reality From Chaos; Will Encrypted Messaging Apps, Like Telegram and Signal, Turn Into Misinformation Hot Spots, The New York Times* B1 (Feb. 4, 2021).

735. *Id.*

736. *See* Popper, *supra* note 578, at B1.

737. *See* Daisuke Wakabayashi, *YouTube Bars a Right-Wing Host for Making False Covid Claims, The New York Times* B6 (Jan. 27, 2022).

738. *Id.*

739. *Id.*

740. *Id.*; *see also* Dave Sebastian, *YouTube to Pull Videos Containing Vaccine Falsehoods, The Wall Street Journal* A7 (Sept. 30, 2021).

741. *See* Paige Leskin, *Facebook Is Scrambling to Squash Online Groups That Are Planning Anti-Quarantine Protests in States That Are in Lockdown—But They're Popping Up Faster Than the Company Can Stop Them*, Business Insider, msn.com (Apr. 22, 2020).

742. *See* Thompson & Isaac, *supra* note 597.

been removed from Telegram (information which the site regards as "harmful"), the site has not banned the organization.[743] Telegram regards Hamas's posts as a "unique source of first-hand information for researchers, journalists and fact checkers."[744] Thus, it is unwilling to ban Hamas outright from its platform.[745]

Of course, the problem with platforms that cater to particular political perspectives is that they allow conservatives (or, liberals, for that matter) to silo themselves into isolated communities.[746] In other words, it allows them to function in "echo chambers" where they encounter only views that agree with their own.[747] For example, the Proud Boys and Q'anon conspiracy theorists have moved away from traditional social media platforms where they can be deplatformed.[748] As groups silo themselves into their own communities, where they speak only to themselves, there is a risk of aggravating "political polarization and social divisiveness" and allowing misinformation to circulate freely and without challenge.[749] Some argue that this siloization is positive because it gets extremist groups off of traditional social media platforms where they can connect with new sympathizers and disseminate their messages to millions of people.[750] At the same time, it makes it harder for law enforcement to track them.[751] However, Telegram has a group chat function that allows up to 200,000 people to participate.[752] The apps also propose messages that users can forward to others, including social media platforms, and one message was forwarded 14,000 times.[753] Some apps (WhatsApp) have restricted forwarding to prevent so much forwarding.[754] While Signal allows forward-

---

743. *Id.*

744. *Id.*

745. *Id.*

746. *See* Chen & Roose, *supra* note 750, at B7.

747. *See Trump's Social Platform Will Join a Crowded Field, supra* note 683, at B1.

748. *See* Chen & Roose, *supra* note 750, at B7.

749. *See* Singer & Confessore, *supra* note 710, at B3.

750. *See* Chen & Roose, *supra* note 750, at B7.

751. *See* Ellen Nakashima, Mark Berman & Matthew D. LaPlante, *Purges Force Extremists Off Social Media Sites. That Can Complicate Investigators Work, The Washington Post* (Jan. 17, 2021).

752. *Id.*

753. *Id.*

754. *Id.*

ing, messages can only go to five persons at a time.[755] Also, in response to social media attempts to limit their funding, some right wing groups have started their own funding websites.[756]

1. ALGORITHMS

Coming into greater focus today are the algorithms that social media platforms use to keep individuals engaged with their platforms.[757] As one commentator noted, "these platforms are incredibly sophisticated at learning our habits and keeping us engaged in ways that are not necessarily healthy for us or our communities."[758] For individuals on the far left, algorithms feed individuals with information that support and enhance their pre-existing views.[759] Likewise for those on the right.[760] Individuals can resist these algorithms by using devices like YouTube anonymously, as well as by keeping their search browsers in incognito mode.[761]

There is a risk that social media platform algorithms will help spread disinformation and potentially radicalize users of those platforms.[762] A Facebook study described a test involving a woman with strong conservative but not extremist views.[763] The test woman purportedly showed a preference for mainstream news sources, liked groups that mocked liberals, endorsed Christianity, and liked Melania Trump.[764] Over the course of a couple of days, Facebook began recommending extremist content to her.[765]

---

755. *Id.*

756. *See The Alt-Right Finds a New Enemy, supra* note 523.

757. *See* Fisher, *supra* note 586, at B3.

758. *Id.*

759. *Id.*

760. *See* Alan Suderman & Joshua Goodman, *Facebook Had Its Own Insurrection Jan. 6, Courier-Journal* 15A (Oct. 24, 2021).

761. *See* Fisher, *supra* note 586, at B3.

762. *See* Suderman & Goodman, *supra* note 776 at15A.

763. *Id.*

764. *Id.*

765. *Id.*

2. INTERNET ATTACKS

In addition to the restrictions placed by social media companies on their platforms, there have also been "attacks" on websites designed to take those websites down or render them non-functional.[766] Whether these attacks are the work of private individuals, or involve the efforts of governments seeking to shield themselves from public disclosure of embarrassing facts, is unclear. The attacks are accomplished by essentially overwhelming a system (although not necessarily compromising confidential information on the system), in an effort to make them nonfunctional, and the goal is to silence the speaker's message.[767] For example, following its release of classified governmental documents, WikiLeaks website was aggressively attacked by internet hackers,[768] and governments moved to cut off its internet access.[769]

---

766. *See* Neal Conan, *"Operation Payback" Targets WikiLeaks' Foes*, National Public Radio, Talk of the Nation (Dec. 9, 2010), http://www.npr.org/2010/12/09/131937254/-operation-payback-targets-wikileaks-foes; *See* Eric Pfanner, *Apocalypse in Cyberspace? Its Overdone, The New York Times*, Media Cache (blog) (Jan. 16, 2011), http://www.nytimes.com/2011/01/17/technology/17cache.html?_r=1&scp=pfanner%20apocalypse%20cyber space&st=cse (claiming that China has attacked Google's website); *Corporations Are Drawn Into WikiLeaks Controversy, supra* note 427.

767. *See* NPR Staff, *Attacking Websites Is Surprisingly Easy Social Protest*, National Public Radio, All Things Considered (Dec. 12, 2010), http://www.npr.org/2010/12/12/132013474/social-protest-in-the-cyber-age-is-surprisingly-easy ("Think of a denial-of-service attack like a phone call. When many computers attempt to connect to the same website, it's as if many people are calling the same person. 'Now, when another person tries to call, they're going to get a busy signal,' Nicolas Christin tells NPR's Audie Cornish. Christin is associate director of the Information Networking Institute at Carnegie Mellon University. He says denial-of-service attacks work by replicating that principle, but on a much larger scale. Traditionally, Christin says, a few lone attackers release a worm or virus that infiltrates other computers on the Internet, turning them into a 'zombie network' that repeatedly bombs a single website with data. A single Web user can easily volunteer their computer for the attack, too, by downloading a simple push-button application.").

768. *See Hackers Overwhelm WikiLeaks Servers, supra* note 447 ("'"The website WikiLeaks is having trouble staying online. The site, which recently released a large amount of sensitive State Department correspondence, has had to switch servers a number times in the last few weeks due to 'denial of service' attacks.") http://www.npr.org/2010/12/03/131790969/Hackers-Overwhelm-WikiLeaks-Servers.

769. *See* Richard G. Satter & Peter Svensson, *WikiLeaks Puts Up Battle to Stay Online, The Courier-Journal*, at A4 (Dec. 4, 2010). ("Like a fugitive moving from house to house, WikiLeaks changed the name of its Web site after a U.S. company stopped directing traffic to its wikileaks.org. French officials then moved to oust it from its new home.").

Similar attacks and denials of service have hardly been limited to WikiLeaks. When the Electronic Frontier Foundation (EFF) condemned Hackers who had attacked websites in support of WikiLeaks, the hackers attacked the EFF's website.[770] There is reason to believe that governments have been involved in some of these website attacks.[771] Hacking and denials of service issues have been common in Russia. For example, some allege that pro-Putin forces attacked a newspaper's website, causing the site to crash.[772]

Of course, Web attacks and denials of service cut both ways. When Amazon, PayPal and Visa decided to cut their ties to WikiLeaks, so-called "Hacktivists" attacked the websites of those companies.[773] Some view the hack attacks as a protest against increasing governmental and corporate control of the internet,[774] and as an attempt to make it clear that those who interfere with internet communications will pay a penalty.[775] The Hacktivists promised to continue their attacks as long as the government, or other private interests, continued to try to suppress WikiLeaks.[776]

Over time, Web attacks have become increasingly sophisticated.[777] Some websites offer free software that protestors can download and install

770. *See id.* ("Recently, the Electronic Frontier Foundation was the target of a denial-of-service attack. EFF condemned the anonymous hackers who support WikiLeaks for attacking the websites of Amazon, PayPal, Visa and MasterCard. So, the anonymous hackers turned around and attacked EFF's website.").

771. *See Apocalypse in Cyberspace?, supra* note 782.

772. *See Web Strike Blamed on Pro-Putin Youth, supra* note 248, at A11.

773. *See "Operation Payback" Targets WikiLeaks' Foes, supra* note 782 ("Supporters of WikiLeaks launched attacks and shut down websites for major credit card companies. Visa, MasterCard and PayPal were all targets in "Operation Payback." Some internet security watchers are calling it a cyberwar—with limitless targets and innumerable, anonymous aggressors."); *Apocalypse in Cyberspace?, supra* note 782.

774. *See* Noam Cohen, *Hackers Find a Rallying Cry in WikiLeaks, The New York Times*, at A1 (Dec. 10, 2010).

775. *Id.*, at A1 & A11 ("'This is kind of the shot heard round the world—this is Lexington,' said John Perry Barlow, a co-founder of the Electronic Frontier Foundation, a civil liberties organization that advocates for a freer Internet.").

776. *See Operation Payback, supra* note 782 ("Groups with monikers like Anonymous and Operation Payback are taking credit, and vow to continue as long as the U.S. and other governments put pressure on WikiLeaks and its allies.").

777. *See Hackers Find a Rallying Cry, supra* note 790, at A11 ("The coordination and the tactics developed in those campaigns appeared to make this week's attacks more powerful, allowing what analysts believe is a small group to enlist thousands of activists to bom-

on their computers.[778] At least one of these websites has produced numerous versions of its attack software.[779] Moreover, some software contains programming that allows a central server to automatically activate and utilize the downloader's computer without the need for human intervention.[780] In other words, the central server can launch attacks remotely utilizing potentially hundreds of computers all over the world. Some fear that internet hackers have become a potent force[781] who can challenge what they perceive to be objectionable communications and actions.[782] For the moment, at least, the advantage seems to lie with the attackers.[783]

The WikiLeaks denial of service attacks are illustrative. Those attacks were coordinated from a central website which issued commands to attack,[784] and had their origins in similar attacks on behalf of a Swedish group.[785] These attacks on private companies can be regarded as simply another means of social protest.[786] As one commentator noted, attacks "are so easy to carry out and relatively difficult to defend against."[787] In

---

bard Web sites with traffic, making them at least temporarily inaccessible. Experts say the group appears to have used more sophisticated software this time that allowed supporters to repeatedly visit the sites at a specific time when the command was given.").

778. *Id.*, at A11 ("The software used to coordinate the attacks is being downloaded about 1,000 times per hour with about one-third of those downloads coming from the United States.").

779. *Id.*

780. *Id.* ("Recently the software was improved so that a command could be sent to a supporter's computers and the attack would begin—no human needed.").

781. *Id.*

782. *Id.*

783. *Id.* ("'Home field advantage' goes to the attacker," said Gunter Ollmann, vice president of research at Dambalia, an Atlanta-based firm that specializes in Internet protection. 'With a little bit of coordination and growing numbers of participants, these things will continue to happen regularly.'").

784. *Id.* (The Anonymous Web site would sometimes contain the simple command to "Fire Now.").

785. *Id.*, at A11 ("The campaigns are part of Operation Payback, created in the summer to defend a file-sharing site in Sweden that counts itself part of the mission of keeping the Internet unfettered and unfiltered and that was singled out by authorities. 'We could move against enemies of WikiLeaks so easily because there was already a network up and running, there was already a chat room for people to meet in,' said Gregg Housh, an activist who has been involved in Anonymous campaigns....").

786. *See Attacking Websites Is Surprisingly Easy, supra* note 783.

787. *Id.* (quoting Nicolas Christin, Associate Director of Information Networking at Carnegie Mellon University).

addition as the attacks gain momentum and publicity on social media sites, others join the attack.[788] However, some commentators claim that these denials of service have been over dramatized by the media.[789] For example, although Amazon was attacked after it denied service to WikiLeaks, the company claims that it successfully defended itself against the attacks.[790]

3. NET NEUTRALITY

Private individuals can also threaten internet communication in other ways. One issue has been the problem of "net neutrality" and network security firewalls[791] which have the potential to limit access to the full internet.[792] Some have argued that internet search engines discriminate on the basis of content, and that search engines should be required to ensure "search neutrality." For example, President Trump has argued that Google intentionally suppresses positive stories about his administration.[793]

Part of the problem is that one company (Google) controls much of the search market worldwide. In 2009, it was estimated that Google controlled 71% the search market in the United States, and up to 90% of the market in the United Kingdom.[794] By 2018, it was estimated that Google controlled up to 90% of all searches.[795]

Google searches are based on algorithms developed by the company which it maintains are proprietary and therefore it does not reveal.[796]

---

788. *Id.* ("With so many people targeting WikiLeaks, there's been less need for an army of "zombie" computers. Thanks to social media, word of the attacks spread quickly—while recruiting more of the living to the cause.").

789. *See Apocalypse in Cyberspace?, supra* note 782.

790. *See Amazon Cites Terms of Use, supra* note 561.

791. *See* Jesdanun, *supra*, note 15, at D5.

792. *See* Adam Raff, *Search, but You May Not Find, The New York Times*, Op-Ed, at A27 (Dec. 28, 2009) ("The Federal Communications Commission has proposed 'network neutrality' rules which would prohibit Internet service providers from discriminating against or charging premiums for certain services or applications on the Web.").

793. *See* Daisuke Wakabayashi, *Google's Secrets Revealed (Sort of): Trump Says the Company's Search Engine Is Rigged. The Reality Is Far More Complex, The New York Times* B1 (Sept. 6, 2018).

794. *See* Raff, *supra* note 808.

795. *See* Wakabayashi, *supra* note 809.

796. *See id.*

However, even "a minor tweak to its algorithm can redirect huge amounts of web traffic."[797] Algorithms can consider a variety of factors, including "Page Rank" which suggests that a web page's value can be determined by examining how many web sites are linked to it. The algorithm can also consider other factors such as "how often and where the keywords bring searches for show up on a specific page, how recently the page was created (a sign of the freshness of the information) and the location of the person making the search."[798] Google disclaims the idea that political ideology factors into its algorithm.[799] However, the Company hires "raters," approximately 10,000 of them worldwide, to give it feedback on whether its search results "deliver expertise, authoritativeness and trustworthiness."[800] Moreover, its engineers tend to be white or Asian, and male, and therefore subtle biases could enter into the search results.[801]

In addition to making advertising revenue from the Web, Google also receives hundreds of billions of dollars per year related to its search results and sponsored links.[802] This money comes from companies that offer travel information, shopping services or that review local restaurants and businesses.[803] As a result, some claim that Google controls search results, and favors itself, through "penalties"[804] as well as through "preferential placements."[805] However, it is not clear that internet search engines nec-

797. *See id.*

798. *See id.*, at B3.

799. *See id.*

800. *See id.*

801. *See id.*

802. *See* Raff, *supra* note 808.

803. *See* Wakabayashi, *supra* note 809, at B3.

804. *See id.* ("One way that Google exploits its control is by imposing covert 'penalties' that can strike legitimate and useful Web sites, removing them entirely from its search results or placing them so far down the rankings that they will in all likelihood never be found. For three years, my company's vertical search and price-comparison site, Foundem, was 'effectively' disappeared from the Internet in this way.").

805. *See id.* ("Another way that Google exploits its control is through preferential placement. With the introduction in 2007 of what it calls 'universal search,' Google began promoting its own services at or the top of its search results, bypassing the algorithms it uses to rank the services of others. Google now favors its own price-comparison results for product queries, its own map results for geographic queries, its own news results for topical queries, and its own YouTube results for video queries. And Google's stated plans for universal search make it clear that this is only the beginning.").

essarily discriminate against particular ideologies or viewpoints. Indeed, many searches come back with a lot of results that include both conservative and liberal viewpoints.[806]

In any event, the problems presented by net neutrality have led some commentators to claim that search neutrality rules are needed to prevent the world from "heading toward a bleakly uniform world of Google everything—Google Travel, Google Finance, Google Insurance, Google Real Estate, Google Telecoms and, of course, Google Books."[807] Some argue that this situation suggests a need for "search neutrality": the "FCC needs to look beyond network neutrality and include 'search neutrality': the principle that search engines should have no editorial policies other than that their results be comprehensive, impartial and based solely on relevance."[808]

To some extent, the absence of neutrality is a problem that can be handled by individual interest groups. One of the big advantages of the internet is that it allows groups of like-mind individuals to find each other and to work together. The absence of net neutrality can make it more difficult for like-minded individuals to find each other. Once they do, however, it is relatively easy for them to remain in touch. Individuals with special interests can establish listservs to communicate with others of similar interests. In addition, once an individual has found a website, the website can be bookmarked and quickly retrieved.

In 2018, the State of California adopted its own net neutrality law.[809] The U.S. government immediately sued California seeking to block the law.

Finally, copyright issues may limit the potential of the internet as well. For example, the United States Department of Justice shut down the file-sharing website Megaupload Ltd. on the theory that it was operat-

---

806. *See id.* ("As they exist today, they [search engines] are the opposite of an echo chamber—you go looking for something, and a cacophony comes back. The big players promise, even boast, about the number of pages scanned to provide the results for a search.").

807. *See id.*

808. *See id.*

809. *See* Dina Kesbeh, *Justice Department Sues California Over Net Neutrality Law*, National Public Radio (Oct. 1, 2018). https://www.npr.org/2018/10/01/653216821/u-s-justice-department-sues-california-over-net-neutrality-law.

ing in violation of copyright laws.[810] Megaupload, which had 180 million registered users and 50 million visitors per day, raised troubling issues for such "cloud" or storage sites.[811] For individuals who had stored their own material on Megaupload, it was unclear how or whether they would be able to get the information back.[812] Interestingly, some other file-sharing websites have successfully defended themselves using the "fair use" defense.[813] A larger threat was posed by the Stop Online Piracy Act (SOPA) which would have given media companies the ability to shut down Web sites that illegally allow downloads of television shows and movies.[814] Individuals protested against SOPA on the Web, with the protests including a 24-hour shutdown of Wikipedia,[815] and politicians began to back away from their support for the legislation.[816] A similar French effort was also met with significant opposition.[817] Content owners are always free to bring their own litigation against offending websites.[818]

Of course, private individuals can also repress internet communications through such methods as threats and physical violence. For example, when a Saudi Arabia man issued Tweets regarding the Prophet Muhammad, private individuals offered rewards for the man's execution.[819] Ultimately, the man was forced to flee his home and his country.[820]

---

810. *See* Geoffrey A. Fowler, *Megaupload's Ripple Effect, The Wall Street Journal*, at B1 (Jan. 25, 2012).

811. *See id.*

812. *Id.*

813. *Id.* at B2.

814. See Jenna Wortham, *Protest on Web Takes on 2 Bills, Using Shutdown: Jolt to Tech Industry; Political Coming of Age—Antipiracy Effort Is the Target, The New York Times*, at A1 (Jan. 18, 2012); *see also* Somini Sengupta, *Big Victory on Internet Buoys Lobby, The New York Times*, at B1 (Jan. 27, 2012).

815. *Id.*

816. *See* Guy Raz, Week in News: *The Salvo Against SOPA*, National Public Radio, All Things Considered (Jan. 21, 2012), http://www.npr.org/2012/01/21/145576381/week-in-news-the-salvo-against-sopa ("This past week, the twin anti-piracy bills known as SOPA and PIPA were dealt perhaps a fatal blow by a popular uprising instigated by major technology companies.").

817. *See* Eric Pfanner, *Should Online Scofflaws Be Denied Web Access?, The New York Times*, at B4 (Apr. 13, 2009).

818. *Id.*

819. *See* Ellen Knickmeyer, *Saudi Tweets Spark Outrage, Death Threats, The Wall Street Journal*, at A7 (Feb. 9, 2012).

820. *Id.*

CHAPTER IX

DISINFORMATION

Earlier chapters examined how the internet has enabled ordinary people to engage in mass communication, circumventing the traditional gatekeepers of communication, and leading to enhanced participation in democratic movements and debates. However, the internet is a double-edged sword in the sense that the same forces (ease of access to the internet and the ability to disseminate information widely) that have enabled ordinary individuals to achieve greater political participation has allowed individuals to undercut or subvert the political process by disseminating disinformation. Of course, the internet can also be used for other nefarious purposes: to perpetrate fraud,[1] disseminate child pornography[2] and evidence of child sexual abuse,[3] recruit criminals or terrorists,[4] and spew

1. *See* Stacy Cowley & Lananh Nguyen, *Fraud Is Flourishing on Zelle. Banks Say It's Not Their Issue, The New York Times* B1 (Mar. 7, 2022).

2. *See* Jeff Horowitz & Katherine Blunt, *Instagram Links Pedophile Network, The Wall Street Journal* A1 (June 28, 2023); *see also* Alexa Corse, *Twitter Found to Have Missed Images of Child Sexual Abuse, The Wall Street Journal* B1 (June 6, 2023).

3. *See* Gabriel J.X. Dance & Michael H. Miller, *Reports of Online Videos of Child Sexual Abuse Climb by Millions, The New York Times* A18 (Feb. 9, 2020).

4. *See* Justin Schenck, Newley Purnell & Jeff Horowitz, *Facebook Staff Flags Traffickers, Cartels. Company Response Is Weak, Wall Street Journal* A1 (Sept. 17, 2021).

hate speech and vitriol.[5] In addition, there are claims that social media platforms are targeting perceived weaknesses in teen brains.[6]

This chapter focuses on disinformation which has become a major problem for the political process,[7] and the evidence shows that disinformation can spread faster than truthful information on social media and penetrate more deeply.[8] Disinformation was 70% more likely to be retweeted, and true stories took six times as long to reach people on social media.[9] As a result, elections can be polluted by conspiracy theories, claims of election fraud, and other false claims, and social media often is the vehicle by which disinformation is spread. There are a variety of reasons why disinformation is spread: to promote a political or ideological position; to draw social media users to particular websites for advertising purposes; and sometimes simply for the entertainment of those who disseminate it.[10] Political disinformation can be used to "distort elections, divert attention from other societal issues or instill fear."[11]

Examples of misinformation and disinformation abound. For example, following the death of George Floyd in Minneapolis, rumors circulated that he was not actually dead, and there were allegations that the billion-

---

5. *See* Tiffany Hsu, Stuart A. Thompson & Steven Lee Myers, *Elections and Disinformation Collide is Year Ripe for Chaos, The New York Times* A1 (Jan. 23, 2024); Kevin Roose & Ali Winston, *Web's Far Right Can Hear Itself as Trump Talks: Cheering the Spread of Once-Fringe Views, The New York Times* A17 (Nov. 5, 2018); *See* Ross Sorkin, *Social Media and Standards Regulations don't yet match reality, The New York Times* C6 (Nov. 6, 2018), at C6; *see also* Amanda Hess, *Feeds Fill With Hate For Actress, The New York Times* C1 & C5 (May 20, 2022) (discussing vitriol directed at Amber Heard during her defamation suit against Johnny Depp.); Steven Lee Myers & Stuart A. Thompson, *Hate on Web Is Expanding From Fringes, The New York Times* B1 (June 1, 2020).

6. *See* Jeff Horowitz, *Meta Targeted Teen Brains, States Allege, The Wall Street Journal* B-4 (Nov. 27, 2023); *see also* Mary Clare Jalonick, *Senators seek to protect kids online, Courier-Journal* 12A (May 5, 2023); Ryan Tracy & John D. McKinnon, *Facebook Accused of Ignoring Data on Instagram's Impact, The Wall Street Journal* A7 (Oct. 1, 2021).

7. *See* Hsu, Thompson & Myers, *supra* note 5, at A1; *see also* Steven Lee Myers & Sheera Frenkel, *Exploding Online, Disinformation Is Now a Fixture of US. Politics, The New York Times* C7 (Oct. 21, 2022).

8. *See* Alina Polianskaya, *Fake News Travels Much Further and Faster Than Real News on Social Media, Study Finds, The Independent* 1 (Mar. 9, 2018).

9. *Id.*

10. *See* Sarah E. Needleman, *Users Adopt New Tactics to Spread Disinformation, The Wall Street Journal* B4 (Oct. 25, 2019).

11. *Id.*

aire investor George Soros was funding protests against police brutality.[12] In 2019, a tweet falsely suggested that Colorado's election system had been hacked.[13] State officials knew that the tweet was a lie because it showed a type of voting machine that was not used in Colorado.[14] Likewise, on President Biden's presidential inauguration day, information circulated that the inauguration was a prerecorded hoax that had actually been filmed in a Hollywood studio rather than at the US Capitol.[15]

Especially in the U.S., which has become politically polarized, false narratives are commonplace.[16] During the Covid-19 pandemic, a considerable amount of disinformation was disseminated regarding the severity of the pandemic and the vaccines used to combat it,[17] including anti-vaccine information,[18] with one post receiving more than 3 million views.[19] One doctor, an advocate for natural health cures, claimed that Covid vaccines alter a recipient's genetic code and do not have an on/off switch.[20] His posts received some 400,000 views on Facebook,[21] appeared on dozens of blogs,[22] and he had 300,000 followers on Twitter,[23] and another 400,000 on YouTube.[24] There was also a claim that Russia was distributing disinformation suggesting that 5G cellphone networks cause serious adverse

---

12. *See* Davey Alba, *'All of It Is Toxic': A Surge in Protest Misinformation, the New York Times* B1 (June 2, 2020).

13. *See* Nick Corasaniti & Davey Alba, *Facing a Deluge of Misinformation, Colorado Takes the Offensive Against It, The New York Times* A20 (Oct. 21, 2020).

14. *Id.*

15. *See* Kevin Roose, *Reclaiming Reality From Chaos; How the Biden Administration Can Help Wean Americans from the Scourge of Hoaxes and Lies, The New York Times* B1 (Feb. 4, 2021).

16. *See* Hsu, Thompson & Myers, *supra* note 5, at A1.

17. *See* Sam Schechner, Jeff Horwitz & Emily Glazer, *Mark Zuckerberg's Vaccine Plan Was No Match for Facebook, The Wall Street Journal* B1 & B4 (Sept.18–19, 2021).

18. *See* Neil MacFarhquhar, *Moving On From 'Stop the Steal,' Far Right Now Vilifies Vaccines, The New York Times* A1 (Mar. 27, 2021); Andrew Restuccia & Sarah E. Needleman. Biden, *Facebook Escalate Barbs on Misinformation, The Wall Street Journal* A6 (July 19, 2021).

19. *See* Schechner, Horwitz & Glazer, *supra* note 17, at B1.

20. *See* Sheera Frenkel, *Disinformation Is Big Business for One Doctor, The New York Times* 1 (July 25, 2021).

21. *See id.*, at 1.

22. *Id.*

23. *Id.*, at16.

24. *Id.*

health effects.[25] Some of this disinformation has gone viral.[26] In one case, a Twitter account post, by a person with only 40 followers, was distributed 16,000 times on Twitter and another 350,000 times on Facebook.[27] A Trump post on his social media platform, Truth Social, coursed through the internet with reposts on Facebook and Twitter.

Disinformation is also rampant in the European Union.[28] For example, in the lead-up to the 2024 European Union elections, there was considerable disinformation regarding European farm policy.[29] There were claims in Italy that the E.U. planned to ban animal breeding, and that the government was causing droughts by demolishing dams, as well as claims that the E.U. was destroying crop fields, forcing reductions in agricultural production, and trying to replace farmers with A.I. robots.[30] There were also claims the E.U. was promoting lab-grown meat, and the consumption of insects, in an effort to combat environmental pollution.[31] In the U.K., following a stabbing attack on three children, false information circulated regarding the identity of the attacker.[32]

The problem of disinformation is complicated by the development of artificial intelligence, including the existence of bots and chatbots[33] which permit the creation of false narratives,[34] and lead to their amplification.[35] For example, "news stories" can be generated by AI,[36] and OpenAI's GPT-2

---

25. *See* William J. Broad, *Russia Wants U.S. to Dread 5G Cellphones, The New York Times* A1 (May 13, 2019).

26. *See* Sapna Maheshware, *How Fake News Goes Viral: A Case Study, The New York Times* A1 (Nov. 22, 2016).

27. *Id.*

28. *See* Tiffany Hsu, *Disinformation Around E.U. Elections Is Fueled by a 'Convergence of Anger,' The New York Times* A6 (July 8, 2024).

29. *Id.*

30. *Id.*

31. *Id.*

32. *See* Megan Specia, *Disinformation Fuels Far-Right Riot After U.K. Stabbing, The New York Times* A8 (Aug. 1, 2024).

33. *See* Hsu, Thompson & Myers, *supra* note 5, at A1.

34. *Id.*

35. *See* Molly Wood, Stephanie Hughes & Shaheen Ainpour, *How Social Media Bots Can Amplify Fake News*, Marketplace (Feb. 27, 2018) https://www.marketplace.org/2018/02/27/how-social-media-bots-can-amplify-fake-news/.

36. *See* Asa Fitch, *Beware of Fake Articles, Courtesy of AI, The Wall Street Journal* R8 (Oct. 14, 2019).

can produce fictional articles that sound genuine.[37] During Argentinian elections, A.I. was used to generate a poster depicting a presidential candidate who "exudes authority and determination."[38] His opponent used A.I. to depict him as "Chinese communist leader and himself as a cuddly cartoon lion."[39] In addition, A.I. videos were created depicting candidates saying things that they didn't say.[40]

Interestingly, while 83% of readers viewed a genuine article as credible, 72% regarded GPT-2's fictional articles as credible as well.[41] At the present time, there are limitations to this type of AI: "the effectiveness of these text-generation tools as propaganda machines was limited because they can't incorporate political context well enough to score points with target audiences. Even if AI can produce a real-looking article, ... a machine can't grasp, say, the dynamics of a feud between two politicians and craft a false story that discredits one of them in a nuanced way."[42] Also, sometimes AI goes off on "strange tangents,"[43] and sometimes gives itself away.[44] However, the fear is that AI will progress to the point that it can eliminate these problems, [45] and create convincing videos depicting individuals saying things that they never said (e.g., a fake video of former President Barack Obama where he defends himself against a conspiracy theory).[46]

Deepfakes have become a common problem that has been exacerbated by the "explosion of artificial-intelligence technology that makes it easier than ever to deceive people on the internet."[47] For example, during the 2023 New Hampshire Democratic primary, thousands of vot-

---

37. *Id.*

38. *See* Jack Nicas & Lucia Cholakian Herrera, *Argentina's Presidential Race Becomes the Wild West of A.I., The New York Times* A1 (Nov. 16, 2023).

39. *Id.*

40. *Id.*

41. *See Beware of Fake Articles, Courtesy of AI, supra* note 36.

42. *Id.* (Paraphrasing a statement by Yoav Shoham, co-founder of AI21).

43. *Id.*

44. *See* Cade Metz & Scott Blumenthal, *How A.I. Could Be Weaponized to Spread Disinformation, The New York Times* A1 (June 10, 2019).

45. *See Beware of Fake Articles, supra* note 36, at R8; *How A.I. Could Be Weaponized to Spread Disinformation, supra* note 44.

46. *See* Stuart A. Thompson & Sapna Maheshwari, *A.I. Mimicry Puts Fakery on TikTok, The New York Times* B1 (Oct. 13, 3023).

47. *See* Robert McMillan, Alexa Corse & Dustin Volz, *New AI Deepfakes Complicate 2024 Votes, The Wall Street Journal* A4 (Feb. 16, 2024).

ers received a phone call from a person who claimed to be President Joe Biden which discouraged eligible voters from going to the polls, and also sought to discourage independents from voting in the Republican presidential primary.[48]

A. DISINFORMATION IS NOT A NEW PHENOMENON

Although disinformation receives a great deal of attention today, it is hardly a new phenomenon. In fact, disinformation has existed since virtually the beginning of time.[49] In ancient Rome, Octavian purportedly engaged in a campaign of disinformation against Marc Anthony.[50] Following Gutenberg's development of the printing press in the 1400s, fictitious stories were circulated depicting Jews as drinking the blood of Christian children.[51] In the sixteenth and seventeenth centuries, disinformation was widely circulated in both France and Italy.[52]

Disinformation was also present in the American colonies. In the eighteenth century, a fake letter, falsely attributed to George Washington, suggested that Washington was "miserable" during the Revolutionary War and believed that the war was a "mistake."[53] In 1782, Benjamin Franklin purportedly created a counterfeit issue of his newspaper which included false stories about "Indians mercilessly scalping the family members of colonists."[54]

---

48. *Id.*

49. *See* Emma M. Savino, *Fake News: No One Is Liable, and That Is a Problem*, 65 Buffalo L. Rev. 1101, 1120–1121 (2017); Jacob Soll, *The Long and Brutal History of Fake News, Politico* (Dec. 18, 2016). https://www.politico.com/magazine/story/2016/12/fake-news-history-long-violent-214535.

50. *See* James Titcomb & James Carson, *What Exactly Is It—And How Can You Spot It?, The Telegraph* (Apr. 7, 2018).

51. *See* Amy Kristin Sanders, Rachel L. Jones & Xiran Liu, *Stemming the Tide of Fake News: A Global Study of Decisions to Regulate*, 8 J. Int'l Media & Ent. Law 205 (2019–2020) (citing a Politico report: Jacob Soll, *The Long and Brutal History of Fake News, Politico* (Dec. 18, 2016), https://www.politico.com/magazine/story/2016/12/fake-news-history-long-violent-214535).

52. *Id.*

53. *See* Carol A. Watson, *Information Literacy in a Fake/False News World: An Overview of the Characteristics of Fakes News and its Historical Developments*, 46 Int'l J. Info. Literacy 93 (2018).

54. *Id.*

Some believe that disinformation played a role in forcing the U.S.'s withdrawal from the Vietnam War.[55] News organizations portrayed the 1968 Tet Offensive as a defeat for American forces when in fact the U.S. eventually obtained a decisive victory.[56] However, the negative press coverage led to a loss of public support for the war as well as for President Johnson who decided not to run for reelection.[57] One commentator described the reporting as "journalistic malpractice."[58]

Disinformation has not been limited to politics. For example, the so-called "Great Moon Hoax"[59] involved a series of articles published in 1835 by *The New York Sun*.[60] The series suggested that there was an alien civilization on the moon, described as having bat-like wings,[61] and was regarded as true by 90% of those who read it.[62] There was also Orson Welles' 1938 radio broadcast which allegedly fooled millions of Americans into believing his frighteningly realistic, carefully detailed, and false account of a real-time Martian invasion.[63] The broadcast actually involved nothing more than a dramatic over-the-air performance of a science-fiction novel.[64] Due to a competing program airing at the same time, many listeners tuned into the radio broadcast after it had begun and did not hear the opening disclaimer that the broadcast was nothing more than a fictional depiction being presented by Orson Welles and the Mercury Theater Company.[65] By the time Welles became aware of the misunderstanding

---

55. *See* William J. Luti, *Did Fake News Lose the Vietnam War?, The Wall Street Journal* A15 (Jan. 30, 2018).
56. *Id.*
57. *Id.*
58. *Id.*
59. Savino, *supra* note 49, at 1120.
60. *Id.*
61. *Id.*
62. *Id.*
63. *See* Welles Scares Nation, HISTORY (last visited Oct. 13, 2017), http://www.history.com/this-day-in-history/welles-scares-nation.
64. *Id.*
65. *Id.*

and came on the air to emphasize that the account was fictitious, it was too late.[66] People were panicking.[67]

B. THE EXPLOSION OF DISINFORMATION IN MODERN TIMES

The internet has been a game changer regarding the transmission of disinformation. Even though disinformation has always existed, the phenomenon has exploded in recent years due to the growth of new technologies.[68] As noted in earlier chapters, for most of human history, ordinary people had limited ability to engage in mass communication. The internet enabled ordinary people to engage in mass communication and has purportedly led to a flood of disinformation. As one commentator noted, "digging up large-scale misinformation on Facebook was as easy as finding baby photos or birthday greetings."[69] Indeed, Twitter (now X) accounts are routinely used to spew propaganda and misinformation.[70] Social media platforms present a particular problem because they allow disinformation to be "shared" with thousands (sometimes millions) of

66. *Id.* ("Perhaps as many as a million radio listeners believed that a real Martian invasion was underway. Panic broke out across the country. In New Jersey, terrified civilians jammed highways seeking to escape the alien marauders. People begged police for gas masks to save them from the toxic gas and asked electric companies to turn off the power so that the Martians wouldn't see their lights."); *see also* Jessica Stone-Erdman, *Just the (Alternative) Facts, Ma'am: The Status of Fake News Under the First Amendment*, 16 First Amendment L. Rev. 416 (2017).

67. *Id.*

68. For example, there has been a wave of fake online obituaries. *See* Andrew Keh & Stuart A. Thompson, *A Tragic Fall or Murder? 'Obituary Pirates" Twist a Man's Fate, The New York Times* A1 (Jan. 28, 2024).

69. *See* Roose, *supra* note 15, at B1.

70. *See* Farhad Manjoo, *How Twitter Is Being Gamed to Feed Misinformation, The New York Times* B-1 & B-7 (June 1, 2017) ("But the biggest problem with Twitter's place in the news is its role in the production and dissemination of propaganda and misinformation."). This article offers the example of a conspiracy theory suggesting that the murder of a staffer at the Democratic National Committee was linked to the leak of Clinton campaign emails. *Id.* at B-7.

other people.[71] For example, one piece of false information was shared at least 16,000 times on Twitter and more than 350,000 times on Facebook.[72]

In addition, "bots" have become increasingly commonplace on the internet in what one commentator described as a "'Cambrian explosion' of robotics technologies"[73] involving millions and millions of bot accounts and bot messages.[74] One estimate suggests that there are as many as 48 million Twitter accounts that are run by bots rather than by human beings, and which accounted for as much as twenty-five percent of all tweets in the 2016 presidential election.[75] A second estimate concluded that there as many as 91 million fake accounts on Facebook, and 24 million bots on Instagram.[76] A Pew Research Center study suggested that nearly two-thirds of all tweeted links were shared by bots and contained links to news and current events.[77] At one point, "YouTube had as much traffic from bots masquerading as people as it did from real human visitors."[78] And, of course, both can easily spread both disinformation and offensive speech. Disinformation is likely to get worse with the advent of AI.[79] Moreover, there are fears that chatbots will eventually be able to

---

71. *See* Sapna Maheshwari, *How Fake News Goes Viral: A Case Study, The New York Times* (Nov. 22, 2016).

72. *Id.*

73. *See* Manjoo, *supra* note 70, at 295.

74. *See* Ashley Fox, *Automated Political Speech: Regulating Social Media Bots in the Political Sphere*, 18 First Amendment L. Rev. 114 (2020); Michael Newberg, *As Many as 48 Million Twitter Accounts Aren't People, Says Study*, CNBC (Mar. 10, 2017, 1:09 PM), https://www.cnbc.com/2017/03/10/nearly-48-million-twitter-accounts-could-be-bots-says-study.html; *see also* Jack Nicas, *Does Facebook Really Know How Many Fake Accounts It Has?*, N.Y. Times (Jan. 30, 2019), https://www.nytimes.com/2019/01/30/technology/facebook-fake-accounts.html.

75. *See* Fox, *supra* note 74, at 117.

76. *Id.*

77. *See* Stefan Wojcik, *5 Things to Know about Bots on Twitter*, Pew Research Center, Factank (Apr. 9, 2018).

78. *See* Michael H. Keller, *The Business of Serving Up YouTube Views: Streams Are for Sale, Eyes Not Included, The New York Times* A18 (Aug. 12, 2018).

79. *See* Hsu, Thompson & Myers, *supra* note 5, at A1; *See also* Ali Swenson & Matt O'Brien, *Poll: AI Will Add to Election Misinformation, Courier-Journal* 6A (Nov. 5, 2023).

notice and respond to cues in the environment,[80] and that hackers will be able to trick AI systems into spewing out troubling or obscene thoughts.[81]

Perhaps the poster child for fake news on the internet is an incident that occurred at a pizzeria, Comet Ping Pong.[82] The incident was preceded by a slew of "fake" online allegations, suggesting that former presidential candidate Hillary Clinton and her campaign manager were operating a child sex ring out of the restaurant.[83] The allegations included online posts, purportedly depicting pictures of children who were alleged "victims" of the sex ring.[84] Even though the allegations were untrue, the pizzeria received 30 to 40 threatening phone calls in a single weekend, and a man entered the pizzeria and fired a rifle, believing that he was acting to protect the children.[85] Likewise, even though Bill Gates (through his foundation) has spent $250 million to slow the spread of Covid-19, information was disseminated suggesting that Gates had unleashed the virus on civilization and that he wanted to surveil the population with microchip implants.[86] During the 2008 presidential campaign, the idea circulated that then vice-presidential candidate Sarah Palin did not know whether Africa was a country or a continent. Norman Mailer referred to such rumors as "factoids" or invented truths because they provided "such deep comfort to powerfully held convictions that belief in them is well-nigh irresistible."[87]

All social media platforms, including Twitter (now X) have been used to disseminate disinformation.[88] For example, rumors circulated that for-

80. *See* Oliver Whang, *Human Power to Process Cues May Be Next Frontier for Bots, The New York Times* A1 (Mar. 28, 2023).

81. *See* Matt O'Brien, *Event Will Let Hackers Test Limits of AI, Courier-Journal* 9A (May 11, 2023).

82. *See* Jennifer Ludden, *Armed Man Threatens D.C. Pizzeria Targeted by Fake News Stories*, National Public Radio, *All Things Considered* (Dec. 5, 2016).

83. *Id.*

84. *Id.*

85. *Id.*

86. *See* Daisuke Wakabayashi, Davey Alba & Marc Tracy, *Fake Theories Put the Blame on Bill Gates, The New York Times* A1 (Apr. 18, 2020).

87. *See* Richard Bernstein, *Looking for the Real Man Behind "Citizen Kane" Letter from America, International Herald Tribune* 2 (Jan. 29, 2009).

88. *See* Manjoo, *supra* note 70, at B-1 & B-7 ("But the biggest problem with Twitter's place in the news is its role in the production and dissemination of propaganda and misinformation."). This article offers the example of a conspiracy theory suggesting that the

mer President (then candidate) Barack Obama was not born in the United States and was not eligible for the presidency,[89] and that (as President) he had decided to ban schoolchildren from reciting the Pledge of Allegiance.[90] During the 2016 presidential campaign, a false rumor circulated that Pope Francis had endorsed Donald Trump.[91] Following Trump's election, false claims circulated that he had won the election by a landslide.[92]

Disinformation is particularly evident on social networking platforms like Facebook which has nearly two billion users worldwide.[93] In the U.S. alone, Facebook is "used by more than 200 million people ... each month, out of a total population of 320 million," and it "reaches approximately 67% of U.S. adults."[94] Facebook users spend an average of over fifty minutes a day on the site.[95] About 44% of U.S. adults say they get their news from Facebook. In fact, digital sources of news were widely used in 2016: "[a]bout 65% of U.S. adults [said] ... they learned about the election in a past week from digital sources. About 48% said they did so from news sites or apps and 44% from social networking sites."[96] Regarding the 2016 election, the Twitter Data Science Team found some 50,000 Russia-linked accounts that were spreading disinformation, and it also found that disinformation was being spread, not only by Republican supporters, but also by Democratic partisans.[97]

A rise in the level of disinformation may also be attributable to a decline in coverage by traditional newspapers. This decline is discussed more fully in a later chapter. For example, newspaper reporting on scientific information, including information related to climate change, has

---

murder of a staffer at the Democratic National Committee was linked to the leak of Clinton campaign emails. *Id.* at B-7.

89. *See* Anand Giridharadas, *Democracy 2.0 awaits an Upgrade, International Herald Tribune* 2 (Sept. 12, 2009).

90. *See How Twitter is Being Gamed to Feed Misinformation, supra* note 70, at B-1 & B-7.

91. *See* Dr. Joel Timmer, *Fighting Falsity: Fake News, Facebook and the First Amendment*, 35 Cardozo Arts & Ent. L.J. 669, 674 (2017); Stone-Erdman, *supra* note 53, at 410.

92. *Id.*

93. *See* Timmer, *supra* note 91, at 672.

94. *Id.* at 672–673.

95. *Id.* at 673.

96. *Id.*

97. *Id.*

declined in traditional newspapers, but such information has increased on the internet,[98] including claims that climate change is a "myth."[99] The internet also contains claims that vaccines cause autism, and that the moon landing, as well as the shootings in Parkland, Florida, and Las Vegas, Nevada, were hoaxes.[100] Such misinformation is circulated online, not only by individuals, but also by bots.[101] Indeed, one study indicated that false information was 70% more likely to be retweeted than accurate information in online fora.[102]

In 2018, there "were doctored photos of Latin American migrants headed towards the United States border. There were easily disprovable lies about the woman who accused Justice Brett M. Kavanaugh of sexual assault, cooked up by partisans with bad faith agendas."[103] Indeed, "every time major political events dominated the news cycle, Facebook was overrun by hoaxers and conspiracy theorists, who used the platform to sow discord, spin falsehoods and stir up tribal anger."[104] There were also conspiracy theories regarding QAnon, "a conspiracy theory about 'deep state' traitors plotting against the President (then President Donald Trump)."[105] Those theories began online, including on Facebook and Twitter.[106]

President Donald Trump routinely uses the term "fake news" to refer to articles or allegations critical of him.[107] Also, Trump attacks the media, not only in his public speeches, but also through his Twitter account.[108] Trump has gone so far as to refer to the media as "very dishonest peo-

---

98. *See* Alan Burdick, *Alternative Realities, and Real Good News, The New York Times* D3 (Nov. 20, 2018).

99. *Id.*

100. *Id.*

101. *Id.*: *see also* Joe Sonka, *Twitter Bots Spread Fake News About Election, The Courier-Journal* A1 (Nov. 12, 2019).

102. *See* Burdick, *supra* note 98, at D3.

103. *See* Kevin Roose, *Facebook Had a Good Election, But It Can't Let Up on Vigilance, The New York Times*, The Shift B1 (Nov. 8, 2018).

104. *Id.*

105. *See* Mike McIntire & Kevin Roose, *Web Delusion Oozes Offline to Real World, The New York Times* A1 (Feb. 10, 2020).

106. *Id.*

107. Emily Cochrane, *Trump Says Social Media Censoring Conservative Voices, Boston Globe* A (Aug. 19, 2018).

108. *See* Frank Bruni, *The News Isn't Fake. But It's Flawed, The New York Times, The New York Times*, Opinion 3 (May 20, 2018).

ple," has alleged that certain news stories constitute "fake news"[109] and has claimed that reporters' "sources don't exist,"[110] especially regarding allegations made against then U.S. Supreme Court nominee Brett Kavanaugh.[111] As one commentator claimed, "Trump has waged relentless attacks on news coverage that he does not like, and has long expressed hostility toward traditional press freedoms."[112] Trump's lawyer, Rudy Giuliani, has even gone so far as to question whether there really is such a thing as "truth." In response to a commentator's statement that "truth is truth," Giuliani responded ""No, it isn't truth. Truth isn't truth."[113] In an earlier interview, Giuliani flatly asserted that facts "are in the eye of the beholder."[114]

Because the internet is global in nature, individuals have the capacity to distribute information across international borders. As a result, during the 2016 presidential election, some believe that Russian operatives attempted to influence the outcome of the election in favor of Donald Trump.[115] During the mid-term elections in the U.S., a conservative talk show host allegedly shared a video of broken voting machines in Arizona.[116] The video, which was shared approximately 20,000 times and liked more than 30,000 times, suggested a false narrative of "widespread voting shenanigans."[117]

But disinformation is also sometimes invoked by U.S. political campaigns against their opponents. For example, it is alleged that Democratic

109. *See* Cochrane, *supra* note 107.

110. *See* Bruni, *supra* note 108.

111. *See* Peter Baker, *'It Was All Fake,' Trump Says in Kavanaugh Ploy, The New York Times* A29 (Nov. 7, 2018). Trump stated "The accuser of Brett Kavanaugh, a man who is a fine man, the accuser admitted she never met him, she never saw him, he never touched her, talked to her, he had nothing to do with her, she made up the story." *Id.* However, Trump's allegation was misleading because, although one woman (Munro-Leighton) did recant her allegations against Kavanaugh, Trump implied that another woman (Christine Blasey-Ford) had recanted. *Id.*

112. *See* Bruni, *supra* note 108.

113. *See* William Goldschlag & Dan Janison, *"Truth Isn't Truth," and That's a Trap for Trump, Giuliani Says, Newsday* (Aug. 20, 2018).

114. *Id.*

115. *See* Stephen Budiansky, *The Coming War for Cyberspace, The Wall Street Journal* C5 (July 15–16, 2017) ("An army of Russia-based human and automated attackers ("robo-trolls") deluged the United States with pro-Trump disinformation ...")

116. *See* Sheera Frenkel & Steven Lee Myers, *Misinformation Flowed During Election, but Les Seemed to Stick, The New York Times* B5 (Nov. 10, 2022).

117. *Id.*

party officials tried to use Russian-style disinformation tactics in their effort to defeat senatorial candidate Roy Moore.[118] Purportedly, those officials created fake Russian Twitter accounts, and a fake Facebook page allegedly established by conservative Alabamans to oppose Mr. Moore.[119] A second fake Facebook page had purportedly been created by Baptists who described Mr. Moore as an ally in their effort to ban alcohol sales in the State of Alabama.[120] A progressive activist described the disinformation campaign as a "moral imperative."[121]

Disinformation has also been prevalent in other political campaigns. During the 2020 election in Pennsylvania, tweets falsely asserted that Pennsylvania would not accept mail-in ballots, that ballots might not have been counted in the prior election, and that Democrat senatorial candidate John Fetterman had tattoos of a notorious street gang on his body.[122] Other disinformation alleged that a Republican candidate had stated that Iran had the right idea about how to treat women.[123] This disinformation was part of a "deluge of false or misleading posts, photographs and videos on social media, as well as increasingly partisan, bitter and at times unhinged claims on television, radio and live streams."[124] After candidate Fetterman had a stroke, a video was released magnifying the extent of his impairment.[125] One post purported to show a Republican candidate (Fetterman's opponent, Oz) kissing the star of Donald Trump on the Hollywood Walk of Fame (when the candidate was actually kissing his own star).[126] As noted, there was also a false tweet indicating that the Colorado election system had been hacked.[127]

The problem of fake news is hardly limited to the United States. Europe has also been hit with disinformation, including allegations that Sweden

---

118. *See* Jim Rutenberg, *Fake News From Within Is on the Rise, The New York Times* B1 & B5 (Jan. 14, 2019).

119. *Id.*

120. *Id.*

121. *Id.*

122. *See* Steven Lee Myers, *With Push of a Button, Lies Flood a Swing State, The New York Times* A1 (Nov. 1, 2022).

123. *Id.*

124. *Id.*

125. *Id.*

126. *Id.*

127. *See* Corasaniti & Alba, *supra* note 13, at A20.

supports the Islamic State, and that the EU has drafted rules regulating the ethnicity of snowmen.[128] In addition, there are allegations that the Russians tried to interfere with French elections by spreading disinformation.[129] Germany, in particular, has been besieged by fake news, much of which is believed to come from Russia.[130] There are also claims that Russia is distributing disinformation designed to undercut Ukrainian officials.[131]

In the UK, during elections held in 2019, the British were awash in disinformation.[132] Although some of the disinformation came from foreigners, trying to meddle in UK elections, a significant amount of the disinformation came from British political parties and candidates.[133] For example, anti-Muslim posts contained disinformation in an effort to encourage Hindus to vote against the Labour party.[134] As in many other countries, some young people rarely watch established news outlets, and instead obtain their "news" from sources like Twitter, Facebook, Instagram, and YouTube.[135] With a large number of individual Facebook posts, it is hard for Facebook users to know what content is accurate and what content involves disinformation.[136] However, it was not clear whether (and to what extent) voters were being swayed by disinformation.[137]

In Brazil, during the 2018 presidential campaign, fake news was spread over WhatsApp, a smartphone messaging app owned by Facebook[138]

---

128. *See* Mark Scott & Melissa Eddy, *Europe Combats New Enemy of Political Unity: Fake News, The New York Times International* A8 (Feb. 21, 2017).

129. *See* Peter Baker & Steve Erlanger, *Moscow Seeks to Sow Division in the West; Officials Say It Is Waging a War of Disinformation to Win Allies in Ukraine, International New York Times* 1 (June 8, 2015).

130. *See* Scott & Eddy, *supra* note 128, at A8.

131. *See* Steven L. Myers, *Russia's Fake Journalist Web, The New York Times* B1 (Mar. 22, 2024).

132. *See* Adam Satariano & Amie Tsang, *In Britain, Disinformation Ahead of Vote Comes Largely From Within, The New York Times International* A13 (Dec. 11, 2019).

133. *Id.*

134. *Id.*

135. *Id.*

136. *Id.*

137. *Id.*

138. *See* Mike Issac & Kevin Roose, *Fake News Deluges WhatsApp in Brazil, The New York Times* B1 (Oct. 20, 2018).

which was used by 44% of the Brazilian public.[139] One widely circulated message listed the name of a candidate next to the number 17.[140] This message was significant because Brazilians vote by entering a candidate's number in a voting machine.[141] The difficulty was that this particular candidate had not been assigned the number 17; that number had been assigned to a different candidate.[142] As a result, there was a risk that the message would encourage supporters of the first candidate to enter the number 17, thinking that they were voting for the candidate mentioned in the message, but they would in fact be voting for someone else.

Such deception (as in the Brazilian election) was common and was aided by the fact that WhatsApp is more trusted as well as widely used (by more than a billion people worldwide),[143] especially since it enables individuals to send encrypted messages.[144] However, the platform is more of a texting app rather than a social media network,[145] and it is especially valuable to various groups, including migrants, dissidents and political activists who fear persecution.[146] Given the privateness and secrecy, disinformation can spread more easily on WhatsApp.[147] Moreover, given the familiarity between users, disinformation may be more trusted.[148] In any event, the app is more trusted because it is regarded as more personal, and frequently involves closed communications between smaller groups of people.[149] However, the app is often used to spread fake news. A Brazilian study found that, of some 100,000 WhatsApp messages more than half contained misleading or false information.[150] including a rumor that billionaire George Soros was funding efforts to interfere in the Brazilian

---

139. *Id.* at B3; *see also* Mike Issac, *For Social Media, an Election Day Test, The New York Times*, The Week in Tech B3 (Nov. 12, 2018).

140. *See Fake News Deluges WhatsApp, supra* note 138, at B1.

141. *Id.*

142. *Id.*

143. *See For Social Media, an Election Day Test, supra* note 139.

144. *See* Farhad Manjoo, *Psst. WhatsApp Needs Fixing. Pass It On, The New York Times* B1 (Oct. 25, 2018).

145. *Id.*

146. *Id.*, at B7.

147. *Id.*

148. *Id.*

149. *See Fake News Deluges WhatsApp, supra* note 138, at B3.

150. *Id.*; *see also For Social Media, an Election Day Test, supra* note 139.

election.[151] Since WhatsApp is an end-to-end encrypted service, outsiders cannot see the content of messages, and therefore there are fewer opportunities to correct disinformation.[152] Even if Facebook's fact checkers could see the disinformation, many Brazilians distrust the "fact checkers" who they view "as part of a nefarious effort by big corporations like Facebook to shield Brazilians from the truth."[153] WhatsApp did try to slow down the flow of misinformation by banning suspicious accounts and by sending cease-and-desist orders to offending individuals and companies.[154]

WhatsApp has also been used to spread disinformation in Myanmar,[155] as well as in India.[156] In India, WhatsApp had 300 million users which was more users than Facebook.[157] In the lead-up to national elections, both WhatsApp and Indian governmental officials tried to stop the spread of disinformation with little effect.[158] In 2019, Facebook removed hundreds of posts, as well as fake accounts, that were spreading disinformation.[159] Some of the accounts were linked to the Pakistani military.[160]

There are allegations that Iran has been actively spreading disinformation online, referred to as a "disinformation assembly line," through fake personas and attacking Iran's adversaries.[161] There were posts on "emotionally charged topics like race relations and Donald Trump."[162] Some allege

---

151. *Id.*

152. *Id.*

153. *Id.*

154. *Id.*

155. *See* Max Fisher, *Social Re-engineering, From Myanmar to Germany, The New York Times*, Tech We're Using B5 (Nov. 8, 2018).

156. *See* Newley Purnell, *Fake News Roils WhatsApp in India, The Wall Street Journal* A1 (Apr. 7, 2019).

157. *Id.*

158. *Id.*

159. *See* Newley Purnell, *Facebook Targets Misleading India News, The Wall Street Journal* B4 (Apr. 2, 2019).

160. *Id.*

161. *See* Mike Isaac & Sheera Frenkel, *Facebook Takes Down Iran-Based Network Amid Disinformation, The New York Times* B5 (Oct. 27, 2018); Scott Shane & Ronen Bergman, *A 'Disinformation Assembly Line:' Spreading Fake News to Bolster Iran, The New York Times International* A9 (May 14, 2019).

162. *See Facebook Takes Down, supra* note 161.

that Iran is actively spreading disinformation through fake accounts,[163] as well as through videos and social media, under the name Liberty Front Press.[164] Indeed, a number of social media companies have deleted allegedly fake Iranian accounts (13), as well as a number of Iranian videos (39), blogs (6) and various social media posts.[165] For example, Google took down 284 allegedly fake accounts, including some 652 pages, all of which were purportedly connected to Iran.[166] Iranian actions tended to promote pro-Palestinian and anti-Israeli stories.[167] Some of the accounts were allegedly connected to the Islamic Republic of Iran Broadcasting, and those accounts attracted a substantial number (13,466) of views.[168] In deleting the accounts and posts, social media companies claimed that they were in violation of the platform's policies regarding terms of service.[169] Part of the problem, according to some commentators, is that it is easy to sign up for many social media platforms with a false name.[170]

There are also claims that Russian trolls distribute disinformation in an effort to exacerbate social divisions within the U.S.[171] For example, following the women's march in Washington, D.C., in 2017, Russian trolls purportedly made numerous Twitter posts, including posts by alleged black women who were critical of white feminists, by conservative women who were critical of the march, and by men who mocked it.[172] In addition, the trolls targeted Linda Sarsour, one of the organizers of the march,[173]and an activist for Muslim rights, with nearly 3,000 posts.[174] Some of the posts

---

163. *See* Dustin Volz & Robert McMillan, *Tech Giants Target Iran: YouTube Erases Videos Linked to Propaganda Effort; Twitter, Facebook Also Delete Accounts, The Wall Street Journal* A1 (Aug. 24, 2018).

164. *Id.*

165. *Id.*

166. *Id.* at A2.

167. *Id.* at A1.

168. *Id.* at A2.

169. *Id.*

170. *Id.*

171. *See* Ellen Barry, *Trolls in Russia Schemed to Divide Women's March, The New York Times* A1 (Sept. 19, 2022).

172. *Id.*

173. *Id.*

174. *Id.*

focused on her association with Louis Farrakhan, the controversial Nation of Islam leader.[175] A Russian ad linked Hillary Clinton with Satan.[176]

There are similar claims suggesting that China is trying to influence U.S. elections,[177] as well as to spreading disinformation within China (e.g., likening Hong Kong protestors to ISIS fighters).[178] Some allege that in the U.S., Chinese accounts portray themselves as American supporters of Donald Trump, promote conspiracy theories, try to stoke divisions, and attack President Biden.[179] In the process, China appears to be attempting to connect with partisan divisions within the U.S.[180] The effort, referred to by some as "Spamouflage" does things like promote MAGA and denigrate then President Biden.[181]

Some fear that fake news can lead to violence,[182] as happened in India.[183] One article suggested that Facebook has made Germany more prone to racial violence, and generally caused German communities (where Facebook use was highest) to be more prone to violence.[184] For example, one German firefighter purportedly set a refugee group house on fire,[185] allegedly egged on by Facebook posts which portrayed immigrants as a threat to Germany; posts which purportedly contained "racist vitriol."[186] Likewise, in Sri Lanka, when a video suggested that there was a Muslim plot to wipe out Buddhists in the country (Buddhists constitute a majority

---

175. *Id.*, at A12.

176. *See* Cecilia Kang, Nicholas Fandos & Mike Isaac, *Russia-Financed Ad Linked Clinton and Satan, The New York Times* A1 (Nov. 2, 2017).

177. *See* Tiffany Hsu & Steven Lee Myers, *China's Advancing Efforts To Influence U.S. Election, The New York Times* B1 (Apr. 2, 2024).

178. *See* Kate Conger, *Social Media: China's Disinformation Bullhorn, The New York Times* A1 (Aug. 20, 2019).

179. *See* Hsu & Myers, *supra* note 177, at B1.

180. *Id.*

181. *Id.*

182. *See* Davey Alba, *Anti-Asian Online Posts Set the Stage for Real-World Violence, The New York Times* A13 (Mar. 20, 2021); Amanda Taub & Max Fisher, *Where Facebook Rumors Fuel Thirst for Revenge, The New York Times* A-1 (Apr. 22, 2018).

183. *See Fake News Deluges WhatsApp, supra* note 138, at B3.

184. *See* Taub & Fisher, *supra* note 182, at A8.

185. *Id.* at A1 ("Whenever per-person Facebook use rose to one standard deviation above the national average, attacks on refugees increased by about 50 percent," and "drove one-tenth of all anti-refugee violence.").

186. *Id.* at A8.

of the population),[187] there were Buddhist protests during which a Muslim man was burned to death.[188] Facebook "hoaxes" allegedly incited riots in Myanmar.[189] In addition, Facebook had previously been linked to riots and other violence in Sri Lanka,[190] and some claimed that a Sri Lankan "extremist" had used Facebook as his personal broadcast station to spread paranoia and hatred of the country's Muslin minority.[191] "Fake reports of sectarian violence went viral in India, setting off riots that killed several people and displaced thousands."[192] The same article alleged that "chillingly similar Facebook-linked problems are becoming increasingly visible in wealthy, developed countries like the United States.[193] For example, so-called "fake news" about immigrants to the U.S. has allegedly led to hate crimes against immigrants.[194] It has been alleged that Russia is disseminating "disinformation" in Sweden in order to create social unrest.[195]

C. THE DEMOCRATIC IMPLICATIONS OF DISINFORMATION (AND OTHER HARMS)

In drafting the U.S. Declaration of Independence, Thomas Jefferson implicitly rejected monarchy and the concept of hereditary succession in favor of a democratically elected government: "Governments are instituted among Men, deriving their just powers from the consent of the governed."[196] In construing the U.S. Constitution, the U.S. Supreme Court continues to emphasize democratic values, and has recognized that

---

187. *Id.*

188. *Id.*

189. *See* Max Fisher, *Facebook's Worst Demons Have Come Home to Roost, The New York Times* B-1 & B-6 (Aug. 9, 2018) *Id.* at B1; *see also* Alexandra Stevenson, *Facebook Admits Role Platform Had in Fueling Violence in Myanmar, The New York Times* B2 (Nov. 7, 2018) (suggesting that Facebook's WhatsApp has also led to violence in Myanmar based on allegations, some of which were false).

190. *Id.*

191. *See* Fisher, *supra* note 155, at B5.

192. *Id.*

193. *Id.* at B5.

194. *See Facebook's Worst Demons, supra* note 189, at B5.

195. *See* Stephen Lee Myers, *Sweden Is Not Staying Neutral in Russia's Information War, The New York Times* B4 (Aug. 14, 2023).

196. U.S. Declaration of Independence (July 4, 1776).

freedom of expression and freedom of the press are the essential building blocks of democratic societies:[197] Indeed, the Court has emphatically stated that "Speech concerning public affairs is more than self-expression; it is the essence of self-government"[198] and "'was fashioned to assure unfettered interchange of ideas for the bringing about of political and social changes desired by the people'" so that "changes may be obtained by lawful means."[199]

Disinformation, referred to by some as "fake news," which can sometimes involve just "misinformation," is problematic because it has the potential to undermine the democratic process by deluding the electorate with inaccurate information.[200] Indeed, as one commentator asked "how can the people be well informed in a world where misinformation

---

197. *See* C. Edwin Baker, *Scope of the First Amendment Freedom of Speech*, 25 U.C.L.A. L. Rev. 964 (1978); Robert H. Bork, *Neutral Principles and Some First Amendment Problems*, 47 Ind. L.J. 1 (1971); Thomas I. Emerson, *Toward a General Theory of the First Amendment*, 72 Yale L.J. 877 (1963); Alexander Meiklejohn, *The First Amendment as an Absolute*,1961 Sup. Ct. Rev. 245; Russell L. Weaver &, Catherine Hancock, The First Amendment: Cases, Materials and Problems (Carolina Academic Press, 7th ed., 2023).

198. *Connick v. Myers*, 461 U.S. 138, 145 (1983) (quoting *Garrison v. Louisiana*, 379 U.S. 64, 74–75 (1964)); *see also R.A.V. v. City of St. Paul*, 505 U.S. 377, 423 (1992) (Blackmun, J., concurring) ("core political speech occupies the highest, most protected position."); *see also Roth v. United States*, 354 U.S. 476, 484 (1957) ("The protection given speech and press was fashioned to assure unfettered interchange of ideas for the bringing about of political and social changes desired by the people.").

199. *New York Times, Co. v. Sullivan*, 376 U.S. 254, 269 (1964) (quoting *Stromberg v. California*, 283 U.S. 359). *See also Citizens United v. Federal Election Commission*, 558 U.S. 310, 339 (2010) ("Speech is an essential mechanism of democracy, for it is the means to hold officials accountable to the people. The right of citizens to inquire, to hear, to speak, and to use information to reach consensus is a pre-condition to enlightened self-government and a necessary means to protect it. The First Amendment "'has its fullest and most urgent application' to speech uttered during a campaign for political office.' It is inherent in the nature of the political process that voters must be free to obtain information from diverse sources in order to determine how to cast their votes."); *Virginia v. Black*, 538 U.S. 343, 365 (2003) ("Political speech, of course, is 'at the core of what the First Amendment is designed to protect.'").

200. *See* Alan K. Chen, *Free Speech, Rational Deliberation and Some Truth About Lies*, 62 Wm. & Mary L. Rev. 357 (2020); *Stemming the Tide of Fake News, supra* note 51, at 203; Andrew J. Schuyler, *Regulating Facts: A Procedural Framework for Identifying, Excluding and Deterring the Intentional or Knowing Proliferation of Fake News Online*, 2019 U. Ill. J.L.T.P. 211 (2019).

is intentionally circulated?"[201] And misinformation can have real world consequences: "coordinated disinformation campaigns threaten to exacerbate public health emergencies, stoke ethnic and racial divisions and even undermine democracy itself."[202]

"Fake news"—in the sense of disinformation—is particularly disturbing in nations premised upon democratic principles. If, as the Declaration of Independence flatly declares, the power to govern "derives from the consent of the governed,"[203] and if the government is based on the assumption that the "people, not the government, possess the absolute sovereignty,"[204] freedom of speech and of the press are essential components of the governmental system.[205] As the United States Supreme Court has recognized, "'Speech concerning public affairs is more than self-expression; it is the essence of self-government,'"[206] and is designed to insure the "unfettered interchange of ideas for the bringing about of political and social changes desired by the people.'"[207] Disinformation is

---

201. Schuyler, *supra* note 200, at 212.

202. Steven Lee Myers & Eileen Sullivan, *Disinformation Has Become Another Untouchable Problem in Washington, International New York Times* 1 (July 8, 2022).

203. U.S. DECLARATION OF INDEPENDENCE (July 4, 1776).

204. *New York Times Co. v. Sullivan*, 376 U.S. 254, 274 (1976) (quoting James Madison).

205. *See* Baker, *supra* note 197, at 964; Bork, *supra* note 197; Emerson, *supra* note 197; Meikeljohn, *supra* note 197; THE FIRST AMENDMENT: CASES, MATERIALS AND PROBLEMS, *supra* note 197.

206. *See Connick v. Myers*, 461 U.S. 138, 145 (1983) (quoting *Garrison v. Louisiana*, 379 U.S. 64, 74–75 (1964)); *see also R.A.V. v. City of St. Paul*, 505 U.S. 377, 423 (1992) (Blackmun, J., concurring) ("core political speech occupies the highest, most protected position."); *Roth v. United States*, 354 U.S. 476, 484 (1957) ("The protection given speech and press was fashioned to assure unfettered interchange of ideas for the bringing about of political and social changes desired by the people.").

207. *New York Times, Co. v. Sullivan*, 376 U.S. 254, 269 (1964) (quoting *Stromberg v. California*, 283 U.S. 359); *see also Citizens United v. Federal Election Commission*, 558 U.S. 310, 339 (2010) ("Speech is an essential mechanism of democracy, for it is the means to hold officials accountable to the people. The right of citizens to inquire, to hear, to speak, and to use information to reach consensus is a pre-condition to enlightened self-government and a necessary means to protect it. The First Amendment "'has its fullest and most urgent application' to speech uttered during a campaign for political office.' It is inherent in the nature of the political process that voters must be free to obtain information from diverse sources in order to determine how to cast their votes."); *Virginia v. Black*, 538 U.S. 343, 365 (2003) ("Political speech, of course, is 'at the core of what the First Amendment is designed to protect.'").

troubling because it has the potential to subvert and undermine the democratic process. Indeed, some have argued that the goal of fake news is to destabilize institutions.[208]

Moreover, social media platforms create the possibility for foreign interference in elections because other nations can attempt to stir discontent by spreading disinformation. In the 2018 U.S. elections, some claim that Israel and Nigeria tried to insert false information.[209] However, in some instances, for example the campaign of U.S. Senator Angus King (Maine), politicians are prepared to seek out and respond to the disinformation.[210]

The other problem with disinformation is that it can promote violence. In France, in 2019, there were allegations on social media that the Roma (also known as "gypsies," although that term is regarded as derogatory in Europe) were kidnapping young children in the Paris suburbs.[211] Even though the allegations were false, they precipitated violence against the Roma.[212] In the Middle East, disinformation allegedly inflamed the Israeli-Palestinian conflict prior to the October 7, 2023, Hamas attack on Israel and the subsequent Israeli-Palestinian war.[213] Not only did the Israeli government disseminate disinformation, but that information was widely shared on social media platforms.[214]

D. POLITICIANS AND DISINFORMATION

Although some attribute disinformation to the internet era and the rise of social media,[215] the reality is that the problem runs far deeper. For example, it is not at all uncommon for politicians and governmental officials to lie to the public. Following Edward Snowden's revelation that the U.S.

---

208. *See* Scott & Eddy, *supra* note 128, at A8.

209. *See* Davey Alba, *Campaigns Aren't Ready for Political Fakery Surge, The New York Times* b1 (Dec. 16, 2019).

210. *Id.*

211. *See* Aurelien Breeden, *Rumors of Abduction Flare Up in France, and Roma Become Scapegoats, The New York Times* A9 (Mar. 29, 2019).

212. *Id.*

213. *See* Sheera Frenkel, *Social Media Lies Inflame Israeli-Palestinian Conflict, The New York Times* B4 (May 15, 2021).

214. *Id.*

215. *See* Roose, *supra* note 103, at B1.

government was running a massive cybersurveillance operation, then National Security Agency (NSA) Director James Clapper was asked about the program.[216] In response to a direct question regarding whether the NSA was collecting "any type of data at all on millions or hundreds of millions of Americans," he flatly stated, "No, sir. Not wittingly."[217] Clapper later admitted that he had lied and tried to explain the lie away by stating that it was the "most truthful" or "least untruthful" thing that he could say at the time.[218] About the same time, then President Barack Obama assured the U.S. public that the NSA's cybersurveillance program was not focused on ordinary U.S. citizens, but rather only on individuals who pose a terrorist threat to the United States and on communications of "foreign intelligence value"[219] and foreign intelligence targets.[220] That turned out to be a lie as well. The U.S. government was in fact collecting large amounts of data about virtually everyone.[221] And the lies were significant. If the U.S. citizens are going to exercise oversight and supervisory control over governmental activities like the cybersurveillance operation, they must first know that it exists.

Clapper and Obama are hardly the only politicians who have lied to the American public. Former President Donald Trump may be the all-time champion of disinformation and has been widely denounced as a com-

---

216. *See* Editorial Board, *Edward Snowden, Whistle Blower, The New York Times* A18 (Jan. 2, 2014) ("[Snowdens'] leaks revealed that James Clapper Jr., the director of national intelligence, lied to Congress when testifying in March that the N.S.A. was not collecting data on millions of Americans. (There has been no discussion of punishment for that lie.)); Andrew Rosenthal, *Clapper and Carney Get Slippery on Surveillance, The New York Times*, Taking Note (Oct. 24, 2013); Charlie Savage & Scott Shane, *N.S.A. Leaker Denies Giving Secrets to China, The New York Times* A5 (June 18, 2013) (suggesting that Snowden decided to go public because Director Clapper had lied to the American public regarding the NSA data collection program).

217. *See N.S.A. Leaker Denies Giving Secrets to China, supra* note 216.

218. *See* Rosenthal, *supra* note 216.

219. *See* Scott Shane, *Documents Detail Restrictions on N.S.A. Surveillance, The New York Times* A9 (June 21, 2014).

220. *Id.*

221. *See* Scott Shane, *No Morsel Too Minuscule for All-Consuming NSA: From Spying on Leader of U.N. to tracking Drug Deals, on Ethos of 'Why Not?', The New York Times*, A10 (Nov. 13, 2013); Doug Stanglin; *Snowden Says NSA Can Tap Email Chats, The Courier-Journal*, A3 (Aug. 1, 2013).

pulsive "liar."[222] "The Big Lie," Trump's claim that the 2020 presidential election was stolen is the example that comes most readily to mind.[223] But presidential lying goes well beyond Trump. President Joe Biden is hardly a paragon of virtue when it comes to telling the truth. For example, following the disastrous withdrawal of U.S. troops from Afghanistan, when the media asked President Biden why he did not keep more U.S. troops in the country to help with the withdrawal, Biden flatly stated that his senior military advisors had advised him not to do so.[224] Both Gen. Mark Milley, chairman of the Joint Chiefs of Staff, and Gen. Kenneth McKenzie Jr., head of U.S. Central Command, subsequently disputed Biden's claims in sworn testimony.[225] Secretary of Defense Lloyd Austin flatly agreed with Milley and McKenzie, stating that Biden's military advisers "were in lock step in recommending that the U.S. leave 3,000 to 4,500 troops in Afghanistan."[226] So, either Biden lied, the three officials all perjured themselves under oath or Biden simply did not remember because of his mental acuity problems.

Afghanistan is not the only subject about which Biden lied. When inflation was raging in 2022, and the mid-term elections were on the horizon, Biden tried to tell the American people that the inflation was due to the Ukrainian War,[227] and he frequently referred to inflation as "Putin's

---

222. *See* Roger Cohen, *Robert Mueller in the Age of the Unicorn, International New York Times* 18 (Apr. 22, 2019) (suggesting that White House Counsel Donald McGahn, "wants a contemporaneous record of the truth to protect himself and—God knows—the Republic against Trump's lies."); Thomas Friedland, *America Dodged an Arrow, The International New York Times* (Nov. 11, 2022) (referring to the lies and fantasies of Donald Trump"), 2022 WLNR 36137439; Mara Liasson, *Democrats and Some Republicans Fear How Trump's Election Lies May Affect Democracy*, National Public Radio, All Things Considered (Nov. 5, 2021) https://www.npr.org/2021/11/05/1052968081/democrats-and-some-republicans-fear-how-trumps-election-lies-may-affect-democrac.

223. *See* Tovia Smith, ,*Why Is the "Big Lie" Proving So Hard to Dispel?*, National Public Radio, All Things Considered (Jan. 4. 2022), https://www.npr.org/2022/01/04/1070337968/why-is-the-big-lie-proving-so-hard-to-dispel; *see also* Danny Hakim & Alexandra Berzon, *A Big Lie in a New Package, The International New York Times* 11 (June 9, 2022).

224. *See* Bret Stephens, *An Ethically Challenged Presidency, International New York Times* 21 (Oct. 7, 2021).

225. *Id.*

226. *Id.*

227. *See* Zolan Kannos-Young & Jeanna Smalalek, *White House Struggles to Talk About the "Problem from Hell," International New York Times* (June 10, 2022), 2022 WLNR 18126115.

price hike."[228] In fact, inflation was raging well before Russia invaded Ukraine.[229] However, Biden wasn't about to let the truth get in the way of a good political argument. Likewise, when it was discovered that former President Trump was in possession of classified documents at Mara Lago, Biden denounced Trump's possession of those documents as "totally irresponsible."[230] While he may have forgotten that he had also taken classified documents to unauthorized places (including his garage!), he might also have lied.[231] In denouncing Trump's actions, perhaps Biden simply "forgot" that he had unauthorized possession of classified documents, but he might have lied as well. Moreover, even though it was not technically a "lie," he concealed this information from the public for 68 days.[232]

There are plenty of other examples of political disinformation. The *Wall Street Journal* labeled California Congressman (now, U.S. Senator) Adam Schiff as "disinformation man."[233] According to the report, Intelligence Committee Chairman Devin Nunes tried in 2018 to inform the public about the FBI's alleged abuse of the FISA warrant process in regard to its investigation into Trump's alleged collusion with Russia.[234] In rebuttal, Congressman Schiff, who had full access to all of the intelligence information, made a variety of false statements designed to undercut the Nunes report.[235] Schiff's statements caused the media to denounce the Nunes report as a "joke."[236] The validity of the Nunes report was later confirmed

---

228. *Id.*

229. Jeanna Smalalek, *Democrats Blast Corporate Profits as Inflation Surges, International New York Times* (Jan. 5, 2022), 2022 WLNR 291958.

230. *See* Joseph A. Wulfsohn, *Biden Shamed 'Irresponsible' Trump for Having Classified Socs Before WH Admitted he had Sensitive VP Records*, FoxNews (Jan. 10, 2023). https://www.foxnews.com/media/biden-shamed-irresponsible-trump-classified-docs-before-wh-admitted-sensitive-vp-records.

231. *See* Mariah Espada, *President Biden, His Corvette, and the Latest Stash of Classified Documents*, Time.com (Jan. 12, 2023). https://time.com/6246994/biden-classified-documents-delaware-corvette/.

232. *See* Michael D. Shear, Peter Baker & Katie Rogers, *68 Days of Silence: Why the White House Stayed Mum on Classified Documents, International New York Times* (Jan. 21, 2023), 2023 WLNR 2402675.

233. *See Adam Schiff, Disinformation Man, The Wall Street Journal* A12 (Jan. 21–22, 2023).

234. *Id.*

235. *Id.*

236. *Id.*

by the Justice Department's Inspector General Michael Horowitz.[237] In other words, Schiff lied.

There are allegations that the government affirmatively uses social media to propagandize.[238] Indeed, the U.S. has used fake Twitter accounts to disseminate propaganda regarding Russia, China, and other adversaries.[239] There are also allegations that U.S. officials posed as Iraqis to allege on Twitter that Iran was smuggling drugs into Iraq.[240] While Twitter eventually shut down these accounts, it waited two years before doing so.[241] In other countries, governments also use the internet to propagandize, sometimes intentionally disseminating disinformation.[242] Allegations of such conduct have been made against both China and Russia.[243] For example, China portrays Hong Kong protestors as "violent" and "extreme."[244] Platforms like Facebook sometimes take down such posts when they are posted by foreign governments.[245] But there are hundreds of social media accounts that are used to smear opponents of Prime Minister Benjamin Netanyahu.[246] There are allegations that the accounts spread slander, lies, and rumors.[247]

---

237. *Id.*

238. *See* Hiawatha Bray, *We Ignore Musk's "Twitter Files" at Our Peril, Boston Globe* (Jan. 20. 2023) ("Another discovery: There's no evidence of any "deep state" conspiracy behind Twitter's decision to suppress the New York Post's October 2020 story about the contents of a laptop belonging to President Biden's son Hunter. Twitter executives screwed up that decision all by themselves. They chose to believe a false allegation that the data had been stolen by hackers."), 2023 WLNR 2287522.

239. *Id.*

240. *Id.*

241. *Id.*

242. *See* Conger, *supra* note 178, at A1.

243. *Id.*

244. *Id.*

245. *Id.*

246. *See Ronen Bergman, Fake Accounts Promote Netanyahu Online, Watchdog Says, The New York Times* A8 (Apr. 1, 2019).

247. *Id.*

E. MEDIA BIAS AND AN INFORMED ELECTORATE

But, if society is concerned about disinformation, and its impact on the ability of the electorate to make educated decisions, perhaps it should also be concerned about the media. Just as disinformation can undercut the democratic process, media bias has the potential to mislead the public with limited or deceptive information. A recent poll suggested that two-thirds of likely voters believe that "reporters covering political campaigns try to help the candidate that they want to win."[248] While one journalist denied that this perception was correct, he noted that, although bias is good business, "it's bad for democracy."[249]

Early in U.S. history, President Thomas Jefferson denigrated the press, saying "Nothing can now be believed which is seen in a newspaper," and "Truth itself becomes suspicious by being put into that polluted vehicle."[250] William Randolph Hearst aggressively used his newspapers to campaign for causes that he supported,[251] as well as to promote his preferred views and positions.[252] Prior to the American Revolution, there is evidence that printers used their presses to affect and attempt to control public debates. For example, there are stories about James Franklin (Benjamin Franklin's brother) and his opposition to positions taken by prominent Bostonian Cotton Mather who (to James) represented the Boston "establishment."[253] When Mather advocated for mass inoculations against smallpox,[254]

---

248. *See* Al Cross, *Defending Journalism, Despite Its Mistakes, The Courier-Journal* H1 (July 3, 2011).

249. *Id.*, at H4.

250. Edward Rothstein, *Life and Times of the U.S. Press, International Herald Tribune* 8 (Sept. 23, 2006) (quoting a letter from President Jefferson to John Norvell written in 1807).

251. *See* W.A. SWANBERG. CITIZEN HEARST 100, 119–127 (1961) (hereafter "CITIZEN HEARST").

252. *See* Jerome A. Barron, *Access to the Media—1967 to 2007 and Beyond: A Symposium Honoring Jerome A. Barron's Path-Breaking Article "Access Reconsidered,"* 76 GEO. W. L. REV. 826, 832 (2008).

253. *See* H.W. BRANDS, THE FIRST AMERICAN: THE LIFE AND TIMES OF BENJAMIN FRANKLIN 25 (2000).

254. *Id.* ("The occasion of the attack [by James Franklin against Mather] was an epidemic of smallpox, the first in nearly two decades,—which hiatus was a primary cause of the virulence of this outbreak, in that an unexposed generation had little or no resistance to the disease. For all his obsession with the supernatural, Mather had maintained his

Franklin opposed Mather even though he "knew next to nothing of the etiology of smallpox."[255] He did know that "he despised Mather for what James judged the eminent minister's smugness and his inordinate influence over the life of Boston. If Mather advocated inoculation, the *Courant* [James Franklin's newspaper] must oppose it—and did."[256]

At one point in U.S. history, some newspapers practiced what was described as "yellow journalism" in the sense that those newspapers "sent out squads of reporters to hunt down leads and, if evidence failed to materialize, make up stories."[257] For "yellow journalists," the idea of presenting the news "objectively" was regarded as "only an occasional and tangential goal."[258] Indeed, there were allegations that Hearst intended to drag the U.S. into the Spanish-American War by "printing blatantly fictional content and not caring that it was deliberate fiction."[259] When a photographer allegedly cabled Hearst that no war was taking place, Hearst allegedly responded (some dispute the account): "You furnish the pictures and I'll furnish the war."[260]

Media bias (and dishonesty?) is not simply a thing of the past. Indeed, 75% of Americans believe that the media is responsible for increasing political polarization in this country, and nearly half the country has little or no trust in the media to report the news fairly and accurately.[261] There is a widespread perception that the media spreads disinformation,[262] and that fact encourages people to seek news on social media rather than from the mainstream media.[263] While 40% of those interviewed believe that

---

youthful interest in the natural, and he advocated the novel technique of inoculation to combat the contagion.").

255. *Id.*

256. *Id.*

257. *See* William Grimes, *The Devil's Gentleman, International Herald Tribune* 13 (Oct. 26, 2007).

258. *See* Rothstein, *supra* note 250, at 8

259. *See* Bernstein, *supra* note 87.

260. *See* Rothstein, *supra* note 250, at 8 (noting that the statement may have been apocryphal because the letter in which Hearst allegedly made this statement has never been found).

261. *See* David Klepper, *Poll: Most Fault Media for Division, Courier-Journal* 10A (May 2, 2023).

262. *Id.*

263. *Id.*

the press is doing more to hurt democracy than to promote it, only 20% believe that the press is doing more to protect it.[264]

When discussions of media bias occur, commentators often focus on Fox News, contending that it has a right-wing bias and that it skews the news in favor of that bias.[265] And, indeed, there is evidence indicating that Fox News deliberately disseminated disinformation regarding the outcome of the 2020 election.[266] That view is reinforced by the fact that Fox News entered into a entered into a $787.5 million settlement with Dominion Voting Systems for making allegations that the 2020 presidential election was rigged and that Dominion Voting systems played a role.[267]

Despite the claims of some,[268] media bias is hardly limited to Fox News. For example, there is evidence suggesting that National Public Radio (NPR) has a decidedly left-wing bias.[269] Indeed, NPR's then-fundraiser, Mr. Ron Schiller, was videotaped making disparaging remarks about conservatives.[270] If NPR's bias were limited to its fundraisers, that would not

---

264. *Id.*

265. *See* Frank James, *Jon Stewart 'Defends' Mainstream Media Against Fox News, Sort Of*, National Public Radio, It's All About Politics (June 20, 2011). https://www.npr.org/sections/itsallpolitics/2011/06/20/137298761/jon-stewart-defends-mainstream-media-against-fox-news-sort-of.

266. *Id.*

267. *See* Richard Luscombe, Chris Michael & Andrew Roth, *Moscow Confirms Putin Interview with Tucker Carlson; Kremlin Said Interview Was Granted Because Carlson Was Different from Other 'Exceptionally One-Sided' Western Media, The Guardian* (Feb. 7, 2024).

268. *See* James, *supra* notes 265 ("'The bias of the mainstream media is towards sensationalism, conflict and laziness,' said [Comedian Jon] Stewart as he spelled out what, at least to his mind, differentiated other major news outlets from Fox News, an operation Stewart has repeatedly targeted in his comedy as on an ideological mission.").

269. *See* Brett Zongker, *NPR's Williams Is Fired After Muslim Remarks, The Courier-Journal*, A2 (Oct. 22, 2010).

270. *See* Associated Press, *NPR Chief Executive Quits Over Hidden Camera Video*, National Public Radio (Mar. 9, 2011), http://www.npr.org/blogs/thetwo-way/2011/03/10/134388981/npr-ceo-vivian-schiller-resigns; David Folkenflik, *N.P.R. V.P. Resigns, CEO Rebuked Over Williams' Firing*, National Public Radio, Morning Edition (Jan. 7, 2011), http://www.npr.org/2011/01/07/132726894/npr-v-p-resigns-ceo-rebuked-over-williams-firing; Mark Memmott, *In Video: NPR Exec Slams Tea Party, Questions Need for Federal Funds*, National Public Radio, The Two-Way (Mar. 8, 2011), http://www.npr.org/blogs/thetwo-way/2011/03/09/134358398/in-video-npr-exec-slams-tea-party-questions-need-for-federal-funds; Mark Memmott, *NPR CEO Vivian Schiller Resigns After Board Decides She Should Go*, National Public Radio, The Two-Way (Mar. 9, 2011), http://www.npr.org/blogs/thetwo-way/2011/03/10/134388981/npr-ceo-vivian-schiller-resigns; David Folkenf-

necessarily be a problem. However, the evidence suggests that NPR's left-wing bias goes well beyond its fundraisers. In a detailed analysis, then NPR Senior Correspondent Uri Berliner argued that NPR has "lost its way."[271] He noted that there has been a shift in the demographics of NPR's listening audience. Whereas 26% of NPR listeners described themselves as conservative, 23% "as middle of the road," and 37 percent as liberal in 2011, those numbers had shifted considerably by 2023: only "11 percent described themselves as very or somewhat conservative, 21 percent as middle of the road, and 67 percent of listeners said they were very or somewhat liberal."[272] Berliner claimed that the shift occurred as NPR moved from a neutral news reporting outlet to an advocacy organization.[273] While NPR is concerned about promoting diversity in the racial sense, and in other "woke" ways, it is not terribly interested in ideological diversity.[274] Those allegations are borne out by the facts.[275]

F. RESPONSES TO DISINFORMATION AND OTHER INTERNET PROBLEMS OUTSIDE THE UNITED STATES

The difficulty in trying to deal with disinformation is that the cure may be worse than the disease. Authoritarian regimes have always exercised greater control over the public debate and have routinely attempted to censor and control the flow of information. In democratic countries, the accepted wisdom is that divergent views should be allowed, and governmental censorship should be avoided. In general, in the U.S., the government is not designated as the arbiter of truth!

In many countries, there has been considerable repression of disinformation. For example, in Brazil, individuals who spread false statements

---

lik, *NPR Exec: NPR Would Be Better Off Without Federal Support*, National Public Radio, All Things Considered (Mar. 8, 2011), http://www.npr.org/2011/03/08/134371393/NPR-Exec-NPR-Would-Be-Better-Off-Without-Fed-Support.

271. See Uri Berliner, I've Been at NPR for 25 Years. Here's How We Lost America's Trust, The Free Press (Apr. 11, 2024). https://www.thefp.com/p/npr-editor-how-npr-lost-americas-trust.

272. *Id.*

273. *Id.*

274. *Id.*

275. *See* discussion in chapter 5.

can be prosecuted under an existing law that prohibits individuals from spreading rumors with the "potential to generate panic or unrest."[276] In addition, the legislature has contemplated passage of a new law imposing criminal penalties on those who spread fake news regarding public health, public safety, the economy or the electoral process.[277] In addition, Brazil is developing guidelines for regulating online electoral advertising.[278] In the past, the country has imposed fines on companies (*e.g.*, Google) that fail to delete objectionable online content.[279]

Malaysia has proposed prison terms of up to 10 years, or fines of up to 500,000 ringgit ($127,715), for those who spread false information.[280] The law defines fake news as "any news, information, data and reports which are wholly or partly false, whether in the form of features, visuals or audio recordings or in any other form capable of suggesting words or ideas."[281] If an individual is ordered to remove fake news, and fails to do so, the individual can be fined up to 100,000 ringgit, and up to 3,000 ringgit for each day the material remains available.[282] Of course, critics fear that Malaysia will use this law punitively as a way to punish dissent, especially since the government has stated that any news related to the state fund would be considered "fake" unless it has been verified by governmental officials.[283] In addition, Malaysia has pressured TikTok to control disinformation.[284]

Sweden has gone so far as to create a "Psychological Defense Agency," a branch of the Ministry of Defense, to respond to disinformation/misinformation.[285] In creating the agency, Swedish officials were concerned that "the Kremlin had targeted Sweden with a concerted online campaign on social media and elsewhere to discredit the country and undermine its

---

276. *See* Ernesto Londoño, *Brazil Mounts a Campaign Against Fake News: Fears of Tainting Presidential Race, The New York Times* (Feb. 18, 2018).

277. *Id.*

278. *Id.*

279. *Id.*

280. *See* Yantoultra Ngui, *Malaysia Aims at 'Fake News': Critics Say Proposed Law Seeks to Curb Dissent Before National Elections, The Wall Street Journal* A6 (Mar. 27, 2018).

281. *Id.*

282. *Id.*

283. *Id.*

284. *See* Ying Xian Wong, *Malaysia Says App Isn't in Compliance, The Wall Street Journal* B-4 (Oct. 13, 2023).

285. *See* Myers, *supra* note 195, at B-1 & B-4.

bid to join the NATO alliance."[286] The impetus to create the Agency began after Russia's invasion of Crimea, as well as by an extensive disinformation campaign that began in 2021 on social media platforms related to the government's decision to remove the children of an Iraqi immigrant from his custody."[287] The immigrant was portrayed as a Muslim, but was not.[288] There were also allegations that Sweden would not allow a Russian immigrant's children to speak Russian.[289] The allegations gave rise to a new political party.[290] There were also posts relating to the burning of the Quran in Sweden.[291] The agency now has five employees.[292]

At one point, the EU tried to deal with the problem of fake news by establishing a unit, East Stratcom, which examined information to determine whether it is fake, and has the power to take steps to discredit that information.[293] The unit was established because of fears that individuals and governments outside of Europe were targeting European countries with stories and information designed to decrease the public's faith in government.[294] The Unit responded to more than 2,500 news stories, many of which had ties to Russia.[295] Some of these stories targeted European politicians, or attempted to portray Middle Eastern refugees as terrorists or rapists, all with the intent of "fomenting populist anger."[296] Because of the enormity of the problem, East Stratcom felt "outgunned" because it was confronted by an "immense" volume of fake news and has "scant" resources to combat it.[297] Indeed, East Stratcom believes that it would be virtually impossible to unearth all fake news.[298] Members of East Stratcom have received death threats.[299]

---

286. *Id.*
287. *Id.*
288. *Id.*
289. *Id.*
290. *Id.*
291. *Id.*
292. *Id.*
293. *See* Scott & Eddy, *supra* note 128, at A1.
294. *Id.*
295. *Id.*
296. *Id.* at A8.
297. *Id.*
298. *Id.*
299. *Id.*

Similar groups have been created in individual European countries,[300] and Germany is considering the possibility of imposing fines on tech platforms that host fake news.[301] However, there is concern regarding whether response groups like East Stratcom will have much impact. Fake news can enter the news stream quickly,[302] and governmental responses are frequently overwhelmed and much slower.[303]

G. RESPONSES IN THE UNITED STATES

Before we delve into the possible remedies for disinformation in the U.S., it is important to realize that there is a fine line between "persuasive political argument" and "disinformation." For example, in 2023, the Republican National Committee used AI to create a video designed to show the future of the nation if President Biden were re-elected.[304] The video, created entirely by AI, showed boarded-up storefronts, armored military patrols on city streets, and waves of immigrants creating panic.[305] The video served as a persuasive indication of how the RNC saw the future if President Bide was re-elected.[306] Such speech should be protected even if there are efforts to root out disinformation.

In the United States, although many recognize that fake news is a serious problem, as well as the other ills associated with the web (e.g., child pornography and hate speech), there are very few effective legal remedies.

Possible Criminal Prosecutions. Unlike in many countries, where criminal prosecutions are possible, imposing criminal sanctions on offensive speech is generally impermissible in the United States. Within the U.S., there is a general reluctance to allow government to censor political ideas or arguments, as well as to allow it to impose criminal punishments on those ideas or arguments. As the U.S. Supreme Court stated in *Cohen v. California*:[307] "The constitutional right of free expression is powerful med-

300. *Id.*
301. *Id.* at A8.
302. *Id.*
303. *Id.*
304. *See also* Swenson & O'Brien, *supra* note 79, at 6A.
305. *Id.*
306. *Id.*
307. 403 U.S. 15, 24 (1971).

icine in a society as diverse and populous as ours. It is designed and intended to remove governmental restraints from the arena of public discussion, putting the decision as to what views shall be voiced largely into the hands of each of us, in the hope that use of such freedom will ultimately produce a more capable citizenry and more perfect polity and in the belief that no other approach would comport with the premise of individual dignity and choice upon which our political system rests." The Court has reiterated these principles on numerous occasions in a variety of ways.[308] In such a system, the prospect of criminal prosecutions of speech is very disturbing because it can enable governmental repression of views that may not be false, but with which the government simply disagrees.

Regarding disinformation, some commentators have attempted to analyze it under the "marketplace of ideas" metaphor, and have suggested that restrictions on speech might be appropriate in an effort to quell or stamp out disinformation.[309] For example, one scholar stated that to "suggest that the proliferation of fake news represents a breakdown in a market where consumers trade ideas is to presume that fake news concerns ideas about which the public can debate. It doesn't. Fake news does not concern ideas. It concerns facts."[310]

Of course, there are lots of problems with this argument. First, it is not clear that there really is a "marketplace of ideas" in the sense that free and

---

308. Likewise, in *Ashcroft v. American Civil Liberties Union*, 535 U.S. 564, 573 (2002), the Court stated that as "a general matter, the First Amendment means that government has no power to restrict expression because of its message, its ideas, its subject matter, or its content." *See also United States v. Alvarez*, 567 U.S. 709 (2012); *Brown v. Entertainment Merchants Ass'n*, 564 U.S. 756 (2011). Again, from *Cohen v. California*, 403 U.S. 15 (1971): "We cannot indulge the facile assumption that one can forbid particular words without also running a substantial risk of suppressing ideas in the process. Indeed, governments might soon seize upon the censorship of particular words as a convenient guise for banning the expression of unpopular views. We have been able, as noted above, to discern little social benefit that might result from running the risk of opening the door to such grave results." *Id.* at 26. Justice Brandeis powerfully argued for similar principles in a concurring opinion in *Whitney v California*, 274 US 357, 372 (1927), when he stated that the government generally lacks "the power to prohibit dissemination of social, economic and political doctrine which a vast majority of its citizens believes to be false and fraught with evil consequences."

309. *See* Ezra Waldman, *The Marketplace of Fake News*, 20 U. Pa. J. Const. L. 845 (2018).

310. *Id.* at 847.

open debate will lead society to "truth."[311] In any event, in the U.S., there are few formal mechanisms for determining when truth has prevailed.[312] For example, there are no "truth commissions" which are charged with declaring "truth," or with rejecting falsity. In addition, unlike some countries (*e.g.*, France) which make it criminal to deny the truth of certain facts (*e.g.*, the French Gayssot law criminalizes denial of the Holocaust),[313] the First Amendment does not generally allow the U.S. government to formally declare that certain facts must be accepted (or, at least, cannot be denied) on pain of criminal penalty.[314] Moreover, the creation of truth commissions would be constitutionally dubious. Those commissions might be biased in the sense of declaring "facts" which favor one side of the political debate and disadvantage the other side. So, the reality is that the marketplace of ideas does not play a meaningful role in U.S. First Amendment analysis except as a reflection of the idea that all ideas and information must be allowed into the "marketplace." But, under such circumstances, it is difficult to preclude "fake news." How can one reliably determine that news is "fake?" More to the point, is the U.S. society prepared to give government that authority? Presumably not.

Even though the U.S. Supreme Court sometimes discusses and purports to apply the marketplace metaphor, the Court more frequently focuses on democratic process principles,[315] and prohibits government

311. *See* Baker, *supra* note 197.

312. Of course, individuals who perjure themselves in legal proceedings, or who make false statements to governmental officials, can be prosecuted. In addition, it is theoretically possible to recover damages in a defamation action for demonstrably false statements. However, in many cases, the burden of proof is extremely high and generally require far more than proof of falsity. *See New York Times Co. v. Sullivan*, 376 U.S. 254 (1964).

313. *See* Russell L. Weaver, Nicholas Delpierre & Laurence Boissier, *Governmentally Imposed Truth: An Examination of France's Holocaust Denial Law*, 41 TEXAS TECH. U. L. REV. 495–517 (2009).

314. *See id.*

315. Likewise, in its landmark decision in *New York Times Co. v. Sullivan*, 376 U.S. 254 (1964), the Court stated that "'Those who won our independence believed * * * that public discussion is a political duty; and that this should be a fundamental principle of the American government.'" *Id.* at 269 (quoting *Whitney v. California*, 274 U.S. 357, 375–376 (1927) (Brandeis, J., concurring). In *Citizens United v. Federal Election Commission*, 558 U.S. 310, 339 (2010), the Court declared that: "Speech is an essential mechanism of democracy, for it is the means to hold officials accountable to the people. The right of citizens to inquire, to hear, to speak, and to use information to reach consensus is a pre-condition to enlightened

from attempting to control or regulate the content of most speech, particularly political speech.[316] In other words, the marketplace of ideas metaphor does not fully explain the reason why the Court gives freedom of expression a preferred position in the hierarchy of values.[317] And, of course, if government were given the power to prohibit or regulate so-called "fake news," there is a very real risk that the government would use that power to discriminate against ideas that it does not like. In numerous decisions, the Court has made clear that government does not have the power to censor or prohibit ideas.[318]

Moreover, the mere fact that individuals make false statements does not mean that they can be criminally prosecuted. For example, the Stolen Valor Act was a federal statute that made it a crime for individuals to falsely claim to have won the Congressional Medal of Honor. In *United States v. Alvarez*,[319] the Court flatly rejected the proposition that false speech has no value, and therefore should be denied constitutional protection.[320] In doing so, the Court expressed concern that the government might try to create something like the Truth Commission (referencing

---

self-government and a necessary means to protect it. The First Amendment "'has its fullest and most urgent application' to speech uttered during a campaign for political office.' It is inherent in the nature of the political process that voters must be free to obtain information from diverse sources in order to determine how to cast their votes." *See Citizens United v. Federal Election Commission*, 558 U.S. 310, 339 (2010); *see also Virginia v. Black*, 538 U.S. 343, 365 (2003) ("Political speech, of course, is 'at the core of what the First Amendment is designed to protect.'").

316. *See Cohen v. California*, 403 U.S. 15, 24 (1971), the Court stated the principle in the following way: "The constitutional right of free expression is powerful medicine in a society as diverse and populous as ours. It is designed and intended to remove governmental restraints from the arena of public discussion, putting the decision as to what views shall be voiced largely into the hands of each of us, in the hope that use of such freedom will ultimately produce a more capable citizenry and more perfect polity and in the belief that no other approach would comport with the premise of individual dignity and choice upon which our political system rests."

317. *See, e.g., Snyder v. Phelps*, 562 U.S. 443 (2011); *R.A.V. v. City of St. Paul*, 505 U.S. 377 (1992); *Hustler Magazine v. Falwell*, 485 U.S. 46 (1988); *Brandenburg v. Ohio*, 395 U.S. 444 (1969); *Time, Inc. v. Hill*, 385 U.S. 374 (1967); *New York Times Co. v. Sullivan*, 376 U.S. 254 (1964).

318. *See R.A.V. v. City of St. Paul*, 505 U.S. 377 (1992).

319. 567 U.S. 709 (2012).

320. *Id.* at 718. The Court did note that certain types of false speech could be criminally prosecuted such as perjury or filing a false claim with the U.S. government.

George Orwell's Oceania Ministry of Truth), and empower it with the authority to "compile a list of subjects about which false statements are punishable."[321] The Court referred to this type of power as being a "broad censorial power," which the Court viewed as "unprecedented in this Court's cases or in our constitutional tradition," and one which involves "a chill the First Amendment cannot permit if free speech, thought and discourse are to remain a foundation of our freedom."[322]

Alvarez is fully consistent with the Court's general free speech jurisprudence which generally deprives government of the power to control, limit and suppress the range of ideas that the people can hear or consider. In *Ashcroft v. American Civil Liberties Union*,[323] the Court stated that as "a general matter, the First Amendment means that government has no power to restrict expression because of its message, its ideas, its subject matter, or its content."[324] While *Ashcroft's* observations are not entirely correct, in the sense that the government does have the power to prohibit certain types of speech (*e.g.*, child pornography[325] and obscenity),[326] the First Amendment otherwise tends to deprive the government of the power to control either the content or the viewpoints espoused in speech.[327] As a result, when California enacted a law purporting to prohibit the spread of false information regarding Covid-19 vaccines, the law was immediately tied up in litigation.[328]

Some types of false speech (*e.g.*, perjury and the making of false statements to governmental officials) can be prohibited. The difficulty is that, even though perjury can be prosecuted, that crime generally focuses on false statements made in judicial proceedings, and disinformation is published either on the media, or on social platforms, and involve no "false statements" in judicial proceedings or to government officials. Indeed,

---

321. *Id.* at 723 (citing GEORGE ORWELL, NINETEEN EIGHTY-FOUR (1949)).

322. *Id.*

323. 535 U.S. 564, 573 (2002).

324. *See also United States v. Alvarez*, 567 U.S. 709 (2012); *Brown v. Entertainment Merchants Ass'n*, 564 U.S. 756 (2011).

325. *See Ferber v New York*, 458 U.S. 747 (1982).

326. *See Miller v. California*, 413 U.S. 15 (1973).

327. *See R.A.V. v. City of St. Paul*, 505 U.S. 377 (1992),

328. *See* Steven Lee Myers, *Law to Stem Medical Falsities Faces Free Speech Challenge, The New York Times* B1 (Dec. 1, 2022).

much disinformation does not involve any attempt to speak as a government official, or on behalf of or to the government. On the contrary, most such statements are made either on traditional media, or through social media platforms, with no attempt to mislead the government or to mislead the public into believing that the speaker is acting on behalf of the government.

It is also not possible to criminally prosecute disinformation as criminal libel. At one point in history, governments had broad authority to prosecute seditious statements. That authority stemmed from a 1606 English Star Chamber decision in *de Libellis Famosis*,[329] which made it a punishable offense to criticize the government or governmental officials (and, initially, the clergy as well).[330] The crime was premised on the notion that criticism of the government can breed disrespect for governmental as well as for clerical authority. Moreover, since truthful criticism might breed disrespect as effectively as untruthful criticism, truth was not a defense in a seditious libel prosecution. Indeed, because the common law assumed that truthful criticisms were potentially more damaging than false criticisms, truthful criticisms were punished more severely.[331] The problem is that the modern equivalent of seditious libel, prosecutions for criminal libel, are no longer possible in many countries, including the United States.[332]

Injunctions. There is very little chance that the U.S. government, or for that matter state governments, could obtain injunctions designed to protect the public against disinformation on either social media platforms or in the traditional media (although it is conceivable that they might be able to obtain an injunction prohibiting foreign interference in U.S. elections or prohibiting false advertising). In general, U.S. courts have

329. 77 Eng.Rep. 250 (Star Chamber 1606).

330. *See* William T. Mayton, *Seditious Libel and the Lost Guarantee of a Freedom of Expression*, 84 Colum. L. Rev. 91 (1984).

331. The centrality of governmental criticism is attested to in *New York Times v Sullivan*, and in *Derbyshire County Council v. Times Newspaper* [1993] A.C. 534. *Cf.* Ian Loveland, *Defamation of "Government": Taking Lessons for America?* 14 Legal Stud. 206 (1994). Much of the debate regarding free speech concerns its extension to speech in the non-political sphere. Is the exercise of the right to free speech part of the individual's right of self-actualization? This calls for clarification about the foundation of the right.

332. *See Garrison v. Louisiana*, 379 U.S. 64 (1964).

been extremely reluctant to issue prior restraints against speech, including and especially injunctions. For example, in *Near v. Minnesota*,[333] a Minnesota county attorney sought an injunction against what he referred to as a "scandalous, malicious and defamatory" newspaper, *The Saturday Press*, after the newspaper published a series of articles alleging that "a Jewish gangster was in control of gambling, bootlegging, and racketeering in Minneapolis, and that law enforcing officers and agencies were not energetically performing their duties."[334] The mayor of Minneapolis was implicated in the allegations. Even though defamatory speech was not treated as protected speech at that time,[335] and even though it would not receive constitutional protection for many years,[336] the Court viewed the injunction as an unconstitutional prior restraint on speech.[337] Regarding the injunction as impermissible censorship, the Court flatly stated that "Every freeman has an undoubted right to lay what sentiments he pleases before the public; to forbid this, is to destroy the freedom of the press."[338] However, reflecting the law at the time, the Court recognized that, if a newspaper published defamatory material, it could be held liable for damages after the fact: "if he publishes what is improper, mischievous or illegal, he must take the consequence of his own temerity."[339]

The Court subsequently extended the prohibition against injunctions to preclude orders designed to protect national security. In *New York Times Co. v. United States*,[340] also known as the "Pentagon Papers" case, an employee who worked at the U.S. Department of Defense stole a classified document entitled "History of U.S. Decision-Making on Viet Nam Policy." When *The New York Times* and the *Washington Post*, to whom the employee had delivered the documents, sought to publish the documents, the U.S. government sought declaratory and injunctive relief to prevent the publication. Emphasizing that any "system of prior restraints comes to this Court bearing a heavy presumption against its constitu-

333. 283 U.S. 697 (1931).

334. *Id.* at 704.

335. *See Chaplinsky v. New Hampshire*, 315 U.S. 568 (1942).

336. *See New York Times Co. v. Sullivan*, 376 U.S. 253 (1964).

337. *Near*, 283 U.S. at 713–715.

338. *Id.* at 713–714.

339. *Id.* at 714.

340. 403 U.S. 713 (1971).

tional validity," and that any attempt to impose such a restraint must be based on a "heavy burden of justification," the Court held that the government had failed to meet its burden.[341] As a result, the newspapers were free to publish the documents even though they had been stolen.

So, to the extent that government seeks to enjoin disinformation, it will be forced to overcome the prohibition against prior restraints, and its efforts are likely to be thwarted by that doctrine.

Defamation Actions. It may also be difficult for individuals, especially governmental officials or public figures, to recover defamation damages for disinformation. At one point, the Court held that certain categories of speech, including defamation, were not protected under the First Amendment. For example, in *Chaplinsky v. New Hampshire*,[342] the Court flatly stated that defamatory speech receives no First Amendment protection.[343] However, the Court altered its position in *New York Times Co. v. Sullivan*,[344] a case involving allegedly defamatory speech directed at public officials. Previously, most U.S. jurisdictions had used the British common law definition of defamation which was very pro-plaintiff, and placed the burden of proof on the question of truth (*e.g.*, whether the defendant's allegedly defamatory allegations were true or false) on the defendant.[345] Under the Alabama law at issue in the *Sullivan* case, the burden of proof fell on the defendant.[346]

Sullivan dramatically altered the equation, based on what the Court viewed as a "profound national commitment to the principle that debate on public issues should be uninhibited, robust, and wide-open," and the Court recognized that "the public debate may well include vehement, caustic, and sometimes unpleasantly sharp attacks on government and

341. *Id.* at 714.

342. 315 U.S. 568 (1942).

343. *Id.* at 571–572 ("There are certain well-defined and narrowly limited classes of speech, the prevention and punishment of which have never been thought to raise any Constitutional problem. These include the lewd and obscene, the profane, the libelous, and the insulting or 'fighting' words—those which by their very utterance inflict injury or tend to incite an immediate breach of the peace.").

344. 376 U.S. 254 (1964).

345. *See* Russell L. Weaver, Andrew T. Kenyon, David F. Partlett & Clive P. Walker, The Right to Speak Ill: Defamation, Reputation and Free Speech 17–34 (2006) (hereafter "The Right to Speak Ill").

346. *Sullivan*, 376 U.S. at 268.

public officials."[347] Recognizing that "erroneous statement is inevitable in free debate," the Court held that there must be "breathing space" for free expression.[348] As a result, a defamation defendant cannot recover damages simply because a defamatory allegation is untrue.[349] On the contrary, a public official who brings a defamation suit must bear the burden of proof on the question of truth,[350] and must be able to prove not only that defendant's statement was untrue, but that it was made with "actual malice."[351] In other words, plaintiff must prove that defendant knew the statement was false or acted in reckless disregard for whether it was true or false.[352]

In subsequent cases, the Court extended constitutional protections to defamation law suits brought by prominent individuals who did not hold government office. In two decisions, *Curtis Publishing Co. v. Butts*[353] and *Associated Press v. Walker*,[354] the Court extended the actual malice standard to defamation actions brought by "public figures." In other words, just like public officials, public figures may not recover for defamation unless they can prove that defendant made defamatory statements knowing that they were false or acting in reckless disregard for whether they were true or false.

The Court did hold that lower evidentiary standards should apply to defamation actions brought by private individuals. For example, in *Gertz v. Robert Welch, Inc.*,[355] the Court refused to extend the actual malice standard to private individuals even though they may be involved in matters of public interest. Nevertheless, the Court held that courts may not impose liability without proof of fault, and even private individuals may not recover presumed or punitive damages absent proof of actual malice.[356] In *Dun & Bradstreet, Inc. v. Greenmoss Builders, Inc.*,[357] the Court suggested that the

347. *Id.* at 270.
348. *Id.* at 271.
349. *Id.* at 273.
350. *Id.* at 279–280.
351. *Id.*
352. *Id.*
353. 388 U.S. 130 (1967).
354. 388 U.S. 130 (1967).
355. 418 U.S. 323 (1974).
356. *Id.* at 348–349.
357. 472 U.S. 749 (1985).

states have greater latitude to define defamation standards when a case involves a private individual involved in a matter of purely private interest.[358]

Because of these changes in defamation standards, the level of defamation litigation in the United States has dropped to an extremely low level, leaving the print media with broad discretion about what to publish.[359] For most good torts lawyers, defamation litigation is not worth the candle when one can make millions litigating personal injury and wrongful death cases. That said, there has been a significant uptick in defamation litigation over the last year.

So, how do these standards play out in the context of disinformation? On the face of it, one might suspect that defamation damages are recoverable in some cases involving fake news. After all, under the definition of fake news referred to above, the allegations contained in the fake news must be demonstrably false. As a result, the defense of truth disappears.[360] In addition, even though public officials and public figures must satisfy the high bar of the actual malice standard in order to recover damages, one would suspect that some disinformation cases would involve news which is so "made up" that plaintiff might be able to prove that the defendant had the necessary *mens rea*. In other words, defendant knew that the "fake news" was false or at least acted in reckless disregard for truth or falsity. Of course, when private individuals are involved, the proof standards are even lower and therefore it should be even easier to recover, especially if the matter is one that involves purely private matters.

Nevertheless, in particularly outrageous cases, defamation litigation is viable. For example, a successful defamation case was brought against Alex Jones who claimed that a mass killing in Sandy Hook was a hoax.[361] Likewise, Dominion Voting Systems obtained a very large (three-quarters of a billion dollars) defamation settlement against Fox News.

However, defamation plaintiffs may be confronted by a couple of insurmountable obstacles. Because of the extremely democratic nature of the internet—in the sense that virtually anyone can relatively quickly and

358. *Id.* at 760.

359. *See* The Right to Speak Ill, *supra* note 345, at 183–200.

360. *Id.*

361. *See* Elizabeth Williamson, *Facing Damages, Jones Seeks Relief From the 'Deep State,' The New York Times* B15 (Apr. 28, 2022).

easily disseminate information—there is a very real risk that potential defendants may be judgment proof. If the defendant is a media organization, there may be sufficient wealth to recover an adverse judgment even though many media outlets are struggling today. However, if the defamation defendant is an individual who has chosen to disseminate false information, there is a very real risk that the individual may be judgment proof. The other difficulty also stems from the worldwide nature of the internet. Because the internet exists in every country, and because virtually anyone can gain access, it is possible for people all over the world to disseminate fake news. Moreover, information can easily cross-national boundaries so a potential defamation defendant may be in another country. As a result, even if plaintiffs can satisfy the very high standards imposed by U.S. defamation decisions, they may confront very real difficulties in gaining jurisdiction, and they may be forced to litigate in foreign jurisdictions. Even if plaintiffs succeed in obtaining defamation judgments, they may encounter great difficulties in their efforts to enforce those judgments.

Those who are harmed by fake news may have a business tort action available to them. And, indeed, when a case involves purely private interests, courts have even permitted injunctions against speech. For example, in *Schmoldt v. Oakley*,[362] when defendant parked his vehicle outside of plaintiff's dealership, and hung lemons on it, the court concluded that defendant's actions were injurious to plaintiff's business and were engaged in simply for purposes of intimidation or coercion. In these cases, there is a potential conflict between the First Amendment and the potential action for wrongful interference. However, if the allegation made against the plaintiff's business is demonstrably false (*e.g.*, the allegation that a child sexual abuse ring was being run out of the Comet Ping Pong pizzeria), and one can prove that the defendant acted with malice, recovery should be permissible. Of course, the difficulty is whether it will be possible to locate the person who made the false statements, obtain jurisdiction over the individual, and whether he/she is judgment proof.

Another potential basis for challenging disinformation is an action for infliction of mental and emotional distress. In *Hustler Magazine v.*

362. 390 P.3d 882 (Okla. 1964).

Falwell,[363] Hustler Magazine published a satirical advertisement portraying Jerry Falwell, a televangelist who founded a political movement known as The Moral Majority, as having been involved in an incestuous relationship with his mother in an outhouse. Falwell could not sue for defamation because the advertisement made clear that it was satire rather than an assertion of fact.[364] And, in order to recover for intentional infliction of mental and emotional distress, Falwell was required to prove that Hustler made a false statement of fact and did so with actual malice in the *New York Times Co. v. Sullivan* sense.[365] In a subsequent decision, not involving the print media, the Court reaffirmed the *Hustler* decision.[366]

As with a defamation action, it may be possible to satisfy the actual malice standard when a calculated falsehood is involved. Moreover, also like defamation, the courts are likely to apply lower burden of proof standards to suits brought by private individuals. But the same problems that reared their head with regard to defamation cases will arise here: the potential defendant may be impecunious and also may be located outside the U.S. As a result, it may be difficult to bring an action against him/her, and it also may be difficult to collect.

H. CONTENT REGULATION BY SOCIAL MEDIA COMPANIES

Social media platforms (as private entities) are generally regarded as private platforms that have the power to censor speech on their platforms.[367] Indeed, in the U.S., Section 230 of the Communications Decency Act (CDA) explicitly authorizes social media platforms to regulate and censor

363. 485 U.S. 46 (1988).

364. *Id.* at 48.

365. *Id.* at 56.

366. *See Snyder v. Phelps*, 562 U.S. 443 (2011) (refusing to hold individuals liable even though they protested near a dead soldier's funeral, causing mental and emotional distress to the soldier's father).

367. *See* Russell L. Weaver, *Social Media, Section 230, and Free Expression*, 73 Mercer L. Rev. 615, 619 (2022).

information posted on their platforms,[368] and social media platforms have frequently exercised that authority.[369]

Internet companies like Google and Facebook initially did not move aggressively to deal with disinformation.[370] The CDA provides that platforms shall not be liable for "any action voluntarily taken in good faith to restrict access to or availability of material that the provider or user considers to be obscene, lewd, lascivious, filthy, excessively violent, harassing, or otherwise objectionable, whether or not such material is constitutionally protected may censor any information that they deem to be."[371] But as Facebook grew, "so did the hate speech, bullying and other toxic content on the platform."[372] However, Facebook, viewing itself as a "platform," rather than as a "publisher," was reluctant to edit content on its platform.[373] Indeed, Facebook's Chief Executive Mark Zuckerberg has stated that he does not view Facebook as an arbiter of free speech, and that the platform's mission is to "give people a voice."[374] In taking that position, Zuckerberg emphasized that many prominent political figures, including Frederick Douglass, the Rev. Dr. Martin Luther King, Jr., and protestors during the Vietnam War, relied on the First Amendment in the face of governmental attempts to control and censor their speech.[375] He went on to note that "people having the power to express themselves is a new kind of force in the world," and that "the long journey toward greater progress requires confronting ideas that challenge us."[376] He also stated that "we must continue to stand for free expression," and that the public could reach its own conclusions regarding false statements.[377]

---

368. 47 U.S.C. § 230.

369. *See Social Media, Section 230, and Free Expression*, *supra* note 367, at 620–622.

370. *See* Sheera Frenkel, *Nicholas Confessore, Cecilia Kang, Matthew Rosenberg & Jack Nicas, Delay, Deny, Deflect: How Facebook Leaders Leaned Out in Crisis, The New York Times* A1 (Nov. 15, 2018).

371. *Id.*

372. *Id.*

373. *Id.*

374. *See* Cecilia Kang & Mike Isaac, *Zuckerberg Says Facebook Won't Police Political Speech, The New York Times* B1 (Oct. 18, 2019).

375. *Id.*

376. *Id.*

377. *Id.*

At least one commentator has alleged that Facebook's response to fake news has been "agonizingly slow."[378] That response has drawn flak from Facebook employees,[379] and Facebook has come under increasing pressure to "more actively regulate speech on the platform."[380] Facebook, then, in an about fact, started action to deal with misinformation and election interference,[381] Mr. Zuckerberg, Facebook's Chief Executive, indicated that Facebook had established a panel of academics to study social media's impact on elections, and agreed to publish a transparency report showing how many fake accounts had been removed from Facebook.[382] Over time, Facebook took steps to limit who could buy advertisements on its platform, it hired monitors to review posted content, and established a "war room" to root out false information.[383] These measures prompted Mark Zuckerberg, Facebook's chief executive, to declare that Facebook is getting "better and better" at dealing with false information.[384] But, even if Facebook was determined, it faced a daunting task given that Facebook operates all over the world in languages.[385]

As part of its efforts Facebook deleted accounts believed to have engaged in misinformation and political agitation.[386] On or about 2018, Facebook removed 32 pages and accounts from its platform, including some 9,500 posts, which were followed by more than 290,000 Facebook accounts which had promoted some 30 real-world events.[387] The pages and accounts went by such names as "Aztlan Warriors," "Black Elevation," and "Resisters."[388] These fake groups sought to work alongside legitimate groups to organize protests and sow discord, and succeeded in stimulat-

378. *See Facebook's Worst Demons, supra* note 189, at B5.

379. *See* Mike Isaac, Cecilia Kang & Sheera Frenkel, *Facing Furor, Zuckerberg Defends Call on Trump, The New York Times* B1 (June 3, 2020).

380. *See* Kate Conger & Adam Satariano, *Twitter Clamps Down, But Rogue Accounts Turn the Pressure Up, The New York Times* A15 (Nov. 6, 2018).

381. *See* Frenkel & Issac, *supra* note 161, at B2.

382. *Id.*

383. *See* Conger & Satariano, *supra* note 382, at A15.

384. *Id.*

385. *See* Taub & Fisher, *supra* note 182, at A8.

386. *See* Robert McMillan & Deepa Seetharaman, *Facebook Deletes Suspect Accounts, The New York Times* A1 (Aug. 2, 2018).

387. *Id.*

388. *Id.*

ing more than three dozen events in 15 months.[389] In addition, Facebook dramatically expanded its content review division,[390] flagged online disinformation and removed posts if they violated the companies' terms of use policies or local laws.[391] In addition, Facebook announced plans to hire thousands of content moderators and spend hundreds of millions of dollars on content review.[392] Instead of the $150 million that it spent on content moderation in 2016, it spent $220 million in 2017, and far more in 2018.[393] But the number of moderators has varied. While Meta laid off a number of employees assigned to election policy issues in 2022, it claimed that its overall staffing had expanded.[394]

Facebook also requires verification of U.S. citizenship or permanent residency for those who purchase Facebook advertisements in the U.S.[395] For example, in 2023, Meta interrupted a large Chinese disinformation campaign involving some 7,700 accounts and 930 pages, involving disinformation regarding such things as the origin of the Covid-19 pandemic.[396] Facebook also removed 32 other pages and fake accounts.[397] However, there is evidence suggesting that Meta, YouTube and X all recently reduced the size of their content moderation staffs.[398]

Regarding Covid-19, Meta would remove false statements only if they presented a risk of imminent harm.[399] As a result, there were false claims that Meta did not remove.[400] However, after noticing that a high percentage of Meta comments were posted by a small number of users, Meta restricted the number of comments that one user could make (to 13 per

389. *See* Deepa Seetharaman & Robert McMillan, *Fake Accounts Sought Ties to Real Groups, The Wall Street Journal* A4 (Aug. 3, 2018).

390. *See* Deepa Seetharaman, *Facebook Focuses on Policing Content, The Wall Street Journal* B4 (May 16, 2018).

391. *Id.*

392. *Id.*

393. *Id.*

394. *See* McMillan, Corse & Volz, *supra* 47, at A4.

395. *See* Frenkel & Issac, *supra* note 161, at B2.

396. *See* Rohan Goswami, *Meta Says It Has Disrupted a Massive Disinformation Campaign Linked to Chinese Law Enforcement*, CNBC (Aug. 29, 2023).

397. *Id.*

398. *See* Hsu, Thompson & Myers, *supra* note 5, at A6.

399. *See* Schechner, Horwitz & Glazer, *supra* note 17, at B5.

400. *Id.*

hour, down from 300 per hour).[401] In addition, it took steps to demote the prominence of certain material (a step that it took with regard to some 70,000 comments that had been posted over 10 million times).[402] At one point, Twitter would place "caution" labels on disinformation.[403] In regard to a doctor who was regarded as making false Covid claims, Meta banned advertising on his main Facebook page, and removed content that violated Meta terms of use policies.[404]

But it is safe to say that social media platforms have dealt inconsistently with disinformation.[405] After a post falsely depicted a Republican candidate as kissing the star of Donald Trump on the Hollywood Walk of Fame, Facebook noted that it had been "altered" but did not remove it.[406] By contrast, Twitter permanently suspended an account where a false tweet was made regarding mail-in ballots.[407]

Even if social media platforms were determined to deal with disinformation, they would face difficult decisions regarding what content to censor or stifle, and it is not clear how effective companies like Facebook can be in deleting with fake news.[408] Some platforms, for example Meta's Instagram, bans such things as hate speech, and content designed to intimidate voters to deter them from exercising their right to vote.[409] But, in 2019, Facebook decided that it would no longer police disinformation that involved opinion or satire.[410] Thus, Facebook would ignore such content even if its contains falsehoods or disinformation.[411] Some worry that purveyors of disinformation can manipulate the rules by labeling content as "opinion" or "parody" rather than fact.[412]

---

401. *Id.*, at B7.
402. *Id.*
403. *See Disinformation Is Big Business*, *supra* note 20 at A16.
404. *Id.*
405. *See* Myers, *supra* note 122, at A1.
406. *Id.*
407. *Id.*
408. *See* Fisher, *supra* note 155, at B5.
409. *See* Emily Glazer, *Facebook Allows Campaigns to Target Voters*, *The Wall Street Journal* A4 (Jan. 10, 2020).
410. *See* Jeff Horowitz, *Facebook Dials Back Fact Checks*, *The Wall Street Journal* B1 (Oct. 1. 2019).
411. *Id.*
412. *Id.*

In any event, it is not clear that social media companies are equipped to make good decisions regarding content moderation. For example, social media companies faced difficult questions about how to deal with alleged disinformation regarding the Covid-19 vaccine.[413] Some were concerned that disinformation was discouraging Americans from taking the vaccine because of claims that it causes autism or can poison people.[414] In addition, there were concerns that disinformation was discouraging parents from having their children vaccinated for other diseases, leading to the return of certain childhood diseases.[415] As a result, Pinterest attempted to block all searches for the term "vaccines."[416] YouTube banned the account of a radio and Fox News host, Dan Bongino, for violating its Covid-19 misinformation policy.[417] Bongino had claimed that cloth and surgical masks were useless for halting the spread of Covid-19.[418] When Bongino made similar claims on another YouTube channel, YouTube terminated all of his accounts.[419] There was a period when Facebook would remove what it referred to as "vaccine disinformation" that was coming from Russia,[420] would not "recommend" certain content regarding vaccines, and would reject advertisements with false claims.[421] Facebook also took steps to control "low-quality" content by downplaying it, and it has played up "recommended" content.[422]

The more difficult question is whether social media platforms should be deciding what information is "true" and what constitutes "disinformation," and placing themselves in a position of "censoring speech." One arti-

---

413. *See* Barbara Ortutsy, *Social Media Tackle Vaccine Claims, Courier-Journal* 9A (Apr. 6, 2019).

414. *Id.*

415. *Id.*

416. *Id.*

417. *See* Daisuke Wakabayashi, *YouTube Bars a Right-Wing Host for Making False Covid Claims, The New York Times* B6 (Jan. 27, 2022).

418. *Id.*

419. *Id.*

420. *See* Davey Alba, *Facebook Removes Vaccine Disinformation, The New York Times* B2 (Aug. 11, 2021).

421. *See* Barbara Ortutsy, *Social Media Tackle Vaccine Claims, Courier-Journal* 9A (Apr. 6, 2019).

422. *See* Jeff Horowitz, *Facebook Makes Strides to Clean Up Content, The Wall Street Journal* B5 (Nov. 23, 2022).

cle suggests a defect in the system because a physician was allowed to state her misgivings and opposition to some vaccines.[423] But does that mean that all debate regarding the efficacy of vaccines should be squelched? Or might it mean that only "government approved" information regarding vaccines should be allowed? Many might question whether the government should be regarded as the arbitrator of all truth in this area.

In managing Facebook accounts, the company is increasingly relying on artificial intelligence.[424] The use of AI began in 2017,[425] and involved the use of extensive digital fact-checking tools, especially in Europe.[426] The sense is that it's virtually impossible for the platforms to have enough fact-checkers to control disinformation, but the hope is that control is possible through digital mediums,[427] including technology designed to uncover deepfakes.[428] However, some fear that the technology used to create deepfakes will evolve faster than the technology designed to detect it.[429] Facebook alleges that those tools are effective some 98.5% of the time in assisting it in finding fake accounts, nearly 100% of the time in uncovering spam, and also worked well for uncovering nudity.[430] However, other evidence questions the efficacy of using AI for content moderation.[431] AI worked less well in efforts to uncover hate speech because of the need to consider context in making that assessment.[432]

Creators of AI are pledging to limit the use (and abuse) of bots and chatbots in elections.[433] For example, Google plans to preclude it's A.I.

---

423. *Id.*

424. *See* Alex Hern & Olivia Solon, *Facebook Closed 583m Fake Accounts in First Three Months of 2018: Firm's First Quarterly Moderation Report Also Shows Scale of Spam, Hate Speech and Violence, The Guardian* (May 15, 2018).

425. *See* Mark Scott, *As Europe Heads to the Polls, Tech Tackles Fake News, The New York Times* B3 (May 2, 2017).

426. *Id.*

427. *Id.*

428. *See* Cade Metz & Tiffany Hsu, *'Terrified' A.I. Researcher Targets Election Deepfakes, The New York Times* B1 (Apr. 3, 2024).

429. *Id.*

430. *Id.*

431. *See* Hannah Murphy & Madhumita Murgia, *Facebook Delayed at 'Frontier' of AI Policing, FT Weekend* 14 (Nov. 9–10, 2019).

432. *See* Hern & Solon, *supra* note 426.

433. *See* Tiffany Hsu & Cade Metz, *A.I. Creators to Limit Voter Deceit, The New York Times* B1 (Feb. 17, 2024).

chatbot Bard from responding to election-related prompts.[434] Meta is trying (on both Facebook and Instagram) to label A.I.-generated content so that voters know that who they are dealing with.[435] In addition, a number of A.I. creators (Adobe, Amazon, Anthropic, Google, Meta, Microsoft, OpenAI, TikTok and X) signed a pledge to limit and disrupt disruptive A.I. content.[436] In particular, Anthropic pledged to prohibit its technology from being used for political campaigning or lobbying.[437] Synthesia prohibits the use of its technology for "news-like content,"[438] and Stability AI prohibits the use of its technology for illegal or unethical purposes and uses a watermark so that it's content is identifiable.[439] Meta plans to use A.I. tools to help it identify A.I. generated content.[440] Whether any of these efforts will have an appreciable impact on the level of disinformation is unclear. But, as A.I. technology gets better and better (e.g., OpenAI recently announced the creation of Sora, a technology that has the capacity to create very realistic videos), it may be difficult for even the manufacturers to control it.[441]

TikTok has also hired employees to work on content moderation.[442] TikTok hired away employees from Alphabet, Inc., Google, and Twitter.[443] YouTube stopped removing political videos, citing concerns about regulating political speech.[444] In addition, in 2019, Facebook made it clear that it would not police political speech or fact check political advertising.[445] At that time, Facebook refused to take down an advertisement which suggested that then presidential candidate Joe Biden committed corrupt acts in Ukraine (even though CNN and NBCU refused to air it).[446]

---

434. *Id.*
435. *Id.*
436. *Id.*
437. *Id.*
438. *Id.*
439. *Id.*
440. *Id.*
441. *Id.*
442. *See* Georgia Wells & Emily Glazer, *TikTok Pulled Into Election Fray As Both Parties Vie for Youth Vote, The Wall Street Journal* A4 (Jan. 6, 2020).
443. *Id.*
444. *See* McMillan, Corse & Volz, *supra* 47, at A4.
445. *See* Cecilia Kang & Mike Isaac, *supra* note 376, at B1.
446. *Id.*

Before it was purchased by Elon Musk, Twitter took numerous steps to try to control disinformation.[447] For example, it established a team that was charged with ferreting out suspicious content, as well as automated content, and it coordinated closely with the U.S. Department of Homeland Security and the FBI, and created a portal that allowed individuals to easily report misleading tweets.[448] These efforts led Twitter's then head of "trust and safety" to declare that "we are more prepared than we ever have been."[449] Twitter also created a "data science team" that utilized technology to identify "oddities," including noting clusters of accounts that use the same email address or phone number, or that constantly tweet at high-profile accounts.[450] During the 2016 election, the team found that disinformation was being spread, not only by Republican supporters, but also Democratic partisans.[451]

Despite Twitter's efforts, some commentators claim that there was 5% more false content on Twitter than during the 2016 elections, and Twitter admitted that it found some 50 fake accounts which were masquerading as accounts by Democratic officials.[452] There were Tweets that urged men not to vote in the mid-term elections in order to give female votes more power, another which alleged that Immigration and Customs Enforcement Officials would be patrolling voting sites in an effort to locate illegal immigrants, and a third which alleged the need for violence and civil war.[453] By 2018, more than a million users exited the platform because of the number of fake accounts, as well as because of evidence regarding "fake followers" being sold by companies.[454]

Social media platform censorship can have profound implications for the democratic process. For example, in 2019, Democratic presidential candidate Tulsi Gabbard sued Google for allegedly stifling and censor-

---

447. *See Twitter Clamps Down*, *supra* note 382.

448. *Id.*

449. *Id.*

450. *Id.*

451. *Id.*

452. *Id.*

453. *Id.*

454. *See* Nicholas Confessore, Gabriel J.X. Dance & Rich Harris, *A Twitter Purge? Followers Abruptly Exit*, *The New York Times* B1 (Feb. 1, 2018).

ing her campaign speech.[455] Even though Gabbard was an elected official, Google suspended her advertising account shortly after the first Democratic debate.[456] Gabbard claimed that the suspension impaired her ability to raise money and convey her campaign message.[457] The suspension became a particular problem for Gabbard because she received a lot of attention after the debate and she was the most searched for candidate on Google.[458] Google explained the censorship on the basis that its automated systems automatically suspend accounts that have unusual advertiser activity.[459] However, some of her views (e.g., anti-gay) were controversial.[460] Nevertheless, the suspension made it more difficult to raise money and to connect with voters.[461]

YouTube also struggles to control content, including difficulties dealing with "disinformation campaigns, like Russia's efforts during the 2016 election, and language it considers hate speech, including posts by the recently banned Infowars site."[462] YouTube has talked about the possibility of outsourcing it's fact-checking to Wikipedia.[463] YouTube's plan is to use "information cues," which come from an online encyclopedia, which "would appear as captions and article links beneath videos that dealt with topics related to popular conspiracy theories."[464] Of course, this proposed solution is not entirely satisfactory because anyone can edit Wikipedia's content.[465] Moreover, "Wikipedia is not necessarily geared toward breaking news—and conspiracy theories tend to move at lightning speed during times of crisis."[466]

---

455. *See* Daisuke Wakabayashi, *Gabbard Sues Google, Saying It Stifled Her Speech, The New York Times* B3 (July 26, 2019).

456. *Id.*

457. *Id.*

458. *Id.*

459. *Id.*

460. *Id.*

461. *Id.*

462. *See* Keller, *supra* note 78, at 38.

463. *See* John Herrman, *YouTube May Add to the Burdens of Humble Wikipedia, International New York Times* A1 (Mar. 19, 2018).

464. *Id.*

465. *Id.*

466. *Id.*

Sidechat, an anonymous app that is used on college campuses, engages in aggressive content-moderation.[467] It employs a team of 30 content-moderators who review posts around the clock, and it bans accounts that make racist or bigoted posts.[468] A user can be banned for a single "severe" violation of the App's terms of use.[469]

At one point, Facebook created an online library ("The Ad Library") of all advertisements posted on its platform.[470] The idea was to allow ordinary users to see the messages that were being promoted, who was promoting them, and how much they were paying.[471] The idea was to create authenticity and transparency for advertisements.[472] The difficulty is that the system was plagued by technical bugs and constraints that made the library so difficult to use that one commentator referred to it as "useless."[473]

There is evidence suggesting that social media platform began reducing their content-moderation efforts in 2022.[474] After years of adding staff focused on content moderation, as well as investing in technologies designed to assist the moderators, YouTube drastically reduced the size of its content-moderation team.[475] Meta, which owns several platforms (Facebook, WhatsApp. and Instagram), similarly reduced the size of its staff devoted to the problem.[476]

Following Elon Musk's purchase of Twitter (now X), it's approach to disinformation changed dramatically.[477] For one thing, the platform reduced by 50% the number of staff devoted to managing information,[478]

467. *See* Zachary Schermale, *Students Love Sidechat; Colleges Don't, The Courier-Journal* 13A (Mar. 10, 2024).

468. *Id.*

469. *Id.*

470. *See* Matthew Rosenberg, *A Tool That Facebook Built To Combat Disinformation Doesn't Work as Advertised, The New York Times* B1 (July 26, 2019).

471. *Id.*

472. *Id.*

473. *Id.*

474. *See* Steven Lee Myers & Nico Grant, *Fight Against Disinformation, The Front Line Is Being Thinned, The New York Times* A1 (Feb. 15, 2023).

475. *Id.*

476. *Id.*, at A19.

477. *See* Hsu, Thompson & Myers, *supra* note 5, at A1-2.

478. *See* Ryan Mac, Mike Isaac & Kellen Browning, *Twitter's Cuts to Work Force Put It on Brink, The New York Times* A1 (Nov. 19, 2022).

especially election integrity issues,[479] and was faced with a slew of resignations.[480] In addition, X stopped policing Covid misinformation in the sense that it no longer provided corrective information, removed inaccurate information, or banned offending accounts (previously, 97,000 pieces of misleading content had been banned and 11,000 accounts had been suspended).[481] X was warned by EU regulators regarding its more relaxed approach to content-moderation.[482] In 2024, X indicated that it was hiring more "safety staffers," including 100 content moderators.[483]

X did introduce a new system which it called "Community Notes" which allows anyone to post "corrections" on posts.[484] Users can respond by indicating whether the notes were "helpful."[485] Some question whether such notes have much impact: a study found that "the presence of a Community Note did not keep false information from spreading widely. Users who created misleading posts saw no change in their engagement for subsequent posts, suggesting that they paid no penalty for sharing falsehoods."[486] Moreover, since most posts received a "surge of attention" immediately after they are posted, Community Notes may come too late to counteract the disinformation.[487]

Even if one could argue that social media platforms could or should ban "disinformation," it is not clear that they have the capacity to make good decisions regarding what constitutes "disinformation." For example, Facebook's moderators were "overwhelmed" by the total volume of work.[488] Purportedly, Facebook receives more than 6.5 million reports a week regarding allegations of fake or improper accounts.[489] Even though

---

479. *See* Tiffany Hsu & Stuart A. Thompson, *Campaigns to Root Out Falsehoods are Fading, The New York Times* B-2 (Oct. 9, 2023).

480. *See* Mac, Isaac & Browning, *supra* note 480, at A1.

481. *See* Maxwell Adler, *Twitter Says It Stopped Policing Covid Misinformation Under Musk*, Bloomberg News (Nov. 29, 2022).

482. *See* Deepa Seetharaman & Meghan Bobrowsky, *Hands-Off Approach to Twitter Draws a Caution From Regulator, The Wall Street Journal* A1 (Apr. 27, 2022).

483. *See* McMillan, Corse & Volz, *supra* 47, at A4.

484. *See* Hsu & Thompson, *supra* note 523, at B-2.

485. *Id.*

486. *Id.*

487. *Id.*

488. *See* Hern & Solon, *supra* note 426.

489. *Id.*

Facebook had some 35,000 moderators at one point,[490] Facebook's moderators were sometimes forced to make decisions regarding the permissibility of content in as little as 10 seconds.[491] The time pressures inevitably result in bad decisions. As one commentator noted, referring to the way that social media companies handled the Hunter Biden laptop story: "These decisions get made quickly, in the heat of the moment, and it's possible that more contemplation and debate would produce more satisfying choices."[492] For a while, even though there was (and is) some uncertainty regarding the origins of the Covid-19 virus,[493] Facebook banned all claims that the virus was man-made,[494] but it eventually decided to allow such claims.[495] In addition, Facebook purportedly banned references to certain Bible passages, as well as links to Biblehub.com.[496] After investigating, Facebook confirmed that links to Biblehub.com had been banned, eventually admitted that it had acted in error, and purportedly rectified the problem.[497] Facebook even went so far as to ban academics who were doing research on ad transparency and the spread of misinformation on Facebook.[498] It isn't clear that anyone (or any social media platform) should set itself up as an arbiter of "truth."

---

490. *See Facebook Delayed at 'Frontier' of AI Policing, supra* note 475, at 14.

491. *See* Hern & Solon, *supra* note 426.

492. *See* Kevin Roose, *Eyes on 2016, Social Media Tackles 2020, The New York Times* A27 (Oct. 16, 2020).

493. *See* Alina Chan, *Why Covid Probably Started in a Lab, The New York Times*, Sunday Review 6 (June 9, 2024).

494. *See* Thomas Barrabi, *Facebook Ends Ban on Posts Claiming COVID-19 Is Man-Made:*

Facebook Had Previously Insisted the Claim Had Been 'Debunked,' Fox Business (May 26, 2021) https://www.foxbusiness.com/technology/facebook-ends-ban-posts-claiming-covid-19-man-made.

495. *Id.*

496. *See* Julia Marnin, *Fact Check: Is Facebook Banning Bible Passages?*, Newsweek (Jan. 28, 2021) https://www.newsweek.com/fact-check-facebook-banning-bible-passages-1565190.

497. *Id.*

498. *See* James Vincent, *Facebook Bans Academics Who Researched Ad Transparency and Misinformation on Facebook: The Researchers Say Their Work Is Being Silenced*, The Verge (Aug. 4, 2021) https://www.theverge.com/2021/8/4/22609020/facebook-bans-academic-researchers-ad-transparency-misinformation-nyu-ad-observatory-plug-in.

As noted earlier, social media platforms (especially Facebook) censored information regarding the origins of the Covid-19 virus.[499] However, when government documents were declassified in 2023 (several years later), they were inconclusive regarding the origins of the virus.[500] Officials were unable to determine whether the virus leaked from a lab in China, or resulted from natural transmission, and intelligence officials suggested that the trail had "run cold."[501] Nevertheless, Facebook squelched public discussion of the issue.[502]

Of course, there is a risk that censorship decisions by social media platforms will be based on political bias, but it is not clear that posts are censored in that way. For example, there were allegations that Facebook's Chief Executive, Mark Zuckerberg, who strongly supports the idea of immigration reform, was "appalled" by some of Donald Trump's postings regarding immigration.[503] However, he did not move to censor Trump's speech.[504] In addition, Facebook indicated that it would allow political campaigns to post advertisements targeting particular constituencies, and that it would not police the content of those communications.[505] Facebook maintained this position in the face of substantial critics.[506] Facebook justified its approach on free speech grounds, as well as on its support for the democratic process, noting that Facebook did not wish to be in the position of policing what politicians say to constituents, and emphasizing that such advertisements allow campaigns to fundraise, register voters, build crowds for events, and organize volunteers.[507] Facebook argues that its policy is consistent with "global democracy" and is "a vote for the idea that Facebook is a fairly designed playing field that is conducive to healthy

---

499. *Id.*

500. *See* Julian E. Barnes, *Declassified Data on Covid's Origins Is Said to Be Inconclusive, The New York Times* A8 (June 22, 2023).

501. *Id.*

502. *Id.*

503. *See Delay, Deny, Deflect, supra* note 370, at A14.

504. *Id.*

505. *See* Mike Isaac & Cecilia Kang, *Facebook Keeps Policy Protecting Political Ads, The New York Times* B1 (Jan. 10, 2020).

506. *Id.*, at B6.

507. *Id.*, at B1.

political debate, and that whatever problems it has simply reflect the problems that exist in society as a whole."[508]

Facebook notes that tighter rules might limit the ability of "smaller, less well-funded organizations to raise money and organize.[509] However, Facebook provided users with the ability to limit such ads.[510] Facebook did indicate in 2019 that it would cut-off political advertising the week before an election,[511] and that it was taking steps to thwart Russian trolls, and it imposed a verification process that requires political advertisers to register with a U.S. address.[512] In addition, Facebook banned certain types of disinformation (e.g., misinforming potential voters regarding the date of election day).[513] Facebook (as well as its various platforms, including Instagram and Messenger) also prohibited "microtargeting" on political topics; microtargeting involves highly personalized messages on political topics.[514] While Facebook believes that microtargeting is highly effective, it worries that the technique could be used to incite violence or suppress voter turnout.[515] Some critics suggest that Facebook's policies are "anything but neutral" since they favor "candidates who are good at cranking out emotionally charged, hyper partisan content, regardless of their factual accuracy."[516] In announcing that it would not limit political advertising, Facebook noted that it raised far more money from commercial advertising than from other sources.[517]

In its pre-Musk days, Twitter banned all political advertisements from its platform.[518] Google has also chosen to restrict political advertising.[519]

---

508. *See* Kevin Roose, *Facebook Opts to Influence 2020 Election, The New York Times* B4 (Jan. 11, 2020).

509. *See Facebook Keeps Policy Protecting Political Ads, supra* note 507, at B6.

510. *Id.*; *see also Facebook Allows Campaigns to Target Voters, supra* note 411, at A1.

511. *See* Jeff Horowitz, *Facebook Sets Political-Ad Cutoff, The Wall Street Journal* A1 (Sept. 4, 2020).

512. *See Facebook Opts to Influence 2020 Election, supra* note 510, at B4.

513. *Id.*

514. *See* Jeff Horwitz, *Meta Limits Ad Targeting, The Wall Street Journal* A6 (Nov. 10, 2021).

515. *Id.*

516. *See Facebook Opts to Influence 2020 Election, supra* note 510, at B4.

517. *See* Isaac & Kang, *supra* note 507, at B6.

518. *Id.*

519. *See Facebook Opts to Influence 2020 Election, supra* note 510, at B1.

During the 2020 campaign, the Trump campaign spent more than $27 million on Facebook advertising by January, some 10 months before the election, and critics claimed that Facebook's policy allowed him to lie.[520]

Despite the potential for problems with social media content moderation, there may be instances when moderation is appropriate. For example, when a tweet was circulating suggesting that Colorado's election system had been hacked, Colorado's Secretary of State contacted Twitter and arranged for the tweet to be taken down because Colorado was not using the type of machine shown in the tweet.[521] The tweet was taken down within an hour.[522] However, such governmental contacts are complicated by the problems outlined in the prior chapter with government attempting to encourage (pressure, threaten) social media platforms regarding their content moderation decisions. Perhaps a more appropriate response was Colorado's decision to buy responsive advertisements.[523]

Another approach to content-moderation was used at Reddit.[524] Reddit was once viewed as a "free speech paradise" which contained "nonconsensual pornography, overt racism and violent misogyny."[525] Instead of trying to deal with content post-by-post, it decided to shut down thousands of subreddits where its rules had been "consistently broken."[526] For example, Reddit shut down a user group devoted to Donald Trump.[527] In addition, rather than trying to do all of the content-moderation itself, Reddit decided to employ "an army of volunteer moderators."[528] Users who had frequented toxic parts of the sites either reformed their conduct or left the site altogether.[529] All of these actions raise troubling censorship questions.

---

520. *See* Isaac & Kang, *supra* note 507, at B6.

521. *See* Corasaniti & Alba, *supra* note 13, at A20.

522. *Id.*

523. *Id.*

524. *See* Kevin Roose, *How Reddit Subdued Its Trolls and Saved Itself, The New York Times* A21 (Mar. 22, 2024).

525. *Id.*, at A1.

526. *Id.*, at A21.

527. *See* Mike Isaac, *Reddit Bans User Group Devoted to Trump, The New York Times* B1 (June 30, 2020).

528. *See How Reddit Subdued Its Trolls and Saved Itself, supra* note 526, at A21.

529. *Id.*

I. FLAGGING POTENTIAL DISINFORMATION?

One potential solution to the problem of disinformation is to "flag" it as constituting "disinformation," and then perhaps direct the viewer to sources that contain accurate information. For example, some newspapers (e.g., El Pais) have expanded their fact-checking efforts.[530] This approach would be less objectionable than outright suppression of information because the information would still be distributed, but would be met with counter-speech that attempts to set the record straight. For example, TikTok, which has approximately 1.6 billion monthly users, labeled posts related to the midterm elections with links to posts from authoritative sources.[531] In any event, researchers concluded that TikTok failed to catch some 90% of political advertisements, involving false or misleading information.[532] YouTube responded to false information by adjusting its recommendation algorithm and removing videos and livestreams.[533] Meta removed posts that promoted voter suppression or that discouraged people from voting.[534] When Donald Trump called for military action against a protest, and referred to the participants as "thugs," Twitter posted a warning because the tweet purportedly violated Twitter's policy against promoting violence.[535] Essentially, Twitter hid some Trump tweets behind these warning labels.[536]

For a while, Twitter attached fact-checking labels to the posts of others.[537] For example, it attached labels to posts by Zhao Lijian, of China's foreign ministry, who claimed that the Covid-19 pandemic may have started in the U.S. and was brought to China by the U.S. military.[538]

530. *See Delay, Deny, Deflect, supra* note 370, at A1.

531. *See* Frenkel & Myers, *supra* note 116, at B5.

532. *Id.*

533. *Id.*

534. *Id.*

535. *See* Tiffany Hsu & Cecilia Kang, *Facebook's Stand on Trump Prompts Some to Pause Ads, The New York Times* B6 (June 10, 2020).

536. *See* Kate Conger, *A Look Inside Twitter's Move to Flag Trump, The New York Times* A1 (May 31, 2020).

537. *See* Kate Conger & Mike Isaac, *Adding Fact-Checking Labels, Twitter Defies the President, The New York Times* B1 (May 29, 2020)

538. *Id.*

In some respects, efforts to flag or question disinformation might prove to be an effective remedy. For example, in the case of "fake news" on the internet, the reader could be referred to more accurate information. The remedy could also work for false statements by politicians. For example, when President Biden lied about the recommendations from his military advisers regarding the Afghanistan withdrawal, the Biden comments (to the extent that they were reported online) could have been linked to verbatim transcripts of the contrary testimony by his military advisers. The situation might also work to combat media bias. For example, if NPR's reporting about Kavanaugh's were posted online, the flag could refer the reader to the *N.Y. Times* analysis of the allegations or the *Washington Post* article questioning the allegations. In the case of the OPM program on whether NPR is biased, the listener or reader (for someone who read the article online) could be referred to some of the criticisms of NPR.

One way to deal with disinformation is through fact-checking organizations. In 2016, Meta (formerly Facebook) began working with and paying fact-checking organizations.[539] Such organizations use a variety of techniques ranging from "context labels," "accuracy flags," "warning screens," "content removal policies," and "media literacy trainings."[540] For example, an assertion might be labelled as "disputed" or "false."[541] In the first six months of 2023, more than 40 million posts received fact-checking labels.[542] Such labels were attached to statements made by then President Trump regarding the fact that mail-in ballots could lead to a rigged election,[543] as well as to other statements that he made,[544] and a statement that mail-in ballot boxes are not sanitized against Covid-19.[545] Facebook claimed that the statements violated its Civic Integrity Policy

539. *See* Hsu & Thompson, *supra* note 481, at B-2.

540. *Id.*

541. *See* Brendan Nyhan, *Is Facebook's Fact-Checking Effective? Researchers Offer Warnings, The New York Times* B2 (Oct. 24, 2017).

542. *See* Hsu & Thompson, *supra* note 481, at B-2.

543. *See* Jim Rutenberg & Kate Conger, *His Fact Checkers Long Gone, Musk Echoes Voting Lies on X, The New York Times* A1 (Jan. 27, 2024). The labels stated: "Get the facts about mail-in voting. Experts say mail-in ballots are very rarely linked to voter fraud." *Id.*

544. *See* Cecilia Kang, *A Campaign Prepares to Go Public in Its Attack on Facebook's Speech Policies, The New York Times* A15 (June 12, 2020).

545. *See* Kate Conger, *Twitter Flags a Tweet By Trump on Voting, The New York Times* B3 (Aug. 24, 2020).

by discouraging people from voting.[546] In other counties (e.g., India), a website (Alt News) attempts to debunk disinformation regarding a variety of issues (gangs, Covid).[547]

But it is not clear that fact checking or warnings have much impact on what people believe.[548] One study showed that such labels have some impact on believability.[549] For example, following the 2020 presidential election, 30% of the electorate believed that President Biden had prevailed because of fraud.[550] Three years later, after dozens of fact-checking organizations had weighed in on the issue, the numbers had not changed much with 30% of the people still believing that Biden had prevailed because of fraud.[551] As a result, although fact-checking operations blossomed during the pandemic, and after the 2020 election, they seem to be in decline now.[552] X, formerly Twitter, which attached labels to Trumps posts, no longer does so since it get rid of its fact checkers.[553] X now uses "Community Notes" which allows individual users to question the accuracy of information.[554]

The trend towards declining fact-checking is evident, not only in the U.S., but elsewhere.[555] The number of new fact-checking sites being created has declined, and some existing organizations have "gone quiet."[556] Part of the problem is that fact-checking organizations are not always viewed as "neutral" or "unbiased."[557] Because societies have become so polarized, some choose to ignore fact-checking labels as unreliable.[558] As one commentator asked, "Who fact-checks the fact-checkers?"[559]

546. *Id.*

547. *See* Suhasini Raj, *In India, One Website Battles Rampant Online Misinformation, The New York Times* B1 (Sept. 27, 1992).

548. *See* Hsu & Thompson, *supra* note 481, at B-2.

549. *See* Nyhan, *supra* note 543, at B2.

550. *Id.*

551. *Id.*

552. *Id.* ("The number of fact-checking operations at news organizations and elsewhere has stagnated, and perhaps even fallen.").

553. *See His Fact Checkers Long Gone, supra* note 545, at A1.

554. *See* Hsu & Thompson, *supra* note 481, at B1.

555. *Id.*

556. *Id.*, at B-2.

557. *Id.*

558. *Id.*

559. *Id.* (Quoting Yasmin Green, chief executive of Jigsaw).

Similar concerns were raised regarding a fact checking organization in India because one of the organizers is regarded as opinionated and abrasive.[560] Moreover, users may gravitate to other sources.[561]

There are also concerns regarding whether fact-checking labels are (or will be) accurate. Essentially, someone (the social media platform or an independent group) sets themselves up as the "arbiter of truth," and there is no assurance that they will get it right. In addition, there is always that the fact-checking label will itself involve disinformation and point the reader to inaccurate information. In the case of the Hunter Biden laptop story, the media got it wrong. So, any attempt to link the laptop story to articles questioning its validity, would itself constitute disinformation. Likewise, if the Nunes intelligence report were linked to the Schiff denunciation of that report, the responsive speech might again promote disinformation.

J. WILL THE FREE MARKET SOLVE THE PROBLEMS WITH THE INTERNET?

Perhaps the free market will provide the best solution to disinformation and the other problems created by the internet (e.g., the dissemination of things like child pornography and hate speech). Recently, there have been important developments. The first is a move towards decentralization in the social media industry.[562] For many years, the social media environment has been dominated by a small number of large companies.[563] Upset with the content moderation policies of those companies, which they view as furthering political agendas, some have gravitated to decentralized platforms (e.g., Farcaster) or apps (e.g., Bluesky and Mastodon).[564] Some argue that decentralization will create "chaos and challenges," if there is no central content moderator, but some argue that this type of change is needed.[565]

---

560. *See* Suhasini Raj, *supra* note 549, at B5.

561. *Id.*

562. *See* Sriram Krishnan, *Social Media Will Never Be the Same, The New York Times* A18 (July 17, 2023).

563. *Id.*

564. *Id.*

565. *Id.*

There are already platforms (Gab and Parler) which are very lightly moderated.[566] But these sites are allegedly filled with Nazi symbols, racism commentary, and "other extreme content, including calls to violence."[567] Those who object to such sites, including advertisers, can gravitate to other sites.[568] The free market may dictate whether such sites succeed, depending on whether users avoid the sites because of the content, and whether advertisers avoid them as well.[569] The *Epoch Times*, affiliated with the Chinese Falun Gang movement, has fostered a number of right-wing groups.[570]

Of course, advertisers can influence social media platforms as they decide whether to control or delete disinformation and hate speech.[571] For example, in 2020, Ford Motor Co., Clorox Co., and Denny's Corp. all decided to boycott Facebook because of the platform's content-moderation decisions.[572] There is no question but that advertising plays a huge role in the financial model of social media platforms.[573] Indeed, advertising provides 98% of Meta's revenue.[574] In 2021, Meta had approximately 10 million advertisers which netted the platform $114 billion in advertising revenue, approximately 17% of the global advertising market.[575] At the same time, Meta was extremely valuable to its users given that it has 3.5 billion monthly users, generates a substantial return for its advertisers, and has led to increases in ad pricing.[576] As a result, many advertisers (especially small businesses and individuals) believe that they have no

566. *See* Barbara Ortutay, Tom Krisher & Matt O'Brien, *Musk Takes Over Twitter and Faces Social Media Crash Course, Courier-Journal* 6A (Oct. 30, 2022).

567. *Id.*

568. *Id.*

569. *Id.*; *see also* Patience Haggin & Suzanne Vranica, *Twitter Advertisers Are Uneasy, Courier-Journal* B1 (Oct. 28, 2023).

570. *See* Kevin Roose, *How the Epoch Times Created a Giant Influence Machine, The New York Times* A1 (Oct. 26, 2020).

571. *See* Suzanne Vranica, *Facebook Presses to Contain Ad Boycott, The Wall Street Journal* B1 (June 26, 2020).

572. *See* Micah Maidenberg, *Clorox, Denny's, Ford Join Boycott Of Facebook Ads, The Wall Street Journal* B3 (June 30, 2020).

573. *See Meta Delivers for Its Advertisers, The Wall Street Journal*, Heard on the Street B14 (Nov. 3, 2021).

574. See *Facebook's Stand on Trump Prompts Some to Pause Ads, supra* note 537, at B6.

575. *See Meta Delivers for Its Advertisers, supra* note 575.

576. *Id.*

choice but to advertise on Facebook.[577] Some did move their advertising to Google and LinkedIn, but anticipated returning to Facebook because it is "the best option there is right now in terms of cost and scale."[578] One small business owner suggested that Facebook was keeping small businesses alive.[579] Indeed, in some elections, Twitter (now X) has been a dominant influence.[580]

Meta's reliance on advertising provides activist groups with a potential method for forcing Meta to alter its content-moderation practices, and some advertisers have in fact withheld advertising in an effort to pressure Meta.[581] In 2020, some companies (e.g., Coca-Cola and Unilever) halted their advertising on Facebook,[582] and some advertisers balked at Meta's refusal to block Trump's posts which they regarded as aggressive and misleading.[583] Civil rights groups, concerned about the proliferation of harmful material on Facebook, called for a boycott.[584] In response, Facebook stated that its business interests would not be allowed to dictate or control its policies: "we set our policies based on principles rather than business interests."[585] However, the Anti-Defamation League urged advertisers to consider whether their ads were being placed close to hate speech.[586] When that happened, Facebook seemed to back down and exercise greater control.[587] Certainly, other platforms tried to steal advertisers away from Facebook.[588] In response, Facebook started holding daily meetings with advertisers, and suggested that it was doing more to stamp out

577. See *Facebook's Stand on Trump Prompts Some to Pause Ads, supra* note 537, at B6.

578. *Id.* (quoting an executive at an advertising firm).

579. *Id.*

580. *See* Mike Isaac & Sydney Ember, *For Election Day Chatter, Twitter Still Dominated Its Social Media Peers, The New York Times* B4 (Nov. 9, 2016).

581. See *Facebook's Stand on Trump Prompts Some to Pause Ads, supra* note 537, at B6 (citing the example of an advertiser that withheld at $60,000 advertising campaign because of Facebook's unwillingness to censor Trump.).

582. *See* Laura Forman, *Facebook's Politics Aren't Aging Well, The Wall Street Journal* B11 (June 30, 2020).

583. *Id.*

584. *See Facebook Presses to Contain Ad Boycott, supra* note 573, at B1.

585. *Id.*

586. *Id.*

587. *See* Tiffany Hsu & Mike Isaac, *Count Us Out, Facebook, The New York Times* B1 (July 1, 2020).

588. *Id.*

hate speech,[589] and it announced that it would invest billions of dollars in technology and content moderators in an effort to control content.[590]

As of 2020, boycotts and the threat of boycotts had not significantly undercut Facebook's revenue.[591] Indeed, some view Facebook as a "must" placement for advertisements, but some advertisers asked for greater transparency regarding where their ads will be placed.[592] Facebook did pledge to invest more in its efforts to control hate speech.[593]

But the impact of advertising cuts both ways. In 2020, Trump was a major advertiser on Facebook, spending more than $2.8 million on advertising in a single month.[594] There was parallel spending by the Republican National Committee, as well as by the Make American Great Again Committee and President Trump's reelection campaign, making Trump the 10th largest advertiser on Facebook.[595]

The second major development was Elon Musk's purchase of Twitter in 2022 for $44 billion.[596] In making the purchase, Musk declared that Twitter had "extraordinary potential," and confidently asserted that he would unlock that potential.[597] Following the purchase, Musk made some fairly dramatic changes, including changing the name of the company to "X,"[598] getting rid of its well-known blue and white bird logo,[599] and it's iconic

589. *Id.*

590. *Id.*

591. *See Facebook's Politics Aren't Aging Well, supra* note 584, at B11.

592. *See Facebook Presses to Contain Ad Boycott, supra* note 573, at B1.

593. *Id.*

594. *See Facebook's Stand on Trump Prompts Some to Pause Ads, supra* note 537, at B6.

595. *Id.*

596. *See* Kate Conger, *Musk's Ultimatum: Buy In or Get Out, The New York Times* B5 (Nov. 17, 2022); Kate Conger, *Taking Twitter Private Will Allow for a Vast Makeover Without Having To Consider The Concerns of Investors, The New York Times* B1 (Oct. 29, 2022); Erin Griffith, *It's A Happy Day For The Millions of 'Muskies,' Who Are Anticipating Less Moderation And More Innovation, The New York Times* b1 (Oct. 29, 2022); Ryan Mac & Tiffany Hsu, *Bye, Twitter and Hello X: Musk Begins Rebranding, The New York Times* B1 (July 25, 2023).

597. *See* Lauren Hirsch, *'Twitter Has Extraordinary Potential. I Will Unlock It,' The New York Times* B1 (Apr. 15, 2022).

598. *See* Juliana Kim, *Twitter replaces its bird logo with an X as part of Elon Musk's plan for a super App,* National Public Radio, (July 24, 2023). https://www.npr.org/2023/07/23/1189685146/elon-musk-twitter-logo-bird-x.

599. *See* Mac & Hsu, *supra* note 598.

reference to posts as "tweets."[600] In making the purchase, Musk expressed concern about social media platform censorship, and suggested that X would be focused on creating a free speech environment.[601] He declared that "Free speech is the bedrock of a functioning democracy, and Twitter is the digital town square where matters vital to the future of humanity are debated."[602] Finally, he stated that "Unless the woke mind virus, which is fundamentally anti-science, anti-merit, and anti-human in general, is stopped, civilization will never become multiplanetary."[603]

In an effort to implement his vision, Musk promptly dismissed X's content moderator team.[604] Musk also disbanded Twitter's Trust and Safety Council, which was established to help the company respond to "hate speech, child exploitation, suicide, self-harm and other problems on the platform."[605] A number of Twitter employees resigned, purportedly because of Musk's management style.[606] Musk also altered Twitter's verified blue check marks, which were formerly free, and which were awarded to accounts that Twitter deemed "authentic and notable."[607] Musk began charging for Twitter Blue, but those who paid were allowed to post longer tweets and videos.[608] Musk also limited the number of tweets that users would view, but exempted verified accounts (those that pay a subscription

---

600. *Id.*

601. *See* Shira Ovide, *Buying Twitter, Elon Musk Will Face Reality of His Free Speech Talk on Tech, International New York Times* 1 (Apr. 27, 2022) ("Mr. Musk has not been specific about his plans once he becomes Twitter's owner, but he has bristled when the company has removed posts and barred users, and has said Twitter should be a haven for unfettered expression within the bounds of the law.").

602. *Id.*; *see also* Walter Isaacson, *The Real Story of Musk's Twitter Takeover, The Wall Street Journal* C2 (Sept. 2–3, 2023) (suggesting that Musk believes that it would be good for democracy if Twitter stopped trying to restrict what users could say).

603. *See The Real Story of Musk's Twitter Takeover, supra* note 604, at C2.

604. *See* Kate Conger, Ryan Mac & Mike Isaac, *Confusion and Frustration Reign as Elon Musk Cuts Half of Twitter's Staff, International New York Times* 1 (Nov. 7, 2022).

605. *See* Associated Press, *Musk's Twitter has dissolved its Trust and Safety Council*, National Public Radio, Technology (Dec. 12, 2022). https://www.npr.org/2022/12/12/1142399312/twitter-trust-and-safety-council-elon-musk.

606. *See* Micah Maidenberg, *Under Musk, Twitter Now Looks More Like Space X, The Wall Street Journal* B2 (May 13–4, 2023).

607. *See* Alexa Corse, *Musk Created Opening for Rivals, The Wall Street Journal* B9 (July 8–9, 2023).

608. *See* Mark Saltzman, *Best ways to spot fake Twitter accounts, Courier-Journal* 2F (May 7, 2023).

fee); a restriction that he later relaxed.[609] Finally, Musk reinstated Donald Trump's account.[610] As X's Chief Executive, Linda Yaccarino, wrote, "X is enabling an information independence that is uncomfortable for some people. X is standing at a unique and amazing intersection of Free Speech and Main Street—and the X community is powerful and here to welcome you."[611] X refused to "block content that might degrade confidence in democracy," including claims related to the 2020 election.[612] X still curated posts that incited violence, or that contained verifiably false information about voting locations, voter eligibility, and disability information.[613]

Some are doubtful regarding whether Mush's takeover will work out well: "If Twitter wants to pull back from moderating speech on its site, will people be less willing to hang out where they might be harassed by those who disagree with them and swamped by pitches for crypto currency, fake Gucci handbags or pornography?"[614] As one commentator noted, "Few people want to have their social media feeds clogged by spammy advertisements for crypto currency, terrorist recruitment pitches or harassment of children."[615] There are allegations that Twitter was flooded with misinformation on election day, and that there was less curation of misinformation than before Musk purchased the platform.[616]

When Twitter started out, it was a very free-speech oriented social media company.[617] Many years ago, Twitter's then chief executive declared that Twitter is the "free-speech wing of the free-speech party."[618] Observers interpreted that statement to mean that "Twitter would defend people's

609. *Id.*

610. *See* Ayesha Roscoe & Camila Domonowski, *Elon Musk says he's reinstating Trump's Twitter account*, National Public Radio, Weekend Edition Sunday (Nov. 20, 2022) https://www.npr.org/2022/11/20/1138051094/elon-musk-says-hes-reinstating-donald-trumps-twitter-account.

611. *See* Kate Conger & Tiffany Hsu, *Advertisers Say They Do Not Plan Return to X After Musk's Comments, International New York Times* 4 (Dec. 2, 2023).

612. *See His Fact Checkers Long Gone, supra* note 545, at A1.

613. *Id.*

614. *See Advertisers Say They Do Not Plan Return to X, supra* note 613, at 4.

615. *See* Shira Ovide, *If $43 Billion Bid Prevails, Mercurial Billionaire Could Turn Twitter Into a No-Holds-Barred Tool, The New York Times* B6 (Apr. 15, 2022).

616. *See* Tiffany Hsu, *Musk's Twitter Was Fertile Ground for Election Day Misinformation, The New York Times* B5 (Nov. 10, 2022).

617. *See* Ovide, *supra* note 617, at 1.

618. *Id.*

ability to post whatever they wished and be heard by the world."[619] However, faced with a flood of disinformation and other concerning material, Twitter moved towards more aggressive content moderation.[620] As one commentator described it, Twitter had "pages upon pages of rules prohibiting content such as material that promotes child sexual exploitation, coordinated government propaganda, offers of counterfeit goods and tweets 'wishing for someone to fall victim to a serious accident.'"[621] Facebook also moved to control content.[622] Perhaps, they regarded content moderation as essential to their survival. Yik Yak, a social media app which became known for racist, sexist and threatening speech, folded up (although it was restarted in 2021).[623] Some believe that its initial collapse was due to a lack of content moderation.[624]

So, Musk's purchase of Twitter, which he renamed as "X" and "tweets" were renamed "posts,"[625] promised a "back to the future" approach to content moderation. Musk's goal was to transform X into an "everything app" designed to create "unlimited interactivity," including the sharing of social media posts, ordering dinner, transferring money, and creating a "global marketplace for ideas, goods, services and opportunities."[626] In addition, Musk pledged a strong commitment to freedom of expression: "Mr. Musk plans to bring his commitment to a more hands-off approach on speech to a company that has struggled to reconcile freewheeling conversation with content that appeals to advertisers."[627] As a result, Musk stated that he wants "the platform to be a destination for wide-ranging discourse and disagreements."[628] He stated that he hopes that "even my

619. *Id.*

620. *Id.*

621. *Id.*

622. *Id.*

623. *See* Valeriya Safronova, *The Rise and Fall of a Messaging App, The New York Times* A2 (May 28, 2017).

624. *Id.*

625. *See* Kate Conger, *So, What Do We Call That Bird App Now?, The New York Times* B1 & B4 (Aug. 3, 2023).

626. *Id.*, at B4.

627. *See* Cara Lombardo, Meghan Bobrowsky & Georgia Wells, *Musk Strikes Deal to Buy Twitter, The Wall Street Journal* A1 (Apr. 26, 2022).

628. *Id.*

worst critics remain on Twitter, because that is what free speech means."[629] He went to state that, "Given that Twitter serves as the de facto public town square, failing to adhere to free speech principles fundamentally undermines democracy."[630]

A number of users were upset when Musk limited the number of posts that a user could make (a move that was purportedly undertaken to reduce spam and bots on the platform and prevent data scraping), as well as by X's decision to charge for the use of TweetDeck (which allows users to see multiple panels of tweets simultaneously).[631] A number of advertisers, concerned about having their products displayed in proximity to hate speech, withdrew their advertising from X.[632] Prior to Musk's purchase, Twitter reportedly received $4.7 billion in advertising revenue.[633] Over one five week period after the purchase, advertising was down 59%,[634] and appeared to be declining further.[635] Although both General Motors and Volkswagen withdrew their advertising, X saw growth in other areas that Twitter traditionally shied away from (e.g., online gambling and marijuana advertising).[636]

Unquestionably, advertising revenue had a substantial impact on X's bottom line.[637] As the head of a marketing consulting company stated: "There is no advertising value that would offset the reputational risk of going back on the platform."[638] As a result, X was under some financial

---

629. *Id.*

630. *Id.*, at A16.

631. *See* Tim Higgins, *Twitter Rivals Press Amid User Frustration, The Wall Street Journal* B1 (July 5, 2023).

632. *See* Bloomberg Law News, *Threads Poses Legal Challenges for Brands and Corporate Counsel* July 13, 2023) (""Twitter's significant downgrading of its content moderation activities drove a number of brands to suspend their marketing activities on the platform out of fear of being associated with distasteful, if not outright, hate speech.").

633. *See Meta Threads a Fine Needle, The Wall Street Journal*, Heard on the Street B12 (July 7, 2023).

634. *See* Ryan Mac & Tiffany Hsu, *Musk Era Has Ravaged Twitter Ads, The New York Times* B1 (June 6, 2023).

635. *See Meta Threads a Fine Needle, supra* note 635, at B12.

636. *See Musk Era Has Ravaged Twitter Ads, supra* note 636, at B1.

637. *Id.*; *see also* Shira Ovide, *The Ad Empires of Google and Facebook, The New York Times* B2 (Nov. 1 2021); *Facebook Presses to Contain Ad Boycott, supra* note 573, at B1.

638. *See Advertisers Say They Do Not Plan Return to X, supra* note 613, at 4.

stress,[639] and overall value allegedly plummeted by approximately 55% from $44 billion to $19 billion.[640] That alleged decline was not reflected in X's stock price which, by mid-2023, was near the price that Musk had paid ($54.20 per share) to purchase the company.[641] Musk claimed that he has a plan to revive the company by offering new services,[642] and creating an app "where you can basically do anything you want on our system,"[643] including online banking,[644] video messaging,[645] consuming news,[646] paying rent,[647] paying fines,[648] dating,[649] making medical appointments,[650] and job recruiting.[651]

Following a rumor that Musk had endorsed an anti-Semitic conspiracy theory, a number of X advertisers either halted their advertising on the platform or are contemplating doing so.[652] Included are large companies such as IBM, Apple, Disney, and other major companies, involving 200 or more advertising units.[653] The downturn in advertising came at a bad time for X, during the Christmas buying season, involving Black Friday and Cyber Monday.[654] When Musk responded with expletives, many advertisers indicated that they would not return: "At least half a dozen marketing agencies said the brands they represent were standing firm against advertising on X, while others said they had advised advertisers to stop posting

639. *Id.*

640. *See* Ryan Mac, *Since Musk Bought X, Value Has Plummeted to About $19 Billion, the New York Times* B-3 (Oct. 31, 2023). ("X, the company formerly known as Twitter, handed out stock grants to employees that showed it was worth about $19 billion, down about 5 percent from the $44 billion that Elon Musk paid to buy the firm a year ago....")

641. *Id.*

642. *Id.* (Musk "laid out how he believed X could serve as an all-purpose app with an array of features, including dating services and job recruiting.").

643. *Id.*

644. *See* Kim, *supra* note 600.

645. *Id.*

646. *Id.*

647. *Id.*

648. *Id.*

649. *See* Bloomberg, *supra* note 634.

650. *Id.*

651. *Id.*

652. *See* Ryan Mac & Kate Conger, *X May Lose up to $75 Million in Revenue as More Advertisers Pull Out, International New York Times* Nov. 27, 2023).

653. *Id.*

654. *Id.*

anything on the platform. Some temporary spending pauses that advertisers enacted against X are likely to turn into permanent freezes, they added, with Mr. Musk's comments giving them no incentive to return."[655] Afterwards, X hired a new chief executive, Linda Yaccarino, who was charged with helping bring back advertisers.[656] Nevertheless, many believe that X remains the "go-to for tens of millions of Americans, especially for breaking news and politics."[657] Given that X has more than 368 million active users, the platform remains "one of the most popular."[658]

X's confusion has created opportunities for competitors,[659] including Mastodon, Bluesky, Spill[660] and Post.[661] Following Musk's purchase, Tumblr (a rival network) saw an uptick in usage,[662] and Bluesky usage more than doubled.[663] But many questioned whether these other platforms provided an adequate substitute for Twitter.[664] Each had their own problems, including Reddit (siloed by topics), LinkedIn (work focused), Pinterest (focused on hobbies), TikTok (video-centric), and Facebook (it "has its own problems").[665]

A more serious competitor, Meta, entered the market on July 5, 2023, with a similar social media platform called "Threads",[666] which was a spin-off from Instagram,[667] and was designed to create "a prime place

---

655. *See Advertisers Say They Do Not Plan Return to X, supra* note 613, at 4.

656. *See* Corse, *supra* note 2; Tim Higgins, *Can Twitter's Odd Couple Make It Work?, The Wall Street Journal* B1 (June 10–11, 2023).

657. *See Best ways to spot fake Twitter accounts, supra* note 610, at 2F.

658. *Id.*

659. *See Musk Created Opening for Rivals, supra* note 609, at B9 ("the Twitter that Meta Platforms is now competing with is a much different service than the one Elon Musk took over eight months ago—in ways that many users aren't happy about.").

660. *See* Joanna Stern & Ann-Marie Alcantara, *Meta's Threads Gives Twitter Some Real Competition, The Wall Street Journal* B1 (July 7, 2023).

661. *See Meta Threads a Fine Needle, supra* note 635, at B12.

662. *See* Rebecca Fishbein, *Welcome to Tumblr. Now Go Away, International New York Times* (Dec. 13, 2022).

663. *See Meta Threads a Fine Needle, supra* note 635.

664. *See* Brian X. Chen, *Lessons From the Turmoil at Twitter, The New York Times* B1 (Nov 17, 2022).

665. *Id.*

666. *See* Bloomberg, *supra* note 634.

667. *See* Brian X. Chen & Mike Isaac, *How Threads Stacks Up Against Twitter, The New York Times*, Tech Fix B1 (July 13, 2023).

for public, real-time conversations."[668] Meta described Threads as a place "where communities come together to discuss everything from the topics you care about today to what'll be trending tomorrow."[669] Moreover, the goal was to create a more "positive" environment.[670] The Threads app was free and could be downloaded from the Apple or Google app stores, and connected to a user's Instagram account.[671] Basically, the app enables the user to publish short memos.[672] While the app allows users to embed photos, the primary focus is on text[673] although users can post short videos.[674] Unlike Twitter (X), where free accounts were limited to 280 characters, Threads permits 500 characters in a single post (whereas Twitter Blue allowed individuals to post long essays).[675] Also, unlike X, where all posts from an individual appear in reverse chronological order, users see different posts based on their interests (not necessarily in chronological order).[676] However, it appears that Threads (and X, for that matter) are used more by "big brands, celebrities, politicians and media outlets" than by ordinary people as a social network.[677] Initially, Threads was not constructed to allow users to individually message others.[678] Threads contrasts with TikTok and Instagram's Reels which involve lots of videos of celebrities and influencers.[679]

Meta's stated goal in creating Threads was to establish a platform that was "safer" and "less toxic" then X,[680] and it invested heavily in content moderation.[681] Threads made it clear that it would reject both hate speech and sexually explicit posts in an effort to provide "advertisers "with more

668. *Id.*

669. *See* Kelvin Chan, *Meta Looks to Target Twitter With Rival App, Courier-Journal* 6A (July 5, 2023).

670. See *Meta's Threads Gives Twitter Some Real Competition, supra* note 664, at B1.

671. *Id.*

672. *Id.*

673. *Id.*

674. See *Meta's Threads Gives Twitter Some Real Competition, supra* note 664, at B1.

675. *See* Chen, *supra* note 668, at B1.

676. *Id.*

677. *Id.*

678. *Id.*

679. *Id.*

680. *See* Bloomberg, *supra* note 634.

681. *Id.*

comfort concerning the social media environment."[682] Threads signed up more than 30 million users on the first day,[683] 75 million users in the first week,[684] and more than 100 million users in the first month.[685] and various celebrities gravitated to the platform.[686] However, Twitter was much larger than Threads with 535 million monetized monthly users.[687] An independent group, Insider Intelligence, estimated that Twitter has about 363.7 million monthly users.[688] So, while some question whether Threads will be "fatal" to X, it clearly creates a challenge.[689]

Of course, there is no guarantee that Threads will replace X. In 2011, Google rolled out Google+ with the idea of replacing Facebook.[690] Even though Google was a large company with billions of users, the effort failed.[691] By 2018, Google+ was relegated to "the ash heap of history."[692] Complicating the situation is the fact that Threads has limitations. For example, Threads has a limitation of 500 characters per post.[693] For some social media influencers, the Federal Trade Commission imposes mandatory disclosure requirements which must be set forth in the post itself rather than buried in hashtags,[694] and the size requirements coupled with the disclosure requirements may make it difficult to convey one's message in the remaining allotted space.[695]

After an initial surge in new users, Threads usage fell off.[696] In July of 2023, usage was down 70% to 13 million active users, and the number

682. *Id.*

683. *See Musk Created Opening for Rivals, supra* note 609, at B9.

684. *Id.*

685. *See Social Media Will Never Be The Same, supra* note 564, at A18.

686. *See* Yiwen Lu, *What Happened When 15 of Twitter's Top Celebrities Joined Threads. How Active Are They?, The New York Times* B1-2 (July 31, 2023).

687. *See Musk Created Opening for Rivals, supra* note 609, at B9.

688. *Id.*

689. *Id.*

690. *See* Mike Isaac, *Overnight Success of Twitter Rival Threads May Yet Slip Away, The New York Times* A1 (July 12,2023).

691. *Id.*

692. *Id.*

693. *See* Bloomberg, *supra* note 634.

694. *Id.*

695. *Id.*

696. *See* Lindsey Choo, *Threads Is Facing Pressure as Usage Falls, The Wall Street Journal* B1 (July 22–23, 2023).

of minutes per day per user also declined from 19 minutes a day to four minutes a day.[697] Some analysts view the declines as a reflection of the fact that users cannot do as much on Threads as on X.[698] As a result, Threads might seem more "dull" than Instagram, and users may not be posting as frequently as they did on Twitter.[699] Moreover, there appear to be more corporate brands making posts on Threads.[700] To reverse the decline, Threads considered creating new functions, including the ability to have multiple accounts, to edit posts, and to have chronological feed options.[701] In addition, Threads was trying to distinguish itself from Twitter on the basis that it is not encouraging discussions of politics or hard news.[702] In light of these changes, one analyst predicted that Threads would ultimately succeed: "Meta definitely has the patience, they have the money, and they have the engineering talent."[703]

Of course, the free market may also result in greater societal division. For example, after Donald Trump was prohibited from posting on Twitter, he started his own social media network, Truth Social, which was purportedly dedicated to freedom of expression.[704] The platform has led to "a vibrant right-wing ecosystem increasingly brimming with activity."[705] The platform quickly accumulated as many as 1.7 million visitors (albeit small by Facebook and Twitter standards, but larger than platforms like Gab, Parler, Gettr, MeWe and Minds), and Donald Trump now primarily relies on Truth Social to disseminate his message.[706] In addition, the platform has attracted "a coalition of right-wing Americans, including conservative celebrities like Dan Bongino, the radio host and television commentator; political firebrands like Representative Marjorie Taylor Greene of Georgia; and a constellation of conspiracy theory peddlers,

697. *Id.*

698. *Id.*

699. *Id.*

700. *Id.* (Quoting Debra Ahol Williamson described as a principal analysis at Insider Intelligence, a market research firm.)

701. *Id.*

702. *Id.*

703. *Id.*

704. *See* Stuart A. Thompson & Matthew Goldstein, *Truth Social's Influence Grows Despite Its Business Problems, International New York Times* 1 (Nov. 8, 2022).

705. *Id.*

706. *Id.*

far-right influencers and rank-and-file voters."[707] Of course, the problem with platforms like Truth Social is that they encourage people to silo into platforms where they encounter only people who agree with them, and discourages them from engaging with a range of views.

Whether Truth Social will survive Elon Musk's takeover of X is unclear.[708] Truth Social's *raison d'etre*, to provide an outlet for speech being censored by other social media platforms, seems less important as Musk makes X more free-speech friendly.[709] As of April, 2023, Truth Social had 1.3 million installs compared to Twitter's 200 million active users, and even the number of Trump's followers had declined to one million (from the 89 million he once had on Twitter).[710]

K. IS EDUCATION THE ANSWER?

In some countries, initiatives have been started to help educate the population about how to deal with disinformation.[711] In Germany, for example, there are organizations such as the Business Council for Democracy and Weltoffenes Sachsen.[712] In the U.S., there are entities called the Civic Alliance and the Leadership Now Project.[713] In addition, some companies are offering education to their employees.[714] These efforts help educate individuals about how to deal with such things as hate speech and disinformation.[715] Some of these efforts focus on civics and democracy.[716] Organizers make a conscious effort to include only voluntary participants, and to remain free of ideological bias.[717]

---

707. *Id.*

708. *See* Matthew Goldstein, Kenneth P. Vogel & Ryan Mac, *A Musk Takeover of Twitter Could Endanger Trump's Truth Social, The New York Times* B3 (Apr. 23, 2022).

709. *Id.*

710. *Id.*

711. *See* Melissa Eddy, *Disinformation's Impact on the Workplace, The New York Times* A-6 (Oct. 29, 2023).

712. *Id.*

713. *Id.*

714. *Id.*

715. *Id.*

716. *Id.*

717. *Id.*

L. GOVERNMENTAL MANIPULATION OF SOCIAL MEDIA PLATFORM CENSORSHIP

Moreover, there is a very real risk that governmental officials will try to unduly influence the censorship decisions of social media platforms. The Twitter files reveal that the U.S. government has interfered with Twitter in an effort to encourage Twitter to suppress content.[718] The Twitter Files suggest that the FBI warned Twitter "to expect a flood of fake news out of Russia just in time for the election."[719] Indeed, there were approximately 150 emails between Yoel Roth, Twitter's chief in charge of weeding out inappropriate content, and FBI officials over a two year period.[720] Roth admitted that these emails played a role in his decision to quash the Hunter Biden story.[721] The FBI even went so far as to give Twitter officials temporary security clearances, so they could receive classified briefings prior to the 2020 election.[722] In addition, the FBI notified Twitter regarding tweets that it regarded as "suspicious," and suggested that the tweets should be suppressed.[723] If governmental pressure is involved, social media platform censorship may be politically rather than objectively based.

If there is a high level of governmental interference with social media platform content decisions, it is not clear that social media platforms should be treated as private actors for purposes of the First Amendment. For years, congressional committees have called the heads of social media platforms before them, and pressured those companies to engage in more censorship.[724] Whether such pressure is enough to transform the actions of social media companies into state actors is unclear, but there is much more governmental involvement in social media platform censorship, including pressure from the White House. According to information released by Twitter, the Trump Administration asked for help in restricting messages that might encourage panic-buying by consumers at the

---

718. *Id.*
719. *Id.*
720. *Id.*
721. *Id.*
722. *Id.*
723. *Id.*
724. *See* Restuccia & Needleman, *supra* note 18, at A6.

start of the pandemic, while the Biden Administration called for Twitter to silence speakers who dissented from the official government line.[725] Moreover, there is evidence of constant communication between the FBI and Twitter officials responsible for content moderation.[726] In *Missouri v. Biden*,[727] a federal district court concluded that governmental officials had tried to coerce social media companies into censoring content, and held that their content decisions should be treated as state action (rather than private action).

Although Twitter sometimes refused the FBI's requests for censorship, the company was paid $3,415,323 to cover the cost of working with the feds. While it is not unethical for Twitter to be compensated for its efforts, the sheer size of the payment suggests a level of government influence over content decisions.[728] Moreover, there is plenty of evidence showing that the federal government worked the refs like an aggressive football coach, hectoring and goading the company's executives into exercising ever-stricter control over what users are permitted to say.[729] This was true for not only the FBI, but also the White House.[730] Since the US government has the power to make things very unpleasant for companies that resist, the temptation to comply may prove irresistible.[731]

---

725. *See* Bray, *supra* note 238.

726. *Id.*

727. ___ F. Supp.3d ___, 2023 WL 4335270 (W.D. La. 2023).

728. *Id.*

729. *Id.*

730. *See* Jenin Younes & Arrno Kheriaty, *The White House Covid Censorship Machine, The Wall Street Journal* A 17 (Jan. 9, 2023) ("Newly released documents show that the White House played a major role in censoring Americans on social media.").

731. *See* Bray, *supra* note 238.

M. IS A DISINFORMATION BOARD THE SOLUTION?

One possible way to control fake news is to establish systems designed to regulate and control fake news.[732] For example, the Department of Homeland Security (DHS) proposed the creation of a Disinformation Board to respond to false information.[733] In theory, the Board was designed to create a set of standardized practices that could be used by federal agencies to respond to violent threats against the nation.[734] However, the effort was halted when it was met with a firestorm of criticism that led to a suspension of the Board.[735]

Senator Amy Klobuchar suggested an alternate but similar system. Her 2021 proposal was to threaten to remove liability protections from social media platforms if they did not curtail misinformation during public health emergencies.[736] She would have ceded authority regarding health information to the Department of Health and Human Services.[737] Under her proposal, if a company runs afoul of government guidelines, it would lose Section 230 protection and be subject to litigation regarding the posts.[738] The Klobuchar proposal was met by similar objections as the Disinformation Board,[739] and was never enacted.[740]

Should there be a federal disinformation board to deal with disinformation in society? In fact, the creation of such a board would run counter to the U.S.' free speech tradition, which generally denies government the

732. *See* Michael P. Goodyear, *Priam's Folly: United Stats v. Alvarez and the Fake News Trojan Horse*, 73 Stanford L. Rev. (Online) 194 (2021) (suggesting that courts apply a lower standard of review, and that certain public health initiatives be subject to fake news regulation); Schuyler, *supra* note 200, at 240 (suggesting that fake news should be controlled through a notice-and-correction-or-exclusion procedure).

733. *See* Deepa Shivaram, *DHS Pauses a Board Created to Combat Disinformation Amid a Campaign to Discredit It*, National Public Radio, Politics (May 18, 2022), https://www.npr.org/2022/05/18/1099848240/dhs-disinformation-group-pause.

734. See Nicole Seganga, What is DHS' Disinformation Governance Board and why is everyone so mad about it?, CBS News (May 6, 2022). https://www.cbsnews.com/news/what-is-dhs-disinformation-governance-board-and-why-is-everyone-so-mad-about-it/.

735. *See* Shivaram, *supra* note 737.

736. *See* Siabhan Hughes, *Bill Targets Health Misinformation, The Wall Street Journal* A6 (July 23, 2021).

737. *Id.*

738. *Id.*

739. *Id.*

740. *Id.*

ability to regulate the content of speech (except in limited situations). Even if society could agree that we should create and maintain a "disinformation board," it would face questions regarding the scope of the board's authority and jurisdiction. Should the board police disinformation on the internet? Should it intervene and check false statements by public officials like Clapper, Trump, Obama, and Biden? Should it also police media bias and "call it out"?

Of course, the more critical question is whether a disinformation board should be given the power to prohibit, criminalize, sanction or enjoin the dissemination of disinformation. Presumably, any attempt to prohibit the dissemination of disinformation would be treated as a "prior restraint" on speech and would be presumptively unconstitutional.[741] And it seems unlikely that the courts would allow the government to criminalize speech which does not involve fraud, perjury, or some other objective basis for suppression.

Even if we could agree that a disinformation board should exist, would the American people trust the government to determine what speech is false, and to prohibit it? As a general rule, governments do not have the power to ban speech simply because it is false. Moreover, any assertion of authority of this nature would run counter to the idea that false speech is protected. *United States v. Alvarez*[742] involved an individual's false assertion that he won the Congressional Medal of Honor. While *Alvarez* recognized that individuals can be prosecuted for false speech in limited and defined circumstances (e.g., perjury in a judicial proceeding or making false statements to a governmental official or agency),[743] the Court held that he could not be convicted for making a false statement to the effect that he had won the medal.

Alvarez is consistent with the Court's general free speech jurisprudence. If the legitimacy of our governmental system depends on the consent of the governed, it is inconsistent with that system to give government the power to control, limit and suppress the range of ideas that the people can hear or consider. As the U.S. Supreme Court recognized in

741. *See Near v. Minnesota*, 283 U.S. 697 (1931).
742. 567 U.S. 709 (2012).
743. *Id.*

Ashcroft v. American Civil Liberties Union,[744] as "a general matter, the First Amendment means that government has no power to restrict expression because of its message, its ideas, its subject matter, or its content."[745] Likewise, in *Cohen v. California*,[746] the Court flatly recognized that the "constitutional right of free expression ... is designed and intended to remove governmental restraints from the arena of public discussion, putting the decision as to what views shall be voiced largely into the hands of each of us, in the hope that use of such freedom will ultimately produce a more capable citizenry and more perfect polity and in the belief that no other approach would comport with the premise of individual dignity and choice upon which our political system rests." *Cohen* went on to state that it would not "indulge the facile assumption that one can forbid particular words without also running a substantial risk of suppressing ideas in the process. Indeed, governments might soon seize upon the censorship of particular words as a convenient guise for banning the expression of unpopular views."[747]

Of course, the modern aversion to governmental control of speech has deep roots. As previously noted, following Johannes Gutenberg invention of the printing press in the fifteenth century, many kings feared that widespread use of the press might undermine their power, and therefore they sought to control and limit its use.[748] For example, the English government used the decision in *de Libellis Famosis*,[749] to criminally prosecute those who criticized the Crown or religious officials of high station, and it did so in an effort to prosecute, intimidate, and silence governmental critics.[750] Moreover, under English law, a defendant could not rely on the defense of truth; indeed truth was treated as an aggravating factor: "Since maintaining a proper regard for government was the goal of this new offense, it followed that truth was just as reprehensible as falsehood

---

744. 535 U.S. 564, 573 (2002).

745. *See also United States v. Alvarez*, 567 U.S. 709 (2012); *Brown v. Entertainment Merchants Ass'n*, 564 U.S. 756 (2011).

746. 403 U.S. 15, 24 (1971).

747. *Id.* at 26.

748. *See* WEAVER & HANCOCK, *supra* note 197, at 5.

749. 77 Eng. Rep. 250 (Star Chamber 1606).

750. *See Seditious Libel and the Lost Guarantee*, *supra* note 330, at 98.

and was eliminated as a defense."[751] Similar restrictions were imposed in the American colonies where the British prosecuted "criticism directed against the government or public officials" because it was considered to be "a threat against public order and a criminal offense," and again truth was not a defense.[752]

In general, the Court's decisions have suggested that government should have limited authority to control either thought or speech. As the Court stated in *Ashcroft v. American Civil Liberties Union*,[753] "First Amendment freedoms are most in danger when the government seeks to control thought or to justify its laws for that impermissible end. The right to think is the beginning of freedom, and speech must be protected from the government because speech is the beginning of thought." Likewise, in *Virginia v. Black*,[754] the Court stated that the "hallmark of the protection of free speech is to allow free trade in ideas—even ideas that the overwhelming majority of people might find distasteful or discomforting." Professor Emerson argued that the "only justification for suppressing an opinion is that those who seek to suppress it are infallible in their judgment of the truth. But no individual or group can be infallible, particularly in a constantly changing world."[755] As a result, through "the acquisition of new knowledge, the toleration of new ideas, the testing of opinion in open competition, the discipline of rethinking its assumptions, a society will be better able to reach common decisions that will meet the needs and aspirations of its members."[756]

Governmental attempts to regulate disinformation might lead to a number of thorny questions regarding the proper role of government in our constitutional system. If Congress decides to create a Disinformation Board to regulate fake news, would U.S. society feel comfortable giving the Disinformation Board the power to determine which ideas and facts are "true," and which are "false," and to prosecute those who espouse ideas and facts that the Board regards as completely false? Would

---

751. *Id.*

752. *See* Lawrence W. Crispo, Jill M. Slansky & Geanene M. Yriarte, *Jury Nullification: Law Versus Anarchy*, 31 LOY. L.A. L. REV. 1, 7 (1997).

753. 535 U.S. 234, 253 (2002).

754. 538 U.S. 343, 358 (2003).

755. Emerson, *supra* note 197, at 882.

756. *Id.*

we feel comfortable giving the Disinformation Board the power to license news, based on its truth or falsity, and the power to prohibit false facts and ideas? Would it also be allowed the censor the speech of politicians or media organizations? My guess is no.

If the Disinformation Board were given such authority, how would it go about determining what qualifies as disinformation? In order to qualify as false, must something be "completely false," or could something be regarded as disinformation if it is simply biased, slanted in favor of one side of a debate, or presents an incomplete factual picture? Many might fear whether government would exercise such power impartially. For example, suppose that during the Obama Administration, the Disinformation Board had decided that climate change was a "fact," and that climate change denial was fake news. Could the Disinformation Board have criminally prosecuted those who argued that climate change was a hoax? Would the Board have been free to redefine the truth regarding climate change when Donald Trump came to power? In other words, could the Board have changed its definition of the "truth," dismissed all charges against climate change deniers, and criminally prosecuted those who were arguing that climate change is a real phenomenon? Would we, as a society, feel comfortable giving the government to power to declare that facts like these are undeniably true, and subject to criminal sanctions anyone who refuses to accept them? Given that the last three administrations have lied to the American people at various times, would we be comfortable giving them the power to censor disinformation?

Of course, the Disinformation Board might be given the power to prohibit not only "completely false" ideas or facts, but also to prohibit slanted, biased or partially false statements. In other words, the Disinformation Board might be given the power to impose the equivalent of the Federal Communication Commission's "fairness doctrine,"[757] but extend that doctrine beyond broadcasting to all communications, including newspapers, cable television, the internet and satellite communications. If the Board were given the power to prosecute for bias or lack of "fairness," it might have lots to prosecute on both sides of the political spectrum (as the prior

757. *See Red Lion Broadcasting Co. v. Federal Communications Commission*, 395 U.S. 367 (1969) (The "Fairness Doctrine" required that broadcasters' discussion of public issues give fair coverage to both sides of those issues.).

examples illustrate). Those on the left might argue that Fox News and other right-wing commentators should be criminally prosecuted for their biased views and statements. At the same time, those on the right, who believe that the media has a left-wing bias, might argue for the prosecution of a wide swath of left wing journalists. Although I would personally find it offensive to prosecute anyone for simply expressing their ideas, no matter how biased or slanted, if I were forced (at gun point on threat of death) to name a news personality who exhibits extreme bias and lack of objectivity, I would name a particular National Public Radio program host; someone whose work I often find highly offensive because it is so biased and slanted. Would the Disinformation Board be free to criminally prosecute the NPR host for bias and slanted news coverage? Would the host have a defense if there is *some truth* to his statements of fact and articulated ideas? I'm not confident that any of this would be a good idea.

In the final analysis, even though disinformation can distort the democratic process, the Court made clear in decisions like *New York Times, Inc. v. Sullivan*,[758] and *Near v. Minnesota*,[759] that information should not be withheld from the public even though it may contain an element of untruth. In the case of Hunter Biden's laptop, the American people were denied accurate information, during an election, because it was regarded as misinformation. Not only the media, but also the government and social media platforms sought to suppress the Hunter Biden story.

---

758. 376 U.S. 254, 269 (1964).
759. 283 U.S. 697 (1931).

CHAPTER X

THE RISE OF BOTS AND ARTIFICIAL INTELLIGENCE

In addition to the problem of disinformation, the internet has been beset by "bots" in what one commentator described as a "'Cambrian explosion' of robotics technologies"[1] with millions and millions of bot accounts and bot messages.[2] While some bots are designed to communicate information, others are used to perpetuate fraud.[3] Bots should be distinguished from "trolls," which are human beings which have malicious intent, or a "cyborg" which is a human managed account that sometimes employs

1. *See* Farhad Manjoo, *How Twitter Is Being Gamed to Feed Misinformation, The New York Times* B-1 & B-7 (June 1, 2017).

2. *See* Ashley Fox, *Automated Political Speech: Regulating Social Media Bots in the Political Sphere*, 18 First Amendment L. Rev. 114 (2020); Michael Newberg, *As Many as 48 Million Twitter Accounts Aren't People, Says Study*, CNBC (Mar. 10, 2017, 1:09 PM), https://www.cnbc.com/2017/03/10/nearly-48-million-twitter-accounts-could-be-bots-says-study.html; *see also* Jack Nicas, *Does Facebook Really Know How Many Fake Accounts It Has?*, N.Y. Times (Jan. 30, 2019), https://www.nytimes.com/2019/01/30/technology/facebook-fake-accounts.html. At one point, Facebook indicated that it had blocked some 4.5 billion accounts over a nine month period, of which a majority were bot accounts. *See* Jack Nicas, *Why Social Networks Can't Catch the Fakes, The New York Times* B3 (Dec. 14, 2020).

3. *See* Belle Lin, *Bad Chatbots Pose New Threat on Web, The Wall Street Journal*, B1 (Feb. 29, 2024) (describing chatbots like "BadGPT" and "FraudGPT" which cybercriminals use, in conjunction with AI, to send out phishing emails, and to create malware and fake websites.).

bots, both of which can disseminate information.[4] One estimate suggests that there are as many as 48 million Twitter accounts that are run by bots rather than human beings, and which accounted for as much as twenty-five percent of all tweets in the 2016 presidential election.[5] A second estimate concluded that there as many as 91 million fake accounts on Facebook, and 24 million bots on Instagram,[6] and that nearly half of all tweets about Covid-19 were by bots.[7] A Pew Research Center study suggested that nearly two-thirds of all tweeted links were shared by bots and had links to news and current events.[8] The net effect is that, at one point, "YouTube had as much traffic from bots masquerading as people as it did from real human visitors."[9] Bots are flooding the internet with comments, Facebook "likes," and other forms of communication.[10] And, of course, bots can easily spread both disinformation and offensive speech.[11] Some believe that chatbots will become ever more sophisticated.[12]

Some question the data regarding bots.[13] After National Public Radio aired a piece on the subject, suggesting that bots were prevalent on the internet, one commentator found that NPR had no research study to back up its claims.[14] On the contrary, it had simply relied on the assertion of a researcher who was unwilling to share her data on the subject.[15] His conclusion: "Unless we posit that there are more bots than people out there on social media, there needs to be extremely good data to make a claim that half of all conversation about Covid-19 is from bots. The burden of

---

4. *See* Siobhan Roberts, *Was That a Bot Post? Maybe, Maybe Not, The New York Times* B1 (June 16, 2020).

5. *See Automated Political Speech, supra* note 2, at 117.

6. *Id.*

7. *See Was That a Bot Post? Maybe, supra* note 4, at B1.

8. *See* Stefan Wojcik, *5 Things to Know about Bots on Twitter*, Pew Research Center, Factank (Apr. 9, 2018).

9. *See* Michael H. Keller, *The Business of Serving Up YouTube Views: Streams Are for Sale, Eyes Not Included, The New York Times* A18 (Aug. 12, 2018).

10. *Id.*

11. See Kevin Roose, *A.I. Poses "Risk of Extinction," Tech Leaders Warn, The New York Times* A1 (May 31, 2023).

12. *See* Oliver Whang, *Human Power to Process Cues May Be Next Frontier for Bots, The New York Times* A1 (Mar. 28, 2023).

13. *See Was That a Bot Post? Maybe, supra* note 4, at B1.

14. *Id.*

15. *Id.*

proof is huge and has not been met."[16] Another story indicated that 30% to 49% of all tweets regarding Black Lives Matter, and related conspiracy theories, came from bots.[17] These claims were also met with skepticism.[18] One commentator noted that: "Dropping a statistic into the world without any explanation of what kind of content is attached is particularly troubling."[19] There are also questions about whether bots influence the outcome of elections: "The precis: 'Social bots have influenced elections. Does it sound plausible? Yes. Is it scientifically founded? Not at all.'"[20] Indeed, some claim that humans are sometimes mistaken for bots.[21] Moreover, bots may be interacting with each other more than with humans.[22]

The existence of a large number of bots seems to have been proven by a rulemaking proceeding conducted by the U.S. Federal Communications Commission (FCC) regarding whether to repeal its net neutrality requirement. During that rulemaking, the FCC received an absolutely extraordinary number (23 million) of public comments.[23] When the comments were analyzed by a machine learning engineer, the analysis suggested that at least 1.3 million comments were submitted using stolen or misused identities, and that more than 445,000 comments came from Russian or German email accounts.[24] Many fake comments were submitted by bots which were detectable because they involved duplicate comments differentiated only by the substitution of a synonym for a particular word.[25]

---

16. *Id.*
17. *Id.*
18. *Id.*
19. *Id.*
20. *Id.*
21. *Id.*
22. *Id.*, at B1.
23. *See* Jason Tashea, *No Comment: The FCC*, ABA JOURNAL 33 (Aug. 2018).
24. *Id.*
25. *See* Brian X. Chen, *The Internet Trolls Have Won. Get Used to It, The New York Times* B-7 (Aug. 9, 2018); *see also* James V. Grimaldi & Paul Overberg, *Millions Post Comments on Regulations—Many Are Fake, The New York Times* A1 (Dec. 13, 2017).

A. THE RISE OF ARTIFICIAL INTELLIGENCE

Bots are supplemented by AI which involves both natural language processing and machine learning.[26] "ChatGPT is a free chatbot tool, which has become profoundly popular having gained 100 million users within the first two months after its release,[27] and it is capable of answering questions with convincingly human-like responses."[28] It can be used for both political and non-political purposes. For example, if an individual wants to make a pumpkin pie, the individual can inquire regarding the required ingredients.[29] AI can also be used to assist doctors and nurses in making medical decisions,[30] and it has the capacity to recognize objects,[31] write descriptive listings for Facebook Marketplace,[32] analyze the text of articles,[33] and speak to users with spoken responses.[34] For example, one can ask ChatGPT to play the role of a friend, a therapist, or a teacher and chat about relevant things,[35] or it can read a bedtime story to children.[36] The growing importance of AI is underscored by the fact that Microsoft has invested $13 billion in one AI project.[37]

A.I. has produced impressive results.[38] For example, researchers asked an A.I. system to produce a mathematical proof showing that there were

---

26. *See How Meta Platforms Plans to Incorporate AI Into Its Products, The Wall Street Journal* R8 (Oct. 24, 2023) (interview with Meta's Chief Product Officer Chris Cox).

27. *See* Mike Isaac, *Overnight Success of Twitter Rival Threads May Yet Slip Away, The New York Times* A1 (July 12, 2023).

28. *See* Matt O'Brien, *ChatGPT Chief Favors AI Regulations, Courier-Journal* 16A (May 17, 2023).

29. *Id.*

30. *See What Is the Government's Role in Developing—and Regulating—AI?, The Wall Street Journal* R10 (Oct. 24, 2023) (interview with Fei-Fei-Li, co-director of the Stanford Institute for Human-Centered Artificial Intelligence).

31. *See* Kevin Roose, *The New ChatGPT Case "See, Hear and Speak." What's That Like?, The New York Times* B7 (Sept. 29, 2023) (The technology was able to identify a silicone object.).

32. *Id.*

33. *Id.* (describing a mini-fridge as "perfect for those who appreciate a touch of yesteryear in their modern-day homes.").

34. *Id.*

35. *Id.*

36. *Id.*

37. *See* Cade Metz, *Microsoft Says New A.I. Nears Human Insight, The New York Times* A18 (May 17, 2023).

38. *Id.*

infinite prime numbers and asked it to do so in a way that rhymed.[39] The researchers were impressed with the "poetic proof" that resulted.[40] With that and other projects, they found that AI demonstrated a "deep and flexible understanding" of "human concepts and skills."[41] In other words, AI is really good "at analyzing and synthesizing and evaluating and judging text" rather than just "generating it."[42] For example, when they asked the system to create a unicorn using TiKZ (a computer language), it generated a system that could generate one.[43] Even more impressively, when they removed the code that allowed the system to draw the unicorn's head, and asked the system to modify the program so that it could draw a unicorn's head, it was able to do so.[44] The system was also able to write a letter in the voice of Mahatma Gandhi, and a Socratic dialogue that explored the dangers and misuses of L.L.M.s.[45] But there were also failures,[46] and AI can also be used to promote disinformation.[47]

Modern AI is programed with large language models that are not programmed line-by-line.[48] Instead they "learn on their own" by ingesting vast amounts of data and identifying patterns and relationships.[49] However, at this point at least, A.I.'s impact on elections is more theoretical than factual.[50] Nonetheless, nightmare scenarios are predicted by many.[51]

---

39. *Id.*
40. *Id.*
41. *Id.*
42. *Id.*
43. *Id.*
44. *Id.*
45. *Id.*
46. *Id.*
47. *See* O'Brien, *supra* note 28; Stuart A. Thompson & Sapna Maheshwari, *'A.I. Obama' and Fake Newscasters: How A.I. Audio Is Swarming TikTok, The New York Times* A1 (Oct. 13, 2023).
48. *See* Kevin Roose, *A.I.'s Black Boxes Just Got A Little Less Mysterious, The New York Times* B1 (May 22, 2024).
49. *Id.*
50. *See* Shane Goldmacher, Tiffany Hsu & Steven Lee Myers, *A.I.'s Effect on Election Is Still Mostly Theoretical, The New York Times* B1 (May 28, 2024).
51. *Id.*

B. DEEPFAKES

AI can also be used to create so called "deepfakes"[52] which involve videos altered with artificial intelligence.[53] Sophisticated software has made it possible to relatively easily create deepfakes.[54] For example, deepfake technology can be used to graft a digital face onto someone else's body.[55] It can also change images by miscaptioning photos, cutting footage, changing a video's speed or sequence, splitting sound from images, cloning voices, and creating fake text messages.[56] While many of the early deepfakes were not well done, and thus easily recognizable, later ones are becoming increasingly sophisticated.[57]

Deepfakes might be created for nefarious reasons (e.g., by those seeking to "discredit reality and dodge accountability"),[58] but they might also be created to parody someone or something.[59] Some label their deepfakes as manipulated, but others do not.[60] Deepfakes create plausible deniability for what seem like video evidence.[61]

Of course, image manipulation has been possible for decades.[62] At one point, technologies like Photoshop could be used to alter photos.[63] However, modern technology is much more sophisticated and can be used to create fake pornographic depictions of famous actresses, singers, and others that are surprisingly realistic.[64] On various social media platforms, particularly on TikTok, deepfakes flourish.[65] They have been used to create

---

52. *See* Patrick Coffee, *AI Deepfakes Draw Scrutiny in Congress, The Wall Street Journal* A2 (Nov. 7, 2023).

53. *See* Cade Metz, *Spot the Deepfake. (It's Getting Harder.), The New York Times* B1 (Nov. 25, 2019).

54. *Id.*, at B4.

55. *See* Tiffany Hsu, *'Deepfakes' Flourish on TikTok, Raising Alarms, The New York Times* A1 (Nov. 14, 2022).

56. *Id.*

57. *Id.*

58. *Id.*

59. *Id.*

60. *Id.*

61. *Id.*

62. *See* Isiah Poritz, *Deepfake Porn, Political Ads Push States to Curb Rampant AI,* Bloomberg Law (June 22, 2023).

63. *Id.*

64. *Id.*

65. *See 'Deepfakes' Flourish on TikTok, Raising Alarms, supra* note 55, at A1.

fraudulent commercial advertisements on social media platforms,[66] and they have also been used to produce false and deceptive political statements.[67] For example, while she was Speaker of the House, a deepfake was released showing what appeared to be an inebriated Nancy Pelosi.[68] In fact, the original video had simply been slowed down make it appear that Pelosi was slurring her words.

A.I. voice technology has also been used to create videos containing the voices of famous people (Obama and Oprah Winfrey) purportedly saying things that they did not say.[69] In one instance, AI was used to create a video showing individuals endorsing a product.[70] The video was fake, having been created using AI tools.[71] The tools are now good enough that it is possible to clone celebrity voices, alter their mouth movements to match the audio, and even include very persuasive dialogue.[72] For example, Vice-President Kamala Harris was depicted as saying that everyone who was hospitalized for Covid had been vaccinated.[73] In fact, she said exactly the opposite: everyone who had been hospitalized was unvaccinated.[74] In addition, a fake video was released showing President Biden stating that a national draft was being instituted to supply manpower for the Ukrainian War.[75] A fake video showing Donald Trump hugging and kissing Dr. Anthony Fauci was also released.[76] In a video of First Lady Jill Biden at a Philadelphia Eagles game, cheers were replaced with boos.[77]

As technology has become more widely available, deepfake technology is no longer limited to those with sophisticated technology and know-

---

66. *See AI Deepfakes Draw Scrutiny in Congress, supra* note 52, at A2.

67. *See Doctored Nancy Pelosi Video Highlights Threat of "Deepfake" Tech*, CBS News (May 26, 2019). https://www.cbsnews.com/news/doctored-nancy-pelosi-video-highlights-threat-of-deepfake-tech-2019-05-25/.

68. *Id.*

69. *Id.*

70. *See* Stuart A. Thompson, *Fake Videos Just Got Easier for Everyone, The New York Times* B1 (Mar. 13, 2023).

71. *Id.*

72. *Id.*

73. *Id.*

74. *Id.*

75. *Id.*

76. *See Deepfake Porn, Political Ads, supra* note 62.

77. *See 'Deepfakes' Flourish on TikTok, Raising Alarms, supra* note 55, at A1.

how.[78] For example, ElevenLabs has released a "speech-cloning tool that can be trained to replicate voices in seconds."[79] 4chan also uses it for similar purposes.[80] Some of the deepfakes created with these technologies have gone viral.[81] Indeed, deepfakes can be quickly created and at scale.[82] A recent study uncovered some 15,000 deepfakes online, the overwhelming majority of which involved pornographic videos of women.[83]

Some AI system make guesses about what to say after obtaining and examining information from many different sources.[84] When such systems make mistakes, they can be huge: e.g., providing wildly inaccurate flour measurements for the recipe in a cake.[85] One study found that up to 70% of the information provided by AI was inaccurate.[86] Not only was AI inaccurate in terms of planning menus, but also regarding the plots of video games.[87] AI was much more accurate if the user directed it to rely only on known and reliable sources.[88] Of course, deepfakes create many of the same risks that disinformation creates: they have the capacity to sow division or help individuals advance conspiracy theories.[89]

As technology has advanced, it has become increasingly difficult to distinguish human beings from bots and AI.[90] For example, on TikTok, MrBeast (a YouTube star) was shown in a fraudulent advertisement for a surprisingly cheap ($2) iPhone.[91] And, indeed, fraudsters are using AI to make copies of human voices and access bank accounts.[92] In a curious twist, "we have not only seen bots pretending to be human ... but an

78. *See Fake Videos Just Got Easier for Everyone*, *supra* note 70, at B1.

79. *Id.*

80. *Id.*

81. *Id.*

82. *See 'Deepfakes' Flourish on TikTok, Raising Alarms*, *supra* note 77, at A1.

83. *See Deepfake Porn, Political Ads*, *supra* note 62.

84. *See* Brian X. Chen, *A.I. Bots Are So Much Better When You Use This Little Tip*, *The New York Times*, Tech Fix B1 (July 25, 2023).

85. *Id.*

86. *Id.*

87. *Id.*

88. *Id.*

89. *See 'Deepfakes' Flourish on TikTok, Raising Alarms*, *supra* note 77, at A1.

90. *See Deepfake Porn, Political Ads*, *supra* note 62.

91. *See AI Deepfakes Draw Scrutiny in Congress*, *supra* note 52, at A2.

92. *See* Emily Flitter & Stacy Cowley, *A.I. Copies Your Voice, Then Calls Up Your Bank*, *The New York Times* B-1 (Sept. 11, 2023).

increasing number of humans pretending to be bots."[93] If we try to assess the level of public support for a proposition or an issue, bots can deceive us by suggesting that particular ideas have far more support than they actually have.

Social media platforms have differing policies regarding AI and deepfakes. YouTube's misinformation policies ban the distribution of videos that are misleadingly altered.[94] Likewise, TikTok prohibits videos that "mislead users by distorting the truth of events and cause significant harm to the subject of the video."[95] TikTok uses both humans and machines to enforce its policy.[96] Meta and Twitch also ban deepfakes and manipulated videos that deceive users.[97] Meta is developing programs to detect deepfakes.[98]

The quality of the deepfakes can vary.[99] In an interesting parody, a phony AI-created video was posted on Facebook which purported to depict Facebook chief executive Mark Zuckerberg.[100] In the video, Zuckerberg talked about an imaginary scenario: "Imagine this for a second: One man with total control of billions of people's stolen data, all their secrets, their lives, their futures."[101] Zuckerberg goes on to suggest that he owes it all to Spectre (the evil organization portrayed in a James Bond film): "Spectre showed me that whoever controls the data, controls the future."[102] Facebook decided to handle the Zuckerberg video in the same way that it handled the Pelosi video: while the video was initially left up, Facebook committed to rely on its fact checkers to determine whether it should be "filtered" from Facebook's recommended sites.[103]

---

93. *See* Bryan Casey & Mark A. Lemly, *You Might Be a Robot*, 105 Cornell L. Rev. 287, 291 (2020).

94. *Id.*

95. *Id.*

96. *Id.*

97. *Id.*

98. *Id.*

99. *Id.*

100. *See* Cade Metz, *Phony Video Tests Facebook, The New York Times* B7 (June 12, 2019).

101. *Id.*

102. *Id.*

103. *Id.*

C. THE FIRST AMENDMENT AND BOTS

It is tempting to assume that bot speech should be denied First Amendment protection. The U.S. governmental system is grounded in democratic principles. As Thomas Jefferson emphatically stated in the Declaration of Independence, "the power to govern derives from the consent of the governed."[104] If the U.S. is committed to democratic principles, then freedom of expression is the engine that makes democratic governance work. As the U.S. Supreme Court has recognized, "speech concerning public affairs is more than self-expression; it is the essence of self-government.[105] Or, as the Court stated in *Citizens United v. Federal Election Commission*,[106]

> Speech is an essential mechanism of democracy, for it is the means to hold officials accountable to the people. The right of citizens to inquire, to hear, to speak, and to use information to reach consensus is a pre-condition to enlightened self-government and a necessary means to protect it. The First Amendment has its fullest and most urgent application 'to speech uttered during a campaign for political office.' It is inherent in the nature of the political process that voters must be free to obtain information from diverse sources in order to determine how to cast their votes.[107]

The Court has also declared that "maintenance of the opportunity for free political discussion to the end that government may be responsive to the will of the people and that changes may be obtained by lawful means, an opportunity essential to the security of the Republic, is a fundamental principle of our constitutional system."[108]

Of course, at the time that the First Amendment was written and ratified, computers and robotic speech did not exist. Although the printing

---

104. U.S. DECLARATION OF INDEPENDENCE (July 4, 1776).

105. *Garrison v. Louisiana*, 379 U.S. 64, 74 75 (1964); *see also R.A.V. v. City of St. Paul*, 505 U.S. 377, 423 (1992) (Blackmun, J., concurring) ("core political speech occupies the highest, most protected position.").

106. 558 U.S. 310, 339 (2010).

107. *See also Virginia v. Black*, 538 U.S. 343, 365 (2003) ("Political speech, of course, is 'at the core of what the First Amendment is designed to protect.'").

108. *New York Times Co. v. Sullivan*, 376 U.S. 254, 269 (1964) *(quoting Stromberg v. California*, 283 U.S. 359).

press did exist, most modern communications technologies (e.g., radio, television, cable, satellite and the internet) did not. As a result, in formulating and ratifying the First Amendment, eighteenth century Americans would have been focused on the ability of actual people to participate in and influence the political process through oral speech or through printed works created by hand or (more likely) using the Gutenberg press. So, the question is how the First Amendment should be applied to modern technologies like bots which were beyond the contemplation of the founding generation.

Some have argued that bot speech, even if it involves "bot-created content," should be protected under the First Amendment because of its communication value. As one commentator noted, "If the courts focus on the publisher, it would be difficult for AI communicators to receive journalistic protections. If the courts focus on what was published, however, AI communicators have a better chance of succeeding, particularly if their content can be seen as a public good."[109] Another commentator makes a similar argument: "Even though bots are abstract entities, we might think of them as having free speech rights to the extent that they are promoting or promulgating useful information for the rest of us."[110]

The problem with this approach is that it attempts to draw a clear dividing line between human speech and bot speech, a line that does not necessarily exist. In some instances, what seems like bot speech may actually be the speech of human beings.[111] For example, in one case, a Ted Cruz tweet included an embedded button that allowed the receiver to instantly and easily retweet the original Cruz message.[112] A machine controlled when the new tweet would actually be sent.[113] Thus, even though the retweets might have appeared to be bots, because Cruz's original message was retweeted in mass without alteration, the tweets involved the conscious decision of an actual person who was choosing to retweet the message.[114]

---

109. Jared Schroeder, *Are Bots Entitled to Free Speech?*, COLUMBIA JOURNALISM REVIEW (May 24, 2018). https://www.cjr.org/innovations/are-bots-entitled-to-free-speech.php.

110. Matt Field, *Do Social Media Bots Have a Right to Free Speech?*, BULLETIN OF THE ATOMIC SCIENTISTS (Jan. 9, 2019) (quoting Professor Laurent Sacharoff).

111. *See* Casey & Lemly, *supra* note 93, at 289–290.

112. *Id.*, at 289–290.

113. *Id.*, at 290.

114. *Id.*

Through the centuries, much human speech has been disseminated through machines of one kind or another beginning with Gutenberg's development of the printing press in the 1400s. In the last couple of centuries, the use of machines has only increased as humans used radio, television, satellites, and the internet to help make mass communication possible. Radio enabled FDR to broadcast his fireside chats to the American people. Large media companies use both radio and television (and, lately, satellites) to communicate. So, the internet is similar in that it involves technology that allows ordinary people to mass communicate and widely disseminate their ideas. When bots flood social media with ideas, their messages will sometimes reflect the views of a single individual who is simply trying to influence the public debate. In other words, in some instances, bots and the internet provide nothing more than a mechanism by which individuals can distribute their ideas.

A distinction could perhaps be made between bots that simply relay the speech of actual persons as "content communicators" (in the sense that they share existing content) from bots that are "content creators."[115] The latter might involve bots, controlled by artificial intelligence, that can "automatically create tweets without direct human oversight."[116] There is a fear that bots will be able to spread information, and misinformation, with alarming speed."[117] They may be able to "like," "share," "follow," or "retweet" in conjunction with an online account.[118] Moreover, bots that use functions such as "like" or "share" are less likely to reveal their non-human status "by inadvertently using poor grammar or issuing off-color remarks."[119] In this way, bots can create "floods of emotive reactions to headline news" that appear real.[120] But, in the instance of "content-creator" bots, the dividing line between bots and people is not clear-cut. So far at least, bots do not function completely autonomously. On the contrary, someone programs

---

115. *See Automated Political Speech, supra* note 2, at 117–118 (quoting a study by Jared Schroeder).

116. *See* Wojcik, *supra* note 8.

117. Ryan Calo & Madeline Lamo, *We Need to Decide If Robots Are Protected by the First Amendment: Should Bots Be Required to Tell You That They're Not Human? And Would Such a Rule Be a Violation of Free Speech?*, BuzzFeedNews (July 26, 2018).

118. Casey & Lemly, *supra* note 93, at 322.

119. *Id.*, at 322.

120. *Id.*

the bots to intervene in public debates on specific issues, and programs the bots to give a particular type of response.[121] So, even "content-creator" bots involve a mix of human conduct and bot conduct.

Some might object to bots on the ground that they allow individuals who use them to have an outsized influence on the public debate by flooding social media and other online venues with their comments and views. As one commentator noted, "Thanks to the democratization of computer science know-how, state-sponsored 'influence campaigns,' and a profound cheapening of computing power, this category of spoofer is more prolific than ever. Even actors of limited means can now use bots to generate thousands of public comments, put celebrity faces on pornographic videos, inflate friend and follower lists, or maliciously influence the electoral process."[122] As a result, bots can help someone "weaponize" speech by making it appear that certain ideas have much greater support and acceptance than they actually have.[123] And "bots have been used to mislead users; to artificially inflate follower counts, likes, and retweets; and to manufacture consensus on divisive issues. In 2015 and 2016, bots were frequently used to make topics trend on Twitter, creating the false impression that certain stories were of great importance."[124]

The difficulty is that the problem of outsized influence has always existed. Historically, the U.S. media has been controlled by rich individuals or corporations. At one time in the U.S., prominent families controlled the newspaper business, including the Ochs-Sulzbergers (New York), Binghams (Louisville), Chandlers (Los Angeles), Medills (Chicago

121. *See* Molly Wood, Stephanie Hughes & Shaheen Ainpour, *How Social Media Bots Can Amplify Fake News*, Marketplace (Feb. 27, 2018) (quoting Jonathan Morgan) ("Ultimately the decision making always happens by a human because a human being writes the software that's going to operate an account even when it's automated. So somewhere there is a human being saying whenever some account that I already know of posts any message that contains the keyword 'guns,' retweet that tweet.") https://www.marketplace.org/2018/02/27/how-social-media-bots-can-amplify-fake-news/.

122. Casey & Lemly, *supra* note 93, at 307.

123. Jonathan Peters, *The Modern Fight for Media Freedom*, 18 First Amendment L. Rev. 60, 68 (2020).

124. Renee Diresta, *A New Law Makes Bots Identify Themselves—That's the Problem*, Wired (July 24, 2019).https://www.wired.com/story/law-makes-bots-identify-themselves/.

and elsewhere),[125] and Hearsts (various cities).[126] Those who controlled the means of communication were able to bias the news in the direction of their preferred positions. For example, during World War II, the Medills advocated for an isolationist position that some attributed to their dislike for President Franklin Delano Roosevelt.[127] William Randolph Hearst aggressively used his newspapers to campaign for causes that he supported,[128] as well as to promote his preferred views and positions.[129] Prior to the American Revolution, there is evidence that printers similarly used their presses to pursue the interests and positions that they preferred. For example, there are stories about James Franklin (Benjamin Franklin's brother) and his opposition to positions taken by prominent Bostonian Cotton Mather who (to James) represented the Boston "establishment."[130]

Just as the internet has allowed ordinary individuals to engage in mass communication, bots and never technologies may have enabled ordinary people to leverage their influence. It is not clear that such influence should be objectionable. The rich and powerful have always been to exercise outsized influence. Should we privilege only the speech of rich people and corporations who control the traditional media? Even today, there is considerable evidence of media bias, and that includes media outlets who try to portray themselves as neutral and objective (e.g., National Public Radio).[131] So, why shouldn't ordinary individuals be allowed to use technology to help them level the playing field and push their preferred positions? In some respects, bot technology might be regarded as nothing

---

125. *See* Joseph Epstein, *Dynasts of the Daily Press*, reviewing Megan McKinney, *The Magnificent Medills: America's Royal Family of Journalism During a Century of Turbulent Splendor* (2011); Amanda Smith, *Newspaper Titan: The Infamous Life and Monumental Times of Cissy Patterson* (2011), *The New York Times* Book Review Section, at 17 (Oct. 16, 2011).

126. *See* W.A. SWANBERG. CITIZEN HEARST 26, 40, 43–44, 47 & 100 (1961) (hereafter "CITIZEN HEARST").

127. *See id.*, at 14.

128. *See id.*, at 100 & 119–127.

129. *See* Jerome A. Barron, *Access to the Media—1967 to 2007 and Beyond: A Symposium Honoring Jerome A. Barron's Path-Breaking Article "Access Reconsidered,"* 76 GEO. W. L. REV. 826, 832 (2008).

130. *See* H.W. BRANDS, THE FIRST AMERICAN: THE LIFE AND TIMES OF BENJAMIN FRANKLIN 25 (2000).

131. *Id.*

more than a mechanism by which less wealthy individuals can widely disseminate their ideas. Since we are not prepared to limit the power of media outlets, it seems inappropriate to deprive ordinary people of their mass communication machines.

Bot technology has been employed by organizations and activists who are seeking to promote societal change.[132] Those who are disenfranchised sometimes use social media platforms in unusual ways (e.g., tweeting 24 hours a day or posting 1,000 times a day).[133] Bots may be enabling such a high level of activity.

Some might object that bot speech can lead to the widespread dissemination of disinformation. In recent years, as previously noted, there has been a flood of disinformation online,[134] and bots are believed to have played a major role in the circulation of such disinformation.[135] And it is relatively easy to find disinformation online.[136] Indeed, "every time major political events dominated the news cycle, Facebook was overrun by hoaxers and conspiracy theorists, who used the platform to sow discord, spin falsehoods and stir up tribal anger."[137] Bots may have played a significant role in the 2016 presidential election as armies of bots spread false information on fake social media accounts.[138] Common Sense Media, a nonprofit focused on media and technology in relation to children, claims that Facebook and Twitter had a combined total of 100 million bot accounts, and that these accounts wreaked havoc online: "The destructive role of unlabeled Russian bots in the American election is well documented.... Bots played a significant role in attacking high school students victimized by the Parkland, Florida, shooting, in encouraging kids to use electronic cigarettes, in spreading racism online, and in recent human rights violations in Kenya and Mexico." Online bots, which people misperceive as human, "lend false credibility" to various messages, California State Sen. Robert M. Hertzberg (D-Van Nuys) said, and are a major contributor to

---

132. *See Was That a Bot Post? Maybe*, *supra* note 4, at B1.
133. *Id.*
134. *See* Diresta, *supra* note 124.
135. *Id.*
136. *Id.*
137. *Id.*
138. Calo & Lamo, *supra* note 117.

fake news.[139] But the mere presence of disinformation does not provide an adequate basis for suppressing bot speech.

Of course, AI and bots are potentially more alarming if they can not only think independently, but can come up with their own ideas and conclusions. In the 1950s, the mathematician Alan Turing posited that "someday we would develop machines that would learn on their own, rather than merely execute programs."[140] In other words, they would be able to originate ideas and might eventually evolve into something like an adult brain,[141] but they would be capable of learning on their own and essentially leave humans behind.[142] Some claim that we have now reached that point.[143] As MIT psychologist J.C.R. Licklider suggests, the "hope is that, in not too many years, human brains and computing machines will be coupled together very tightly" and "that the resulting partnership will think as no human brain has ever thought and process data in a way not approached by the information handling machines we know today."[144]

Elon Musk has even posited the idea of "a microchip with neural sensors that can be implanted into the brain and allow almost instant sharing of information and signals between us and our computers."[145] Musk's project has advanced to the point that animal studies have been completed and an application has been filed with the U.S. Food and Drug Administration to allow computer chips to be implanted into the brains of humans on a test basis.[146] Musk argues that the "best way to make sure that AI does not turn against us or destroy humanity is to tightly connect it to human agency."[147] Some worry that AI may not "fully understand how and why they produce certain answers, have hallucinations, make false assertions and even seem to express unsettling emotions."[148]

---

139. Kristin Houser, *Should Bots Have a Right to Free Speech? This Non-Profit Thinks So. Does the First Amendment Apply to AIs, Too?, Futurism* (May 25, 2018).

140. *See* Walter Isaacson, *Will AI Help Us or Leave Us Behind, The Wall Street Journal* C3 (May 13–14, 2023).

141. *Id.*

142. *Id.*

143. *Id.*

144. *Id.*

145. *Id.*

146. *Id.*

147. *Id.*

148. *Id.*

Microsoft has suggested that bots are coming close to having AGI (artificial general intelligence).[149] In a recent study, Microsoft engineers found that AI showed a remarkable level of ingenuity in solving difficult problems.[150] Microsoft engineers referred to it as involving a "new kind of intelligence" that is similar to human intelligence.[151] In other words, machines are not simply spitting out preprogrammed answers.[152]

But, at least at this point, it is not clear that AI has achieved independence. AI is frequently used to perform relatively simple tasks (e.g., creating coloring pages for children, explaining the rules of card games, serving as a creative writing coach, and suggesting nonalcoholic drink recipes).[153] But AI frequently makes mistakes. For example, while many have been wowed by ChatGPT, it "often makes things up" (referred to as "hallucinations").[154] Google's A.I. also has a tendency to spew "nonsense."[155] For example, in writing a court brief, ChatGPT cited non-existent precedent.[156] When asked who has done more harm, Stalin or Libertarians, Google's chatbot Gemini indicated that it "is difficult to say definitively."[157] Afterwards, Google released a statement indicating that Gemini is a "creativity and productivity" tool and may not always be accurate or reliable.[158] Indeed, a recent study estimated that AI is erroneous at least 3% of the time and sometimes as much as 27% of the time, and the inaccuracy rate varies with the particular AI technology.[159] When non-summarization

---

149. *See* Cade Metz, *Microsoft Says New A.I. Nears Human Insight, The New York Times* A18 (May 17, 2023).

150. *Id.* (The problem involved how to stack a book, nine eggs, a laptop, a bottle and a nail.) *Id.*

151. *Id.* at A18.

152. *Id.*

153. *See* Kevin Roose, *World Might Not Be Ready, But A.I. 'Agents' Are Here, The New York Times* B1 & B3 (Nov. 13, 2023).

154. *See* Cade Metz, *A.I.-Powered Chatbots May 'Hallucinate' More Often Than Many Realized, The New York Times* B1 (Nov. 7, 2023).

155. *Id.*

156. *Id.*

157. *See* Mailes Kruppa, *Google's Big AI Chatbot Push Leaves It Mired in Controversy, The Wall Street Journal* B1 (Feb. 28, 2024).

158. *Id.*

159. *See A.I.-Powered Chatbots May 'Hallucinate' More Often Than Many Realized, supra* note 170, at B1.

tasks are involved, error rates may be higher.[160] Of course, the gravity of such error rates depends on context with errors being potentially more serious when bots are dealing with medical information, business data, or court documents.[161] Moreover, the likelihood of error may be increased by the fact that AI uses L.L.M. (large language model) to examine enormous amounts of information that it finds in "digital text, Wikipedia articles and online chat logs," and errors can be introduced if the AI relies on untruthful information.[162] AI also relies on "probabilities" in an effort to determine what language to use.[163]

In any event, it is not clear that chatbots will gravitate in favor of independence. Some suggest that we may be moving towards a future in which AI algorithms demonstrate a bias in favor of particular political positions (e.g., progressive, conservative, etc.),[164] and that those biases can influence how ChatGPT composes text. If AI does actually create its own speech, independent of the programmers, then a meaningful distinction might be made between machine speech and human speech.

Social media platforms have taken steps to limit and control bot speech. Indeed, when Musk purchased Twitter, he stated that would "defeat the spam bots or die trying."[165] Bots and spam are problematic for social media platforms because they distort advertising data.[166] One way that Musk has tried to eliminate bots is through Twitter Blue which verifies accounts, but that system encountered resistance because there was a charge.[167] In any event, it is not clear that the system works,[168] or that the level of bot speech declined significantly after Musk's efforts.[169] In some respects, the attack on bots is a bit of a cat and mouse game: as social media platforms

160. *Id.*

161. *Id.*

162. *Id.*

163. *Id.*

164. *See* Christopher Mims, *Help! My Political Beliefs Were Altered by a Chatbot!, The Wall Street Journal* B4 (May 13–14, 2023).

165. *See* Sarah E. Needleman, *Twitter Bots Persist Despite Efforts to Curb Fake Accounts, The Wall Street Journal* B1 (June 13, 2023).

166. *Id.*

167. *Id.*; *see also* Alexa Corse, *Celebrities See Red on Twitter Blue Fees, The Wall Street Journal* A1 (Mar. 31, 2023).

168. *See Twitter Bots Persist Despite Efforts to Curb Fake Accounts, supra* note 181, at B1.

169. *Id.*

get better at detecting and removing bots and spam, the spam and bots get better at hiding themselves.[170]

There is a talk of governmental regulation of AI.[171] Indeed, Sam Altman, the chief executive of Open AI, has openly called for a pause in the development of AI,[172] and has asked government to create AI regulation.[173] He argues that "if this technology goes wrong, it can go quite wrong."[174] So, he wants "to work with government to prevent that from happening."[175] Likewise, Elon Musk called for a pause on AI development,[176] and some of the top tech leaders (Sam Altman of OpenAI, Dennis Hassabis of Google DeepMind and Dario Amodei of Anthropic) have warned that AI presents an "existential" threat to humanity.[177] Gregory Hinton, who formerly worked on AI at Google, resigned and stated that he regretted his life's work.[178]

Both then President Biden and members of Congress have indicated an intent to regulate AI,[179] and there is talk of establishing an independent agency to regulate it.[180] An Executive Order issued by President Biden in 2023 encourages administrative agencies to "use their full range of authorities" to protect consumers from AI.[181] The order goes on to require agencies to "consider emphasizing or clarifying where existing regulations and guidance apply to AI, and requires them to impose safeguards on use of the technology."[182] Although the primary focus of the order seems to

---

170. *Id.*

171. *See* Ryan Tracy, *ChatGPT Creator Issues AI Warning, The Wall Street Journal* A3 (May 17, 2023).

172. *See* Deepa Seetharaman, *Musk, Experts Call for Pause in AI Tech Advances, The Wall Street Journal* B1 (Mar. 20, 2023).

173. *Id.*; *see also* Cecilia Kang, *The Most Important Man in Tech (Right Now), The New York Times* B1 (May 17, 2023).

174. *See* Kang, *supra* note 18, at B1 & B 4.

175. *Id.*

176. *See* Seetharaman, *supra* note 188, at B1.

177. *See A.I. Poses "Risk of Extinction," supra* note 11, at A1.

178. *See* Cade Metz, *He Warns of Risks From A.I. He Helped Create, The New York Times* A1 (May 2, 2023).

179. *See* Kang, *supra* note 188.

180. *Id.*

181. *See* Tonya Riley, *AI Order Puts Agencies Front and Center in Building Safeguards,* Bloomberg Law News (Nov. 14, 2023).

182. *Id.*

be on privacy issues,[183] there are concerns that AI can be used to create and spread disinformation, or take over decisions regarding such things as credit, housing and employment decisions.[184] Nevertheless, all seem to agree that the benefits of AI are enormous.[185]

Some social media platforms are making efforts to identify AI generated speech. Facebook, for example, is using software that helps identify and block bots.[186] TikTok is attaching "AI generated" labels to posts that it identifies as having been created or edited with AI technology,[187] and it requires users to indicate whether their posts involve manipulated media.[188] TikTok prohibits deep fakes of young people and private individuals.[189] YouTube prohibits posters from using A.I. in political ads, and requires other users to label their non-political ads as containing A.I.[190] Facebook uses labels to indicate whether content has been altered.[191] X prohibits as a violation of its policies any content that has been "significantly and deceptively altered, manipulated or fabricated."[192]

Social media platforms are also using AI to track down AI posts as well as to uncover disinformation.[193] For example, ElevenLabs has created an A.I. detection tool.[194] However, there is some doubt about the effectiveness of using AI for this task.[195] For example, PolitiFact used ChatGPT on some 40 instances of disinformation and concluded that AI either made a mistake, refused to answer, or arrived at a different conclusion from the human fact checkers (who purportedly had meticulously researched the issues), and did so at least half of the time.[196] There is increasing talk

---

183. *Id.*

184. *Id.*

185. *See* Kang, *supra* note 188, at B4.

186. *See Why Social Networks Can't Catch the Fakes, supra* note 2, at B3.

187. *See* Tiffany Hsu & Stuart A. Thompson, *Campaigns to Root Out Falsehoods Are Fading, The New York Times* B-2 (Oct. 9, 2023).

188. *See* Thompson & Maheshwari, *supra* note 47, at B4.

189. *Id.*

190. *Id.*

191. *Id.*

192. *Id.*

193. *Id.*

194. *Id.*

195. *Id.*

196. *Id.*

about the need for governmental regulation of AI, especially for dealing with copyright, civil rights, and consumer protection issues.[197] Some argue that AI companies should be required to test their systems and disclose known risks.[198] Of course, there is a concern that AI systems will be able to "self-replicate" or "self-exfiltrate into the wild," and could "manipulate humans into ceding control."[199]

In some instances, individuals may be able to bring privacy actions for appropriation of their name or likeness in deepfakes.[200] Indeed, some states have enacted laws that prohibit deepfakes involving pornography and election influence.[201] However, recovery is unlikely when a public official is satirized or parodied.[202] There is also talk about the possibility of creating a federal law prohibiting unauthorized deepfakes in the commercial context,[203] as well as creating greater rights to one's name and likeness.[204]

A further solution has been proposed by NewsGuard which has created the equivalent of "nutrition labels for news organizations."[205] With a team of approximately 50 journalists and analysts, NewsGuard rates news organizations ranging from *The New York Times* and *The Wall Street Journal* to BuzzFeed, Newsmax, Fox News, The Hill, The Daily Beast and others.[206] The hope is that readers will use the ratings and gravitate to more reliable sites.[207]

---

197. *See* O'Brien, *supra* note 28, at 16A.
198. *Id.*
199. *Id.*
200. *Id.*
201. *See AI Deepfakes Draw Scrutiny in Congress, supra* note 52, at A2.
202. *Id.*
203. *Id.*
204. *Id.*
205. *See* Edmund Lee, *Media Veterans Devise a New Strategy to Combat Online Fakery, The New York Times* B3 (Jan. 17, 2019).
206. *Id.*
207. *Id.*

In 2018, California passed the Bolstering Online Transparency Law (BOT Law) which requires that a bot disclose its identity (as a bot) in any online situation (including social media) involving a commercial transaction or an attempt to influence a vote in an election.[208] The sponsor of the law explained its intent as follows: "The heart of this issue is simple: we need to know if we are having debates with real people or if we're being misled."[209] According to the sponsor, the law was proposed as a way to "'protect democracy' from disingenuous accounts programmed to misinform the public."[210] He added that: "Bots continue to misrepresent public sentiments and perceptions about topics, or to mute dissenting opinions and distract from current events."[211]

When it enacted the law, the California legislature heard evidence that, during the 2016 political campaign, "social media bots accounted for 3.8 million (19 percent) of US election-related tweets. Twitter told a Senate committee that a Russian intelligence agency had 2,752 Twitter accounts, of which 47 percent were bots."[212] "To its supporters, the bot law is a respite in a time of online chaos, a sorely needed defense against the disinformation, misinformation, and filter bubbles that exist on today's sprawling social media platforms. For regulators, it's a chance to do something—to make social media manipulation less of a free-for-all—as the US heads into another election."[213]

It is not clear that the BOT Law can or will be effective in regulating bot speech. One problem is that the law suffers from vagueness and may be unconstitutional. For one thing, it is difficult to know what constitutes an attempt "to influence a vote in an election." In *Minnesota Voters Alliance*

208. § 17941 provides as follows: "(a) It shall be unlawful for any person to use a bot to communicate or interact with another person in California online, with the intent to mislead the other person about its artificial identity for the purpose of knowingly deceiving the person about the content of the communication in order to incentivize a purchase or sale of goods or services in a commercial transaction or to influence a vote in an election."

209. *See Should Bots Have a Right to Free Speech?*, *supra* note 139.

210. *See* Mark Rapazzini, *California's Online BOT Bill*, Heffler Claims Group (July 20, 2020). https://www.hefflerclaims.com/general/california-online-bot-bill/.

211. *Id.*

212. *Id.*

213. Diresta, *supra* note 124.

v. Mansky,[214] the U.S. Supreme Court struck down a Minnesota law that made it a crime to "display campaign material, post signs, ask, solicit, or in any manner try to induce or persuade a voter within a polling place or within 100 feet of the building in which a polling place is situated" to "vote for or refrain from voting for a candidate or ballot question." While the Court agreed with Minnesota that "some forms of advocacy should be excluded from the polling place,"[215] it struck the law down because it was too vague. Minnesota construed the law as banning "only words and symbols that an objectively reasonable observer would perceive as conveying a message about the electoral choices at issue in the polling place."[216] But, the Court found it difficult to determine "what qualifies as an 'issue.'"[217] The Court viewed the state's answer ("any subject on which a political candidate or party has taken a stance") as too broad. [218] As the Court noted, "Candidates for statewide and federal office and major political parties can be expected to take positions on a wide array of subjects of local and national import,"[219] and therefore the restriction was unduly vague.[220]

If the law had been limited to "promoting a group with recognizable political views" concerning the election at hand, the Court concluded that such a limitation would "make matters worse."[221] As the Court noted,

> Any number of associations, educational institutions, businesses, and religious organizations could have an opinion on an "issue confronting voters in a given election." For instance, the American Civil Liberties Union, the AARP, the World Wildlife Fund, and Ben & Jerry's all have stated positions on matters of public concern. If the views of those groups align or conflict with the position of a candidate or party on the ballot, does that mean that their insignia are banned? See *id.*, at 24, n. 15 (representing that

214. 585 U.S. 1 (2018).
215. *Id.*
216. *Id.*
217. *Id.*
218. *Id.*
219. *Id.*
220. *Id.*
221. *Id.*

> "AFL-CIO or Chamber of Commerce apparel" would be banned if those organizations "had objectively recognizable views on an issue in the election at hand"). Take another example: In the run-up to the 2012 election, Presidential candidates of both major parties issued public statements regarding the then-existing policy of the Boy Scouts of America to exclude members on the basis of sexual orientation. Should a Scout leader in 2012 stopping to vote on his way to a troop meeting have been asked to cover up his uniform?[222]

California's BOT Law suffers from as many, if not more, problems than the Minnesota law that was struck down in *Mansky*. What does it mean to "influence" an election? Is one attempting to do so if one criticizes a public official (or, for that matter, praises the official), or must one specifically advocate for the election or defeat of an official? "Is sharing legitimate news stories or voting locations a form of 'influence?'"[223] Is someone attempting to influence an election if he/she makes no reference to a particular candidate or candidates, but praises or is critical of issues on which a candidate (or candidates) have taken explicit positions? Undoubtedly, the California law suffers from all of the same problems evident in the Minnesota law.

But there is another major flaw in the California law: the law defines the term "bot" as "an automated online account where all or substantially all of the actions or posts of that account are not the result of a person."[224] What does that mean? When bots mass distribute information, does that necessarily make it bot speech? At the very least, the law is extremely vague. In the Ted Cruz example, cited above, bots were involved in retweeting the original Cruz Tweet. But, in each instance, the retweet occurred because a human being clicked on the embedded link in order to make that happen. Presumably, that situation meets the definition of something for which "all or substantially of the actions" involve that of a person, and therefore would be exempt from the law. Should it matter that

222. *Id.*

223. Diresta, *supra* note 124.

224. Cal. Bus. & Prof. Code § 17940(a).

the retweets were sent to a machine which decided when and whether to forward them? One would think not.

The law also would seem to be inapplicable when one or more people use robotic technology to widely disseminate their own ideas. If the bots are simply a platform for forwarding the ideas of individual people, then presumably the requirement that the post come from (or substantially all of it from) a human is satisfied, and it would again be offensive to label such speech as nothing more than "bot speech."

Presumably, the California law is directed towards bots that are acting relatively autonomously to distribute information broadly on platforms like social media. In other words, suppose that a bot is programmed to automatically respond when it spots the discussion of particular issues (e.g., vaccines, Black Lives Matter, or other "hot button" matters), and to give a pre-programmed response. Would this type of action be regarded as bot speech under the law? Even here, the distinction between "bot speech" and "human speech" is not so clear. One commentator asks whether it is possible to "imagine any online activity—no matter how automated—that is 'not the result of a [real or corporate] person' at the end of the day."[225]

Suppose that an individual has strong feelings about vaccines, or for that matter, about the BLM movement, and programs computers to respond with his position each time someone posts on these topics. Given the human involvement, would the bot responses be regarded as bot speech or as human speech? Since bots rarely act with complete autonomy, and are usually programmed by individuals to respond on issues that the individuals care about, and to state the preferred positions of those individuals, it is not clear that they fall within the scope of the California law.

To make matters more complicated, at times, there can be interaction between the bots and their human operators. As one commentator noted,

> Malign bots are often automated for some percentage of the time, whether that's intra-day or over their life cycle, particularly if the operator wants to "age" the account so that it doesn't look like it was created for one purpose. But the account is then taken over

225. Casey & Lemley, *supra* note 93.

> by a human operator when it's time to execute an influence operation. Russia's infamous Internet Research Agency accounts, for example, are often carelessly referred to as "bots." In reality, their most effective and well-known personas were largely human-operated. Persona accounts run directly by people are a much more daunting problem than purely automated bots when it comes to mitigating online influence operations.[226]

Russia's Internet Research Agency (IRA) employed so-called "trolls" (essentially, Russian individuals) who posed as Americans and weighed in on controversial issues.[227] These "trolls," purportedly numbering in the thousands, worked 12 hour shifts, and were prepped regarding what to say on U.S. social media and on how to say it.[228] Each troll was expected to produce at least 80 comments per day and to have at least 20 shares per day.[229] Once a troll created a post, he would forward it to one of a "countless" number of fake accounts in an effort to create a large number of "page views."[230] Although some Clinton supporters believe that the Russian efforts tipped the election,[231] it is not clear how much impact these posts had on the U.S. electorate.[232] There were lots of problems with the Clinton campaign, including Clinton's general unpopularity.[233] As one commentator observed regarding the posts, "the audience seemed to grow more jaded and paid less attention to what they wrote."[234]

---

226. Diresta, *supra* note 124.

227. *See* Mike Isaac, *For Social Media, an Election Day Test, The New York Times, The Week in Tech* B3 (Nov. 12, 2018); Anton Troianovski, *A Former Russian Troll Speaks: "It was like being in Orwell's world," The Washington Post* (Feb. 18, 2018).

228. *See* Neil MacFarquhar, *Unrest Spreads, Some Violently, in Middle East, The New York Times*, at A1 (Feb. 17, 2011)

229. *Id.*

230. *Id.*

231. *See* Jonathan Martin & Maggie Haberman, *Moscow's Hand Swirled in U.S., but Whether It Tipped Election is Unclear, the New York Times* A11 (Feb. 19, 2018) (As Clinton's campaign communications director alleged, "Russia succeeded in weakening her [Clinton] enough so that the Comey letter could knock her off.").

232. *See id.* ("And the nation's intelligence agencies say they do not have any way to calculate whether the Russian effort swung the election.").

233. *Id.*

234. *See* MacFarquhar, *supra* note 244.

There are some potential limitations on bot speech. For example, the U.S. government prohibits foreign interference in U.S. elections, and it can prosecute foreigners who attempt to interfere. Whether the U.S. government can get hold of interfering foreigners (e.g., Russian trolls or the handlers of bots) is far from clear. In addition, social media platforms can attempt to aggressively control bots. As private entities, they are not constrained by the First Amendment, and they have greater freedom to regulate bot speech. But, as noted, these companies can control only their own platforms, and bots can roam more freely on the rest of the internet. Moreover, there are so many bots that it is not clear that social media companies can effectively identify and control them.

CHAPTER XI

THE INTERNET'S IMPACT ON TRADITIONAL MEDIA

Not only has the internet had a profound impact on communication, it has also had a major impact on traditional media.

A. THE DECLINE OF TRADITIONAL MEDIA

Not coincidentally, as PCs (and other handheld devices) and the internet have gained in importance, traditional media has declined in importance. Although the media's role as a gatekeeper of information has not disappeared, traditional media is facing a host of challenges, some of them monumental and unprecedented, and to some extent traditional media has been supplanted by other types of online communication.

The present situation stands in stark contrast to the situation that existed in the mid-twentieth century. At that time, many people obtained their news through one of the (then) three major networks (CBS, ABC and NBC).[1] In the absence of cable and satellite television, and the internet, network news programs were able to capture sizeable market shares,

1. *See* Neal Conan, *Should Objectivity Still Be the Standard in News?*, National Public Radio, Talk of the Nation (Nov. 16, 2010), http://www.npr.org/2010/11/16/131361367/should-objectivity-still-be-the-standard-in-news (the transcript involves an interview with Ted Koppel who states that "The need for clear, objective reporting in a world of rising religious fundamentalism, economic interdependence and global ecological problems is probably greater than it ever has been. But we are no longer a national audience receiving

and to play a prominent role in politics and society.[2] In addition, because such a large percentage of the population watched the three networks, their news programs had a homogenizing effect on society and societal attitudes.[3] At one point, a particular CBS anchorman was referred to as "the most trusted name in news."[4]

In modern times, the grip of the major networks has eroded. The three major television networks have now morphed into four,[5] have been supplemented by multiple cable and satellite offerings,[6] and their market share has dropped dramatically.[7] People who do not like the major networks can ignore them altogether, and still have lots of cable and internet options available to them for obtaining news. The array of cable and satellite radio and television channels, as well as blogs and other new internet forms of communication,[8] would have been mind-boggling to Gutenberg. The net effect is that the major networks are faced with "declining revenues" and "plummeting profits,"[9] and no longer have the ability to shape public opinion in the same way that they did decades ago. Even bookstores have fallen on hard times because of competition from e-books and

---

news from a handful of trusted gatekeepers. We're now a million or more clusters of consumers harvesting information from like-minded providers.").

2. *See* Elizabeth Jackson, *How the World Changed During Queen Elizabeth's Reign, Daily Tribune* (Sept. 8, 2022) ("Around the world, television captured the hearts and minds of people looking for entertainment and news alike. Whereas previously many people received their news from radio and newspapers, television became increasingly dominant in the 1950s.").

3. *See Room for Debate: Do We Need Network TV?, The New York Times* (Feb. 27, 2009) (blog), http://roomfordebate.blogs.nytimes.com/2009/02/27/how-network-tv-brought-america-together/.

4. *See* John Nichols, *The Nation: Walter Cronkite America's Anchorman*, National Public Radio (July 20, 2009), http://www.npr.org/templates/story/story.php?storyId=106796633.

5. Fox News has now been added to the mix, and it has at times been controversial. *See* David Folkenflik, *Obama Administration Takes on Fox News*, National Public Radio, All Things Considered (Oct. 14, 2009), http://www.npr.org/templates/story/story.php?storyId=113803593.

6. *See* Associated Press, *Comcast Drives Growth with Pricier Bundles*, National Public Radio (Oct. 27, 2010), http://www.npr.org/templates/story/story.php?storyId=130854321.

7. *See* Sam Schechner, *TV Networks See Key Audience Erode, The Wall Street Journal* B5 (May 27, 2011).

8. *See* Eric A. Taub, *Digital Transmissions Could Transform Radio in the Car and at Home, The New York Times*, at G1 (Oct. 19, 2000).

9. *Room for Debate, supra* note 3.

online book sellers.[10] One of the last major bookstore chains, Barnes & Noble, is struggling to stay afloat.[11] However, the book publishing industry may be saved by cell phone-size editions of books.[12]

Many people are opting for alternate sources of news. Fewer than 3% of Americans obtain their primary news about political campaigns from the print media.[13] For people under 30, the print media is their least important source of information.[14] In any event, the print media is struggling because it is costly to the publisher (and, therefore, to the subscriber) to deliver the news in print form.[15] Moreover, print presents readers with a narrower range of ideas than can be found on the web.[16]

Network newscasts have enjoyed a bit of a resurgence in recent years.[17] Some ascribe this revival to the fact that the newscasts are anchored by single individuals, who are regarded as trusted journalists, as opposed to the "arguing experts" that appear on some cable channels.[18] The resurgence may also be due to the fact that some online organizations are regarded as too partisan, and therefore suffer from a credibility gap, so that people "want someone they trust at the end of the day to explain it [the news] to them.[19] But, even with this "resurgence," network newcasts are only viewed by slightly more than 20 million people, or approximately 6% of the U.S. population.[20]

---

10. *See* L. Gordon Crovitz, *From Gutenberg to Zoobert, The Wall Street Journal*, Information Age, at A15 (Aug. 9, 2010).

11. *See* Alexandra Alter & Tiffany Hsu, *As Barnes & Noble Struggles, Its Founder Takes Heat, The New York Times* A1 (Aug. 13, 2018).

12. *See* Alexandra Alter, *Books You Can Read While You're Texting: Mini-editions Are Cellphone-Size, No Thicker Than a Thumb and Held Horizontally in One Hand, and They Could Transform the American Publishing Industry, The New York Times*, Business Day B1 (Oct. 30, 2018).

13. *See* Farhad Manjoo, *Yesterday's News Today: Deep, Informed, Accurate and Inky, The New York Times*, State of the Art B7 (Mar. 8, 2018).

14. *Id.*

15. *Id.*

16. *Id.*

17. *See* David Bauder, *Evening News Lives: Networks Bring in More Viewers, The Courier-Journal*, at D1 (Oct. 18, 2011).

18. *Id.*

19. *Id.*

20. *Id.*, at D1.

Like network newscasts, local newspapers are also in decline.[21] At one time, newspapers held a dominant position in American society. Most citizens subscribed to one or local newspapers, and local dailies were capable of influencing and shaping public opinion. Because of their prominence, newspapers were able to attract significant resources (primarily through advertising and subscriptions), thereby enabling them to employ large numbers of staff and reporters. Today, the problems confronting daily newspapers are significantly more daunting than those confronted by radio and television networks, and it is not clear how many of them can or will survive in their current form.[22] The internet enables people to read, not only their local newspapers, but to access newspapers (and other news outlets) in quite distant places. Indeed, when Americans travel in Europe (or Europeans travel in the United States), it is possible for them to continue reading their hometown newspapers via the internet.

Because of an increase in online news possibilities, most newspapers have seen a steady decline in their circulation numbers.[23] Overall circulation in the U.S. has dropped by 50% since the year 2000.[24] As one commentator noted, a "stark divide has emerged between a handful of national players that have managed to stabilize their businesses and local outlets for which time is running out."[25] "Local papers have suffered sharper declines in circulation than national outlets and greater incursions into their online advertising businesses from tech giants such

21. *See* Keach Hagey, Lukas L Alpert & Yaryna Serkez, *Local News Fades Out: A Divide Between Newspaper Haves and Have-Nots, The Wall Street Journal* B1 (May 4–5, 2019).

22. *See* Michael J. De la Merced, *Tribune Files for Bankruptcy, The New York Times*, Deal Book Blog (Dec. 8, 2008), http://dealbook.nytimes.com/2008/12/08/tribune-files-for-bankruptcy/ ("It is only the latest—and biggest—sign of duress for the newspaper industry yet. Several newspaper companies have struggled to cope with declining revenues and mounting debt woes."); *see also* David Folkenflik, *Imagining a City Without its Daily Newspaper*, National Public Radio's *Morning Edition* (Feb. 5, 2009), http://www.npr.org/templates/story/story.php?storyId=100256908 ("In cities around the country, such as Atlanta and San Francisco, the major newspaper in town is losing money. Financial analysts say they expect some big dailies to fold, perhaps as soon as this year.").

23. *See* Staff and Wire Dispatches, *Newspaper Circulation Tumbling: ABC Audit Shows Decline Accelerating, The Courier-Journal*, at B6 (Oct. 27, 2009).

24. *See* David Chavern, *Journalism Needs a Lifeline, The Courier-Journal* 1E (Nov. 20, 2022).

25. *See Local News Fades Out, supra* note 21, at B1.

as Alphabet Inc.'s Google and Facebook Inc."[26] Indeed, circulation at local papers has dropped by approximately 41%.[27] As advertising revenue has declined, local news outlets are seeking to generate more online advertising revenue, but the rates for that advertising are lower and large tech companies snag approximately 77% of the advertising.[28] Some local newspapers have tried to sell news content to companies like Google and Facebook, but the profit margins are small.[29] As a result, 1,800 newspapers closed between 2004 and 2018, leaving 200 counties with no newspaper at all and half the counties in the country with only one.[30] Many of those that remain are being snapped up by bargain hunters who are seeking major cost savings in an effort to make the outlets sustainable.[31] Warren Buffet summed up the situation by declaring that newspapers are "toast," and "are going to disappear."[32]

The result is that many cities "have watched their papers slide into bankruptcy, while still others are being served by dailies with newsrooms that have shriveled by half."[33] Some cities went from multiple newspapers to a single newspaper, and some lost their only newspaper or the surviving newspaper's scope of coverage has shrunk dramatically, leaving those cities in "news deserts" because there are no reporters at city council meetings.[34] In recent years, newspaper declines have continued with overall newspaper circulation declining 43% (53% for one big city Florida

26. *Id.*, at B8.
27. *Id.*
28. *Id.*
29. *Id.*
30. *Id.*
31. *Id.*
32. *Id.*
33. *See* Howard Kurtz, *Industry Shudders as Famed Newspaper Closes, The Courier-Journal*, Forum Section, at A7 (March 3, 2009). *The New York Times* summarized the situation in an editorial: "The Rocky Mountain News is dead. The Seattle Post-Intelligencer will publish its last issue Tuesday. The Detroit Free Press has cut home delivery to three days a week. The Star Tribune in Minneapolis and the Inquirer and Daily News in Philadelphia have all declared bankruptcy."; Eric Etheridge, *Why Newspapers Can't Be Saved, But the News Can, The New York Times*, The Opinion Pages, Opinionater (blog) (Mar. 16, 2009), http://opinionator.blogs.nytimes.com/2009/03/16/why-newspapers-cant-be-saved-but-the-news-can/?scp=24&sq=media%20newspapers%20guardians%20democracy&st=cse.
34. *See* Kailey Broussard, *Newspaper Cuts Leave Communities Like Arlington, Texas, Without Vital Local Coverage*, National Public Radio, All Things Considered (Aug. 30,

newspaper),[35] and the *Daily News* recently laid off half of its newsroom staff.[36] The Salt Lake Tribune let go of 34 of its 90 journalists in 2018.[37] After a change in ownership, *am-New York*, a free tabloid paper for subway riders, cuts its newsroom staff by half.[38] However, there are a few exceptions to this trend. For example, *The Daily Sun*, which publishes in a Florida retirement community is actually gaining readership (up 169%), because older readers are more inclined to rely on the print media.[39]

Similar difficulties are being confronted by magazines, a number of which have closed,[40] and many of which are cutting back.[41] Although magazine subscription levels remain high, newsstand sales (which are more profitable than subscriptions) have declined, and advertising revenue has declined significantly.[42] For example, U.S. News and World Report ended the print version of its publication and now publishes solely online.[43] Even the National Enquirer, which one might have assumed would survived well given its sensational nature, is struggling "with ballooning debt, falling revenue and shrinking newsstand sales."[44] Likewise, Condé Nast,

---

2023). https://www.npr.org/2023/08/30/1196874201/newspaper-cuts-leave-communities-like-arlington-texas-without-vital-local-covera.

35. *See* Ted Geltner, *Print Is Dead? Not in This Florida Retirement Enclave, The New York Times* B3 (Sept. 3, 2018).

36. *See* Edmund Lee & Sapna Masheshwari, *Facing Losses, Condé Nast Plans to Put 3 Magazines Up for Sale, The New York Times* (Aug. 1, 2018).

37. *See* Katherine Rosman, *Keeping the Presses Rolling, The New York Times* B8 (May 23, 2019).

38. *See* Marc Tracy, *New Owners of Subway Paper amNew York Halves Newsroom Staff, The New York Times* B5 (Oct. 12, 2019).

39. *See Facing Losses, Condé Nast Plans to Put 3 Magazines Up for Sale, supra* note 36.

40. *See* Jim Zarroli, *As Magazines Hemorrhage Cash, Industry Evolves*, National Public Radio (Jan. 13, 2010), http://www.npr.org/templates/story/story.php?storyId=122529209.

41. *Id.* ("Meanwhile, *Fortune* says its cutting back the number of issues it publishes every year, and *Business Week* was sold for the embarrassingly low price of just $9 million.").

42. *Id.*; *see also* Tanzina Vega, *Magazine Newstand Sales Decline 10%, The New York Times*, at B3 (Feb. 8, 2012).

43. *See* Jeremy W. Peters, *U.S. News & World Report to Become Online Only, The New York Times*, Media Decoder: Behind the Screens, Between the Lines (blog) (Nov. 5, 2010). http://mediadecoder.blogs.nytimes.com/2010/11/05/u-s-news-to-cease-printing-become-online-only/?scp=2&sq=u.s.%20news%20world%20report&st=cse.

44. *See* Lukas I. Alpert, *Tabloid Struggles Despite Publicity: National Enquirer's Ties to Trump Don't Do Much for Performance of Parent Company, The Wall Street Journal* B6 (Apr. 20, 2018).

which owns a host of magazines—Self, Teen Vogue, Bridges, Golf Digest, W, Vogue, Vanity Fair and the New Yorker—has taken a number of steps to trim losses (including laying off some 80 employees), but nevertheless lost $120 million in 2017.[45] The losses have continued, despite a number of (unsuccessful steps) to stem them, including Nast's decision to sell off some of its magazines.[46] There have been some signs of resurgence for some women's magazines.[47]

The obstacles facing newspapers are manifold. In addition to the escalating cost of ink and newsprint, as well as distribution costs, newspapers have been affected by the growth of the internet which has assumed a much greater role in society. As news options have mushroomed on the Web, fewer people feel the need or desire to subscribe to daily newspapers, and fewer advertisers feel compelled to purchase newspaper advertising.[48]

The net effect is that newspaper circulation and newspaper advertising have been declining steadily in recent decades. Throughout the 1990s and the early 2000s, the decline was approximately 1% per year.[49] During the economic downturn of the late 2000s, the decline began to accelerate.[50] In early 2009, newspaper advertising declined by as much as 30 percent,[51] with print circulation declining by 7 percent,[52] and total circulation of all newspaper dailies dropping to 44 million copies a day—the lowest level since the 1940s.[53] Illustrative of the decline is *The Los Angeles Times* which saw total circulation fall from 1.1 million to 657,000 between the years two thousand and two thousand nine.[54] The decline continues as the

---

45. *See* Edmund Lee & Sapna Maheshwari, *Condé Nast to Sell 3 Magazines In Effort to Stanch Ad Losses, The New York Times* A1 (Aug. 2, 2018).

46. *Id.*

47. *See* Russell Adams, *Slide in Magazine Sales Decelerates, The Wall Street Journal*, at B7 (Aug. 10, 2010).

48. *See* Kurtz, *supra* note 33, at A7 (suggesting that advertising revenue fell 18%).

49. *See* Richard Perez-Pena, *Newspaper Circulation Falls by More Than 10%, The New York Times*, at B3 (Oct. 27, 2009).

50. *Id.*

51. *See* Richard Perez-Pena, *Newspaper Ad Revenue Could Fall as Much as 30%, The New York Times*, at B3 (Apr. 15, 2009).

52. *See* Tim Arango, *Fall in Newspaper Sales Accelerates to Pass 7%, The New York Times*, at B3 (Apr. 28, 2009).

53. *See Newspaper Circulation Falls, supra* note 49, at B3.

54. *Id.*

paper laid off 110 employees in 2024.[55] The decline is continuing.[56] *USA Today* has suffered declines in both circulation and advertising.[57]

During the 2008 economic downturn, the signs of economic distress for traditional newspapers were widespread and deep. Many newspapers suffered severe budget shortfalls, and were forced to furlough[58] or reduce staff,[59] lower salaries,[60] suspend retirement contributions,[61] consider reductions in home delivery,[62] or file for bankruptcy protection.[63] For example, the McClatchy Company, which controls approximately thirty daily newspapers and another fifty nondaily papers, laid off 15 percent of its staff.[64] Conde Nast, faced with a steep decline in advertising revenue, engaged in aggressive cost-cutting measures.[65] *The Washington Times* was losing money and its future is uncertain.[66] The industry, as a whole, shed twelve thousand jobs in a recent year.[67]

The pain of the 2008 economic downturn had a major impact on a multitude of publications. *The Rocky Mountain News* closed down

---

55. *See* Farley Elliott, *Mass Layoffs Hit LA Times, California's Biggest Newspaper*, SF Gate (Jan. 18, 2024).

56. *See Newspaper Circulation Tumbling, supra* note 23.

57. *See* Jeremy W. Peters, *USA Today to Remake Itself to Stress Digital Operations, The New York Times*, at B1 (Aug. 28, 2010).

58. *See* Richard Pérez-Pena, *Gannett Plans to Furlough Workers, The New York Times*, at B12 (Jan. 15, 2009) (suggesting that Gannett, the world's largest newspaper chain with 85 daily newspapers in the U.S. alone, was forcing employees to take week-long furloughs in an effort to avoid layoffs). *See id.*(the announcement was made following Gannett's announcement of a sharp drop in earnings and revenue, and amounted to approximately 3,000 jobs).

59.

60. *See* Richard Perez-Pena, *McClatchy Plans to Cut 15% of Staff, The New York Times*, at B5 (Mar. 10, 2009).

61. *See id.*

62.

63. *See* Richard Perez-Pena, *Tribune, Major News Chain, Seeks Bankruptcy Protection, The New York Times* A1 (Dec. 9, 2008).

64. *See McClatchy Plans to Cut 15%, supra* note 60.

65. *See* Stephanie Clifford, *Conde Nast Reports Sharp Drop in Ad Pages, The New York Times*, at B3 (Nov. 12, 2009).

66. *See* Ashley Parker, *Washington Times Faces Uncertainty, The New York Times*, at B1 (Dec. 1, 2010).

67. *See* Kurtz, *supra* note 33, at A7.

because of financial difficulties,[68] and major Chicago[69] and Philadelphia[70] newspapers were either forced into bankruptcy,[71] or faced the possibility of bankruptcy.[72] Two Philadelphia newspapers, *The Inquirer* and the *Daily News*, were both sold at public auction.[73] A number of newspapers folded,[74] and most newspapers saw their circulations drop[75] and those

---

68. *See* Kirk Johnson, *The Rocky Says Goodbye, Taking a Part of its City's Past with It*, *The New York Times*, at A11 (Feb. 28, 2009) ("The Rocky's owner, the E. W. Scripps Company, announced Thursday that the paper, which had been up for sale, had attracted no credible buyers and that its losses—$16 million in 2008—could not be sustained."); Andrew Ross Sarkin, *DealBook: Rocky Mountain News Is Shutting Down*, *The New York Times* (Feb. 26, 2009) ("The Rocky Mountain News in Denver will cease publication on Friday. E.W. Scripps, which owns newspaper, known locally as The Rocky, announced Thursday that it had failed to find a buyer for the daily. Scripps's chief executive, Rich Boehne, said in a statement that The Rocky was "a victim of changing times in our industry and huge economic challenges." Scripps said the newspaper lost $16 million last year."). While the UK's News of the World closed down in 2011, the shutdown was more due to the fact that it's staff had engaged in questionable practices. *See* Cassandra Vinograd, *News of the World Bids Farewell to UK Readers, The Courier-Journal* A 16 (July 10, 2011).

69. *See Tribune, Major News Chain, Seeks Bankruptcy Protection*, *supra* note 63, at A1 (Dec. 9, 2008).

70. Joel Rose, *Philadelphia Newspaper Inc. Files for Chapter 11*, National Public Radio's Morning Edition (Feb. 23, 2009), http://www.npr.org/templates/story/story.php?storyId=101024311 ("As the news industry continues to struggle with falling ad revenues, the publisher of Philadelphia's two major papers—the *Inquirer* and the *Daily News*—has filed for protection from creditors.").

71. *See* Richard Pérez-Pena, *As Cities Go From Two Papers to One, Talk of Zero*, *The New York Times*, at A1 (Mar. 11, 2009) ("The top papers in many markets, like The Star Tribune in Minneapolis, The Philadelphia Inquirer and The New Haven Register, belong to companies that have gone into bankruptcy in the last three months.").

72. *See id.* ("Other publishers, like the Seattle Times Company and MediaNews Group, owner of The Denver Post, The San Jose Mercury News and The Detroit News, are seen as being at risk of bankruptcy. Many newspapers—from The Miami Herald to The Chicago Sun-Times—have been put up for sale, with no buyers on the horizon.").

73. *See* Joseph Plambeck, *Creditors Win Auction for Philadelphia Newspapers*, *The New York Times*, at B3 (Apr. 29, 2010).

74. *See* Brooke Gladstone, *Are Newspapers Dead Yet?*, National Public Radio, On the Media (Jan. 28, 2011) (citing The *Tuscon Citizen, The Rocky Mountain News, The Baltimore Examiner, Kentucky Post, Cincinnati Post, King County Journal*, and *Union City Register Tribune*). http://www.onthemedia.org/2010/jul/16/are-newspapers-dead-yet/transcript/.

75. *Id.* ("If you look at the twenty-five largest newspapers by circulation, a number of those newspapers cut their circulations by 10 to 20 percent in the last year. To me, there's not much of a distinction between having to cut your distribution base that rapidly and going completely out of business.").

that remain have substantial debt,[76] or have slid toward bankruptcy.[77] The Washington Post Company announced that it would sell *Newsweek* because it was losing money.[78] Some of these negative trends began to turn around somewhat in 2011.[79]

Even those newspapers that survived have suffered serious financial reverses, including the *Washington Post*,[80] *Detroit Free Press*,[81] *The Detroit News*,[82] *Seattle Post-Intelligencer*[83] and *San Francisco Chronicle*.[84] The *Seattle Post-Intelligencer*, which desperately sought a purchaser,[85] ultimately decided to discontinue print publication and become an entirely online publication.[86] With the shift, *The Seattle Times*, the *Post-Intelligencer's* chief competitor, returned to profitability.[87] The *San Francisco Chronicle*

---

76. *Id.*

77. *See* Jeremy W. Peters, *American Media Reveals Plans to File Bankruptcy, The New York Times*, at B3 (Nov. 2, 2010).

78. *See* Stephanie Clifford, *As Newsweek Goes on the Block, An Era Fades, The New York Times*, at A1 (May 6, 2010).

79. *See* Brian Stelter, *News Corp.'s Net Income More Than Doubles, Led by Its Cable Networks, The New York Times*, at B4 (Feb. 3, 2011); Tanzina Vega, *Time Warner Raises Dividend as Earnings Beat Forecast, The New York Times*, at B4 (Feb. 3, 2011).

80. Associated Press, *Sharp Decline in Profit at Washington Post Co., The New York Times*, at B2 (Feb. 26, 2009) ("Fourth-quarter profit declined 77 percent at The Washington Post Company despite modest revenue growth led by the company's education and cable television businesses.").

81. *See* Richard Perez-Pena & Mary Chapman, *In a Grand Experiment, 2 Daily Newspapers Now Not So Daily, The New York Times*, at A14 (Mar. 31, 2009).

82. *Id.*

83. *See Rocky Mountain News Is Shutting Down, supra* note 68 ("The San Francisco Chronicle, and it plans to close The Seattle Post-Intelligencer if it finds no buyer for that paper.").

84. Richard Perez-Pena, *Hearst Threatens to End San Francisco Newspaper, The New York Times*, at B9 (Feb. 25, 2009) ("Hearst Corporation said Tuesday that it would close or sell The San Francisco Chronicle unless it could wring concessions from its unions, raising the prospect of San Francisco becoming the largest city in the country to lose its dominant newspaper. Hearst said The Chronicle, which has daily circulation of 339,000, lost more than $50 million in 2008 and will lose more this year. It has had significant losses every year since 2001."); *San Francisco: A No Newspaper Town?*, CNN (Feb. 25, 2009).

85. *See* Kurtz, *supra* note 33, at A7.

86. *See* William Yardley & Richard Perez-Pena, *In Seattle, A Newspaper Loses Its Paper Routes, The New York Times*, A1 (March 17, 2009).

87. *See* Richard Perez-Pena, *Seattle Paper Is Resurgent as a Solo Act, The New York Times*, at B1 (Aug. 10, 2009).

has also been in dire financial straits,[88] and the McClatchy Company lost four million dollars in 2009.[89] Of course, the stock valuations of many newspapers declined significantly, sometimes by as much as 90 percent,[90] and many newspapers were saddled with high debt levels.[91] To some extent these bankruptcies were beneficial because they allowed organizations like the Tribune Co. to reorganize.[92] Even the venerable *New York Times* announced temporary salary cuts.[93]

The stresses on the media continued into 2024.[94] While advertising revenues remained low, the media faced difficulties resulting from a fall in web traffic caused by a withdrawal of support from the tech giants.[95] For example, in 2024, the Los Angeles Times moved to cut approximately 100 jobs which amounted to approximately 20% of its work force, prompting the remaining employees to strike.[96] When the *L.A. Times* was purchased in 2018, it had approximately 400 employees and the new owner hired approximately 150 additional journalists.[97] However, by June 2023, the paper cut 74 jobs (approximately 13 percent of its workforce), and the additional cuts put the paper at or below the number of employees when it was purchased in 2018.[98] Financial losses or job cuts were also announced by *The Washington Post*, *Time Magazine*, *Sports Illustrated*, and *Pitchfork*.[99]

88. *See* Kurtz, *supra* note 33, at A7.

89. *See McClatchy Plans to Cut 15%, supra* note 60.

90. *See Hearst Threatens to End, supra* note 84.

91. *See id.*

92. *See* Shira Ovide, *At Tribune Co., Leaving Behind Bankruptcy and Old Ways, The Wall Street Journal*, at B1 (July 26, 2010).

93. *See* Richard Perez-Pena, *Times Co. Announces Temporary Salary Cuts, The New York Times*, at B6 (Mar. 27, 2009).

94. *See* Katie Robertson & Benjamin Mullin, *Finding Sprouts of Hope in a Gloomy Media Era, The New York Times* B1 (Mar. 23, 2024).

95. *Id.*

96. *See* Benjamin Mullin & Katie Robertson, *Facing Cuts, L.A. Times Is Turbulent With Tension, The New York Times* B1 (Jan. 23, 2024).

97. *Id.*

98. *Id.*

99. *Id.*

The publishing business has also been complicated by the development of artificial intelligence (AI).[100] Historically, newspapers served as a source of information for millions who clicked through newspaper websites.[101] However, Google and Microsoft have created A.I. systems which quickly provide answers to questions in full paragraphs.[102] However, there is a reciprocal relationship between publishers and A.I.[103] A.I. uses newspaper websites to amass content for their answers.[104] Initially, newspapers were content because A.I. drove viewers to their websites, amounting to 50% of all visits to their websites, increasing the value of those websites to advertisers.[105] But A.I. has become more sophisticated, involving text, images, and other media.[106] Many publishers believe that A.I. manufacturers should pay for the use of their content.[107]

Because of these stresses, a number of cities have gone from being multi newspaper cities to single newspaper cities,[108] and some daily newspapers no longer publish every day.[109] Some believe that a few cities will ultimately be left with no newspaper at all.[110]

---

100. *See* Katie Robertson, *Publishers Gird for Threat From A.I., The New York Times* B1 (Mar. 31 2023).

101. *Id.*

102. *Id.*

103. *Id.*

104. *Id.*

105. *Id.*

106. *Id.*

107. *Id.*

108. *See At Tribune Co., supra* note 92, at B1 ("The history of The Seattle Post-Intelligencer stretches back more than two decades before Washington became a state, but after 146 years of publishing, the paper is expected to print its last issue next week, perhaps surviving only in a much smaller online version. The Star Tribune, the leading daily in Minneapolis, is owned by a private equity company that filed for bankruptcy in January. And it is not alone. The Rocky Mountain News shut down two weeks ago, and The Tucson Citizen is expected to fold next week. At least Denver, Seattle and Tucson still have daily papers.").

109. *See* Richard Perez-Pena, *4 Michigan Markets Will Lose Daily Newspapers, as Ailing Industry Tries to Cope, The New York Times*, at B8 (Mar. 24, 2009).

110. *Id.* ("[Some] economists and newspaper executives say it is only a matter of time—and probably not much time at that—before some major American city is left with no prominent local newspaper at all. 'In 2009 and 2010, all the two-newspaper markets will become one-newspaper markets, and you will start to see one-newspaper markets

Some commentators argue that "the sky is falling" view of the media is overblown. Mr. Andrew Garson, former president and publisher of *The Courier-Journal*, thinks that the reported death of traditional newspapers has been overstated.[111] He argues that, despite the high-profile nature of recent newspaper bankruptcies and staff cuts, less than 1 percent of the nation's daily newspapers have closed.[112] By contrast, he noted that 10 percent of car dealerships have closed, and the number of realtors have declined by 15 percent.[113] In addition, he argues that the newspapers that have closed were essentially the second largest newspapers in their jurisdictions, and had been kept alive only because of joint operating agreements,[114] or were already heavily in debt.[115] There may be some validity to these arguments. For example, even before the economic downturn, *The San Francisco Chronicle* was losing money.[116]

Even so, Garson admitted that his then newspaper, *The Courier-Journal*, had suffered declining ad revenue, had been forced to cut expenses during the economic downturn,[117] and had even forced employees to take two weeks of unpaid leave.[118] Even Pulitzer Prize winning newspapers could not escape cutbacks and retrenchments.[119] Part of the problem is that society has undergone dramatic changes as people have shifted from paper

---

become no-newspaper markets,' said Mike Simonton, a senior director at Fitch Ratings, who analyzes the industry.").

111. *See* Arnold Garson, *Despite Recession, Industry Changes, Newspaper Remains Strong, The Courier-Journal*, at H1 (May 17, 2009).

112. *Id.*

113. *Id.*

114. *Id.*

115. *Id.*

116. *See* Richard Perez-Pena, *Bay Area's Main Daily at Impasse, The New York Times*, at B1 (Mar. 30, 2009).

117. *See Despite Recession, Industry Changes, Newspaper Remains Strong, supra* note 111, at H1.

118. *See* Associated Press, *C-J Parent Gannett Orders 2nd Week of Unpaid Leave: Hearld-Leader Announces Layoff of 53 Employees, The Courier-Journal*, at B7 (Mar. 24, 2009).

119. *See* Robert Smith, *Pulitzer High Offset by Low Newspaper Demand*, National Public Radio, Morning Edition (Apr. 21, 2009), http://www.npr.org/templates/story/story.php?storyId=103313118:

> The awards were announced after one of the most depressing years the newspaper industry has ever seen, with layoffs, bankruptcies and closings brought on by the recession and an exodus of readers and advertisers to the Internet.

to digital, and this change has manifested itself in various ways.[120] As one restaurant owner noted, people who ate alone used to read newspapers, and the restaurant would end up with a "huge pile of newspapers by the front doors that people had left behind."[121] Now, people text and e-mail during their meals instead of reading newspapers.[122] Garson argues that *The Courier-Journal* is working to position itself to succeed in lots of different media forms.[123]

Some believe that newspaper staff cutbacks have affected both the quantity and the quality of newspaper coverage. As one reporter noted, "nearly every large paper in the country prints fewer pages and fewer articles, and many have eliminated entire sections. Bureaus in foreign capitals and even Washington have closed, and newspapers have jettisoned film criticism, book reviews and coverage of local news outside their home markets."[124] As the *Chronicle's* Editor-at-Large suggested, cutbacks of this magnitude inevitably affect the ability of newspapers to report the news: "It's objectively true that there's less in the paper.... You can't deny that a loss is a loss."[125] The former editor of the *Buffalo News* suggested that the paper went through "round after round of buyouts" so that it "could no longer cover things the way we used to."[126]

The *Free Press* was honored less than a month after the Detroit paper cut back home delivery to three days a week.

The Pulitzer for editorial cartooning went to Steve Breen of The San Diego Union-Tribune, which was sold last month to a private equity firm after its advertising plunged 40 percent since 2006 and it forced employees to take unpaid furloughs.

...

The awards also follow a difficult year for the Times, which is dealing with the burden of a heavy debt, forcing the distinguished paper to ask employees for pay cuts and seek an infusion of cash from a Mexican billionaire investor.

120. *See Bay Area's Main Daily at Impasse, supra* note 116.

121. *Id.*

122. *Id.*

123. *See Despite Recession, Industry Changes, supra* note 111.

124. *See As Cities Go From Two Papers to One, supra* note 71.

125. *Id.*

126. *See* Marc Tracy, *The Decline of Local News, Dissected By a Newspaper Veteran, The New York Times* B3 (July 16, 2020).

There is evidence suggesting that newspaper staff reductions are affecting the ability of newspapers to cover governmental issues and politics.[127] "Only one TV station in Virginia still has a reporter at the capital. Many newspapers have decided to cover the capital by phone, if at all."[128] A similar situation prevails at the Maryland capital.[129] Symptomatic of the times is the fact that the American Society of Newspaper Editors cancelled a recent convention because too many editors decided to stay home.[130] Some newspapers have laid off copy-editors despite the obvious implications for the quality of the finished news product.[131]

The decline in newspapers is reflected in reporting on science issues.[132] In 1989, more than 90 newspapers maintained weekly science sections.[133] By 2013, that number had fallen to 19 newspapers.[134] Much science information has shifted to online publications, including Aeon, Ars Technica, Gizmodo, Live Science, Nautilus, Quanta, Stat, Undark and Vox, as well as to social media platforms.[135]

By 2023, there were mixed results for print news organizations. Some organizations were trying to directly connect with their readers and were seeing an increase in readership.[136] *The Atlantic*, for example, had seen a 10% increase in subscriptions.[137] Rural newspapers were struggling to

---

127. Marc Fisher, *Bloggers Can't Fill the Gap Left by Shrinking Press Corps, The Courier-Journal*, Forum Section, at A7 (quoting Virginia's Lieutenant Governor as saying "What you want is an informed and engaged population, but with less manpower and less space, there just isn't the opportunity to talk about many topics that lie beneath the marquee issues.").

128. *Id.*

129. *Id.* (suggesting that the number of reporters covering the Maryland legislature has declined by half over the last two years).

130. *See* Kurtz, *supra* note 33, at A7.

131. *See Newspaper Layoffs*, National Public Radio, On the Media (July 24, 2009), http://www.onthemedia.org/2009/jul/24/neswpaper-leighoffs/transcript/.

132. *See* Alan Burdick, *Alternative Realities, and Real Good News, The New York Times* D3 (Nov. 20, 2018).

133. *Id.*

134. *Id.*

135. *Id.*

136. *See* Mike Isaac, Katie Robertson & Nico Grant, *Silicon Valley Ditches News, Shaking an Unstable Industry, The New York Times* B1 (Oct. 21, 2023).

137. *Id.*

survive, with some closing.[138] In addition, the McClatchy newspaper chain (which owned the *Miami Herald* and *Kansas City Star*) slid into bankruptcy.[139]

In Britain, local newspapers remained in full-scale retreat, placing journalists on leave and suspending print and online production.[140] Indeed, advertising revenue had dropped to almost zero, and some newspapers were even enlisting volunteers to deliver their product to customers.[141] While there was an uptick in visits to news sites, those visits did not produce large amounts of revenue since many local British newspapers do not have pay walls.[142] Newsquest, which owns 165 publications in the UK, furloughed approximately 2,500 employees.[143]

The bottom line is that newspapers, as a gatekeeper to communication, are in full scale retreat. As newspaper subscriptions have declined, and fewer and fewer young people read hard-copy newspapers, hope for a revival fades. The net effect is that many newspapers are desperately seeking new economic models.[144] While tens of millions of people still read print newspapers, many now read their news entirely online,[145] and journalism students are understandably fearful regarding their career prospects.[146] The problem for the traditional print media is that they have higher operating costs related to ink, paper and news print distribution

138. *See* Leah Willingham, *Newspaper Shuts in Declining Coal County, Louisville Courier-Journal* 13A (July 31, 2023).

139. *See* Nathan Boney, *McClatchy newspapers file for bankruptcy, Courier-Journal* A28 (Feb. 14, 2020).

140. *See* Claire Moses, *Newspapers in Britain Struggle With Fewer Ads but More Readers, The New York Times* B3 (May 4, 2020).

141. *Id.*

142. *Id.*

143. *Id.*

144. *See A Newspaper Loses Its Paper Routes, supra* note 86 ("Other newspapers have closed and many more are threatened. But the transition to an all-digital product for The P-I will be especially closely watched in an industry that is fast losing revenue and is casting around for a new economic model.").

145. *See As Cities Go From Two Papers to One, supra* note 71.

146. *See* Sarah McCammon, *Journalism Students Uneasy About Job Prospects*, National Public Radio, All Things Considered (Feb. 26, 2009), http://www.npr.org/templates/story/story.php?storyId=100253844.

than online publishers.[147] Nevertheless, some investors regard the current situation as an investment opportunity and are seeking to snap up distressed media outlets in hopes of finding a new way forward.[148]

B. MEDIA EFFORTS TO SURVIVE

In an effort to adapt and survive in the modern environment, media outlets have taken a number of relatively drastic steps. For example, *The Christian Science Monitor* and *The Kentucky Post* jettisoned their print versions and now publish completely online.[149] Other newspapers, in an effort to save money, no longer publish on a daily basis,[150] have significantly downsized,[151] or are sharing material with competitors.[152] *The Washington Post* saw significant declines, and was forced to eliminate its Saturday print edition, Sunday Source section, and its Book World section (which continues, but not as a separate section).[153] *The New York Times* took out a large loan,[154] eliminated a quarterly dividend to conserve cash, folded its Metro section into the first section of the paper,[155] and reduced newsroom staff.[156] News Corp., which owns a variety of newspapers—including *The Wall Street Journal*, *New York Post*, and *Newsday*—marked down the value of its newspaper unit by $3 billion.[157] One newspaper accepted

---

147. *See* Richard Perez-Pena & Tim Arango, *Adding Fees and Fences on Media Sites*, *The New York Times*, at B1 (Dec. 28, 2009).

148. *See* Julie Creswell, *For a Few, Papers Seem a Timely Bet*, *The New York Times*, at B1 (Sept. 22, 2010).

149. *See* Richard Perez-Pena, *Detroit Newspapers May Sharply Cut Home Delivery*, *The New York Times* B3 (Dec. 13, 2008).

150. *Id.* (referring to The Detroit Free Press, The Detroit News, and other smaller newspapers).

151. *See As Cities Go From Two Papers to One*, *supra* note 71 ("Advance Publications said last fall that it might shut down *The Star-Ledger*, the dominant paper in New Jersey, but a set of cutbacks and union concessions kept the paper alive in much-downsized form.").

152. *See Id.*

153. *See* Kurtz, *supra* note 33, at A7.

154. *Id.* (*The New York Times* has borrowed $250 million from a Mexican financier at 14 percent interest....").

155. *Id.*

156. *See* Richard Perez-Pena, *Times Moves to Trim 100 in Newsroom*, *The New York Times*, at B1 (Oct. 20, 2009).

157. *See* Kurtz, *supra* note 33, at A7.

a governmental credit guarantee despite obvious implications for the paper's independence and impartiality.[158] The *San Francisco Chronicle* reduced its newsroom staff by 300 people or about 50 percent.[159] Other major newspapers reduced their staffs by 20 percent or more, including *The Washington Post* and *Los Angeles Times*.[160] In addition, the New York Times Co. threatened to shut down *The Boston Globe* which it had purchased for a record price some years earlier.[161] It ultimately decided to keep the paper open, but only after forcing *Boston Globe* workers to accept pay reductions.[162] In 2009, it ordered temporary pay cuts for employees of *The New York Times*.[163] The Time, Inc. media conglomerate was ultimately broken apart and sold in pieces.[164]

In the UK, Newsquest, which owns some 165 publications, is moving towards an all online publication environment.[165] While Newsquest is planning to impose a pay wall, it is a relatively loose one so that a reader must access 40 articles in 30 days before the pay wall kicks in.[166]

---

158. *See* Holly Ramer, *New Hampshire Aids Paper, The Courier-Journal*, at A13 (Nov. 15, 2009).

159. *See* Kurtz, *supra* note 33, at A7 (*quoting San Francisco Chronicle* Editor-at-Large Phil Bronstein).

160. *See As Cities Go From Two Papers to One, supra* note 71:

> The steady trickle of downsizing that sapped American papers for almost a decade has become a flood in the last few years. The Los Angeles Times still has one of the largest news staffs in the country, about 600 people, but it was twice as big in the late 1990s. The Washington Post had a newsroom of more than 900 six years ago, and has fewer than 700 now. The Gannett Company, the largest newspaper publisher in the country, eliminated more than 8,300 jobs in 2007 and 2008, or 22 percent of the total.
>
> On Wednesday, The Miami Herald, once the celebrated flagship of the Knight Ridder chain, said it would trim an additional 19 percent of its already diminished staff.

161. *See* Verena Dobnik, *Insiders: Boston Threat a Warning to Newspapers, The Courier-Journal*, at A2 (Apr. 5, 2009).

162. *See* Richard Perez-Pena, *Boston Globe Workers Reverse Course and Agree to Cuts, The New York Times*, at B5 (July 21, 2009).

163. *See Times Co. Announces Temporary Salary Cuts, supra* note 93.

164. *See* Sridhar Pappu & Jay Stowe, *The End of a Media Dynasty: An Oral History of How the Once-Dominant Time Inc. Ended Up on the Scrap Heap, The New York Times*, Business Section, B2 (May 20, 2018).

165. *See* Moses, *supra* note 140.

166. *Id.*

By 2018, despite aggressive efforts to adapt to a changing environment, the print media was still in decline. In New York City alone, the *Daily News*, once the largest circulation newspaper in the country,[167] cut its already diminished staff in half.[168] The reductions were motivated by the fact that it had lost millions of dollars as advertising and readership had declined.[169] Nevertheless, the scope of the cuts was staggering as the newspaper fired more than 40 newsroom employees, including 25 of its 34 sports journalists, and one-half of its editors, and these reductions came on top of other recent staff cuts.[170] *The Village Voice* ceased operations, as did two online sites (Gothamist and DNA Info).[171] However, one of those web sites was ultimately revived by WNYC Radio.[172] In New Orleans, *The Times-Picayune* newspaper purchased *The Advocate*.[173] Even though *The Times-Picayune kept The Advocate*'s brand, website, archives, and subscriber list, it laid off all 65 staff members.[174]

2019 was no better.[175] News room employment decreased by nearly 8,000, some media outlets decreased coverage, and some local newspapers disappeared.[176]

For many publishers, their future may be on the Web as online readership continues to grow.[177] Between 2007 and 2009, total online readership grew from 60 million visitors a month to 72 million visitors a month,[178] and some European newspapers were acquiring significant profit on Web

167. *See* Jaclyn Peiser, *Daily News, Lean but Brassy New York Staple, Cuts Staff in Half, The New York Times* A-1 (July 24, 2018).

168. *See* Jaclyn Peiser, *Website Revs Up, With Magazine's Help, to Cover More Next York News, The New York Times*, Business Section B3 (Sept. 27, 2018).

169. *See Lean but Brassy, supra* note 167, at A19.

170. *See id.* at A1.

171. *See id.* A19.

172. *Id.*

173. *See* Campbell Robertson, *Venerable Paper Meets End With a 'Let Them Eat Cake,' The New York Times* A1 (May 13, 2019).

174. *Id.*

175. *See* David Folkenflik, *A Year of Bad News for the New Industry*, National Public Radio, Weekend Edition Sunday (Dec. 29, 2019). https://www.npr.org/2019/12/29/792146686/a-year-of-bad-news-for-the-news-industry.

176. *Id.*

177. *See Newspaper Circulation Falls, supra* note 49, at B3.

178. *Id.*

publications.[179] *USA Today*, which had lost its status as the nation's most widely circulated newspaper, was trying to dramatically increase its digital presence, as well as to target mobile phone and tablet markets.[180] MSNBC.com was aggressively using the Web to expand the scope of its coverage.[181] In order to document the effects of the recent recession, MSNBC.com placed a reporter in Elkhart, Indiana, to blog, as well as to post videos and Twitter messages about the effects of the recession.[182] The *Daily News* decided to move towards more digital reporting.[183] In 2018, a new online New York City newspaper, *The City*, sprang up,[184] and the John S. And James L. Knight Foundation and the Lenfest Institute for Journalism created a $20 million fund to help "accelerate the digital transformation of major metro newsrooms around the nation."[185]

In order to deal with staff cutbacks, newspapers took a number of actions. *The Los Angeles Times*, for example, was considering the possibility of using the internet to allow newspaper readers to obtain "customized" newspapers tailored to their interests.[186] By doing so, the *Times* hoped to create targeted advertising for each customer.[187] Some newspapers have entered into joint operating agreements under which they share production and delivery expenses,[188] or they share articles, photo-

179. *See* Eric Pfanner, *European Newspapers Find Creative Ways to Thrive in the Internet Age, The New York Times*, at B4 (Mar. 30, 2009).

180. *See USA Today to Remake Itself, supra* note 57.

181. *See* Brian Stelter, *News Site Keeps Focus on Town's Recession, The New York Times*, at B1 (Aug. 10, 2009).

182. *Id.*

183. *See Lean but Brassy, supra* note 167, at A19.

184. *See* Peiser, *supra* note 167.

185. *Id.*

186. *See* Tim Arango, *An Effort to Attract More Readers By Offering Print-at-Home, The New York Times*, at B6 (Mar. 9, 2009) ("The service, which allows readers to pick and choose only the stories that interest them, is among the many maneuvers that newspapers across the country are making to respond to the changes the Internet has wrought on their businesses.").

187. *Id.* ("MediaNews has been working with a technology company—Mr. Vandevanter would not say which one—to develop a proprietary printer for a reader's home. It would receive and print a subscriber's customized newspaper—with targeted advertising.").

188. *See Seattle Paper is Resurgent as a Solo Act, supra* note 87.

graphs and other news content with other newspapers.[189] Rather than having multiple papers commit staff to a single story, one newspaper might assume responsibility for the task, but share the end product with other newspapers. This trend is motivated by two considerations: the fact that newsroom staffs have shrunk in recent years,[190] and the fact that Associated Press content is regarded as too expensive.[191] Under these joint agreements, newspapers do not necessarily share all of their content (*e.g.*, a newspaper might reserve the right to publish special investigative series without sharing the content with other papers).[192]

Another trend is for newspapers and broadcasters to rely on outside sources for more of their news content.[193] In other words, rather than maintaining a large staff of employees to prepare content, a newspaper might purchase that content from other sources such as stringers or freelance writers. The primary motivation, as with the sharing agreements, is to save money. Unlike permanent employees, for which companies usually provide a variety of fringe benefits (*e.g.*, health care, pension, vacation, sick leave), most stringers and free lance writers are paid on a per assignment basis. Such outsourcing may have implications for quality. As one prominent newspaper reported, "News comes from more and more outlets, about which readers know less and less."[194] While the media has always relied on freelance journalists, as well as on the Associated Press and Reuters, "a raft of smaller news outlets have cropped up in the last few years, selling or simply giving news reports to the traditional media—groups like Pro-Publica, Global Post, *Politico* and Kaiser Health News."[195] Some fear that these outside organizations may have biases (as if

189. *See* Richard Perez-Pena, *5 Big Papers to Share Articles and Photos*, *The New York Times*, at B7 (Feb. 19, 2009) (discussing an agreement between *The Daily News* (New York), the *Star-Ledger* (Newark), *The Buffalo News*, *The Record* (Hackensack, N.J.), and *The Times Union* (Albany, New York).

190. *See id.*

191. *See id.*

192. *See id.*

193. *See* Richard Perez-Pena, *As Shrinking Newsrooms Use Upstarts' Content, Vetting Questions Arise*, *The New York Times*, at B6 (Jan. 18, 2010).

194. *See id.*

195. *Id.*

existing media outlets do not?),[196] or may engage in less professional journalism.[197] Nevertheless, financial considerations are forcing newspapers to look more closely at such arrangements.

News Corporation, which owns publications in the United States, Australia and the United Kingdom, is trying to re-use content from one location in other locations in order to save money.[198] In order to do so, News Corporation has been hiring journalists to transform the language of articles from the usage in one jurisdiction to that of another jurisdiction (*e.g.*, shifting from using British English to American English, or vice-versa, as appropriate).[199]

A major problem for newspapers is that advertising, usually the largest revenue source for newspapers, is declining,[200] and is declining so quickly that newspapers cannot cut their budgets quickly enough to remain profitable.[201] A significant percentage of advertising has migrated to the Web,[202] or to other electronic competitors (*e.g.*, cable television).[203] For example,

---

196. *See id.*, at B6 (Jan. 18, 2010) ("Some of these issues came to a head recently, when the Washington Post published an article from a newly formed news organization, The Fiscal Times, about the debate over federal spending without disclosing that the group's financial backer is Peter G. Peterson, who has an abiding interest in the issue and ties to experts cited in the article. . . .").

197. *See id.*, at B6 (Jan. 18, 2010) (suggesting, thus far, that the quality has been good, but arguing that there "'are going to be some newsrooms, I can guarantee you, they're going to get garbage and they're going to print it,' said Kelly McBride, ethics group leader at the Poynter Institute, a school for journalists in St. Petersburg, Florida.").

198. *See* Tim Arango, *News Corp. Setting Up an Internal Wire Service, The New York Times*, at B5 (Sept. 14, 2009).

199. *Id.*

200. *See* Richard Perez-Pena, *McClatchy to Cut 15% of Staff, The New York Times*, Media, (Mar. 9, 2009) https://www.nytimes.com/2009/03/10/business/media/10mcclatchy.html ("The entire industry has experienced a sharp drop in ad revenue, particularly in two of the most important states for McClatchy, California and Florida.").

201. *See* Russell Adams, *Rocky Mountain News Shuts Down: Scripps Fails to Find Buyer for Denver Newspaper; Dailies at Risk in Other Metropolitan Markets, The New York Times*, at B1 (Feb. 27, 2009); *see also Venerable Paper Meets End With a 'Let Them Eat Cake,' supra* note 173, at A1.

202. *See* Richard Pérez-Pena, *Papers Facing Worst Year for Ad Revenue, The New York Times*, at C3 (Jun. 23, 2008).

203. *See* Brian Stelter, *Cable Networks Trying to Build on Their Gains in Ratings, The New York Times*, at C5 (May 26, 2008) ("In the 18- to 49-year-old demographic highly favored by advertisers, ABC, CBS and NBC each recorded double-digit declines, while Fox showed a slight uptick of 2 percent over last year, according to Nielsen Media Research.

even Twitter made a significant percentage of its income off advertising.[204] Over just the last couple of years, newspaper advertising has dropped by 25 percent.[205] Today, instead of scouring the local daily newspaper for job openings, many applicants conduct their job searches online using services like Monster.com[206] or Hotjobs.com,[207] obviating the need to buy comparatively expensive newspapers and search through newspaper classified advertisements.[208] In addition, many people are using Craigslist[209] to buy and sell goods,[210] thereby eliminating the need to purchase comparatively expensive newspaper ads.[211] As one industry observer noted, "Web sites like Craigslist have been to classified ads what the internal combustion engine was to horse-drawn buggies."[212] Even blogs are beginning

---

During the same time frame, ad-supported cable channels showed a 9 percent audience gain."). During the 2012 political campaign, cable news networks gained market share vis-a-vis television news. *See* Brian Stelter, *For Campaign News, Most Turn to Cable, The New York Times*, at B3 (Feb. 8, 2012).

204. *See* Bob Garfield, *The Point of Twitter*, National Public Radio, On the Media (Nov. 26, 2010), http://www.onthemedia.org/2010/nov/26/the-point-of-twitter/transcript/.

205. *See As Cities Go From Two Papers to One, supra* note 71 ("Ad revenue, the industry's lifeblood, has dropped about 25 percent in the last two years (by comparison, automotive revenue for Detroit's Big Three fell about 15 percent during the same period, although it has accelerated recently), and that slide, accelerated by the recession, shows no sign of leveling off in 2009.").

206. *See* http://www.monster.com/.

207. *See* http://hotjobs.yahoo.com/.

208. *See* Felicity Barringer, *HELP WANTED: Newspapers Seek Cyber Partners to Fight On-Line Ads, The New York Times* (Aug. 30, 1999).

209. http://www.craigslist.org/about/sites.

210. *See Craigslist Meets the Capitalists, The New York Times* (Dec. 8, 2006) (blog), http://dealbook.nytimes.com/2006/12/08/craigslist-meets-the-capitalists/ (noting that Craigslist "is doubling in size every year, as measured by page views and listings.").

211. *See Imagining a City Without Its Daily Newspaper, supra* note 22:

> A few blocks away, at a cigar bar in the city's financial center, an out-of-work IT professional named Bruce Salisbury is drawing deeply while surfing the Web on his laptop. 'Right now, I'm looking for a new position,' he says, 'and the thought hasn't even occurred to me to pick up the *Hartford Courant* to look in the jobs section. Everything is online. It's online; it's fast; it's immediate.' People are becoming more like Salisbury every day. That's threatening to papers like the *Courant*, which is the nation's oldest continuously published newspaper—older even than the Declaration of Independence.

http://www.npr.org/templates/story/story.php?storyId=100256908.

212. *See As Cities Go From Two Papers to One, supra* note 71.

to attract advertising revenue.[213] Although most bloggers do not attract enough revenue to allow them to quit their day jobs, some do.[214]

Newspapers also seek to attract online advertising, but there is less online newspaper advertising than print advertising although it is rapidly gaining ground on print advertising.[215] The difficulty is that the online and print advertising that exists is not sufficient to support traditional newspapers in their historical form and at historical staffing levels.[216] Most advertising (77%) gravitated away from local newspapers to tech companies like Facebook and Google.[217]

News organizations were able to stimulate some online advertising revenue by linking themselves to large social media platforms like Apple News Plus.[218] The hope was that the links would allow publishers to reach a broader audience.[219] By 2019, these partnerships were become relatively common.[220] By 2020, news sites obtained approximately 11.5% of their web traffic by linking to social media networks.[221] Traffic from Facebook and Twitter were major components (with TikTok, Snapchat and Instagram generating negligible traffic).[222] However, as social media platforms have moved to de-emphasize their links to news organizations, that traffic (and the associated advertising) have decreased.[223] Google seems to remain a player in this arena for now, and news organizations strategize

---

213. *See* Claire Cain Miller, *Ad Shift Throws Blogs a Business Line: Small Web-Based Media Networks Attract Big-Ticket Marketers, The New York Times*, at B1 (Sept. 14, 2009).

214. *Id.*

215. *See* Julie Bosman, *Online Newspaper Ads Gaining Ground on Print, The New York Times*, at C3 (Jun. 6, 2006) (while print advertising is still larger than online advertising, "newspaper print ad spending in the first three months of 2006 increased only 0.3 percent, to $10.5 billion, over the corresponding period last year. At the same time, spending for online advertising surged 35 percent.").

216. *See As Cities Go From Two Papers to One*, *supra* note 71 ("But no one yet has unlocked the puzzle of supporting a large newsroom purely on digital revenue....").

217. *See* Alexandra Bruell & Keach Hagey, *Facebook Rethinks Deals to Pay for News, The Wall Street Journal* B4 (June 10, 2022).

218. *See Silicon Valley Ditches News, Shaking an Unstable Industry supra* note 136, at B1.

219. *Id.*

220. *See* Edmund Lee, *Old Media Gambles on a Deal With Apple, The New York Times* B1 (Apr. 3, 2019).

221. *See Silicon Valley Ditches News, Shaking an Unstable Industry supra* note 136, at B1.

222. *Id.*

223. *Id.*

about how to use Google to drive viewers to their web sites.[224] However, even Google is beginning to de-emphasize news and laid off 45 workers in its news department.[225] In addition, Google has begun to utilize AI which may also decrease traffic to news organizations.[226]

Another possibility is for newspapers to accept donation. For example, Craig Newmark, the founder of Craigslist, gave a $2.5 million gift to New York Public Radio, $20 million to CUNY's graduate school, and another $20 million to the Markup (a website devoted to investigative technology.[227] In addition, a website has been established that allows individuals to donate to their newspapers,[228] but it is hard to believe that voluntary donations will be sufficient to save existing newspapers. In a desperate search for ways to make money and remain viable,[229] some have suggested radical solutions (*e.g.*, government subsidies and tax exemptions for newspapers).[230]

News outlets have also been trying to charge access fees for their online content.[231] A few U.S. newspapers have been successful in charging for content,[232] as have some European newspapers,[233] and the technology that

224. *Id.*

225. *Id.*

226. *Id.*

227. David Streitfeld, *How a Villain to Newspapers Is Trying to Save Journalism, The New York Times* B1 (Oct. 18, 2018).

228. *See* Bob Garfield, *Getting Desperate*, National Public Radio, On the Media (Feb. 20, 2009), http://www.onthemedia.org/2009/feb/20/getting-desperate/transcript/.

229. *See* Eric Pfanner, *German Publisher Lays Out Plan to Save Newspapers from the Internet; A German Plan to Save Newspapers from Death by Internet: Springer Offers Strategy for Publishers and Net Firms to Work Together, International Herald Tribune*, at 21 (Dec. 7, 2009).

230. *See* Bob Garfield, *Government Intervention to Save Journalism*, National Public Radio, On the Media (Jan. 28, 2011), http://www.onthemedia.org/2011/jan/28/government-intervention-to-save-journalism/transcript/.

231. *See* David Carr, *Papers Push to Get Out of a Box, The New York Times*, The Media Equation, at B1 (Apr. 13, 2009) (discussing the Associated Press's effort to be paid for reuse of its content by other organizations such as Google); Michael Moran, *No Such Thing as Free News*, National Public Radio (Apr. 21, 2009), http://www.npr.org/templates/story/story.php?storyId=103316249.

232. *See* Perez-Pena & Arango, *supra* note 147.

233. *See European Newspapers Find Creative Ways, supra* note 179.

would support charges is readily available.[234] Among the newspapers that do charge are *The Wall Street Journal* and the *Financial Times,*[235] as well as some of their subsidiaries,[236] and *The New York Times*[237] and *The Washington Post.*[238] In 2019, for a basic monthly subscription, *The New York Times* charged $15 a month, *The Washington Post* charged $10, and *The Wall Street Journal* charged $39.[239] Among those three, *The Washington Post* has 1.5 million digital subscribers, *The New York Times* has 3.4 million, and *The Wall Street* Journal has 1.7 million.[240] Those three have been much more successful at converting online viewers into digital subscribers with *The New York Times* converting 3.6% and *The Wall Street Journal* converting 4.5%.[241]

Although *The Wall Street Journal* has nearly one million subscribers, the *Financial Times* has only slightly more than 100,000.[242] The *Financial Times* remains profitable because it charges $300 for a subscription and $100 more for the print edition, and has even been able to increase revenue from subscriptions.[243] Some suggest that the *Financial Times'* strategy of charging for content was a wise one,[244] but that the *Financial Times'* success is primarily due to the nature of the publication (as a provider of specialized financial information).[245] A similar approach has worked

---

234. *See* David Folkenflik, *Jeff Jarvis: Rewriting Media's Business Model (Again)*, National Public Radio, All Things Considered (Oct. 6, 2009), http://www.npr.org/templates/story/story.php?storyId=113512103.

235. *See* Eric Pfanner, *The Paper That Doesn't Want to Be Free, The Courier-Journal*, at B1 (Aug. 17, 2009).

236. *Id.*

237. *See Local News Fades Out, supra* note 21, at B8.

238. *Id.*

239. *Id.*

240. *Id.*

241. *Id.*

242. *See The Paper That Doesn't Want to be Free, supra* note 235, at B7.

243. *Id.*

244. *Id.* ("The growth of paid online services under the Financial Times banner shows that the paper was right to maintain pay walls at a time when other media companies were yielding to the Silicon Valley mantra that 'information wants to be free,' said Tim Luckhurst, a journalism professor at the University of Kent in Britain and a former editor of The Scotsman.").

245. *Id.* ("For other online publishers seeking to charge readers, the big question is whether consumers would be willing to pay for general news, as opposed to specialized

for *The Information*, which focuses on Silicon Valley, is advertisement free, charges $399 a year, and generated $20 million in sales by the end of 2020.[246]

The Wall Street Journal, one of the few financially profitable newspapers,[247] adopted more of an intermediate approach to charging for content. Although it charged for its online content right from the start,[248] it placed approximately 70% of its content outside the paywall, including sports coverage, arts and entertainment articles, and selected stories.[249] "It's a pretty standard strategy for business, rights. I mean, you allow people to come in, sample your wares, but then say, if you want it all folks, you have to pay."[250] Although some of *The Journal's* business and financial news are freely available online, most of it is behind the paywall.[251] *The Journal* rarely attempts to charge for popular mainstream stories that can readily be found on free websites.[252] But even this approach has limits since it is possible to find *The Journal's* content on the Web through targeted internet searches.[253] *The Financial Times* recently modified its policy to permit "micropayments" that allow users to purchase individual articles rather than require a full subscription.[254]

---

financial news. Some analysts doubt it, but Mr. Ridding [Chief Executive of the *Financial Times*] said he thought they might.").

246. *See* Edmund Lee, *Maybe Information Doesn't Want to Be Free, The New York Times*, Sunday Business 1 (Feb. 9, 2020).

247. *See* Edmund Lee, *Who Is Going to Save Newspapers?; At the Wall Street Journal, Leaders Battle over the Future, and the Newsroom Is Divided, The New York Times, Sunday Business* 1 (Apr. 11, 2021).

248. *See* Bob Garfield, *Should Newspapers Charge for Content Online?*, National Public Radio, On the Media (Jan. 28, 2011), http://www.onthemedia.org/2011/jan/28/should-newspapers-charge-for-content-online/ ("Alan Murray is the Deputy Managing Editor and Executive Editor online for The Journal. Murray says from day one The Journal has charged its readers for online content. "Way back in 1996, a decision was made that we thought our content was valuable, and if people wanted it they were going to have to pay for it.").

249. *Id.*

250. *Id.* (Quoting Alan Murray).

251. *Id.*

252. *Id.*

253. *See The Paper That Doesn't Want to be Free, supra* note 235.

254. *See Id.*

Whether other news outlets will be able to successfully charge for their content, is far less clear. Few have been able to do so.[255] For example, The Gannett Corp. has been much less successful at converting viewers to subscribers, having only a 0.4% success rate.[256] *The Dallas Morning News* began charging for content in 2011, but it only had 30,000 digital subscribers and obtained only 5.6% of its circulation revenue from digital subscriptions.[257] In 2019, it laid off more than 170 employees.[258] By contrast, *The Minneapolis Star Tribune* had approximately 60,000 digital only subscribers which generated about $200 million per year.[259] The paper has remained profitable and supports a staff of 250,[260] but it projects that it will need 150,000 digital subscribers to remain profitable over the long term.[261] *The Boston Globe* has 110,000 digital subscribers which it charges $1 per day, and 35% of its subscribers come from outside its area. *The Daily News* had an online penetration of 23 million readers, but has not achieved success in its effort to change for content.[262] The paper was sold for $1 and lost $23.6 million in 2017.[263]

At least one commentator has argued that each news outlet must determine what is unique and valuable to its particular readership (*e.g.*, a Houston newspaper might choose to charge for content related to the oil industry),[264] and doubts whether newspapers can survive based solely on online advertising.[265]

For most newspapers and media outlets, there is a delicate balance between charging for online content, which can generate subscriptions

---

255. *See* Perez-Pena & Arango, *supra* note 140 ("Newspapers ... are weighing whether to ask online readers to pay for at least some of what they offer, as a handful of papers, like the Wall Street Journal and the Financial Times, already do.").

256. *See Local News Fades Out, supra* note 21, at B8.

257. *Id.*

258. *Id.*

259. *Id.*

260. *Id.*

261. *Id.*

262. *See Lean but Brassy, supra* note 167, at A19.

263. *Id.*

264. *Id.*

265. *Id.* (quoting Mr. Alan Murray of *The Wall Street Journal*: "It's going to be extremely difficult to support a robust news gathering operation on advertising alone, so they're going to have to find other sources of revenue.").

and income, and risking the possibility of discouraging online advertisers by limiting online traffic through paywalls.[266] Many publishers have decided that they cannot risk the possibility of alienating online advertisers who constitute a significant source of their online income.[267] Alan Rusbridger, former Editor of *The Guardian* newspaper, argues that "the future is going to be a world in which everyone—and by everyone I mean everything in science, academics, politics—is going to be open and linked and collaborative."[268] He doubts that newspapers can simply "withdraw from that world."[269] At the time of his statement, *The Guardian* was making approximately 40 million British Pounds per year from subscriptions.[270] However, even Rusbridger questioned whether *The Guardian* could survive long-term based solely on online advertising revenue, and he suggested that newspapers may ultimately be forced to enter into more collaborative relationships.[271]

For a while, *The Courier-Journal* allowed online readers to access a limited number of articles, and individual articles can be accessed only for a period of one week. After that, only abstracts were available for free, and readers were charged for viewing the full text of archived articles.[272] Now *The Courier-Journal* gives free access to some articles, but places others behind pay walls. *The New York Times* twice attempted to impose paywalls without success.[273] Undeterred, *The New York Times* has moved again in

---

266. *See The Paper That Doesn't Want to be Free, supra* note 235, at B7.

267. *Id.*

268. *See Should Newspapers Charge for Online Content?, supra* note 238.

269. *Id.*

270. *Id.*

271. *Id.* ("But I think we shouldn't lose sight of the ... way the rest of the Web is going, I think there are effort-saving and therefore money-saving ideas there to do with collaborating and linking and using networks and not trying to do everything ourselves.").

272. *See, e.g.*, http://pqasb.pqarchiver.com/courier_journal/access/2221997001.html?FMT=ABS&date=Dec+26%2C+2010.

273. *See* David Folkenflik, *"New York Times" Considers Risk and New Revenue*, National Public Radio (July 19, 2009), http://www.npr.org/templates/story/story.php?storyId=106774623.

that direction,[274] as have a number of French publishers.[275] For a while, *The New York Times* gave online readers free access to a limited number of articles per month, but attempted to charge for reading additional articles.[276] Rupert Murdoch's other newspapers have flirted with the idea of charging for online content.[277] As Murdoch recently stated, "Quality journalism is not cheap, and an industry that gives away its content is simply cannibalizing its ability to produce good reporting.... We intend to charge for all our news Web sites."[278] Amazon markets the Kindle and charges subscription fees to download news.[279]

Whether *The New York Times* or Murdoch (or any other newspaper) will succeed in charging for their online content is far from clear. Because so many publishers offer free online content, a single publisher (or groups of publishers) may not be able to successfully impose charges without seeing large numbers of readers migrate to other Web sites.[280] People can simply "Google" the information they seek.[281] Part of the problem is that online content has tended to be free, and there is the potential for consumer resistance,[282] which has forced most media outlets to move cau-

274. *See* Melissa Block, *The New York Times to Reinstitute Pay Wall*, National Public Radio, All Things Considered (Jan. 20, 2010), http://www.npr.org/templates/story/story.php?storyId=122777083.

275. *See* Eric Pfanner, *French Publishers Plan Digital Newstand: Online and Mobile Users Would Reach Content Via a Single Paid-Access Site, International Herald Tribune*, at 16 (Dec. 6, 2010).

276. *See* David Folkenflik, *"New York Times Unveils Metered Online Pay Wall*, National Public Radio, All Things Considered (Mar. 17, 2011), http://www.npr.org/2011/03/17/134621239/new-york-times-unveils-metered-online-paywall ("The *Times* is unveiling a metered system under which the paper's most loyal readers would pay for access to the website, though most casual online readers would not pay a cent. Print subscribers would also continue to receive unfettered access at no additional cost.").

277. *See* David Carr, *The Media Equation: For Murdoch, It's Try, Try Again, The New York Times*, at B1 (Aug. 10, 2009).

278. *Id.*

279. *See "New York Times" Considers Risk and New Revenue, supra* note 263.

280. *See The New York Times to Reinstitute Pay Wall, supra* note 264 (interviewing Professor Jay Rosen of New York University).

281. *See* Brooke Gladstone, *Google's Quest to Save Newspapers*, National Public Radio, On the Media (Jan. 28, 2011), http://www.onthemedia.org/2010/jul/16/googles-quest-to-save-newspapers/transcript/.

282. *See The New York Times to Reinstitute Pay Wall, supra* note 264 ("Over more than a decade, consumers became accustomed to the sweet, steady flow of free news, pictures,

tiously in deciding to impose fees.[283] Some new technologies provide the media with an easy method to charge for content,[284] and some French newspapers charge.[285]

The imposition of fees might ultimately benefit new online publishers: "Arianna Huffington, cofounder and editor in chief of *The Huffington Post*, predicted that much of the talk of media's mining the Web for new revenue would never become reality—and that if it did, free sites like hers would benefit. Some of the plans now being laid might work, she said, but many of them would just alienate the internet users who click from one site to another, wherever links and their curiosity take them."[286] However, preliminary estimates suggest that *The New York Times*' efforts to charge for content seem to be bearing fruit: the paper's new model was greeted by an increase in profits and an increase in the number of subscribers.[287] Google is working to create new ways to access news information.[288] "Living Stories" groups a variety of articles on centralized topics, and "Fast Flip" provides an online cache of magazine pages so that a reader can simply flip through them.[289] Traditional newspapers and magazines benefit from this arrangement through advertising on the Google system.[290]

Magazines are facing comparable issues. For example, *Time* magazine decided to limit access to free online content by providing only summa-

---

videos and music on the Internet. Paying was for suckers and old fogeys. Content, like wild horses, wanted to be free.").

283. *Id.* ("Industry experts have their doubts, saying that pay systems might work, but in limited ways and only for some sites. Publishers who sounded early this year as though they were raring to go have not yet taken the leap, and the executives who advocate change tend to range from vague to cautious in making any predictions about fundamentally changing the finances of their battered businesses.").

284. *See* Brad Stone & Stephanie Clifford, *In Apple Tablet, Print Media Hope for a Payday, The New York Times*, at B1 (Jan. 26, 2010).

285. *See* Jeremy Kirk, *UK, French Newspapers to Charge for Content*, CIO.com, (Mar. 26, 2010). http://www.cio.com/article/588284/UK_French_Newspapers_to_Charge_for_Content.

286. *See Adding Fees and Fences on Media Sites, supra* note 147.

287. *See* NPR Staff, *The News Tip: Don't Listen to Naysayers*, National Public Radio, Weekend Edition Sunday (Oct. 30, 2011), http://www.npr.org/2011/10/30/141834659/the-news-tip-don't-listen-to-pay-wall-naysayers.

288. *See Google's Quest to Save Newspapers, supra* note 271.

289. *Id.*

290. *Id.*

ries and requiring readers to pay subscription fees in order to obtain full access.[291] *Newsweek* posted its cover online, along with small excerpts from certain articles, and invited interested individuals to purchase the magazine if they wish to read more.[292] In addition, it has undergone a complete redesign.[293] However, certain high-end "niche" magazines are doing well.[294] Included are magazines like Adventure Journal, Mountain Gazette, Summit Journal and Ori.[295] Often, these magazines are lavish affairs with lots of photographs and are designed as coffee table displays.[296] Moreover, most are produced by small at-home operations.[297]

Some have argued that news websites should shift to local news coverage, and should enter into alliances with other local Web-based news organizations. In addition, one commentator has argued that websites should blur the line between amateur and professional news gathering,[298] disclose their personal beliefs and biases, and conduct their reporting in full public view.[299] Others question whether the market for hyper-local reporting is sufficient to sustain the market.[300]

At the same time that newspapers are under threat, traditional television broadcasters are under pressure as well. Advertising revenue at the major networks has suffered a significant decline.[301] The decline is directly attributable to competition from cable television which has been steadily attracting viewers away from traditional television, lowering viewing levels, and ultimately making it more difficult for traditional television to

291. *See* Jeremy W. Peters, *Time Moves to Limit Free Content Online, The New York Times*, at B3 (July 8, 2010).

292. *Id.*

293. *See* Jeremy W. Peters, *From a Subdued Tina Brown, A Quiet Restart of Newsweek, The New York Times*, at B1 (Feb. 24, 2011).

294. *See* John Branch, *High-End Outdoors Magazines Are Thriving in Print, The New York Times* B1 (June 23, 2024).

295. *Id.*

296. *Id.*

297. *Id.*

298. *See Rewriting Media's Business Model (Again), supra* note 234.

299. *Id.*

300. *Id.*

301. *See* Tim Arango, *Broadcast TV Struggles to Stay Viable, The New York Times*, at A1 (Feb. 28, 2009) ("CBS, home to '60 Minutes,' ... is having a better year in prime time than any other network. And yet, as at the other networks, profits have declined sharply at CBS.").

justify high advertising rates.[302] At it's peak, the cable industry attracted as many as 100 million viewers.[303] The 2008 recession also affected the broadcaster advertising rates.[304] As the recession abated, advertising revenues recovered somewhat.[305] But even cable television companies have been challenged as new streaming services have popped up (e.g., Fubo and Sling), encouraging consumers to eliminate their cable subscriptions.[306] Cable companies have lost an average of 5 million viewers per year, and total subscriptions now cover only 75 million people.[307] Cable companies are scrambling to respond by coming up with new "bundles" to attract customers.[308]

Some believe that the broadcasting industry may be in the midst of a "revolution." In an editorial, *The New York Times* quotes internet observer Clay Shirky who noted that many traditional media outlets have fallen by the wayside,[309] and observed that "this is what a revolution looks like."[310] He argues that "the old stuff gets broken faster than the new stuff is put in its place. The importance of any given experiment isn't apparent at the moment it appears; big changes stall, small changes spread. Even the revolutionaries can't predict what will happen. Agreements on all sides that core institutions must be protected are rendered meaningless by the very

---

302. *Id.* ("CBS reported that for the fourth quarter of last year, as the recession deepened, operating income in its television segment declined 40 percent, even though it was by far the most-watched network.... And Disney's broadcasting business had a 60 percent drop in operating income."); *see also* Suzanne Vranica & Ethan Smith, *Internet Radio Wants More Ad Dollars, The Wall Street Journal*, at B4 (Dec. 22, 2011).

303. *See* Benjamin Mullen, *Cable TV is on Life Support, But a New Bundle is Coming Alive, The New York Times* B-3 (Sept. 14, 2023).

304. *Id.*

305. *See* Stuart Elliott, *Still Counting on the Power of Television, The New York Times*, at B5 (Dec. 7, 2010).

306. *See* Mullen, *supra* note 289, at B-1 ("As cord cutting accelerates across the country, with millions of Americans dropping their traditional cable-TV packages each year, it threatens to upend yhr psy-TV bundle, a linch-pin of the media industry for decades.").

307. *Id.*

308. *Id.*

309. *See Why Newspapers Can't Be Saved, But the News Can, supra* note 33 ("The Rocky Mountain News is dead. The Seattle Post-Intelligencer will publish its last issue Tuesday. The Detroit Free Press has cut home delivery to three days a week. The Star Tribune in Minneapolis and the Inquirer and Daily News in Philadelphia have all declared bankruptcy.").

310. *Id.*

people doing the agreeing.... Ancient social bargains, once disrupted, can neither be mended nor quickly replaced, since any such bargain takes decades to solidify."[311]

Shirky goes on to note that some argue that the traditional media can be resuscitated with a "digital facelift."[312] Some frame the issue in the following way: "Now that newspapers are starting to drop dead, the survivors are rapidly shuffling through these ideas again, desperate to stop the bleeding, "demanding to know 'If the old model is broken, what will work in its place?'"[313] Sharky's answer is "nothing."[314]

---

311. *Id.* He went on to note that:

> And so it is today. When someone demands to know how we are going to replace newspapers, they are really demanding to be told that we are not living through a revolution. They are demanding to be told that old systems won't break before new systems are in place. They are demanding to be told that ancient social bargains aren't in peril, that core institutions will be spared, that new methods of spreading information will improve previous practice rather than upending it. They are demanding to be lied to. There are fewer and fewer people who can convincingly tell such a lie.

Id; see also Brooke Gladstone, *Newspaper of the Future*, National Public Radio, On the Media (Jan. 28, 2011), http://www.onthemedia.org/2011/jan/28/newspaper-of-the-future/transcript/ (quoting Yochai Benkler, described as author of The Wealth of Networks).

312. *Id.*, again quoting Sharky:

> The curious thing about the various plans hatched in the '90s is that they were, at base, all the same plan: "Here's how we're going to preserve the old forms of organization in a world of cheap perfect copies!" The details differed, but the core assumption behind all imagined outcomes ... was that the organizational form of the newspaper, as a general-purpose vehicle for publishing a variety of news and opinion, was basically sound, and only needed a digital facelift.
>
> Now that newspapers are starting to drop dead, the survivors are rapidly shuffling through these ideas again, desperate to stop the bleeding, "demanding to know 'If the old model is broken, what will work in its place?'

Id.

313. *Id.* (Quoting Sharky).

314. *Id.*, Sharky states that:

> Nothing will work. There is no general model for newspapers to replace the one the internet just broke.
>
> With the old economics destroyed, organizational forms perfected for industrial production have to be replaced with structures optimized for digital data. It makes increasingly less sense even to talk about a publishing industry, because the core problem publishing solves—the incredible difficulty, complexity, and expense of making something available to the public—has stopped being a problem.

Id.

Nevertheless, Shirky is optimistic about the future of the media, but he sees a future that is far different from the present and that may be entirely online.[315] As people spend more and more time connected to the Web, online advertising will necessarily increase.[316] For some publications, for example *The New York Times*, digital advertising revenue is rapidly approaching equivalence to print advertising revenue.[317] Even there, while print advertising has declined, digital advertising has increased, so that overall advertising revenue has remained flat.[318] The bright spot for newspapers is that the rates for digital advertising are generally higher than the rates for print advertising.[319]

The future of the media is also complicated by the development of AI. New technologies, particularly Google and Microsoft's intelligence tools, allow individuals to submit search inquiries in "full paragraphs" rather than as a list of links.[320] However, there is a risk that these new AI tools

---

315. *Id. The New York Times* editorial states that:

> Shirky, like many Internet enthusiasts, is future-positive. For him, it's time to get on with the revolution. Forget about saving newspapers. Instead, experiment with new ways of doing journalism in the digital era.
>
> There is one possible answer to the question "If the old model is broken, what will work in its place?" The answer is: Nothing will work, but everything might. Now is the time for experiments, lots and lots of experiments, each of which will seem as minor at launch as craigslist did, as Wikipedia did . . .
>
> Any experiment . . . designed to provide new models for journalism is going to be an improvement over hiding from the real, especially in a year when, for many papers, the unthinkable future is already in the past.
>
> For the next few decades, journalism will be made up of overlapping special cases. Many of these models will rely on amateurs as researchers and writers. Many of these models will rely on sponsorship or grants or endowments instead of revenues. Many of these models will rely on excitable 14 year olds distributing the results. Many of these models will fail. No one experiment is going to replace what we are now losing with the demise of news on paper, but over time, the collection of new experiments that do work might give us the journalism we need.

Id.

316. *See* Eric Pfanner, *Internet Companies and Ad Agencies Go From Old Enemies to New Friends*, *The New York Times*, at B7 (July 4, 2009). http://www.nytimes.com/2009/07/04/business/media/04digital.html?scp=1&sq=internet%20companies%20ad%20agencies&st=cse.

317. *See* Martin Peers, *Mixed Ad Message From Newspaper*, *The Wall Street Journal*, Heard on the Street, at B12 (July 29, 2010).

318. *Id.*

319. *Id.*

320. *See Publishers Gird for Threat from A.I.*, *supra* note 100.

will further undercut the viability of existing media outlets.[321] Some have referred to this as the "Wikipedia-ization" of information.[322] Previously, search engines would use links to direct readers to media sites for the answers.[323]

A couple of trends run counter to these conclusions. For one thing, CNN decided in 2017 to increase the level of its investigative reporting.[324] In addition to bringing existing reporters into an investigative unit, CNN decided to hire at least 12 more reporters.[325] The unit was being advised by two Pulitzer Prize winning editors (Carl Bernstein and James Steele).[326]

Some billionaires have purchased newspapers, creating hope their business acumen might make the publications profitable.[327] Jeff Bezos paid $250 million for *The Washington Post*, Dr. Patrick Soon-Shiong paid $500 million for the *Los Angeles Times*, and Marc Benioff bought Time Magazine for $190 million.[328] But the billionaires have not been able to operate their media purchases at a profit, losing millions, "wealth doesn't insulate an owner from the serious challenges plaguing many media companies."[329]

Some online groups have obtained funding through grants. The City raised nearly $8.5 million in grants, with $2.5 million each coming from the Leon Levy Foundation, the Charles H. Revson Foundation, and Craig Newmark (the founder of Craigslist).[330] ProPublica decided to expand its local reporting network and is funding projects on government accountability.[331]

In Britain, in an effort to assist newspapers, the government has taken several actions. For one thing, the government eliminated a tax on e-books

---

321. *Id.*

322. *Id.*

323. *Id.*

324. *See* David Folkenflik, *CNN Beefs Up Investigative Reporting*, National Public Radio, Media (Jan. 30, 2017).

325. *Id.*

326. *Id.*

327. *See* Benjamin Mullin & Katie Robertson, *Billionaires Hope to Profit in Media. It's Not Working, The New York Times* B1 (Jan. 19, 2024).

328. *Id.*

329. *Id.*

330. *See* Peiser, *supra* note 167.

331. *Id.*

and e-newspapers,[332] and it announced plans to spend 35 million British pounds on advertising by the National Health Service.[333] However, neither action was expected to stem the slide.[334] While 35 million in advertising revenue is a substantial amount, British newspapers are losing hundreds of millions of pounds, and the advertising revenue was not spread equally among all newspapers.[335] As a result, despite the efforts, many were predicting that the UK would still be left with newspaper "black holes."[336]

In some countries (e.g., Canada and Australia), governments have started requiring social media platforms (e.g., Meta Platforms) to compensate news outlets for linking to their content.[337] In that way, social media outlets would be required to help finance news gathering activities.[338] In the U.S., some have called for Congress to enact the Journalism Competition and Preservation Act which has a similar objective.[339]

These proposals have not been well-received by tech companies. For example, Google and Facebook have threatened to block Australian users,[340] arguing that their companies already help news outlet by directing traffic to their websites (making them more attractive for potential advertisers).[341] While the companies seem willing to pay for content (for example, they pay news outlets in France), they object to the idea that the government would set the price if the parties could not agree.[342] When Canada tried to implement such an approach, Meta responded by blocking access on its site to news links.[343] Many social media platforms

332. *See* Moses, *supra* note 140.

333. *Id.*

334. *Id.*

335. *Id.*

336. *Id.*

337. *See* Livia Albeck-Ripka, *Australia to Make Facebook And Google Pay News Outlets, The New York Times* B4 (Apr. 21. 2020); Paul Vieira, *Meta Acts to Block News in Canada, The Wall Street Journal* B4 (Aug. 2, 2023).

338. *Id.*

339. *See Journalism Needs a Lifeline, supra* note 24, at 1E.

340. *See* Damien Cave, *Google and Facebook Balk As Australia Gets Tough, The New York Times* B1 Jan. 23, 2021).

341. *Id.*

342. *Id.*, at B3.

343. *See* Livia Albeck-Ripka, *Australia to Make Facebook And Google Pay News Outlets, The New York Times* B4 (Apr. 21. 2020); Paul Vieira, *Meta Acts to Block News in Canada, The Wall Street Journal* B4 (Aug. 2, 2023).

have started reducing their links to the news industry.[344] As a result, news outlets like BuzzFeed News have disappeared.[345] Moreover, Meta has re-thought its decision to pay for news.[346] Previously, Facebook paid as much as $15 million to the *Washington Post*, $20 million to the *New York Times*, and $10 million to the *Wall Street Journal*.[347] Facebook paid because it maintained a selection of free articles for its users, and it agreed to pay the publishers for using their content.[348]

One interesting development is that some homeless individuals have started "street" newspapers that are traditional printed papers.[349] Many of these new papers are nonprofit organizations that survive based on newspaper sales, as well as based on grants and donations.[350] Included are publications such as *Street Roots* (Portland, Oregon) which has a circulation of 16,000, *Real Change* (Seattle, Washington) which has a circulation of 72,000 and a street sales force of more than one hundred people, and *Street Sense* (Washington, D.C.).[351]

In Japan, online publications have struggled to survive in competition with the traditional media.[352] The online publication JanJan News was ultimately forced to shut down most of its operation.[353] Japan's situation may be explained by reference to Japanese culture and it's experience may not be transferable to the United States or Europe.[354]

---

344. *See Silicon Valley Ditches News, Shaking an Unstable Industry supra* note 136, at B1.

345. *See* Benjamin Mullin & Katie Robertson, *A Web Pioneer, BuzzFeed News Will Shut Down, The New York Times* A1 (Apr. 21, 2023); *see also* Bobby Allyn, *Digital news sites fight to survive as online ad dollars dry up*, National Public Radio, All Things Considered (May 2, 2023).

346. *See Facebook Rethinks Deals to Pay for News, supra* not 227, at B4.

347. *Id.*

348. *Id.*

349. *See* Janie Lorber, *Extra, Extra! Homeless Lift Street Papers, And Attitudes, The New York Times*, at B5 (Apr. 13, 2009).

350. *Id.*

351. *Id.*

352. *See* Martin Fackler, *Ink Gushes in Japan's Media Landscape, The New York Times*, at A14 (June 21, 2010) ("No online journalism of any kind has yet posed a significant challenge to Japan's monolithic but sclerotic news media.").

353. *Id.*

354. *Id.*

C. WILL THE INTERNET LEAD TO THE DEMISE OF THE "WATCHDOG OF DEMOCRACY?"

Some commentators worry that the decline of traditional media, and the rise of the internet, will have troubling implications for the democratic system. Large newspapers have historically played a "watchdog" role in society by investigating and challenging the government.[355] Perhaps the most famous example of this watchdog function is provided by Woodward and Bernstein's Watergate investigation for *The Washington Post*; an investigation that ultimately led to President Richard Nixon's resignation from the presidency.[356] But numerous other examples abound, and investigative reporting is a proud tradition among American newspapers.[357]

Newspapers were able to conduct investigations because they maintained paid staffs who could devote time and effort to investigative journalism. As advertising revenue has declined, some newspapers no longer have sufficient resources to support strong investigative reporting.[358] As traditional media continues to decline, and more news organizations move online, there is a risk that investigative journalism will decline still further. This possibility has caused some commentators to express concern that there will be a net loss to democracy if newspapers are no longer available to perform their investigative function, and can no longer serve

---

355. *See* Irving Fang, A History of Mass Communication: Six Information Revolutions 56 (1997) (referring to articles "awakening the nation to governmental corruption, the greed of industrialists, and the need for pure food laws and child labor laws.").

356. *See* Alicia C. Shepard, *Deep Throat's Legacy to Journalism*, National Public Radio (Dec. 19, 2008). http://www.npr.org/templates/story/story.php?storyId=98532461.

357. *See Imagining a City Without Its Daily Newspaper, supra* note 22:

> So let's let the *[Hartford] Courant* stand in for all papers facing tough times and take a moment to imagine Connecticut without it. For one thing, former Gov. John Rowland wouldn't have faced corruption charges a few years back. Richard Blumenthal, the state's longtime attorney general, says the *Courant*'s tenacious coverage compelled authorities to investigate Rowland. He describes the *Courant*'s reporting as 'old-fashioned muckraking, finding out that there was corruption. The bad guys go to prison; the system's changed, reformed—you know, the sort of basic American tableau of what a good newspaper does at its best.' Hartford's mayor has just been indicted on bribery charges, and the *Courant* was out ahead on that, too. The paper has exposed polluters and the deployment of mentally ill soldiers to Iraq. But it's not just pursuing hard news.

358. *See No Such Thing as Free News, supra* note 231.

as a check against governmental misconduct and abuse.[359] As a former Executive Editor of the *Miami Herald* put it: "nobody else will step in and do the occasionally extraordinary reporting that newspapers do. The difference that a good newspaper makes to the quality of life in any community is vital. It's like a healthy heart."[360] Nicholas Lemann, Dean of Columbia University's School of Journalism, agrees, arguing that: "In a world where content is free, original newsgathering doesn't happen. We really need to face up to the fact that this is going to be lost."[361] Steve Coll, former Managing Editor of *The Washington Post*, has argued that traditional newspapers provide certain essential advantages to reporting: "audiences of a global scale," the "independence that comes with scale," legal departments and deep pockets and an imperviousness to threat, particularly in these libel-shopping, globalized days."[362] In addition, traditional organizations help train journalists and give them the time to do quality work.[363]

The difficulty is that many people, especially young people, are moving away from traditional media outlets towards online news sources.[364] As a result, the number of online news outlets is growing.[365] One commentator worries that these online sources tend to present opinions first and then facts.[366] He argues that real journalism takes time and that runs counter to the speed of the internet: "Real life is slow; it takes professionals time to figure out what happened, and how it fits into context. Technology is

---

359. *See* Kurtz, *supra* note 33, at A7; *As Cities Go From Two Papers to One*, *supra* note 71 ("For more than two centuries, newspapers have been the indispensable source of public information and a check on the abuses of government and other powerful interests. And they still reach a vast and growing audience.").

360. *Id.* (*quoting* former *Miami Herald* Executive Editor Tom Fiedler).

361. *See* Kurtz, *supra* note 33, at A7 (quoting Dean Nicholas Lemann, Columbia University, School of Journalism).

362. *See* Brooke Gladstone, *Stopping the Presses*, National Public Radio, On the Media (Feb. 20, 2009), http://www.onthemedia.org/2009/feb/20/stopping-the-press/transcript/.

363. *Id.* (quoting Steve Coll, former Managing Editor, *The Washington Post*) ("And the other thing they have is the ability to protect journalists from anything other than the perfection of their work over a long period of time and to give them the language training and the area studies that the best of them will employ to do the work that matters and work that lasts.").

364. *See* Sapna Maheshwari, *Instagram Grows as a News Source, Reluctantly, The New York Times* A1 (Feb. 23, 2024).

365. *Id.*

366. *See* Manjoo, *supra* note 12, at B7.

fast. Smartphones and social networks are giving us facts about the news much faster than we can make sense of them, letting speculation and misinformation fill the gap."[367]

While the internet is a very democratic medium, in the sense that it has enabled ordinary people to communicate on a mass scale, the critical question is whether online publications can adequately replace the investigative role of newspapers. As newspapers close or reduce staffs, the net number of reporters is necessarily reduced. For example, when the *Rocky Mountain News* closed, more than 200 reporters lost their jobs, and the community lost a newspaper that was trying to do "special projects that took in-depth looks at the issues of most concern to the citizens of Denver."[368]

Increasingly, unable to fund their own reporters, some newspapers are relying on wire services for information.[369] One micro story suggested that the death of a newspaper could lower election turnouts and increase the chances that incumbents would be reelected.[370] Interestingly, the public seems not to be excessively concerned about the possible loss of this "watchdog." Although 43% of responders in one study indicated that civic life in their community would be harmed if local newspapers closed, only 33% indicated that they would miss their local paper.[371]

Although, individuals can undertake investigations on their own, it is not clear that individuals will choose to devote their free time to such investigations. Moreover, online allegations, not backed up by the imprimatur of newspapers (or by the status of radio or television stations), may not be considered "reliable" or taken seriously by the public. As the Dean of Columbia University's School of Journalism stated, "If you don't have

---

367. *Id.*

368. *See* Brooke Gladstone, *Rocky Mountain Bye*, National Public Radio, On the Media (Mar. 6, 2009) (quoting Rich Boehne), http://www.onthemedia.org/2009/mar/06/rocky-mountain-bye/transcript/.

369. *See No Such Thing as Free News*, *supra* note 231 ("National Public Radio and the web-based Pro Publica re among the last bastions of objective international news reporting and analysis. And those newspapers still standing increasingly rely on dispatches from the Associated Press and Reuters, the public utilities of the journalism world.").

370. *See* Bob Garfield, *Paper Trail*, National Public Radio, On the Media (Apr. 3, 2009), http://www.onthemedia.org/2009/apr/03/paper-trail/transcript/.

371. *See* Bob Garfield, *A Shrug Goodbye*, National Public Radio, On the Media (Mar. 13, 2009), http://www.onthemedia.org/2009/mar/13/a-shrug-goodbye/transcript/.

people out working as full-time reporters, there's this category of information that's not going to appear magically out of nowhere."[372] For example, one reporter questioned the reliability of social media that reported on uprisings in Iran.[373]

Some of the concerns about the future of newspapers miss the point. The critical question is not whether traditional ink and paper publications will survive, but whether the traditional investigative function will continue. As one commentator noted, "I think that the policy should not necessarily be to try to preserve ink printed on newsprint and thrown on people's doorsteps every morning, because what's important here is not that method of delivering the information. It's all of the reporting and organizing of information that goes on in newsrooms."[374] Matthew Yglesias, a blogger and a fellow with the Center for American Progress Action Fund, agrees: "The question is, do you want to try to channel [your efforts] into this dying model that isn't exactly working any more, or is it more important to find ways to fund new kinds of institutions?"[375]

Traditional media makes less and less sense in an online world. News magazines have traditionally operated on a weekly news cycle,[376] and most newspapers have published one edition a day. In an internet era, when information moves quickly, almost instantaneously, a weekly model (and even, to some extent, a daily model) runs the risk of being dangerously out-of-date. As a result, many young people have gravitated to the Web and away from traditional media for their news information.[377]

As the traditional media declines, new forms of investigative journalism are springing up online, and there are many non-traditional media outlets conducting investigations (*e.g.*, the Drudge Report).[378] Of course,

---

372. *Id.*

373. *See* Frank James, *Which Tweets From Iran Are True?*, National Public Radio, The Two Way (June 17, 2009) http://www.npr.org/blogs/thetwo-way/2009/06/which_tweats_from_iran_are_tru.html.

374. *The Paper Trail, supra* note 370 (quoting Professor Sam Schulhofer-Wohl, Princeton University).

375. *See Stopping the Presses, supra* note 362.

376. *See* David Carr, *Newsweek's Journalism of Fourth and Long, The New York Times*, Week in Review, at 1 (May 24, 2009).

377. *See* Brian Stelter, *Youths Are Watching But Less Often on TV, The New York Times*, at B1 (Feb. 9, 2012).

378. *See* http://www.drudgereport.com/.

online newspapers are not entirely new phenomenons,[379] having existed for some time,[380] and some online publications began entirely online rather than shifting from print to online. In recent years, approximately 400 local news sites have been established.[381] However, the local news sites tend to be located in big cities and in more affluent areas.[382]

The trend towards online investigative journalism is no doubt influenced by significant staff reductions at a number of traditional newspapers. As those cuts occurred, a number of experienced staff were fired or laid off. Rather than change careers, some experienced journalists decided to continue doing journalistic work. Without the resources or market to justify a print edition, they decided to work online. Online publications have the advantage that they can be sent to computers and iPhones and can be updated during the course of the day.[383] Illustrative of this new approach is GlobalPost whose staff includes former journalists from *Newsday*, the *Boston Globe*, and the *Los Angeles Times*.[384]

Online investigative journalism may actually have "watchdog" advantages over traditional newspapers. As noted earlier, newspapers have biases that can affect their reporting on matters of public interest. As Andrew Garson of *The Courier-Journal* admits, his newspaper has a liberal bias.[385] While Garson denies that the paper's bias affects its news reporting (as opposed to its editorial views),[386] that is not necessarily the case.[387] So, democracy may actually benefit if journalism shifts from a single newspaper with monopolistic control (as is the case in some cities) to

---

379. *See* A HISTORY OF MASS COMMUNICATION, *supra* note 355, at 234.

380. *Id.*

381. *See Local News Fades Out*, *supra* note 21, at B8.

382. *Id.*

383. *See* Claire Cain Miller, *At Tech Blog, Combining Strategies, The New York Times*, at B1 (July 12, 2010).

384. *Id.*

385. *See* Arnold Garson, *Editorial: The Politics of a Newspaper, The Courier-Journal*, H4 (Aug. 2, 2009).

386. *Id.*

387. *See Stopping the Presses*, *supra* note 362 (quoting Matthew Yglesias) ("You know, ... even if we keep having coverage from abroad, coverage of national politics, it's going to have a different kind of tone. It's going to be animated by a different set of values. And so, to the extent that we appreciate the current tone and values, there will be a loss. I don't think that those values and that approach are necessarily all they're cracked up to be all the time...").

multiple online news entities offering a variety of perspectives.[388] These online entities may be more likely to present diverse perspectives on the issues of the day.[389]

The "new media" includes a variety of models, including "smaller groups, those devoted to journalism, those operating out of universities, those operating from advocacy groups and think tanks, all these things are already happening."[390] As local news coverage in New York City declined, *The City*,[391] an online news site devoted to local coverage emerged.[392] Run by a former city editor at the *Daily News*, *The City* was planning to hire 15 journalists to focus on local issues such as "transportation, politics, affordable housing, health care, education and climate change."[393] The goal was to "reconnect people to civil activity," and to focus on stories that "bubble up from communities."[394] In an innovative step, the web site teamed up with *New York* magazine to make some of its content available on that magazine's website.[395] In return the magazine provided the website with technological infrastructure and office space.[396]

Blogs have also emerged as a source of news. Included are blogs which are one-person operations, as well as large organizations like the *Huffington Post*[397] and the *Daily Beast* that publish blog posts by unpaid bloggers.[398] There are also "hyperlocal" blogs (focused on "50 to 60,000 people who have common interests such as the school system, parks, or the local tax base"). These "hyperlocal" blogs often focus on issues that may be

---

388. *See Id.* (quoting Matthew Yglesias) ("Then a time came with, I think, the invention of television and radio that a lot of newspapers started collapsing, and we had the kind of one-newspaper model. And that let a newspaper in a city, and particularly the newspaper in the biggest city, acquire a sort of authoritativeness, and it made the press very powerful vis-a-vis other kinds of actors in politics and in the business world, which in some ways was good because it's a check on other large powers.").

389. *Id.*

390. *Id.*

391. https://www.thecity.nyc/.

392. *See* Peiser, *supra* note 167.

393. *Id.*

394. *Id.*

395. *Id.*

396. *Id.*

397. https://www.huffpost.com/.

398. *See No Such Thing as Free News*, *supra* note 231.

overlooked by larger and more traditional news organizations,[399] and sometimes they collaborate with traditional newspapers.[400] Included are websites such as EveryBlock, Outside.in, PlaceBlogger and Patch.[401] These sites might attempt to alert readers to government data reports, local arrests, restaurant reviews, and house sales.[402] EveryBlock was started with a grant in excess of $1 million, and has spread to several cities.[403] Because of small audiences,[404] some hyper-local blogs can have difficulty generating significant advertising revenue,[405] but there is hope that local businesses will eventually provide financial support for such sites.[406]

There is also a tendency to distribute news through subscription newsletters that focus on niches areas with broad appeal.[407] Included are Puck, Punchbowl News, The Anker, and Semafor, which often display on platforms such as Substack, The Free Press and The Bulwark.[408] These newsletters "have attracted top journalists by putting them at the heart of the enterprise, sometimes as part owners of the companies."[409] Puck employs 14 reporters who write about politics, finance, and media.[410] These new startups derive revenue from advertisements, paid subscriptions and sponsored events.[411] Punchbowl News, another newsletter, with 30 employees, aggressively covers Congress and aggressively reports on Capitol Hill and has expanded to cover the financial services industry.[412] The Chief Executive, Anna Palmer, indicated that the newsletter does not

---

399. *See* Bob Garfield, *Is Hyperlocal the Future of News?*, National Public Radio, On the Media (Jan. 28, 2011), http://www.onthemedia.org/2010/jul/16/is-hyperlocal-the-future-of-news/transcript/ (quoting Mary Ann Giordano, Deputy Metro Editor, *The New York Times*).

400. *Id.*

401. *See* Claire Cain Miller & Brad Stone, *News Without Newspapers: "Hyperlocal" Updates From Blogs, Police, And Even Reporters, The New York Times*, at B1 (Apr. 13, 2009).

402. *Id.*

403. *Id.*

404. *Id.*

405. *Id.*

406. *Id.*

407. *See Finding Sprouts of Hope in a Gloomy Media Era, supra* note 94.

408. *Id.*

409. *Id.*

410. *Id.*

411. *Id.*

412. *Id.*

simply focus on interesting stories, but rather on information that subscribers need to do their jobs.[413] While the morning newsletter is free, a subscription to its other newsletters costs $350 a year, and a subscription to its policy reporting costs $1,200 a year.[414] With this model, Punchbowl has been profitable and generated $20 million in revenue in 2023.[415] The Gadfly, which focuses on entertainment, has seven employees, publishes several newsletters, and is also profitable.[416] Semafor has 75 employees and produces newsletters focused on global niches, including election tracking.[417] Puck, which has approximately 40 employees and 40,000 paid subscribers, focuses on entertainment and finance.[418] Of course, because these newsletters are sometimes based upon star writers that their subscribers follow, there is a risk of losing subscriptions and profitability if those writers move on.[419]

Instagram is also developing as a news source.[420] An Instagram poster (Mosheh Oinounou), who used to work for CBS, Fox News, and Bloomberg News, has started Mo News which he prepares after reading a number of major newspapers and in excess of a dozen newsletters each morning.[421] He also does daily podcasts with his co-host (Jill Wagner), has three employees, and has developed an Instagram following of 436,000.[422] Some believe that consumers, critical and skeptical of traditional media outlets, have gravitated to sites like Mo News.[423] In general, these new news sites promise to be nonpartisan, and they source content from major news outlets and add their own analysis.[424] Another site, News Not Noise, has 650,000 followers, and is run by a former CNN White House correspondent.[425] Because of sites like these, 16% of Americans regularly obtain

413. *Id.*
414. *Id.*
415. *Id.*
416. *Id.*
417. *Id.*
418. *Id.*
419. *Id.*
420. *See Instagram Grows as a News Source, supra* note 364, at A13.
421. *Id.*
422. *Id.*
423. *Id.*, at A13.
424. *Id.*
425. *Id.*

news on Instagram.[426] Other comparable sites include MeidasTouch, A More Perfect Union, @Impact and @Betches_News.[427]

Some journalists are leaving established news outlets to start their own subscription newsletters.[428] For example, one journalist used Substack to create a newsletter, Platformer, about the tech industry.[429] These journalists write about a variety of issues, ranging from climate issues, sports, history, economics, and Hollywood.[430] Some of these journalists make $100,000 a year on their newsletters, and have tens of thousands of followers.[431] Substack takes a 10 percent cut for hosting the newsletters.[432]

Instagram also hosts a number of "news influencers."[433] For example, a former high school teacher attracted more than 1 million followers by explaining the fundamentals of government.[434] She views herself more as a teacher than a journalist.[435] Many of these Instagram accounts are supported by advertisements and subscriptions.[436] However, Instagram and its parent company Meta have been reluctant to promote or recommend news sites that contain political content, causing "shares" of such content to fall 26 percent.[437]

But it is far from clear that online journalism will be able to replace traditional print journalism. For one thing, while newsroom employment has decreased from 71,000 employees to 39,000, employment in digital newsrooms has increased far less (from 7,400 to 13,000 employees).[438] Moreover, some question whether online investigative units investigate as well as traditional print investigative units: "As news organizations evolved to a digital landscape dominated by apps and social platforms,

---

426. *Id.*

427. *Id.*

428. *See* Marc Tracy, *Some Journalists Are Leaving the Internet for Your Inbox, The New York Times* B3 (Sept. 24, 2020).

429. *Id.*

430. *Id.*

431. *Id.*

432. *Id.*

433. *See Instagram Grows as a News Source, supra* note 364, at A13.

434. *Id.*

435. *Id.*

436. *Id.*

437. *Id.*

438. *See Local News Fades Out, supra* note 21, at B8.

they felt more pressure to push news out faster. Now, after something breaks, we're all buzzed with the alert, often before most of the facts are in."[439] And some argue that there are benefits to waiting for the print version of the media: "when it showed up on my front door, hundreds of experienced professionals had done the hard work for me."[440] And the concern is that too many people were getting their news from Facebook and Twitter: "Just about every problem we battle in understanding the news today—and every one we will battle tomorrow—is exacerbated by plugging into the social media herd. Twitter and Facebook reward speed over depth, hot takes over facts and seasoned propagandists over well-meaning analyzers of news."[441]

Moreover, the development of blog-based newspapers may further undermine traditional newspapers and news organizations.[442] *Huffington Post* and *Daily Beast*[443] bloggers work for free, and some of them are professional journalists:[444] "By joining the fray on these sites, journalists and their cousins in the punditocracy undermine the very newspapers and magazines that value their work enough to actually pay for it."[445]

1. WIKILEAKS AND OTHER LEAKS ORGANIZATIONS

Other types of organizations are also developing online, including WikiLeaks.[446] WikiLeaks is difficult to precisely categorize, but it investigates and publishes articles about government and institutions, and it leaks confidential and classified documents to the public and sometimes to the press.[447] WikiLeaks attracted worldwide attention, including both praise and condemnation, for its leaks of classified U.S. government documents. Despite the criticism, WikiLeaks fervently embraces its image as a leaker of information. On its website, WikiLeaks asks this simple but

---

439. *See* Manjoo, *supra* note 12, at B7.
440. *Id.*
441. *Id.*
442. *See No Such Thing as Free News*, *supra* note 231.
443. https://www.thedailybeast.com/.
444. *Id.*
445. *Id.*
446. http://mirror.wikileaks.info/.
447. *See id.*

poignant question "Have documents the world needs to see?"[448] It then goes on to proclaim that "We help you safely get the truth out,"[449] and exhorts the public to help WikiLeaks in this effort: "Disclosed documents are classified, censored or otherwise opaque to the public record. We rely on readers to alert their communities and press to the revelations here. Go to it!"[450]

WikiLeaks has attracted considerable controversy, created diplomatic uproar[451] and has forced U.S. governmental officials to scramble to deal with diplomatic and political pressures.[452] For example, WikiLeaks released video footage of U.S. helicopters in Iraq killing some eighteen people.[453] In November 2010, WikiLeaks created a worldwide uproar when it claimed to have gained possession of a quarter-of-a-million classified diplomatic documents.[454] These documents dealt with U.S. diplomacy, including secret bargaining, contained candid views of foreign leaders, and discussed foreign nuclear and terrorist threats.[455] Although WikiLeaks initially released only a few hundred of the documents (a very small percentage of the total number),[456] it followed that disclosure with additional releases,[457] dealing with an incredible array of information

---

448. http://mirror.wikileaks.info/; *see also* Raphale G. Satter & Michael Weissenstein, *WikiLeaks' War Records Reveal Grim Accounts: Iraqis Accused of Torture Slayings, The Courier-Journal*, at A5 (Oct. 23, 2010).

449. *Id.*

450. *Id.*

451. *See* Scott Shane, *WikiLeaks Prompts New Round of Diplomatic Uproar: Envoys Fear for Sources' Safety as Reporters Sift Newly Released Cables for Revelations, The New York Times*, at A11 (Sept. 1, 2011).

452. *See* Eric Schmitt & Helene Cooper, *Document Leak Adds to Pressure on White House: Policy Faces Scrutiny, The New York Times*, at A1 (July 27, 2010).

453. Michael H. Keller, *The Business of Serving Up YouTube Views: Streams Are for Sale, Eyes Not Included, The New York Times* A18 (Aug. 12, 2018).

454. *See* Dina Temple Raston, *WikiLeaks Release Reveals Messier Side of Diplomacy*, National Public Radio (Nov. 28, 2010).

455. *See* Scott Shane & Andrew W. Lehren, *Leaked Cables Offer Raw Look at U.S. Diplomacy, The New York Times*, at A1 (Nov. 29, 2010).

456. *See* Ray Somaiya & Alan Cowell, *WikiLeaks Founder Said to Fear "Illegal Rendition" to U.S., The New York Times*, A6 (Jan. 12, 2001).

457. *See* David Folkenflik, *WikiLeaks: An Editor-in-Chief or Prolific Source?*, National Public Radio, Weekend Edition Saturday (July 31, 2010), http://www.npr.org/templates/story/story.php?storyId=128870288 (discussing the release of some 90,000 classified documents relating to the Afghanistan war).

dating back to 1966, some of which might allegedly harm U.S. relations with foreign officials.[458] Some documents raised questions about the safety of Australia's air safety system,[459] dealt with a standoff between the U.S. and Pakistan over nuclear fuel transfers, discussed the possibility that North Korea and South Korea might reunite, as well as a host of other topics,[460] including internal details regarding the Israeli-Palestinian peace talks,[461] bargaining about how to remove prisoners from Guantanamo Bay,[462] and concerns about Pakistan.[463] In addition, the documents included some embarrassing revelations related to Prince Henry of the United Kingdom.[464] The documents also detailed purported torture and murder by Iraqi forces,[465] the beginning and conduct of the Iraq War,[466] and a tale of intrigue related to the Nazis, a famous Impressionist painting and sunken treasure.[467] Some documents raised questions regarding the Securities and Exchange Commission's regulation of the financial industry.[468]

---

458. *See Leaked Cables Offer Raw Look, supra* note 455.

459. *See WikiLeaks Prompts New Round of Diplomatic Uproar, supra* note 451.

460. *See* Dina Temple Raston, *supra* note 454; *See Leaked Cables Offer Raw Look, supra* note 455.

461. *See* Ethan Bronner, *Leaked Documents Open a Door on Mideast Peace Talks, The New York Times*, A4 (Jan. 25, 2011).

462. *See* Charles Savage & Andrew W. Lehren, *Cables Depict U.S. Haggling to Clear Guantanamo*, National Public Radio (Nov. 29, 2010), http://www.nytimes.com/2010/11/30/world/americas/30gitmo.html?scp=1&sq=cables%20depict%20U.S.&st=cse.

463. *See* Jane Perlez, David E. Sanger & Eric Schmitt, *STATE SECRET'S DAY: Wary Dance With Pakistan in Nuclear World, The New York Times*, at A1 (Dec. 1, 2010).

464. *See* Alan Cowell, *WikiLeaks and a Royal Off the Cuff, The International Herald Tribune*, at 2 (Dec. 4–5, 2010).

465. *See WikiLeaks' War Records, supra* note 448.

466. *See* Bill Chappell, *WikiLeaks Begins Exposing 400,000 U.S. Documents About the Iraq War*, National Public Radio, The Two-Way (Oct. 22, 2010), http://www.npr.org/blogs/thetwo-way/2010/10/22/130760662/wikileaks-begins-exposing-400-000-u-s-documents-about-the-iraq-war.

467. *See* Kim Severson & Robbie Brown, *WikiLeaks Cables Make Appearance in a Tale of Sunken Treasure and Nazi Theft, The New York Times*, at A10 (Jan. 7, 2011) (suggesting that an American ambassador to Spain "offered to assist Spain in the fight over the sunken treasure. In return, ... Spain was to help get a Madrid museum to return the 1897 Pissaro painting valued at as much as $20 million, to a California family that says it was illegally taken by Nazis in Germany.").

468. *See* Andrew Ross Sorkin, *A WikiLeaks Problem for Enforcers, The New York Times*, at B1 (Dec. 21, 2010).

Some of the information released by WikiLeaks was not only classified, but sensitive and potentially damaging to U.S. relations with foreign nations and foreign leaders.[469] For example, some documents contained criticisms by U.S. officials of foreign leaders,[470] including Afghan President Hamid Karzai,[471] and suggested that Afghan leaders were corrupt.[472] The leaked documents also contained critical views of then Prime Minister Sylvio Berlusconi of Italy,[473] unflattering references to a number of

---

469. *See* Dina Temple Raston, *supra* note 454:

> The cables also detail recent meetings with the Yemeni president after U.S. strikes in his country against alleged terrorists. President Ali Abdullah Saleh says he will tell the Yemeni parliament that the bombs that fell were Yemeni, not American ones. He jokes about smuggling in his country and says he's concerned about drugs and weapons, but doesn't object to "good whiskey" being smuggled in. He's the ruler of a conservative Muslim country.
>
> The released cables also talk about Afghan President Hamid Karzai's half-brother, Ahmed Wali Karzai. American officials met with him in late 2009 and early 2010. U.S. diplomats made clear in their cables that they don't trust him. In the middle of a cable back to Washington, they put in the following: "Note: While we must deal with AWK as the head of the Provincial Council, he is widely understood to be corrupt and a narcotics trafficker."
>
> Another cable reads: Karzai "demonstrated that he will dissemble when it suits his needs." It says he clearly did not appear to "understand the level of our knowledge of his activities. We will need to monitor his activity closely, and deliver a recurring, transparent message to him about the limits of American tolerance."
>
> The concern is that if he didn't know the level of American surveillance before, he knows it now—thanks to the release of these dispatches.

470. *See WikiLeaks Prompts New Round of Diplomatic Uproar, supra* note 451.

471. *See* Helene Cooper & Carlotta Gall, *Cables Depict a Roller-Coaster Trajectory for Karzai, From Exalted to Baffling, The New York Times*, A10 (Dec. 3, 2010) ("Oman's foreign minister says that he is 'losing confidence' in him. A British diplomat says Britain feels 'deep frustration' with him, while an Australian official complains that he 'ignores reality.' A diplomat from the United Arab Emirates says Afghanistan would be better off without him. NATO's Secretary General speculates that he has a split personality.").

472. *See* Scott Shane, Mark Mazetti & Dexter Filkins, *State's Secrets Day 5; Pervasive Afghan Graft, Starting at Top, The New York Times*, at A1 (Dec. 3, 2010) ("From hundreds of diplomatic cables, Afghanistan emerges as a looking-glass land where bribery, extortion and embezzlement are the norm and the honest man is a distinct outlier.").

473. *See* Rachel Donadio & Celestine Bohlen, *Caustic U.S. Views of Berlusconi Churn Italy's Politics, The New York Times*, A11 (Dec. 3, 2010) ("Preparing President Obama for a meeting with Mr. Berlusconi in June 2009, Elizabeth Dibble, the deputy chief of mission at the United States Embassy in Rome, warned that some in the American government

world leaders,[474] indications that Palestinian leaders were saying one thing in private and another (inconsistent) thing in public,[475] and secret information regarding Swiss bank accounts.[476] The cables also offered considerable insight into China's efforts to control internet usage, including its attempts to pressure Google to help censor internet content.[477] U.S.-Mexico relations were severely strained by some of the disclosures.[478]

Some of the information in the WikiLeaks disclosures may have played a role in bringing about the Arab Spring revolts, including the demise of Tunisia's President Zine e-Abidine Ben Ali. The Tunisian revolt was rooted in a number of concerns, including allegations of corrupt practices by the President's family.[479] Among the disclosed WikiLeaks documents was a cable from the U.S. Embassy in Tunisia discussing corruption in the Tunisian government, and suggesting that the President's wife's family had benefitted handsomely from his position.[480] Some of the WikiLeaks documents were also published by a Tunisian website, TuniLeaks, and were posted on the same day as the WikiLeaks disclosure (suggesting collaboration between WikiLeaks and TuniLeaks).[481] These documents included allegations that the former President's family was receiving

---

regarded the Italian leader as 'feckless, vain and ineffective as a modern European leader.' Dealing with him, she said 'requires a careful balance of close consideration.'").

474. *See WikiLeaks Begins Exposing 400,000 U.S. Documents, supra* note 466 ("The German chancellor is referred to as Angela 'Teflon' Merkel. Karzai is said to be 'driven by paranoia.' North Korean leader Kim Jong Il is said to suffer from epilepsy. Libyan leader Moammar Gadhafi's full-time nurse is called a 'hot blond.' That's part of the reason why Secretary of State Hillary Clinton and top State Department officials around the world have been on the phones calling foreign leaders to prepare them for the disclosures.").

475. *See Leaked Documents Open a Door, supra* note 461, at A4.

476. *See* Reuters, *Former Swiss Banker is Arrested in WikiLeaks Case, After a Conviction, The New York Times*, at B3 (Jan. 20, 2011).

477. *See* James Glanz & John Markoff, *Vast Hacking by a China Fearful of the Web: Cables Depict Google Shock, Censorship and Cyberattacks, The New York Times*, at A1 (Dec. 5, 2010).

478. *See* Mary Beth Sherdan, *US-Mexico Relations Hit Bottom Over WikiLeaks, The Sydney Morning Herald*, at. 25 (Mar. 5–6, 2011).

479. *See* David Kirkpatrick, *Beyond Tunisia Unrest, Rage Over Wealth of Ruling Family, The New York Times*, at A10 (Jan. 14, 2011).

480. *Id.*

481. *See* Scott Shane, *Cables From American Diplomats Portray U.S. Ambivalence on Tunisia, The New York Times*, at 11 (Jan. 16, 2011).

benefits, and that bribery was commonplace.[482] Thus, the WikiLeaks disclosures regarding Tunisia, coupled with the TuniLeaks disclosures, may have helped spark the Tunisian revolt.[483]

WikiLeaks has become increasingly sophisticated about how it releases leaked documents. For example, in addition to publishing documents on its own website, WikiLeaks has distributed them to traditional news outlets such as *The New York Times*, Germany's *Der Spiegel* magazine, Britain's *Guardian* newspaper,[484] France's *Le Monde* newspaper[485] and Spain's *El Pais* newspaper.[486] In all, WikiLeaks worked with more than fifty local partners, including the *Daily Taraf* in Turkey, *Expresso* in Portugal, and *The Hindu* in India.[487] A number of these relationships have since frayed.[488]

In the early disclosures, there were so many documents and so much information that researchers had difficulty digesting it all even though it was likely that the leaked documents might have implications for business and private interests as well as government.[489] WikiLeaks offered *The Guardian*, a British newspaper, 500,000 military dispatches from Afghanistan and Iraq,[490] but did so only after extracting a promise that the documents would not be released before a specified date.[491] The publications that received the documents worked together to sort through and verify the documents.[492]

This type of cooperation, between internet-based sources and traditional media, is becomingly increasingly common. During the uprising in Tunisia, when Al Jazeera was not allowed into the country, Al Jazeera

---

482. *Id.*

483. *See id.* ("Those cables, from the cache obtained by the anti-secrecy organization WikiLeaks and made public in recent weeks, helped fuel the anger on the streets and culminated Friday with Mr. Ben Ali's flight after 23 years in power.").

484. *See* Dina Temple Raston, *supra* note 454.

485. *See WikiLeaks Founder Said to Fear "Illegal Rendition" to U.S.*, *supra* note 456, at A6.

486. *See WikiLeaks Cables Make Appearance in a Tale of Sunken Treasure*, *supra* note 467, at A10.

487. *See* Brian Stelter & Noam Cohen, *In WikiLeaks' Growth, Some Control Is Lost: Mad Scramble to Be First to Reveal Secrets*, *The New York Times*, at A11 (Apr. 27, 2011).

488. *Id.*

489. *Id.*

490. *See* Keller, *supra* note 453.

491. *Id.*

492. *Id.*

"scoured Facebook and YouTube for newly uploaded material."[493] In other words, rather than just competing with each other, internet organizations and traditional media organizations were beginning to cooperate with each other.[494]

The WikiLeaks case underscores the power of the internet as a communications medium. In the 1960s, when Daniel Ellsberg turned the so-called "Pentagon Papers"—stolen from the U.S. Department of Defense—over to *The New York Times* and the *Washington Post*,[495] communication methods were much less dynamic. In that case, although the lower courts enjoined publication of the Pentagon Papers, the U.S. Supreme Court ultimately lifted the injunction and allowed both papers to publish them.[496] The Court concluded that, while the government had the right to classify the documents, and also had the right to bring criminal sanctions against those who stole the documents, the First Amendment precluded the government from prohibiting publication.

WikiLeaks' disclosure of classified documents is the *Pentagon Papers* case on steroids, and is different from that case in two important respects. First, the scale of the WikiLeaks disclosure was unprecedented. Indeed, it was virtually impossible for a single newspaper (or a group of newspapers) to have reprinted so many documents in the time that it took WikiLeaks to post them online. Second, the speed of the disclosure was also unprecedented. Had the Pentagon Papers been published by *The New York Times*, the entire world could eventually have gained access to them, but the distribution process would have been slow and ponderous given that *The New York Times* was not available on the internet at that time. As a result, those who wanted to review *The New York Times*' account of the Pentagon Papers would have had to wait until they could obtain a copy of the newspaper, or they were able to review another newspaper's summary or republication of the contents of the report. Because of the internet, WikiLeaks was able to reveal a quarter-of-a-million documents

493. *See* Brian Stelter, *Televising the Revolution: Al Jazeera Hopes Reports from Egypt Open Doors in U.S., The New York Times*, at B8 (Feb. 7, 2011).

494. *Id.*

495. *See New York Times Company v. United States*, 403 U.S. 713 (1971).

496. *Id.*

instantaneously to the entire world with the click of a computer mouse.[497] Interestingly, with regard to its own employees, the U.S. government took the position that the leaked documents should still be regarded as "classified" and should not be read by those who did not have the required security clearance.[498] Thus, although virtually anyone in the world could have read the leaked documents, government employees were precluded from reading them unless they had the necessary security clearance.

WikiLeaks' efforts to work with other news organizations to publish the stolen documents is one that evolved over time. In 2008, WikiLeaks simply released documents directly to the media,[499] but the media did not aggressively report on the released documents.[500] Subsequently, WikiLeaks tried releasing a journalistic style video[501] which seemed to have greater impact.[502] Later disclosures involved a partnership with traditional newspapers, and was quite successful, producing extensive newspaper coverage.[503] Rather than simply revealing the documents to the entire world, simultaneously, WikiLeaks made strategic disclosures to particular media outlets in an effort to produce the greatest possible impact and coverage.[504]

---

497. *See Pervasive Afghan Graft, supra* note 472, at A1 & A10 ("It is hardly news that predatory corruption, fueled by a booming illicit narcotics industry, is rampant at every level of Afghan society.... But the collection of confidential diplomatic cables obtained by WikiLeaks and made available to a number of publications, offers a fresh sense of its pervasive nature, its overwhelming scale, and the dispiriting challenge it poses to American officials who have made shoring up support for the Afghan government a cornerstone of America's counter-insurgency strategy in Afghanistan.").

498. *See* Eric Lipton, *Don't Look, Don't Read: Government Tells Workers to Avert Eyes From Leaks, The New York Times*, at A20 (Dec. 5, 2010).

499. *See* David Carr, *WikiLeaks Taps Power of the Press, The New York Times*, at B1 (Dec. 13, 2010).

500. *Id.* ("Think back to 2008, when WikiLeaks simply released documents that suggested the government of Kenya had looted its country. The follow-up in the mainstream media was decidedly muted.").

501. *Id.* ("Then last spring, WikiLeaks adopted a more journalistic approach—editing and annotating a 2007 video from Baghdad in which an Apache helicopter fired on men who appeared to be unarmed, including two employees of Reuters.").

502. *Id.* ("The reviews were mixed, with some suggesting that the video had been edited to political ends, but the disclosure received much more attention in the press.").

503. *Id.*

504. *Id.* ("Julian Assange, WikiLeaks's founder and guiding spirit, apparently began to understand that scarcity, not ubiquity, drives coverage of events. Instead of just pulling

WikiLeaks became somewhat derailed for a while because of legal problems. Sweden sought to extradite WikiLeaks' founder, Julian Assange, and he was forced to remain in England.[505] In addition, some of WikiLeaks' participants defected to other organizations.[506] These defections closed down some of the complex computer systems that WikiLeaks used to maintain secrecy and process information.[507] For at least a time, WikiLeaks was not open for "public business."[508] In addition, there were indications that U.S. governmental officials were intent on prosecuting Assange.[509] Those charges were eventually resolved.

However, WikiLeaks has continued to be player in the news and information business. For example, during the 2016 presidential campaign, WikiLeaks participated in stealing internal emails from the Democratic National Committee.[510] Many of these emails were written by John Podesta, Hillary Clinton's campaign chairman.[511] Even after the election, WikiLeaks continued to wield considerable impact. In 2017, Wikileaks released a massive trove of documents which it claimed revealed how the U.S. Central Intelligence Agency "hacks smart phones, computer operating systems, message applications and internet-connected televisions."[512] The CIA disclosure involved some 8,761 documents;[513] something that the Chairman of the House Intelligence Committee described as "very, very

---

back the blankets for all to see, he began to limit the disclosures to those who would add value through presentation, editing and additional reporting.").

505. *See* David Carr, *WikiLeaks' Founder, In a Gilded British Cage, The New York Times*, The Media Equation, at B1 (Sept. 26, 2011).

506. *See* Ravi Somaiya, *Former WikiLeaks Colleagues Forming New Web Site, OpenLeaks, The New York Times*, at A10 (Feb. 7, 2011).

507. *Id.*

508. *Id.*

509. *See* Julian E. Barnes, Adam Goldman & Charlie Savage, *Assange's Path From Agitator to U.S. Target, The New York Times* A1 (Nov. 17, 2018).

510. *See* Shane Harris & Paul Sonne, *WikiLeaks Dumps CIA Spy Trove, The Wall Street Journal*, A1 (Mar. 8, 2017).

511. *See* Matthew Rosenberg, Scott Shane & Adam Goldman, *C.I.A. Rushes to Limit WikiLeaks Damage: F.B.I. Suspects Insider in Hunt for Leak, The New York Times* A9 (Mar. 19, 2017).

512. *See*, *WikiLeaks Dumps CIA Spy Trove, supra* note 510, at A1; Rosenberg, Shane & Goldman, *supra* note 511.

513. *See* Rosenberg, Shane & Goldman, *supra* note 511.

serious."[514] The release was potentially damaging to the CIA because some of it contained information regarding how the CIA hacks computers and other devices, including some highly technical details, as well as about which programs and companies collaborate with the CIA.[515] As a result, disclosure of the information had the potential to "jeopardize ongoing intelligence gathering operations."[516] WikiLeaks even threatened to release the "source code" that the CIA was using,[517] and some of the documents discussed malicious software components that the CIA had uncovered from other sources.[518] WikiLeaks' asserted justification for releasing the documents was to provoke a public debate on their permissibility and justifiability.[519] Afterwards, the CIA scrambled to uncover the source of the leaked information in an effort to contain the damage.[520]

WikiLeaks has also spawned new "leaks" organizations. Perhaps the most important new organization is "OpenLeaks,"[521] which was founded by former WikiLeaks associates,[522] but operates on a different model. Rather than posting documents on its own website, OpenLeaks works directly with existing media and human rights organizations and connects the leakers with organizations who (in turn) publish the documents.[523] OpenLeaks plans to be more open and transparent than WikiLeaks, and less focused on one individual or personality.[524]

Some of the new WikiLeaks-inspired organizations focus on specific topics (*e.g.*, environmental issues, whistleblowers, or particular areas of the world)[525] These new websites are arguably consistent with Julian Assange's original vision for WikiLeaks: his hope that "mass leaking"

---

514. *Id.*
515. *Id.*
516. *Id.*
517. *Id.*
518. *Id.*
519. *Id.*
520. *See* Rosenberg, Shane & Goldman, *supra* note 511, at A9.
521. *Id.*
522. *See* Ravi Somaiya, *WikiLeaks Angry About Former Staff Member's Book, The New York Times*, A9 (Feb. 11, 2011) (the former associate is Mr. Daniel Domscheit-Berg who is described as a German computer scientist).
523. *See Former WikiLeaks Colleagues Forming New Web Site, supra* note 489.
524. *Id.*
525. *Id.*

would leave governments "exquisitely vulnerable to those who seek to replace them with more open forms of governance."[526] In Russia, the group Anonymous claims that it was able to hack into the e-mail accounts of the Nashi organization (which has been described as a Kremlin-financed youth group),[527] and it released what it claimed were hundreds of Nashi e-mails that offered a "rare peek into a world of pro-Kremlin bloggers and hackers who are paid to flatter Prime Minister Vladimir Putin and smear his political rivals.[528]

In addition to the "leaks" organizations, there are a number of other organizations that are conducting investigations and doing traditional news reporting online.[529] These online publications have grown in "number, size, financing and credibility," and now exist in many cities.[530] Moreover, the Pulitzer Prize is now open to online publications,[531] with *ProPublica* being the first online publisher to win the award.[532] *Talking Points Memo* won the Polk Award for legal reporting,[533] and the Voice of San Diego won an investigative award from the organization Investigative Reporters and

---

526. *Id.*

527. *See* Alan Cullison, *Web Strike Blamed on Pro-Putin Youth, The Wall Street Journal*, A11 (Feb. 10, 2012).

528. *Id.*

529. *See* David Gura, *Online News Organizations Compete for Pulitzers*, National Public Radio, Morning Edition (Apr. 20, 2009), http://www.npr.org/templates/story/story.php?storyId=103222044.

530. *See* Richard Perez-Pena, *In Chicago, Ex-Editor Fights Back, The New York Times*, at B1 (Nov. 23, 2009) ("At the earliest local news sites, like The New Haven Independent and Voice of San Diego, both started in 2005, even the top editors had worked at smaller organizations, or had been free-lancers or had worked in other cities.... Later, there were major exceptions like MinnPost in Minneapolis-St. Paul and the St. Louis Beacon, both run primarily by journalists who had worked for the big papers in those markets....").

531. *Id.*

532. *See* Michel Martin, *Pulitzer Awards First Prize to New Media Outlet*, National Public Radio, Tell Me More (Apr. 13, 2010), http://www.npr.org/templates/story/story.php?storyId=125902373 ("The Pulitzer Prizes, journalism's most prestigious awards, were issued yesterday. Among the winners was Sheri Fink, a physician turned reporter who investigated wrongful death allegations against doctors in New Orleans after Hurricane Katrina for the online news organization *ProPublica*.").

533. *See* Noam Cohen, *Blogger, Sans Pajamas, Rakes Muck and a Prize, The New York Times*, at C1 (Feb. 25, 2008).

Editors.[534] Many of the online news organizations are financially viable. Some bloggers are earning $10,000 to $200,000 a year in income, and therefore the economic basis exists to fund online journalism.[535]

Politico, an online news organization which has teamed up with Reuters news service,[536] is conducting aggressive investigative reporting. *Politico* now has 200 employees, and it hosted one of the Republican presidential primary debates, and started the website 2012 Live to cover the election.[537] 2012 Live publishes extensive information about candidates and local political leaders.[538] During the 2010 elections, traffic at its website reached two million to six million hits a month (which is still relatively small compared to the 20 million hits per month that CNN.com receives, and 15 million hits per month for NYTimes.com).[539] *Politico* expressly proclaims that its mission "is to carve out an even bigger place in the news media landscape" and "to take a leap forward in front of everyone else."[540] During the presidential campaign leading up to the 2012 presidential election, *Politico*[541] published an article claiming that Republican presidential candidate Herman Cain had sexually abused two female colleagues while he was the head of the National Restaurant Association.[542] It also broke stories, involving News Corps political contribu-

---

534. *See* Alex Cohen, *Nonprofit News Site Wins Coveted Media Award*, National Public Radio, All Things Considered (Apr. 7, 2009), http://www.npr.org/templates/story/story.php?storyId=102851849.

535. *See* Bob Garfield, *Post-Newspaper Journalism*, National Public Radio, On the Media (Aug. 21, 2009) (quoting Professor Jeff Jarvis, City University of New York), http://www.onthemedia.org/2009/aug/21/post-newspaper-journalism/transcript/.

536. *See* Richard Perez-Pena, *Politico and Reuters Forge a News Distribution Alliance, The New York Times*, at B4 (Dec. 15, 2008).

537. *See* Jeremy W. Peters, *Political Blogs Are Ready to Flood the Campaign Trail, The New York Times*, at A1 (Jan. 30, 2011).

538. *Id.*

539. *Id.*

540. *Id.* (quoting Mr. VandeHei, *Politico's* Executive Editor and co-founder).

541. http://www.politico.com/.

542. *See* Jonathan Martin, Maggie Haberman, Anna Palmer & Kenneth P. Vogel, *Herman Cain Accused by Two Women of Inappropriate Behavior, Politico* (Oct. 31, 2011). http://www.politico.com/news/stories/1011/67194.html

tions,[543] presidential candidate Jon Huntsman's past,[544] President Obama's handlers' treatment of Muslim women,[545] legislation that allowed corporations to pay large bonuses,[546] and the effort to stop Sarah Palin from running for president.[547]

Other similar organizations are doing significant political reporting. Although *Talking Points Memo*[548] had only a single reporter in 2008,[549] it employed six a year later,[550] and was planning to expand to 15 reporters.[551] Its goal was to compete with *Politico*, as well as with traditional newspapers such as *The New York Times* and *The Washington Post*, and it was receiving about 1.4 million hits per month on its website.[552] *Talking Points Memo* played a lead role in investigating allegations against former U.S. Attorney General, Alberto Gonzalez.[553] In that investigation, *Talking Points Memo* received lots of "tips" from the public.[554] *Real Clear Politics*

543. *See* Frank James, *News Corps. Contributions Raise Eyebrows*, National Public Radio, Its All Politics (Oct. 1, 2010), http://www.npr.org/blogs/itsallpolitics/2010/10/01/130261968/news-corp-s-gop-contributions-raise-eyebrows.

544. *See* Scott Horsley, *Before Politics, Huntsman Aspired to Rock Star Fame*, National Public Radio, All Things Considered (Oct. 12, 2011), http://www.npr.org/2011/10/12/141276651/before-politics-huntsman-aspired-to-rock-star-fame.

545. *See* Melissa Block, *Paper: Muslim Women Sidelined at Obama Rally*, National Public Radio, All Things Considered (June 18, 2008), http://www.npr.org/templates/story/story.php?storyId=91658107.

546. *See* Michele Norris, *Sen. Dodd and the A.I.G. Bonus Loophole*, National Public Radio, All Things Considered, (Mar. 19, 2009), http://www.npr.org/templates/story/story.php?storyId=102128215.

547. *See* Frank James, *Stop Sarah Palin Movement Underway in GOP: Politico*, National Public Radio, Its All Politics (Nov. 1, 2010), http://www.npr.org/blogs/itsallpolitics/2010/11/01/130977276/stop-sarah-palin-movement-underway-in-gop-politico.

548. https://talkingpointsmemo.com/.

549. *See Political Blogs are Ready to Flood the Campaign Trail, supra* note 537.

550. *See* Kurtz, *supra* note 33, at A7.

551. *See Political Blogs Are Ready to Flood the Campaign Trail, supra* note 537.

552. *See id.*

553. *See* Liane Hansen, *New Website Texas Tribune Thrives, But How?*, National Public Radio, Weekend Edition Sunday (Aug. 15, 2010), http://www.npr.org/templates/story/story.php?storyId=129210695 ("Josh Marshall, the editor and publisher of *Talking Points Memo*, an online news and opinion site, was the first person to identify and reveal the full scope of the politicization of the Justice Department under former Attorney General Alberto Gonzalez").

554. *See* Noam Cohen, *A Wiki Takes Aim at Obama, The New York Times*, Link by Link, at B8 (Apr. 4, 2011); https://www.crossroadsgps.org/.

was also actively involved in covering the 2012 election.[555] Like its online competitors, *Real Clear Politics* doubled the size of its reporting staff to six (and, possibly, eight) reporters, and its goal was to put "as many reporters in the field as we can," and to "become part of the conversation."[556] In 2012, it was receiving about 2.6 million hits per month on its website.[557] Other comparable organizations include Politics Daily, started by AOL, and NationalJournal.com.[558]

The Huffington Post expanded from 60 employees in 2008 to more than 200 employees by 2011.[559] Although it was originally focused on the aggregation of information and commentary, it later decided to emphasize original reporting.[560] A significant percentage of that reporting is political in nature.[561] Like Facebook and Twitter, *Huffington Post* relies on writers who work for free.[562] Indeed, some "content farms" like Demand Media, pay very little ($10 to $20 a story).[563] Presumably, many who provide this content are motivated by a desire to showcase their work, or to influence the political process.[564] *The Huffington Post* recently expanded its operation to France with the opening of *Le Huffington Post*.[565]

New online newspapers take many different forms. The *Texas Tribune* focuses on Texas state government, and ignores unrelated news stories (even major ones).[566] The publication, which started with 12 employees

---

555. *See Political Blogs Are Ready to Flood the Campaign Trail*, *supra* note 537.

556. *Id.* (quoting Mr. John McIntyre, Chief Executive and co-founder).

557. *Id.*

558. *Id.*

559. *Id.*

560. *Id.*

561. *Id.*

562. *See* NPR Staff, *Is Writing Online Without Pay Worth It?*, National Public Radio, Morning Edition (Feb. 15, 2011), http://www.npr.org/2011/02/15/133759724/is-writing-online-without-pay-worth-it.

563. *Id.*

564. *Id.*

565. *See* Elaine Sciolino, *Editor Is the Story as the French Huffington Post Starts, The New York Times*, at B2 (Jan. 24, 2012).

566. *See* David Carr, *News Erupts, and So Does a Web Debut, The New York Times*, at B1 (Nov. 9. 2009) ("On Thursday afternoon, when word came about the shootings that left 13 people dead at Fort Hood, just up the road from Austin, it seemed like a made-to-order test for The Texas Tribune, a brand new 12-person Web-based newsroom. They scrambled the jets, made plans, and then—stayed put. The big coverage on the site, TexasTribune.org,

in its Web-based organization,[567] emphasizes investigative reporting,[568] and is a not-for-profit organization that operates on a business model which emphasizes premium content, as well as memberships and corporate sponsorships.[569] The organization began with $3.7 million that was donated by a venture capitalist, and others, as well as grants from the Houston Endowment ($500,000) and the James L. Knight Foundation ($250,000).[570] In addition to its daily reporting, the Texas Tribune hosts blogs and databases on various issues (*e.g.*, spending by lawmakers, donations by PACs and lobbying expenditures).[571] It is not clear whether the *Texas Tribune's* financial model is viable.[572] However, the organization was able to attract the former editor and publisher of *Texas Monthly Magazine* as its CEO and editor-in-chief, and to attract other well-respected reporters and an accomplished editor.[573] The publication claims that its goal is to hold "politicians accountable," and it does that through news stories, video interviews, original audio stories, and the posting of raw data.[574]

Other online investigative services have also popped up,[575] and are breaking significant stories.[576] A former Managing Editor of the *Chicago*

---

on Friday was [about] the 50 highest paid state employees and an exclusive about a state representative who had switched parties. The Texas Tribune was conceived and devised to cover the politics and policy of Texas state government.").

567. *Id.*

568. *See New Website Texas Tribune Thrives, But How?*, *supra* note 553 ("One of the most intriguing news start-ups in the past few years is the Texas Tribune, an Austin-based website that emphasizes explanatory and investigative reporting. Wealthy venture capitalist John Thornton decided the decline of newspapers in his state meant there was room for a new, not-for-profit player to cover the state's political and power scene.").

569. *Id.*

570. *See News Erupts, and So Does a Web Debut*, *supra* note 566, at B1 & B8.

571. *Id.*, at B8.

572. *See New Website Texas Tribune Thrives, But How?*, *supra* note 553.

573. *Id.*

574. *Id.*

575. *See* David Carr, *After a Year of Ruin, Some Hope*, *The New York Times*, at B1 (Dec. 21, 2009) (noting that "in the past year, many sites have added muscle and resources to the pursuit of news. Everyone knows about the reporting assets and influence of *Politico* (Politico.com), but you know that things have changed when Gawker (gawker.com), the attitudinous Manhattan media blog, is hiring the kind of reporters who pick up the phone.").

576. *Id.* ("Let's remember that news of the biggest media merger story of the year—Comcast-NBC Universal—arrived in The Wrap (www.thewrap.com), a Hollywood media site that is less than a year old.").

Tribune (ousted after a dispute) founded a rival paper the *Chicago News Cooperative* that is completely online and directly competes with the *Tribune*.[577] However, it closed in 2012. New online publications have also opened in Washington, D.C., and Texas as well.[578] Similarly, *In Denver Times*,[579] was established as a for profit operation by former journalists for the *Rocky Mountain Times* which closed down, and seeks to pursue a financial model based on monthly pledge amounts from readers.[580] Although the organization gave anyone access to breaking news stories, only subscribers could access news updates on their iPhones and BlackBerrys and could chat online with other readers and columnists.[581]

Other online models are similarly revolutionary. For example, *Global Voices* works with volunteer bloggers and other individuals all over the world to report information.[582] The organization, which is operated as an independent nonprofit, is funded by grants from foundations and donations by private individuals.[583] The organization publishes blog posts and articles, as well as cell phones photos and videos, on sites such as Facebook, Twitter and YouTube.[584] Because of its reliance on volunteers in the affected countries, *Global Voices* was able to provide timely reports on the unrest in Tunisia and Libya, as well as the tsunami that hit Japan.[585] In addition, the organization provides links to other articles that the posters or bloggers may be relying on.[586]

---

577. Perez-Pena, *supra* note 513.

578. *Id.* ("Last month, Jim Brady, formerly the editor in charge of The Washington Post's Web site, was named to head a local news site in Washington, to begin publishing early next year. The Texas Tribune, a site dedicated to that state's government and politics, started operations this month with a staff of editors and reporters drawn mostly from leading news sources around the state.").

579. http://www.indenvertimes.com/.

580. *See* David Folkenflik, *Newspapers Wade Into an Online-Only Future*, National Public Radio, All Things Considered (Mar. 20, 2009), http://www.npr.org/templates/story/story.php?storyId=102162128.

581. *Id.*

582. *See* Jennifer Preston, *When Unrest Stirs, Bloggers Are Already in Place, The New York Times*, at B3 (Mar. 14, 2011).

583. *Id.*

584. *Id.*

585. *Id.*

586. *Id.*

Another news organization that has developed is "Democracy Now!," a nonprofit organization that produces a daily newscast,[587] which is streamed over the Web,[588] and aired through nearly 1,000 other media outlets such as public, community and college radio stations, public access television stations, some PBS affiliates, and the noncommercial satellite networks Free Speech TV and Link TV.[589] Although Democracy Now! reports on the latest news developments, it devotes significant coverage to "struggles for justice and the effects of American foreign policy."[590] Democracy Now! has made a name for itself covering antiwar protests,[591] as well as discussions of alleged torture by U.S. governmental officials,[592] the execution of a Georgia inmate,[593] and the Occupy Wall Street movement.[594]

Some online publications deal with special interest issues. For example, *PolitiFact*, an online publication run by *The St. Petersburg Times*, runs truth and accuracy checks on arguments and claims made by politicians.[595] Gawker.com addresses media issues, and Jezebel focuses on women's interest issues.[596] Jezebel's readers are 97% female, its site receives more than 37 million hits a month,[597] and its articles have been described as both "incendiary" and "cutting."[598]

There are also a number of microblogs. In New Orleans, some of these microblogs work in conjunction with *The Times-Picayune* and other mainstream media to provide coverage that exceeds the capacity of the traditional media.[599] The New Orleans system was started by a citizen

---

587. *See* Brian Stelter, *A Grass Roots Newscast Gives a Voice to Struggles, The New York Times*, at B3 (Oct. 24, 2011).

588. www.democracynow.org.

589. *See A Grass Roots Newscast, supra* note 587.

590. *Id.*

591. *Id.*

592. *Id.*

593. *Id.*

594. *Id.*

595. *See* David Carr, *Journalist, Provocateur, Maybe Both, The New York Times*, The Media Equation, at B1 (July 26, 2010).

596. *See* Jennifer Mascia, *A Web Site That's Not Afraid to Pick a Fight, The New York Times*, at B1 (July 12, 2010).

597. *Id.*

598. *Id.*

599. *See* Bob Garfield, *New and Old Media in Post-Katrina New Orleans*, National Public Radio, On the Media (Sept. 10, 2010), http://www.onthemedia.org/2010/sep/10/new

journalist.[600] MinnPost.com provides coverage of Minnesota, *Voice of San Diego* provides coverage of San Diego issues, Kaiser Health News provides coverage of health care issues, and *ProPublica* provides national and local investigative reporting.[601] Some of these organizations are nonprofits which receive contributions from readers, and the *Voice of San Diego* is funded by a venture capitalist.[602] *The Voice of San Diego* does not attempt to cover all stories, but is rather focused on important stories not being covered by others or stories that it feels that it can report better than other news organizations.[603] In winning a coveted investigative award, the *Voice* acted on a tip that was sent to all media organizations, but that only it decided to pursue.[604]

Online newspapers and broadcasts have considerable advantages over traditional print newspapers. The obvious advantage is that online newspapers eliminate many fixed costs because they do not require ink and paper, and do not require physical delivery of the finished print product by ground transport. Another advantage is that online papers can be more current with the news because they can be updated on an almost immediate basis.[605] Finally, online newspapers offer the possibility of interactivity in the sense that readers can participate in online fora where they can express criticism, support or opposition to a published article piece.[606]

However, online publishers are facing challenges as social media platforms de-emphasize news content.[607]

-and-old-media-in-post-katrina-new-orleans/transcript/ ("Writer and organizer Nathan Rothstein wrote about the partnership forged between new and old media in Katrina's wake. He says the circumstances allowed a unique pattern to develop between bloggers, mainstream media and public policy").

600. *Id.*

601. *See* Bob Garfield, *The Road to Non-Profit*, National Public Radio, On the Media (Aug. 21, 2009), http://www.onthemedia.org/2009/aug/21/the-road-to-non-profit/transcript/.

602. *Id.*

603. *See Nonprofit News Site Wins Coveted Media Award*, *supra* note 534.

604. *Id.*

605. *See A Web Site That's Not Afraid to Pick a Fight*, *supra* note 596.

606. *Id.*

607. *See Digital News Sites Fight to Survive as Online Ad Dollars Dry Up*, *supra* note 345.

D. THE FUTURE OF HARD COPY NEWSPAPERS

Despite the decided economic advantages of the Web, hard-copy newspapers will not necessarily disappear. The Occupy Wall Street Movement, for example, functioned in a very high-tech manner, but some protestors created a hard-copy newspaper to accompany the movement[608] (there is no "official" newspaper because "nothing is official in the world of Occupy Wall Street).[609] Some in the Occupy movement believed that a hard copy paper had special value in this context: "newspapers convey a sense of place, of actually being there, that digital media can't. When is the last time that somebody handed you a Web site?"[610] As one of the producers of the newspaper noted, "A newspaper is tactile, engages all of the senses, and leads to more immersive reading than what people might do online."[611] In addition, unlike a protest sign, a newspaper can provide a more detailed analysis of a protest's grievances and history.[612] Likewise, during the Arab Spring protests in the Middle East, a hard-copy newspaper was published by protestors in Cairo.[613]

As traditional newspapers attempt to stay afloat, they have increasingly begun to offer their content online. Many traditional newspapers are also beginning to offer interactivity as part of their service,[614] thereby allowing readers to participate in discussions, publish their ideas, and engage in discussion with other readers.[615] The difficulty with these interactive solutions is that the newspapers still set the agenda by publishing (online) an article and by giving readers the opportunity to respond to that article.

---

608. David Carr, *A Protest's Ink-Stained Fingers, The New York Times*, The Media Equation, at B1 (Oct. 10, 2011).

609. *See id.*

610. *See id.*, at B3.

611. *Id.*, at B3 (as an attendee at the protests stated, "A Web site will come and go, but this could be here 100 years from now if the mold doesn't get to it.").

612. *See A Protest's Ink-Stained Fingers, supra* note 608, at B3.

613. *Id.*, at B3.

614. *Id.*

615. *Id.* ("The *interactive* newspaper creates a living editorial page and a living *op-ed* page (the opinion page opposite the editorial page) unlike anything exists on paper today. It resembles an Internet chat line or list serves that runs parallel *threads* (ongoing discussions on a topic) on several topics at once. Many discussions are linked to news and editorial content.").

In other words, readers are not necessarily initiating their own discussion fora on topics that interest them.

One might suspect that the future of many existing newspapers will be entirely online. Just as much retail business is shifting from bricks and mortar stores to online shopping, more and more newspapers may be forced to publish online, and the media may morph into a different form as it has done in the past.[616] In the same way that online stores have significant cost advantages over bricks and mortar stores (because they do not have to pay for an expensive storefront location, or as much staffing), online newspapers have significant cost advantages over traditional print newspapers, and these cost variances make online publications much more cost efficient.

The precise nature or form that new online publications will take is not entirely clear. News Corp. has taken steps to develop an iPad-only newspaper, *The Daily*.[617] The content is refreshed each morning, and subscribers are charged $40 per year.[618] In addition to providing news content, *The Daily* provides photographs, video and other interactive features,[619] and it can tailor content to an individual reader's interests.[620] Freed from print, and print distribution problems, News Crop. is able to produce *The Daily* for the relatively cheap cost of $500,000 per year.[621] Of course, the question remains whether the public is willing to pay anything for this online news content.[622]

The *Atlantic Monthly* provides an interesting example of a traditional print publication that shifted to online publication and thereby resusci-

---

616. *See* A History of Mass Communication, *supra* note 355, at 51–53 (suggesting that printing presses have followed different economic models over the centuries. At one point, many printers made their money primarily from accepting printing jobs. Over time, printers developed newspapers, journals and various types of newsletters to provide themselves with an assured audience. These publications included trade presses and the so-called "penny press" (an inexpensive paper for the working man that drew its name from the fact that the original papers sold for only a single penny).

617. *See* Jeremy W. Peters & Brian Stelter, *News Corp. Heralds Debut of The Daily, an iPad-Only Newspaper, The New York Times*, at B1 (Feb. 3, 2011).

618. *Id.*

619. *Id.*

620. *Id.* at B4.

621. *Id.*

622. *Id.*

tated itself.[623] The magazine, which had lost money for more than a decade, realized a $1.8 million profit in 2010 by moving online.[624] Previously, the magazine had attempted various other solutions, all of which failed,[625] and then it settled on the idea of an aggressive online presence. While the magazine still publishes a print version,[626] it has hired bloggers who brought devoted readers with them.[627] In addition, although the *Atlantic Monthly's* advertising sales staff is given monthly sales targets, no distinction is made between print and digital advertising.[628] As a result, total digital advertising rose by 70 percent in a single year,[629] and now accounts for 40 percent of the company's total advertising revenue.[630]

Other traditional newspapers and magazines have begun to make, or have made, the move from ink and print versions to completely online versions.[631] Blender Magazine decided to stop publishing a print version of its magazine and moved online,[632] but it ultimately closed down in 2009. The *Seattle Post-Intelligencer*,[633] which was not viable as a traditional print newspaper, also moved its publication online.[634] In doing so,

---

623. *See* Jeremy W. Peters, *Web Focus Helps Revitalize the Atlantic, The New York Times*, at B1 (Dec. 13, 2010).

624. *Id.*

625. *Id.*, at B4 ("Grappling with a solution, Mr. Bradley [the magazine's owner] went through what he called his Inspector Clouseau phase, likening himself to the hapless Pink Panther detective. He tried going out on sales calls with his advertising staff, only to find that his presence in meetings was a distraction. He sank money into printing the magazine on higher quality paper, only to find that it was a waste. He raised the price of a subscription. He lowered the price of a subscription.").

626. *Id.* at B1.

627. *Id.* at B4 ("He [Mr. Bennett] and Mr. Bradley set out to assemble a team of bloggers who were known quantities and could attract a devoted following. They lured Andrew Sullivan away from the New Republic in what proved to be a major coup. Today, Mr. Sullivan's blog, The Daily Dish, accounts for about a quarter of The Atlantic.com's monthly unique visitors, which reached 4.8 million in October.").

628. *Id.*

629. *Id.* at B4.

630. *Id.*

631. *See A Newspaper Loses Its Paper Routes, supra* note 86.

632. *See* Stephanie Clifford, *Print Version of Blender Magazine Will Cease Publication, The New York Times*, at B6 (Mar. 27, 2009).

633. https://www.seattlepi.com/.

634. *See Newspapers Wade Into an Online-Only Future, supra* note 580.

the paper dramatically reduced its staff from 165 people to 20 people,[635] thereby raising questions about whether the staff reduction would affect the quality and scope of the organization's reporting.[636] In the process, the *Post-Intelligencer* made a conscious decision not to function like a traditional newspaper, in the sense that it would attempt to comprehensively cover all issues, claiming that "few people come to our Web site and try to re-create the experience of reading a newspaper" and reading the publication "cover-to-cover."[637] Instead, the *Post-Intelligencer* covers a more limited range of topics where it has something to say.[638] Nevertheless, the *Post-Intelligencer* has been able to cover a variety of topics, including sports, transportation, courts and local government, and to publish online links to stories in other publications, photo galleries, and comments from civic leaders.[639]

The distinction between print and online newspapers has played out in other ways as well. As Joel Kramer, CEO of the *MinnPost*, another online publication, noted, it is simply not feasible for a Web-based publication to replicate a traditional print-based newspaper.[640] Kramer described the *MinnPost* as more akin to a news magazine since "most stories we don't cover every day."[641] In addition, the tone is different. As Kramer notes regarding the *MinnPost*, "Our writers have much more freedom to be analytical—they combine news with commentary."[642] In addition, the *MinnPost* survives based on foundation grants, reader donations and revenue from online advertising.[643]

Similarly, when the *Cincinnati Post* died, the Scripps Co. (owner of the *Post*) started an online publication, *KYPost.com*[644] which has a limited focus because it centers on the Northern Kentucky suburbs of Cin-

---

635. *See A Newspaper Loses Its Paper Routes, supra* note 86.

636. The publication can be found at Seattlepi.com.

637. *See Newspapers Wade Into an Online-Only Future, supra* note 580.

638. *Id.* (the article goes on to note that the MinnPost in the Minneapolis-Twin Cities area, does the same thing).

639. *See Newspapers Wade Into an Online-Only Future, supra* note 580.

640. *Id.*

641. *Id.*

642. *Id.*

643. *Id.*

644. www.KYPost.com.

cinnati.[645] The publication features regional stories prepared by employees of the Scripps-owned television station, and it also covers very local news and community events.[646] The publication does not have a classified advertisements section.[647]

Of course, since both the *MinnPost* and *Post-Intelligencer* have traditional print-based newspapers in their cities (Minneapolis-St. Paul has both the *St. Paul Pioneer Press* and the *Minneapolis Star Tribune*), it is arguably unnecessary for them to cover as many topics as traditional newspapers. Nevertheless, it is not clear that online publishers can create a comprehensive publication based solely on online advertisements. Although the *Post-Intelligencer* saves the cost of printing and hard copy distribution, advertisers may not be as willing to pay for online advertising as they are for hard copy advertising.[648] Of course, if a traditional print-based publication did not exist in Seattle, advertisers might be willing to pay more for online advertising, and it would be interesting to see if the online publishers would then feel compelled to expand the scope of their coverage.[649] One interesting side-effect of the *Post-Intelligencer's* shift to online publication is that the prospects for its former rival, *The Seattle Times*, have improved given the decline in competition.[650]

So, the fundamental question raised at the beginning of this chapter (whether online investigative reporting services can adequately replace traditional newspapers?) remains unanswered. Some are doubtful.[651] Mr. Joel Kramer, who formerly worked for *The Star Tribune* and now edits an online journal, *MinnPost.com*, questions whether online journals can completely replace traditional newspapers: "'It would be a terrible thing for any city for the dominant paper to go under, because that's who does

---

645. *See Newspapers Wade Into an Online Only Future*, *supra* note 580.

646. *Id.*

647. *Id.*

648. *See Newspapers Wade Into an Online Only Future*, *supra* note 580.

649. *Id.* ("It's worth remembering that in each of these big cities—Seattle, Minneapolis, Denver, Cincinnati—a dominant daily is still limping along. Perhaps the real test for the value of these online news sites will arrive once the final edition of the last big paper in town rolls off the presses.").

650. *See* Perez-Pena, *supra* note 86.

651. *See After a Year of Ruin*, *supra* note 575 ("Blog and new-media sites are cartoonishly written off as places where people write up the soup they just ate. . . .").

the bulk of the serious reporting.'"[652] He notes that: "'Places like us would spring up, ... but they wouldn't be nearly as big. We can tweak the papers and compete with them, but we can't replace them.'"[653]

Others disagree with Kramer and believe that virtually all serious reporting will eventually migrate to the internet. Jeff Jarvis of the City University of New York's graduate school of journalism argues that the "death of a newspaper should result in an explosion of much smaller news sources online, producing at least as much coverage as the paper did ... Those sources might be less polished, but they would be competitive, ending the monopolies many newspapers have long enjoyed."[654] The head of *Talking Points Memo* (TPM), an online investigative website, admits that online investigative reporting cannot now replace the investigative journalism being done by print reporters: "If all the big papers disappeared right now and we replaced them with 50 TPMs, it wouldn't come close to doing the job."[655] However, he believes that online journalism will evolve to fill that void, noting that the industry is "in a broader transformation where models like ours and others are going to evolve that can fill the void."[656]

In the long run, most traditional newspapers may be forced to follow *The Seattle Post-Intelligencer* model, and abandon their print versions in favor of an online distribution system. Indeed, they may have no choice.[657] As Professor Jarvis of City University of New York noted, many money-losing papers should "have the guts to shut down print and go online," and it "will have to be a much smaller product, but that's where we're headed anyway."[658]

---

652. *See As Cities Go From Two Papers to One, supra* note 71.

653. *Id.*

654. *See Id.* (quoting Jeff Jarvis, City University of New York's graduate school of journalism).

655. *See* Kurtz, *supra* note 33, at A7 (quoting John Marshall of *Talking Points Memo* website).

656. *Id.*

657. *See As Cities Go From Two Papers to One, supra* note 71 ("Industry executives who once scoffed at the idea of an Internet-only product now concede that they are probably headed in that direction, but the consensus is that newspapers going all digital would become drastically smaller news sources for the foreseeable future.").

658. *Id.* (quoting Jeff Jarvis, City University of New York's graduate school of journalism).

If newspapers decide to move completely online, they will then be forced to decide whether to charge for the content, to survive based solely on advertising,[659] or to employ some other model (*e.g.*, grants).[660] For the moment, at least, print-based newspapers seem to have more resources available to them than online papers do.[661] However, in another interesting twist, some online newspapers are beginning to work cooperatively with print-based newspapers. For example, the *Chicago News Cooperative* works with *The New York Times* to produce a two-page section for distribution as part of the *Times'* Chicago edition.[662]

As a "watchdog of democracy," online publications have significant advantages over print publications in terms of speed and sometimes range of coverage. Online publications permit greater coverage of local issues. For example, Steven Berlin Johnson founded an online publication (FEED) and also started a hyperlocal news service entitled *outside.in.*[663] Other hyperlocal sites include EveryBlock, Placeblogger and Patch.[664] In the 1980s, it might have taken long periods for information to make it to the end user, but now similar information can be distributed almost instantaneously.[665] In addition, Johnson argues that internet-based coverage can provide more micro coverage that cannot be provided by a large daily newspaper. Indeed, traditional newspapers have not historically provided sufficient coverage of local issues,[666] but blogs and online news

---

659. *See As Cities Go From Two Papers to One, supra* note 71.

660. *See Local News Fades Out, supra* note 21, at B8.

661. Perez-Pena, *supra* note 513, at B1.

662. *See id.*

663. *See Why Newspapers Can't Be Saved, But the News Can, supra* note 33.

664. See *News Without Newspapers, supra* note 401, at B1.

665. *See Why Newspapers Can't Be Saved, But the News Can, supra* note 33 ("In the old days, it might have taken months for details from a John Sculley keynote to make to the College Hill Bookstore; now the lag is seconds, with dozens of people liveblogging every passing phrase from a Jobs speech. There are 8,000-word dissections of each new release of OS X at Ars Technica, written with attention to detail and technical sophistication that far exceeds anything a traditional newspaper would ever attempt. Writers like Jon Gruber or Don Norman regularly post intricate critiques of user interface issues. (I probably read twenty mini-essays about Safari's new tab design.").

666. *Id*:

> When people talk about the civic damage that a community suffers by losing its newspaper, one of the key things that people point to is the loss of local news coverage. But I suspect in ten years, when we look back at traditional local cov-

services are capable of providing that coverage.[667] In other words, society might be losing the traditional "guardian" or "watchdog of democracy," but it may be picking up a new and somewhat different type of watchdog.

E. THE "RELIABILITY" OF ONLINE PUBLICATIONS

Whether the new forms of media will be as "reliable" as traditional media is unclear. Some online publications claim to adhere to the same journalistic standards as traditional news outlets, including fact and source checking and an emphasis on objective reporting.[668] Of course, there are numerous

---

erage, it will look much more like MacWorld circa 1987. I adore the City section of *New York Times*, but every Sunday when I pick it up, there are only three or four stories in the whole section that I find interesting or relevant to my life—out of probably twenty stories total. And yet every week in my neighborhood there are easily twenty stories that I would be interested in reading: a mugging three blocks from my house; a new deli opening; a house sale; the baseball team at my kid's school winning a big game. *The New York Times* can't cover those things in a print paper not because of some journalistic failing on their part, but rather because the economics are all wrong: there are only a few thousand people potentially interested in those news events, in a city of 8 million people. There are metro area stories that matter to everyone in a city: mayoral races, school cuts, big snowstorms. But most of what we care about in our local experience lives in the long tail. We've never thought of it as a failing of the newspaper that its metro section didn't report on a deli closing, because it wasn't even conceivable that a big centralized paper could cover an event with such a small radius of interest.

667. *Id*:

But of course, that's what the Web can do. That's one of the main reasons we created outside.in, because I found myself waking up in the morning and turning to local Brooklyn bloggers like Brownstoner, who were suddenly covering local news with a granularity that the Times had never attempted. Two years later, there are close to a thousand bloggers writing about Brooklyn: there are multiple blogs devoted to the Atlantic Yards real estate development; dozens following the Brooklyn foodie scene; music blogs, politics blogs, parenting blogs. The Times itself is now launching local Brooklyn blogs, which is great. As we get better at organizing all that content—both by selecting the best of it, and by sorting it geographically—our standards about what constitutes good local coverage are going to improve. We're going to go through the same evolution that I did from reading two-month-old news in MacWorld, to expecting an instantaneous liveblog of a keynote announcement. Five years from now, if someone gets mugged within a half mile of my house, and I don't get an email alert about it within three hours, it will be a sign that something is broken.

668. *See When Unrest Stirs*, *supra* note 582.

questions about the extent to which the traditional media reports fairly or objectively.[669] Even the famed anchorman Walter Cronkite expressed concerns about whether the modern media was responsible and of high-quality,[670] and he raised questions regarding the dominance of large media corporations.[671] Some believe that these corporations are more interested in commerce and entertainment than in civics and democracy.[672]

Given the range of internet-devices available, an array of non-journalists can communicate or publish information, but not all of this information will necessarily be reliable. For example, as noted, Egyptian protestors used devices like Twitter to communicate information about the protests occurring there, but there was evidence suggesting that some of the Twitter posts were unreliable.[673]

Undoubtedly, some online publications attempt to adhere, and do in fact adhere, to traditional journalistic standards, and are as reliable as traditional newspapers. That may be particularly true of online newspapers that hire significant numbers of former print journalists. Nevertheless, there have been significant problems regarding the credibility and reliability of some internet communications, and the technology exists to alter pictures and other documents.[674] In other words, because of the democratic nature of the internet, allegations can come from a variety of sources, and it can sometimes be difficult to discern whether an online publisher is a

---

669. *Id.*

670. *See* Nichols, *supra* note 4 ("So it should come as little surprise that what worried Cronkite in the last years of his life was the collapse of journalistic quality and responsibility.").

671. *Id.*

672. *Id.*

673. *See* Steve Inskeep, *Twitter Helped to Distort Egyptian Protests*, National Public Radio, Morning Edition (Aug. 12, 2011), http://www.npr.org/2011/08/12/139570720/twitter-created-echo-chamber-during-egyptian-protests ("I was actually in and around Tahrir, and there was supposed to be a big protest [and] some of the folks on the Twitter-verse [were] claiming that there were hundreds of police security directly shooting even live rounds in the air at people.... I was actually watching [and] I didn't observe any sort of live rounds or anything ").

674. *See* Peter Wayner, *Stretching the Truth Just Became Easier (and Cheaper): Free Software Allows Anyone to Tweak a Picture, Whether by Expanding a Background or Deleting a Blemish, The New York Times*, at B7 (Jan. 31, 2008).

"journalist" as opposed to a "political activist" or both.[675] Video images can be altered, "old" images can be passed off as "new" ones,[676] and information can be disseminated simply as a hoax (as happened with a fake Twitter message regarding Pittsburgh Steelers Quarterback Ben Roethlisberger that were picked up and republished by various media outlets, even though the information had been published by a radio host in order to raise questions about Twitter and call attention to his show).[677]

Moreover, the internet has already shifted the industry to a 24-hour news cycle (in the sense that stories and information are constantly being updated rather than being published once a day) with the inevitable accuracy problems attendant to quicker publication.[678] For example, in their haste to report the event, some news organizations falsely reported that Congresswoman Gabrielle Giffords had been assassinated (instead of wounded) during the Tucson attack on her.[679]

Examples of the blend between "political activists" and "citizen journalists" abound. For example, Andrew Breitbart (now deceased) wrote frequently about such issues as government, journalism, and Hollywood.[680] In July of 2010, the United States Department of Agriculture forced a Georgia official, Ms. Shirley Sherrod, to resign because of statements that

---

675. *See Journalist, Provocateur, supra* note 595, at B2: ("Where once there was a pretty bright line between journalist and political operative, there is now a kind of continuum, with politicians becoming media providers in their own right, and pundits, entertainers and journalists often driving political discussions.").

676. *See* Jennifer Preston & Brian Stelter, *Cellphone Cameras Become World's Eyes and Ears on Protests Across the Middle East, The New York Times*, at A11 (Feb. 19, 2011) ("Authenticating them [Internet-posted video images] remains a challenge, since photos can be easily altered by computers and old videos can resurface again, purporting to be new.").

677. *See* Brooke Gladstone, *The Great Ben Roethlisberger Hoax*, National Public Radio, On the Media (Sept. 23, 2010), http://www.onthemedia.org/2010/sep/03/the-great-ben-roethlisberger-hoax/. There have been other Web hoaxes as well. See Tamara Ikenberg, In Web Hoaxes, Even Experts Bitten By Rumor Bug, *The Courier-Journal*, at A1 (Aug. 23, 2010).

678. *See* Bob Garfield, *The Rush to Report*, National Public Radio, On the Media (Jan. 21, 2011), http://www.onthemedia.org/2011/jan/21/the-rush-to-report/transcript/.

679. *Id.*

680. *See* Jeremy W. Peters, *The Right's Blogger Provocateur, The New York Times* B1 (June 26, 2011).

she allegedly made some twenty-four years earlier.[681] The demand for the resignation was prompted by a video that was posted on a conservative website biggovernment.com that purportedly showed her making racially discriminatory statements.[682] The video was posted by Breitbart.[683] Before demanding the resignation, Agriculture officials did not conduct a thorough investigation, and instead reacted quickly in an effort to engage in damage control.[684] As it turns out, Sherrod's statements were highly edited and taken out of context.[685] Eventually, both the Secretary of Agriculture and President Obama apologized to Ms. Sherrod, and the Department offered to give her job back.[686] Of course, part of the problem is that the traditional media did not conduct an adequate investigation before picking up and publishing the internet allegations against Ms. Sherrod,[687] and

---

681. *See* Michael Martin, *"Shop Talk": The Sherrod Shuffle*, National Public Radio, Tell Me More (July 23, 2010), http://www.npr.org/templates/story/story.php?storyId=128720704.

682. *Id.*

683. *See Journalist, Provocateur, supra* note 595.

684. *See* Tony Cox, *Assessing the Media's Role in Sherrod Scandal*, National Public Radio, Talk of the Nation (July 26, 2010), http://www.npr.org/templates/story/story.php?storyId=128776192 (quoting Ted Koppel, veteran journalist, as saying that "But what happened right after that was that there clearly was some kind of a panic at the White House and a fear that this story of a black woman having said something that was prejudicial toward the white farmer that she was supposed to be serving, that would somehow rear up and bite this administration in the behind. And so the necessity to do something immediately, I think, did as much to create the ridiculous and almost tragic events of that day as anything that our colleagues in the media did.").

685. *See* Brian Stelter, *When Race Is the Issue, Misleading Coverage Sets Off an Uproar: Accusations Can Take Root Online, Then Move to TV or Radio, The New York Times*, at B1 (July 26, 2010); *"Shop Talk": The Sherrod Shuffle, supra* note 681 ("But just as quickly as she had been demonized, the story took a dramatic turn. Speaking in her own defense, Sherrod explained that the video was edited to mislead the viewer and that she not only was not racist in her job performance but had indeed helped the white farmer in question and had used the speech as a lesson in personal redemption from racial prejudice. Additionally, the incident happened 24 years ago, before her employment with the USDA. The apologies flowed in. She was offered a new job in the Agriculture Department and became the latest poster child for a media out of control, which is where we begin our conversation today.").

686. *See "Shop Talk": The Sherrod Shuffle, supra* note 681.

687. *See* Cox, *supra* note 684 ("The media did not cover itself with glory. We did rather poorly. But I must say that the political reaction and we can talk more about that if you want to, Tony, because it flows out of things that have happened over the last 10, 20 years, but the political pressure was what created that storm.").

it may have taken shortcuts because of the pace of information coming from the internet, and a perceived need to respond quickly.[688] Breitbart also caused controversy when he published video clips suggesting that the Acorn organization provided advice to an activist who was posing as a pimp.[689]

Some commentators also view the WikiLeaks disclosures as showing a lack of discretion because the released documents had the potential to harm individuals and governmental interests,[690] as well as to disrupt American operations, place confidential sources in danger,[691] and damage diplomatic relations.[692] In some countries, the disclosure could have meant imprisonment or death for the people mentioned in the disclosures.[693] In general, the newspapers and magazines that worked with WikiLeaks were very careful about such issues, including restrictions on information that might endanger people,[694] as well as militarily-important information.[695]

---

688. *Id.* ("I think people these days, particularly our colleagues in cable television but also in the various blogs and on the Internet, are in a desperate rush to be first with the obvious. And frequently, they haven't done enough homework, spent enough time trying to figure out what is going on, and this was a perfect example. Poor Ms. Sherrod, whose name I predict will not even be remembered by most people a month from now, was a victim of the worst intersection of the shoddiest kind of journalism and the shoddiest kind of politics.").

689. *See Journalist, Provocateur, supra* note 595.

690. *See WikiLeaks Taps Power of the Press, supra* note 499, at B8 ("And by publishing only a portion of the documents, rather than spilling information willy-nilly and recklessly endangering lives, WikiLeaks could also strike a posture of responsibility, an approach that seems to run counter to Mr. Assange's own core anarchism.").

691. *See Leaked Cables Offer Raw Look, supra* note 455; Sharon Theimer, *WikiLeaks Release Has Given Hit List to al-Qaida, U.S. Says, The Courier-Journal*, A5 (Dec. 7, 2011).

692. *See* Alan Cowell, *Cables Elicit Mistrust, But Also Shrugs, International Herald Tribune*, at 1 (Dec. 4–5, 2010) (suggesting that the WikiLeaks disclosures may result in "closing doors to United States diplomats, turning candor to reticence and leaving many people leery of baring their souls and secrets to American officials.").

693. *See* Keller, *supra* note 453.

694. *See id.*, at 34 ("From the beginning, we agreed that in our articles and in any documents we published from the secret archive, we would excise material that could put lives at risk.... Guided by reporters with extensive experience in the field, we redacted the names of ordinary citizens, local officials, activists, academics and others who had spoken to American soldiers or diplomats.").

695. *Id.* ("If a dispatch noted that Aircraft A had left Location B at a certain time and arrived at Location C at a certain time, Chivers edited it out on the off chance that this could teach enemy forces something useful about the capabilities of that aircraft.").

The WikiLeaks website was not as discreet in its disclosures,[696] and some argued that the disclosures provided only an incomplete and distorted view of the situations discussed.[697] Of course, the WikiLeaks disclosures also provided great insight into how government functions, and its disclosures arguably served the public interest.

Eventually, the public may be forced to distinguish between different types of internet publications based on their accuracy and reliability.[698] If so, such differentiation would not be surprising. In England, for example, distinctions are made between the "quality press" and the "tabloids." There is no reason why similar distinctions cannot, or will not, be made by the public regarding online publications. In other words, the public may tend to treat both conservative and liberal bloggers with skepticism and gravitate toward those online publications that are associated with quality reporting.

F. THE INTERNET AND THE CHANGING RELATIONSHIP BETWEEN THE MEDIA AND THE PUBLIC

As the internet matures, a new relationship is developing between the public and the media. Historically, the media has held all of the power, and has employed an enormous capacity to shape public opinion. As a result, individuals who challenged the media did so at their own risk. Indeed, as an old adage states, one should never "pick a fight with someone who buys ink by the barrel."[699] Since the media (be it radio, televi-

---

696. *Id.*, at 37 ("I talked to Assange by phone a few times and heard out his complaints. He was angry that we declined to link our online coverage of the War Logs to the WikiLeaks Web site, a decision we made because we feared—rightly, as it turned out—that its trove would contain the names of low-level informants and make them Taliban targets.").

697. *See Leaked Cables Offer Raw Look, supra* note 455.

698. *See When Race Is the Issue, supra* note 685, at B1 ("Bit is an open question whether conservative media outlets risk damage to their credibility when obscure or misleading stories are blown out of proportion and when what amounts to political opposition research is presented as news.").

699. *See* Katharine Q. Seelye, *Answering Back to the News Media, Using the Internet, The New York Times*, at C1 (Jan. 2. 2006) (the article goes on to note that, "Even when subjects of news stories felt they had been misunderstood or badly treated, they were unlikely to take on reporters or publishers, believing that the power of the press gave the press the final word.").

sion or newspapers) controlled the dominant means of communication, an aggrieved individual was forced to use one of the existing media to respond to an attack. Although an individual might try to circumvent the traditional media by creating posters or fliers, and distributing them, such methods involved a much less effective method of communication.

In the internet-era, the playing field between the media and ordinary individuals has been leveled a bit, and one can more rationally pick a fight with a media outlet—even one that is buying "ink by the barrel." Through the internet, those attacked by traditional media can respond in unconventional ways using blogs, e-mails and their own websites.[700] As one journalist noted, "Subjects of newspaper articles and news broadcasts now fight back with the same methods reporters use to generate articles and broadcasts—taping interviews, gathering e-mail exchanges, taking notes on phone conversations—and publishing them on their own Web sites."[701]

Individual challenges to the media take many different forms. In one case, an interviewee who was concerned about the way his interview might be portrayed by a publication, chose to take the offensive through the internet by publishing e-mail exchanges between himself and the journalist.[702] Interestingly, the interviewee did so even though he had originally requested that the contents of the interview be kept private.[703] Likewise, when Nightline interviewed a member of the Discovery Institute about intelligent design, the Institute published the unedited transcript of the interview on its website in an effort to reveal the "predictable

---

700. *See id.* ("The Internet, and especially the amplifying power of blogs, is changing that. Unhappy subjects discovered a decade ago that they could use their Web sites to correct the record or deconstruct articles to expose what they perceived as a journalist's bias or wrongheaded narration.").

701. *See id.* ("This new weapon in the media wars is shifting the center of gravity in the way that news is gathered and presented, and it carries implications for the future of journalism.").

702. *See id.* ("An early example of turning the tables occurred in 2001, when David D. Kirkpatrick, who then covered the publishing industry for *The New York Times*, wrote an article about Dave Eggers, author of "A Heartbreaking Work of Staggering Genius." Mr. Eggers posted a 10,000-word response on his Web site complaining about the tone of the piece, and included their e-mail exchanges, which Mr. Kirkpatrick had asked be kept private.").

703. *See id.*

tone" of some of Nightline's questions.[704] The Institute accompanied the transcript with the following exhortation from Rob Crowther, the Institute's spokesman: "'Here's your chance to go behind the scenes with the gatekeepers of the national media to see how they screen out viewpoints and information that don't fit their stereotypes.'"[705]

There are additional reasons why traditional media outlets may not hold the upper-hand vis-a-vis private individuals today. One advantage of the traditional media is that it has an established audience that it can regularly and easily reach.[706] Internet-based communications have the potential to reach a much-broader audience: "the power of blogs is exponential; blog posts can be linked and replicated instantly across the Web, creating a snowball effect that often breaks through to the mainstream media."[707] This situation led Dean Thomas Kunkel of the Philip Merrill College of Journalism at the University of Maryland to remark that "reporters had created a kind of 'Wild West atmosphere' in cyberspace.'"[708] Reporters more frequently use e-mail, and therefore journalists must "start thinking a couple of moves ahead because you're leaving a paper trail. And the truth squad mentality of some bloggers means you are apt to have your own questions thrown back at you."[709] In addition, blogs and other new media forms have a "longer shelf life than most traditional news media articles. A newspaper reporter's original article is likely to disappear from the free Web site after a few days and become inaccessible unless purchased from the newspaper's archives, while the blogger's version of events remains available forever."[710] In addition, there is a tendency on the part of some internet responders to publish first and thereby beat the traditional media to the punch.[711]

---

704. *See id.*
705. *See id.*
706. *See id.*
707. *See id.*
708. *See id.*
709. *See id.*
710. *See id.*
711. *See id.*:

> Earlier this year, Edward Nawotka, a book critic based in Austin, Tex., described in The Texas Observer an interview he had conducted via e-mail with Ann Coulter, the conservative writer, a couple of years ago. She sent him a 2,000-word response by e-mail, which he then asked her to trim so he could include it in a

These changes may actually have a positive effect on the media. Some commentators suggest that internet responses to traditional media are forcing the media to be more transparent in the way that it reports the news.[712] In some instances, in addition to publishing summaries of newsmaker interviews, journalists are also publishing the actual transcripts or their notes on interviews on the internet.[713]

G. MEDIA CONVERGENCE

Another trend that the internet has fostered is a movement toward media convergence,[714] and that movement has had a dramatic effect on communication. The convergence extends to all types of media, including the traditional press, broadcasters, satellite communications, cable communications, and the internet. Today, the saying goes, that "a screen is a screen" as "the old dividing lines between television, radio, Web and print disap-

---

daily e-mail newsletter—only to discover that she had already posted her entire response on her Web site. Another example occurred in 1999, when "20/20," the ABC News program, interviewed officials from a company called Metabolife International. The company acquired footage of the interview and posted it on its Web site before the program was shown.... [T]he company bought advertisements in newspapers urging readers to watch the footage. "People do it all the time," said Rebecca MacKinnon, a former CNN correspondent who is now a research fellow at the Berkman Center for Internet and Society at Harvard Law School, where she studies the effect of blogging on journalism. Interview subjects are "annoyed that they're quoted out of context, or they did a half-hour interview and only one sentence got used. Or sometimes they're just flattered that a reporter called them," she said. "If you're one of a growing number of people with a blog, you now have a place where you can set the record straight."

712. *See id.*

713. *See id.* ("Some news outlets are posting transcripts of their interviews with newsmakers, and some reporters are posting their own material. Stephen Baker, a senior writer at BusinessWeek, has posted not only transcripts from his interviews but also his own notes on his Web site, saying he likes to involve his readers in the journalistic process. 'Sometimes I say to my readers, Here's my interview. What story would you have written?' said Mr. Baker, who writes about technology. Journalism, he added, used to be a clear-cut 'before and after process,' much like making a meal; the cooking was done privately in the kitchen and then the meal was served. Now, he said, 'every aspect of it is scrutinized.'").

714. *See* David Carr, *New Rules for the Way We Watch, The New York Times*, The Media Equation, at B1 (Dec. 26, 2011).

pear within the four corners of a tablet."[715] As a result, "CNBC and *The Wall Street Journal* are not in different businesses anymore."[716]

An interesting synergy has developed between the media and online news sources. In some instances, even though ideas and protests may originate on the internet, they are picked up by the traditional media, and thereby transferred to the broader population. In addition, at times, traditional media has been able to influence the content of material that is posted on the internet. Indeed, there is evidence suggesting that internet users respond more quickly to stories that are initially broadcast on traditional media than to issues or concerns that begin solely on the internet.[717] And, of course, the internet is used for communicating all sorts of ideas or messages, many of which have nothing to do with politics or democracy.[718] Internet-based communications regarding social topics probably dwarf the quantity of communication related to political topics.[719] Nevertheless, as we will see, the internet has proved to be an effective medium for influencing the course of politics and political discourse.

As newspapers struggle to survive, they have increasingly been forced to compete directly on the medium (the internet) that has caused them so many problems.[720] More and more newspapers have encouraged "readers" to view their product online.[721] Obviously, some newspapers like the

---

715. *Id.*

716. *Id.*

717. *See* Natasha Singer, *Why Some Twitter Posts Catch On, and Some Don't, The New York Times*, at A4 (Feb. 6, 2011).

718. *Id.*

719. *Id.*

720. *See, e.g.*, the *New York Time's* website: www.nytimes.com; *but see* David Carr, *Newspaper Shuns Web, and Thrives, The New York Times*, at B1 (Dec. 21, 2008) (suggesting that TriCity News in Monmouth County, N.J., is "prospering precisely because it aggressively ignores the Web." The owner suggests that: "I don't understand how putting content on the Web would do anything but help destroy our paper.") http://www.nytimes.com/2008/12/22/business/media/22carr.html.

721. *See Detroit Newspapers May Sharply Cut Home Delivery, supra* note 149 (citing the example of The Detroit News and The Detroit Free Press which are both available for free online); Jeremy W. Peters, *The News, in Bright Bits: Small But Feisty, The Week Grows as Others Lag, The Courier-Journal*, at B1 (Mar. 14, 2011) (noting that The Week now attracted one million visitors to its website at the end of 2010)).

Seattle Post-Intelligencer's have moved entirely online.[722] Even newspapers that continue to offer print editions now offer Facebook pages, iPhone apps, and Twitter feeds, and many new magazines are starting as online only publications,[723] are focused on competing on the internet, and sometimes provide online content that is not available in the print version of their publications.[724] In some instances, newspapers show live versions of local press conferences by governmental officials or other prominent citizens,[725] and conduct online question and answer sessions.[726]

As they try to respond to the challenges of the internet, newspapers and magazines are altering their content in order to be more responsive and competitive. For example, at least one magazine has moved to a format whereby it publishes relatively short articles (rather than lengthy dissertations), and much of its content is culled from the internet and other news organizations.[727] In addition, many newspapers now offer video podcasts to supplement their text so that the print medium is beginning to merge in important respects with television and radio.[728] For example, News Corporation now publishes the *Daily Tablet* which is a Tablet only news publication,[729] but the publication has struggled for various reasons.[730]

---

722. *See A Newspaper Loses Its Paper Routes, supra* note 86 ("The Seattle Post-Intelligencer will produce its last printed edition on Tuesday and become an Internet-only news source, the Hearst Corporation said on Monday, making it by far the largest American newspaper to take that leap.").

723. *See* Zarroli, *supra* note 40.

724. *See, e.g.*, www.nytimes.com (*The New York Times*' website); www.courier-journal.com (*The Courier-Journal's* website).

725. *The Courier-Journal* newspaper now regularly shows news conferences live. For example, it might show former University of Louisville basketball coach Rick Pitino's news conferences live.

726. For example, *The Courier-Journal's* reporters now sometimes do the functional equivalent of press conferences. For example, some of the paper's sports reporters sometimes conduct question and answer sessions online where they take questions on current sports issues.

727. *See The News, in Bright Bits, supra* note 721, at B1.

728. At the time of writing, a podcast of Coach Rick Pitino (University of Louisville's basketball coach) could be viewed on *The Courier-Journal* website. www.courier-journal.com.

729. *See* Amy Chozick, *After a Year, Tablet Daily Is a Struggle, The New York Times*, at B1 (Feb. 6, 2012).

730. *Id.*

Although magazine publishers were once perceived as being behind the times in integrating technology, some magazine publishers are now working to anticipate and prepare for new technologies.[731] "Two magazines—*Esquire* and *GQ*—have developed iPhone versions, while *Wired* and *Sports Illustrated* have made mockups of tablet versions of their print editions."[732] In anticipation of the Apple Tablet, many media outlets geared their content for use on the Tablet.[733] In other words, media outlets have embraced "tools of the [internet] insurgency," are "not waiting for the much-hyped Apple table to land next year before coming up with content that might soar on the device,"[734] and are making every effort to ensure that they can compete in an online format.[735]

Of course, as viewers migrate to the internet, they are free to expand their choices for news options. Since many newspapers now offer online content, including *The New York Times*,[736] the *Washington Post*,[737] and *USA Today*,[738] brand loyalty to a hometown newspaper is required only for very local types of coverage (*e.g.*, sports coverage and coverage of local events and local political issues that might not be covered, or covered as well, at a national level). Even "news" matters such as weather coverage, can be obtained online from national or international sources.[739]

Media convergence is hardly limited to newspapers. The internet has allowed radio and television to assert an online presence so that much traditional broadcast information can be found online, including television

---

731. *See* Stephanie Clifford, *Magazines Get Ready for Tablets*, *The New York Times*, at B1 (Dec. 16, 2009).

732. *Id.*

733. *See After a Year of Ruin*, *supra* note 575.

734. *Id.*

735. *Id.* ("Captains of old-school magazine narrative like David Grange at Esquire and Terry McDonnell at Sports Illustrated are moving very aggressively to refashion their brands for a tablet world.... When the iPhone is put on steroids, consumers will again be able to touch, flip and navigate serendipitously across things they want to see or learn about. And if publishers are able to move out of the nomenclature of 'subscriptions' for content and into the universe of 'applications,' there may be some gold in those hills.").

736. *See* www.nytimes.com.

737. *See* www.washingtonpost.com.

738. *See* www.usatoday.com.

739. *See* www.weather.com.

programs.[740] Like newspapers, many traditional broadcasters are placing their content online in both print[741] and audio versions.[742] Local radio[743] and television stations[744] are doing so as well. Indeed, hundreds of online radio stations exist that broadcast only online.[745] Formerly, individuals might be forced to pay for cable television service in order to watch networks like ESPN (the cable sports network). Today, they have the option to obtain sports updates, as well as to watch football and basketball games in real time online.[746] As time passes, it becomes increasingly difficult to make clear distinctions between the internet, newspapers, broadcasters and other mediums. However, television's rush to the Web has been slowed by television manufacturers who did not initially move aggressively to produce the necessary technology.[747] That has now changed.

Convergence is also occurring in the radio industry. Radio (like all other mediums) can have an online presence that includes print content.[748] While some of this print content reflects material that was previously broadcast on air, some does not. The other major change is the method by which radio content is accessed. Historically, if individuals wanted to listen to a "radio" station, they would turn on a radio and access it over traditional broadcast frequencies. Today, a significant number of new and existing radio stations are broadcasting over the internet.[749] Indeed, as long ago as 2009, there were nearly 16,000 internet radio stations available online.[750] As a recent article concluded, "Early fans of the

740. *See* www.hulu.com; *see also* Brian Stelter, *Comcast Introduces a Streaming TV Service*, *The New York Times*, at B2 (Dec. 16, 2009).

741. *See, e.g.*, www.npr.org (National Public Radio); www.pbs.org (Public Broadcasting Service).

742. *Id.*

743. *See, e.g.*, www.wfpl.org (Louisville's public radio station, WFPL).

744. *See, e.g.*, www.wave3.com (Louisville-based television station).

745. *See* Matthew Friedman, *Nine Years and Still Waiting: While Congress Continues to Hold Off on Amending Copyright Law for the Digital Age, Commercial Industry Has Largely Moved On*, Villanova Sports & Ent. L.J. 637, 660 (2010).

746. *See* www.espn.com (ESPN's website).

747. *See* Matt Richtel, *What Convergence? TV's Hesitant March to the Net*, *The New York Times*, at B1 (Feb. 16, 2009).

748. *See* www.npr.org.

749. *See* Eric A. Taub, *When the Web Is in Reach; So Is a Radio Universe*, *The New York Times*, at B7 (Dec. 31, 2009).

750. *Id.*

iPhone bemoaned that, unlike many of its competitors, their favorite "do anything" device couldn't do one obvious thing: play local radio stations. They didn't get it. FM tuners are passé. Why include tuner technology to play a few dozen stations when you can harness thousands of radio stations over the Internet?"[751] Many people now use smart phones to access the internet and to access radio.[752]

Of course, the advantage of internet radio is that it can be accessed from anywhere. With traditional broadcast stations, it was necessary to be located within the broadcast radius of a radio station in order to hear it.[753] During trips away from home, it was difficult or impossible to access one's local station, and sometimes difficult to keep up with news from one's home country. Today, most radio stations stream online so that it is possible to listen to the exact same radio stations in Europe (or Asia or Africa) that one listens to at home.[754]

The new internet-based "radio" broadcasters run the gamut in terms of organizational structure. Some new "broadcasters" are individuals operating out of their own homes or even their basements,[755] and it is possible to find internet radio for virtually any type of music, as well as political radio focusing on topics from the right to the left.[756] Indeed, the dynamics are such that an individual can effectively create his/her own internet radio station (although this option is usually more focused on music than on political speech).[757] In addition, no longer must a user access an internet radio station through a personal computer.[758] It is possible to access internet radio through an iPhone or through special devices designed to

---

751. *Id.*

752. *See* David Lieberman, *Radio Finding New Life on Smart Phones, The Courier-Journal*, at D5 (Dec. 27, 2009).

753. *See When the Web Is in Reach; So Is a Radio Universe, supra* note 749.

754. *Id.*

755. *Id.*

756. *Id.* ("Literally thousands of genres of Internet radio exist, from oldies, classical and religious to ultraradical talk, from the right and left. The first trick is finding them, and the next is playing them. Fortunately, with a little information, both tasks are rather easy.").

757. *Id.* ("Livio Radio's wireless line includes its AARP, NPR and Pandora models. Pandora's music service allows listeners to "create" a radio station based on an artist or genre they like. Then, Pandora automatically plays other music that the service believes fits the same category.").

758. *Id.*

pick up internet stations.[759] Despite the internet competition, traditional radio stations have faired well as they broadcast over both the airwaves and the internet.[760]

Even some of the new online publishers are moving toward media convergence. *Politico*, an online journal, is beginning to produce and air video programming in competition with news organizations such as CNN and CNBC.[761] *The Huffington Post* is also moving to enter the market with plans to offer twelve hours of video programming per day.[762] Even traditional publishers and news services are moving in this direction with organizations such as Reuters examining the possibility of creating online video content.[763] Google is encouraging publishers to create "Google Hangouts."[764]

Media conglomerates have tried to respond to the convergence problem by purchasing their own cable networks,[765] and in that way have been able to retain a degree of market control.[766] For example, *The New York Times* has moved aggressively into the cable and electronic markets.[767] However, existing media organizations have hardly been able to corral those markets as others, including greeting card manufacturers, have also

---

759. *Id; see also* Lieberman, *supra* note 750.

760. *See* Nick Wingfield, *In the Stream of Internet Radio, Music Stations Hold Their Own: Venturing Online, but Also Playing to Their Traditional Strengths, The New York Times* B1 (Nov. 9, 2015).

761. *See* Brian Stelter, *Print News Media Go Live with Video Programming, The New York Times*, at B1 (Feb. 6, 2012).

762. *Id.*

763. *Id.*

764. *Id.*

765. *See* Bill Carter, *For CBS, a QVC Merger Unlocks Door to Cable, The New York Times*, at 35 (July 4, 1994).

766. *See* Michael K. Powell, *New Rules, Old Rhetoric, The New York Times*, at A17 (July 28, 2003) ("Some say the problem is media concentration, and point out that only five companies control 80 percent of what we see and hear. In reality, those five companies own only 25 percent of more than 300 broadcast, satellite and cable channels, but because of their popularity, 80 percent of the viewing audience chooses to watch them. Popularity is not synonymous with monopoly.").

767. *See* William Glaberson, *Times Company Plans More Shift to Electronic Media, The New York Times* (Dec. 7, 1994), http://www.nytimes.com/1994/12/07/business/the-media-business-times-company-plans-shift-to-more-electronic-media.html.

entered the cable and satellite markets.[768] Nevertheless, even cable television may be going the way of the dinosaurs. With the development of online programming, consumers have less need for cable television, and more and more people are giving up both cable and satellite television.[769] Viewers interested in movies can find ample content online (at cheaper prices!) through companies like Netflix[770] and Blockbuster.[771] In addition, some cable companies are beginning to move their content online. For example, Comcast recently began offering a streaming service available to its subscribers.[772] There is also iSoftware TV which is an online television streaming service which boasts that it offers 3,000 channels.[773]

Media convergence has raised a number of important issues in the free speech arena. Historically, the U.S. Supreme Court has made clear distinctions between the various types of media. For example, the print media received the highest level of protection, so that prior restraints on newspapers have repeatedly been struck down as unconstitutional,[774] and governments have historically had little ability to regulate newspaper content aside from certain limited categories of speech.[775] By contrast, the broadcast media has received far fewer protections. As new methods of communication were developed in recent centuries, including broadcast technology, they were dealt with in medium-specific ways.[776] For example, in the United States, Congress created the Federal Communications Commission (FCC) and gave it the power to regulate wire and radio transmissions.[777] As part of the FCC's mandate, the government

768. *See* Geraldine Fabrikant, *Hallmark to Enter Cable TV in $1 Billion Cencom Deal, The New York Times*, at 33 (Sept. 21, 1991).

769. *See* Renee Montagne, *More TV Watchers Give Up Cable, Satellite*, National public Radio, Morning Edition (Aug. 11, 2011). https://www.npr.org/2011/08/11/139519303/business-news.

770. www.Netflix.com.

771. www.Blockbuster.com.

772. *See Comcast Introduces a Streaming TV Service, supra* note 740.

773. http://isoftwaretv.com/?hop=linkdreamz#.

774. *See* Russell L. Weaver, Understanding the First Amendment § 501. (Carolina Academic Press, 8th Ed., 2023).

775. *See id.*, at §§ 2.01–4.04.

776. *See FCC v. Pacifica Foundation*, 438 U.S. 726 (1978) (upholding FCC order relating to a radio station's broadcast of George Carlin's *Filthy Words* satire); *Red Lion Broadcasting Co. v. FCC*, 395 U.S. 367 (1969) (commenting on the scarcity of broadcast licenses).

777. 47 U.S.C. § 151.

maintained ownership of all radio waves, and created a licensing scheme designed to allocate the use of those airwaves.[778] Congress also gave the FCC the power to regulate wire and radio transmissions as needed for the public interest, convenience and necessity.[779]

Congress and the FCC's regulation of wire and radio broadcasts has extended not only to questions of *who* may communicate over the airwaves, but to some extent *what* they can communicate. For example, Congress has imposed the requirement that broadcasters allocate § 501. equal time to qualified political candidates.[780] At one point, the FCC also imposed the so-called Fairness Doctrine which mandated content-based restrictions on broadcasters. The Fairness Doctrine contained two separate and distinct components. The first, the political attack prong, required broadcasters to provide a right of reply to any person or group they attacked. The Fairness Doctrine also contained a requirement that broadcasters give adequate coverage to public issues, and required that this coverage accurately reflects opposing viewpoints. In *Red Lion Broadcasting Co. v. Federal Communications Commission*,[781] the Court upheld the Fairness Doctrine, concluding that the broadcast media could be treated differently than the print media because of the limited number of broadcasting bands available, and the fact that those who are allocated those bandwidths could be treated as trustees of those airwaves.[782] The Court refused to apply strict scrutiny, and simply asserted the public's right "to receive suitable access to social, political, esthetic, moral, and other ideas."[783] Likewise, in *FCC v. Pacifica Foundation*,[784] the Court held that the FCC could impose another content-based restriction: it could regulate the hours at which indecent programs are broadcast.

None of the restrictions that have been imposed on broadcasters would have been upheld had they been imposed on newspapers.[785] Aside from

778. 47 U.S.C. § 301.

779. *See* 47 U.S.C. § 303.

780. *See* 47 U.S.C. § 315.

781. 395 U.S. 367 (1969).

782. *Id.*

783. *Id.*

784. *See FCC v. Pacifica Foundation*, 438 U.S. 726 (1978) (upholding FCC order relating to a radio station's broadcast of George Carlin's *Filthy Words* satire).

785. *See Miami Herald Publishing Co. v. Tornillo*, 418 U.S. 241 (1974).

broadcasters, content-based and viewpoint-based restrictions on speech are regarded as presumptively unconstitutional.[786] In particular, Congress (and the states) cannot prohibit "indecent" speech which is not obscene,[787] and the Court struck down a state law that required newspapers to provide a right of reply to those they attacked.[788]

In an internet era, when we are seeing media convergence, the distinction between newspapers and broadcasters may make little sense. As broadcasters have developed print editions, and print newspapers have developed online content with video and audio capability, meaningful distinctions between the different methods of communication make less sense, and the justifications for treating them differently have less force. When the ability to communicate is easy and limitless, scarcity principles have little meaning or application.

As the internet grows in significance, and some newspapers publish entirely online, legitimate questions are raised regarding how they should be treated for First Amendment purposes. Are online newspapers to be regarded as the "press" in the same sense that traditional newspapers have been regarded as the press? What about bloggers? Should they be treated as the "press" as well? All of these issues will ultimately have to be resolved by the courts.

Those newspapers that continue to offer print versions are beginning to shift their publications in a more democratic direction in response to the internet challenge. For example, some newspapers (*e.g.*, *The Courier-Journal* newspaper in Louisville, Kentucky), in their online versions, have permitted the creation of fora whereby ordinary individuals can communicate their views to each other, and can comment on articles.[789] As a result, ordinary people are able to air their views about the issues raised in the article, and have increased ability to participate in the political process. Of course, even this type of access does not entirely eliminate the newspaper's gatekeeper role. Before an individual can comment on an article, the paper's editors must decide that the issue is newsworthy and write about it.

786. *See R.A.V. v. City of St. Paul*, 505 U.S. 377 (1992).

787. *See Reno v. American Civil Liberties Union*, 521 U.S. 844 (1997).

788. *See id.*

789. *See* www.courier-journal.com.

If the paper's editors choose to ignore ideas or positions with which they disagree, there is no forum through which ideas can be discussed.

At least one newspaper is actively using citizen access as a way to increase circulation. When *The Journal Inquirer* of Manchester, Connecticut, decided to offer free online content, its print circulation declined dramatically.[790] In an effort to attract online viewers, the paper included a link to SeeClickFix.com[791] on its website.[792] SeeClickFix.com allows citizens to contract local governmental officials, comment on complaints registered by other citizens, and receive responses from governmental officials.[793] The website, and the paper's articles related to issues raised on that website, have attracted considerable attention from readers. As Doug Hardy, Associate Editor and internet supervisor for the *Journal Inquirer*, noted: "You look back at some of the stuff you've done over the years as a journalist, and you go, 'I've written some important stories; no one ever called or wrote,' Mr. Hardy said. 'I've just gotten tons and tons of response to some of the stories I've written' using SeeClickFix."[794] In addition, the *Journal Inquirer's* use of SeeClickFix.com has moved local officials to action. As Mr. Hardy noted, "'We printed a paragraph from a woman's complaint about a deteriorated mill building in Vernon,' Mr. Hardy wrote in an e-mail message. 'I got responses from the mayor, town administrator and the architect who is redeveloping the building—all within 24 hours.' The *Journal Inquirer* had written about the mill before but had never received such a response."[795]

The difficulty is that many newspapers are not making money online and have little prospect of doing so in the future.[796] Like traditional newspapers, most online papers generate the bulk of their revenue through advertising, and need to encourage broad readership in order to incentiv-

---

790. *See* Daniel E. Slotnik, *News Sites Dabble with a Tool for Nudging Local Officials, The New York Times*, at B1 (Jan. 4, 2010).

791. https://seeclickfix.com/.

792. *See* Slotnik, *supra* note 790.

793. *Id.*; *see also* http://www.journalinquirer.com/.

794. *Id.*

795. *Id.*

796. *See Newspaper Shuns Web, and Thrives, supra* note 720, at B1.

ize advertisers. Some argue that this strategy is a mistake.[797] Indeed, there is some doubt about whether an advertising-based economic model can succeed,[798] and some traditional newspapers are searching for a new business model,[799] especially since private ownership looks increasingly unviable.[800]

797. *See* Kurtz, *supra* note 33, at A7 (suggesting that Nicholas Lemann, Dean, Columbia University, School of Journalism, believes that newspapers made a mistake in deciding to offer their content for free online).

798. *See* Perez-Pena & Arango, *supra* note 140.

799. *See* Kurtz, *supra* note 33, at A7 ("some analysts say newspapers must find a way to charge for online content—perhaps through 'micropayments'" of the kind popularized by iTunes, which offers songs for downloading at 99 cents apiece. Others say papers must go the nonprofit route, relying on donors to raise endowments, much like universities.").

800. *See id.*:

> Private owners, freed from the short-term pressures of Wall Street, were once seen as potential saviors [for troubled newspapers]. But that was before the debt-laden Tribune Co. filed for bankruptcy in December, a year after being bought by Chicago real-estate mogul Sam Zell, and before Philadelphia Newspapers LLC, which was bought by public relations executive Brian Tierney in 2006 and which owns the *Inquirer* and the *Daily News*, did the same last week.

INDEX